Ruby Cookbook™

Other resources from O'Reilly

Related titles
Ajax Hacks™
Ajax Design Patterns
Head Rush Ajax

Rails Cookbook™
Ruby on Rails: Up and Running

oreilly.com
oreilly.com is more than a complete catalog of O'Reilly books. You'll also find links to news, events, articles, weblogs, sample chapters, and code examples.

oreillynet.com is the essential portal for developers interested in open and emerging technologies, including new platforms, programming languages, and operating systems.

Conferences
O'Reilly brings diverse innovators together to nurture the ideas that spark revolutionary industries. We specialize in documenting the latest tools and systems, translating the innovator's knowledge into useful skills for those in the trenches. Visit *conferences.oreilly.com* for our upcoming events.

Safari Bookshelf (*safari.oreilly.com*) is the premier online reference library for programmers and IT professionals. Conduct searches across more than 1,000 books. Subscribers can zero in on answers to time-critical questions in a matter of seconds. Read the books on your Bookshelf from cover to cover or simply flip to the page you need. Try it today for free.

Ruby Cookbook™

Lucas Carlson and Leonard Richardson

O'REILLY®

Beijing · Cambridge · Farnham · Köln · Paris · Sebastopol · Taipei · Tokyo

Ruby Cookbook
by Lucas Carlson and Leonard Richardson

Published by O'Reilly Media, Inc., 1005 Gravenstein Highway North, Sebastopol, CA 95472.

O'Reilly books may be purchased for educational, business, or sales promotional use. Online editions are also available for most titles (*safari.oreilly.com*). For more information, contact our corporate/institutional sales department: (800) 998-9938 or *corporate@oreilly.com*.

Editor: Mike Loukides	**Cover Designer:** Karen Montgomery
Production Editor: Colleen Gorman	**Interior Designer:** David Futato
Proofreader: Colleen Gorman	**Illustrators:** Robert Romano and Jessamyn Read
Indexer: Johnna VanHoose Dinse	

Printing History:

July 2006:	First Edition.

ISBN: 0-596-52369-6
[M]

For Tess, who sat by me the whole time.
For John and Rael, the best programmers I know.

—Lucas Carlson

For Sumana.

—Leonard Richardson

Table of Contents

Preface

Life Is Short

This is a book of recipes: solutions to common problems, copy-and-paste code snippets, explanations, examples, and short tutorials.

This book is meant to save you time. Time, as they say, is money, but a span of time is also a piece of your life. Our lives are better spent creating new things than fighting our own errors, or trying to solve problems that have already been solved. We present this book in the hope that the time it saves, distributed across all its readers, will greatly outweigh the time we spent creating it.

The Ruby programming language is itself a wonderful time-saving tool. It makes you more productive than other programming languages because you spend more time making the computer do what you want, and less wrestling with the language. But there are many ways for a Ruby programmer to spend time without accomplishing anything, and we've encountered them all:

- Time spent writing Ruby implementations of common algorithms.
- Time spent *debugging* Ruby implementations of common algorithms.
- Time spent discovering and working around Ruby-specific pitfalls.
- Time spent on repetitive tasks (including repetitive programming tasks!) that could be automated.
- Time spent duplicating work that someone else has already made publicly available.
- Time spent searching for a library that does X.
- Time spent evaluating and deciding between the many libraries that do X.
- Time spent learning how to use a library because of poor or outdated documentation.
- Time lost staying away from a useful technology because it seems intimidating.

We, and the many contributors to this book, recall vividly our own wasted hours and days. We've distilled our experiences into this book so that you don't waste your time—or at least so you enjoyably waste it on *more* interesting problems.

Our other goal is to expand your interests. If you come to this book wanting to generate algorithmic music with Ruby then, yes, Recipe 12.14 will save you time over starting from scratch. It's more likely that you'd never considered the possibility until now. Every recipe in this book was developed and written with these two goals in mind: to save you time, and to keep your brain active with new ideas.

Audience

This cookbook is aimed at people who know at least a little bit of Ruby, *or* who know a fair amount about programming in general. This isn't a Ruby tutorial (see the Resources section below for some real tutorials), but if you're already familiar with a few other programming languages, you should be able to pick up Ruby by reading through the first 10 chapters of this book and typing in the code listings as you go.

We've included recipes suitable for all skill levels, from those who are just starting out with Ruby, to experts who need an occasional reference. We focus mainly on generic programming techniques, but we also cover specific application frameworks (like Ruby on Rails and GUI libraries) and best practices (like unit testing).

Even if you just plan to use this book as a reference, we recommend that you skim through it once to get a picture of the problems we solve. This is a big book but it doesn't solve every problem. If you pick it up and you can't find a solution to your problem, or one that nudges you in the right direction, then you've *lost* time.

If you skim through this book once beforehand, you'll get a fair idea of the problems we cover in this book, and you'll get a better hit rate. You'll know when this book can help you; and when you should consult other books, do a web search, ask a friend, or get help some other way.

The Structure of This Book

Each of this book's 23 chapters focuses on a kind of programming or a particular data type. This overview of the chapters should give you a picture of how we divided up the recipes. Each chapter also has its own, somewhat lengthier introduction, which gives a more detailed view of its recipes. At the very least, we recommend you skim the chapter introductions and the table of contents.

We start with six chapters covering Ruby's built-in data structures.

- Chapter 1, *Strings*, contains recipes for building, processing, and manipulating strings of text. We devote a few recipes specifically to regular expressions (Recipes 1.17 through 1.19), but our focus is on Ruby-specific issues, and regular expressions are a very general tool. If you haven't encountered them yet, or just find them intimidating, we recommend you go through an online tutorial or *Mastering Regular Expressions* by Jeffrey Friedl (O'Reilly).

- Chapter 2, *Numbers*, covers the representation of different types of numbers: real numbers, complex numbers, arbitrary-precision decimals, and so on. It also includes Ruby implementations of common mathematical and statistical algorithms, and explains some Ruby quirks you'll run into if you create your own numeric types (Recipes 2.13 and 2.14).

- Chapter 3, *Date and Time*, covers Ruby's two interfaces for dealing with time: the one based on the C time library, which may be familiar to you from other programming languages, and the one implemented in pure Ruby, which is more idiomatic.

- Chapter 4, *Arrays*, introduces the array, Ruby's simplest compound data type. Many of an array's methods are actually methods of the Enumerable mixin; this means you can apply many of these recipes to hashes and other data types. Some features of Enumerable are covered in this chapter (Recipes 4.4 and 4.6), and some are covered in Chapter 7.

- Chapter 5, *Hashes*, covers the hash, Ruby's other basic compound data type. Hashes make it easy to associate objects with names and find them later (hashes are sometimes called "lookup tables" or "dictionaries," two telling names). It's easy to use hashes along with arrays to build deep and complex data structures.

- Chapter 6, *Files and Directories*, covers techniques for reading, writing, and manipulating files. Ruby's file access interface is based on the standard C file libraries, so it may look familiar to you. This chapter also covers Ruby's standard libraries for searching and manipulating the filesystem; many of these recipes show up again in Chapter 23.

The first six chapters deal with specific algorithmic problems. The next four are more abstract: they're about Ruby idiom and philosophy. If you can't get the Ruby language itself to do what you want, or you're having trouble writing Ruby code that looks the way Ruby "should" look, the recipes in these chapters may help.

- Chapter 7, *Code Blocks and Iteration*, contains recipes that explore the possibilities of Ruby's code blocks (also known as *closures*).

- Chapter 8, *Objects and Classes*, covers Ruby's take on object-oriented programming. It contains recipes for writing different types of classes and methods, and a few recipes that demonstrate capabilities of all Ruby objects (such as freezing and cloning).

- Chapter 9, *Modules and Namespaces*, covers Ruby's modules. These constructs are used to "mix" new behavior into existing classes and to segregate functionality into different namespaces.

- Chapter 10, *Reflection and Metaprogramming*, covers techniques for programatically exploring and modifying Ruby class definitions.

Chapter 6 covers basic file access, but doesn't touch much on specific file formats. We devote three chapters to popular ways of storing data.

- Chapter 11, *XML and HTML*, shows how to handle the most popular data interchange formats. The chapter deals mostly with parsing other people's XML documents and web pages (but see Recipe 11.9).

- Chapter 12, *Graphics and Other File Formats*, covers data interchange formats other than XML and HTML, with a special focus on generating and manipulating graphics.

- Chapter 13, *Databases and Persistence*, covers the best Ruby interfaces to data storage formats, whether you're serializing Ruby objects to disk, or storing structured data in a database. This chapter demonstrates everything from different ways of serializing data and indexing text, to the Ruby client libraries for popular SQL databases, to full-blown abstraction layers like ActiveRecord that save you from having to write SQL at all.

Currently the most popular use of Ruby is in network applications (mostly through Ruby on Rails). We devote three chapters to different types of applications:

- Chapter 14, *Internet Services*, kicks off our networking coverage by illustrating a wide variety of clients and servers written with Ruby libraries.

- Chapter 15, *Web Development: Ruby on Rails*, covers the web application framework that's been driving so much of Ruby's recent popularity.

- Chapter 16, *Web Services and Distributed Programming*, covers two techniques for sharing information between computers during a Ruby program. In order to use a web service, you make an HTTP request of a program on some other computer, usually one you don't control. Ruby's DRb library lets you share Ruby data structures between programs running on a set of computers, all of which you control.

We then have three chapters on the auxilliary tasks that surround the main programming work of a project.

- Chapter 17, *Testing, Debugging, Optimizing, and Documenting*, focuses mainly on handling exception conditions and creating unit tests for your code. There are also several recipes on the processes of debugging and optimization.

- Chapter 18, *Packaging and Distributing Software*, mainly deals with Ruby's Gem packaging system and the RubyForge server that hosts many gem files. Many recipes in other chapters require that you install a particular gem, so if you're not familiar with gems, we recommend you read Recipe 18.2 in particular. The chapter also shows you how to create and distribute gems for your own projects.

- Chapter 19, *Automating Tasks with Rake*, covers the most popular Ruby build tool. With Rake, you can script common tasks like running unit tests or packaging your code as a gem. Though it's usually used in Ruby projects, it's a general-purpose build language that you can use wherever you might use Make.

We close the book with four chapters on miscellaneous topics.

- Chapter 20, *Multitasking and Multithreading*, shows how to use threads to do more than one thing at once, and how to use Unix subprocesses to run external commands.

- Chapter 21, *User Interface*, covers user interfaces (apart from the web interface, which was covered in Chapter 15). We discuss the command-line interface, character-based GUIs with Curses and HighLine, GUI toolkits for various platforms, and more obscure kinds of user interface (Recipe 21.11).

- Chapter 22, *Extending Ruby with Other Languages*, focuses on hooking up Ruby to other languages, either for performance or to get access to more libraries. Most of the chapter focuses on getting access to C libraries, but there is one recipe about JRuby, the Ruby implementation that runs on the Java Virtual Machine (Recipe 22.5).

- Chapter 23, *System Administration*, is full of self-contained programs for doing administrative tasks, usually using techniques from other chapters. The recipes have a heavy focus on Unix administration, but there are some resources for Windows users (including Recipe 23.2), and some cross-platform scripts.

How the Code Listings Work

Learning from a cookbook means performing the recipes. Some of our recipes define big chunks of Ruby code that you can simply plop into your program and use without really understanding them (Recipe 19.8 is a good example). But most of the recipes demonstrate techniques, and the best way to learn a technique is to practice it.

We wrote the recipes, and their code listings, with this in mind. Most of our listings act like unit tests for the concepts described in the recipe: they poke at objects and show you the results.

Now, a Ruby installation comes with an interactive interpreter called irb. Within an irb session, you can type in lines of Ruby code and see the output immediately. You don't have to create a Ruby program file and run it through the interpreter.

Most of our recipes are presented in a form that you can type or copy/paste directly into an irb session. To study a recipe in depth, we recommend that you start an irb session and run through the code listings as you read it. You'll have a deeper understanding of the concept if you do it yourself than if you just read about it. Once you're done, you can experiment further with the objects you defined while running the code listings.

Sometimes we want to draw your attention to the expected result of a Ruby expression. We do this with a Ruby comment containing an ASCII arrow that points to the expected value of the expression. This is the same arrow irb uses to tell you the value of every expression you type.

We also use textual comments to explain some pieces of code. Here's a fragment of Ruby code that I've formatted with comments as I would in a recipe:

```
1 + 2                         # => 3

# On a long line, the expected value goes on a new line:
Math.sqrt(1 + 2 + 3 + 4 + 5 + 6 + 7 + 8 + 9 + 10)
# => 7.41619848709566
```

To display the expected *output* of a Ruby expression, we use a comment that has no ASCII arrow, and that always goes on a new line:

```
puts "This string is self-referential."
# This string is self-referential.
```

If you type these two snippets of code into irb, ignoring the comments, you can check back against the text and verify that you got the same results we did:

```
$ irb
irb(main):001:0> 1 + 2
=> 3
irb(main):002:0> Math.sqrt(1 + 2 + 3 + 4 + 5 + 6 + 7 + 8 + 9 + 10)
=> 7.41619848709566
irb(main):003:0> puts "This string is self-referential."
This string is self-referential.
=> nil
```

If you're reading this book in electronic form, you can copy and paste the code fragments into irb. The Ruby interpreter will ignore the comments, but you can use them to make sure your answers match ours, without having to look back at the text. (But you should know that typing in the code yourself, at least the first time, is better for comprehension.)

```
$ irb
irb(main):001:0> 1 + 2        # => 3
=> 3
irb(main):002:0>
irb(main):003:0* # On a long line, the expected value goes on a new line:
irb(main):004:0* Math.sqrt(1 + 2 + 3 + 4 + 5 + 6 + 7 + 8 + 9 + 10)
=> 7.41619848709566
irb(main):005:0> # => 7.41619848709566
irb(main):006:0*
irb(main):007:0* puts "This string is self-referential."
This string is self-referential.
=> nil
irb(main):008:0> # This string is self-referential.
```

We don't cut corners. Most of our recipes demonstrate a complete irb session from start to finish, and they include any imports or initialization necessary to illustrate the point we're trying to make. If you run the code exactly as it is in the recipe, you should get the same results we did.[*] This fits in with our philosophy that code samples should

---

[*] When a program's behavior depends on the current time, the random number generator, or the presence of certain files on disk, you might not get the exact same results we did, but it should be similar.

be unit tests for the underlying concepts. In fact, we tested our code samples like unit tests, with a Ruby script that parses recipe texts and runs the code listings.

The irb session technique doesn't always work. Rails recipes have to run within Rails. Curses recipes take over the screen and don't play well with irb. So sometimes we show you standalone files. We present them in the following format:

```
#!/usr/bin/ruby -w
# sample_ruby_file.rb: A sample file

1 + 2
Math.sqrt(1 + 2 + 3 + 4 + 5 + 6 + 7 + 8 + 9 + 10)
puts "This string is self-referential."
```

Whenever possible, we'll also show what you'll get when you run this program: maybe a screenshot of a GUI program, or a record of the program's output when run from the Unix command line:

```
$ ruby sample_ruby_file.rb
This string is self-referential.
```

Note that the output of sample_ruby_file.rb looks different from the same code entered into irb. Here, there's no trace of the addition and the square root operations, because they produce no output.

Installing the Software

Ruby comes preinstalled on Mac OS X and most Linux installations. Windows doesn't come with Ruby, but it's easy to get it with the One-Click Installer: see *http://rubyforge.org/projects/rubyinstaller/*.

If you're on a Unix/Linux system and you don't have Ruby installed (or you want to upgrade), your distribution's package system may make a Ruby package available. On Debian GNU/Linux, it's available as the package ruby-[version]: for instance, ruby-1.8 or ruby-1.9. Red Hat Linux calls it ruby; so does the DarwinParts system on Mac OS X.

If all else fails, download the Ruby source code and compile it yourself. You can get the Ruby source code through FTP or HTTP by visiting *http://www.ruby-lang.org/*.

Many of the recipes in this book require that you install third-party libraries in the form of Ruby gems. In general, we prefer standalone solutions (using only the Ruby standard library) to solutions that use gems, and gem-based solutions to ones that require other kinds of third-party software.

If you're not familiar with gems, consult Chapter 18 as needed. To get started, all you need to know is that you first download the Rubygems library from *http://rubyforge.org/projects/rubygems/* (choose the latest release from that page). Unpack the tarball or ZIP file, change into the rubygems-[version] directory, and run this command as the superuser:

```
$ ruby setup.rb
```

The Rubygems library is included in the Windows One-Click Installer, so you don't have to worry about this step on Windows.

Once you've got the Rubygems library installed, it's easy to install many other pieces of Ruby code. When a recipe says something like "Ruby on Rails is available as the rails gem," you can issue the following command from the command line (again, as the superuser):

```
$ gem install rails --include-dependencies
```

The RubyGems library will download the rails gem (and any other gems on which it depends) and automatically install them. You should then be able to run the code in the recipe, exactly as it appears.

The three most useful gems for new Ruby installations are rails (if you intend to create Rails applications) and the two gems provided by the Ruby Facets project: facets_core and facets_more. The Facets Core library extends the classes of the Ruby standard library with generally useful methods. The Facets More library adds entirely new classes and modules. The Ruby Facets homepage (*http://facets.rubyforge.org/*) has a complete reference.

Some Ruby libraries (especially older ones) are not packaged as gems. Most of the nongem libraries mentioned in this book have entries in the Ruby Application Archive (*http://raa.ruby-lang.org/*), a directory of Ruby programs and libraries. In most cases you can download a tarball or ZIP file from the RAA, and install it with the technique described in Recipe 18.8.

Platform Differences, Version Differences, and Other Headaches

Except where noted, the recipes describe cross-platform concepts, and the code itself should run the same way on Windows, Linux, and Mac OS X. Most of the platform differences and platform-specific recipes show up in the final chapters: Chapter 20, Chapter 21, and Chapter 23 (but see the introduction to Chapter 6 for a note about Windows filenames).

We wrote and tested the recipes using Ruby version 1.8.4 and Rails version 1.1.2, the latest stable versions as of the time of writing. In a couple of places we mention code changes you should make if you're running Ruby 1.9 (the latest unstable version as of the time of writing) or 2.0.

Despite our best efforts, this book may contain unflagged platform-specific code, not to mention plain old bugs. We apologize for these in advance of their discovery. If you have problems with a recipe, check out the eratta for this book (see below).

In several recipes in this book, we modify standard Ruby classes like `Array` to add new methods (see, for instance, Recipe 1.10, which defines a new method called `String#capitalize_first_letter`). These methods are then available to every instance of that class in your program. This is a fairly common technique in Ruby: both Rails and the Facets Core library mentioned above do it. It's somewhat controversial, though, and it can cause problems (see Recipe 8.4 for an in-depth discussion), so we felt we should mention it here in the Preface, even though it might be too technical for people who are new to Ruby.

If you don't want to modify the standard classes, you can put the methods we demonstrate into a subclass, or define them in the `Kernel` namespace: that is, define `capitalize_first_letter_of_string` instead of reopening `String` and defining `capitalize_first_letter` inside it.

Other Resources

If you need to learn Ruby, the standard reference is *Programming Ruby: The Pragmatic Programmer's Guide* by Dave Thomas, Chad Fowler, and Andy Hunt (Pragmatic Programmers). The first edition is available online in HTML format (*http://www.rubycentral.com/book/*), but it's out of date. The second edition is much better and is available as a printed book or as PDF (*http://www.pragmaticprogrammer.com/titles/ruby/*). It's a much better idea to buy the second edition and use the first edition as a handy reference than to try to read the first edition.

"Why's (Poignant) Guide to Ruby," by "why the lucky stiff," teaches Ruby with stories, like an English primer. Excellent for creative beginners (*http://poignantguide.net/ruby/*).

For Rails, the standard book is *Agile Web Development with Rails* by Dave Thomas, David Hansson, Leon Breedt, and Mike Clark (Pragmatic Programmers). There are also two books like this one that focus exclusively on Rails: *Rails Cookbook* by Rob Orsini (O'Reilly) and *Rails Recipes* by Chad Fowler (Pragmatic Programmers).

Some common Ruby pitfalls are explained in the Ruby FAQ (*http://www.rubycentral.com/faq/*, starting in Section 4) and in "Things That Newcomers to Ruby Should Know" (*http://www.glue.umd.edu/~billtj/ruby.html*).

Many people come to Ruby already knowing one or more programming languages. You might find it frustrating to learn Ruby with a big book that thinks it has to teach you programming *and* Ruby. For such people, we recommend Ruby creator Yukihiro Matsumoto's "Ruby User's Guide" (*http://www.ruby-doc.org/docs/UsersGuide/rg/*). It's a short read, and it focuses on what makes Ruby different from other programming languages. Its terminology is a little out of date, and it presents its code samples through the obsolete `eval.rb` program (use `irb` instead), but it's the best short introduction we know of.

There are a few articles especially for Java programmers who want to learn Ruby: Jim Weirich's "10 Things Every Java Programmer Should Know About Ruby" (*http://onestepback.org/articles/10things/*), Francis Hwang's blog entry "Coming to Ruby from Java" (*http://fhwang.net/blog/40.html*), and Chris Williams's collection of links, "From Java to Ruby (With Love)" (*http://cwilliams.textdriven.com/pages/java_to_ruby*) Despite the names, C++ programmers will also benefit from much of what's in these pieces.

The Ruby Bookshelf (*http://books.rubyveil.com/books/Bookshelf/Introduction/Bookshelf*) has produced a number of free books on Ruby, including many of the ones mentioned above, in an easy-to-read HTML format.

Finally, Ruby's built-in modules, classes, and methods come with excellent documentation (much of it originally written for *Programming Ruby*). You can read this documentation online at *http://www.ruby-doc.org/core/* and *http://www.ruby-doc.org/stdlib/*. You can also look it up on your own Ruby installation by using the `ri` command. Pass in the name of a class or method, and `ri` will give you the corresponding documentation. Here are a few examples:

```
$ ri Array             # A class
$ ri Array.new         # A class method
$ ri Array#compact     # An instance method
```

Conventions Used in This Book

The following typographical conventions are used in this book:

Plain text
> Indicates menu titles, menu options, menu buttons, and keyboard accelerators (such as Alt and Ctrl).

Italic
> Indicates new terms, URLs, email addresses, and Unix utilities.

Constant width
> Indicates commands, options, switches, variables, attributes, keys, functions, types, classes, namespaces, methods, modules, properties, parameters, values, objects, events, event handlers, XML tags, HTML tags, macros, programs, libraries, filenames, pathnames, directories, the contents of files, or the output from commands.

Constant width bold
> Shows commands or other text that should be typed literally by the user.

Constant width italic
> Shows text that should be replaced with user-supplied values.

Using Code Examples

This book is here to help you get your job done. In general, you may use the code in this book in your programs and documentation. You do not need to contact us for permission unless you're reproducing a significant portion of the code. For example, writing a program that uses several chunks of code from this book does not require permission. Selling or distributing a CD-ROM of examples from O'Reilly books *does* require permission. Answering a question by citing this book and quoting example code does not require permission. Incorporating a significant amount of example code from this book into your product's documentation *does* require permission.

We appreciate, but do not require, attribution. An attribution usually includes the title, author, publisher, and ISBN. For example: "*Ruby Cookbook*, by Lucas Carlson and Leonard Richardson. Copyright 2006 O'Reilly Media, Inc., 0-596-52369-6."

If you feel your use of code examples falls outside fair use or the permission given above, feel free to contact us at *permissions@oreilly.com*.

Comments and Questions

Please address comments and questions concerning this book to the publisher:

O'Reilly Media, Inc.
1005 Gravenstein Highway North
Sebastopol, CA 95472
800-998-9938 (in the United States or Canada)
707-829-0515 (international or local)
707-829-0104 (fax)

We have a web page for this book, where we list errata, examples, and any additional information. You can access this page at:

http://www.oreilly.com/catalog/rubyckbk

To comment or ask technical questions about this book, send email to:

bookquestions@oreilly.com

For more information about our books, conferences, Resource Centers, and the O'Reilly Network, see our web site at:

http://www.oreilly.com

Acknowledgments

First we'd like to thank our editor, Michael Loukides, for his help and for acquiescing to our use of his name in recipe code samples, even when we turned him into a talking frog. The production editor, Colleen Gorman, was also very helpful.

This book would have taken longer to write and been less interesting without our contributing authors, who, collectively, wrote over 60 of these recipes. The roll of names includes: Steve Arniel, Ben Bleything, Antonio Cangiano, Mauro Cicio, Maurice Codik, Thomas Enebo, Pat Eyler, Bill Froelich, Rod Gaither, Ben Giddings, Michael Granger, James Edward Gray II, Stefan Lang, Kevin Marshall, Matthew Palmer Chetan Patil, Alun ap Rhisiart, Garrett Rooney, John-Mason Shackelford, Phil Tomson, and John Wells. They saved us time by lending their knowledge of various Ruby topics, and they enriched the book with their ideas.

This book would be of appallingly low quality were it not for our technical reviewers, who spotted dozens of bugs, platform-specific problems, and conceptual errors: John N. Alegre, Dave Burt, Bill Dolinar, Simen Edvardsen, Shane Emmons, Edward Faulkner, Dan Fitzpatrick, Bill Guindon, Stephen Hildrey, Meador Inge, Eric Jacoboni, Julian I. Kamil, Randy Kramer, Alex LeDonne, Steven Lumos, Keith Rosenblatt, Gene Tani, and R Vrajmohan.

Finally, to the programmers and writers of the Ruby community; from the celebrities like Yukihiro Matsumoto, Dave Thomas, Chad Fowler, and "why", to the hundreds of unsung heroes whose work went into the libraries we demonstrate throughout the book, and whose skill and patience bring more people into the Ruby community all the time.

## CHAPTER 1

Strings

Ruby is a programmer-friendly language. If you are already familiar with object-oriented programming, Ruby should quickly become second nature. If you've struggled with learning object-oriented programming or are not familiar with it, Ruby should make more sense to you than other object-oriented languages because Ruby's methods are consistently named, concise, and generally act the way you expect.

Throughout this book, we demonstrate concepts through interactive Ruby sessions. Strings are a good place to start because not only are they a useful data type, they're easy to create and use. They provide a simple introduction to Ruby, a point of comparison between Ruby and other languages you might know, and an approachable way to introduce important Ruby concepts like duck typing (see Recipe 1.12), open classes (demonstrated in Recipe 1.10), symbols (Recipe 1.7), and even Ruby gems (Recipe 1.20).

If you use Mac OS X or a Unix environment with Ruby installed, go to your command line right now and type `irb`. If you're using Windows, you can download and install the One-Click Installer from *http://rubyforge.org/projects/rubyinstaller/*, and do the same from a command prompt (you can also run the `fxri` program, if that's more comfortable for you). You've now entered an interactive Ruby shell, and you can follow along with the code samples in most of this book's recipes.

Strings in Ruby are much like strings in other dynamic languages like Perl, Python and PHP. They're not too much different from strings in Java and C. Ruby strings are dynamic, mutable, and flexible. Get started with strings by typing this line into your interactive Ruby session:

```
string = "My first string"
```

You should see some output that looks like this:

```
=> "My first string"
```

You typed in a Ruby expression that created a string "My first string", and assigned it to the variable `string`. The value of that expression is just the new value of `string`, which is what your interactive Ruby session printed out on the right side of the arrow. Throughout this book, we'll represent this kind of interaction in the following form:[*]

```
string = "My first string"              # => "My first string"
```

In Ruby, everything that can be assigned to a variable is an object. Here, the variable `string` points to an object of class `String`. That class defines over a hundred built-in methods: named pieces of code that examine and manipulate the string. We'll explore some of these throughout the chapter, and indeed the entire book. Let's try out one now: `String#length`, which returns the number of bytes in a string. Here's a Ruby method call:

```
string.length                           # => 15
```

Many programming languages make you put parentheses after a method call:

```
string.length( )                        # => 15
```

In Ruby, parentheses are almost always optional. They're especially optional in this-case, since we're not passing any arguments into `String#length`. If you're passing arguments into a method, it's often more readable to enclose the argument list in parentheses:

```
string.count 'i'                        # => 2   # "i" occurs twice.
string.count('i')                       # => 2
```

The return value of a method call is itself an object. In the case of `String#length`, the return value is the number 15, an instance of the `Fixnum` class. We can call a method on this object as well:

```
string.length.next                      # => 16
```

Let's take a more complicated case: a string that contains non-ASCII characters. This string contains the French phrase "il était une fois," encoded as UTF-8:[†]

```
french_string = "il \xc3\xa9tait une fois"   # => "il \303\251tait une fois"
```

Many programming languages (notably Java) treat a string as a series of characters. Ruby treats a string as a series of bytes. The French string contains 14 letters and 3 spaces, so you might think Ruby would say the length of the string is 17. But one of the letters (the e with acute accent) is represented as two bytes, and that's what Ruby counts:

```
french_string.length                    # => 18
```

For more on handling different encodings, see Recipe 1.14 and Recipe 11.12. For more on this specific problem, see Recipe 1.8

You can represent special characters in strings (like the binary data in the French string) with string escaping. Ruby does different types of string escaping depending

---

[*] Yes, this was covered in the Preface, but not everyone reads the Preface.

[†] "\xc3\xa9" is a Ruby string representation of the UTF-8 encoding of the Unicode character é.

on how you create the string. When you enclose a string in double quotes, you can encode binary data into the string (as in the French example above), and you can encode newlines with the code "\n", as in other programming languages:

```
puts "This string\ncontains a newline"
# This string
# contains a newline
```

When you enclose a string in single quotes, the only special codes you can use are "\'" to get a literal single quote, and "\\" to get a literal backslash:

```
puts 'it may look like this string contains a newline\nbut it doesn\'t'
# it may look like this string contains a newline\nbut it doesn't

puts 'Here is a backslash: \\'
# Here is a backslash: \
```

This is covered in more detail in Recipe 1.5. Also see Recipes 1.2 and 1.3 for more examples of the more spectacular substitutions double-quoted strings can do.

Another useful way to initialize strings is with the "here documents" style:

```
long_string = <<EOF
Here is a long string
With many paragraphs
EOF
# => "Here is a long string\nWith many paragraphs\n"

puts long_string
# Here is a long string
# With many paragraphs
```

Like most of Ruby's built-in classes, Ruby's strings define the same functionality in several different ways, so that you can use the idiom you prefer. Say you want to get a substring of a larger string (as in Recipe 1.13). If you're an object-oriented programming purist, you can use the String#slice method:

```
string                           # => "My first string"
string.slice(3, 5)               # => "first"
```

But if you're coming from C, and you think of a string as an array of bytes, Ruby can accommodate you. Selecting a single byte from a string returns that byte as a number.

```
string.chr + string.chr + string.chr + string.chr + string.chr
# => "first"
```

And if you come from Python, and you like that language's slice notation, you can just as easily chop up the string that way:

```
string[3, 5]                     # => "first"
```

Unlike in most programming languages, Ruby strings are mutable: you can change them after they are declared. Below we see the difference between the methods String#upcase and String#upcase!:

```
string.upcase                    # => "MY FIRST STRING"
string                           # => "My first string"
```

```
string.upcase!                          # => "MY FIRST STRING"
string                                  # => "MY FIRST STRING"
```

This is one of Ruby's syntactical conventions. "Dangerous" methods (generally those that modify their object in place) usually have an exclamation mark at the end of their name. Another syntactical convention is that *predicates*, methods that return a true/false value, have a question mark at the end of their name (as in some varieties of Lisp):

```
string.empty?                           # => false
string.include? 'MY'                    # => true
```

This use of English punctuation to provide the programmer with information is an example of Matz's design philosophy: that Ruby is a language primarily for humans to read and write, and secondarily for computers to interpret.

An interactive Ruby session is an indispensable tool for learning and experimenting with these methods. Again, we encourage you to type the sample code shown in these recipes into an irb or fxri session, and try to build upon the examples as your knowledge of Ruby grows.

Here are some extra resources for using strings in Ruby:

- You can get information about any built-in Ruby method with the ri command; for instance, to see more about the String#upcase! method, issue the command ri "String#upcase!" from the command line.
- "why the lucky stiff" has written an excellent introduction to installing Ruby, and using irb and ri: *http://poignantguide.net/ruby/expansion-pak-1.html*
- For more information about the design philosophy behind Ruby, read an interview with Yukihiro "Matz" Matsumoto, creator of Ruby: *http://www.artima.com/intv/ruby.html*

1.1 Building a String from Parts

Problem

You want to iterate over a data structure, building a string from it as you do.

Solution

There are two efficient solutions. The simplest solution is to start with an empty string, and repeatedly append substrings onto it with the << operator:

```
hash = { "key1" => "val1", "key2" => "val2" }
string = ""
hash.each { |k,v| string << "#{k} is #{v}\n" }
puts string
# key1 is val1
# key2 is val2
```

This variant of the simple solution is slightly more efficient, but harder to read:

```
string = ""
hash.each { |k,v| string << k << " is " << v << "\n" }
```

If your data structure is an array, or easily transformed into an array, it's usually more efficient to use Array#join:

```
puts hash.keys.join("\n") + "\n"
# key1
# key2
```

Discussion

In languages like Python and Java, it's very inefficient to build a string by starting with an empty string and adding each substring onto the end. In those languages, strings are immutable, so adding one string to another builds an entirely new string. Doing this multiple times creates a huge number of intermediary strings, each of which is only used as a stepping stone to the next string. This wastes time and memory.

In those languages, the most efficient way to build a string is always to put the substrings into an array or another mutable data structure, one that expands dynamically rather than by implicitly creating entirely new objects. Once you're done processing the substrings, you get a single string with the equivalent of Ruby's Array#join. In Java, this is the purpose of the StringBuffer class.

In Ruby, though, strings are just as mutable as arrays. Just like arrays, they can expand as needed, without using much time or memory. The fastest solution to this problem in Ruby is usually to forgo a holding array and tack the substrings directly onto a base string. Sometimes using Array#join is faster, but it's usually pretty close, and the << construction is generally easier to understand.

If efficiency is important to you, don't build a new string when you can append items onto an existing string. Constructs like str << 'a' + 'b' or str << "#{var1} #{var2}" create new strings that are immediately subsumed into the larger string. This is exactly what you're trying to avoid. Use str << var1 << ' ' << var2 instead.

On the other hand, you shouldn't modify strings that aren't yours. Sometimes safety requires that you create a new string. When you define a method that takes a string as an argument, you shouldn't modify that string by appending other strings onto it, unless that's really the point of the method (and unless the method's name ends in an exclamation point, so that callers know it modifies objects in place).

Another caveat: Array#join does not work precisely the same way as repeated appends to a string. Array#join accepts a separator string that it inserts *between* every two elements of the array. Unlike a simple string-building iteration over an array, it will not insert the separator string after the last element in the array. This example illustrates the difference:

```
data = ['1', '2', '3']
s = ''
```

```
data.each { |x| s << x << ' and a '}
s                                       # => "1 and a 2 and a 3 and a "
data.join(' and a ')                    # => "1 and a 2 and a 3"
```

To simulate the behavior of Array#join across an iteration, you can use Enumerable#each_with_index and omit the separator on the last index. This only works if you know how long the Enumerable is going to be:

```
s = ""
data.each_with_index { |x, i| s << x; s << "|" if i < data.length-1 }
s                                       # => "1|2|3"
```

1.2   Substituting Variables into Strings

Problem

You want to create a string that contains a representation of a Ruby variable or expression.

Solution

Within the string, enclose the variable or expression in curly brackets and prefix it with a hash character.

```
number = 5
"The number is #{number}."                  # => "The number is 5."
"The number is #{5}."                        # => "The number is 5."
"The number after #{number} is #{number.next}."
# => "The number after 5 is 6."
"The number prior to #{number} is #{number-1}."
# => "The number prior to 5 is 4."
"We're ##{number}!"                          # => "We're #5!"
```

Discussion

When you define a string by putting it in double quotes, Ruby scans it for special substitution codes. The most common case, so common that you might not even think about it, is that Ruby substitutes a single newline character every time a string contains slash followed by the letter n ("\n").

Ruby supports more complex string substitutions as well. Any text kept within the brackets of the special marker #{} (that is, #{text in here}) is interpreted as a Ruby expression. The result of that expression is substituted into the string that gets created. If the result of the expression is not a string, Ruby calls its to_s method and uses that instead.

Once such a string is created, it is indistinguishable from a string created without using the string interpolation feature:

```
"#{number}" == '5'                          # => true
```

You can use string interpolation to run even large chunks of Ruby code inside a string. This extreme example defines a class within a string; its result is the return value of a method defined in the class. You should never have any reason to do this, but it shows the power of this feature.

```
%{Here is #{class InstantClass
    def bar
        "some text"
    end
  end
  InstantClass.new.bar
}.}
# => "Here is some text."
```

The code run in string interpolations runs in the same context as any other Ruby code in the same location. To take the example above, the `InstantClass` class has now been defined like any other class, and can be used outside the string that defines it.

If a string interpolation calls a method that has side effects, the side effects are triggered. If a string definition sets a variable, that variable is accessible afterwards. It's bad form to rely on this behavior, but you should be aware of it:

```
"I've set x to #{x = 5; x += 1}."    # => "I've set x to 6."
x                                     # => 6
```

To avoid triggering string interpolation, escape the hash characters or put the string in single quotes.

```
"\#{foo}"                             # => "\#{foo}"
'#{foo}'                              # => "\#{foo}"
```

The "here document" construct is an alternative to the %{} construct, which is sometimes more readable. It lets you define a multiline string that only ends when the Ruby parser encounters a certain string on a line by itself:

```
name = "Mr. Lorum"
email = <<END
Dear #{name},

Unfortunately we cannot process your insurance claim at this
time. This is because we are a bakery, not an insurance company.

Signed,
 Nil, Null, and None
 Bakers to Her Majesty the Singleton
END
```

Ruby is pretty flexible about the string you can use to end the "here document":

```
<<end_of_poem
There once was a man from Peru
Whose limericks stopped on line two
end_of_poem
# => "There once was a man from Peru\nWhose limericks stopped on line two\n"
```

See Also

- You can use the technique described in Recipe 1.3, "Substituting Variables into an Existing String," to define a template string or object, and substitute in variables later

1.3 Substituting Variables into an Existing String

Problem

You want to create a string that contains Ruby expressions or variable substitutions, without actually performing the substitutions. You plan to substitute values into the string later, possibly multiple times with different values each time.

Solution

There are two good solutions: printf-style strings, and ERB templates.

Ruby supports a printf-style string format like C's and Python's. Put printf directives into a string and it becomes a template. You can interpolate values into it later using the modulus operator:

```
template = 'Oceania has always been at war with %s.'
template % 'Eurasia'  # => "Oceania has always been at war with Eurasia."
template % 'Eastasia'  # => "Oceania has always been at war with Eastasia."

'To 2 decimal places: %.2f' % Math::PI     # => "To 2 decimal places: 3.14"
'Zero-padded: %.5d' % Math::PI             # => "Zero-padded: 00003"
```

An ERB template looks something like JSP or PHP code. Most of it is treated as a normal string, but certain control sequences are executed as Ruby code. The control sequence is replaced with either the output of the Ruby code, or the value of its last expression:

```
require 'erb'

template = ERB.new %q{Chunky <%= food %>!}
food = "bacon"
template.result(binding)                      # => "Chunky bacon!"
food = "peanut butter"
template.result(binding)                      # => "Chunky peanut butter!"
```

You can omit the call to Kernel#binding if you're not in an irb session:

```
puts template.result
# Chunky peanut butter!
```

You may recognize this format from the .rhtml files used by Rails views: they use ERB behind the scenes.

Discussion

An ERB template can reference variables like food before they're defined. When you call ERB#result, or ERB#run, the template is executed according to the current values of those variables.

Like JSP and PHP code, ERB templates can contain loops and conditionals. Here's a more sophisticated template:

```
template = %q{
<% if problems.empty? %>
  Looks like your code is clean!
<% else %>
  I found the following possible problems with your code:
  <% problems.each do |problem, line| %>
    * <%= problem %> on line <%= line %>
  <% end %>
<% end %>}.gsub(/^\s+/, '')
template = ERB.new(template, nil, '<>')

problems = [["Use of is_a? instead of duck typing", 23],
            ["eval() is usually dangerous", 44]]
template.run(binding)
# I found the following possible problems with your code:
# * Use of is_a? instead of duck typing on line 23
# * eval() is usually dangerous on line 44

problems = []
template.run(binding)
# Looks like your code is clean!
```

ERB is sophisticated, but neither it nor the printf-style strings look like the simple Ruby string substitutions described in Recipe 1.2. There's an alternative. If you use single quotes instead of double quotes to define a string with substitutions, the substitutions won't be activated. You can then use this string as a template with eval:

```
class String
  def substitute(binding=TOPLEVEL_BINDING)
    eval(%{"#{self}"}, binding)
  end
end

template = %q{Chunky #{food}!}                 # => "Chunky \#{food}!"

food = 'bacon'
template.substitute(binding)                    # => "Chunky bacon!"
food = 'peanut butter'
template.substitute(binding)                    # => "Chunky peanut butter!"
```

You must be very careful when using eval: if you use a variable in the wrong way, you could give an attacker the ability to run arbitrary Ruby code in your eval statement. That won't happen in this example since any possible value of food gets stuck into a string definition before it's interpolated:

```
food = '#{system("dir")}'
puts template.substitute(binding)
# Chunky #{system("dir")}!
```

See Also

- This recipe gives basic examples of ERB templates; for more complex examples, see the documentation of the ERB class (*http://www.ruby-doc.org/stdlib/libdoc/ erb/rdoc/classes/ERB.html*)
- Recipe 1.2, "Substituting Variables into Strings"
- Recipe 10.12, "Evaluating Code in an Earlier Context," has more about `Binding` objects

1.4   Reversing a String by Words or Characters

Problem

The letters (or words) of your string are in the wrong order.

Solution

To create a new string that contains a reversed version of your original string, use the reverse method. To reverse a string in place, use the reverse! method.

```
s = ".sdrawkcab si gnirts sihT"
s.reverse                         # => "This string is backwards."
s                                 # => ".sdrawkcab si gnirts sihT"

s.reverse!                        # => "This string is backwards."
s                                 # => "This string is backwards."
```

To reverse the order of the words in a string, split the string into a list of whitespace-separated words, then join the list back into a string.

```
s = "order. wrong the in are words These"
s.split(/(\s+)/).reverse!.join('')   # => "These words are in the wrong order."
s.split(/\b/).reverse!.join('')      # => "These words are in the wrong. order"
```

Discussion

The `String#split` method takes a regular expression to use as a separator. Each time the separator matches part of the string, the portion of the string before the separator goes into a list. split then resumes scanning the rest of the string. The result is a list of strings found between instances of the separator. The regular expression /(\s+)/ matches one or more whitespace characters; this splits the string on word boundaries, which works for us because we want to reverse the order of the words.

The regular expression \b matches a word boundary. This is not the same as matching whitespace, because it also matches punctuation. Note the difference in punctuation between the two final examples in the Solution.

Because the regular expression /(\s+)/ includes a set of parentheses, the separator strings themselves are included in the returned list. Therefore, when we join the strings back together, we've preserved whitespace. This example shows the difference between including the parentheses and omitting them:

```
"Three little  words".split(/\s+/)   # => ["Three", "little", "words"]
"Three little  words".split(/(\s+)/)
# => ["Three", " ", "little", "  ", "words"]
```

See Also

- Recipe 1.9, "Processing a String One Word at a Time," has some regular expressions for alternative definitions of "word"
- Recipe 1.11, "Managing Whitespace"
- Recipe 1.17, "Matching Strings with Regular Expressions"

1.5   Representing Unprintable Characters

Problem

You need to make reference to a control character, a strange UTF-8 character, or some other character that's not on your keyboard.

Solution

Ruby gives you a number of escaping mechanisms to refer to unprintable characters. By using one of these mechanisms within a double-quoted string, you can put any binary character into the string.

You can reference any any binary character by encoding its octal representation into the format "\000", or its hexadecimal representation into the format "\x00".

```
octal = "\000\001\010\020"
octal.each_byte { |x| puts x }
# 0
# 1
# 8
# 16

hexadecimal = "\x00\x01\x10\x20"
hexadecimal.each_byte { |x| puts x }
# 0
# 1
# 16
# 32
```

This makes it possible to represent UTF-8 characters even when you can't type them or display them in your terminal. Try running this program, and then opening the generated file *smiley.html* in your web browser:

```
open('smiley.html', 'wb') do |f|
  f << '<meta http-equiv="Content-Type" content="text/html;charset=UTF-8">'
  f << "\xe2\x98\xBA"
end
```

The most common unprintable characters (such as newline) have special mneumonic aliases consisting of a backslash and a letter.

```
"\a" == "\x07"  # => true  # ASCII 0x07 = BEL (Sound system bell)
"\b" == "\x08"  # => true  # ASCII 0x08 = BS (Backspace)
"\e" == "\x1b"  # => true  # ASCII 0x1B = ESC (Escape)
"\f" == "\x0c"  # => true  # ASCII 0x0C = FF (Form feed)
"\n" == "\x0a"  # => true  # ASCII 0x0A = LF (Newline/line feed)
"\r" == "\x0d"  # => true  # ASCII 0x0D = CR (Carriage return)
"\t" == "\x09"  # => true  # ASCII 0x09 = HT (Tab/horizontal tab)
"\v" == "\x0b"  # => true  # ASCII 0x0B = VT (Vertical tab)
```

Discussion

Ruby stores a string as a sequence of bytes. It makes no difference whether those bytes are printable ASCII characters, binary characters, or a mix of the two.

When Ruby prints out a human-readable string representation of a binary character, it uses the character's \xxx octal representation. Characters with special \x mneumonics are printed as the mneumonic. Printable characters are output as their printable representation, even if another representation was used to create the string.

```
"\x10\x11\xfe\xff"           # => "\020\021\376\377"
"\x48\145\x6c\x6c\157\x0a"   # => "Hello\n"
```

To avoid confusion with the mneumonic characters, a literal backslash in a string is represented by two backslashes. For instance, the two-character string consisting of a backslash and the 14th letter of the alphabet is represented as "\\n".

```
"\\".size          # => 1
"\\" == "\x5c"     # => true
"\\n"[0] == ?\\    # => true
"\\n"[1] == ?n     # => true
"\\n" =~ /\n/      # => nil
```

Ruby also provides special shortcuts for representing keyboard sequences like Control-C. "\C-_x_" represents the sequence you get by holding down the control key and hitting the *x* key, and "\M-_x_" represents the sequence you get by holding down the Alt (or Meta) key and hitting the *x* key:

```
"\C-a\C-b\C-c"     # => "\001\002\003"
"\M-a\M-b\M-c"     # => "\341\342\343"
```

Shorthand representations of binary characters can be used whenever Ruby expects a character. For instance, you can get the decimal byte number of a special character by prefixing it with ?, and you can use shorthand representations in regular expression character ranges.

```
?\C-a                                  # => 1
?\M-z                                  # => 250

contains_control_chars = /[\C-a-\C-^]/
'Foobar' =~ contains_control_chars     # => nil
"Foo\C-zbar" =~ contains_control_chars # => 3

contains_upper_chars = /[\x80-\xff]/
'Foobar' =~ contains_upper_chars       # => nil
"Foo\212bar" =~ contains_upper_chars   # => 3
```

Here's a sinister application that scans logged keystrokes for special characters:

```
def snoop_on_keylog(input)
  input.each_byte  do |b|
    case b
      when ?\C-c; puts 'Control-C: stopped a process?'
      when ?\C-z; puts 'Control-Z: suspended a process?'
      when ?\n;   puts 'Newline.'
      when ?\M-x; puts 'Meta-x: using Emacs?'
    end
  end
end

snoop_on_keylog("ls -ltR\003emacsHello\012\370rot13-other-window\012\032")
# Control-C: stopped a process?
# Newline.
# Meta-x: using Emacs?
# Newline.
# Control-Z: suspended a process?
```

Special characters are only interpreted in strings delimited by double quotes, or strings created with %{} or %Q{}. They are not interpreted in strings delimited by single quotes, or strings created with %q{}. You can take advantage of this feature when you need to display special characters to the end-user, or create a string containing a lot of backslashes.

```
puts "foo\tbar"
# foo     bar
puts %{foo\tbar}
# foo     bar
puts %Q{foo\tbar}
# foo     bar

puts 'foo\tbar'
# foo\tbar
puts %q{foo\tbar}
# foo\tbar
```

If you come to Ruby from Python, this feature can take advantage of you, making you wonder why the special characters in your single-quoted strings aren't treated as special. If you need to create a string with special characters and a lot of embedded double quotes, use the %{} construct.

1.6   Converting Between Characters and Values

Problem

You want to see the ASCII code for a character, or transform an ASCII code into a string.

Solution

To see the ASCII code for a specific character as an integer, use the ? operator:

```
?a                      # => 97
?!                      # => 33
?\n                     # => 10
```

To see the integer value of a particular in a string, access it as though it were an element of an array:

```
'a'[0]                  # => 97
'bad sound'[1]          # => 97
```

To see the ASCII character corresponding to a given number, call its #chr method. This returns a string containing only one character:

```
97.chr                  # => "a"
33.chr                  # => "!"
10.chr                  # => "\n"
0.chr                   # => "\000"
256.chr                 # RangeError: 256 out of char range
```

Discussion

Though not technically an array, a string acts a lot like like an array of Fixnum objects: one Fixnum for each byte in the string. Accessing a single element of the "array" yields a Fixnum for the corresponding byte: for textual strings, this is an ASCII code. Calling String#each_byte lets you iterate over the Fixnum objects that make up a string.

See Also

- Recipe 1.8, "Processing a String One Character at a Time"

1.7   Converting Between Strings and Symbols

Problem

You want to get a string containing the label of a Ruby symbol, or get the Ruby symbol that corresponds to a given string.

Solution

To turn a symbol into a string, use `Symbol#to_s`, or `Symbol#id2name`, for which `to_s` is an alias.

```
:a_symbol.to_s              # => "a_symbol"
:AnotherSymbol.id2name      # => "AnotherSymbol"
:"Yet another symbol!".to_s # => "Yet another symbol!"
```

You usually reference a symbol by just typing its name. If you're given a string in code and need to get the corresponding symbol, you can use `String.intern`:

```
:dodecahedron.object_id          # => 4565262
symbol_name = "dodecahedron"
symbol_name.intern               # => :dodecahedron
symbol_name.intern.object_id     # => 4565262
```

Discussion

A `Symbol` is about the most basic Ruby object you can create. It's just a name and an internal ID. Symbols are useful becase a given symbol name refers to the same object throughout a Ruby program.

Symbols are often more efficient than strings. Two strings with the same contents are two different objects (one of the strings might be modified later on, and become different), but for any given name there is only one `Symbol` object. This can save both time and memory.

```
"string".object_id  # => 1503030
"string".object_id  # => 1500330
:symbol.object_id   # => 4569358
:symbol.object_id   # => 4569358
```

If you have *n* references to a name, you can keep all those references with only one symbol, using only one object's worth of memory. With strings, the same code would use *n* different objects, all containing the same data. It's also faster to compare two symbols than to compare two strings, because Ruby only has to check the object IDs.

```
"string1" == "string2"  # => false
:symbol1 == :symbol2    # => false
```

Finally, to quote Ruby hacker Jim Weirich on when to use a string versus a symbol:

- If the contents (the sequence of characters) of the object are important, use a string.
- If the identity of the object is important, use a symbol.

See Also

- See Recipe 5.1, "Using Symbols as Hash Keys" for one use of symbols
- Recipe 8.12, "Simulating Keyword Arguments," has another

- Chapter 10, especially Recipe 10.4, "Getting a Reference to a Method" and Recipe 10.10, "Avoiding Boilerplate Code with Metaprogramming"
- See *http://glu.ttono.us/articles/2005/08/19/understanding-ruby-symbols* for a symbol primer

1.8   Processing a String One Character at a Time

Problem

You want to process each character of a string individually.

Solution

If you're processing an ASCII document, then each byte corresponds to one character. Use String#each_byte to yield each byte of a string as a number, which you can turn into a one-character string:

```
'foobar'.each_byte { |x| puts "#{x} = #{x.chr}" }
# 102 = f
# 111 = o
# 111 = o
# 98 = b
# 97 = a
# 114 = r
```

Use String#scan to yield each character of a string as a new one-character string:

```
'foobar'.scan( /./ ) { |c| puts c }
# f
# o
# o
# b
# a
# r
```

Discussion

Since a string is a sequence of bytes, you might think that the String#each method would iterate over the sequence, the way Array#each does. But String#each is actually used to split a string on a given record separator (by default, the newline):

```
"foo\nbar".each { |x| puts x }
# foo
# bar
```

The string equivalent of Array#each method is actually each_byte. A string stores its characters as a sequence of Fixnum objects, and each_bytes yields that sequence.

String#each_byte is faster than String#scan, so if you're processing an ASCII file, you might want to use String#each_byte and convert to a string every number passed into the code block (as seen in the Solution).

`String#scan` works by applying a given regular expression to a string, and yielding each match to the code block you provide. The regular expression /./ matches every character in the string, in turn.

If you have the `$KCODE` variable set correctly, then the `scan` technique will work on UTF-8 strings as well. This is the simplest way to sneak a notion of "character" into Ruby's byte-based strings.

Here's a Ruby string containing the UTF-8 encoding of the French phrase "ça va":

```
french = "\xc3\xa7a va"
```

Even if your terminal can't properly display the character "ç", you can see how the behavior of `String#scan` changes when you make the regular expression Unicode-aware, or set `$KCODE` so that Ruby handles all strings as UTF-8:

```
french.scan(/./) { |c| puts c }
#
#
# a
#
# v
# a

french.scan(/./u) { |c| puts c }
# ç
# a
#
# v
# a

$KCODE = 'u'
french.scan(/./) { |c| puts c }
# ç
# a
#
# v
# a
```

Once Ruby knows to treat strings as UTF-8 instead of ASCII, it starts treating the two bytes representing the "ç" as a single character. Even if you can't see UTF-8, you can write programs that handle it correctly.

See Also

- Recipe 11.12, "Converting from One Encoding to Another"

1.9   Processing a String One Word at a Time

Problem

You want to split a piece of text into words, and operate on each word.

Solution

First decide what you mean by "word." What separates one word from another? Only whitespace? Whitespace or punctuation? Is "johnny-come-lately" one word or three? Build a regular expression that matches a single word according to whatever definition you need (there are some samples are in the Discussion).

Then pass that regular expression into `String#scan`. Every word it finds, it will yield to a code block. The `word_count` method defined below takes a piece of text and creates a histogram of word frequencies. Its regular expression considers a "word" to be a string of Ruby identifier characters: letters, numbers, and underscores.

```
class String
  def word_count
    frequencies = Hash.new(0)
    downcase.scan(/\w+/) { |word| frequencies[word] += 1 }
   return frequencies
  end
end

%{Dogs dogs dog dog dogs.}.word_count
# => {"dogs"=>3, "dog"=>2}
%{"I have no shame," I said.}.word_count
# => {"no"=>1, "shame"=>1, "have"=>1, "said"=>1, "i"=>2}
```

Discussion

The regular expression /\w+/ is nice and simple, but you can probably do better for your application's definition of "word." You probably don't consider two words separated by an underscore to be a single word. Some English words, like "pan-fried" and "fo'c'sle", contain embedded punctuation. Here are a few more definitions of "word" in regular expression form:

```
# Just like /\w+/, but doesn't consider underscore part of a word.
/[0-9A-Za-z]/

# Anything that's not whitespace is a word.
/[^\S]+/

# Accept dashes and apostrophes as parts of words.
/[-'\w]+/

# A pretty good heuristic for matching English words.
/(\w+([-'.]\w+)*/
```

The last one deserves some explanation. It matches embedded punctuation within a word, but not at the edges. "Work-in-progress" is recognized as a single word, and "—-never—-" is recognized as the word "never" surrounded by punctuation. This regular expression can even pick out abbreviations and acronyms such as "Ph.D" and "U.N.C.L.E.", though it can't distinguish between the final period of an acronym and the period that ends a sentence. This means that "E.F.F." will be recognized as the word "E.F.F" and then a nonword period.

Let's rewrite our word_count method to use that regular expression. We can't use the original implementation, because its code block takes only one argument. String#scan passes its code block one argument for each match group in the regular expression, and our improved regular expression has two match groups. The first match group is the one that actually contains the word. So we must rewrite word_count so that its code block takes two arguments, and ignores the second one:

```
class String
  def word_count
    frequencies = Hash.new(0)
    downcase.scan(/(\w+([-'.]\w+)*)/) { |word, ignore| frequencies[word] += 1 }
    return frequencies
  end
end

%{"That F.B.I. fella--he's quite the man-about-town."}.word_count
# => {"quite"=>1, "f.b.i"=>1, "the"=>1, "fella"=>1, "that"=>1,
#     "man-about-town"=>1, "he's"=>1}
```

Note that the "\w" character set matches different things depending on the value of $KCODE. By default, "\w" matches only characters that are part of ASCII words:

```
french = "il \xc3\xa9tait une fois"
french.word_count
# => {"fois"=>1, "une"=>1, "tait"=>1, "il"=>1}
```

If you turn on Ruby's UTF-8 support, the "\w" character set matches more characters:

```
$KCODE='u'
french.word_count
# => {"fois"=>1, "une"=>1, "était"=>1, "il"=>1}
```

The regular expression group \b matches a word *boundary*: that is, the last part of a word before a piece of whitespace or punctuation. This is useful for String#split (see Recipe 1.4), but not so useful for String#scan.

See Also

- Recipe 1.4, "Reversing a String by Words or Characters"
- The Facets core library defines a String#each_word method, using the regular expression /([-'\w]+)/

1.10 Changing the Case of a String

Problem

Your string is in the wrong case, or no particular case at all.

Solution

The `String` class provides a variety of case-shifting methods:

```
s = 'HELLO, I am not here. I WENT to tHe MaRKEt.'
s.upcase          # => "HELLO, I AM NOT HERE. I WENT TO THE MARKET."
s.downcase        # => "hello, i am not here. i went to the market."
s.swapcase        # => "hello, i AM NOT HERE. i went TO ThE mArKeT."
s.capitalize      # => "Hello, i am not here. i went to the market."
```

Discussion

The `upcase` and `downcase` methods force all letters in the string to upper- or lower-case, respectively. The `swapcase` method transforms uppercase letters into lowercase letters and vice versa. The `capitalize` method makes the first character of the string uppercase, if it's a letter, and makes all other letters in the string lowercase.

All four methods have corresponding methods that modify a string in place rather than creating a new one: `upcase!`, `downcase!`, `swapcase!`, and `capitalize!`. Assuming you don't need the original string, these methods will save memory, especially if the string is large.

```
un_banged = 'Hello world.'
un_banged.upcase    # => "HELLO WORLD."
un_banged           # => "Hello world."

banged = 'Hello world.'
banged.upcase!      # => "HELLO WORLD."
banged              # => "HELLO WORLD."
```

To capitalize a string without lowercasing the rest of the string (for instance, because the string contains proper nouns), you can modify the first character of the string in place. This corresponds to the `capitalize!` method. If you want something more like `capitalize`, you can create a new string out of the old one.

```
class String
  def capitalize_first_letter
    self[0].chr.capitalize + self[1, size]
  end

  def capitalize_first_letter!
    unless self[0] == (c = self[0,1].upcase[0])
      self[0] = c
      self
    end
    # Return nil if no change was made, like upcase! et al.
  end
end

s = 'i told Alice. She remembers now.'
s.capitalize_first_letter     # => "I told Alice. She remembers now."
s                             # => "i told Alice. She remembers now."
s.capitalize_first_letter!
s                             # => "I told Alice. She remembers now."
```

To change the case of specific letters while leaving the rest alone, you can use the `tr` or `tr!` methods, which translate one character into another:

```
'LOWERCASE ALL VOWELS'.tr('AEIOU', 'aeiou')
# => "LoWeRCaSe aLL VoWeLS"

'Swap case of ALL VOWELS'.tr('AEIOUaeiou', 'aeiouAEIOU')
# => "SwAp cAsE Of aLL VoWeLS"
```

See Also

- Recipe 1.18, "Replacing Multiple Patterns in a Single Pass"
- The Facets Core library adds a `String#camelcase` method; it also defines the case predicates `String#lowercase?` and `String#uppercase?`

1.11 Managing Whitespace

Problem

Your string contains too much whitespace, not enough whitespace, or the wrong kind of whitespace.

Solution

Use `strip` to remove whitespace from the beginning and end of a string:

```
" \tWhitespace at beginning and end. \t\n\n".strip
```

Add whitespace to one or both ends of a string with `ljust`, `rjust`, and `center`:

```
s = "Some text."
s.center(15)
s.ljust(15)
s.rjust(15)
```

Use the gsub method with a string or regular expression to make more complex changes, such as to replace one type of whitespace with another.

```
#Normalize Ruby source code by replacing tabs with spaces
rubyCode.gsub("\t", "    ")

#Transform Windows-style newlines to Unix-style newlines
"Line one\n\rLine two\n\r".gsub(\n\r", "\n")
# => "Line one\nLine two\n"

#Transform all runs of whitespace into a single space character
"\n\rThis string\t\t\tuses\n all\tsorts\nof whitespace.".gsub(/\s+/," ")
# => " This string uses all sorts of whitespace."
```

Discussion

What counts as whitespace? Any of these five characters: space, tab (\t), newline (\n), linefeed (\r), and form feed (\f). The regular expression /\s/ matches any one character from that set. The `strip` method strips any combination of those characters from the beginning or end of a string.

In rare cases you may need to handle oddball "space" characters like backspace (\b or \010) and vertical tab (\v or \012). These are not part of the \s character group in a regular expression, so use a custom character group to catch these characters.

```
" \bIt's whitespace, Jim,\vbut not as we know it.\n".gsub(/[\s\b\v]+/, " ")
# => "It's whitespace, Jim, but not as we know it."
```

To remove whitespace from only one end of a string, use the `lstrip` or `rstrip` method:

```
s = "   Whitespace madness! "
s.lstrip                           # => "Whitespace madness! "
s.rstrip                           # => "   Whitespace madness!"
```

The methods for adding whitespace to a string (center, ljust, and rjust) take a single argument: the total length of the string they should return, counting the original string and any added whitespace. If center can't center a string perfectly, it'll put one extra space on the right:

```
"four".center(5)                   # => "four "
"four".center(6)                   # => " four "
```

Like most string-modifying methods, `strip`, `gsub`, `lstrip`, and `rstrip` have counterparts `strip!`, `gsub!`, `lstrip!`, and `rstrip!`, which modify the string in place.

1.12 Testing Whether an Object Is String-Like

Problem

You want to see whether you can treat an object as a string.

Solution

Check whether the object defines the to_str method.

```
'A string'.respond_to? :to_str     # => true
Exception.new.respond_to? :to_str  # => true
4.respond_to? :to_str              # => false
```

More generally, check whether the object defines the specific method of String you're thinking about calling. If the object defines that method, the right thing to do is usually to go ahead and call the method. This will make your code work in more places:

```
def join_to_successor(s)
  raise ArgumentError, 'No successor method!' unless s.respond_to? :succ
  return "#{s}#{s.succ}"
end

join_to_successor('a')             # => "ab"
join_to_successor(4)               # => "45"
```

```
join_to_successor(4.01)
# ArgumentError: No successor method!
```

If I'd checked s.is_a? String instead of s.respond_to? :succ, then I wouldn't have been able to call join_to_successor on an integer.

Discussion

This is the simplest example of Ruby's philosophy of "duck typing:" if an object quacks like a duck (or acts like a string), just go ahead and treat it as a duck (or a string). Whenever possible, you should treat objects according to the methods they define rather than the classes from which they inherit or the modules they include.

Calling obj.is_a? String will tell you whether an object derives from the String class, but it will overlook objects that, though intended to be used as strings, don't inherit from String.

Exceptions, for instance, are essentially strings that have extra information associated with them. But they don't subclass class name "String". Code that uses is_a? String to check for stringness will overlook the essential stringness of Exceptions. Many add-on Ruby modules define other classes that can act as strings: code that calls is_a? String will break when given an instance of one of those classes.

The idea to take to heart here is the general rule of duck typing: to see whether provided data implements a certain method, use respond_to? instead of checking the class. This lets a future user (possibly yourself!) create new classes that offer the same capability, without being tied down to the preexisting class structure. All you have to do is make the method names match up.

See Also

- Chapter 8, especially the chapter introduction and Recipe 8.3, "Checking Class or Module Membership"

1.13   Getting the Parts of a String You Want

Problem

You want only certain pieces of a string.

Solution

To get a substring of a string, call its slice method, or use the array index operator (that is, call the [ ] method). Either method accepts a Range describing which characters to retrieve, or two Fixnum arguments: the index at which to start, and the length of the substring to be extracted.

```
s = 'My kingdom for a string!'
s.slice(3,7)                            # => "kingdom"
```

```
s[3,7]                        # => "kingdom"
s[0,3]                        # => "My "
s[11, 5]                      # => "for a"
s[11, 17]                     # => "for a string!"
```

To get the first portion of a string that matches a regular expression, pass the regular expression into slice or [ ]:

```
s[/.ing/]                     # => "king"
s[/str.*/]                    # => "string!"
```

Discussion

To access a specific byte of a string as a Fixnum, pass only one argument (the zero-based index of the character) into String#slice or [ ] method. To access a specific byte as a single-character string, pass in its index and the number 1.

```
s.slice(3)                    # => 107
s[3]                          # => 107
107.chr                       # => "k"
s.slice(3,1)                  # => "k"
s[3,1]                        # => "k"
```

To count from the end of the string instead of the beginning, use negative indexes:

```
s.slice(-7,3)                 # => "str"
s[-7,6]                       # => "string"
```

If the length of your proposed substring exceeds the length of the string, slice or [ ] will return the entire string after that point. This leads to a simple shortcut for getting the rightmost portion of a string:

```
s[15...s.length]              # => "a string!"
```

See Also

- Recipe 1.9, "Processing a String One Word at a Time"
- Recipe 1.17, "Matching Strings with Regular Expressions"

1.14 Handling International Encodings

Problem

You need to handle strings that contain nonASCII characters: probably Unicode characters encoded in UTF-8.

Solution

To use Unicode in Ruby, simply add the following to the beginning of code.

```
$KCODE='u'
require 'jcode'
```

You can also invoke the Ruby interpreter with arguments that do the same thing:

```
$ ruby -Ku -rjcode
```

If you use a Unix environment, you can add the arguments to the shebang line of your Ruby application:

```
#!/usr/bin/ruby -Ku -rjcode
```

The jcode library overrides most of the methods of String and makes them capable of handling multibyte text. The exceptions are String#length, String#count, and String#size, which are not overridden. Instead jcode defines three new methods: String#jlength, string#jcount, and String#jsize.

Discussion

Consider a UTF-8 string that encodes six Unicode characters: efbca1 (A), efbca2 (B), and so on up to UTF-8 efbca6 (F):

```
string = "\xef\xbc\xa1" + "\xef\xbc\xa2" + "\xef\xbc\xa3" +
         "\xef\xbc\xa4" + "\xef\xbc\xa5" + "\xef\xbc\xa6"
```

The string contains 18 bytes that encode 6 characters:

```
string.size                              # => 18
string.jsize                             # => 6
```

String#count is a method that takes a strong of bytes, and counts how many times those bytes occurs in the string. String#jcount takes a string of *characters* and counts how many times those characters occur in the string:

```
string.count "\xef\xbc\xa2"              # => 13
string.jcount "\xef\xbc\xa2"             # => 1
```

String#count treats "\xef\xbc\xa2" as three separate bytes, and counts the number of times each of those bytes shows up in the string. String#jcount treats the same string as a single character, and looks for that character in the string, finding it only once.

```
"\xef\xbc\xa2".length                    # => 3
"\xef\xbc\xa2".jlength                    # => 1
```

Apart from these differences, Ruby handles most Unicode behind the scenes. Once you have your data in UTF-8 format, you really don't have to worry. Given that Ruby's creator Yukihiro Matsumoto is Japanese, it is no wonder that Ruby handles Unicode so elegantly.

See Also

- If you have text in some other encoding and need to convert it to UTF-8, use the iconv library, as described in Recipe 11.2, "Extracting Data from a Document's Tree Structure"

- There are several online search engines for Unicode characters; two good ones are at *http://isthisthingon.org/unicode/* and *http://www.fileformat.info/info/unicode/char/search.htm*

1.15 Word-Wrapping Lines of Text

Problem

You want to turn a string full of miscellaneous whitespace into a string formatted with linebreaks at appropriate intervals, so that the text can be displayed in a window or sent as an email.

Solution

The simplest way to add newlines to a piece of text is to use a regular expression like the following.

```
def wrap(s, width=78)
  s.gsub(/(.{1,#{width}})(\s+|\Z)/, "\\1\n")
end

wrap("This text is too short to be wrapped.")
# => "This text is too short to be wrapped.\n"

puts wrap("This text is not too short to be wrapped.", 20)
# This text is not too
# short to be wrapped.

puts wrap("These ten-character columns are stifling my creativity!", 10)
# These
# ten-character
# columns
# are
# stifling
# my
# creativity!
```

Discussion

The code given in the Solution preserves the original formatting of the string, inserting additional line breaks where necessary. This works well when you want to preserve the existing formatting while squishing everything into a smaller space:

```
poetry = %q{It is an ancient Mariner,
And he stoppeth one of three.
"By thy long beard and glittering eye,
Now wherefore stopp'st thou me?}

puts wrap(poetry, 20)
# It is an ancient
# Mariner,
# And he stoppeth one
# of three.
# "By thy long beard
# and glittering eye,
# Now wherefore
# stopp'st thou me?
```

But sometimes the existing whitespace isn't important, and preserving it makes the result look bad:

```
prose = %q{I find myself alone these days, more often than not,
watching the rain run down nearby windows. How long has it been
raining? The newspapers now print the total, but no one reads them
anymore.}

puts wrap(prose, 60)
# I find myself alone these days, more often than not,
# watching the rain run down nearby windows. How long has it
# been
# raining? The newspapers now print the total, but no one
# reads them
# anymore.
```

Looks pretty ragged. In this case, we want to get replace the original newlines with new ones. The simplest way to do this is to preprocess the string with another regular expression:

```
def reformat_wrapped(s, width=78)
  s.gsub(/\s+/, " ").gsub(/(.{1,#{width}})( |\Z)/, "\\1\n")
end
```

But regular expressions are relatively slow; it's much more efficient to tear the string apart into words and rebuild it:

```
def reformat_wrapped(s, width=78)
  lines = []
  line = ""
  s.split(/\s+/).each do |word|
    if line.size + word.size >= width
      lines << line
      line = word
    elsif line.empty?
      line = word
    else
      line << " " << word
    end
  end
  lines << line if line
  return lines.join "\n"
end

puts reformat_wrapped(prose, 60)
# I find myself alone these days, more often than not,
# watching the rain run down nearby windows. How long has it
# been raining? The newspapers now print the total, but no one
# reads them anymore.
```

See Also

- The Facets Core library defines String#word_wrap and String#word_wrap! methods

1.16 Generating a Succession of Strings

Problem

You want to iterate over a series of alphabetically-increasing strings as you would over a series of numbers.

Solution

If you know both the start and end points of your succession, you can simply create a range and use Range#each, as you would for numbers:

```
('aa'..'ag').each { |x| puts x }
# aa
# ab
# ac
# ad
# ae
# af
# ag
```

The method that generates the successor of a given string is String#succ. If you don't know the end point of your succession, you can define a generator that uses succ, and break from the generator when you're done.

```
def endless_string_succession(start)
  while true
    yield start
    start = start.succ
  end
end
```

This code iterates over an endless succession of strings, stopping when the last two letters are the same:

```
endless_string_succession('fol') do |x|
  puts x
  break if x[-1] == x[-2]
end
# fol
# fom
# fon
# foo
```

Discussion

Imagine a string as an odometer. Each character position of the string has a separate dial, and the current odometer reading is your string. Each dial always shows the same kind of character. A dial that starts out showing a number will always show a number. A character that starts out showing an uppercase letter will always show an uppercase letter.

The string succession operation increments the odometer. It moves the rightmost dial forward one space. This might make, the rightmost dial wrap around to the beginning: if that happens, the dial directly to its left is also moved forward one space. This might make *that* dial wrap around to the beginning, and so on:

```ruby
'89999'.succ                        # => "90000"
'nzzzz'.succ                        # => "oaaaa"
```

When the leftmost dial wraps around, a new dial is added to the left of the odometer. The new dial is always of the same type as the old leftmost dial. If the old leftmost dial showed capital letters, then so will the new leftmost dial:

```ruby
'Zzz'.succ                          # => "AAaa"
```

Lowercase letters wrap around from "z" to "a". If the first character is a lowercase letter, then when it wraps around, an "a" is added on to the beginning of the string:

```ruby
'z'.succ                            # => "aa"
'aa'.succ                           # =>  "ab"
'zz'.succ                           # => "aaa"
```

Uppercase letters work in the same way: "Z" becomes "A". Lowercase and uppercase letters never mix.

```ruby
'AA'.succ       # =>  "AB"
'AZ'.succ                           # =>   "BA"
'ZZ'.succ # => "AAA"
'aZ'.succ                           # =>   "bA"
'Zz'.succ                           # =>  "AAa"
```

Digits in a string are treated as numbers, and wrap around from 9 to 0, just like a car odometer.

```ruby
'foo19'.succ                # => "foo20"
'foo99'.succ                        # => "fop00"
'99'.succ                           # => "100"
'9Z99'.succ  # => "10A00"
```

Characters other than alphanumerics are not incremented unless they are the only characters in the string. They are simply ignored when calculating the succession, and reproduced in the same positions in the new string. This lets you build formatting into the strings you want to increment.

```ruby
'10-99'.succ                        # => "11-00"
```

When nonalphanumerics are the only characters in the string, they are incremented according to ASCII order. Eventually an alphanumeric will show up, and the rules for strings containing alphanumerics will take over.

```ruby
'a-a'.succ                          # => "a-b"
'z-z'.succ                          # => "aa-a"
'Hello!'.succ # => "Hellp!"
%q{'zz'}.succ                       # => "'aaa'"
%q{z'zz'}.succ                      # => "aa'aa'"
'$$$$'.succ                         # => "$$$%"
```

```
s = '!@-'
13.times { puts s = s.succ }
                                        # !@.
                                        # !@/
                                        # !@0
                                        # !@1
                                        # !@2
                                        # ...
                                        # !@8
                                        # !@9
                                        # !@10
```

There's no reverse version of String#succ. Matz, and the community as a whole, think there's not enough demand for such a method to justify the work necessary to handle all the edge cases. If you need to iterate over a succession of strings in reverse, your best bet is to transform the range into an array and iterate over that in reverse:

```
("a".."e").to_a.reverse_each { |x| puts x }
                                        # e
                                        # d
                                        # c
                                        # b
                                        # a
```

See Also

- Recipe 2.15, "Generating a Sequence of Numbers"
- Recipe 3.4, "Iterating Over Dates"

1.17   Matching Strings with Regular Expressions

Problem

You want to know whether or not a string matches a certain pattern.

Solution

You can usually describe the pattern as a regular expression. The =~ operator tests a string against a regular expression:

```
string = 'This is a 30-character string.'

if string =~ /([0-9]+)-character/ and $1.to_i == string.length
  "Yes, there are #$1 characters in that string."
end
# => "Yes, there are 30 characters in that string."
```

You can also use Regexp#match:

```
match = Regexp.compile('([0-9]+)-character').match(string)
if match && match[1].to_i == string.length
  "Yes, there are #{match[1]} characters in that string."
end
# => "Yes, there are 30 characters in that string."
```

You can check a string against a series of regular expressions with a case statement:

```
string = "123"

case string
when /^[a-zA-Z]+$/
  "Letters"
when /^[0-9]+$/
  "Numbers"
else
  "Mixed"
end
# => "Numbers"
```

Discussion

Regular expressions are a cryptic but powerful minilanguage for string matching and substring extraction. They've been around for a long time in Unix utilities like sed, but Perl was the first general-purpose programming language to include them. Now almost all modern languages have support for Perl-style regular expression.

Ruby provides several ways of initializing regular expressions. The following are all equivalent and create equivalent Regexp objects:

```
/something/
Regexp.new("something")
Regexp.compile("something")
%r{something}
```

The following modifiers are also of note.

Regexp::IGNORECASE	i	Makes matches case-insensitive.
Regexp::MULTILINE	m	Normally, a regexp matches against a single line of a string. This will cause a regexp to treat line breaks like any other character.
Regexp::EXTENDED	x	This modifier lets you space out your regular expressions with whitespace and comments, making them more legible.

Here's how to use these modifiers to create regular expressions:

```
/something/mxi
Regexp.new('something',
           Regexp::EXTENDED + Regexp::IGNORECASE + Regexp::MULTILINE)
%r{something}mxi
```

Here's how the modifiers work:

```
case_insensitive = /mangy/i
case_insensitive =~ "I'm mangy!"                 # => 4
case_insensitive =~ "Mangy Jones, at your service." # => 0

multiline = /a.b/m
multiline =~ "banana\nbanana"                     # => 5
/a.b/ =~ "banana\nbanana"                         # => nil
```

```
# But note:
/a\nb/ =~ "banana\nbanana"                              # => 5

extended = %r{ \ was       # Match " was"
                \s         # Match one whitespace character
                a          # Match "a" }xi
extended =~ "What was Alfred doing here?"               # => 4
extended =~ "My, that was a yummy mango."               # => 8
extended =~ "It was\n\n\na fool's errand"               # => nil
```

See Also

- *Mastering Regular Expressions* by Jeffrey Friedl (O'Reilly) gives a concise introduction to regular expressions, with many real-world examples
- RegExLib.com provides a searchable database of regular expressions (*http://regexlib.com/default.aspx*)
- A Ruby-centric regular expression tutorial (*http://www.regular-expressions.info/ruby.html*)
- ri Regexp
- Recipe 1.19, "Validating an Email Address"

1.18 Replacing Multiple Patterns in a Single Pass

Problem

You want to perform multiple, simultaneous search-and-replace operations on a string.

Solution

Use the Regexp.union method to aggregate the regular expressions you want to match into one big regular expression that matches any of them. Pass the big regular expression into String#gsub, along with a code block that takes a MatchData object. You can detect which of your search terms actually triggered the regexp match, and choose the appropriate replacement term:

```
class String
  def mgsub(key_value_pairs=[].freeze)
    regexp_fragments = key_value_pairs.collect { |k,v| k }
    gsub(Regexp.union(*regexp_fragments)) do |match|
      key_value_pairs.detect{|k,v| k =~ match}[1]
    end
  end
end
```

Here's a simple example:

```
"GO HOME!".mgsub([[/.*GO/i, 'Home'], [/home/i, 'is where the heart is']])
# => "Home is where the heart is!"
```

This example replaces all letters with pound signs, and all pound signs with the letter P:

```
"Here is number #123".mgsub([[/[a-z]/i, '#'], [/#/, 'P']])
# => "#### ## ###### P123"
```

Discussion

The naive solution is to simply string together multiple gsub calls. The following examples, copied from the solution, show why this is often a bad idea:

```
"GO HOME!".gsub(/.*GO/i, 'Home').gsub(/home/i, 'is where the heart is')
# => "is where the heart is is where the heart is!"

"Here is number #123".gsub(/[a-z]/i, "#").gsub(/#/, "P")
# => "PPPP PP PPPPPP P123"
```

In both cases, our replacement strings turned out to match the search term of a later gsub call. Our replacement strings were themselves subject to search-and-replace. In the first example, the conflict can be fixed by reversing the order of the substitutions. The second example shows a case where reversing the order won't help. You need to do all your replacements in a single pass over the string.

The mgsub method will take a hash, but it's safer to pass in an array of key-value pairs. This is because elements in a hash come out in no particular order, so you can't control the order of substution. Here's a demonstration of the problem:

```
"between".mgsub(/ee/ => 'AA', /e/ => 'E')      # Bad code
# => "bEtwEEn"

"between".mgsub([[/ee/, 'AA'], [/e/, 'E']])     # Good code
# => "bEtwAAn"
```

In the second example, the first substitution runs first. In the first example, it runs second (and doesn't find anything to replace) because of a quirk of Ruby's Hash implementation.

If performance is important, you may want to rethink how you implement mgsub. The more search and replace terms you add to the array of key-value pairs, the longer it will take, because the detect method performs a set of regular expression checks for every match found in the string.

See Also

- Recipe 1.17, "Matching Strings with Regular Expressions"
- Confused by the *regexp_fragments syntax in the call to Regexp.union? Take a look at Recipe 8.11, "Accepting or Passing a Variable Number of Arguments"

1.19 Validating an Email Address

Problem

You need to see whether an email address is valid.

Solution

Here's a sampling of valid email addresses you might encounter:

```
test_addresses = [ #The following are valid addresses according to RFC822.
                   'joe@example.com', 'joe.bloggs@mail.example.com',
                   'joe+ruby-mail@example.com', 'joe(and-mary)@example.museum',
                   'joe@localhost',
```

Here are some invalid email addresses you might encounter:

```
                   # Complete the list with some invalid addresses
                   'joe', 'joe@', '@example.com',
                   'joe@example@example.com',
                   'joe and mary@example.com' ]
```

And here are some regular expressions that do an okay job of filtering out bad email addresses. The first one does very basic checking for ill-formed addresses:

```
valid = '[^ @]+' # Exclude characters always invalid in email addresses
username_and_machine = /^#{valid}@#{valid}$/

test_addresses.collect { |i| i =~ username_and_machine }
# => [0, 0, 0, 0, 0, nil, nil, nil, nil, nil]
```

The second one prohibits the use of local-network addresses like "joe@localhost". Most applications should prohibit such addresses.

```
username_and_machine_with_tld = /^#{valid}@#{valid}\.#{valid}$/

test_addresses.collect { |i| i =~ username_and_machine_with_tld }
# => [0, 0, 0, 0, nil, nil, nil, nil, nil, nil]
```

However, the odds are good that you're solving the wrong problem.

Discussion

Most email address validation is done with naive regular expressions like the ones given above. Unfortunately, these regular expressions are usually written too strictly, and reject many email addresses. This is a common source of frustration for people with unusual email addresses like *joe(and-mary)@example.museum*, or people taking advantage of special features of email, as in *joe+ruby-mail@example.com*. The regular expressions given above err on the opposite side: they'll accept some syntactically invalid email addresses, but they won't reject valid addresses.

Why not give a simple regular expression that always works? Because there's no such thing. The definition of the syntax is anything but simple. Perl hacker Paul Warren defined an 6343-character regular expression for Perl's Mail::RFC822::Address module, and even it needs some preprocessing to accept absolutely every allowable email address. Warren's regular expression will work unaltered in Ruby, but if you really want it, you should go online and find it, because it would be foolish to try to type it in.

Check validity, not correctness

Even given a regular expression or other tool that infallibly separates the RFC822-compliant email addresses from the others, you can't check the *validity* of an email address just by looking at it; you can only check its syntactic correctness.

It's easy to mistype your username or domain name, giving out a perfectly valid email address that belongs to someone else. It's trivial for a malicious user to make up a valid email address that doesn't work at all—I did it earlier with the *joe@example.com* nonsense. *!@* is a valid email address according to the regexp test, but no one in this universe uses it. You can't even compare the top-level domain of an address against a static list, because new top-level domains are always being added. Syntactic validation of email addresses is an enormous amount of work that only solves a small portion of the problem.

The only way to be certain that an email address is valid is to successfully send email to it. The only way to be certain that an email address is the *right* one is to send email to it and get the recipient to respond. You need to weigh this additional work (yours and the user's) against the real value of a verified email address.

It used to be that a user's email address was closely associated with their online identity: most people had only the email address their ISP gave them. Thanks to today's free web-based email, that's no longer true. Email verification no longer works to prevent duplicate accounts or to stop antisocial behavior online—if it ever did.

This is not to say that it's never useful to have a user's working email address, or that there's no problem if people mistype their email addresses. To improve the quality of the addresses your users enter, without rejecting valid addresses, you can do three things beyond verifying with the permissive regular expressions given above:

1. Use a second naive regular expression, more restrictive than the ones given above, but don't prohibit addresses that don't match. Only use the second regular expression to advise the user that they may have mistyped their email address. This is not as useful as it seems, because most typos involve changing one letter for another, rather than introducing nonalphanumerics where they don't belong.

   ```
   def probably_valid?(email)
    valid = '[A-Za-z\d.+-]+' #Commonly encountered email address characters
    (email =~ /#{valid}@#{valid}\.#{valid}/) == 0
   end

   #These give the correct result.
   probably_valid? 'joe@example.com'                  # => true
   probably_valid? 'joe+ruby-mail@example.com'        # => true
   probably_valid? 'joe.bloggs@mail.example.com'      # => true
   probably_valid? 'joe@examplecom'                   # => false
   probably_valid? 'joe+ruby-mail@example.com'        # => true
   probably_valid? 'joe@localhost'                    # => false
   ```

```
# This address is valid, but probably_valid thinks it's not.
probably_valid? 'joe(and-mary)@example.museum'   # => false

# This address is valid, but certainly wrong.
probably_valid? 'joe@example.cpm'                 # => true
```

2. Extract from the alleged email address the hostname (the "example.com" of *joe@example.com*), and do a DNS lookup to see if that hostname accepts email. A hostname that has an MX DNS record is set up to receive mail. The following code will catch most domain name misspellings, but it won't catch any username misspellings. It's also not guaranteed to parse the hostname correctly, again because of the complexity of RFC822.

```
require 'resolv'
def valid_email_host?(email)
  hostname = email[(email =~ /@/)+1..email.length]
  valid = true
  begin
    Resolv::DNS.new.getresource(hostname, Resolv::DNS::Resource::IN::MX)
  rescue Resolv::ResolvError
    valid = false
  end
  return valid
end

#example.com is a real domain, but it won't accept mail
valid_email_host?('joe@example.com')            # => false

#lcqkxjvoem.mil is not a real domain.
valid_email_host?('joe@lcqkxjvoem.mil')         # => false

#oreilly.com exists and accepts mail, though there might not be a 'joe' there.
valid_email_host?('joe@oreilly.com')            # => true
```

3. Send email to the address the user input, and ask the user to verify receipt. For instance, the email might contain a verification URL for the user to click on. This is the only way to guarantee that the user entered a valid email address that they control. See Recipes 14.5 and 15.19 for this.

This is overkill much of the time. It requires that you add special workflow to your application, it significantly raises the barriers to use of your application, and it won't always work. Some users have spam filters that will treat your test mail as junk, or whitelist email systems that reject all email from unknown sources. Unless you really need a user's working email address for your application to work, very simple email validation should suffice.

See Also

- Recipe 14.5, "Sending Mail"
- Recipe 15.19, "Sending Mail with Rails"
- See the amazing colossal regular expression for email addresses at *http://www.ex-parrot.com/~pdw/Mail-RFC822-Address.html*

1.20   Classifying Text with a Bayesian Analyzer

Problem

You want to classify chunks of text by example: an email message is either spam or not spam, a joke is either funny or not funny, and so on.

Solution

Use Lucas Carlson's Classifier library, available as the classifier gem. It provides a naive Bayesian classifier, and one that implements Latent Semantic Indexing, a more advanced technique.

The interface for the naive Bayesian classifier is very straightforward. You create a Classifier::Bayes object with some classifications, and train it on text chunks whose classification is known:

```
require 'rubygems'
require 'classifier'

classifier = Classifier::Bayes.new('Spam', 'Not spam')

classifier.train_spam 'are you in the market for viagra? we sell viagra'
classifier.train_not_spam 'hi there, are we still on for lunch?'
```

You can then feed the classifier text chunks whose classification is unknown, and have it guess:

```
classifier.classify "we sell the cheapest viagra on the market"
# => "Spam"
classifier.classify "lunch sounds great"
# => "Not spam"
```

Discussion

Bayesian analysis is based on probablities. When you train the classifier, you are giving it a set of words and the classifier keeps track of how often words show up in each category. In the simple spam filter built in the Solution, the frequency hash looks like the @categories variable below:

```
classifier
# => #<Classifier::Bayes:0xb7cec7c8
#      @categories={:"Not spam"=>
#                     { :lunch=>1, :for=>1, :there=>1,
#                       :"?"=>1, :still=>1, :","=>1 },
#                   :Spam=>
#                     { :market=>1, :for=>1, :viagra=>2, :"?"=>1, :sell=>1 }
#                   },
#      @total_words=12>
```

These hashes are used to build probability calculations. Note that since we mentioned the word "viagra" twice in spam messages, there is a 2 in the "Spam" frequency hash for that word. That makes it more spam-like than other words like "for" (which also shows up in nonspam) or "sell" (which only shows up once in spam). The classifier can apply these probabilities to previously unseen text and guess at a classification for it.

The more text you use to train the classifier, the better it becomes at guessing. If you can verify the classifier's guesses (for instance, by asking the user whether a message really was spam), you should use that information to train the classifier with new data as it comes in.

To save the state of the classifier for later use, you can use Madeleine persistence (Recipe 13.3), which writes the state of your classifier to your hard drive.

A few more notes about this type of classifier. A Bayesian classifier supports as many categories as you want. "Spam" and "Not spam" are the most common, but you are not limited to two. You can also use the generic train method instead of calling train_[category_name]. Here's a classifier that has three categories and uses the generic train method:

```
classifier = Classifier::Bayes.new('Interesting', 'Funny', 'Dramatic')

classifier.train 'Interesting', "Leaving reminds us of what we can part
  with and what we can't, then offers us something new to look forward
  to, to dream about."
classifier.train 'Funny', "Knock knock. Who's there? Boo boo. Boo boo
  who? Don't cry, it is only a joke."
classifier.train 'Dramatic', 'I love you! I hate you! Get out right
  now.'

classifier.classify 'what!'
# => "Dramatic"
classifier.classify "who's on first?"
# => "Funny"
classifier.classify 'perchance to dream'
# => "Interesting"
```

It's also possible to "untrain" a category if you make a mistake or change your mind later.

```
classifier.untrain_funny "boo"
classifier.untrain "Dramatic", "out"
```

See Also

- Recipe 13.3, "Persisting Objects with Madeleine"
- The README file for the Classifier library has an example of an LSI classifier
- Bishop (*http://bishop.rubyforge.org/*) is another Bayesian classifier, a port of Python's Reverend; it's available as the bishop gem
- *http://en.wikipedia.org/wiki/Naive_Bayes_classifier*
- *http://en.wikipedia.org/wiki/Latent_Semantic_Analysis*

## CHAPTER 2

Numbers

Numbers are as fundamental to computing as breath is to human life. Even programs that have nothing to do with math need to count the items in a data structure, display average running times, or use numbers as a source of randomness. Ruby makes it easy to represent numbers, letting you breathe easy and tackle the harder problems of programming.

An issue that comes up when you're programming with numbers is that there are several different implementations of "number," optimized for different purposes: 32-bit integers, floating-point numbers, and so on. Ruby tries to hide these details from you, but it's important to know about them because they often manifest as mysteriously incorrect calculations.*

The first distinction is between small numbers and large ones. If you've used other programming languages, you probably know that you must use different data types to hold small numbers and large numbers (assuming that the language supports large numbers at all). Ruby has different classes for small numbers (Fixnum) and large numbers (Bignum), but you don't usually have to worry about the difference. When you type in a number, Ruby sees how big it is and creates an object of the appropriate class.

```
1000.class                  # => Fixnum
10000000000.class           # => Bignum
(2**30 - 1).class           # => Fixnum
(2**30).class               # => Bignum
```

When you perform arithmetic, Ruby automatically does any needed conversions. You don't have to worry about the difference between small and large numbers:†

```
small = 1000
big = small ** 5            # => 1000000000000000
```

---

* See, for instance, the Discussion section of Recipe 2.11, where it's revealed that Matrix#inverse doesn't work correctly on a matrix full of integers. This is because Matrix#inverse uses division, and integer division works differently from floating-point division.

† Python also has this feature.

```
big.class                          # => Bignum
smaller = big / big                # => 1
smaller.class                      # => Fixnum
```

The other major distinction is between whole numbers (integers) and fractional numbers. Like all modern programming languages, Ruby implements the IEEE floating-point standard for representing fractional numbers. If you type a number that includes a decimal point, Ruby creates a `Float` object instead of a `Fixnum` or `Bignum`:

```
0.01.class                         # => Float
1.0.class                          # => Float
10000000000.00000000001.class      # => Float
```

But floating-point numbers are imprecise (see Recipe 2.2), and they have their own size limits, so Ruby also provides a class that can represent any number with a finite decimal expansion (Recipe 2.3). There's also a class for numbers like two-thirds, which have an infinite decimal expansion (Recipe 2.4), and a class for complex or "irrational" numbers (Recipe 2.12).

Every kind of number in Ruby has its own class (`Integer`, `Bignum`, `Complex`, and so on), which inherits from the `Numeric` class. All these classes implement the basic arithmetic operations, and in most cases you can mix and match numbers of different types (see Recipe 8.9 for more on how this works). You can reopen these classes to add new capabilities to numbers (see, for instance, Recipe 2.17), but you can't usefully subclass them.

Ruby provides simple ways of generating random numbers (Recipe 2.5) and sequences of numbers (Recipe 2.15). This chapter also covers some simple mathematical algorithms (Recipes 2.7 and 2.11) and statistics (Recipe 2.8).

2.1 Parsing a Number from a String

Problem

Given a string that contains some representation of a number, you want to get the corresponding integer or floating-point value.

Solution

Use `String#to_i` to turn a string into an integer. Use `String#to_f` to turn a string into a floating-point number.

```
'400'.to_i                 # => 400
'3.14'.to_f                # => 3.14
'1.602e-19'.to_f           # => 1.602e-19
```

Discussion

Unlike Perl and PHP, Ruby does not automatically make a number out of a string that contains a number. You must explicitly call a conversion method that tells Ruby *how* you want the string to be converted.

Along with `to_i` and `to_f`, there are other ways to convert strings into numbers. If you have a string that represents a hex or octal string, you can call `String#hex` or `String#oct` to get the decimal equivalent. This is the same as passing the base of the number into `to_i`:

```
'405'.oct                       # => 261
'405'.to_i(8)                   # => 261
'405'.hex                       # => 1029
'405'.to_i(16)                  # => 1029
'fed'.hex                       # => 4077
'fed'.to_i(16)                  # => 4077
```

If `to_i`, `to_f`, hex, or oct find a character that can't be part of the kind of number they're looking for, they stop processing the string at that character and return the number so far. If the string's first character is unusable, the result is zero.

```
"13: a baker's dozen".to_i                              # => 13
'1001 Nights'.to_i                                      # => 1001
'The 1000 Nights and a Night'.to_i                      # => 0
'60.50  Misc. Agricultural Equipment'.to_f             # => 60.5
'$60.50'.to_f                                           # => 0.0
'Feed the monster!'.hex                                 # => 65261
'I fed the monster at Canoga Park Waterslides'.hex     # => 0
'0xA2Z'.hex                                             # => 162
'-10'.oct                                               # => -8
'-109'.oct                                              # => -8
'3.14'.to_i                                             # => 3
```

Note especially that last example: the decimal point is just one more character that stops processing of a string representing an integer.

If you want an exception when a string can't be completely parsed as a number, use `Integer( )` or `Float( )`:

```
Integer('1001')                             # => 1001
Integer('1001 nights')
# ArgumentError: invalid value for Integer: "1001 nights"

Float('99.44')                              # => 99.44
Float('99.44% pure')
# ArgumentError: invalid value for Float(): "99.44% pure"
```

To extract a number from within a larger string, use a regular expression. The `NumberParser` class below contains regular expressions for extracting floating-point strings, as well as decimal, octal, and hexadecimal numbers. Its `extract_numbers` method uses `String#scan` to find all the numbers of a certain type in a string.

```
class NumberParser
  @@number_regexps = {
    :to_i => /([+-]?[0-9]+)/,
    :to_f => /([+-]?([0-9]*\.)?[0-9]+(e[+-]?[0-9]+)?)/i,
    :oct => /([+-]?[0-7]+)/,
    :hex => /\b([+-]?(0x)?[0-9a-f]+)\b/i
    #The \b characters prevent every letter A-F in a word from being
    #considered a hexadecimal number.
  }

  def NumberParser.re(parsing_method=:to_i)
    re = @@number_regexps[parsing_method]
    raise ArgumentError, "No regexp for #{parsing_method.inspect}!" unless re
    return re
  end

  def extract(s, parsing_method=:to_i)
    numbers = []
    s.scan(NumberParser.re(parsing_method)) do |match|
      numbers << match[0].send(parsing_method)
    end
    numbers
  end
end
```

Here it is in action:

```
p = NumberParser.new

pw = "Today's numbers are 104 and 391."
NumberParser.re(:to_i).match(pw).captures            # => ["104"]
p.extract(pw, :to_i)                                 # => [104, 391]

p.extract('The 1000 nights and a night')            # => [1000]
p.extract('$60.50', :to_f)                           # => [60.5]
p.extract('I fed the monster at Canoga Park Waterslides', :hex)
# => [4077]
p.extract('In octal, fifteen is 017.', :oct)         # => [15]

p.extract('From 0 to 10e60 in -2.4 seconds', :to_f)
# => [0.0, 1.0e+61, -2.4]
p.extract('From 0 to 10e60 in -2.4 seconds')
# => [0, 10, 60, -2, 4]
```

If you want to extract more than one kind of number from a string, the most reliable
strategy is to stop using regular expressions and start using the scanf module, a free
third-party module that provides a parser similar to C's scanf function.

```
require 'scanf'
s = '0x10 4.44 10'.scanf('%x %f %d')                 # => [16, 4.44, 10]
```

See Also

- Recipe 2.6, "Converting Between Numeric Bases"

- Recipe 8.9, "Converting and Coercing Objects to Different Types"
- The scanf module (*http://www.rubyhacker.com/code/scanf/*)

2.2   Comparing Floating-Point Numbers

Problem

Floating-point numbers are not suitable for exact comparison. Often, two numbers that should be equal are actually slightly different. The Ruby interpreter can make seemingly nonsensical assertions when floating-point numbers are involved:

```
1.8 + 0.1              # => 1.9
1.8 + 0.1 == 1.9       # => false
1.8 + 0.1 > 1.9        # => true
```

You want to do comparison operations approximately, so that floating-point numbers infintesimally close together can be treated equally.

Solution

You can avoid this problem altogether by using BigDecimal numbers instead of floats (see Recipe 2.3). BigDecimal numbers are completely precise, and work as well as as floats for representing numbers that are relatively small and have few decimal places: everyday numbers like the prices of fruits. But math on BigDecimal numbers is much slower than math on floats. Databases have native support for floating-point numbers, but not for BigDecimals. And floating-point numbers are simpler to create (simply type 10.2 in an interactive Ruby shell to get a Float object). BigDecimals can't totally replace floats, and when you use floats it would be nice not to have to worry about tiny differences between numbers when doing comparisons.

But how tiny is "tiny"? How large can the difference be between two numbers before they should stop being considered equal? As numbers get larger, so does the range of floating-point values that can reasonably be expected to model that number. 1.1 is probably not "approximately equal" to 1.2, but $10^{20} + 0.1$ is probably "approximately equal" to $10^{20} + 0.2$.

The best solution is probably to compare the relative magnitudes of large numbers, and the absolute magnitudes of small numbers. The following code accepts both two thresholds: a relative threshold and an absolute threshold. Both default to Float::EPSILON, the smallest possible difference between two Float objects. Two floats are considered approximately equal if they are within absolute_epsilon of each other, or if the difference between them is relative_epsilon times the magnitude of the larger one.

```
class Float
  def approx(other, relative_epsilon=Float::EPSILON, epsilon=Float::EPSILON)
    difference = other - self
    return true if difference.abs <= epsilon
```

```
      relative_error = (difference / (self > other ? self : other)).abs
      return relative_error <= relative_epsilon
    end
  end

100.2.approx(100.1 + 0.1)                  # => true
10e10.approx(10e10+1e-5)                    # => true
100.0.approx(100+1e-5)                      # => false
```

Discussion

Floating-point math is very precise but, due to the underlying storage mechanism for Float objects, not very accurate. Many real numbers (such as 1.9) can't be represented by the floating-point standard. Any attempt to represent such a number will end up using one of the nearby numbers that does have a floating-point representation.

You don't normally see the difference between 1.9 and 1.8 + 0.1, because Float#to_s rounds them both off to "1.9". You can see the difference by using Kernel#printf to display the two expressions to many decimal places:

```
printf("%.55f", 1.9)
# 1.8999999999999999111821580299874767661094665527343750000
printf("%.55f", 1.8 + 0.1)
# 1.9000000000000001332267629550187848508358001708984375000
```

Both numbers straddle 1.9 from opposite ends, unable to accurately represent the number they should both equal. Note that the difference between the two numbers is precisely Float::EPSILON:

```
Float::EPSILON                              # => 2.22044604925031e-16
(1.8 + 0.1) - 1.9                           # => 2.22044604925031e-16
```

This EPSILON's worth of inaccuracy is often too small to matter, but it does when you're doing comparisons. 1.9+Float::EPSILON is not equal to 1.9-Float::EPSILON, even if (in this case) both are attempts to represent the same number. This is why most floating-point numbers are compared in relative terms.

The most efficient way to do a relative comparison is to see whether the two numbers differ by more than an specified error range, using code like this:

```
class Float
  def absolute_approx(other, epsilon=Float::EPSILON)
    return (other-self).abs <= epsilon
  end
end

(1.8 + 0.1).absolute_approx(1.9)            # => true
10e10.absolute_approx(10e10+1e-5)           # => false
```

The default value of epsilon works well for numbers close to 0, but for larger numbers the default value of epsilon will be too small. Any other value of epsilon you might specify will only work well within a certain range.

Thus, Float#approx, the recommended solution, compares both absolute and relative magnitude. As numbers get bigger, so does the allowable margin of error for two numbers to be considered "equal." Its default relative_epsilon allows numbers between 2 and 3 to differ by twice the value of Float::EPSILON. Numbers between 3 and 4 can differ by three times the value of Float::EPSILON, and so on.

A very small value of relative_epsilon is good for mathematical operations, but if your data comes from a real-world source like a scientific instrument, you can increase it. For instance, a Ruby script may track changes in temperature read from a thermometer that's only 99.9% accurate. In this case, relative_epsilon can be set to 0.001, and everything beyond that point discarded as noise.

```
98.6.approx(98.66)                    # => false
98.6.approx(98.66, 0.001)             # => true
```

See Also

- Recipe 2.3, "Representing Numbers to Arbitrary Precision," has more information on BigDecimal numbers
- If you need to represent a fraction with an infinite decimal expansion, use a Rational number (see Recipe 2.4, "Representing Rational Numbers")
- "Comparing floating point numbers" by Bruce Dawson has an excellent (albeit C-centric) overview of the tradeoffs involved in different ways of doing floating-point comparisons (*http://www.cygnus-software.com/papers/comparingfloats/ comparingfloats.htm*)

2.3 Representing Numbers to Arbitrary Precision

Problem

You're doing high-precision arithmetic, and floating-point numbers are not precise enough.

Solution

A BigDecimal number can represent a real number to an arbitrary number of decimal places.

```
require 'bigdecimal'

BigDecimal("10").to_s                 # => "0.1E2"
BigDecimal("1000").to_s               # => "0.1E4"
BigDecimal("1000").to_s("F")          # => "1000.0"

BigDecimal("0.123456789").to_s        # => "0.123456789E0"
```

Compare how Float and BigDecimal store the same high-precision number:

```
nm = "0.123456789012345678901234567890123456789"
nm.to_f                  # => 0.123456789012346
```

```
BigDecimal(nm).to_s
# => "0.12345678901234567890123456789012345678901234567890E0"
```

Discussion

BigDecimal numbers store numbers in scientific notation format. A BigDecimal consists of a sign (positive or negative), an arbitrarily large decimal fraction, and an arbitrarily large exponent. This is similar to the way floating-point numbers are stored, but a double-precision floating-point implementation like Ruby's cannot represent an exponent less than Float::MIN_EXP (−1021) or greater than Float::MAX_EXP (1024). Float objects also can't represent numbers at a greater precision than Float::EPSILON, or about $2.2*10^{-16}$.

You can use BigDecimal#split to split a BigDecimal object into the parts of its scientific-notation representation. It returns an array of four numbers: the sign (1 for positive numbers, −1 for negative numbers), the fraction (as a string), the base of the exponent (which is always 10), and the exponent itself.

```
BigDecimal("105000").split
# => [1, "105", 10, 6]
# That is, 0.105*(10**6)

BigDecimal("-0.005").split
# => [-1, "5", 10, -2]
# That is, -1 * (0.5*(10**-2))
```

A good way to test different precision settings is to create an infinitely repeating decimal like 2/3, and see how much of it gets stored. By default, BigDecimals give 16 digits of precision, roughly comparable to what a Float can give.

```
(BigDecimal("2") / BigDecimal("3")).to_s
# => "0.6666666666666667E0"


2.0/3
# => 0.666666666666667
```

You can store additional significant digits by passing in a second argument n to the BigDecimal constructor. BigDecimal precision is allocated in chunks of four decimal digits. Values of n from 1 to 4 make a BigDecimal use the default precision of 16 digits. Values from 5 to 8 give 20 digits of precision, values from 9 to 12 give 24 digits, and so on:

```
def two_thirds(precision)
  (BigDecimal("2", precision) / BigDecimal("3")).to_s
end

two_thirds(1)                          # => "0.6666666666666667E0"
two_thirds(4)                          # => "0.6666666666666667E0"
two_thirds(5)                          # => "0.66666666666666666667E0"
two_thirds(9)                          # => "0.666666666666666666666667E0"
two_thirds(13)                         # => "0.6666666666666666666666666667E0"
```

Not all of a number's significant digits may be used. For instance, Ruby considers BigDecimal("2") and BigDecimal("2.000000000000") to be equal, even though the second one has many more significant digits.

You can inspect the precision of a number with BigDecimal#precs. This method returns an array of two elements: the number of significant digits actually being used, and the toal number of significant digits. Again, since significant digits are allocated in blocks of four, both of these numbers will be multiples of four.

```
BigDecimal("2").precs                  # => [4, 8]
BigDecimal("2.000000000000").precs     # => [4, 20]
BigDecimal("2.000000000001").precs     # => [16, 20]
```

If you use the standard arithmetic operators on BigDecimals, the result is a BigDecimal accurate to the largest possible number of digits. Dividing or multiplying one BigDecimal by another yields a BigDecimal with more digits of precision than either of its parents, just as would happen on a pocket calculator.

```
(a = BigDecimal("2.01")).precs         # => [8, 8]
(b = BigDecimal("3.01")).precs         # => [8, 8]

(product = a * b).to_s("F")            # => "6.0501"
product.precs                          # => [8, 24]
```

To specify the number of significant digits that should be retained in an arithmetic operation, you can use the methods add, sub, mul, and div instead of the arithmetic operators.

```
two_thirds = (BigDecimal("2", 13) / 3)
two_thirds.to_s          # => "0.6666666666666666666666666666666666667E0"

(two_thirds + 1).to_s    # => "0.1666666666666666666666666666666666667E1"

two_thirds.add(1, 1).to_s    # => "0.2E1"
two_thirds.add(1, 4).to_s    # => "0.1667E1"
```

Either way, BigDecimal math is significantly slower than floating-point math. Not only are BigDecimals allowed to have more significant digits than floats, but BigDecimals are stored as an array of decimal digits, while floats are stored in a binary encoding and manipulated with binary arithmetic.

The BigMath module in the Ruby standard library defines methods for performing arbitrary-precision mathematical operations on BigDecimal objects. It defines power-related methods like sqrt, log, and exp, and trigonometric methods like sin, cos, and atan.

All of these methods take as an argument a number prec indicating how many digits of precision to retain. They may return a BigDecimal with more than prec significant digits, but only prec of those digits are guaranteed to be accurate.

```
require 'bigdecimal/math'
include BigMath
```

```
two = BigDecimal("2")
BigMath::sqrt(two, 10).to_s("F")     # => "1.4142135623730950488016883515"
```

That code gives 28 decimal places, but only 10 are guaranteed accurate (because we passed in an n of 10), and only 24 are actually accurate. The square root of 2 to 28 decimal places is actually 1.4142135623730950488016887242. We can get rid of the inaccurate digits with `BigDecimal#round`:

```
BigMath::sqrt(two, 10).round(10).to_s("F") # => "1.4142135624"
```

We can also get a more precise number by increasing n:

```
BigMath::sqrt(two, 28).round(28).to_s("F")     # => "1.4142135623730950488016887242"
```

`BigMath` also annotates `BigDecimal` with class methods `BigDecimal.PI` and `BigDecimal.E`. These methods construct `BigDecimals` of those transcendental numbers at any level of precision.

```
Math::PI                       # => 3.14159265358979
Math::PI.class                 # => Float
BigDecimal.PI(1).to_s          # => "0.31415926535897932364198143965603E1"
BigDecimal.PI(20).to_s
# => "0.3141592653589793238462643383279502883919859293521427E1"
```

See Also

- At the time of writing, `BigMath::log` was very slow for `BigDecimals` larger than about 10; see Recipe 2.7, "Taking Logarithms," for a much faster implementation
- See Recipe 2.4, "Representing Rational Numbers," if you need to exactly represent a rational number with an infinite decimal expansion, like 2/3
- The `BigDecimal` library reference is extremely useful; if you look at the generated RDoc for the Ruby standard library, `BigDecimal` looks almost undocumented, but it actually has a comprehensive reference file (in English and Japanese): it's just not in RDoc format, so it doesn't get picked up; this document is available in the Ruby source package, or do a web search for "BigDecimal: An extension library for Ruby"

2.4   Representing Rational Numbers

Problem

You want to precisely represent a rational number like 2/3, one that has no finite decimal expansion.

Solution

Use a `Rational` object; it represents a rational number as an integer numerator and denominator.

```
float = 2.0/3.0                          # => 0.666666666666667
float * 100                              # => 66.6666666666667
float * 100 / 42                         # => 1.58730158730159

require 'rational'
rational = Rational(2, 3)                # => Rational(2, 3)
rational.to_f                            # => 0.666666666666667
rational * 100                           # => Rational(200, 3)
rational * 100 / 42                      # => Rational(100, 63)
```

Discussion

Rational objects can store numbers that can't be represented in any other form, and arithmetic on Rational objects is completely precise.

Since the numerator and denominator of a Rational can be Bignums, a Rational object can also represent numbers larger and smaller than those you can represent in floating-point. But math on BigDecimal objects is faster than on Rationals. BigDecimal objects are also usually easier to work with than Rationals, because most of us think of numbers in terms of their decimal expansions.

You should only use Rational objects when you need to represent rational numbers with perfect accuracy. When you do, be sure to use only Rationals, Fixnums, and Bignums in your calculations. Don't use any BigDecimals or floating-point numbers: arithmetic operations between a Rational and those types will return floating-point numbers, and you'll have lost precision forever.

```
10 + Rational(2,3)                       # => Rational(32, 3)
require 'bigdecimal'
BigDecimal('10') + Rational(2,3)         # => 10.6666666666667
```

The methods in Ruby's Math module implement operations like square root, which usually give irrational results. When you pass a Rational number into one of the methods in the Math module, you get a floating-point number back:

```
Math::sqrt(Rational(2,3))                # => 0.816496580927726
Math::sqrt(Rational(25,1))               # => 5.0
Math::log10(Rational(100, 1))            # => 2.0
```

The mathn library adds miscellaneous functionality to Ruby's math functions. Among other things, it modifies the Math::sqrt method so that if you pass in a square number, you get a Fixnum back instead of a Float. This preserves precision whenever possible:

```
require 'mathn'
Math::sqrt(Rational(2,3))                # => 0.816496580927726
Math::sqrt(Rational(25,1))               # => 5
Math::sqrt(25)                           # => 5
Math::sqrt(25.0)                         # => 5.0
```

See Also

- The `rfloat` third-party library lets you use a `Float`-like interface that's actually backed by `Rational` (*http://blade.nagaokaut.ac.jp/~sinara/ruby/rfloat/*)
- RCR 320 proposes better interoperability between `Rationals` and floating-point numbers, including a `Rational#approximate` method that will let you convert the floating-point number 0.1 into Rational(1, 10) (*http://www.rcrchive.net/rcr/show/320*)

2.5   Generating Random Numbers

Problem

You want to generate pseudorandom numbers, select items from a data structure at random, or repeatedly generate the same "random" numbers for testing purposes.

Solution

Use the `Kernel#rand` function with no arguments to select a psuedorandom floating-point number from a uniform distribution between 0 and 1.

```
rand                              # => 0.517297883846589
rand                              # => 0.946962603814814
```

Pass in a single integer argument *n* to `Kernel#rand`, and it returns an integer between 0 and *n–1*:

```
rand(5)                          # => 0
rand(5)                          # => 4
rand(5)                          # => 3
rand(1000)                       # => 39
```

Discussion

You can use the single-argument form of `Kernel#rand` to build many common tasks based on randomness. For instance, this code selects a random item from an array.

```
a = ['item1', 'item2', 'item3']
a[rand(a.size)]                  # => "item3"
```

To select a random key or value from a hash, turn the keys or values into an array and select one at random.

```
m = { :key1 => 'value1',
      :key2 => 'value2',
      :key3 => 'value3' }
values = m.values
values[rand(values.size)]        # => "value1"
```

This code generates pronounceable nonsense words:

```
def random_word
  letters = { ?v => 'aeiou',
              ?c => 'bcdfghjklmnprstvwyz' }
  word = ''
  'cvcvcvc'.each_byte do |x|
    source = letters[x]
    word << source[rand(source.length)].chr
  end
  return word
end

random_word                          # => "josuyip"
random_word                          # => "haramic"
```

The Ruby interpreter initializes its random number generator on startup, using a seed derived from the current time and the process number. To reliably generate the same random numbers over and over again, you can set the random number seed manually by calling the Kernel#srand function with the integer argument of your choice. This is useful when you're writing automated tests of "random" functionality:

```
#Some random numbers based on process number and current time
rand(1000)                           # => 187
rand(1000)                           # => 551
rand(1000)                           # => 911

#Start the seed with the number 1
srand 1
rand(1000)                           # => 37
rand(1000)                           # => 235
rand(1000)                           # => 908

#Reset the seed to its previous state
srand 1
rand(1000)                           # => 37
rand(1000)                           # => 235
rand(1000)                           # => 908
```

See Also

- Recipe 4.10, "Shuffling an Array"
- Recipe 5.11, "Choosing Randomly from a Weighted List"
- Recipe 6.9, "Picking a Random Line from a File"
- The Facets library implements many methods for making random selections from data structures: Array#pick, Array#rand_subset, Hash#rand_pair, and so on; it also defines String.random for generating random strings
- Christian Neukirchen's rand.rb also implements many random selection methods (*http://chneukirchen.org/blog/static/projects/rand.html*)

2.6 Converting Between Numeric Bases

Problem

You want to convert numbers from one base to another.

Solution

You can convert specific binary, octal, or hexadecimal numbers to decimal by representing them with the 0b, 0o, or 0x prefixes:

```
0b100                           # => 4
0o100                           # => 64
0x100                           # => 256
```

You can also convert between decimal numbers and string representations of those numbers in any base from 2 to 36. Simply pass the base into String#to_i or Integer#to_s.

Here are some conversions between string representations of numbers in various bases, and the corresponding decimal numbers:

```
"1045".to_i(10)                 # => 1045
"-1001001".to_i(2)              # => -73
"abc".to_i(16)                  # => 2748
"abc".to_i(20)                  # => 4232
"number".to_i(36)               # => 1442151747
"zz1z".to_i(36)                 # => 1678391
"abcdef".to_i(16)               # => 11259375
"AbCdEf".to_i(16)               # => 11259375
```

Here are some reverse conversions of decimal numbers to the strings that represent those numbers in various bases:

```
42.to_s(10)                     # => "42"
-100.to_s(2)                    # => "-1100100"
255.to_s(16)                    # => "ff"
1442151747.to_s(36)             # => "number"
```

Some invalid conversions:

```
"6".to_i(2)                     # => 0
"0".to_i(1)                     # ArgumentError: illegal radix 1
40.to_s(37)                     # ArgumentError: illegal radix 37
```

Discussion

String#to_i can parse and Integer#to_s can create a string representation in every common integer base: from binary (the familiar base 2, which uses only the digits 0 and 1) to hexatridecimal (base 36). Hexatridecimal uses the digits 0–9 and the letters a–z; it's sometimes used to generate alphanumeric mneumonics for long numbers.

The only commonly used counting systems with bases higher than 36 are the variants of base-64 encoding used in applications like MIME mail attachments. These usually encode strings, not numbers; to encode a string in MIME-style base-64, use the base64 library.

See Also

- Recipe 12.5, "Adding Graphical Context with Sparklines," and Recipe 14.5, "Sending Mail," show how to use the base64 library

2.7 Taking Logarithms

Problem

You want to take the logarithm of a number, possibly a huge one.

Solution

Math.log calculates the natural log of a number: that is, the log base e.

```
Math.log(1)                    # => 0.0
Math.log(Math::E)              # => 1.0
Math.log(10)                   # => 2.30258509299405
Math::E ** Math.log(25)        # => 25.0
```

Math.log10 calculates the log base 10 of a number:

```
Math.log10(1)                  # => 0.0
Math.log10(10)                 # => 1.0
Math.log10(10.1)               # => 1.00432137378264
Math.log10(1000)               # => 3.0
10 ** Math.log10(25)           # => 25.0
```

To calculate a logarithm in some other base, use the fact that, for any bases b_1 and b_2, $\log_{b1}(x) = \log_{b2}(x) / \log_{b2}(k)$.

```
module Math
  def Math.logb(num, base)
    log(num) / log(base)
  end
end
```

Discussion

A logarithm function inverts an exponentiation function. The log base k of x, or $\log_k(x)$, is the number that gives x when raised to the k power. That is, Math.log10(1000)==3.0 because 10 cubed is 1000.Math.log(Math::E)==1 because e to the first power is e.

The logarithm functions for all numeric bases are related (you can get from one base to another by dividing by a constant factor), but they're used for different purposes.

Scientific applications often use the natural log: this is the fastest log implementation in Ruby. The log base 10 is often used to visualize datasets that span many orders of magnitude, such as the pH scale for acidity and the Richter scale for earthquake intensity. Analyses of algorithms often use the log base 2, or binary logarithm.

If you intend to do a lot of algorithms in a base that Ruby doesn't support natively, you can speed up the calculation by precalculating the dividend:

```
dividend = Math.log(2)
(1..6).collect { |x| Math.log(x) / dividend }
# => [0.0, 1.0, 1.58496250072116, 2.0, 2.32192809488736, 2.58496250072116]
```

The logarithm functions in `Math` will only accept integers or floating-point numbers, not `BigDecimal` or `Bignum` objects. This is inconvenient since logarithms are often used to make extremely large numbers managable. The `BigMath` module has a function to take the natural logarithm of a `BigDecimal` number, but it's very slow.

Here's a fast drop-in replacement for `BigMath::log` that exploits the logarithmic identity `log(x*y) == log(x) + log(y)`. It decomposes a `BigDecimal` into three much smaller numbers, and operates on those numbers. This avoids the cases that give `BigMath::log` such poor performance.

```
require 'bigdecimal'
require 'bigdecimal/math'
require 'bigdecimal/util'

module BigMath
  alias :log_slow :log
  def log(x, prec)
    if x <= 0 || prec <= 0
      raise ArgumentError, "Zero or negative argument for log"
    end
    return x if x.infinite? || x.nan?
    sign, fraction, power, exponent = x.split
    fraction = BigDecimal(".#{fraction}")
    power = power.to_s.to_d
    log_slow(fraction, prec) + (log_slow(power, prec) * exponent)
  end
end
```

Like `BigMath::log`, this implementation returns a `BigMath` accurate to at least `prec` digits, but containing some additional digits which might not be accurate. To avoid giving the impression that the result is more accurate than it is, you can round the number to `prec` digits with `BigDecimal#round`.

```
include BigMath

number = BigDecimal("1234.5678")
Math.log(number)                      # => 7.11847622829779

prec = 50
BigMath.log_slow(number, prec).round(prec).to_s("F")
# => "7.1184762282977862925087925363870818413407321414145175"
```

```
BigMath.log(number, prec).round(prec).to_s("F")
# => "7.1184762282977862925087925363870818413407321441451751"
BigMath.log(number ** 1000, prec).round(prec).to_s("F")
# => "7118.4762282977862925087925363870818413407321441451751611"
```

As before, calculate a log other than the natural log by dividing by `BigMath.log(base)` or `BigMath.log_slow(base)`.

```
huge_number = BigDecimal("1000") ** 1000
base = BigDecimal("10")
(BigMath.log(huge_number, 100) / BigMath.log(base, 100)).to_f
# => 3000.0
```

How does it work? The internal representation of a `BigDecimal` is as a number in scientific notation: `fraction * 10**power`. Because `log(x*y) = log(x) + log(y)`, the log of such a number is `log(fraction) + log(10**power)`.

`10**power` is just 10 multiplied by itself power times (that is, `10*10*10*...*10`). Again, `log(x*y) = log(x) + log(y)`, so `log(10*10*10*...*10) = log(10)+log(10) + log(10)+...+log(10)`, or `log(10)*`power. This means we can take the logarithm of a huge `BigDecimal` by taking the logarithm of its (very small) fractional portion and the logarithm of 10.

See Also

- Mathematicians used to spend years constructing tables of logarithms for scientific and engineering applications; so if you find yourself doing a boring job, be glad you don't have to do that (see *http://en.wikipedia.org/wiki/Logarithm#Tables_of_logarithms*)

2.8   Finding Mean, Median, and Mode

Problem

You want to find the average of an array of numbers: its mean, median, or mode.

Solution

Usually when people speak of the "average" of a set of numbers they're referring to its mean, or arithmetic mean. The mean is the sum of the elements divided by the number of elements.

```
def mean(array)
  array.inject(0) { |sum, x| sum += x } / array.size.to_f
end

mean([1,2,3,4])                        # => 2.5
mean([100,100,100,100.1])              # => 100.025
mean([-100, 100])                      # => 0.0
mean([3,3,3,3])                        # => 3.0
```

The median is the item x such that half the items in the array are greater than x and the other half are less than x. Consider a sorted array: if it contains an odd number of elements, the median is the one in the middle. If the array contains an even number of elements, the median is defined as the mean of the two middle elements.

```
def median(array, already_sorted=false)
  return nil if array.empty?
  array = array.sort unless already_sorted
  m_pos = array.size / 2
  return array.size % 2 == 1 ? array[m_pos] : mean(array[m_pos-1..m_pos])
end
```

```
median([1,2,3,4,5])                    # => 3
median([5,3,2,1,4])                    # => 3
median([1,2,3,4])                      # => 2.5
median([1,1,2,3,4])                    # => 2
median([2,3,-100,100])                 # => 2.5
median([1, 1, 10, 100, 1000])          # => 10
```

The mode is the single most popular item in the array. If a list contains no repeated items, it is not considered to have a mode. If an array contains multiple items at the maximum frequency, it is "multimodal." Depending on your application, you might handle each mode separately, or you might just pick one arbitrarily.

```
def modes(array, find_all=true)
  histogram = array.inject(Hash.new(0)) { |h, n| h[n] += 1; h }
  modes = nil
  histogram.each_pair do |item, times|
    modes << item if modes && times == modes[0] and find_all
    modes = [times, item] if (!modes && times>1) or (modes && times>modes[0])
  end
  return modes ? modes[1...modes.size] : modes
end
```

```
modes([1,2,3,4])                       # => nil
modes([1,1,2,3,4])                     # => [1]
modes([1,1,2,2,3,4])                   # => [1, 2]
modes([1,1,2,2,3,4,4])                 # => [1, 2, 4]
modes([1,1,2,2,3,4,4], false)          # => [1]
modes([1,1,2,2,3,4,4,4,4,4])           # => [4]
```

Discussion

The mean is the most popular type of average. It's simple to calculate and to understand. The implementation of mean given above always returns a floating-point number object. It's a good general-purpose implementation because it lets you pass in an array of Fixnums and get a fractional average, instead of one rounded to the nearest integer. If you want to find the mean of an array of BigDecimal or Rational objects, you should use an implementation of mean that omits the final to_f call:

```
def mean_without_float_conversion(array)
  array.inject(0) { |x, sum| sum += x } / array.size
end
```

```
require 'rational'
numbers = [Rational(2,3), Rational(3,4), Rational(6,7)]
mean(numbers)
# => 0.757936507936508
mean_without_float_conversion(numbers)
# => Rational(191, 252)
```

The median is mainly useful when a small proportion of outliers in the dataset would make the mean misleading. For instance, government statistics usually show "median household income" instead of "mean household income." Otherwise, a few super-wealthy households would make everyone else look much richer than they are. The example below demonstrates how the mean can be skewed by a few very high or very low outliers.

```
mean([1, 100, 100000])          # => 33367.0
median([1, 100, 100000])        # => 100

mean([1, 100, -1000000])        # => -333299.666666667
median([1, 100, -1000000])      # => 1
```

The mode is the only definition of "average" that can be applied to arrays of arbitrary objects. Since the mean is calculated using arithmetic, an array can only be said to have a mean if all of its members are numeric. The median involves only comparisons, except when the array contains an even number of elements: then, calculating the median requires that you calculate the mean.

If you defined some other way to take the median of an array with an even number of elements, you could take the median of Arrays of strings:

```
median(["a", "z", "b", "l", "m", "j", "b"])
# => "j"
median(["a", "b", "c", "d"])
# TypeError: String can't be coerced into Fixnum
```

The standard deviation

A concept related to the mean is the standard deviation, a quantity that measures how close the dataset as a whole is to the mean. When a mean is distorted by high or low outliers, the corresponding standard deviation is high. When the numbers in a dataset cluster closely around the mean, the standard deviation is low. You won't be fooled by a misleading mean if you also look at the standard deviation.

```
def mean_and_standard_deviation(array)
  m = mean(array)
  variance = array.inject(0) { |variance, x| variance += (x - m) ** 2 }
  return m, Math.sqrt(variance/(array.size-1))
end

#All the items in the list are close to the mean, so the standard
#deviation is low.
mean_and_standard_deviation([1,2,3,1,1,2,1])
# => [1.57142857142857, 0.786795792469443]
```

```
#The outlier increases the mean, but also increases the standard deviation.
mean_and_standard_deviation([1,2,3,1,1,2,1000])
# => [144.285714285714, 377.33526837801]
```

A good rule of thumb is that two-thirds (about 68 percent) of the items in a dataset are within one standard deviation of the mean, and almost all (about 95 percent) of the items are within two standard deviations of the mean.

See Also

- "Programmers Need to Learn Statistics or I Will Kill Them All," by Zed Shaw (*http://www.zedshaw.com/blog/programming/programmer_stats.html*)
- More Ruby implementations of simple statistical measures (*http://dada.perl.it/shootout/moments.ruby.html*)
- To do more complex statistical analysis in Ruby, try the Ruby bindings to the GNU Scientific Library (*http://ruby-gsl.sourceforge.net/*)
- The Stats class in the Mongrel web server (*http://mongrel.rubyforge.org*) implements other algorithms for calculating mean and standard deviation, which are faster if you need to repeatedly calculate the mean of a growing series

2.9   Converting Between Degrees and Radians

Problem

The trigonometry functions in Ruby's Math library take input in radians (2π radians in a circle). Most real-world applications measure angles in degrees (360 degrees in a circle). You want an easy way to do trigonometry with degrees.

Solution

The simplest solution is to define a conversion method in Numeric that will convert a number of degrees into radians.

```
class Numeric
  def degrees
    self * Math::PI / 180
  end
end
```

You can then treat any numeric object as a number of degrees and convert it into the corresponding number of radians, by calling its degrees method. Trigonometry on the result will work as you'd expect:

```
90.degrees                      # => 1.5707963267949
Math::tan(45.degrees)           # => 1.0
Math::cos(90.degrees)           # => 6.12303176911189e-17
Math::sin(90.degrees)           # => 1.0
Math::sin(89.9.degrees)         # => 0.999998476913288

Math::sin(45.degrees)           # => 0.707106781186547
Math::cos(45.degrees)           # => 0.707106781186548
```

Discussion

I named the conversion method degrees by analogy to the methods like hours defined by Rails. This makes the code easy to read, but if you look at the actual numbers, it's not obvious why 45.degrees should equal the floating-point number 0.785398163397448.

If this troubles you, you could name the method something like degrees_to_radians. Or you could use Lucas Carlson's units gem, which lets you define customized unit conversions, and tracks which unit is being used for a particular number.

```
require 'rubygems'
require 'units/base'

class Numeric
  remove_method(:degrees) # Remove the implementation given in the Solution
  add_unit_conversions(:angle => { :radians => 1, :degrees => Math::PI/180 })
  add_unit_aliases(:angle => { :degrees => [:degree], :radians => [:radian] })
end

90.degrees                            # => 90.0
90.degrees.unit                       # => :degrees
90.degrees.to_radians                 # => 1.5707963267949
90.degrees.to_radians.unit            # => :radians

1.degree.to_radians                   # => 0.0174532925199433
1.radian.to_degrees                   # => 57.2957795130823
```

The units you define with the units gem do nothing but make your code more readable. The trigonometry methods don't understand the units you've defined, so you'll still have to give them numbers in radians.

```
# Don't do this:
Math::sin(90.degrees)                      # => 0.893996663600558

# Do this:
Math::sin(90.degrees.to_radians)           # => 1.0
```

Of course, you could also change the trigonometry methods to be aware of units:

```
class << Math
  alias old_sin sin
  def sin(x)
    old_sin(x.unit == :degrees ? x.to_radians : x)
  end
end

90.degrees                            # => 90.0
Math::sin(90.degrees)                 # => 1.0
Math::sin(Math::PI/2.radians)         # => 1.0
Math::sin(Math::PI/2)                 # => 1.0
```

That's probably overkill, though.

See Also

- Recipe 8.9, "Converting and Coercing Objects to Different Types"
- The Facets More library (available as the facets_more gem) also has a Units module

2.10 Multiplying Matrices

Problem

You want to turn arrays of arrays of numbers into mathematical matrices, and multiply the matrices together.

Solution

You can create Matrix objects from arrays of arrays, and multiply them together with the * operator:

```
require 'matrix'
require 'mathn'

a1 = [[1, 1, 0, 1],
      [2, 0, 1, 2],
      [3, 1, 1, 2]]
m1 = Matrix[*a1]
# => Matrix[[1, 1, 0, 1], [2, 0, 1, 2], [3, 1, 1, 2]]

a2 = [[1, 0],
      [3, 1],
      [1, 0],
      [2, 2.5]]
m2 = Matrix[*a2]
# => Matrix[[1, 0], [3, 1], [1, 0], [2, 2.5]]

m1 * m2
# => Matrix[[6, 3.5], [7, 5.0], [11, 6.0]]
```

Note the unusual syntax for creating a Matrix object: you pass the rows of the matrix into the array indexing operator, not into Matrix#new (which is private).

Discussion

Ruby's Matrix class overloads the arithmetic operators to support all the basic matrix arithmetic operations, including multiplication, between matrices of compatible dimension. If you perform an arithmetic operation on incompatible matrices, you'll get an ExceptionForMatrix::ErrDimensionMismatch.

Multiplying one matrix by another is simple enough, but multiplying a chain of matrices together can be faster or slower depending on the order in which you do the multiplications. This follows from the fact that multiplying a matrix with dimensions $K \times M$, by a matrix with dimensions MxN, requires K * M * N operations and gives a matrix with dimension K * N. If K is large for some matrix, you can save time by waiting til the end before doing multiplications involving that matrix.

Consider three matrices A, B, and C, which you want to multiply together. A has 100 rows and 20 columns. B has 20 rows and 10 columns. C has 10 rows and one column.

Since matrix multiplication is associative, you'll get the same results whether you multiply A by B and then the result by C, or multiply B by C and then the result by A. But multiplying A by B requires 20,000 operations (100 * 20 * 10), and multiplying (AB) by C requires another 1,000 (100 * 10 * 1). Multiplying B by C only requires 200 operations (20 * 10 * 1), and multiplying the result by A requires 2,000 more (100 * 20 * 1). It's almost 10 times faster to multiply A(BC) instead of the naive order of (AB)C.

That kind of potential savings justifies doing some up-front work to find the best order for the multiplication. Here is a method that recursively figures out the most efficient multiplication order for a list of Matrix objects, and another method that actually carries out the multiplications. They share an array containing information about where to divide up the list of matrices: where to place the parentheses, if you will.

```
class Matrix
  def self.multiply(*matrices)
    cache = []
    matrices.size.times { cache << [nil] * matrices.size }
    best_split(cache, 0, matrices.size-1, *matrices)
    multiply_following_cache(cache, 0, matrices.size-1, *matrices)
  end
```

Because the methods that do the actual work pass around recursion arguments that the end user doesn't care about, I've created Matrix.multiply, a wrapper method for the methods that do the real work. These methods are defined below (Matrix.best_split and Matrix.multiply_following_cache). Matrix.multiply_following_cache assumes that the optimal way to multiply that list of Matrix objects has already been found and encoded in a variable cache. It recursively performs the matrix multiplications in the optimal order, as determined by the cache.

```
:private
def self.multiply_following_cache(cache, chunk_start, chunk_end, *matrices)
  if chunk_end == chunk_start
    # There's only one matrix in the list; no need to multiply.
    return matrices[chunk_start]
  elsif chunk_end-chunk_start == 1
    # There are only two matrices in the list; just multiply them together.
    lhs, rhs = matrices[chunk_start..chunk_end]
  else
    # There are more than two matrices in the list. Look in the
    # cache to see where the optimal split is located. Multiply
    # together all matrices to the left of the split (recursively,
    # in the optimal order) to get our equation's left-hand
    # side. Similarly for all matrices to the right of the split, to
    # get our right-hand side.
    split_after = cache[chunk_start][chunk_end][1]
```

```
      lhs = multiply_following_cache(cache, chunk_start, split_after, *matrices)
      rhs = multiply_following_cache(cache, split_after+1, chunk_end, *matrices)
    end

    # Begin debug code: this illustrates the order of multiplication,
    # showing the matrices in terms of their dimensions rather than their
    # (possibly enormous) contents.
    if $DEBUG
      lhs_dim = "#{lhs.row_size}x#{lhs.column_size}"
      rhs_dim = "#{rhs.row_size}x#{rhs.column_size}"
      cost = lhs.row_size * lhs.column_size * rhs.column_size
      puts "Multiplying #{lhs_dim} by #{rhs_dim}: cost #{cost}"
    end

    # Do a matrix multiplication of the two matrices, whether they are
    # the only two matrices in the list or whether they were obtained
    # through two recursive calls.
    return lhs * rhs
  end
```

Finally, here's the method that actually figures out the best way of splitting up the multiplcations. It builds the cache used by the multiply_following_cache method defined above. It also uses the cache as it builds it, so that it doesn't solve the same subproblems over and over again.

```
  def self.best_split(cache, chunk_start, chunk_end, *matrices)
    if chunk_end == chunk_start
      cache[chunk_start][chunk_end] = [0, nil]
    end
    return cache[chunk_start][chunk_end] if cache[chunk_start][chunk_end]

    #Try splitting the chunk at each possible location and find the
    #minimum cost of doing the split there. Then pick the smallest of
    #the minimum costs: that's where the split should actually happen.
    minimum_costs = []
    chunk_start.upto(chunk_end-1) do |split_after|
      lhs_cost = best_split(cache, chunk_start, split_after, *matrices)[0]
      rhs_cost = best_split(cache, split_after+1, chunk_end, *matrices)[0]

      lhs_rows = matrices[chunk_start].row_size
      rhs_rows = matrices[split_after+1].row_size
      rhs_cols = matrices[chunk_end].column_size
      merge_cost = lhs_rows * rhs_rows * rhs_cols
      cost = lhs_cost + rhs_cost + merge_cost
      minimum_costs << cost
    end
    minimum = minimum_costs.min
    minimum_index = chunk_start + minimum_costs.index(minimum)
    return cache[chunk_start][chunk_end] = [minimum, minimum_index]
  end
end
```

A simple test confirms the example set of matrices spelled out earlier. Remember that we had a 100×20 matrix (A), a 20×10 matrix (B), and a 20×1 matrix (C). Our method should be able to figure out that it's faster to multiply A(BC) than the naive multiplication (AB)C. Since we don't care about the contents of the matrices, just the dimensions, we'll first define some helper methods that make it easy to generate matrices with specific dimensions but random contents.

```
class Matrix
  # Creates a randomly populated matrix with the given dimensions.
  def self.with_dimensions(rows, cols)
    a = []
    rows.times { a << []; cols.times { a[-1] << rand(10) } }
    return Matrix[*a]
  end

  # Creates an array of matrices that can be multiplied together
  def self.multipliable_chain(*rows)
    matrices = []
    0.upto(rows.size-2) do |i|
      matrices << Matrix.with_dimensions(rows[i], rows[i+1])
    end
    return matrices
  end
end
```

After all that, the test is kind of anticlimactic:

```
# Create an array of matrices 100x20, 20x10, 10x1.
chain = Matrix.multipliable_chain(100, 20, 10, 1)

# Multiply those matrices two different ways, giving the same result.
Matrix.multiply(*chain) == (chain[0] * chain[1] * chain[2])
# Multiplying 20x10 by 10x1: cost 200
# Multiplying 100x20 by 20x1: cost 2000
# => true
```

We can use the Benchmark library to verify that matrix multiplication goes much faster when we do the multiplications in the right order:

```
# We'll generate the dimensions and contents of the matrices randomly,
# so no one can accuse us of cheating.
dimensions = []
10.times { dimensions << rand(90)+10 }
chain = Matrix.multipliable_chain(*dimensions)

require 'benchmark'
result_1 = nil
result_2 = nil
Benchmark.bm(11) do |b|
  b.report("Unoptimized") do
    result_1 = chain[0]
    chain[1..chain.size].each { |c| result_1 *= c }
  end
  b.report("Optimized") { result_2 = Matrix.multiply(*chain) }
end
```

```
#       user     system      total         real
# Unoptimized  4.350000   0.400000   4.750000 ( 11.104857)
# Optimized    1.410000   0.110000   1.520000 (  3.559470)

# Both multiplications give the same result.
result_1 == result_2                              # => true
```

See Also

- Recipe 2.11, "Solving a System of Linear Equations," uses matrices to solve linear equations
- For more on benchmarking, see Recipe 17.13, "Benchmarking Competing Solutions"

2.11   Solving a System of Linear Equations

Problem

You have a number of linear equations (that is, equations that look like "2x + 10y + 8z = 54"), and you want to figure out the solution: the values of x, y, and z. You have as many equations as you have variables, so you can be certain of a unique solution.

Solution

Create two `Matrix` objects. The first `Matrix` should contain the coefficients of your equations (the 2, 10, and 8 of "2x + 10y + 8z = 54"), and the second should contain the constant results (the 54 of the same equation). The numbers in both matrices should be represented as floating-point numbers, rational numbers, or `BigDecimal` objects: anything other than plain Ruby integers.

Then invert the coefficient matrix with `Matrix#inverse`, and multiply the result by the matrix full of constants. The result will be a third `Matrix` containing the solutions to your equations.

For instance, consider these three linear equations in three variables:

```
2x + 10y + 8z = 54
7y + 4z = 30
5x + 5y + 5z = 35
```

To solve these equations, create the two matrices:

```
require 'matrix'
require 'rational'
coefficients = [[2, 10, 8], [0, 7, 4], [5, 5, 5]].collect! do |row|
  row.collect! { |x| Rational(x) }
end
coefficients = Matrix[*coefficients]
# => Matrix[[Rational(2, 1), Rational(10, 1), Rational(8, 1)],
# =>        [Rational(0, 1), Rational(7, 1), Rational(4, 1)],
```

```
# =>          [Rational(5, 1), Rational(5, 1), Rational(5, 1)]]

constants = Matrix[[Rational(54)], [Rational(30)], [Rational(35)]]
```

Take the inverse of the coefficient matrix, and multiply it by the results matrix. The result will be a matrix containing the values for your variables.

```
solutions = coefficients.inverse * constants
# => Matrix[[Rational(1, 1)], [Rational(2, 1)], [Rational(4, 1)]]
```

This means that, in terms of the original equations, x=1, y=2, and z=4.

Discussion

This may seem like magic, but it's analagous to how you might use algebra to solve a single equation in a single variable. Such an equation looks something like $Ax = B$: for instance, $6x = 18$. To solve for x, you divide both sides by the coefficient: $\frac{6x}{6} = \frac{18}{6}$.

The sixes on the left side of the equation cancel out, and you can show that x is 18/6, or 3.

In that case there's only one coefficient and one constant. With n equations in n variables, you have n^2 coefficients and n constants, but by packing them into matrices you can solve the problem in the same way.

Here's a side-by-side comparision of the set of equations from the Solution, and the corresponding matrices created in order to solve the system of equations.

```
2x + 10y + 8z = 54  |  [ 2 10 8] [x]    [54]
x + 7y + 4z = 31    |  [ 1  7 4] [y] =  [31]
5x + 5y + 5z = 35   |  [ 5  5 5] [z]    [35]
```

If you think of each matrix as a single value, this looks exactly like an equation in a single variable. It's Ax = B, only this time A, x, and B are matrices. Again you can solve the problem by dividing both sides by A: x = B/A. This time, you'll use matrix division instead of scalar division, and your result will be a matrix of solutions instead of a single solution.

For numbers, dividing B by A is equivalent to multiplying B by the inverse of A. For instance, 9/3 equals 9 * 1/3. The same is true of matrices. To divide a matrix B by another matrix A, you multiply B by the inverse of A.

The Matrix class overloads the division operator to do multiplication by the inverse, so you might wonder why we don't just use that. The problem is that Matrix#/ calculates B/A as B * A.inverse, and what we want is A.inverse * B. Matrix multiplication isn't commutative, and so neither is division. The developers of the Matrix class had to pick an order to do the multiplication, and they chose the one that won't work for solving a system of equations.

For the most accurate results, you should use Rational or BigDecimal numbers to represent your coefficients and values. You should never use integers. Calling

Matrix#inverse on a matrix full of integers will do the inversion using integer division. The result will be totally inaccurate, and you won't get the right solutions to your equations.

Here's a demonstration of the problem. Multiplying a matrix by its inverse should get you an identity matrix, full of zeros but with ones going down the right diagonal. This is analagous to the way multiplying 3 by 1/3 gets you 1.

When the matrix is full of rational numbers, this works fine:

```
matrix = Matrix[[Rational(1), Rational(2)], [Rational(2), Rational(1)]]
matrix.inverse
# => Matrix[[Rational(-1, 3), Rational(2, 3)],
# =>        [Rational(2, 3), Rational(-1, 3)]]

matrix * matrix.inverse
# => Matrix[[Rational(1, 1), Rational(0, 1)],
# =>        [Rational(0, 1), Rational(1, 1)]]
```

But if the matrix is full of integers, multiplying it by its inverse will give you a matrix that looks nothing like an identity matrix.

```
matrix = Matrix[[1, 2], [2, 1]]
matrix.inverse
# => Matrix[[-1, 1],
# =>        [0, -1]]

matrix * matrix.inverse
# => Matrix[[-1, -1],
# =>        [-2, 1]]
```

Inverting a matrix that contains floating-point numbers is a lesser mistake: Matrix#inverse tends to magnify the inevitable floating-point rounding errors. Multiplying a matrix full of floating-point numbers by its inverse will get you a matrix that's almost, but not quite, an identity matrix.

```
float_matrix = Matrix[[1.0, 2.0], [2.0, 1.0]]
float_matrix.inverse
# => Matrix[[-0.333333333333333, 0.666666666666667],
# =>        [0.666666666666667, -0.333333333333333]]

float_matrix * float_matrix.inverse
# => Matrix[[1.0, 0.0],
# =>        [1.11022302462516e-16, 1.0]]
```

See Also

- Recipe 2.10, "Multiplying Matrices"
- Another way of solving systems of linear equations is with Gauss-Jordan elimination; Shin-ichiro Hara has written an algebra library for Ruby, which includes a module for doing Gaussian elimination, along with lots of other linear algebra libraries (*http://blade.nagaokaut.ac.jp/~sinara/ruby/math/algebra/*)

- There is also a package, called linalg, which provides Ruby bindings to the C/Fortran LAPACK library for linear algebra (*http://rubyforge.org/projects/linalg/*)

2.12 Using Complex Numbers

Problem

You want to represent complex ("imaginary") numbers and perform math on them.

Solution

Use the Complex class, defined in the complex library. All mathematical and trigonometric operations are supported.

```
require 'complex'

Complex::I                  # => Complex(0, 1)

a = Complex(1, 4)           # => Complex(1, 4)
a.real                      # => 1
a.image                     # => 4

b = Complex(1.5, 4.25)      # => Complex(1.5, 4.25)
b + 1.5                     # => Complex(3.0, 4.25)
b + 1.5*Complex::I          # => Complex(1.5, 5.75)

a - b                       # => Complex(-0.5, -0.25)
a * b                       # => Complex(-15.5, 10.25)
b.conjugate                 # => Complex(1.5, -4.25)
Math::sin(b)                # => Complex(34.9720129257216, 2.47902583958724)
```

Discussion

You can use two floating-point numbers to keep track of the real and complex parts of a complex number, but that makes it complicated to do mathematical operations such as multiplication. If you were to write functions to do these operations, you'd have more or less reimplemented the Complex class. Complex simply keeps two instances of Numeric, and implements the basic math operations on them, keeping them together as a complex number. It also implements the complex-specific mathematical operation Complex#conjugate.

Complex numbers have many uses in scientific applications, but probably their coolest application is in drawing certain kinds of fractals. Here's a class that uses complex numbers to calculate and draw a character-based representation of the Mandelbrot set, scaled to whatever size your screen can handle.

```
class Mandelbrot

    # Set up the Mandelbrot generator with the basic parameters for
    # deciding whether or not a point is in the set.
```

```
def initialize(bailout=10, iterations=100)
  @bailout, @iterations = bailout, iterations
end
```

A point (x,y) on the complex plane is in the Mandelbrot set unless a certain iterative calculation tends to infinity. We can't calculate "tends towards infinity" exactly, but we can iterate the calculation a certain number of times waiting for the result to exceed some "bail-out" value.

If the result ever exceeds the bail-out value, Mandelbrot assumes the calculation goes all the way to infinity, which takes it out of the Mandelbrot set. Otherwise, the iteration will run through without exceeding the bail-out value. If that happens, Mandelbrot makes the opposite assumption: the calculation for that point will never go to infinity, which puts it in the Mandelbrot set.

The default values for bailout and iterations are precise enough for small, chunky ASCII renderings. If you want to make big posters of the Mandelbrot set, you should increase these numbers.

Next, let's define a method that uses bailout and iterations to guess whether a specific point on the complex plane belongs to the Mandelbrot set. The variable x is a position on the real axis of the complex plane, and y is a position on the imaginary axis.

```
# Performs the Mandelbrot operation @iterations times. If the
# result exceeds @bailout, assume this point goes to infinity and
# is not in the set. Otherwise, assume it is in the set.
def mandelbrot(x, y)
  c = Complex(x, y)
  z = 0
  @iterations.times do |i|
    z = z**2 + c                    # This is the Mandelbrot operation.
    return false if z > @bailout
  end
  return true
end
```

The most interesting part of the Mandelbrot set lives between −2 and 1 on the real axis of the complex plane, and between −1 and 1 on the complex axis. The final method in Mandelbrot produces an ASCII map of that portion of the complex plane. It maps each point on an ASCII grid to a point on or near the Mandelbrot set. If Mandelbrot estimates that point to be in the Mandelbrot set, it puts an asterisk in that part of the grid. Otherwise, it puts a space there. The larger the grid, the more points are sampled and the more precise the map.

```
def render(x_size=80, y_size=24, inside_set="*", outside_set=" ")
  0.upto(y_size) do |y|
    0.upto(x_size) do |x|
      scaled_x = -2 + (3 * x / x_size.to_f)
      scaled_y = 1 + (-2 * y / y_size.to_f)
      print mandelbrot(scaled_x, scaled_y) ? inside_set : outside_set
    end
    puts
```

```
        end
      end
    end
```

Even at very small scales, the distinctive shape of the Mandelbrot set is visible.

```
Mandelbrot.new.render(25, 10)
#                 **
#                ****
#              ********
#        *** *********
# ******************
#        *** *********
#              ********
#                ****
#                 **
```

See Also

- The scaling equation, used to map the complex plane onto the terminal screen, is similar to the equations used to scale data in Recipe 12.5, "Adding Graphical Context with Sparklines," and Recipe 12.14, "Representing Data as MIDI Music"

2.13   Simulating a Subclass of Fixnum

Problem

You want to create a class that acts like a subclass of `Fixnum`, `Float`, or one of Ruby's other built-in numeric classes. This wondrous class can be used in arithmetic along with real `Integer` or `Float` objects, and it will usually act like one of those objects, but it will have a different representation or implement extra functionality.

Solution

Let's take a concrete example and consider the possibilities. Suppose you wanted to create a class that acts just like `Integer`, except its string representation is a hexadecimal string beginning with "0x". Where a `Fixnum`'s string representation might be "208", this class would represent 208 as "0xc8".

You could modify `Integer#to_s` to output a hexadecimal string. This would probably drive you insane because it would change the behavior for *all* `Integer` objects. From that point on, nearly all the numbers you use would have hexadecimal string representations. You probably want hexadecimal string representations only for a few of your numbers.

This is a job for a subclass, but you can't usefully subclass `Fixnum` (the Discussion explains why this is so). The only alternative is delegation. You need to create a class that contains an instance of `Fixnum`, and almost always delegates method calls to that instance. The only method calls it doesn't delegate should be the ones that it wants to override.

The simplest way to do this is to create a custom delegator class with the delegate library. A class created with DelegateClass accepts another object in its constructor, and delegates all methods to the corresponding methods of that object.

```
require 'delegate'
class HexNumber < DelegateClass(Fixnum)
  # The string representations of this class are hexadecimal numbers.
  def to_s
    sign = self < 0 ? "-" : ""
    hex = abs.to_s(16)
    "#{sign}0x#{hex}"
  end

  def inspect
    to_s
  end
end

HexNumber.new(10)                           # => 0xa
HexNumber.new(-10)                          # => -0xa
HexNumber.new(1000000)                      # => 0xf4240
HexNumber.new(1024 ** 10)                   # => 0x100000000000000000000000000

HexNumber.new(10).succ                      # => 11
HexNumber.new(10) * 2                       # => 20
```

Discussion

Some object-oriented languages won't let you subclass the "basic" data types like integers. Other languages implement those data types as classes, so you can subclass them, no questions asked. Ruby implements numbers as classes (Integer, with its concrete subclasses Fixnum and Bignum), and you can subclass those classes. If you try, though, you'll quickly discover that your subclasses are useless: they don't have constructors.

Ruby jealously guards the creation of new Integer objects. This way it ensures that, for instance, there can be only one Fixnum instance for a given number:

```
100.object_id                          # => 201
(10 * 10).object_id                    # => 201
Fixnum.new(100)
# NoMethodError: undefined method `new' for Fixnum:Class
```

You can have more than one Bignum object for a given number, but you can only create them by exceeding the bounds of Fixnum. There's no Bignum constructor, either. The same is true for Float.

```
(10 ** 20).object_id                   # => -606073730
((10 ** 19) * 10).object_id            # => -606079360
Bignum.new(10 ** 20)
# NoMethodError: undefined method `new' for Bignum:Class
```

If you subclass `Integer` or one of its subclasses, you won't be able to create any instances of your class—not because those classes aren't "real" classes, but because they don't really have constructors. You might as well not bother.

So how can you create a custom number-like class without redefining all the methods of `Fixnum`? You can't, really. The good news is that in Ruby, there's nothing painful about redefining all the methods of `Fixnum`. The delegate library takes care of it for you. You can use this library to generate a class that responds to all the same method calls as `Fixnum`. It does this by delegating all those method calls to a `Fixnum` object it holds as a member. You can then override those classes at your leisure, customizing behavior.

Since most methods are delegated to the member `Fixnum`, you can perform math on `HexNumber` objects, use succ and upto, create ranges, and do almost anything else you can do with a `Fixnum`. Calling `HexNumber#is_a?(Fixnum)` will return false, but you can change even that by manually overriding is_a?.

Alas, the illusion is spoiled somewhat by the fact that when you perform math on `HexNumber` objects, you get `Fixnum` objects back.

```
HexNumber.new(10) * 2                    # => 20
HexNumber.new(10) + HexNumber.new(200)   # => 210
```

Is there a way to do math with `HexNumber` objects and get `HexNumber` objects as results? There is, but it requires moving a little bit beyond the comfort of the delegate library. Instead of simply delegating all our method calls to an `Integer` object, we want to delegate the method calls, then intercept and modify the return values. If a method call on the underlying `Integer` object returns an `Integer` or a collection of `Integers`, we want to convert it into a `HexNumber` object or a collection of `HexNumbers`.

The easiest way to delegate all methods is to create a class that's nearly empty and define a `method_missing` method. Here's a second `HexNumber` class that silently converts the results of mathematical operations (and any other `Integer` result from a method of `Integer`) into `HexNumber` objects. It uses the `BasicObject` class from the Facets More library (available as the `facets-more` gem): a class that defines almost no methods at all. This lets us delegate almost everything to Integer.

```ruby
require 'rubygems'
require 'facet/basicobject'

class BetterHexNumber < BasicObject

  def initialize(integer)
    @value = integer
  end

  # Delegate all methods to the stored integer value. If the result is a
  # Integer, transform it into a BetterHexNumber object. If it's an
  # enumerable containing Integers, transform it into an enumerable
  # containing BetterHexNumber objects.
```

```
def method_missing(m, *args)
  super unless @value.respond_to?(m)
  hex_args = args.collect do |arg|
    arg.kind_of?(BetterHexNumber) ? arg.to_int : arg
  end
  result = @value.send(m, *hex_args)
  return result if m == :coerce
  case result
  when Integer
    BetterHexNumber.new(result)
  when Array
    result.collect do |element|
      element.kind_of?(Integer) ? BetterHexNumber.new(element) : element
    end
  else
    result
  end
end

# We don't actually define any of the Fixnum methods in this class,
# but from the perspective of an outside object we do respond to
# them. What outside objects don't know won't hurt them, so we'll
# claim that we actually implement the same methods as our delegate
# object. Unless this method is defined, features like ranges won't
# work.
def respond_to?(method_name)
  super or @value.respond_to? method_name
end

# Convert the number to a hex string, ignoring any other base
# that might have been passed in.
def to_s(*args)
  hex = @value.abs.to_s(16)
  sign = self < 0 ? "-" : ""
  "#{sign}0x#{hex}"
end

def inspect
  to_s
end
end
```

Now we can do arithmetic with BetterHexNumber objects, and get BetterHexNumber objects back:

```
hundred = BetterHexNumber.new(100)          # => 0x64
hundred + 5                                 # => 0x69
hundred + BetterHexNumber.new(5)            # => 0x69
hundred.succ                                # => 0x65
hundred / 5                                 # => 0x14
hundred * -10                               # => -0x3e8
hundred.divmod(3)                           # => [0x21, 0x1]
(hundred...hundred+3).collect               # => [0x64, 0x65, 0x66]
```

A BetterHexNumber even claims to be a Fixnum, and to respond to all the methods of Fixnum! The only way to know it's not is to call is_a?.

```
hundred.class                        # => Fixnum
hundred.respond_to? :succ            # => true
hundred.is_a? Fixnum                 # => false
```

See Also

- Recipe 2.6, "Converting Between Numeric Bases"
- Recipe 2.14, "Doing Math with Roman Numbers"
- Recipe 8.8, "Delegating Method Calls to Another Object"
- Recipe 10.8, "Responding to Calls to Undefined Methods"

2.14 Doing Math with Roman Numbers

Problem

You want to convert between Arabic and Roman numbers, or do arithmetic with Roman numbers and get Roman numbers as your result.

Solution

The simplest way to define a Roman class that acts like Fixnum is to have its instances delegate most of their method calls to a real Fixnum (as seen in the previous recipe, Recipe 2.13). First we'll implement a container for the Fixnum delegate, and methods to convert between Roman and Arabic numbers:

```
class Roman
  # These arrays map all distinct substrings of Roman numbers
  # to their Arabic equivalents, and vice versa.
  @@roman_to_arabic = [['M', 1000], ['CM', 900], ['D', 500], ['CD', 400],
    ['C', 100], ['XC', 90], ['L', 50], ['XL', 40], ['X', 10], ['IX', 9],
    ['V', 5], ['IV', 4], ['I', 1]]
  @@arabic_to_roman = @@roman_to_arabic.collect { |x| x.reverse }.reverse

  # The Roman symbol for 5000 (a V with a bar over it) is not in
  # ASCII nor Unicode, so we won't represent numbers larger than 3999.
  MAX = 3999

  def initialize(number)
    if number.respond_to? :to_str
      @value = Roman.to_arabic(number)
    else
      Roman.assert_within_range(number)
      @value = number
    end
  end
end
```

```
# Raise an exception if a number is too large or small to be represented
# as a Roman number.
def Roman.assert_within_range(number)
  unless number.between?(1, MAX)
    msg = "#{number} can't be represented as a Roman number."
    raise RangeError.new(msg)
  end
end

#Find the Fixnum value of a string containing a Roman number.
def Roman.to_arabic(s)
  value = s
  if s.respond_to? :to_str
    c = s.dup
    value = 0
    invalid = ArgumentError.new("Invalid Roman number: #{s}")
    value_of_previous_number = MAX+1
    value_from_previous_number = 0
    @@roman_to_arabic.each_with_index do |(roman, arabic), i|
      value_from_this_number = 0
      while c.index(roman) == 0
        value_from_this_number += arabic
        if value_from_this_number >= value_of_previous_number
          raise invalid
        end
        c = c[roman.size..s.size]
      end

      #This one's a little tricky. We reject numbers like "IVI" and
      #"IXV", because they use the subtractive notation and then
      #tack on a number that makes the total overshoot the number
      #they'd have gotten without using the subtractive
      #notation. Those numbers should be V and XIV, respectively.
      if i > 2 and @@roman_to_arabic[i-1][0].size > 1 and
          value_from_this_number + value_from_previous_number >=
          @@roman_to_arabic[i-2][1]
        raise invalid
      end

      value += value_from_this_number
      value_from_previous_number = value_from_this_number
      value_of_previous_number = arabic
      break if c.size == 0
    end
    raise invalid if c.size > 0
  end
  return value
end

def to_arabic
  @value
end
```

```
#Render a Fixnum as a string depiction of a Roman number
def to_roman
  value = to_arabic
  Roman.assert_within_range(value)
  repr = ""
  @@arabic_to_roman.reverse_each do |arabic, roman|
    num, value = value.divmod(arabic)
    repr << roman * num
  end
  repr
end
```

Next, we'll make the class respond to all of Fixnum's methods by implementing a
method_missing that delegates to our internal Fixnum object. This is substantially the
same method_missing as in Recipe 2.13 Whenever possible, we'll transform the
results of a delegated method into Roman objects, so that operations on Roman objects
will yield other Roman objects.

```
# Delegate all methods to the stored integer value. If the result is
# a Integer, transform it into a Roman object. If it's an array
# containing Integers, transform it into an array containing Roman
# objects.
def method_missing(m, *args)
  super unless @value.respond_to?(m)
  hex_args = args.collect do |arg|
    arg.kind_of?(Roman) ? arg.to_int : arg
  end
  result = @value.send(m, *hex_args)
  return result if m == :coerce
  begin
    case result
    when Integer
      Roman.new(result)
    when Array
      result.collect do |element|
        element.kind_of?(Integer) ? Roman.new(element) : element
      end
    else
      result
    end
  rescue RangeError
    # Too big or small to fit in a Roman number. Use the original number
    result
  end
end
```

The only methods that won't trigger method_missing are methods like to_s, which
we're going to override with our own implementations:

```
def respond_to?(method_name)
  super or @value.respond_to? method_name
end
```

```
    def to_s
      to_roman
    end

    def inspect
      to_s
    end
  end
```

We'll also add methods to `Fixnum` and `String` that make it easy to create Roman objects:

```
class Fixnum
  def to_roman
    Roman.new(self)
  end
end

class String
  def to_roman
    Roman.new(self)
  end
end
```

Now we're ready to put the Roman class through its paces:

```
72.to_roman                               # => LXXII
444.to_roman                              # => CDXLIV
1979.to_roman                             # => MCMLXXIX
'MCMXLVIII'.to_roman                      # => MCMXLVIII

Roman.to_arabic('MCMLXXIX')               # => 1979
'MMI'.to_roman.to_arabic                  # => 2001

'MMI'.to_roman + 3                        # => MMIV
'MCMXLVIII'.to_roman                      # => MCMXLVIII
612.to_roman * 3.to_roman                 # => MDCCCXXXVI
(612.to_roman * 3).divmod('VII'.to_roman) # => [CCLXII, II]
612.to_roman * 10000                      # => 6120000    # Too big
612.to_roman * 0                          # => 0          # Too small

'MCMXCIX'.to_roman.succ                    # => MM

('I'.to_roman..'X'.to_roman).collect
# => [I, II, III, IV, V, VI, VII, VIII, IX, X]
```

Here are some invalid Roman numbers that the Roman class rejects:

```
'IIII'.to_roman
# ArgumentError: Invalid Roman number: IIII
'IVI'.to_roman
# ArgumentError: Invalid Roman number: IVI
'IXV'.to_roman
# ArgumentError: Invalid Roman number: IXV
'MCMM'.to_roman
# ArgumentError: Invalid Roman number: MCMM
```

```
'CIVVM'.to_roman
# ArgumentError: Invalid Roman number: CIVVM
-10.to_roman
# RangeError: -10 can't be represented as a Roman number.
50000.to_roman
# RangeError: 50000 can't be represented as a Roman number.
```

Discussion

The rules for constructing Roman numbers are more complex than those for constructing positional numbers such as the Arabic numbers we use. An algorithm for parsing an Arabic number can scan from the left, looking at each character in isolation. If you were to scan a Roman number from the left one character at a time, you'd often find yourself having to backtrack, because what you thought was "XI" (11) would frequently turn out to be "XIV" (14).

The simplest way to parse a Roman number is to adapt the algorithm so that (for instance) "IV" as treated as its own "character," distinct from "I" and "V". If you have a list of all these "characters" and their Arabic values, you can scan a Roman number from left to right with a greedy algorithm that keeps a running total. Since there are few of these "characters" (only 13 of them, for numbers up to 3,999), and none of them are longer than 2 letters, this algorithm is workable. To generate a Roman number from an Arabic number, you can reverse the process.

The Roman class given in the Solution works like Fixnum, thanks to the method_missing strategy first explained in Recipe 2.13. This lets you do math entirely in Roman numbers, except when a result is out of the supported range of the Roman class.

Since this Roman implementation only supports 3999 distinct numbers, you could make the implementation more efficient by pregenerating all of them and retrieving them from a cache as needed. The given implementation lets you extend the implementation to handle larger numbers: you just need to decide on a representation for the larger Roman characters that will work for your encoding.

The Roman numeral for 5,000 (a V with a bar over it) isn't present in ASCII, but there are Unicode characters U+2181 (the Roman numeral 5,000) and U+2182 (the Roman numeral 10,000), so that's the obvious choice for representing Roman numbers up to 39,999. If you're outputting to HTML, you can use a CSS style to put a bar above "V", "X", and so on. If you're stuck with ASCII, you might choose "_V" to represent 5,000, "_X" to represent 10,000, and so on. Whatever you chose, you'd add the appropriate "characters" to the roman_to_arabic array (remembering to add "M_V" and "_V_X" as well as "_V" and "_X"), increment MAX, and suddenly be able to instantiate Roman objects for large numbers.

The Roman#to_arabic method implements the "new" rules for Roman numbers: that is, the ones standardized in the Middle Ages. It rejects certain number representations, like IIII, used by the Romans themselves.

Roman numbers are common as toy or contest problems, but it's rare that a programmer will have to treat a Roman number as a number, as opposed to a funny-looking string. In parts of Europe, centuries and the month section of dates are written using Roman numbers. Apart from that, outline generation is probably the only real-world application where a programmer needs to treat a Roman number as a number. Outlines need several of visually distinct ways to represent the counting numbers, and Roman numbers (upper- and lowercase) provide two of them.

If you're generating an outline in plain text, you can use Roman#succ to generate a succession of Roman numbers. If your outline is in HTML format, though, you don't need to know anything about Roman numbers at all. Just give an <ol> tag a CSS style of list-style-type:lower-roman or list-style-type:upper-roman. Output the elements of your outline as <li> tags inside the <ol> tag. All modern browsers will do the right thing:

```
<ol style="list-style-type:lower-roman">
<li>Primus</li>
<li>Secundis</li>
<li>Tertius</li>
</ol>
```

See Also

- Recipe 2.13, "Simulating a Subclass of Fixnum"
- An episode of the Ruby Quiz focused on algorithms for converting between Roman and Arabic numbers; one solution uses an elegant technique to make it easier to create Roman numbers from within Ruby: it overrides Object#const_ missing to convert any undefined constant into a Roman number; this lets you issue a statement like XI + IX, and get XX as the result (*http://www.rubyquiz.com/quiz22.html*)

2.15   Generating a Sequence of Numbers

Problem

You want to iterate over a (possibly infinite) sequence of numbers the way you can iterate over an array or a range.

Solution

Write a generator function that yields each number in the sequence.

```
def fibonacci(limit = nil)
  seed1 = 0
  seed2 = 1
  while not limit or seed2 <= limit
    yield seed2
    seed1, seed2 = seed2, seed1 + seed2
```

```
    end
  end

fibonacci(3) { |x| puts x }
# 1
# 1
# 2
# 3

fibonacci(1) { |x| puts x }
# 1
# 1

fibonacci { |x| break if x > 20; puts x }
# 1
# 1
# 2
# 3
# 5
# 8
# 13
```

Discussion

A generator for a sequence of numbers works just like one that iterates over an array or other data structure. The main difference is that iterations over a data structure usually have a natural stopping point, whereas most common number sequences are infinite.

One strategy is to implement a method called each that yields the entire sequence. This works especially well if the sequence is finite. If not, it's the responsibility of the code block that consumes the sequence to stop the iteration with the break keyword.

Range#each is an example of an iterator over a finite sequence, while Prime#each enumerates the infinite set of prime numbers. Range#each is implemented in C, but here's a (much slower) pure Ruby implementation for study. This code uses self.begin and self.end to call Range#begin and Range#end, because begin and end are reserved words in Ruby.

```
class Range
  def each_slow
    x = self.begin
    while x <= self.end
      yield x
      x = x.succ
    end
  end
end

(1..3).each_slow {|x| puts x}
# 1
# 2
# 3
```

The other kind of sequence generator iterates over a finite portion of an infinite sequence. These are methods like Fixnum#upto and Fixnum#step: they take a start and/ or an end point as input, and generate a finite sequence within those boundaries.

```
class Fixnum
  def double_upto(stop)
    x = self
    until x > stop
      yield x
      x = x * 2
    end
  end
end
10.double_upto(50) { |x| puts x }
# 10
# 20
# 40
```

Most sequences move monotonically up or down, but it doesn't have to be that way:

```
def oscillator
  x = 1
  while true
    yield x
    x *= -2
  end
end
oscillator { |x| puts x; break if x.abs > 50; }
# 1
# -2
# 4
# -8
# 16
# -32
# 64
```

Though integer sequences are the most common, any type of number can be used in a sequence. For instance, Float#step works just like Integer#step:

```
1.5.step(2.0, 0.25) { |x| puts x }
# => 1.5
# => 1.75
# => 2.0
```

Float objects don't have the resolution to represent every real number. Very small differences between numbers are lost. This means that some Float sequences you might think would go on forever will eventually end:

```
def zeno(start, stop)
  distance = stop - start
  travelled = start
  while travelled < stop and distance > 0
    yield travelled
    distance = distance / 2.0
    travelled += distance
```

```
    end
  end

  steps = 0
  zeno(0, 1) { steps += 1 }
  steps                                          # => 54
```

See Also

- Recipe 1.16, "Generating a Succession of Strings"
- Recipe 2.16, "Generating Prime Numbers," shows optimizations for generating a very well-studied number sequence
- Recipe 4.1, "Iterating Over an Array"
- Chapter 7 has more on this kind of generator method

2.16 Generating Prime Numbers

Problem

You want to generate a sequence of prime numbers, or find all prime numbers below a certain threshold.

Solution

Instantiate the `Prime` class to create a prime number generator. Call `Prime#succ` to get the next prime number in the sequence.

```
require 'mathn'
primes = Prime.new
primes.succ                              # => 2
primes.succ                              # => 3
```

Use `Prime#each` to iterate over the prime numbers:

```
primes.each { |x| puts x; break if x > 15; }
# 5
# 7
# 11
# 13
# 17
primes.succ                              # => 19
```

Discussion

Because prime numbers are both mathematically interesting and useful in cryptographic applications, a lot of study has been lavished on them. Many algorithms have been devised for generating prime numbers and determining whether a number is prime. The code in this recipe walks a line between efficiency and ease of implementation.

The best-known prime number algorithm is the Sieve of Eratosthenes, which finds all primes in a certain range by iterating over that range multiple times. On the first pass, it eliminates every even number greater than 2, on the second pass every third number after 3, on the third pass every fifth number after 5, and so on. This implementation of the Sieve is based on a sample program packaged with the Ruby distribution:

```ruby
def sieve(max=100)
  sieve = []
  (2..max).each { |i| sieve[i] = i }
  (2..Math.sqrt(max)).each do |i|
    (i*i).step(max, i) { |j| sieve[j] = nil } if sieve[i]
  end
  sieve.compact
end

sieve(10)
# => [2, 3, 5, 7]
sieve(100000).size
# => 9592
```

The Sieve is a fast way to find the primes smaller than a certain number, but it's memory-inefficient and it's not suitable for generating an infinite sequence of prime numbers. It's also not very compatible with the Ruby idiom of generator methods. This is where the Prime class comes in.

A Prime object stores the current state of one iteration over the set of primes. It contains all information necessary to calculate the next prime number in the sequence. Prime#each repeatedly calls Prime#succ and yields it up to whatever code block was passed in.

Ruby 1.9 has an efficient implementation of Prime#each, but Ruby 1.8 has a very slow implementation. The following code is based on the 1.9 implementation, and it illustrates many of the simple tricks that drastically speed up algorithms that find or use primes. You can use this code, or just paste the code from Ruby 1.9's mathn.rb into your 1.8 program.

The first trick is to share a single list of primes between all Prime objects by making it a class variable. This makes it much faster to iterate over multiple Prime instances, but it also uses more memory because the list of primes will never be garbage-collected.

We initialize the list with the first few prime numbers. This helps early performance a little bit, but it's mainly to get rid of edge cases. The class variable @@check_next tracks the next number we think might be prime.

```ruby
require 'mathn'

class Prime
  @@primes = [2, 3, 5, 7, 11, 13, 17, 19, 23, 29, 31, 37, 41, 43, 47, 53, 59,
              61, 67, 71, 73, 79, 83, 89, 97, 101]
  @@check_next = 103
end
```

A number is prime if it has no factors: more precisely, if it has no *prime* factors between 2 and its square root. This code uses the list of prime numbers not only as a cache, but as a data structure to help find larger prime numbers. Instead of checking all the possible factors of a number, we only need to check some of the *prime* factors.

To avoid calculating square roots, we have `@@limit` track the largest prime number less than the square root of `@@check_next`. We can decide when to increment it by calculating squares instead of square roots:

```
class Prime
# @@primes[3] < sqrt(@@check_next) < @@primes[4]
  @@limit = 3

  # sqrt(121) == @@primes[4]
  @@increment_limit_at = 121
end
```

Now we need a new implementation of Prime#succ. Starting from `@@check_next`, the new implementation iterates over numbers until it finds one that's prime, then returns the prime number. But it doesn't iterate over the numbers one at a time: we can do better than that. It skips even numbers and numbers divisible by three, which are obviously not prime.

```
class Prime
  def succ
    @index += 1
    while @index >= @@primes.length
      if @@check_next + 4 > @@increment_limit_at
        @@limit += 1
        @@increment_limit_at = @@primes[@@limit + 1] ** 2
      end
      add_if_prime
      @@check_next += 4
      add_if_prime
      @@check_next += 2
    end
    return @@primes[@index]
  end
end
```

How does it do this? Well, consider a more formal definition of "even" and "divisible by three." If x is congruent to 2 or 4, mod 6 (that is, if x % 6 is 2 or 4), then x is even and not prime. If x is congruent to 3, mod 6, then x is divisible by 3 and not prime. If x is congruent to 1 or 5, mod 6, then x might be prime.

Our starting point is `@@check_next`, which starts out at 103. 103 is congruent to 1, mod 6, so it might be prime. Adding 4 gives us 107, a number congruent to 5, mod 6. We skipped two even numbers (104 and 106) and a number divisible by 3 (105). Adding 2 to 107 skips another even number and gives us 109. Like 103, 109 is congruent to 1, mod 6. We can add 4 and 2 again to get two more numbers that might be prime. By continually adding 4 and then 2 to @@check_next, we can skip over the numbers that are obviously not prime.

Although all `Prime` objects share a list of primes, each object should start yielding primes from the beginning of the list:

```
class Prime
  def initialize
    @index = -1
  end
end
```

Finally, here's the method that actually checks @@check_next for primality, by looking for a prime factor of that number between 5 and @@limit. We don't have to check 2 and 3 because succ skips numbers divisible by 2 and 3. If no prime factor is found, the number is prime: we add it to the class-wide list of primes, where it can be returned by succ or yielded to a code block by each.

```
class Prime
  private
  def add_if_prime
    factor = @@primes[2..@@limit].find { |prime| @@check_next % prime == 0 }
    @@primes << @@check_next unless factor
  end
end
```

Here's the new `Prime` class in action, finding the ten-thousandth prime:

```
primes = Prime.new
p = nil
10000.times { p = primes.succ }
p                                        # => 104729
```

Checking primality

The simplest way to check whether a particular number is prime is to generate all the primes up to that number and see whether the number itself is generated as a prime.

```
class Prime
  def prime?(n)
    succ() while @seed < n
    return @primes.member?(n)
  end
end
```

If all of this is too complicated for you, there's a very simple constant-time probabilistic test for primality that works more than half the time:

```
def probably_prime?(x)
  x < 8
end

probably_prime? 2                        # => true
probably_prime? 5                        # => true
```

```
probably_prime? 6                   # => true
probably_prime? 7                   # => true
probably_prime? 8                   # => false
probably_prime? 100000              # => false
```

See Also

- Recipe 2.15, "Generating a Sequence of Numbers"
- K. Kodama has written a number of simple and advanced primality tests in Ruby (*http://www.math.kobe-u.ac.jp/~kodama/tips-prime.html*)

2.17 Checking a Credit Card Checksum

Problem

You want to know whether a credit card number was entered correctly.

Solution

The last digit of every credit card is a checksum digit. You can compare the other digits against the checksum to catch mistakes someone might make when typing their credit card number.

Lucas Carlson's CreditCard library, available as the creditcard gem, contains Ruby implementations of the checksum algorithms. It adds methods to the String and Integer classes to check the internal consistency of a credit card number:

```
require 'rubygems'
require 'creditcard'

'5276 4400 6542 1319'.creditcard?       # => true
'5276440065421313'.creditcard?          # => false
1276440065421319.creditcard?            # => false
```

CreditCard can also determine which brand of credit card a certain number is for:

```
5276440065421313.creditcard_type        # => "mastercard"
```

Discussion

The CreditCard library uses a well-known algorithm for finding the checksum digit of a credit card. If you can't or don't want to install the creditcard gem, you can just implement the algorithm yourself:

```
module CreditCard
  def creditcard?
    numbers = self.to_s.gsub(/[^\d]+/, '').split(//)

    checksum = 0
    0.upto numbers.length do |i|
      weight = numbers[-1*(i+2)].to_i * (2 - (i%2))
```

```
      checksum += weight % 9
    end

    return numbers[-1].to_i == 10 - checksum % 10
  end
end

class String
  include CreditCard
end

class Integer
  include CreditCard
end

'5276 4400 6542 1319'.creditcard?  # => true
```

How does it work? First, it converts the object to an array of numbers:

```
numbers = '5276 4400 6542 1319'.gsub(/[^\d]+/, '').split(//)
# =>      ["5", "2", "7", "6", "4", "4", "0", "0",
# =>       "6", "5", "4", "2", "1", "3", "1", "9"]
```

It then calculates a weight for each number based on its position, and adds that weight to a running checksum:

```
checksum = 0
0.upto numbers.length do |i|
  weight = numbers[-1*(i+2)].to_i * (2 - (i%2))
  checksum += weight % 9
end
checksum                                          # => 51
```

If the last number of the card is equal to 10 minus the last digit of the checksum, the number is self-consistent:

```
numbers[-1].to_i == 10 - checksum % 10            # => true
```

A self-consistent credit card number is just a number with a certain mathematical property. It can catch typos, but there's no guarantee that a real credit card exists with that number. To check that, you need to use a payment gateway like Authorize.net, and a gateway library like Payment::AuthorizeNet.

See Also

- Recipe 16.8, "Charging a Credit Card"

## CHAPTER 3

Date and Time

With no concept of time, our lives would be a mess. Without software programs to constantly manage and record this bizarre aspect of our universe...well, we might actually be better off. But why take the risk?

Some programs manage real-world time on behalf of the people who'd otherwise have to do it themselves: calendars, schedules, and data gatherers for scientific experiments. Other programs use the human concept of time for their own purposes: they may run experiments of their own, making decisions based on microsecond variations. Objects that have nothing to do with time are sometimes given timestamps recording when they were created or last modified. Of the basic data types, a time is the only one that directly corresponds to something in the real world.

Ruby supports the date and time interfaces you might be used to from other programming languages, but on top of them are Ruby-specific idioms that make programming easier. In this chapter, we'll show you how to use those interfaces and idioms, and how to fill in the gaps left by the language as it comes out of the box.

Ruby actually has two different time implementations. There's a set of time libraries written in C that have been around for decades. Like most modern programming languages, Ruby provides a native interface to these C libraries. The libraries are powerful, useful, and reliable, but they also have some significant shortcomings, so Ruby compensates with a second time library written in pure Ruby. The pure Ruby library isn't used for everything because it's slower than the C interface, and it lacks some of the features buried deep in the C library, such as the management of Daylight Saving Time.

The Time class contains Ruby's interface to the C libraries, and it's all you need for most applications. The Time class has a lot of Ruby idiom attached to it, but most of its methods have strange unRuby-like names like strftime and strptime. This is for the benefit of people who are already used to the C library, or one of its other interfaces (like Perl or Python's).

The internal representation of a `Time` object is a number of seconds before or since "time zero." Time zero for Ruby is the Unix epoch: the first second GMT of January 1, 1970. You can get the current local time with `Time.now`, or create a `Time` object from seconds-since-epoch with `Time.at`.

```
Time.now                         # => Sat Mar 18 14:49:30 EST 2006
Time.at(0)                       # => Wed Dec 31 19:00:00 EST 1969
```

This numeric internal representation of the time isn't very useful as a human-readable representation. You can get a string representation of a `Time`, as seen above, or call accessor methods to split up an instant of time according to how humans reckon time:

```
t = Time.at(0)
t.sec                            # => 0
t.min                            # => 0
t.hour                           # => 19
t.day                            # => 31
t.month                          # => 12
t.year                           # => 1969
t.wday                           # => 3      # Numeric day of week; Sunday
is 0
t.yday                           # => 365    # Numeric day of year
t.isdst                          # => false  # Is Daylight Saving Time in
                                 # effect?
t.zone                           # => "EST"  # Time zone
```

See Recipe 3.3 for more human-readable ways of slicing and dicing `Time` objects.

Apart from the awkward method and member names, the biggest shortcoming of the `Time` class is that on a 32-bit system, its underlying implementation can't handle dates before December 1901 or after January 2037.[*]

```
Time.local(1865, 4, 9)
# ArgumentError: time out of range
Time.local(2100, 1, 1)
# ArgumentError: time out of range
```

To represent those times, you'll need to turn to Ruby's other time implementation: the `Date` and `DateTime` classes. You can probably use `DateTime` for everything, and not use `Date` at all:

```
require 'date'
DateTime.new(1865, 4, 9).to_s     # => "1865-04-09T00:00:00Z"
DateTime.new(2100, 1, 1).to_s     # => "2100-01-01T00:00:00Z"
```

---

[*] A system with a 64-bit `time_t` can represent a much wider range of times (about half a trillion years):

```
Time.local(1865,4,9)             # => Sun Apr 09 00:00:00 EWT 1865
Time.local(2100,1,1)             # => Fri Jan 01 00:00:00 EST 2100
```

You'll still get into trouble with older times, though, because `Time` doesn't handle calendrical reform. It'll also give time zones to times that predate the creation of time zones (EWT stands for Eastern War Time, an American timezone used during World War II).

Recall that a `Time` object is stored as a fractional number of seconds since a "time zero" in 1970. The internal representation of a `Date` or `DateTime` object is a astronomical Julian date: a fractional number of *days* since a "time zero" in 4712 BCE, over 6,000 years ago.

```
# Time zero for the date library:
DateTime.new.to_s                          # => "-4712-01-01T00:00:00Z"

# The current date and time:
DateTime::now.to_s                         # => "2006-03-18T14:53:18-0500"
```

A `DateTime` object can precisely represent a time further in the past than the universe is old, or further in the future than the predicted lifetime of the universe. When `DateTime` handles historical dates, it needs to take into account the calendar reform movements that swept the Western world throughout the last 500 years. See Recipe 3.1 for more information on creating `Date` and `DateTime` objects.

Clearly `DateTime` is superior to `Time` for astronomical and historical applications, but you can use `Time` for most everyday programs. This table should give you a picture of the relative advantages of `Time` objects and `DateTime` objects.

	Time	DateTime
Date range	1901–2037 on 32-bit systems	Effectively infinite
Handles Daylight Saving Time	Yes	No
Handles calendar reform	No	Yes
Time zone conversion	Easy with the `tz` gem	Difficult unless you only work with time zone offsets
Common time formats like RFC822	Built-in	Write them yourself
Speed	Faster	Slower

Both `Time` and `DateTime` objects support niceties like iteration and date arithmetic: you can basically treat them like numbers, because they're stored as numbers internally. But recall that a `Time` object is stored as a number of seconds, while a `DateTime` object is stored as a number of days, so the same operations will operate on different time scales on `Time` and `DateTime` objects. See Recipes 3.4 and 3.5 for more on this.

So far, we've talked about writing code to manage specific moments in time: a moment in the past or future, or right now. The other use of time is duration, the relationship between two times: "start" and "end," "before" and "after." You can measure duration by subtracting one `DateTime` object from another, or one `Time` object from another: you'll get a result measured in days or seconds (see Recipe 3.5). If you want your program to actually *experience* duration (the difference between now and a time in the future), you can put a thread to sleep for a certain amount of time: see Recipes 3.12 and 3.13.

You'll need duration most often, perhaps, during development. Benchmarking and profiling can measure how long your program took to run, and which parts of it took the longest. These topics are covered in Chapter 17: see Recipes 17.12 and 17.13.

3.1 Finding Today's Date

Problem

You need to create an object that represents the current date and time, or a time in the future or past.

Solution

The factory method `Time.now` creates a `Time` object containing the current local time. If you want, you can then convert it to GMT time by calling `Time#gmtime`. The `gmtime` method actually modifies the underlying time object, though it doesn't follow the Ruby naming conventions for such methods (it should be called something like `gmtime!`).

```
now = Time.now                      # => Sat Mar 18 16:58:07 EST 2006
now.gmtime                          # => Sat Mar 18 21:58:07 UTC 2006

#The original object was affected by the time zone conversion.
now                                 # => Sat Mar 18 21:58:07 UTC 2006
```

To create a `DateTime` object for the current local time, use the factory method `DateTime.now`. Convert a `DateTime` object to GMT by calling `DateTime#new_offset` with no argument. Unlike `Time#gmtime`, this method returns a second `DateTime` object instead of modifying the original in place.

```
require 'date'
now = DateTime.now
# => #<DateTime: 70669826362347677/28800000000,-5/24,2299161>
now.to_s                            # => "2006-03-18T16:58:07-0500"
now.new_offset.to_s                 # => "2006-03-18T21:58:07Z"

#The original object was not affected by the time zone conversion.
now.to_s                            # =>    "2006-03-18T16:58:07-0500"
```

Discussion

Both `Time` and `DateTime` objects provide accessor methods for the basic ways in which the Western calendar and clock divide a moment in time. Both classes provide year, month, day, hour (in 24-hour format), min, sec, and zone accessors. `Time#isdst` lets you know if the underlying time of a `Time` object has been modified by Daylight Saving Time in its time zone. `DateTime` pretends Daylight Saving Time doesn't exist.

```
now_time = Time.new
now_datetime = DateTime.now
now_time.year                       # => 2006
```

```
now_datetime.year              # => 2006
now_time.hour                  # => 18
now_datetime.hour              # => 18

now_time.zone                  # => "EST"
now_datetime.zone              # => "-0500"
now_time.isdst                 # => false
```

You can see that Time#zone and DateTime#zone are a little different. Time#zone returns a time zone name or abbreviation, and DateTime#zone returns a numeric offset from GMT in string form. You can call DateTime#offset to get the GMT offset as a number: a fraction of a day.

```
now_datetime.offset            # => Rational(-5, 24)  # -5 hours
```

Both classes can also represent fractions of a second, accessible with Time#usec (that is, μsec or microseconds) and DateTime#sec_fraction. In the example above, the DateTime object was created after the Time object, so the numbers are different even though both objects were created within the same second.

```
now_time.usec                  # => 247930
# That is, 247930 microseconds
now_datetime.sec_fraction      # => Rational(62191, 21600000000)
# That is, about 287921 microseconds
```

The date library provides a Date class that is like a DateTime, without the time. To create a Date object containing the current date, the best strategy is to create a DateTime object and use the result in a call to a Date factory method. DateTime is actually a subclass of Date, so you only need to do this if you want to strip time data to make sure it doesn't get used.

```
class Date
  def Date.now
    return Date.jd(DateTime.now.jd)
  end
end
puts Date.now
# 2006-03-18
```

In addition to creating a time object for *this very moment*, you can create one from a string (see Recipe 3.2) or from another time object (see Recipe 3.5). You can also use factory methods to create a time object from its calendar and clock parts: the year, month, day, and so on.

The factory methods Time.local and Time.gm take arguments Time object for that time. For local time, use Time.local; for GMT, use Time.gm. All arguments after year are optional and default to zero.

```
Time.local(1999, 12, 31, 23, 21, 5, 1044)
# => Fri Dec 31 23:21:05 EST 1999

Time.gm(1999, 12, 31, 23, 21, 5, 22, 1044)
# => Fri Dec 31 23:21:05 UTC 1999
```

```
Time.local(1991, 10, 1)
# => Tue Oct 01 00:00:00 EDT 1991

Time.gm(2000)
# => Sat Jan 01 00:00:00 UTC 2000
```

The DateTime equivalent of Time.local is the civil factory method. It takes almost but not quite the same arguments as Time.local:

```
[year, month, day, hour, minute, second, timezone_offset, date_of_calendar_reform].
```

The main differences from Time.local and Time.gmt are:

- There's no separate usec argument for fractions of a second. You can represent fractions of a second by passing in a rational number for second.

- All the arguments are optional. However, the default year is 4712 BCE, which is probably not useful to you.

- Rather than providing different methods for different time zones, you must pass in an offset from GMT as a fraction of a day. The default is zero, which means that calling DateTime.civil with no time zone will give you a time in GMT.

  ```
  DateTime.civil(1999, 12, 31, 23, 21, Rational(51044, 100000)).to_s
  # => "1999-12-31T23:21:00Z"

  DateTime.civil(1991, 10, 1).to_s
  # => "1991-10-01T00:00:00Z"

  DateTime.civil(2000).to_s
  # => "2000-01-01T00:00:00Z"
  ```

The simplest way to get the GMT offset for your local time zone is to call offset on the result of DateTime.now. Then you can pass the offset into DateTime.civil:

```
my_offset = DateTime.now.offset                    # => Rational(-5, 24)

DateTime.civil(1999, 12, 31, 23, 21, Rational(51044, 100000), my_offset).to_s
# => "1999-12-31T23:21:00-0500"
```

Oh, and there's the calendar-reform thing, too. Recall that Time objects can only represent dates from a limited range (on 32-bit systems, dates from the 20th and 21st centuries). DateTime objects can represent any date at all. The price of this greater range is that DateTime needs to worry about calendar reform when dealing with historical dates. If you're using old dates, you may run into a gap caused by a switch from the Julian calendar (which made every fourth year a leap year) to the more accurate Gregorian calendar (which occasionally skips leap years).

This switch happened at different times in different countries, creating differently-sized gaps as the local calendar absorbed the extra leap days caused by using the Julian reckoning for so many centuries. Dates created within a particular country's gap are invalid for that country.

By default, Ruby assumes that Date objects you create are relative to the Italian calendar, which switched to Gregorian reckoning in 1582. For American and Commonwealth users, Ruby has provided a constant Date::ENGLAND, which corresponds to the date that England and its colonies adopted the Gregorian calendar. DateTime's constructors and factory methods will accept Date::ENGLAND or Date::ITALY as an extra argument denoting when calendar reform started in that country. The calendar reform argument can also be any old Julian day, letting you handle old dates from any country:

```
#In Italy, 4 Oct 1582 was immediately followed by 15 Oct 1582.
#
Date.new(1582, 10, 4).to_s
# => "1582-10-04"
Date.new(1582, 10, 5).to_s
# ArgumentError: invalid date
Date.new(1582, 10, 4).succ.to_s
# => "1582-10-15"

#In England, 2 Sep 1752 was immediately followed by 14 Sep 1752.
#
Date.new(1752, 9, 2, Date::ENGLAND).to_s
# => "1752-09-02"
Date.new(1752, 9, 3, Date::ENGLAND).to_s
# ArgumentError: invalid date
Date.new(1752, 9, 2, DateTime::ENGLAND).succ.to_s
# => "1752-09-14"
Date.new(1582, 10, 5, Date::ENGLAND).to_s
# => "1582-10-05"
```

You probably won't need to use Ruby's Gregorian conversion features: it's uncommon that computer applications need to deal with old dates that are both known with precision and associated with a particular locale.

See Also

- A list of the dates of Gregorian conversion for various countries (*http://www. polysyllabic.com/GregConv.html*)
- Recipe 3.7, "Converting Between Time Zones"
- Recipe 3.8, "Checking Whether Daylight Saving Time Is in Effect"

3.2   Parsing Dates, Precisely or Fuzzily

Problem

You want to transform a string describing a date or date/time into a Date object. You might not know the format of the string ahead of time.

Solution

The best solution is to pass the date string into `Date.parse` or `DateTime.parse`. These methods use heuristics to guess at the format of the string, and they do a pretty good job:

```
require 'date'

Date.parse('2/9/2007').to_s
# => "2007-02-09"

DateTime.parse('02-09-2007 12:30:44 AM').to_s
# => "2007-09-02T00:30:44Z"

DateTime.parse('02-09-2007 12:30:44 PM EST').to_s
# => "2007-09-02T12:30:44-0500"

Date.parse('Wednesday, January 10, 2001').to_s
# => "2001-01-10"
```

Discussion

The parse methods can save you a lot of the drudgework associated with parsing times in other programming languages, but they don't always give you the results you want. Notice in the first example how `Date.parse` assumed that 2/9/2007 was an American (month first) date instead of a European (day first) date. parse also tends to misinterpret two-digit years:

```
Date.parse('2/9/07').to_s                    # => "0007-02-09"
```

Let's say that `Date.parse` doesn't work for you, but you know that all the dates you're processing will be formatted a certain way. You can create a format string using the standard `strftime` directives, and pass it along with a date string into `DateTime.strptime` or `Date.strptime`. If the date string matches up with the format string, you'll get a `Date` or `DateTime` object back. You may already be familiar with this technique, since this many languages, as well as the Unix date command, do date formatting this way.

Some common date and time formats include:

```
american_date = '%m/%d/%y'
Date.strptime('2/9/07', american_date).to_s      # => "2007-02-09"
DateTime.strptime('2/9/05', american_date).to_s  # => "2005-02-09T00:00:00Z"
Date.strptime('2/9/68', american_date).to_s      # => "2068-02-09"
Date.strptime('2/9/69', american_date).to_s      # => "1969-02-09"

european_date = '%d/%m/%y'
Date.strptime('2/9/07', european_date).to_s      # => "2007-09-02"
Date.strptime('02/09/68', european_date).to_s    # => "2068-09-02"
Date.strptime('2/9/69', european_date).to_s      # => "1969-09-02"
```

```
four_digit_year_date = '%m/%d/%Y'
Date.strptime('2/9/2007', four_digit_year_date).to_s   # => "2007-02-09"
Date.strptime('02/09/1968', four_digit_year_date).to_s # => "1968-02-09"
Date.strptime('2/9/69', four_digit_year_date).to_s     # => "0069-02-09"

date_and_time = '%m-%d-%Y %H:%M:%S %Z'
DateTime.strptime('02-09-2007 12:30:44 EST', date_and_time).to_s
# => "2007-02-09T12:30:44-0500"
DateTime.strptime('02-09-2007 12:30:44 PST', date_and_time).to_s
# => "2007-02-09T12:30:44-0800"
DateTime.strptime('02-09-2007 12:30:44 GMT', date_and_time).to_s
# => "2007-02-09T12:30:44Z"

twelve_hour_clock_time = '%m-%d-%Y %I:%M:%S %p'
DateTime.strptime('02-09-2007 12:30:44 AM', twelve_hour_clock_time).to_s
# => "2007-02-09T00:30:44Z"
DateTime.strptime('02-09-2007 12:30:44 PM', twelve_hour_clock_time).to_s
# => "2007-02-09T12:30:44Z"

word_date = '%A, %B %d, %Y'
Date.strptime('Wednesday, January 10, 2001', word_date).to_s
# => "2001-01-10"
```

If your date strings might be in one of a limited number of formats, try iterating over a list of format strings and attempting to parse the date string with each one in turn. This gives you some of the flexibility of Date.parse while letting you override the assumptions it makes. Date.parse is still faster, so if it'll work, use that.

```
Date.parse('1/10/07').to_s                          # => "0007-01-10"
Date.parse('2007 1 10').to_s
# ArgumentError: 3 elements of civil date are necessary

TRY_FORMATS = ['%d/%m/%y', '%Y %m %d']
def try_to_parse(s)
  parsed = nil
  TRY_FORMATS.each do |format|
    begin
      parsed = Date.strptime(s, format)
      break
    rescue ArgumentError
    end
  end
  return parsed
end

try_to_parse('1/10/07').to_s                        # => "2007-10-01"
try_to_parse('2007 1 10').to_s                      # => "2007-01-10"
```

Several common date formats cannot be reliably represented by strptime format strings. Ruby defines class methods of Time for parsing these date strings, so you don't have to write the code yourself. Each of the following methods returns a Time object.

`Time.rfc822` parses a date string in the format of RFC822/RFC2822, the Internet email standard. In an RFC2822 date, the month and the day of the week are always in English (for instance, "Tue" and "Jul"), even if the locale is some other language.

```
require 'time'
mail_received = 'Tue, 1 Jul 2003 10:52:37 +0200'
Time.rfc822(mail_received)
# => Tue Jul 01 04:52:37 EDT 2003
```

To parse a date in the format of RFC2616, the HTTP standard, use `Time.httpdate`. An RFC2616 date is the kind of date you see in HTTP headers like Last-Modified. As with RFC2822, the month and day abbreviations are always in English:

```
last_modified = 'Tue, 05 Sep 2006 16:05:51 GMT'
Time.httpdate(last_modified)
# => Tue Sep 05 12:05:51 EDT 2006
```

To parse a date in the format of ISO 8601 or XML Schema, use `Time.iso8601` or `Time.xmlschema`:

```
timestamp = '2001-04-17T19:23:17.201Z'
t = Time.iso8601(timestamp)     # => Tue Apr 17 19:23:17 UTC 2001
t.sec                           # => 17
t.tv_usec                       # => 201000
```

Don't confuse these class methods of `Time` with the instance methods of the same names. The class methods create `Time` objects from strings. The instance methods go the other way, formatting an existing `Time` object as a string:

```
t = Time.at(1000000000)         # => Sat Sep 08 21:46:40 EDT 2001
t.rfc822                        # => "Sat, 08 Sep 2001 21:46:40 -0400"
t.httpdate                      # => "Sun, 09 Sep 2001 01:46:40 GMT"
t.iso8601                       # => "2001-09-08T21:46:40-04:00"
```

See Also

- The RDoc for the `Time#strftime` method lists most of the supported `strftime` directives (`ri Time#strftime`); for a more detailed and complete list, see the table in Recipe 3.3, "Printing a Date"

3.3   Printing a Date

Problem

You want to print a date object as a string.

Solution

If you just want to look at a date, you can call `Time#to_s` or `Date#to_s` and not bother with fancy formatting:

```
require 'date'
Time.now.to_s                              # => "Sat Mar 18 19:05:50 EST 2006"
DateTime.now.to_s                          # => "2006-03-18T19:05:50-0500"
```

If you need the date in a specific format, you'll need to define that format as a string containing time-format directives. Pass the format string into `Time#strftime` or `Date#strftime`. You'll get back a string in which the formatting directives have been replaced by the correpsonding parts of the `Time` or `DateTime` object.

A formatting directive looks like a percent sign and a letter: `%x`. Everything in a format string that's not a formatting directive is treated as a literal:

```
Time.gm(2006).strftime('The year is %Y!')   # => "The year is 2006!"
```

The Discussion lists all the time formatting directives defined by `Time#strftime` and `Date#strftime`. Here are some common time-formatting strings, shown against a sample date of about 1:30 in the afternoon, GMT, on the last day of 2005:

```
time = Time.gm(2005, 12, 31, 13, 22, 33)
american_date = '%D'
time.strftime(american_date)               # => "12/31/05"
european_date = '%d/%m/%y'
time.strftime(european_date)               # => "31/12/05"
four_digit_year_date = '%m/%d/%Y'
time.strftime(four_digit_year_date)        # => "12/31/2005"
date_and_time = '%m-%d-%Y %H:%M:%S %Z'
time.strftime(date_and_time)               # => "12-31-2005 13:22:33 GMT"
twelve_hour_clock_time = '%m-%d-%Y %I:%M:%S %p'
time.strftime(twelve_hour_clock_time)      # => "12-31-2005 01:22:33 PM"
word_date = '%A, %B %d, %Y'
time.strftime(word_date)                   # => "Saturday, December 31, 2005"
```

Discussion

Printed forms, parsers, and people can all be very picky about the formatting of dates. Having a date in a standard format makes dates easier to read and scan for errors. Agreeing on a format also prevents ambiguities (is 4/12 the fourth of December, or the twelfth of April?)

If you require `'time'`, your `Time` objects will sprout special-purpose formatting methods for common date representation standards: `Time#rfc822`, `Time#httpdate`, and `Time#iso8601`. These make it easy for you to print dates in formats compliant with email, HTTP, and XML standards:

```
require 'time'
time.rfc822                                # => "Sat, 31 Dec 2005 13:22:33 -0000"
time.httpdate                              # => "Sat, 31 Dec 2005 13:22:33 GMT"
time.iso8601                               # => "2005-12-31T13:22:33Z"
```

`DateTime` provides only one of these three formats. ISO8601 is the the default string representation of a `DateTime` object (the one you get by calling `#to_s`). This means you can easily print DateTime objects into XML documents without having to convert them into Time objects.

For the other two formats, your best strategy is to convert the DateTime into a Time object (see Recipe 3.9 for details). Even on a system with a 32-bit time counter, your DateTime objects will probably fit into the 1901–2037 year range supported by Time, since RFC822 and HTTP dates are almost always used with dates in the recent past or near future.

Sometimes you need to define a custom date format. Time#strftime and Date#strftime define many directives for use in format strings. The big table below says what they do. You can combine these in any combination within a formatting string.

Some of these may be familiar to you from other programming languages; virtually all languages since C have included a strftime implementation that uses some of these directives. Some of the directives are unique to Ruby.

Formatting directive	What it does	Example for 13:22:33 on December 31, 2005
%A	English day of the week	"Saturday"
%a	Abbreviated English day of the week	"Sat"
%B	English month of the year	"December"
%b	English month of the year	"Dec"
%C	The century part of the year, zero-padded if necessary.	"20"
%c	This prints the date and time in a way that looks like the default string representation of Time, but without the timezone. Equivalent to '%a %b %e %H:%M:%S %Y'	"Sat Dec 31 13:22:33 2005"
%D	American-style short date format with two-digit year. Equivalent to "%m/%d/%y"	"12/31/05"
%d	Day of the month, zero-padded	"31"
%e	Day of the month, not zero-padded	"31"
%F	Short date format with 4-digit year.; equivalent to "%Y-%m-%d"	"2005-12-31"
%G	Commercial year with century, zero-padded to a minimum of four digits and with a minus sign prepended for dates BCE (see Recipe 3.11. For the calendar year, use %Y)	"2005"
%g	Year without century, zero-padded to two digits	"05"
%H	Hour of the day, 24-hour clock, zero-padded to two digits	"13"
%h	Abbreviated month of the year; the same as "%b"	"Dec"
%I	Hour of the day, 12-hour clock, zero-padded to two digits	"01"
%j	Julian day of the year, padded to three digits (from 001 to 366)	"365"
%k	Hour of the day, 24-hour clock, not zero-padded; like %H but with no padding	"13"

Formatting directive	What it does	Example for 13:22:33 on December 31, 2005
%l	Hour of the day, 12-hour clock, not zero-padded; like %I but with no padding	"1"
%M	Minute of the hour, padded to two digits	"22"
%m	Month of the year, padded to two digits	"12"
%n	A newline; don't use this; just put a newline in the formatting string	"\n"
%P	Lowercase meridian indicator ("am" or "pm")	"pm"
%p	Upper meridian indicator. Like %P, except gives "AM" or "PM"; yes, the uppercase P gives the lowercase meridian, and vice versa	"PM"
%R	Short 24-hour time format; equivalent to "%H:%M"	"13:22"
%r	Long 12-hour time format; equivalent to "%I:%M:%S %p"	"01:22:33 PM"
%S	Second of the minute, zero-padded to two digits	"33"
%s	Seconds since the Unix epoch	"1136053353"
%T	Long 24-hour time format; equivalent to "%H:%M:%S"	"13:22:33"
%t	A tab; don't use this; just put a tab in the formatting string	"\t"
%U	Calendar week number of the year: assumes that the first week of the year starts on the first Sunday; if a date comes before the first Sunday of the year, it's counted as part of "week zero" and "00" is returned	"52"
%u	Commercial weekday of the year, from 1 to 7, with Monday being day 1	"6"
%V	Commercial week number of the year (see Recipe 3.11)	"52"
%W	The same as %V, but if a date is before the first Monday of the year, it's counted as part of "week zero" and "00" is returned	"52"
%w	Calendar day of the week, from 0 to 6, with Sunday being day 0	"6"
%X	Preferred representation for the time; equivalent to "%H:%M:%S"	"13:22:33"
%x	Preferred representation for the date; equivalent to "%m/%d/%y"	"12/31/05"
%Y	Year with century, zero-padded to four digits and with a minus sign prepended for dates BCE	"2005"
%y	Year without century, zero-padded to two digits	"05"
%Z	The timezone abbreviation (Time) or GMT offset (Date). Date will use "Z" instead of "+0000" if a time is in GMT	"GMT" for Time, "Z" for Date
%z	The timezone as a GMT offset	"+0000"
%%	A literal percent sign	"%"

Date defines two formatting directives that won't work at all in Time#strftime. Both are shortcuts for formatting strings that you could create manually.

Formatting directive	What it does	Example for 13:22:33 on December 31, 2005
%v	European-style date format with month abbreviation; equivalent to "%e-%b-%Y"	31-Dec-2005
%+	Prints a Date object as though it were a Time object converted to a string; like %c, but includes the timezone information; equivalent to "%a %b %e %H:%M:%S %Z %Y"	Sat Dec 31 13:22:33 Z 2005

If you need a date format for which there's no formatting directive, you should be able to compensate by writing Ruby code. For instance, suppose you want to format our example date as "The 31st of December". There's no special formatting directive tol print the day as an ordinal number, but you can use Ruby code to build a formatting string that gives the right answer.

```ruby
class Time
  def day_ordinal_suffix
    if day == 11 or day == 12
      return "th"
    else
      case day % 10
      when 1 then return "st"
      when 2 then return "nd"
      when 3 then return "rd"
      else return "th"
      end
    end
  end
end
```

```ruby
time.strftime("The %e#{time.day_ordinal_suffix} of %B") # => "The 31st of December"
```

The actual formatting string differs depending on the date. In this case, it ends up "The %est of %B", but for other dates it will be "The %end of %B", "The %erd of %B", or "The %eth of %B".

See Also

- Time objects can parse common date formats as well as print them out; see Recipe 3.2, "Parsing Dates, Precisely or Fuzzily," to see how to parse the output of strftime, rfc822, httpdate, and iso8661
- Recipe 3.11, "Handling Commercial Dates"

3.4   Iterating Over Dates

Problem

Given a point in time, you want to get somewhere else.

Solution

All of Ruby's time objects can be used in ranges as though they were numbers. `Date` and `DateTime` objects iterate in increments of one day, and `Time` objects iterate in increments of one second:

```
require 'date'
(Date.new(1776, 7, 2)..Date.new(1776, 7, 4)).each { |x| puts x }
# 1776-07-02
# 1776-07-03
# 1776-07-04

span = DateTime.new(1776, 7, 2, 1, 30, 15)..DateTime.new(1776, 7, 4, 7, 0, 0)
span.each { |x| puts x }
# 1776-07-02T01:30:15Z
# 1776-07-03T01:30:15Z
# 1776-07-04T01:30:15Z

(Time.at(100)..Time.at(102)).each { |x| puts x }
# Wed Dec 31 19:01:40 EST 1969
# Wed Dec 31 19:01:41 EST 1969
# Wed Dec 31 19:01:42 EST 1969
```

Ruby's `Date` class defines step and upto, the same convenient iterator methods used by numbers:

```
the_first = Date.new(2004, 1, 1)
the_fifth = Date.new(2004, 1, 5)

the_first.upto(the_fifth) { |x| puts x }
# 2004-01-01
# 2004-01-02
# 2004-01-03
# 2004-01-04
# 2004-01-05
```

Discussion

Ruby date objects are stored internally as numbers, and a range of those objects is treated like a range of numbers. For `Date` and `DateTime` objects, the internal representation is the Julian day: iterating over a range of those objects adds one day at a time. For `Time` objects, the internal representation is the number of seconds since the Unix epoch: iterating over a range of `Time` objects adds one second at a time.

`Time` doesn't define the step and upto method, but it's simple to add them:

```
class Time
  def step(other_time, increment)
    raise ArgumentError, "step can't be 0" if increment == 0
    increasing = self < other_time
    if (increasing && increment < 0) || (!increasing && increment > 0)
      yield self
      return
```

```
      end
      d = self
      begin
        yield d
        d += increment
      end while (increasing ? d <= other_time : d >= other_time)
  end

  def upto(other_time)
    step(other_time, 1) { |x| yield x }
  end
end

the_first = Time.local(2004, 1, 1)
the_second = Time.local(2004, 1, 2)
the_first.step(the_second, 60 * 60 * 6) { |x| puts x }
# Thu Jan 01 00:00:00 EST 2004
# Thu Jan 01 06:00:00 EST 2004
# Thu Jan 01 12:00:00 EST 2004
# Thu Jan 01 18:00:00 EST 2004
# Fri Jan 02 00:00:00 EST 2004

the_first.upto(the_first) { |x| puts x }
# Thu Jan 01 00:00:00 EST 2004
```

See Also

- Recipe 2.15, "Generating a Sequence of Numbers"

3.5   Doing Date Arithmetic

Problem

You want to find how much time has elapsed between two dates, or add a number to a date to get an earlier or later date.

Solution

Adding or subtracting a Time object and a number adds or subtracts that number of seconds. Adding or subtracting a Date object and a number adds or subtracts that number of days:

```
require 'date'
y2k = Time.gm(2000, 1, 1)          # => Sat Jan 01 00:00:00 UTC 2000
y2k + 1                            # => Sat Jan 01 00:00:01 UTC 2000
y2k - 1                            # => Fri Dec 31 23:59:59 UTC 1999
y2k + (60 * 60 * 24 * 365)         # => Sun Dec 31 00:00:00 UTC 2000

y2k_dt = DateTime.new(2000, 1, 1)
(y2k_dt + 1).to_s                  # => "2000-01-02T00:00:00Z"
(y2k_dt - 1).to_s                  # => "1999-12-31T00:00:00Z"
```

```
(y2k_dt + 0.5).to_s                      # => "2000-01-01T12:00:00Z"
(y2k_dt + 365).to_s                      # => "2000-12-31T00:00:00Z"
```

Subtracting one `Time` from another gives the interval between the dates, in seconds. Subtracting one `Date` from another gives the interval in days:

```
day_one = Time.gm(1999, 12, 31)
day_two = Time.gm(2000, 1, 1)
day_two - day_one                        # => 86400.0
day_one - day_two                        # => -86400.0

day_one = DateTime.new(1999, 12, 31)
day_two = DateTime.new(2000, 1, 1)
day_two - day_one                        # => Rational(1, 1)
day_one - day_two                        # => Rational(-1, 1)

# Compare times from now and 10 seconds in the future.
before_time = Time.now
before_datetime = DateTime.now
sleep(10)
Time.now - before_time                   # => 10.003414
DateTime.now - before_datetime           # => Rational(5001557, 43200000000)
```

The activesupport gem, a prerequisite of Ruby on Rails, defines many useful functions on `Numeric` and `Time` for navigating through time:[*]

```
require 'rubygems'
require 'active_support'

10.days.ago                              # => Wed Mar 08 19:54:17 EST 2006
1.month.from_now                         # => Mon Apr 17 20:54:17 EDT 2006
2.weeks.since(Time.local(2006, 1, 1))    # => Sun Jan 15 00:00:00 EST 2006

y2k - 1.day                              # => Fri Dec 31 00:00:00 UTC 1999
y2k + 6.3.years                          # => Thu Apr 20 01:48:00 UTC 2006
6.3.years.since y2k                      # => Thu Apr 20 01:48:00 UTC 2006
```

Discussion

Ruby's date arithmetic takes advantage of the fact that Ruby's time objects are stored internally as numbers. Additions to dates and differences between dates are handled by adding to and subtracting the underlying numbers. This is why adding 1 to a `Time` adds one second and adding 1 to a `DateTime` adds one day: a `Time` is stored as a number of seconds since a time zero, and a `Date` or `DateTime` is stored as a number of days since a (different) time zero.

Not every arithmetic operation makes sense for dates: you could "multiply two dates" by multiplying the underlying numbers, but that would have no meaning in terms of real time, so Ruby doesn't define those operators. Once a number takes on

---

[*] So does the Facets More library.

aspects of the real world, there are limitations to what you can legitimately do to that number.

Here's a shortcut for adding or subtracting big chunks of time: using the right- or left-shift operators on a Date or DateTime object will add or subtract a certain number number of months from the date.

```
(y2k_dt >> 1).to_s                    # => "2000-02-01T00:00:00Z"
(y2k_dt << 1).to_s                    # => "1999-12-01T00:00:00Z"
```

You can get similar behavior with activesupport's Numeric#month method, but that method assumes that a "month" is 30 days long, instead of dealing with the lengths of specific months:

```
y2k + 1.month                         # => Mon Jan 31 00:00:00 UTC 2000
y2k - 1.month                         # => Thu Dec 02 00:00:00 UTC 1999
```

By contrast, if you end up in a month that doesn't have enough days (for instance, you start on the 31st and then shift to a month that only has 30 days), the standard library will use the last day of the new month:

```
# Thirty days hath September...
halloween = Date.new(2000, 10, 31)
(halloween << 1).to_s                 # => "2000-09-30"
(halloween >> 1).to_s                 # => "2000-11-30"
(halloween >> 2).to_s                 # => "2000-12-31"

leap_year_day = Date.new(1996, 2, 29)
(leap_year_day << 1).to_s             # => "1996-01-29"
(leap_year_day >> 1).to_s             # => "1996-03-29"
(leap_year_day >> 12).to_s            # => "1997-02-28"
(leap_year_day << 12 * 4).to_s        # => "1992-02-29"
```

See Also

- Recipe 3.4, "Iterating Over Dates"
- Recipe 3.6, "Counting the Days Since an Arbitrary Date"
- The RDoc for Rails' ActiveSupport::CoreExtensions::Numeric::Time module (*http://api.rubyonrails.com/classes/ActiveSupport/CoreExtensions/Numeric/Time.html*)

3.6   Counting the Days Since an Arbitrary Date

Problem

You want to see how many days have elapsed since a particular date, or how many remain until a date in the future.

Solution

Subtract the earlier date from the later one. If you're using `Time` objects, the result will be a floating-point number of seconds, so divide by the number of seconds in a day:

```
def last_modified(file)
  t1 = File.stat(file).ctime
  t2 = Time.now
  elapsed = (t2-t1)/(60*60*24)
  puts "#{file} was last modified #{elapsed} days ago."
end

last_modified("/etc/passwd")
# /etc/passwd was last modified 125.873605469919 days ago.
last_modified("/home/leonardr/")
# /home/leonardr/ was last modified 0.113293513796296 days ago.
```

If you're using `DateTime` objects, the result will be a rational number. You'll probably want to convert it to an integer or floating-point number for display:

```
require 'date'
def advent_calendar(date=DateTime.now)
  christmas = DateTime.new(date.year, 12, 25)
  christmas = DateTime.new(date.year+1, 12, 25) if date > christmas
  difference = (christmas-date).to_i
  if difference == 0
    puts "Today is Christmas."
  else
    puts "Only #{difference} day#{"s" unless difference==1} until Christmas."
  end
end

advent_calendar(DateTime.new(2006, 12, 24))
# Only 1 day until Christmas.
advent_calendar(DateTime.new(2006, 12, 25))
# Today is Christmas.
advent_calendar(DateTime.new(2006, 12, 26))
# Only 364 days until Christmas.
```

Discussion

Since times are stored internally as numbers, subtracting one from another will give you a number. Since both numbers measure the same thing (time elapsed since some "time zero"), that number will actually mean something: it'll be the number of seconds or days that separate the two times on the timeline.

Of course, this works with other time intervals as well. To display a difference in hours, for `Time` objects divide the difference by the number of seconds in an hour (3,600, or `1.hour` if you're using Rails). For `DateTime` objects, divide by the number of days in an hour (that is, multiply the difference by 24):

```
sent = DateTime.new(2006, 10, 4, 3, 15)
received = DateTime.new(2006, 10, 5, 16, 33)
```

```
elapsed = (received-sent) * 24
puts "You responded to my email #{elapsed.to_f} hours after I sent it."
# You responded to my email 37.3 hours after I sent it.
```

You can even use `divmod` on a time interval to hack it down into smaller and smaller pieces. Once when I was in college, I wrote a script that displayed how much time remained until the finals I should have been studying for. This method gives you a countdown of the days, hours, minutes, and seconds until some scheduled event:

```
require 'date'
def remaining(date, event)
  intervals = [["day", 1], ["hour", 24], ["minute", 60], ["second", 60]]
  elapsed = DateTime.now - date
  tense = elapsed > 0 ? "since" : "until"
  interval = 1.0
  parts = intervals.collect do |name, new_interval|
    interval /= new_interval
    number, elapsed = elapsed.abs.divmod(interval)
  "#{number.to_i} #{name}#{"s" unless number == 1}"
  end
  puts "#{parts.join(", ")} #{tense} #{event}."
end

remaining(DateTime.new(2006, 4, 15, 0, 0, 0, DateTime.now.offset),
          "the book deadline")
# 27 days, 4 hours, 16 minutes, 9 seconds until the book deadline.
remaining(DateTime.new(1999, 4, 23, 8, 0, 0, DateTime.now.offset),
          "the Math 114A final")
# 2521 days, 11 hours, 43 minutes, 50 seconds since the Math 114A final.
```

See Also

*   Recipe 3.5, "Doing Date Arithmetic"

3.7   Converting Between Time Zones

Problem

You want to change a time object so that it represents the same moment of time in some other time zone.

Solution

The most common time zone conversions are the conversion of system local time to UTC, and the conversion of UTC to local time. These conversions are easy for both `Time` and `DateTime` objects.

The `Time#gmtime` method modifies a `Time` object in place, converting it to UTC. The `Time#localtime` method converts in the opposite direction:

```
now = Time.now              # => Sat Mar 18 20:15:58 EST 2006
now = now.gmtime            # => Sun Mar 19 01:15:58 UTC 2006
now = now.localtime         # => Sat Mar 18 20:15:58 EST 2006
```

The DateTime.new_offset method converts a DateTime object from one time zone to another. You must pass in the dstination time zone's offset from UTC; to convert local time to UTC, pass in zero. Since DateTime objects are immutable, this method creates a new object identical to the old DateTime object, except for the time zone offset:

```
require 'date'
local = DateTime.now
local.to_s                  # => "2006-03-18T20:15:58-0500"
utc = local.new_offset(0)
utc.to_s                    # => "2006-03-19T01:15:58Z"
```

To convert a UTC DateTime object to local time, you'll need to call DateTime#new_offset and pass in the numeric offset for your local time zone. The easiest way to get this offset is to call offset on a DateTime object known to be in local time. The offset will usually be a rational number with a denominator of 24:

```
local = DateTime.now
utc = local.new_offset

local.offset                # => Rational(-5, 24)
local_from_utc = utc.new_offset(local.offset)
local_from_utc.to_s         # => "2006-03-18T20:15:58-0500"
local == local_from_utc     # => true
```

Discussion

Time objects created with Time.at, Time.local, Time.mktime, Time.new, and Time.now are created using the current system time zone. Time objects created with Time.gm and Time.utc are created using the UTC time zone. Time objects can represent any time zone, but it's difficult to use a time zone with Time other than local time or UTC.

Suppose you need to convert local time to some time zone other than UTC. If you know the UTC offset for the destination time zone, you can represent it as a fraction of a day and pass it into DateTime#new_offset:

```
#Convert local (Eastern) time to Pacific time
eastern = DateTime.now
eastern.to_s                # => "2006-03-18T20:15:58-0500"

pacific_offset = Rational(-7, 24)
pacific = eastern.new_offset(pacific_offset)
pacific.to_s                # => "2006-03-18T18:15:58-0700"
```

DateTime#new_offset can convert between arbitrary time zone offsets, so for time zone conversions, it's easiest to use DateTime objects and convert back to Time objects if necessary. But DateTime objects only understand time zones in terms of numeric UTC offsets. How can you convert a date and time to UTC when all you know is that the time zone is called "WET", "Zulu", or "Asia/Taskent"?

On Unix systems, you can temporarily change the "system" time zone for the current process. The C library underlying the Time class knows about an enormous number of time zones (this "zoneinfo" database is usually located in /usr/share/ zoneinfo/, if you want to look at the available time zones). You can tap this knowledge by setting the environment variable TZ to an appropriate value, forcing the Time class to act as though your computer were in some other time zone. Here's a method that uses this trick to convert a Time object to any time zone supported by the underlying C library:

```ruby
class Time
  def convert_zone(to_zone)
    original_zone = ENV["TZ"]
    utc_time = dup.gmtime
    ENV["TZ"] = to_zone
    to_zone_time = utc_time.localtime
    ENV["TZ"] = original_zone
    return to_zone_time
  end
end
```

Let's do a number of conversions of a local (Eastern) time to other time zones across the world:

```ruby
t = Time.at(1000000000)            # => Sat Sep 08 21:46:40 EDT 2001

t.convert_zone("US/Pacific")       # => Sat Sep 08 18:46:40 PDT 2001

t.convert_zone("US/Alaska")        # => Sat Sep 08 17:46:40 AKDT 2001
t.convert_zone("UTC")              # => Sun Sep 09 01:46:40 UTC 2001
t.convert_zone("Turkey")           # => Sun Sep 09 04:46:40 EEST 2001
```

Note that some time zones, like India's, are half an hour offset from most others:

```ruby
t.convert_zone("Asia/Calcutta")    # => Sun Sep 09 07:16:40 IST 2001
```

By setting the TZ environment variable before creating a Time object, you can represent the time in any time zone. The following code converts Lagos time to Singapore time, regardless of the "real" underlying time zone.

```ruby
ENV["TZ"] = "Africa/Lagos"
t = Time.at(1000000000)            # => Sun Sep 09 02:46:40 WAT 2001
ENV["TZ"] = nil

t.convert_zone("Singapore")        # => Sun Sep 09 09:46:40 SGT 2001

# Just to prove it's the same time as before:
t.convert_zone("US/Eastern")       # => Sat Sep 08 21:46:40 EDT 2001
```

Since the TZ environment variable is global to a process, you'll run into problems if you have multiple threads trying to convert time zones at once.

See Also

- Recipe 3.9, "Converting Between Time and DateTime Objects"
- Recipe 3.8, "Checking Whether Daylight Saving Time Is in Effect"
- Information on the "zoneinfo" database (*http://www.twinsun.com/tz/tz-link.htm*)

3.8 Checking Whether Daylight Saving Time Is in Effect

Problem

You want to see whether the current time in your locale is normal time or Daylight Saving/Summer Time.

Solution

Create a `Time` object and check its `isdst` method:

```
Time.local(2006, 1, 1)           # => Sun Jan 01 00:00:00 EST 2006
Time.local(2006, 1, 1).isdst     # => false
Time.local(2006, 10, 1)          # => Sun Oct 01 00:00:00 EDT 2006
Time.local(2006, 10, 1).isdst    # => true
```

Discussion

Time objects representing UTC times will always return false when `isdst` is called, because UTC is the same year-round. Other `Time` objects will consult the daylight saving time rules for the time locale used to create the `Time` object. This is usually the sysem locale on the computer you used to create it: see Recipe 3.7 for information on changing it. The following code demonstrates some of the rules pertaining to Daylight Saving Time across the United States:

```
eastern = Time.local(2006, 10, 1)   # => Sun Oct 01 00:00:00 EDT 2006
eastern.isdst                       # => true

ENV['TZ'] = 'US/Pacific'
pacific = Time.local(2006, 10, 1)   # => Sun Oct 01 00:00:00 PDT 2006
pacific.isdst                       # => true

# Except for the Navajo Nation, Arizona doesn't use Daylight Saving Time.
ENV['TZ'] = 'America/Phoenix'
arizona = Time.local(2006, 10, 1)   # => Sun Oct 01 00:00:00 MST 2006
arizona.isdst                       # => false

# Finally, restore the original time zone.
ENV['TZ'] = nil
```

The C library on which Ruby's `Time` class is based handles the complex rules for Daylight Saving Time across the history of a particular time zone or locale. For instance,

Daylight Saving Time was mandated across the U.S. in 1918, but abandoned in most locales shortly afterwards. The "zoneinfo" file used by the C library contains this information, along with many other rules:

```
# Daylight saving first took effect on March 31, 1918.
Time.local(1918, 3, 31).isdst       # => false
Time.local(1918, 4, 1).isdst        # => true
Time.local(1919, 4, 1).isdst        # => true

# The federal law was repealed later in 1919, but some places
# continued to use Daylight Saving Time.
ENV['TZ'] = 'US/Pacific'
Time.local(1920, 4, 1)              # => Thu Apr 01 00:00:00 PST 1920

ENV['TZ'] = nil
Time.local(1920, 4, 1)              # => Thu Apr 01 00:00:00 EDT 1920

# Daylight Saving Time was reintroduced during the Second World War.
Time.local(1942,2,9)               # => Mon Feb 09 00:00:00 EST 1942
Time.local(1942,2,10)              # => Tue Feb 10 00:00:00 EWT 1942
# EWT stands for "Eastern War Time"
```

A U.S. law passed in 2005 expands Daylight Saving Time into March and November, beginning in 2007. Depending on how old your zoneinfo file is, Time objects you create for dates in 2007 and beyond might or might not reflect the new law.

```
Time.local(2007, 3, 13)            # => Tue Mar 13 00:00:00 EDT 2007
# Your computer may incorrectly claim this time is EST.
```

This illustrates a general point. There's nothing your elected officials love more than passing laws, so you shouldn't rely on isdst to be accurate for any Time objects that represent times a year or more into the future. When that time actually comes around, Daylight Saving Time might obey different rules in your locale.

The Date class isn't based on the C library, and knows nothing about time zones or locales, so it also knows nothing about Daylight Saving Time.

See Also

- Recipe 3.7, "Converting Between Time Zones"
- Information on the "zoneinfo" database (*http://www.twinsun.com/tz/tz-link.htm*)

3.9 Converting Between Time and DateTime Objects

Problem

You're working with both DateTime and Time objects, created from Ruby's two standard date/time libraries. You can't mix these objects in comparisons, iterations, or date arithmetic because they're incompatible. You want to convert all the objects into one form or another so that you can treat them all the same way.

Solution

To convert a Time object to a DateTime, you'll need some code like this:

```ruby
require 'date'
class Time
  def to_datetime
    # Convert seconds + microseconds into a fractional number of seconds
    seconds = sec + Rational(usec, 10**6)

    # Convert a UTC offset measured in minutes to one measured in a
    # fraction of a day.
    offset = Rational(utc_offset, 60 * 60 * 24)
    DateTime.new(year, month, day, hour, min, seconds, offset)
  end
end

time = Time.gm(2000, 6, 4, 10, 30, 22, 4010)
# => Sun Jun 04 10:30:22 UTC 2000
time.to_datetime.to_s
# => "2000-06-04T10:30:22Z"
```

Converting a DateTime to a Time is similar; you just need to decide whether you want the Time object to use local time or GMT. This code adds the conversion method to Date, the superclass of DateTime, so it will work on both Date and DateTime objects.

```ruby
class Date
  def to_gm_time
    to_time(new_offset, :gm)
  end

  def to_local_time
    to_time(new_offset(DateTime.now.offset-offset), :local)
  end

  private
  def to_time(dest, method)
    #Convert a fraction of a day to a number of microseconds
    usec = (dest.sec_fraction * 60 * 60 * 24 * (10**6)).to_i
    Time.send(method, dest.year, dest.month, dest.day, dest.hour, dest.min,
              dest.sec, usec)
  end
end

(datetime = DateTime.new(1990, 10, 1, 22, 16, Rational(41,2))).to_s
# => "1990-10-01T22:16:20Z"
datetime.to_gm_time
# => Mon Oct 01 22:16:20 UTC 1990
datetime.to_local_time
# => Mon Oct 01 17:16:20 EDT 1990
```

Discussion

Ruby's two ways of representing dates and times don't coexist very well. But since neither can be a total substitute for the other, you'll probably use them both during your Ruby career. The conversion methods let you get around incompatibilities by simply converting one type to the other:

```
time < datetime
# ArgumentError: comparison of Time with DateTime failed
time.to_datetime < datetime
# => false
time < datetime.to_gm_time
# => false

time - datetime
# TypeError: can't convert DateTime into Float
(time.to_datetime - datetime).to_f
# => 3533.50973962975                    # Measured in days
time - datetime.to_gm_time
# => 305295241.50401                     # Measured in seconds
```

The methods defined above are reversible: you can convert back and forth between Date and DateTime objects without losing accuracy.

```
time                                     # => Sun Jun 04 10:30:22 UTC 2000
time.usec                                # => 4010

time.to_datetime.to_gm_time             # => Sun Jun 04 10:30:22 UTC 2000
time.to_datetime.to_gm_time.usec        # => 4010

datetime.to_s                            # => "1990-10-01T22:16:20Z"
datetime.to_gm_time.to_datetime.to_s     # => "1990-10-01T22:16:20Z"
```

Once you can convert between Time and DateTime objects, it's simple to write code that normalizes a mixed array, so that all its elements end up being of the same type. This method tries to turn a mixed array into an array containing only Time objects. If it encounters a date that won't fit within the constraints of the Time class, it starts over and converts the array into an array of DateTime objects instead (thus losing any information about Daylight Saving Time):

```
def normalize_time_types(array)
  # Don't do anything if all the objects are already of the same type.
  first_class = array[0].class
  first_class = first_class.super if first_class == DateTime
  return unless array.detect { |x| !x.is_a?(first_class) }

  normalized = array.collect do |t|
    if t.is_a?(Date)
      begin
        t.to_local_time
      rescue ArgumentError # Time out of range; convert to DateTimes instead.
        convert_to = DateTime
        break
```

```
        end
      else
        t
      end
    end

    unless normalized
      normalized = array.collect { |t| t.is_a?(Time) ? t.to_datetime : t }
    end
    return normalized
  end
```

When all objects in a mixed array can be represented as either `Time` or `DateTime` objects, this method makes them all `Time` objects:

```
mixed_array = [Time.now, DateTime.now]
# => [Sat Mar 18 22:17:10 EST 2006,
#      #<DateTime: 23556610914534571/9600000000,-5/24,2299161>]
normalize_time_types(mixed_array)
# => [Sat Mar 18 22:17:10 EST 2006, Sun Mar 19 03:17:10 EST 2006]
```

If one of the `DateTime` objects can't be represented as a `Time`, `normalize_time_types` turns all the objects into `DateTime` instances. This code is run on a system with a 32-bit time counter:

```
mixed_array << DateTime.civil(1776, 7, 4)
normalize_time_types(mixed_array).collect { |x| x.to_s }
# => ["2006-03-18T22:17:10-0500", "2006-03-18T22:17:10-0500",
# =>  "1776-07-04T00:00:00Z"]
```

See Also

• Recipe 3.1, "Finding Today's Date"

3.10   Finding the Day of the Week

Problem

You want to find the day of the week for a certain date.

Solution

Use the `wday` method (supported by both `Time` and `DateTime`) to find the day of the week as a number between 0 and 6. Sunday is day zero.

The following code yields to a code block the date of every Sunday between two dates. It uses `wday` to find the first Sunday following the start date (keeping in mind that the first date may itself be a Sunday). Then it adds seven days at a time to get subsequent Sundays:

```
def every_sunday(d1, d2)
  # You can use 1.day instead of 60*60*24 if you're using Rails.
```

```
    one_day = d1.is_a?(Time) ? 60*60*24 : 1
    sunday = d1 + ((7-d1.wday) % 7) * one_day
    while sunday < d2
      yield sunday
      sunday += one_day * 7
    end
  end

  def print_every_sunday(d1, d2)
    every_sunday(d1, d2) { |sunday| puts sunday.strftime("%x")}
  end

  print_every_sunday(Time.local(2006, 1, 1), Time.local(2006, 2, 4))
  # 01/01/06
  # 01/08/06
  # 01/15/06
  # 01/22/06
  # 01/29/06
```

Discussion

The most commonly used parts of a time are its calendar and clock readings: year, day, hour, and so on. Time and DateTime let you access these, but they also give you access to a few other aspects of a time: the Julian day of the year (yday), and, more usefully, the day of the week (wday).

The every_sunday method will accept either two Time objects or two DateTime objects. The only difference is the number you need to add to an object to increment it by one day. If you're only going to be using one kind of object, you can simplify the code a little.

To get the day of the week as an English string, use the strftime directives %A and %a:

```
t = Time.local(2006, 1, 1)
t.strftime("%A %A %A!")              # => "Sunday Sunday Sunday!"
t.strftime("%a %a %a!")              # => "Sun Sun Sun!"
```

You can find the day of the week and the day of the year, but Ruby has no built-in method for finding the week of the year (there is a method to find the *commercial* week of the year; see Recipe 3.11). If you need such a method, it's not hard to create one using the day of the year and the day of the week. This code defines a week method in a module, which it mixes in to both Date and Time:

```
require 'date'
module Week
  def week
    (yday + 7 - wday) / 7
  end
end

class Date
  include Week
end
```

```
class Time
  include Week
end

saturday = DateTime.new(2005, 1, 1)
saturday.week                          # => 0
(saturday+1).week                      # => 1    #Sunday, January 2
(saturday-1).week                      # => 52   #Friday, December 31
```

See Also

- Recipe 3.3, "Printing a Date"
- Recipe 3.5, "Doing Date Arithmetic"
- Recipe 3.11, "Handling Commercial Dates"

3.11 Handling Commercial Dates

Problem

When writing a business or financial application, you need to deal with commercial dates instead of civil or calendar dates.

Solution

DateTime offers some methods for working with commercial dates. Date#cwday gives the commercial day of the week, Date#cweek gives the commercial week of the year, and Date#cwyear gives the commercial year.

Consider January 1, 2006. This was the first day of calendar 2006, but since it was a Sunday, it was the last day of commercial 2005:

```
require 'date'
sunday = DateTime.new(2006, 1, 1)
sunday.year                            # => 2006
sunday.cwyear                          # => 2005
sunday.cweek                           # => 52
sunday.wday                            # => 0
sunday.cwday                           # => 7
```

Commercial 2006 started on the first *weekday* in 2006:

```
monday = sunday + 1
monday.cwyear                          # => 2006
monday.cweek                           # => 1
```

Discussion

Unless you're writing an application that needs to use commercial dates, you probably don't care about this, but it's kind of interesting (if you think dates are interesting). The commercial week starts on Monday, not Sunday, because Sunday's part of the weekend. DateTime#cwday is just like DateTime#wday, except it gives Sunday a value of seven instead of zero.

This means that DateTime#cwday has a range from one to seven instead of from zero to six:

```ruby
(sunday...sunday+7).each do |d|
  puts "#{d.strftime("%a")} #{d.wday} #{d.cwday}"
end
# Sun 0 7
# Mon 1 1
# Tue 2 2
# Wed 3 3
# Thu 4 4
# Fri 5 5
# Sat 6 6
```

The cweek and cwyear methods have to do with the commercial year, which starts on the first Monday of a year. Any days before the first Monday are considered part of the previous commercial year. The example given in the Solution demonstrates this: January 1, 2006 was a Sunday, so by the commercial reckoning it was part of the last week of 2005.

See Also

- See Recipe 3.3, "Printing a Date," for the strftime directives used to print parts of commercial dates

3.12   Running a Code Block Periodically

Problem

You want to run some Ruby code (such as a call to a shell command) repeatedly at a certain interval.

Solution

Create a method that runs a code block, then sleeps until it's time to run the block again:

```ruby
def every_n_seconds(n)
  loop do
    before = Time.now
    yield
    interval = n-(Time.now-before)
    sleep(interval) if interval > 0
  end
end
```

```
every_n_seconds(5) do
  puts "At the beep, the time will be #{Time.now.strftime("%X")}... beep!"
end
# At the beep, the time will be 12:21:28... beep!
# At the beep, the time will be 12:21:33... beep!
# At the beep, the time will be 12:21:38... beep!
# ...
```

Discussion

There are two main times when you'd want to run some code periodically. The first is when you actually want something to happen at a particular interval: say you're appending your status to a log file every 10 seconds. The other is when you would prefer for something to happen continuously, but putting it in a tight loop would be bad for system performance. In this case, you compromise by putting some slack time in the loop so that your code isn't *always* running.

The implementation of every_n_seconds deducts from the sleep time the time spent running the code block. This ensures that calls to the code block are spaced evenly apart, as close to the desired interval as possible. If you tell every_n_seconds to call a code block every five seconds, but the code block takes four seconds to run, every_n_seconds only sleeps for one second. If the code block takes six seconds to run, every_n_seconds won't sleep at all: it'll come back from a call to the code block, and immediately yield to the block again.

If you always want to sleep for a certain interval, no matter how long the code block takes to run, you can simplify the code:

```
def every_n_seconds(n)
  loop do
    yield
    sleep(n)
  end
end
```

In most cases, you don't want every_n_seconds to take over the main loop of your program. Here's a version of every_n_seconds that spawns a separate thread to run your task. If your code block stops the loop by with the break keyword, the thread stops running:

```
def every_n_seconds(n)
  thread = Thread.new do
    while true
      before = Time.now
      yield
      interval = n-(Time.now-before)
      sleep(interval) if interval > 0
    end
  end
  return thread
end
```

In this snippet, I use every_n_seconds to spy on a file, waiting for people to modify it:

```
def monitor_changes(file, resolution=1)
  last_change = Time.now
  every_n_seconds(resolution) do
    check = File.stat(file).ctime
    if check > last_change
      yield file
      last_change = check
    elsif Time.now - last_change > 60
      puts "Nothing's happened for a minute, I'm bored."
      break
    end
  end
end
```

That example might give output like this, if someone on the system is working on the file /tmp/foo:

```
thread = monitor_changes("/tmp/foo") { |file| puts "Someone changed #{file}!" }
# "Someone changed /tmp/foo!"
# "Someone changed /tmp/foo!"
# "Nothing's happened for a minute; I'm bored."
thread.status                    # => false
```

See Also

- Recipe 3.13, "Waiting a Certain Amount of Time"
- Recipe 23.4, "Running Periodic Tasks Without cron or at"

3.13 Waiting a Certain Amount of Time

Problem

You want to pause your program, or a single thread of it, for a specific amount of time.

Solution

The Kernel#sleep method takes a floating-point number and puts the current thread to sleep for some (possibly fractional) number of seconds:

```
3.downto(1) { |i| puts "#{i}..."; sleep(1) }; puts "Go!"
# 3...
# 2...
# 1...
# Go!

Time.new                    # => Sat Mar 18 21:17:58 EST 2006
sleep(10)
```

```
Time.new                   # => Sat Mar 18 21:18:08 EST 2006
sleep(1)
Time.new                   # => Sat Mar 18 21:18:09 EST 2006

# Sleep for less then a second.
Time.new.usec              # => 377185
sleep(0.1)
Time.new.usec              # => 479230
```

Discussion

Timers are often used when a program needs to interact with a source much slower than a computer's CPU: a network pipe, or human eyes and hands. Rather than constantly poll for new data, a Ruby program can sleep for a fraction of a second between each poll, giving other programs on the CPU a chance to run. That's not much time by human standards, but sleeping for a fraction of a second at a time can greatly improve a system's overall performance.

You can pass any floating-point number to sleep, but that gives an exaggerated picture of how finely you can control a thread's sleeping time. For instance, you can't sleep for 10^{-50} seconds, because it's physically impossible (that's less than the Planck time). You can't sleep for Float::EPSILON seconds, because that's almost certainly less than the resolution of your computer's timer.

You probably can't even reliably sleep for a microsecond, even though most modern computer clocks have microsecond precision. By the time your sleep command is processed by the Ruby interpreter and the thread actually starts waiting for its timer to go off, some small amount of time has already elapsed. At very small intervals, this time can be greater than the time you asked Ruby to sleep in the first place.

Here's a simple benchmark that shows how long sleep on your system will actually make a thread sleep. It starts with a sleep interval of one second, which is fairly accurate. It then sleeps for shorter and shorter intervals, with lessening accuracy each time:

```
interval = 1.0
10.times do |x|
  t1 = Time.new
  sleep(interval)
  actual = Time.new - t1

  difference = (actual-interval).abs
  percent_difference = difference / interval * 100
  printf("Expected: %.9f Actual: %.6f Difference: %.6f (%.2f%%)\n",
         interval, actual, difference, percent_difference)

  interval /= 10
end
# Expected: 1.000000000 Actual: 0.999420 Difference: 0.000580 (0.06%)
# Expected: 0.100000000 Actual: 0.099824 Difference: 0.000176 (0.18%)
# Expected: 0.010000000 Actual: 0.009912 Difference: 0.000088 (0.88%)
# Expected: 0.001000000 Actual: 0.001026 Difference: 0.000026 (2.60%)
```

```
# Expected: 0.000100000 Actual: 0.000913 Difference: 0.000813 (813.00%)
# Expected: 0.000010000 Actual: 0.000971 Difference: 0.000961 (9610.00%)
# Expected: 0.000001000 Actual: 0.000975 Difference: 0.000974 (97400.00%)
# Expected: 0.000000100 Actual: 0.000015 Difference: 0.000015 (14900.00%)
# Expected: 0.000000010 Actual: 0.000024 Difference: 0.000024 (239900.00%)
# Expected: 0.000000001 Actual: 0.000016 Difference: 0.000016 (1599900.00%)
```

A small amount of the reported time comes from overhead, caused by creating the second Time object, but not enough to affect these results. On my system, if I tell Ruby to sleep for a millisecond, the time spent running the sleep call greatly exceeds the time I wanted to sleep in the first place! According to this benchmark, the shortest length of time for which I can expect sleep to accurately sleep is about 1/100 of a second.

You might think to get better sleep resolution by putting the CPU into a tight loop with a certain number of repetitions. Apart from the obvious problems (this hurts system performance, and the same loop will run faster over time since computers are always getting faster), this isn't even reliable.

The operating system doesn't know you're trying to run a timing loop: it just sees you using the CPU, and it can interrupt your loop at any time, for any length of time, to let some other process use the CPU. Unless you're on an embedded operating system where you can control exactly what the CPU does, the only reliable way to wait for a specific period of time is with sleep.

Waking up early

The sleep method will end early if the thread that calls it has its run method called. If you want a thread to sleep until another thread wakes it up, use Thread.stop:

```
alarm = Thread.new(self) { sleep(5); Thread.main.wakeup }
puts "Going to sleep for 1000 seconds at #{Time.new}..."
sleep(10000); puts "Woke up at #{Time.new}!"
# Going to sleep for 1000 seconds at Thu Oct 27 14:45:14 PDT 2005...
# Woke up at Thu Oct 27 14:45:19 PDT 2005!

alarm = Thread.new(self) { sleep(5); Thread.main.wakeup }
puts "Goodbye, cruel world!";
Thread.stop;
puts "I'm back; how'd that happen?"
# Goodbye, cruel world!
# I'm back; how'd that happen?
```

See Also

- Recipe 3.12, "Running a Code Block Periodically"
- Chapter 20
- The Morse Code example in Recipe 21.11, "Making Your Keyboard Lights Blink," displays an interesting use of sleep

3.14 Adding a Timeout to a Long-Running Operation

Problem

You're running some code that might take a long time to complete, or might never complete at all. You want to interrupt the code if it takes too long.

Solution

Use the built-in timeout library. The Timeout.timeout method takes a code block and a deadline (in seconds). If the code block finishes running in time, it returns true. If the deadline passes and the code block is still running, Timeout.timeout terminates the code block and raises an exception.

The following code would never finish running were it not for the timeout call. But after five seconds, timeout raises a Timeout::Error and execution halts:

```
# This code will sleep forever... OR WILL IT?
require 'timeout'
before = Time.now
begin
  status = Timeout.timeout(5) { sleep }
rescue Timeout::Error
  puts "I only slept for #{Time.now-before} seconds."
end
# I only slept for 5.035492 seconds.
```

Discussion

Sometimes you must make a network connection or take some other action that might be incredibly slow, or that might never complete at all. With a timeout, you can impose an upper limit on how long that operation can take. If it fails, you can try it again later, or forge ahead without the information you were trying to get. Even when you can't recover, you can report your failure and gracefully exit the program, rather than sitting around forever waiting for the operation to complete.

By default, Timeout.timeout raises a Timeout::Error. You can pass in a custom exception class as the second argument to Timeout.timeout: this saves you from having to rescue the Timeout:Error just so you can raise some other error that your application knows how to handle.

If the code block had side effects, they will still be visible after the timeout kills the code block:

```
def count_for_five_seconds
  $counter = 0
  begin
    Timeout::timeout(5) { loop { $counter += 1 } }
  rescue Timeout::Error
    puts "I can count to #{$counter} in 5 seconds."
```

```
    end
  end

count_for_five_seconds
# I can count to 2532825 in 5 seconds.
$counter                                # => 2532825
```

This may mean that your dataset is now in an inconsistent state.

See Also

- `ri Timeout`
- Recipe 3.13, "Waiting a Certain Amount of Time"
- Recipe 14.1, "Grabbing the Contents of a Web Page"

## CHAPTER 4

Arrays

Like all high-level languages, Ruby has built-in support for *arrays*, objects that contain ordered lists of other objects. You can use arrays (often in conjunction with hashes) to build and use complex data structures without having to define any custom classes.

An array in Ruby is an ordered list of *elements*. Each element is a reference to some object, the way a Ruby variable is a reference to some object. For convenience, throughout this book we usually talk about arrays as though the array elements were the actual objects, not references to the objects. Since Ruby (unlike languages like C) gives no way of manipulating object references directly, the distinction rarely matters.

The simplest way to create a new array is to put a comma-separated list of object references between square brackets. The object references can be predefined variables (my_var), anonymous objects created on the spot ('my string', 4.7, or MyClass.new), or expressions (a + b, object.method). A single array can contain references to objects of many different types:

```
a1 = []                             # => []
a2 = [1, 2, 3]                      # => [1, 2, 3]
a3 = [1, 2, 3, 'a', 'b', 'c', nil]  # => [1, 2, 3, "a", "b", "c", nil]

n1 = 4
n2 = 6
sum_and_difference = [n1, n2, n1+n2, n1-n2]
# => [4, 6, 10, -2]
```

If your array contains only strings, you may find it simpler to build your array by enclosing the strings in the w{} syntax, separated by whitespace. This saves you from having to write all those quotes and comma:

```
%w{1 2 3}                           # => ["1", "2", "3"]
%w{The rat sat
   on the mat}
# => ["The", "rat", "sat", "on", "the", "mat"]
```

The << operator is the simplest way to add a value to an array. Ruby dynamically resizes arrays as elements are added and removed.

```
a = [1, 2, 3]          # => [1, 2, 3]
a << 4.0               # => [1, 2, 3, 4.0]
a << 'five'            # => [1, 2, 3, 4.0, "five"]
```

An array element can be any object reference, including a reference to another array. An array can even contain a reference to itself, though this is usually a bad idea, since it can send your code into infinite loops.

```
a = [1,2,3]            # => [1, 2, 3]
a << [4, 5, 6]         # => [1, 2, 3, [4, 5, 6]]
a << a                 # => [1, 2, 3, [4, 5, 6], [...]]
```

As in most other programming languages, the elements of an array are numbered with *indexes* starting from zero. An array element can be looked up by passing its index into the array index operator [ ]. The first element of an array can be accessed with a[0], the second with a[1], and so on.

Negative indexes count from the end of the array: the last element of an array can be accessed with a[-1], the second-to-last with a[-2], and so on. See Recipe 4.13 for more ways of using the array indexing operator.

The size of an array is available through the Array#size method. Because the index numbering starts from zero, the index of the last element of an array is the size of the array, minus one.

```
a = [1, 2, 3, [4, 5, 6]]
a.size                 # => 4
a << a                 # => [1, 2, 3, [4, 5, 6], [...]]
a.size                 # => 5

a[0]                   # => 1
a[3]                   # => [4, 5, 6]
a[3][0]                # => 4
a[3].size              # => 3

a[-2]                  # => [4, 5, 6]
a[-1]                  # => [1, 2, 3, [4, 5, 6], [...]]
a[a.size-1]            # => [1, 2, 3, [4, 5, 6], [...]]

a[-1][-1]              # => [1, 2, 3, [4, 5, 6], [...]]
a[-1][-1][-1]          # => [1, 2, 3, [4, 5, 6], [...]]
```

All languages with arrays have constructs for iterating over them (even if it's just a for loop). Languages like Java and Python have general iterator methods similar to Ruby's, but they're usually used for iterating over arrays. In Ruby, iterators are the standard way of traversing all data structures: array iterators are just their simplest manifestation.

Ruby's array iterators deserve special study because they're Ruby's simplest and most accessible iterator methods. If you come to Ruby from another language, you'll probably start off thinking of iterator methods as letting you treat aspects of a data structure "like an array." Recipe 4.1 covers the basic array iterator methods, including ones in the Enumerable module that you'll encounter over and over again in different contexts.

The Set class, included in Ruby's standard library, is a useful alternative to the Array class for many basic algorithms. A Ruby set models a mathematical set: sets are not ordered, and cannot contain more than one reference to the same object. For more about sets, see Recipes 4.14 and 4.15.

4.1 Iterating Over an Array

Problem

You want to perform some operation on each item in an array.

Solution

Iterate over the array with Enumerable#each. Put into a block the code you want to execute for each item in the array.

```
[1, 2, 3, 4].each { |x| puts x }
# 1
# 2
# 3
# 4
```

If you want to produce a new array based on a transformation of some other array, use Enumerable#collect along with a block that takes one element and transforms it:

```
[1, 2, 3, 4].collect { |x| x ** 2 }          # => [1, 4, 9, 16]
```

Discussion

Ruby supports for loops and the other iteration constructs found in most modern programming languages, but its prefered idiom is a code block fed to an method like each or collect.

Methods like each and collect are called *generators* or *iterators*: they iterate over a data structure, yielding one element at a time to whatever code block you've attached. Once your code block completes, they continue the iteration and yield the next item in the data structure (according to whatever definition of "next" the generator supports). These methods are covered in detail in Chapter 7.

In a method like each, the return value of the code block, if any, is ignored. Methods like collect take a more active role. After they yield an element of a data structure to a code block, they use the return value in some way. The collect method uses the return value of its attached block as an element in a new array.

Although commonly used in arrays, the collect method is actually defined in the Enumerable module, which the Array class includes. Many other Ruby classes (Hash and Range are just two) include the Enumerable methods; it's a sort of baseline for Ruby objects that provide iterators. Though Enumerable does not define the each method, it must be defined by any class that includes Enumerable, so you'll see that method a lot, too. This is covered in Recipe 9.4.

If you need to have the array indexes along with the array elements, use Enumerable#each_with_index.

```
['a', 'b', 'c'].each_with_index do |item, index|
  puts "At position #{index}: #{item}"
end
# At position 0: a
# At position 1: b
# At position 2: c
```

Ruby's Array class also defines several generators not seen in Enumerable. For instance, to iterate over a list in reverse order, use the reverse_each method:

```
[1, 2, 3, 4].reverse_each { |x| puts x }
# 4
# 3
# 2
# 1
```

Enumerable#collect has a destructive equivalent: Array#collect!, also known as Arary#map! (a helpful alias for Python programmers). This method acts just like collect, but instead of creating a new array to hold the return values of its calls to the code block, it *replaces* each item in the old array with the corresponding value from the code block. This saves memory and time, but it destroys the old array:

```
array = ['a', 'b', 'c']
array.collect! { |x| x.upcase }
array                            # => ["A", "B", "C"]
array.map! { |x| x.downcase }
array                            # => ["a", "b", "c"]
```

If you need to skip certain elements of an array, you can use the iterator methods Range#step and Integer#upto instead of Array#each. These methods generate a sequence of numbers that you can use as successive indexes into an array.

```
array = ['junk', 'junk', 'junk', 'val1', 'val2']
3.upto(array.length-1) { |i| puts "Value #{array[i]}" }
# Value val1
# Value val2

array = ['1', 'a', '2', 'b', '3', 'c']
(0..array.length-1).step(2) do |i|
  puts "Letter #{array[i]} is #{array[i+1]}"
end
# Letter 1 is a
# Letter 2 is b
# Letter 3 is c
```

Like most other programming languages, Ruby lets you define for, while, and until loops—but you shouldn't need them very often. The for construct is equivalent to each, whether it's applied to an array or a range:

```
for element in ['a', 'b', 'c']
  puts element
end
# a
# b
# c

for element in (1..3)
  puts element
end
# 1
# 2
# 3
```

The while and until constructs take a boolean expression and execute the loop while the expression is true (while) or until it becomes true (until). All three of the following code snippets generate the same output:

```
array = ['cherry', 'strawberry', 'orange']

for index in (0...array.length)
  puts "At position #{index}: #{array[index]}"
end

index = 0
while index < array.length
  puts "At position #{index}: #{array[index]}"
  index += 1
end

index = 0
until index == array.length
  puts "At position #{index}: #{array[index]}"
  index += 1
end

# At position 0: cherry
# At position 1: strawberry
# At position 2: orange
```

These constructs don't make for very idiomatic Ruby. You should only need to use them when you're iterating over a data structure in a way that doesn't already have an iterator method (for instance, if you're traversing a custom tree structure). Even then, it's more idiomatic if you only use them to define your own iterator methods.

The following code is a hybrid of each and each_reverse. It switches back and forth between iterating from the beginning of an array and iterating from its end.

```
array = [1,2,3,4,5]
new_array = []
front_index = 0
```

```
back_index = array.length-1
while front_index <= back_index
  new_array << array[front_index]
  front_index += 1
  if front_index <= back_index
   new_array << array[back_index]
    back_index -= 1
  end
end
new_array                              # => [1, 5, 2, 4, 3]
```

That code works, but it becomes reusable when defined as an iterator. Put it into the
Array class, and it becomes a universally accessible way of doing iteration, the col-
league of each and reverse_each:

```
class Array
 def each_from_both_sides
    front_index = 0
    back_index = self.length-1
    while front_index <= back_index
      yield self[front_index]
      front_index += 1
      if front_index <= back_index
    yield self[back_index]
        back_index -= 1
      end
    end
  end
end

new_array = []
[1,2,3,4,5].each_from_both_sides { |x| new_array << x }
new_array                         # => [1, 5, 2, 4, 3]
```

This "burning the candle at both ends" behavior can also be defined as a collect-
type method: one which constructs a new array out of multiple calls to the attached
code block. The implementation below delegates the actual iteration to the each_
from_both_sides method defined above:

```
class Array
  def collect_from_both_sides
    new_array = []
    each_from_both_sides { |x| new_array << yield(x) }
    return new_array
  end
end

["ham", "eggs", "and"].collect_from_both_sides { |x| x.capitalize }
# => ["Ham", "And", "Eggs"]
```

See Also

• Chapter 7, especially Recipe 7.5, "Writing an Iterator Over a Data Structure,"
  and Recipe 7.9, "Looping Through Multiple Iterables in Parallel"

4.2 Rearranging Values Without Using Temporary Variables

Problem

You want to rearrange a number of variables, or assign the elements of an array to individual variables.

Solution

Use a single assignment statement. Put the destination variables on the left-hand side, and line each one up with a variable (or expression) on the right side.

A simple swap:

```
a = 1
b = 2
a, b = b, a
a                                    # => 2
b                                    # => 1
```

A more complex rearrangement:

```
a, b, c = :red, :green, :blue
c, a, b = a, b, c
a                                    # => :green
b                                    # => :blue
c                                    # => :red
```

You can split out an array into its components:

```
array = [:red, :green, :blue]
c, a, b = array
a                                    # => :green
b                                    # => :blue
c                                    # => :red
```

You can even use the splat operator to extract items from the front of the array:

```
a, b, *c = [12, 14, 178, 89, 90]
a                                    # => 12
b                                    # => 14
c                                    # => [178, 89, 90]
```

Discussion

Ruby assignment statements are very versatile. When you put a comma-separated list of variables on the left-hand side of an assignment statement, it's equivalent to assigning each variable in the list the corresponding right-hand value. Not only does this make your code more compact and readable, it frees you from having to keep track of temporary variables when you swap variables.

Ruby works behind the scenes to allocate temporary storage space for variables that would otherwise be overwritten, so you don't have to do it yourself. You don't have to write this kind of code in Ruby:

```
a, b = 1, 2
x = a
a = b
b = x
```

The right-hand side of the assignment statement can get almost arbitrarily complicated:

```
a, b = 5, 10
a, b = b/a, a-1                 # => [2, 4]

a, b, c = 'A', 'B', 'C'
a, b, c = [a, b], { b => c }, a
a                               # => ["A", "B"]
b                               # => {"B"=>"C"}
c                               # => "A"
```

If there are more variables on the left side of the equal sign than on the right side, the extra variables on the left side get assigned nil. This is usually an unwanted side effect.

```
a, b = 1, 2
a, b = b
a                               # => 2
b                               # => nil
```

One final nugget of code that is interesting enough to mention even though it has no legitimate use in Ruby: it doesn't save enough memory to be useful, and it's slower than doing a swap with an assignment. It's possible to swap two integer variables using bitwise XOR, without using any additional storage space at all (not even implicitly):

```
a, b = rand(1000), rand(1000)   # => [595, 742]
a = a ^ b                       # => 181
b = b ^ a                       # => 595
a = a ^ b                       # => 742

[a, b]                          # => [742, 595]
```

In terms of the cookbook metaphor, this final snippet is a dessert—no nutritional value, but it sure is tasty.

4.3 Stripping Duplicate Elements from an Array

Problem

You want to strip all duplicate elements from an array, or prevent duplicate elements from being added in the first place.

Solution

Use Array#uniq to create a new array, based on an existing array but with no duplicate elements. Array#uniq! strips duplicate elements from an existing array.

```
survey_results = [1, 2, 7, 1, 1, 5, 2, 5, 1]
distinct_answers = survey_results.uniq          # => [1, 2, 7, 5]
survey_results.uniq!
survey_results                                   # => [1, 2, 7, 5]
```

To ensure that duplicate values never get into your list, use a Set instead of an array. If you try to add a duplicate element to a Set, nothing will happen.

```
require 'set'
survey_results = [1, 2, 7, 1, 1, 5, 2, 5, 1]
distinct_answers = survey_results.to_set
# => #<Set: {5, 1, 7, 2}>

games = [["Alice", "Bob"], ["Carol", "Ted"],
         ["Alice", "Mallory"], ["Ted", "Bob"]]
players = games.inject(Set.new) { |set, game| game.each { |p| set << p }; set }
# => #<Set: {"Alice", "Mallory", "Ted", "Carol", "Bob"}>

players << "Ted"
# => #<Set: {"Alice", "Mallory", "Ted", "Carol", "Bob"}>
```

Discussion

The common element between these two solutions is the hash (see Chapter 5). Array#uniq iterates over an array, using each element as a key in a hash that it always checks to see if it encountered an element earlier in the iteration. A Set keeps the same kind of hash from the beginning, and rejects elements already in the hash. You see something that acts like an array, but it won't accept duplicates. In either case, two objects are considered "duplicates" if they have the same result for ==.

The return value of Array#uniq is itself an array, and nothing prevents you from adding duplicate elements to it later on. If you want to start enforcing uniqueness in perpetuity, you should turn the array into a Set instead of calling uniq. Requiring the set library will define a new method Enumerable#to_set, which does this.

Array#uniq preserves the original order of the array (that is, the first instance of an object remains in its original location), but a Set has no order, because its internal implementation is a hash. To get array-like order in a Set, combine this recipe with Recipe 5.8 and subclass Set to use an OrderedHash:

```
class OrderedSet < Set
  def initialize
    @hash ||= OrderedHash.new
  end
end
```

Needing to strip all instances of a particular value from an array is a problem that often comes up. Ruby provides Array#delete for this task, and Array#compact for the special case of removing nil values.

```
a = [1, 2, nil, 3, 3, nil, nil, nil, 5]
a.compact                              # => [1, 2, 3, 3, 5]

a.delete(3)
a                                      # => [1, 2, nil, nil, nil, nil, 5]
```

4.4   Reversing an Array

Problem

Your array is the wrong way around: the last item should be first and the first should be last.

Solution

Use reverse to create a new array with the items reversed. Internal subarrays will not themselves be reversed.

```
[1,2,3].reverse                        # => [3, 2, 1]
[1,[2,3,4],5].reverse                  # => [5, [2, 3, 4], 1]
```

Discussion

Like many operations on basic Ruby types, reverse has a corresponding method, reverse!, which reverses an array in place:

```
a = [1,2,3]
a.reverse!
a                                      # => [3, 2, 1]
```

Don't reverse an array if you just need to iterate over it backwards. Don't use a for loop either; the reverse_each iterator is more idiomatic.

See Also

- Recipe 1.4, "Reversing a String by Words or Characters"
- Recipe 4.1, "Iterating Over an Array," talks about using Array#reverse_each to iterate over an array in reverse order
- Recipe 4.2, "Rearranging Values Without Using Temporary Variables"

4.5   Sorting an Array

Problem

You want to sort an array of objects, possibly according to some custom notion of what "sorting" means.

Solution

Homogeneous arrays of common data types, like strings or numbers, can be sorted "naturally" by just calling Array#sort:

```
[5.01, -5, 0, 5].sort                        # => [-5, 0, 5, 5.01]
["Utahraptor", "Ankylosaur", "Maiasaur"].sort
# => ["Ankylosaur", "Maiasaur", "Utahraptor"]
```

To sort objects based on one of their data members, or by the results of a method call, use Array#sort_by. This code sorts an array of arrays by size, regardless of their contents:

```
arrays = [[1,2,3], [100], [10,20]]
arrays.sort_by { |x| x.size }                 # => [[100], [10, 20], [1, 2, 3]]
```

To do a more general sort, create a code block that compares the relevant aspect of any two given objects. Pass this block into the sort method of the array you want to sort.

This code sorts an array of numbers in ascending numeric order, except that the number 42 will always be at the end of the list:

```
[1, 100, 42, 23, 26, 10000].sort do |x, y|
  x == 42 ? 1 :  x <=> y
end
# => [1, 23, 26, 100, 10000, 42]
```

Discussion

If there is one "canonical" way to sort a particular class of object, then you can have that class implement the <=> comparison operator. This is how Ruby automatically knows how to sort numbers in ascending order and strings in ascending ASCII order: Numeric and String both implement the comparison operator.

The sort_by method sorts an array using a Schwartzian transform (see Recipe 4.6 for an in-depth discussion). This is the most useful customized sort, because it's fast and easy to define. In this example, we use sort_by to sort on any one of an object's fields.

```
class Animal
  attr_reader :name, :eyes, :appendages

  def initialize(name, eyes, appendages)
   @name, @eyes, @appendages = name, eyes, appendages
  end

  def inspect
    @name
  end
end

animals = [Animal.new("octopus", 2, 8),
           Animal.new("spider", 6, 8),
           Animal.new("bee", 5, 6),
           Animal.new("elephant", 2, 4),
           Animal.new("crab", 2, 10)]
```

```
animals.sort_by { |x| x.eyes }
# => [octopus, elephant, crab, bee, spider]

animals.sort_by { |x| x.appendages  }
# => [elephant, bee, octopus, spider, crab]
```

If you pass a block into sort, Ruby calls the block to make comparisons instead of using the comparison operator. This is the most general possible sort, and it's useful for cases where sort_by won't work.

The comparison operator and a sort code block both take one argument: an object against which to compare self. A call to <=> (or a sort code block) should return –1 if self is "less than" the given object (and should therefore show up before it in a sorted list). It should return 1 if self is "greater than" the given object (and should show up after it in a sorted list), and 0 if the objects are "equal" (and it doesn't matter which one shows up first). You can usually avoid remembering this by delegating the return value to some other object's <=> implementation.

See Also

- Recipe 4.6, "Ignoring Case When Sorting Strings," covers the workings of the Schwartzian Transform
- Recipe 4.7, "Making Sure a Sorted Array Stays Sorted"
- Recipe 4.10, "Shuffling an Array"
- If you need to find the minimum or maximum item in a list according to some criteria, don't sort it just to save writing some code; see Recipe 4.11, "Getting the N Smallest Items of an Array," for other options

4.6   Ignoring Case When Sorting Strings

Problem

When you sort a list of strings, the strings beginning with uppercase letters sort before the strings beginning with lowercase letters.

```
list = ["Albania", "anteater", "zorilla", "Zaire"]
list.sort
# => ["Albania", "Zaire", "anteater", "zorilla"]
```

You want an alphabetical sort, regardless of case.

Solution

Use Array#sort_by. This is both the fastest and the shortest solution.

```
list.sort_by { |x| x.downcase  }
# => ["Albania", "anteater", "Zaire", "zorilla"]
```

Discussion

The `Array#sort_by` method was introduced in Recipe 4.5, but it's worth discussing in detail because it's so useful. It uses a technique called a Schwartzian Transform. This common technique is like writing the following Ruby code (but it's a lot faster, because it's implemented in C):

```
list.collect { |s| [s.downcase, s] }.sort.collect { |subarray| subarray[1] }
```

It works like this: Ruby creates a new array containing two-element subarrays. Each subarray contains a value of `String#downcase`, along with the original string. This new array is sorted, and then the original strings (now sorted by their values for `String#downcase`) are recovered from the subarrays. `String#downcase` is called only once for each string.

A sort is the most common occurance of this pattern, but it shows up whenever an algorithm calls a particular method on the same objects over and over again. If you're not sorting, you can't use Ruby's internal Schwartzian Transform, but you can save time by caching, or *memoizing*, the results of each distinct method call.

If you need to implement a Schwartzian Transform in Ruby, it's faster to use a hash than an array:

```
m = {}
list.sort { |x,y| (m[x] ||= x.downcase) <=> (m[y] ||= y.downcase) }
```

This technique is especially important if the method you need to call has side effects. You certainly don't want to call such methods more than once!

See Also

- The Ruby FAQ, question 9.15
- Recipe 4.5, "Sorting an Array"

4.7 Making Sure a Sorted Array Stays Sorted

Problem

You want to make sure an array stays sorted, even as you replace its elements or add new elements to it.

Solution

Subclass `Array` and override the methods that add items to the array. The new implementations add every new item to a position that maintains the sortedness of the array.

As you can see below, there are a lot of these methods. If you can guarantee that a particular method will never be called, you can get away with not overriding it.

```
class SortedArray < Array

  def initialize(*args, &sort_by)
    @sort_by = sort_by || Proc.new { |x,y| x <=> y }
    super(*args)
    sort! &sort_by
  end

  def insert(i, v)
    # The next line could be further optimized to perform a
    # binary search.
    insert_before = index(find { |x| @sort_by.call(x, v) == 1 })
    super(insert_before ? insert_before : -1, v)
  end

  def <<(v)
    insert(0, v)
  end

  alias push <<
  alias unshift <<
```

Some methods, like collect!, can modify the items in an array, taking them out of
sort order. Some methods, like flatten!, can add new elements to strange places in
an array. Rather than figuring out a way to implement these methods in a way that
preserves the sortedness of the array, we'll just let them run and then re-sort the
array.*

```
  ["collect!", "flatten!", "[]="].each do |method_name|
    module_eval %{
      def #{method_name}(*args)
        super
        sort! &@sort_by
      end
    }
  end

  def reverse!
    #Do nothing; reversing the array would disorder it.
  end
end
```

A SortedArray created from an unsorted array will end up sorted:

```
a = SortedArray.new([3,2,1])          # => [1, 2, 3]
```

Discussion

Many methods of Array are much faster on sorted arrays, so it's often useful to
expend some overhead on keeping an array sorted over time. Removing items from a

---

* We can't use define_method to define these methods because in Ruby 1.8 you can't use define_method to create a method that takes a block argument. See Chapter 10 for more on this.

sorted array won't unsort it, but adding or modifying items can. Keeping a sorted array sorted means intercepting and reimplementing every sneaky way of putting objects into the array.

The SortedArray constructor accepts any code block you can pass into Array#sort, and keeps the array sorted according to that code block. The default code block uses the comparison operator (<=>) used by sort.

```
unsorted= ["b", "aa", "a", "cccc", "1", "zzzzz", "k", "z"]
strings_by_alpha = SortedArray.new(unsorted)
# => ["1", "a", "aa", "b", "cccc", "k", "z", "zzzzz"]
strings_by_length = SortedArray.new(unsorted) do |x,y|
  x.length <=> y.length
end
# => ["b", "z", "a", "k", "1", "aa", "cccc", "zzzzz"]
```

The methods that add elements to an array specify where in the array they operate: push operates on the end of the array, and insert operates on a specified spot. SortedArray responds to these methods but it ignores the caller's request to put elements in a certain place. Every new element is inserted into a position that keeps the array sorted.

```
a << -1                       # => [-1, 1, 2, 3]
a << 1.5                      # => [-1, 1, 1.5, 2, 3]
a.push(2.5)                   # => [-1, 1, 1.5, 2, 2.5, 3]
a.unshift(1.6)                # => [-1, 1, 1.5, 1.6, 2, 2.5, 3]
```

For methods like collect! and array assignment ([]=) that allow complex changes to an array, the simplest solution is to allow the changes to go through and then re-sort:

```
a = SortedArray.new([10, 6, 4, -4, 200, 100])
# => [-4, 4, 6, 10, 100, 200]
a.collect! { |x| x * -1 }     # => [-200, -100, -10, -6, -4, 4]

a[3] = 25
a                             # => [-200, -100, -10, -4, 4, 25]
# That is, -6 has been replaced by 25 and the array has been re-sorted.

a[1..2] = [6000, 10, 600, 6]
a                             # => [-200, -4, 4, 6, 10, 25, 600, 6000]
# That is, -100 and -10 have been replaced by 6000, 10, 600, and 6,
# and the array has been re-sorted.
```

But with a little more work, we can write a more efficient implementation of array assignment that gives the same behavior. What happens when you run a command like a[0] = 10 on a SortedArray? The first element in the SortedArray is replaced by 10, and the SortedArray is re-sorted. This is equivalent to removing the first element in the array, then adding the value 10 to a place in the array that keeps it sorted.

Array#[]= implements three different types of array assignment, but all three can be modeled as a series of removals followed by a series of insertions. We can use this fact to implement a more efficient version of SortedArray#[]=:.

```
class SortedArray
  def []=(*args)
    if args.size == 3
      #e.g. "a[6,3] = [1,2,3]"
      start, length, value = args
      slice! Range.new(start, start+length, true)
      (value.respond_to? :each) ? value.each { |x| self << x } : self << value
    elsif args.size == 2
      index, value = args
      if index.is_a? Numeric
        #e.g. "a[0] = 10" (the most common form of array assignment)
        delete_at(index)
        self << value
      elsif index.is_a? Range
        #e.g. "a[0..3] = [1,2,3]"
        slice! index
        (value.respond_to? :each) ? value.each { |x| self << x } : self << value
      else
        #Not supported. Delegate to superclass; will probably give an error.
        super
        sort!(&sort_by)
      end
    else
      #Not supported. Delegate to superclass; will probably give an error.
      super
      sort!(&sort_by)
    end
  end
end
```

Just as before, the sort will be maintained even when you use array assignment to replace some of a SortedArray's elements with other objects. But this implementation doesn't have to re-sort the array every time.

```
a = SortedArray.new([1,2,3,4,5,6])
a[0] = 10
a                                    # => [2, 3, 4, 5, 6, 10]

a[0, 2] = [100, 200]
a                                    # => [4, 5, 6, 10, 100, 200]

a[1..2] = [-4, 6]
a                                    # => [-4, 4, 6, 10, 100, 200]
```

It's possible to subvert the sortedness of a SortedArray by modifying an object in place in a way that changes its sort order. Since the SortedArray never hears about the change to this object, it has no way of updating itself to move that object to its new sort position:[*]

---

[*] One alternative is to modify SortedArray[] so that when you look up an element of the array, you actually get a delegate object that intercepts all of the element's method calls, and re-sorts the array whenever the user calls a method that modifies the element in place. This is probably overkill.

```
stripes = SortedArray.new(["aardwolf", "zebrafish"])
stripes[1].upcase!
stripes                                 # => ["aardwolf", "ZEBRAFISH"]
stripes.sort!                           # => ["ZEBRAFISH", "aardwolf"]
```

If this bothers you, you can make a SortedArray keep frozen copies of objects instead of the objects themselves. This solution hurts performance and uses more memory, but it will also prevent objects from being modified after being put into the SortedArray. This code adds a convenience method to Object that makes a frozen copy of the object:

```
class Object
  def to_frozen
    f = self
    unless frozen?
      begin
        f = dup.freeze
      rescue TypeError
        #This object can't be duped (e.g. Fixnum); fortunately,
        #it usually can't be modified either
      end
    end
    return f
  end
end
```

The FrozenCopySortedArray stores frozen copies of objects instead of the objects themselves:

```
class FrozenCopySortedArray < SortedArray
  def insert(i, v)
    insert_before = index(find { |x| x > v })
    super(insert_before ? insert_before : -1, v.to_frozen)
  end

  ["initialize", "collect!", "flatten!"].each do |method_name|
    define_method(method_name) do
      super
      each_with_index { |x, i| self[i] = x.to_frozen }
      # No need to sort; by doing an assignment to every element
      # in the array, we've made #insert keep the array sorted.
    end
  end
end

stripes = SortedArray.new(["aardwolf", "zebrafish"])
stripes[1].upcase!
# TypeError: can't modify frozen string
```

Unlike a regular array, which can have elements of arbitrarily different data classes, all the elements of a SortedArray must be mutually comparable. For instance, you can mix integers and floating-point numbers within a SortedArray, but you can't mix integers and strings. Any data set that would cause Array#sort to fail makes an invalid SortedArray:

```
[1, "string"].sort
# ArgumentError: comparison of Fixnum with String failed

a = SortedArray.new([1])
a << "string"
# ArgumentError: comparison of Fixnum with String failed
```

One other pitfall: operations that create a new object, such as |=, +=, and to_a will turn an SortedArray into a (possibly unsorted) array.

```
a = SortedArray.new([3, 2, 1])        # => [1, 2, 3]
a += [1, -10]                          # => [1, 2, 3, 1, -10]
a.class                                # => Array
```

The simplest way to avoid this is to override these methods to transform the resulting array back into a SortedArray:

```
class SortedArray
  def + (other_array)
    SortedArray.new(super)
  end
end
```

See Also

- Recipe 4.11, "Getting the N Smallest Items of an Array," uses a SortedArray
- If you're going to do a lot of insertions and removals, a red-black tree may be faster than a SortedArray; you can choose from a pure Ruby implementation (*http://www.germane-software.com/software/Utilities/RBTree/*) and one that uses a C extension for speed (*http://www.geocities.co.jp/SiliconValley-PaloAlto/3388/rbtree/README.html*)

4.8   Summing the Items of an Array

Problem

You want to add together many objects in an array.

Solution

There are two good ways to accomplish this in Ruby. Plain vanilla iteration is a simple way to approach the problem:

```
collection = [1, 2, 3, 4, 5]
sum = 0
collection.each {|i| sum += i}
sum                                    # => 15
```

However this is such a common action that Ruby has a special iterator method called inject, which saves a little code:

```
collection = [1, 2, 3, 4, 5]
collection.inject(0) {|sum, i| sum + i}        # => 15
```

Discussion

Notice that in the inject solution, we didn't need to define the variable total variable outside the scope of iteration. Instead, its scope moved into the iteration. In the example above, the initial value for total is the first argument to inject. We changed the += to + because the block given to inject is evaluated on each value of the collection, and the total variable is set to its output every time.

You can think of the inject example as equivalent to the following code:

```
collection = [1, 2, 3, 4, 5]
sum = 0
sum = sum + 1
sum = sum + 2
sum = sum + 3
sum = sum + 4
sum = sum + 5
```

Although inject is the preferred way of summing over a collection, inject is generally a few times slower than each. The speed difference does not grow exponentially, so you don't need to always be worrying about it as you write code. But after the fact, it's a good idea to look for inject calls in crucial spots that you can change to use faster iteration methods like each.

Nothing stops you from using other kinds of operators in your inject code blocks. For example, you could multiply:

```
collection = [1, 2, 3, 4, 5]
collection.inject(1) {|total, i| total * i}      # => 120
```

Many of the other recipes in this book use inject to build data structures or run calculations on them.

See Also

- Recipe 2.8, "Finding Mean, Median, and Mode"
- Recipe 4.12, "Building Up a Hash Using Injection"
- Recipe 5.12, "Building a Histogram"

4.9   Sorting an Array by Frequency of Appearance

Problem

You want to sort an array so that its least-frequently-appearing items come first.

Solution

Build a histogram of the frequencies of the objects in the array, then use it as a lookup table in conjunction with the sort_by method.

The following method puts the least frequently-appearing objects first. Objects that have the same frequency are sorted normally, with the comparison operator.

```
module Enumerable
  def sort_by_frequency
    histogram = inject(Hash.new(0)) { |hash, x| hash[x] += 1; hash}
    sort_by { |x| [histogram[x], x] }
  end
end

[1,2,3,4,1,2,4,8,1,4,9,16].sort_by_frequency
# => [3, 8, 9, 16, 2, 2, 1, 1, 1, 4, 4, 4]
```

Discussion

The sort_by_frequency method uses sort_by, a method introduced in Recipe 4.5 and described in detail in Recipe 4.6. The technique here is a little different from other uses of sort_by, because it sorts by two different criteria. We want to first compare the relative frequencies of two items. If the relative frequencies are equal, we want to compare the items themselves. That way, all the instances of a given item will show up together in the sorted list.

The block you pass to Enumerable#sort_by can return only a single sort key for each object, but that sort key can be an array. Ruby compares two arrays by comparing their corresponding elements, one at a time. As soon as an element of one array is different from an element of another, the comparison stops, returning the comparison of the two different elements. If one of the arrays runs out of elements, the longer one sorts first. Here are some quick examples:

```
[1,2] <=> [0,2]                    # => 1
[1,2] <=> [1,2]                    # => 0
[1,2] <=> [2,2]                    # => -1
[1,2] <=> [1,1]                    # => 1
[1,2] <=> [1,3]                    # => -1
[1,2] <=> [1]                      # => 1
[1,2] <=> [3]                      # => -1
[1,2] <=> [0,1,2]                  # => 1
[1,2] <=> []                       # => 1
```

In our case, all the arrays contain two elements: the relative frequency of an object in the array, and the object itself. If two objects have different frequencies, the first elements of their arrays will differ, and the items will be sorted based on their frequencies. If two items have the same frequency, the first element of each array will be the same. The comparison method will move on to the second array element, which means the two objects will be sorted based on their values.

If you don't mind elements with the same frequency showing up in an unsorted order, you can speed up the sort a little by comparing only the histogram frequencies:

```
module Enumerable
  def sort_by_frequency_faster
    histogram = inject(Hash.new(0)) { |hash, x| hash[x] += 1; hash}
    sort_by { |x| histogram[x] }
  end
end
```

```
[1,2,3,4,1,2,4,8,1,4,9,16].sort_by_frequency_faster
# => [16, 8, 3, 9, 2, 2, 4, 1, 1, 4, 4, 1]
```

To sort the list so that the most-frequently-appearing items show up first, either invert the result of sort_by_frequency, or multiply the histogram values by –1 when passing them into sort_by:

```
module Enumerable
  def sort_by_frequency_descending
    histogram = inject(Hash.new(0)) { |hash, x| hash[x] += 1; hash}
    sort_by { |x| [histogram[x] * -1, x]}
  end
end
```

```
[1,2,3,4,1,2,4,8,1,4,9,16].sort_by_frequency_descending
# => [1, 1, 1, 4, 4, 4, 2, 2, 3, 8, 9, 16]
```

If you want to sort a list by the frequency of its elements, but not have repeated elements actually show up in the sorted list, you can run the list through Array#uniq after sorting it. However, since the keys of the histogram are just the distinct elements of the array, it's more efficient to sort the keys of the histogram and return those:

```
module Enumerable
  def sort_distinct_by_frequency
    histogram = inject(Hash.new(0)) { |hash, x| hash[x] += 1; hash }
    histogram.keys.sort_by { |x| [histogram[x], x] }
  end
end
```

```
[1,2,3,4,1,2,4,8,1,4,9,16].sort_distinct_by_frequency
# => [3, 8, 9, 16, 2, 1, 4]
```

See Also

- Recipe 4.5, "Sorting an Array"
- Recipe 5.12, "Building a Histogram"

4.10   Shuffling an Array

Problem

You want to put the elements of an array in random order.

Solution

The simplest way to shuffle an array (in Ruby 1.8 and above) is to sort it randomly:

```
[1,2,3].sort_by { rand }    # => [1, 3, 2]
```

This is not the fastest way, though.

Discussion

It's hard to beat a random sort for brevity of code, but it does a lot of extra work. Like any general sort, a random sort will do about *n log n* variable swaps. But to shuffle a list, it suffices to put a randomly selected element in each position of the list. This can be done with only *n* variable swaps.

```
class Array
  def shuffle!
    each_index do |i|
      j = rand(length-i) + i
      self[j], self[i] = self[i], self[j]
    end
  end

  def shuffle
    dup.shuffle!
  end
end
```

If you're shuffling a very large list, either Array#shuffle or Array#shuffle! will be significantly faster than a random sort. Here's a real-world example of shuffling using Array#shuffle:

```
class Card
  def initialize(suit, rank)
    @suit = suit
    @rank = rank
  end

  def to_s
    "#{@suit} of #{@rank}"
  end
end

class Deck < Array
  attr_reader :cards
  @@suits = %w{Spades Hearts Clubs Diamonds}
  @@ranks = %w{Ace 2 3 4 5 6 7 8 9 10 Jack Queen King}

  def initialize
    @@suits.each { |suit| @@ranks.each { |rank| self << Card.new(rank, suit) } }
  end
end
```

```
deck = Deck.new
deck.collect { |card| card.to_s }
# => ["Ace of Spades", "2 of Spades", "3 of Spades", "4 of Spades", ... ]

deck.shuffle!
deck.collect { |card| card.to_s }
# => ["6 of Clubs", "8 of Diamonds", "2 of Hearts", "5 of Clubs", ... ]
```

See Also

- Recipe 2.5, "Generating Random Numbers"
- The Facets Core library provides implementations of `Array#shuffle` and `Array#shuffle!`

4.11   Getting the N Smallest Items of an Array

Problem

You want to find the smallest few items in an array, or the largest, or the most extreme according to some other measure.

Solution

If you only need to find the single smallest item according to some measure, use `Enumerable#min`. By default, it uses the `<=>` method to see whether one item is "smaller" than another, but you can override this by passing in a code block.

```
[3, 5, 11, 16].min
# => 3
["three", "five", "eleven", "sixteen"].min
# => "eleven"
["three", "five", "eleven", "sixteen"].min { |x,y| x.size <=> y.size }
# => "five"
```

Similarly, if you need to find the single largest item, use `Enumerable#max`.

```
[3, 5, 11, 16].max
# => 16
["three", "five", "eleven", "sixteen"].max
# => "three"
["three", "five", "eleven", "sixteen"].max { |x,y| x.size <=> y.size }
# => "sixteen"
```

By default, arrays are sorted by their natural order: numbers are sorted by value, strings by their position in the ASCII collating sequence (basically alphabetical order, but all lowercase characters precede all uppercase characters). Hence, in the previous examples, "three" is the largest string, and "eleven" the smallest.

It gets more complicated when you need to get a number of the smallest or largest elements according to some measurement: say, the top 5 or the bottom 10. The simplest solution is to sort the list and skim the items you want off of the top or bottom.

```
l = [1, 60, 21, 100, -5, 20, 60, 22, 85, 91, 4, 66]
sorted = l.sort

#The top 5
sorted[-5...sorted.size]
# => [60, 66, 85, 91, 100]

#The bottom 5
sorted[0...5]
# => [-5, 1, 4, 20, 21]
```

Despite the simplicity of this technique, it's inefficient to sort the entire list unless the number of items you want to extract approaches the size of the list.

Discussion

The min and max methods work by picking the first element of the array as a "champion," then iterating over the rest of the list trying to find an element that can beat the current champion on the appropriate metric. When it finds one, that element becomes the new champion. An element that can beat the old champion can also beat any of the other contenders seen up to that point, so one run through the list suffices to find the maximum or minimum.

The naive solution to finding more than one smallest item is to repeat this process multiple times. Iterate over the Array once to find the smallest item, then iterate over it again to find the next-smallest item, and so on. This is naive for the same reason a bubble sort is naive: you're repeating many of your comparisons more times than necessary. Indeed, if you run this algorithm once for every item in the array (trying to find the n smallest items in an array of *n* items), you get a bubble sort.

Sorting the list beforehand is better when you need to find more than a small fraction of the items in the list, but it's possible to do better. After all, you don't really want to sort the whole list: you just want to sort the bottom of the list to find the smallest items. You don't care if the other elements are unsorted because you're not interested in those elements anyway.

To sort only the smallest elements, you can keep a sorted "stable" of champions, and kick the largest champion out of the stable whenever you find an element that's smaller. If you encounter a number that's too large to enter the stable, you can ignore it from that point on. This process rapidly cuts down on the number of elements you must consider, making this approach faster than doing a sort.

The SortedList class from Recipe 4.7 is useful for this task. The min_n method below creates a SortedList "stable" that keeps its elements sorted based on the same block being used to find the minimum. It keeps the stable at a certain size by kicking out the largest item in the stable whenever a smaller item is found. The max_n method works similarly, but the comparisons are reversed, and the smallest element in the stable is kicked out when a larger element is found.

```
module Enumerable
  def min_n(n, &block)
    block = Proc.new { |x,y| x <=> y } if block == nil
    stable = SortedArray.new(&block)
    each do |x|
      stable << x if stable.size < n or block.call(x, stable[-1]) == -1
      stable.pop until stable.size <= n
    end
    return stable
  end

  def max_n(n, &block)
    block = Proc.new { |x,y| x <=> y } if block == nil
    stable = SortedArray.new(&block)
    each do |x|
      stable << x if stable.size < n or block.call(x, stable[0]) == 1
      stable.shift until stable.size <= n
    end
    return stable
  end
end

l = [1, 60, 21, 100, -5, 20, 60, 22, 85, 91, 4, 66]
l.max_n(5)
# => [60, 66, 85, 91, 100]
l.min_n(5)
# => [-5, 1, 4, 20, 21]

l.min_n(5) { |x,y| x.abs <=> y.abs }
# => [1, 4, -5, 20, 21]
```

See Also

- Recipe 4.7, "Making Sure a Sorted Array Stays Sorted"

4.12 Building Up a Hash Using Injection

Problem

You want to create a hash from the values in an array.

Solution

As seen in Recipe 4.8, the most straightforward way to solve this kind of problem is to use Enumerable#inject. The inject method takes one parameter (the object to build up, in this case a hash), and a block specifying the action to take on each item. The block takes two parameters: the object being built up (the hash), and one of the items from the array.

Here's a straightforward use of inject to build a hash out of an array of key-value pairs:

```
collection = [ [1, 'one'], [2, 'two'], [3, 'three'],
               [4, 'four'], [5, 'five']
             ]
collection.inject({}) do |hash, value|
  hash[value.first] = value.last
  hash
end
# => {5=>"five", 1=>"one", 2=>"two", 3=>"three", 4=>"four"}
```

Discussion

Why is there that somewhat incongrous expression hash at the end of the inject block above? Because the next time it calls the block, inject uses the value it got from the block the last time it called the block. When you're using inject to build a data structure, the last line of code in the block should evaluate to the object you're building up: in this case, our hash.

This is probably the most common inject-related gotcha. Here's some code that doesn't work:

```
collection.dup.inject({}) { |hash, value| hash[value.first] = value.last }
# IndexError: index 3 out of string
```

Why doesn't this work? Because hash assignment returns the assigned value, not the hash.

```
Hash.new["key"] = "some value"                          # => "some value"
```

In the broken example above, when inject calls the code block for the second and subsequent times, it does not pass the hash as the code block's first argument. It passes in the last value to be assigned to the hash. In this case, that's a string (maybe "one" or "four"). The hash has been lost forever, and the inject block crashes when it tries to treat a string as a hash.

Hash#update can be used like hash assignment, except it returns the hash instead of the assigned value (and it's slower). So this code will work:

```
collection.inject({}) do |hash, value|
  hash.update value.first => value.last
end
# => {5=>"five", 1=>"ontwo", 2=>"two", 3=>"three", 4=>"four"}
```

Ryan Carver came up with a more sophisticated way of building a hash out of an array: define a general method for all arrays called to_h.

```
class Array
  def to_h(default=nil)
    Hash[ *inject([]) { |a, value| a.push value, default || yield(value) } ]
  end
end
```

The magic of this method is that you can provide a code block to customize how keys in the array are mapped to values.

```
a = [1, 2, 3]

a.to_h(true)
# => {1=>true, 2=>true, 3=>true}

a.to_h { |value| [value * -1, value * 2] }
# => {1=>[-1, 2], 2=>[-2, 4], 3=>[-3, 6]}
```

References

- Recipe 5.3, "Adding Elements to a Hash"
- Recipe 5.12, "Building a Histogram"
- The original definition of `Array#to_h`: (*http://fivesevensix.com/posts/2005/05/20/ array-to_h*)

4.13   Extracting Portions of Arrays

Problem

Given an array, you want to retrieve the elements of the array that occupy certain positions or have certain properties. You might to do this in a way that removes the matching elements from the original array.

Solution

To gather a chunk of an array without modifying it, use the array retrieval operator `Array#[]`, or its alias `Array#slice`.

The array retrieval operator has three forms, which are the same as the corresponding forms for substring accesses. The simplest and most common form is `array[index]`. It takes a number as input, treats it as an index into the array, and returns the element at that index. If the input is negative, it counts from the end of the array. If the array is smaller than the index, it returns `nil`. If performance is a big consideration for you, `Array#at` will do the same thing, and it's a little faster than `Array#[]`:

```
a = ("a".."h").to_a         # => ["a", "b", "c", "d", "e", "f", "g", "h"]

a[0]                        # => "a"
a[1]                        # => "b"

a.at(1)                     # => "b"
a.slice(1)                  # => "b"
a[-1]                       # => "h"
a[-2]                       # => "g"
a[1000]                     # => nil
a[-1000]                    # => nil
```

The second form is `array[range]`. This form retrieves every element identified by an index in the given range, and returns those elements as a new array.

A range in which both numbers are negative will retrieve elements counting from the end of the array. You can mix positive and negative indices where that makes sense:

```
a[2..5]              # => ["c", "d", "e", "f"]
a[2...5]             # => ["c", "d", "e"]
a[0..0]              # => ["a"]
a[1..-4]             # => ["b", "c", "d", "e"]
a[5..1000]           # => ["f", "g", "h"]

a[2..0]              # => []
a[0...0]             # => []

a[-3..2]             # => []
```

The third form is `array[start_index, length]`. This is equivalent to `array[range.new(start_index...start_index+length)]`.

```
a[2, 4]              # => ["c", "d", "e", "f"]
a[2, 3]              # => ["c", "d", "e"]
a[0, 1]              # => ["a"]
a[1, 2]              # => ["b", "c"]
a[-4, 2]             # => ["e", "f"]
a[5, 1000]           # => ["f", "g", "h"]
```

To remove a slice from the array, use `Array#slice!`. This method takes the same arguments and returns the same results as `Array#slice`, but as a side effect, the objects it retrieves are removed from the array.

```
a.slice!(2..5)       # => ["c", "d", "e", "f"]
a                    # => ["a", "b", "g", "h"]

a.slice!(0)          # => "a"
a                    # => ["b", "g", "h"]

a.slice!(1,2)        # => ["g", "h"]
a                    # => ["b"]
```

Discussion

The `Array` methods `[]`, `slice`, and `slice!` work well if you need to extract one particular elements, or a set of adjacent elements. There are two other main possibilities: you might need to retrieve the elements at an arbitrary set of indexes, or (a catch-all) you might need to retrieve all elements with a certain property that can be determined with a code block.

To nondestructively gather the elements at particular indexes in an array, pass in any number of indices to `Array#values_at`. Results will be returned in a new array, in the same order they were requested.

```
a = ("a".."h").to_a   # => ["a", "b", "c", "d", "e", "f", "g", "h"]
a.values_at(0)        # => ["a"]
```

```
a.values_at(1, 0, -2)          # => ["b", "a", "g"]
a.values_at(4, 6, 6, 7, 4, 0, 3)# => ["e", "g", "g", "h", "e", "a", "d"].
```

Enumerable#find_all finds all elements in an array (or other class with Enumerable mixed in) for which the specified code block returns true. Enumerable#reject will find all elements for which the specified code block returns false.

```
a.find_all { |x| x < "e" }     # => ["a", "b", "c", "d"]
a.reject { |x| x < "e" }       # => ["e", "f", "g", "h"]
```

To find all elements in an array that match a regular expression, you can use Enumerable#grep instead of defining a block that does the regular expression match:

```
a.grep /[aeiou]/               # => ["a", "e"]
a.grep /[^g]/                  # => ["a", "b", "c", "d", "e", "f", "h"]
```

It's a little tricky to implement a destructive version of Array#values_at, because removing one element from an array changes the indexes of all subsequent elements. We can let Ruby do the work, though, by replacing each element we want to remove with a dummy object that we know cannot already be present in the array. We can then use the C-backed method Array#delete to remove all instances of the dummy object from the array. This is much faster than using Array#slice! to remove elements one at a time, because each call to Array#slice! forces Ruby to rearrange the array to be contiguous.

If you know that your array contains no nil values, you can set your undesired values to nil, then use use Array#compress! to remove them. The solution below is more general.

```
class Array
  def strip_values_at!(*args)
    #For each mentioned index, replace its value with a dummy object.
    values = []
    dummy = Object.new
    args.each do |i|
      if i < size
        values << self[i]
        self[i] = dummy
      end
    #Strip out the dummy object.
    delete(dummy)
    return values
  end
end

a = ("a".."h").to_a
a.strip_values_at!(1, 0, -2)            # => ["b", "a", "g"]
a                                       # => ["c", "d", "e", "f", "h"]

a.strip_values_at!(1000)                # => []
a                                       # => ["c", "d", "e", "f", "h"]
```

`Array#reject!` removes all items from an array that match a code block, but it doesn't return the removed items, so it won't do for a destructive equivalent of `Enumerable#find_all`. This implementation of a method called `extract!` picks up where `Array#reject!` leaves off:

```ruby
class Array
  def extract!
    ary = self.dup
    self.reject! { |x| yield x }
    ary - self
  end
end

a = ("a".."h").to_a
a.extract! { |x| x < "e" && x != "b" }    # => ["a", "c", "d"]
a                                         # => ["b", "e", "f", "g", "h"]
```

Finally, a convenience method called `grep_extract!` provides a method that destructively approximates the behavior of `Enumerable#grep`.

```ruby
class Array
  def grep_extract!(re)
    extract! { |x| re.match(x) }
  end
end

a = ("a".."h").to_a
a.grep_extract!(/[aeiou]/)                # => ["a", "e"]
a                                         # => ["b", "c", "d", "f", "g", "h"]
```

See Also

- Strings support the array lookup operator, `slice`, `slice!`, and all the methods of Enumerable, so you can treat them like arrays in many respects; see Recipe 1.13, "Getting the Parts of a String You Want"

4.14 Computing Set Operations on Arrays

Problem

You want to find the union, intersection, difference, or Cartesian product of two arrays, or the complement of a single array with respect to some universe.

Solution

Array objects have overloaded arithmetic and logical operators to provide the three simplest set operations:

```ruby
#Union
[1,2,3] | [1,4,5]          # => [1, 2, 3, 4, 5]
```

```
#Intersection
[1,2,3] & [1,4,5]          # => [1]

#Difference
[1,2,3] - [1,4,5]          # => [2, 3]
```

Set objects overload the same operators, as well as the exclusive-or operator (^). If you already have Arrays, though, it's more efficient to deconstruct the XOR operation into its three component operations.

```
require 'set'
a = [1,2,3]
b = [3,4,5]
a.to_set ^ b.to_set        # => #<Set: {5, 1, 2, 4}>
(a | b) - (a & b)          # => [1, 2, 4, 5]
```

Discussion

Set objects are intended to model mathematical sets: where arrays are ordered and can contain duplicate entries, Sets model an unordered collection of unique items. Set not only overrides operators for set operations, it provides English-language aliases for the three most common operators: Set#union, Set#intersection, and Set#difference. An array can only perform a set operation on another array, but a Set can perform a set operation on any Enumerable.

```
array = [1,2,3]
set = [3,4,5].to_s
array & set                # => TypeError: can't convert Set into Array
set & array                # => #<Set: {3}>
```

You might think that Set objects would be optimized for set operations, but they're actually optimized for constant-time membership checks (internally, a Set is based on a hash). Set union is faster when the left-hand object is a Set object, but intersection and difference are significantly faster when both objects are arrays. It's not worth it to convert arrays into Sets just so you can say you performed set operations on Set objects.

The union and intersection set operations remove duplicate entries from arrays. The difference operation does not remove duplicate entries from an array except as part of a subtraction.

```
[3,3] & [3,3]              # => [3]
[3,3] | [3,3]              # => [3]
[1,2,3,3] - [1]            # => [2, 3, 3]
[1,2,3,3] - [3]            # => [1, 2]
[1,2,3,3] - [2,2,3]        # => [1]
```

Complement

If you want the complement of an array with respect to some small universe, create that universe and use the difference operation:

```
u = [:red, :orange, :yellow, :green, :blue, :indigo, :violet]
a = [:red, :blue]
u - a                      # => [:orange, :yellow, :green, :indigo, :violet]
```

More often, the relevant universe is infinite (the set of natural numbers) or extremely large (the set of three-letter strings). The best strategy here is to define a generator and use it to iterate through the complement. Be sure to break when you're done; you don't want to iterate over an infinite set.

```ruby
def natural_numbers_except(exclude)
  exclude_map = {}
  exclude.each { |x| exclude_map[x] = true }
  x = 1
  while true
    yield x unless exclude_map[x]
    x = x.succ
  end
end

natural_numbers_except([2,3,6,7]) do |x|
  break if x > 10
  puts x
end
# 1
# 4
# 5
# 8
# 9
# 10
```

Cartesian product

To get the Cartesian product of two arrays, write a nested iteration over both lists and append each pair of items to a new array. This code is attached to Enumerable so you can also use it with Sets or any other Enumerable.

```ruby
module Enumberable
  def cartesian(other)
    res = []
    each { |x| other.each { |y| res << [x, y] } }
    return res
  end
end

[1,2,3].cartesian(["a",5,6])
# => [[1, "a"], [1, 5], [1, 6],
#     [2, "a"], [2, 5], [2, 6],
#     [3, "a"], [3, 5], [3, 6]
```

This version uses Enumerable#inject to make the code more concise; however, the original version is more efficient.

```ruby
module Enumerable
  def cartesian(other)
    inject([]) { |res, x| other.inject(res) { |res, y| res << [x,y] } }
  end
end
```

See Also

- See Recipe 2.5, "Generating Random Numbers," for an example (constructing a deck of cards from suits and ranks) that could benefit from a function to calculate the Cartesian product
- Recipe 2.10, "Multiplying Matrices"

4.15   Partitioning or Classifying a Set

Problem

You want to partition a Set or array based on some attribute of its elements. All elements that go "together" in some code-specific sense should be grouped together in distinct data structures. For instance, if you're partitioning by color, all the green objects in a Set should be grouped together, separate from the group of all the red objects in the Set.

Solution

Use Set#divide, passing in a code block that returns the partition of the object it's passed. The result will be a new Set containing a number of partitioned subsets of your original Set.

The code block can accept either a single argument or two arguments.* The single-argument version examines each object to see which subset it should go into.

```
require 'set'
s = Set.new((1..10).collect)
# => #<Set: {5, 6, 1, 7, 2, 8, 3, 9, 4, 10}>

# Divide the set into the "true" subset and the "false" subset: that
# is, the "less than 5" subset and the "not less than 5" subset.
s.divide { |x| x < 5 }
# => #<Set: {#<Set: {5, 6, 7, 8, 9, 10}>, #<Set: {1, 2, 3, 4}>}>

# Divide the set into the "0" subset and the "1" subset: that is, the
# "even" subset and the "odd" subset.
s.divide { |x| x % 2 }
# => #<Set: {#<Set: {6, 2, 8, 4, 10}>, #<Set: {5, 1, 7, 3, 9}>}>

s = Set.new([1, 2, 3, 'a', 'b', 'c', -1.0, -2.0, -3.0])
# Divide the set into the "String subset, the "Fixnum" subset, and the
# "Float" subset.
s.divide { |x| x.class }
# => #<Set: {#<Set: {"a", "b", "c"}>,
```

---

* This is analogous to the one-argument code block passed into Enumerable#sort_by and the two-argument code block passed into Array#sort.

```
# =>          #<Set: {1, 2, 3}>,
# =>          #<Set: {-1.0, -3.0, -2.0}>}>
```

For the two-argument code block version of Set#divide, the code block should return true if both the arguments it has been passed should be put into the same subset.

```
s = [1, 2, 3, -1, -2, -4].to_set

# Divide the set into sets of numbers with the same absolute value.
s.divide { |x,y| x.abs == y.abs }
# => #<Set: {#<Set: {-1, 1}>,
# =>          #<Set: {2, -2}>,
# =>          #<Set: {-4}>,
# =>          #<Set: {3}>}>

# Divide the set into sets of adjacent numbers
s.divide { |x,y| (x-y).abs == 1 }
# => #<Set: {#<Set: {1, 2, 3}>,
# =>          #<Set: {-1}>,
# =>          #<Set: {-4, -3}>}>
```

If you want to classify the subsets by the values they have in common, use Set#classify instead of Set#divide. It works like Set#divide, but it returns a hash that maps the names of the subsets to the subsets themselves.

```
s.classify { |x| x.class }
# => {String=>#<Set: {"a", "b", "c"}>,
# =>   Fixnum=>#<Set: {1, 2, 3}>,
# =>   Float=>#<Set: {-1.0, -3.0, -2.0}>}
```

Discussion

The version of Set#divide that takes a two-argument code block uses the tsort library to turn the Set into a directed graph. The nodes in the graph are the items in the Set. Two nodes x and y in the graph are connected with a vertex (one-way arrow) if the code block returns true when passed |x,y|. For the Set and the two-argument code block given in the example above, the graph looks like Figure 4-1.

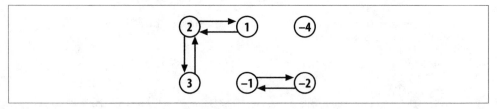

Figure 4-1. The set {1, 2, 3, -1, -2, -4} graphed according to the code block that checks adjacency

The Set partitions returned by Set#divide are the *strongly connected components* of this graph, obtained by iterating over TSort#each_strongly_connected_component. A strongly connected component is a set of nodes such that, starting from any node in the component, you can follow the one-way arrows and get to any other node in the component.

Visually speaking, the strongly connected components are the "clumps" in the graph. 1 and 3 are in the same strongly connected component as 2, because starting from 3 you can follow one-way arrows through 2 and get to 1. Starting from 1, you can follow one-way arrows through 2 and get to 3. This makes 1, 2, and 3 part of the same Set partition, even though there are no direct connections between 1 and 3.

In most real-world scenarios (including all the examples above), the one-way arrows will be symmetrical: if the code returns true for |x,y|, it will also return true for |y,x|. Set#divide will work even if this isn't true. Consider a Set and a divide code block like the following:

```
connections = { 1 => 2, 2 => 3, 3 => 1, 4 => 1 }
[1,2,3,4].to_set.divide { |x,y| connections[x] == y }
# => #<Set: {#<Set: {1, 2, 3}>, #<Set: {4}>}>
```

The corresponding graph looks like Figure 4-2.

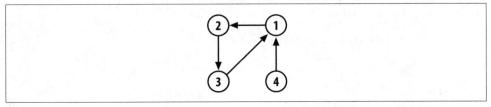

Figure 4-2. The set {1,2,3,4} graphed according to the connection hash

You can get to any other node from 4 by following one-way arrows, but you can't get to 4 from any of the other nodes. This puts 4 is in a strongly connected component—and a Set partition—all by itself. 1, 2, and 3 form a second strongly connected component—and a second Set partition—because you can get from any of them to any of them by following one-way arrows.

Implementation for arrays

If you're starting with an array instead of a Set, it's easy to simulate Set#classify (and the single-argument block form of Set#divide) with a hash. In fact, the code below is almost identical to the current Ruby implementation of Set#classify.

```
class Array
  def classify
    require 'set'
    h = {}
    each do |i|
      x = yield(i)
      (h[x] ||= self.class.new) << i
    end
    h
  end
end
```

```
  def divide(&block)
    Set.new(classify(&block).values)
  end
end

[1,1,2,6,6,7,101].divide { |x| x % 2 }
# => #<Set: {[2, 6, 6], [1, 1, 7, 101]}>
```

There's no simple way to implement a version of Array#divide that takes a two-argument block. The TSort class is Set-like, in that it won't create two different nodes for the same object. The simplest solution is to convert the array into a Set to remove any duplicate values, divide the Set normally, then convert the partitioned subsets into arrays, adding back the duplicate values as you go:

```
class Array
  def divide(&block)
    if block.arity == 2
      counts = inject({}) { |h, x| h[x] ||= 0; h[x] += 1; h}
      to_set.divide(&block).inject([]) do |divided, set|
        divided << set.inject([]) do |partition, e|
          counts[e].times { partition << e }
          partition
        end
      end
    else
      Set.new(classify(&block).values)
    end
  end
end

[1,1,2,6,6,7,101].divide { |x,y| (x-y).abs == 1 }
# => [[101], [1, 1, 2], [6, 6, 7]]
```

Is it worth it? You decide.

## CHAPTER 5

Hashes

Hashes and arrays are the two basic "aggregate" data types supported by most modern programming lagnguages. The basic interface of a hash is similar to that of an array. The difference is that while an array stores items according to a numeric index, the index of a hash can be any object at all.

Arrays and strings have been built into programming languages for decades, but built-in hashes are a relatively recent development. Now that they're around, it's hard to live without them: they're at least as useful as arrays.

You can create a Hash by calling `Hash.new` or by using one of the special sytaxes `Hash[]` or `{}`. With the `Hash[]` syntax, you pass in the initial elements as comma-separated object references. With the `{}` syntax, you pass in the initial contents as comma-separated key-value pairs.

```
empty = Hash.new                    # => {}
empty = {}                          # => {}
numbers = { 'two' => 2, 'eight' => 8} # => {"two"=>2, "eight"=>8}
numbers = Hash['two', 2, 'eight', 8]  # => {"two"=>2, "eight"=>8}
```

Once the hash is created, you can do hash lookups and element assignments using the same syntax you would use to view and modify array elements:

```
numbers["two"]                      # => 2
numbers["ten"] = 10                 # => 10
numbers                             # => {"two"=>2, "eight"=>8, "ten"=>10}
```

You can get an array containing the keys or values of a hash with `Hash#keys` or `Hash#values`. You can get the entire hash as an array with `Hash#to_a`:

```
numbers.keys                        # => ["two", "eight", "ten"]
numbers.values                      # => [2, 8, 10]
numbers.to_a                        # => [["two", 2], ["eight", 8], ["ten", 10]]
```

Like an array, a hash contains references to objects, not copies of them. Modifications to the original objects will affect all references to them:

```
motto = "Don't tread on me"
flag = { :motto => motto,
```

```
        :picture => "rattlesnake.png"}
motto.upcase!
flag[:motto]                              # => "DON'T TREAD ON ME"
```

The defining feature of an array is its ordering. Each element of an array is assigned a Fixnum object as its key. The keys start from zero and there can never be gaps. In contrast, a hash has no natural ordering, since its keys can be any objects at all. This feature make hashes useful for storing lightly structured data or key-value pairs.

Consider some simple data for a person in an address book. For a side-by-side comparison I'll represent identical data as an array, then as a hash:

```
a = ["Maury", "Momento", "123 Elm St.", "West Covina", "CA"]
h = { :first_name => "Maury",
      :last_name => "Momento",
      :address => "123 Elm St."
      :city => "West Covina",
      :state => "CA" }
```

The array version is more concise, and if you know the numeric index, you can retrieve any element from it in constant time. The problem is knowing the index, and knowing what it means. Other than inspecting the records, there's no way to know whether the element at index 1 is a last name or a first name. Worse, if the array format changes to add an apartment number between the street address and city, all code that uses a[3] or a[4] will need to have its index changed.

The hash version doesn't have these problems. The last name will always be at :last_name, and it's easy (for a human, anyway) to know what :last_name means. Most of the time, hash lookups take no longer than array lookups.

The main advantage of a hash is that it's often easier to find what you're looking for. Checking whether an array contains a certain value might require scanning the entire array. To see whether a hash contains a value for a certain key, you only need to look up that key. The set library (as seen in the previous chapter) exploits this behavior to implement a class that looks like an array, but has the performance characteristics of a hash.

The downside of using a hash is that since it has no natural ordering, it can't be sorted except by turning it into an array first. There's also no guarantee of order when you iterate over a hash. Here's a contrasting case, in which an array is obviously the right choice:

```
a = [1, 4, 9, 16]
h = { :one_squared => 1, two_squared => 4, three_squared => 9,
      :four_squared => 16 }
```

In this case, there's a numeric order to the entries, and giving them additional labels distracts more than it helps.

A hash in Ruby is actually implemented as an array. When you look up a key in a hash (either to see what's associated with that key, or to associate a value with the key), Ruby calculates the *hash code* of the key by calling its hash method. The result is used as a numeric index in the array. Recipe 5.5 will help you with the most common problem related to hash codes.

The performance of a hash depends a lot on the fact that it's very rare for two objects to have the same hash code. If all objects in a hash had the same hash code, a hash would be much slower than an array. Code like this would be a very bad idea:

```ruby
class BadIdea
  def hash
    100
  end
end
```

Except for strings and other built-in objects, most objects have a hash code equivalent to their internal object ID. As seen above, you can override Object#hash to change this, but the only time you should need to do this is if your class also overrides Object#==. If two objects are considered equal, they should also have the same hash code; otherwise, they will behave strangely when you put them into hashes. Code like the fragment below is a very good idea:

```ruby
class StringHolder
  attr_reader :string
  def initialize(s)
    @string = s
  end

  def ==(other)
    @string == other.string
  end

  def hash
    @string.hash
  end
end
a = StringHolder.new("The same string.")
b = StringHolder.new("The same string.")
a == b                                      # => true
a.hash                                      # => -1007666862
b.hash                                      # => -1007666862
```

5.1 Using Symbols as Hash Keys

Credit: Ben Giddings

Problem

When using a hash, you want the slight optimization you can get by using symbols as keys instead of strings.

Solution

Whenever you would otherwise use a quoted string, use a symbol instead. A symbol can be created by either using a colon in front of a word, like :keyname, or by transforming a string to a symbol using String#intern.

```
people = Hash.new
people[:nickname] = 'Matz'
people[:language] = 'Japanese'
people['last name'.intern] = 'Matsumoto'
people[:nickname]                                # => "Matz"
people['nickname'.intern]                        # => "Matz"
```

Discussion

While 'name' and 'name' appear exactly identical, they're actually different. Each time you create a quoted string in Ruby, you create a unique object. You can see this by looking at the object_id method.

```
'name'.object_id                                 # => -605973716
'name'.object_id                                 # => -605976356
'name'.object_id                                 # => -605978996
```

By comparison, each instance of a symbol refers to a single object.

```
:name.object_id                                  # => 878862
:name.object_id                                  # => 878862
'name'.intern.object_id                          # => 878862
'name'.intern.object_id                          # => 878862
```

Using symbols instead of strings saves memory and time. It saves memory because there's only one symbol instance, instead of many string instances. If you have many hashes that contain the same keys, the memory savings adds up.

Using symbols as hash keys is faster because the hash value of a symbol is simply its object ID. If you use strings in a hash, Ruby must calculate the hash value of a string each time it's used as a hash key.

See Also

- Recipe 1.7, "Converting Between Strings and Symbols"

5.2 Creating a Hash with a Default Value

Credit: Ben Giddings

Problem

You're using a hash, and you don't want to get nil as a value when you look up a key that isn't present in the hash. You want to get some more convenient value instead, possibly one calculated dynamically.

Solution

A normal hash has a default value of `nil`:

```
h = Hash.new
h[1]                                      # => nil
h['do you have this string?']             # => nil
```

There are two ways of creating default values for hashes. If you want the default value to be the same object for every hash key, pass that value into the `Hash` constructor.

```
h = Hash.new("nope")
h[1]                                      # => "nope"
h['do you have this string?']             # => "nope"
```

If you want the default value for a missing key to depend on the key or the current state of the hash, pass a code block into the hash constructor. The block will be called each time someone requests a missing key.

```
h = Hash.new { |hash, key| (key.respond_to? :to_str) ? "nope" : nil }
h[1]                                      # => nil
h['do you have this string']              # => "nope"
```

Discussion

The first type of custom default value is most useful when you want a default value of zero. For example, this form can be used to calculate the frequency of certain words in a paragraph of text:

```
text = 'The rain in Spain falls mainly in the plain.'
word_count_hash = Hash.new 0              # => {}
text.split(/\W+/).each { |word| word_count_hash[word.downcase] += 1 }
word_count_hash
# => {"rain"=>1, "plain"=>1, "in"=>2, "mainly"=>1, "falls"=>1,
#     "the"=>2, "spain"=>1}
```

What if you wanted to make lists of the words starting with a given character? Your first attempt might look like this:

```
first_letter_hash = Hash.new []
text.split(/\W+/).each { |word| first_letter_hash[word[0,1].downcase] << word }
first_letter_hash
                                          # => {}
first_letter_hash["m"]
# => ["The", "rain", "in", "Spain", "falls", "mainly", "in", "the", "plain"]
```

What's going on here? All those words don't start with "m"....

What happened is that the array you passed into the `Hash` constructor is being used for *every* default value. `first_letter_hash["m"]` is now a reference to that array, as is `first_letter_hash["f"]` and even `first_letter_hash[1006]`.

This is a case where you need to pass in a block to the `Hash` constructor. The block is run every time the `Hash` can't find a key. This way you can create a different array each time.

```
first_letter_hash = Hash.new { |hash, key| hash[key] = [] }
text.split(/\W+/).each { |word| first_letter_hash[word[0,1].downcase] << word }
first_letter_hash
# => {"m"=>["mainly"], "p"=>["plain"], "f"=>["falls"], "r"=>["rain"],
#     "s"=>["Spain"], "i"=>["in", "in"], "t"=>["The", "the"]}
first_letter_hash["m"]
# => ["mainly"]
```

When a letter can't be found in the hash, Ruby calls the block passed into the Hash constructor. That block puts a new array into the hash, using the missing letter as the key. Now the letter is bound to a unique array, and words can be added to that array normally.

Note that if you want to add the array to the hash so it can be used later, you must assign it within the block of the Hash constructor. Otherwise you'll get a new, empty array every time you access first_letter_hash["m"]. The words you want to append to the array will be lost.

See Also

- This technique is used in recipes like Recipe 5.6, "Keeping Multiple Values for the Same Hash Key," and Recipe 5.12, "Building a Histogram"

5.3   Adding Elements to a Hash

Problem

You have some items, loose or in some other data structure, which you want to put into an existing hash.

Solution

To add a single key-value pair, assign the value to the element lookup expression for the key: that is, call hash[key] = value. Assignment will override any previous value stored for that key.

```
h = {}
h["Greensleeves"] = "all my joy"
h                                       # => {"Greensleeves"=>"all my joy"}
h["Greensleeves"] = "my delight"
h                                       # => {"Greensleeves"=>"my delight"}
```

Discussion

When you use a string as a hash key, the string is transparently copied and the copy is frozen. This is to avoid confusion should you modify the string in place, then try to use its original form to do a hash lookup:

```
key = "Modify me if you can"
h = { key => 1 }
```

```
key.upcase!                                 # => "MODIFY ME IF YOU CAN"
h[key]                                      # => nil
h["Modify me if you can"]                   # => 1

h.keys                                      # => ["Modify me if you can"]
h.keys[0].upcase!
# TypeError: can't modify frozen string
```

To add an array of key-value pairs to a hash, either iterate over the array with Array#each, or pass the hash into Array#inject. Using inject is slower but the code is more concise.

```
squares = [[1,1], [2,4], [3,9]]

results = {}
squares.each { |k,v| results[k] = v }
results                              # => {1=>1, 2=>4, 3=>9}

squares.inject({}) { |h, kv| h[kv[0]] = kv[1]; h }
# => {1=>1, 2=>4, 3=>9}
```

To turn a flat array into the key-value pairs of a hash, iterate over the array elements two at a time:

```
class Array
  def into_hash(h)
    unless size % 2 == 0
      raise StandardError, "Expected array with even number of elements"
    end
    0.step(size-1, 2) { |x| h[self[x]] = self[x+1] }
    h
  end
end

squares = [1,1,2,3,4,9]
results = {}
squares.into_hash(results)           # => {1=>1, 2=>3, 4=>9}

[1,1,2].into_hash(results)
# StandardError: Expected array with even number of elements
```

To insert into a hash every key-value from another hash, use Hash#merge!. If a key is present in both hashes when a.merge!(b) is called, the value in b takes precedence over the value in a.

```
squares = { 1 => 1, 2 => 4, 3 => 9}
cubes = { 3 => 27, 4 => 256, 5 => 3125}
squares.merge!(cubes)
squares                              # =>{5=>3125, 1=>1, 2=>4, 3=>27, 4=>256}
cubes                                # =>{5=>3125, 3=>27, 4=>256}
```

Hash#merge! also has a nondestructive version, Hash#merge, which creates a new Hash with elements from both parent hashes. Again, the hash passed in as an argument takes precedence.

To completely replace the entire contents of one hash with the contents of another, use Hash#replace.

```
squares = { 1 => 1, 2 => 4, 3 => 9}
cubes = { 1 => 1, 2 => 8, 3 => 27}
squares.replace(cubes)
squares                              # => {1=>1, 2=>8, 3=>27}
```

This is different from simply assigning the cubes hash to the squares variable name, because cubes and squares are still separate hashes: they just happen to contain the same elements right now. Changing cubes won't affect squares:

```
cubes[4] = 64
squares                              # => {1=>1, 2=>8, 3=>27}
```

Hash#replace is useful for reverting a Hash to known default values.

```
defaults = {:verbose => true, :help_level => :beginner }
args = {}
requests.each do |request|
  args.replace(defaults)
  request.process(args) #The process method might modify the args Hash.
end
```

See Also

- Recipe 4.12, "Building Up a Hash Using Injection," has more about the inject method
- Recipe 5.1, "Using Symbols as Hash Keys," for a way to save memory when constructing certain types of hashes
- Recipe 5.5, "Using an Array or Other Modifiable Object as a Hash Key," talks about how to avoid another common case of confusion when a hash key is modified

5.4   Removing Elements from a Hash

Problem

Certain elements of your hash have got to go!

Solution

Most of the time you want to remove a specific element of a hash. To do that, pass the key into Hash#delete.

```
h = {}
h[1] = 10
h                                    # => {1=>10}
h.delete(1)
h                                    # => {}
```

Discussion

Don't try to delete an element from a hash by mapping it to nil. It's true that, by default, you get nil when you look up a key that's not in the hash, but there's a difference between a key that's missing from the hash and a key that's present but mapped to nil. Hash#has_key? will see a key mapped to nil, as will Hash#each and all other methods except for a simple fetch:

```
h = {}
h[5]                                  # => nil
h[5] = 10
h[5]                                  # => 10
h[5] = nil
h[5]                                  # => nil
h.keys                                # => [5]
h.delete(5)
h.keys                                # => []
```

Hash#delete works well when you need to remove elements on an ad hoc basis, but sometimes you need to go through the whole hash looking for things to remove. Use the Hash#delete_if iterator to delete key-value pairs for which a certain code block returns true (Hash#reject works the same way, but it works on a copy of the Hash). The following code deletes all key-value pairs with a certain value:

```
class Hash
  def delete_value(value)
    delete_if { |k,v| v == value }
  end
end

h = {'apple' => 'green', 'potato' => 'red', 'sun' => 'yellow',
     'katydid' => 'green' }
h.delete_value('green')
h                                     # => {"sun"=>"yellow", "potato"=>"red"}
```

This code implements the opposite of Hash#merge; it extracts one hash from another:

```
class Hash
  def remove_hash(other_hash)
    delete_if { |k,v| other_hash[k] == v }
  end
end

squares = { 1 => 1, 2 => 4, 3 => 9 }
doubles = { 1 => 2, 2 => 4, 3 => 6 }
squares.remove_hash(doubles)
squares                               # => {1=>1, 3=>9}
```

Finally, to wipe out the entire contents of a Hash, use Hash#clear:

```
h = {}
1.upto(1000) { |x| h[x] = x }
h.keys.size                           # => 1000
h.clear
h                                     # => {}
```

See Also

- Recipe 5.3, "Adding Elements to a Hash"
- Recipe 5.7, "Iterating Over a Hash"

5.5   Using an Array or Other Modifiable Object as a Hash Key

Problem

You want to use a modifiable built-in object (an array or a hash, but not a string) as a key in a hash, even while you modify the object in place. A naive solution tends to lose hash values once the keys are modified:

```
coordinates = [10, 5]
treasure_map = { coordinates => 'jewels' }
treasure_map[coordinates]                   # => "jewels"

# Add a z-coordinate to indicate how deep the treasure is buried.
coordinates << -5

coordinates                                 # => [10, 5, -5]
treasure_map[coordinates]                   # => nil
                                            # Oh no!
```

Solution

The easiest solution is to call the Hash#rehash method every time you modify one of the hash's keys. Hash#rehash will repair the broken treasure map defined above:

```
treasure_map.rehash
treasure_map[coordinates]                   # => "jewels"
```

If this is too much code, you might consider changing the definition of the object you use as a hash key, so that modifications don't affect the way the hash treats it.

Suppose you want a reliably hashable Array class. If you want this behavior universally, you can reopen the Array class and redefine hash to give you the new behavior. But it's safer to define a subclass of Array that implements a reliable-hashing mixin, and to use that subclass only for the Arrays you want to use as hash keys:

```
module ReliablyHashable
 def hash
    return object_id
  end
end

class ReliablyHashableArray < Array
  include ReliablyHashable
end
```

It's now possible to keep track of the jewels:

```
coordinates = ReliablyHashableArray.new([10,5])
treasure_map = { coordinates => 'jewels' }
treasure_map[coordinates]                    # => "jewels"

# Add a z-coordinate to indicate how deep the treasure is buried.
coordinates.push(-5)

treasure_map[coordinates]                    # => "jewels"
```

Discussion

Ruby performs hash lookups using not the key object itself but the object's *hash code* (an integer obtained from the key by calling its hash method). The default implementation of hash, in Object, uses an object's internal ID as its hash code. Array, Hash, and String override this method to provide different behavior.

In the initial example, the hash code of [10,5] is 41 and the hash code of [10,5,–5] is –83. The mapping of the coordinate list to 'jewels' is still present (it'll still show up in an iteration over each_pair), but once you change the coordinate list, you can no longer use that variable as a key.

You may also run into this problem when you use a hash or a string as a hash key, and then modify the key in place. This happens because the hash implementations of many built-in classes try to make sure that two objects that are "the same" (for instance, two distinct arrays with the same contents, or two distinct but identical strings) get the same hash value. When coordinates is [10,5], it has a hash code of 41, like any other Array containing [10,5]. When coordinates is [10,5,–5] it has a hash code of –83, like any other Array with those contents.

Because of the potential for confusion, some languages don't let you use arrays or hashes as hash keys at all. Ruby lets you do it, but you have to face the consequences if the key changes. Fortunately, you can dodge the consequences by overriding hash to work the way you want.

Since an object's internal ID never changes, the Object implementation is what you want to get reliable hashing. To get it back, you'll have to override or subclass the hash method of Array or Hash (depending on what type of key you're having trouble with).

The implementations of hash given in the solution violate the principle that different representations of the same data should have the same hash code. This means that two ReliablyHashableArray objects will have different hash codes even if they have the same contents. For instance:

```
a = [1,2]
b = a.clone
a.hash                                        # => 11
b.hash                                        # => 11
```

```
a   = ReliablyHashableArray.new([1,2])
b = a.clone
a.hash                                          # => -606031406
b.hash                                          # => -606034266
```

If you want a particular value in a hash to be accessible by two different arrays with the same contents, then you must key it to a regular array instead of a ReliablyHashableArray. You can't have it both ways. If an object is to have the same hash key as its earlier self, it can't also have the same hash key as another representation of its current state.

Another solution is to freeze your hash keys. Any frozen object can be reliably used as a hash key, since you can't do anything to a frozen object that would cause its hash code to change. Ruby uses this solution: when you use a string as a hash key, Ruby copies the string, freezes the copy, and uses *that* as the actual hash key.

See Also

- Recipe 8.15, "Freezing an Object to Prevent Changes"

5.6   Keeping Multiple Values for the Same Hash Key

Problem

You want to build a hash that might have duplicate values for some keys.

Solution

The simplest way is to create a hash that initializes missing values to empty arrays. You can then append items onto the automatically created arrays:

```
hash = Hash.new { |hash, key| hash[key] = [] }

raw_data = [ [1, 'a'], [1, 'b'], [1, 'c'],
             [2, 'a'], [2, ['b', 'c']],
             [3, 'c'] ]
raw_data.each { |x,y| hash[x] << y }
hash
# => {1=>["a", "b", "c"], 2=>["a", ["b", "c"]], 3=>["c"]}
```

Discussion

A hash maps any given key to only one value, but that value can be an array. This is a common phenomenon when reading data structures from the outside world. For instance, a list of tasks with associated priorities may contain multiple items with the same priority. Simply reading the tasks into a hash keyed on priority would create key collisions, and obliterate all but one task with any given priority.

It's possible to subclass Hash to act like a normal hash until a key collision occurs, and then start keeping an array of values for the key that suffered the collision:

```
class MultiValuedHash < Hash
  def []=(key, value)
    if has_key?(key)
      super(key, [value, self[key]].flatten)
    else
      super
    end
  end
end

hash = MultiValuedHash.new
raw_data.each { |x,y|  hash[x] = y }
hash
# => {1=>["c", "b", "a"], 2=>["b", "c", "a"], 3=>"c"}
```

This saves a little bit of memory, but it's harder to write code for this class than for one that always keeps values in an array. There's also no way of knowing whether a value [1,2,3] is a single array value or three numeric values.

See Also

- Recipe 5.2, "Creating a Hash with a Default Value," explains the technique of the dynamic default value in more detail, and explains why you must initalize the empty list within a code block—never within the arguments to Hash.new

5.7   Iterating Over a Hash

Problem

You want to iterate over a hash's key-value pairs as though it were an array.

Solution

Most likely, the iterator you want is Hash#each_pair or Hash#each. These methods yield every key-value pair in the hash:

```
hash = { 1 => 'one', [1,2] => 'two', 'three' => 'three' }

hash.each_pair { |key, value| puts "#{key.inspect} maps to #{value}"}
# [1, 2] maps to two
# "three" maps to three
# 1 maps to one
```

Note that each and each_pair return the key-value pairs in an apparently random order.

Discussion

Hash#each_pair and Hash#each let you iterate over a hash as though it were an array full of key-value pairs. Hash#each_pair is more commonly used and slightly more efficient, but Hash#each is more array-like. Hash also provides several other iteration methods that can be more efficient than each.

Use Hash#each_key if you only need the keys of a hash. In this example, a list has been stored as a hash to allow for quick lookups (this is how the Set class works). The values are irrelevant, but each_key can be used to iterate over the keys:

```
active_toggles = { 'super' => true, 'meta' => true, 'hyper' => true }
active_toggles.each_key { |active| puts active }
# hyper
# meta
# super
```

Use Hash#each_value if you only need the values of a hash. In this example, each_value is used to summarize the results of a survey. Here it's the keys that are irrelevant:

```
favorite_colors = { 'Alice' => :red, 'Bob' => :violet, 'Mallory' => :blue,
                    'Carol' => :blue, 'Dave' => :violet }

summary = Hash.new 0
favorite_colors.each_value { |x| summary[x] += 1 }
summary
# => {:red=>1, :violet=>2, :blue=>2}
```

Don't iterate over Hash#each_value looking for a particular value: it's simpler and faster to use has_value? instead.

```
hash = {}
1.upto(10) { |x| hash[x] = x * x }
hash.has_value? 49              # => true
hash.has_value? 81              # => true
hash.has_value? 50             # => false
```

Removing unprocessed elements from a hash during an iteration prevents those items from being part of the iteration. However, adding elements to a hash during an iteration will not make them part of the iteration.

Don't modify the keyset of a hash during an iteration, or you'll get undefined results and possibly a RuntimeError:

```
1.upto(100) { |x| hash[x] = true }
hash.keys { |k| hash[k * 2] = true }
# RuntimeError: hash modified during iteration
```

Using an array as intermediary

An alternative to using the hash iterators is to get an array of the keys, values, or key-value pairs in the hash, and then work on the array. You can do this with the keys, values, and to_a methods, respectively:

```
hash = {1 => 2, 2 => 2, 3 => 10}
hash.keys                       # => [1, 2, 3]
hash.values                     # => [2, 2, 10]
hash.to_a                       # => [[1, 2], [2, 2], [3, 10]]
```

The most common use of keys and values is to iterate over a hash in a specific order. All of Hash's iterators return items in a seemingly random order. If you want to iterate over a hash in a certain order, the best strategy is usually to create an array from some portion of the hash, sort the array, then iterate over it.

The most common case is to iterate over a hash according to some property of the keys. To do this, sort the result of Hash#keys. Use the original hash to look up the value for a key, if necessary.

```
extensions = { 'Alice' => '104', 'Carol' => '210', 'Bob' => '110' }
extensions.keys.sort.each do |k|
  puts "#{k} can be reached at extension ##{extensions[k]}"
end
# Alice can be reached at extension #104
# Bob can be reached at extension #110
# Carol can be reached at extension #210
```

Hash#values gives you the values of a hash, but that's not useful for iterating because it's so expensive to find the key for a corresponding value (and if you *only* wanted the values, you'd use each_value).

Hash#sort and Hash#sort_by turn a hash into an array of two-element subarrays (one for each key-value pair), then sort the array of arrays however you like. Your custom sort method can sort on the values, on the values and the keys, or on some relationship between key and value. You can then iterate over the sorted array the same as you would with the Hash.each iterator.

This code sorts a to-do list by priority, then alphabetically:

```
to_do = { 'Clean car' => 5, 'Take kangaroo to vet' => 3,
          'Realign plasma conduit' => 3 }
to_do.sort_by { |task, priority| [priority, task] }.each { |k,v| puts k }
# Realign plasma conduit
# Take kangaroo to vet
# Clean car
```

This code sorts a hash full of number pairs according to the magnitude of the difference between the key and the value:

```
transform_results = { 4 => 8, 9 => 9, 10 => 6, 2 => 7, 6 => 5 }
by_size_of_difference = transform_results.sort_by { |x, y| (x-y).abs }
by_size_of_difference.each { |x, y| puts "f(#{x})=#{y}: difference #{y-x}" }
# f(9)=9: difference 0
# f(6)=5: difference -1
# f(10)=6: difference -4
# f(4)=8: difference 4
# f(2)=7: difference 5
```

See Also

- See Recipe 5.8, "Iterating Over a Hash in Insertion Order," for a more complex iterator

- Recipe 5.12, "Building a Histogram"
- Recipe 5.13, "Remapping the Keys and Values of a Hash"

5.8   Iterating Over a Hash in Insertion Order

Problem

Iterations over a hash happen in a seemingly random order. Sorting the keys or values only works if the keys or values are all mutually comparable. You'd like to iterate over a hash in the order in which the elements were added to the hash.

Solution

Use the orderedhash library (see below for how to get it). Its OrderedHash class acts like a hash, but it keeps the elements of the hash in insertion order.

```
require 'orderedhash'
h = OrderedHash.new
h[1] = 1
h["second"] = 2
h[:third] = 3

h.keys                                      # => [1, "second", :third]
h.values                                    # => [1, 2, 3]
h.each { |k,v| puts "The #{k} counting number is #{v}" }
# The 1 counting number is 1
# The second counting number is 2
# The third counting number is 3
```

Discussion

OrderedHash is a subclass of Hash that also keeps an array of the keys in insertion order. When you add a key-value pair to the hash, OrderedHash modifies both the underlying hash and the array. When you ask for a specific hash element, you're using the hash. When you ask for the keys or the values, the data comes from the array, and you get it in insertion order.

Since OrderedHash is a real hash, it supports all the normal hash operations. But any operation that modifies an OrderedHash may also modify the internal array, so it's slower than just using a hash. OrderedHash#delete is especially slow, since it must perform a linear search of the internal array to find the key being deleted. Hash#delete runs in constant time, but OrderedHash#delete takes time proportionate to the size of the hash.

See Also

- You can get OrderedHash from the RAA at *http://raa.ruby-lang.org/project/ orderedhash/*; it's not available as a gem, and it has no setup.rb script, so you'll need to distribute orderedhash.rb with your project, or copy it into your Ruby library path

- There is a queuehash gem that provides much the same functionality, but it has worse performance than OrderedHash

5.9   Printing a Hash

Credit: Ben Giddings

Problem

You want to print out the contents of a Hash, but Kernel#puts doesn't give very useful results.

```
h = {}
h[:name] = "Robert"
h[:nickname] = "Bob"
h[:age] = 43
h[:email_addresses] = {:home => "bob@example.com",
                       :work => "robert@example.com"}
h
# => {:email_addresses=>["bob@example.com", "robert@example.com"],
#     :nickname=>"Bob", :name=>"Robert", :age=>43}
puts h
# nicknameBobage43nameRobertemail_addresseshomebob@example.comworkrobert@example.com
puts h[:email_addresses]
# homebob@example.comworkrobert@example.com
```

Solution

 In other recipes, we sometimes reformat the results or output of Ruby statements so they'll look better on the printed page. In this recipe, you'll see raw, unretouched output, so you can compare different ways of printing hashes.

The easiest way to print a hash is to use Kernel#p. Kernel#p prints out the "inspected" version of its arguments: the string you get by calling inspect on the hash. The "inspected" version of an object often looks like Ruby source code for creating the object, so it's usually readable:

```
p h[:email_addresses]
# {:home=>"bob@example.com", :work=>"robert@example.com"}
```

For small hashes intended for manual inspection, this may be all you need. However, there are two difficulties. One is that Kernel#p only prints to stdout. The second is that the printed version contains no newlines, making it difficult to read large hashes.

```
p h
# {:nickname=>"Bob", :age=>43, :name=>"Robert", :email_addresses=>{:home=>
# "bob@example.com", :work=>"robert@example.com"}}
```

When the hash you're trying to print is too large, the pp ("pretty-print") module produces very readable results:

```
require 'pp'
pp h[:email_addresses]
# {:home=>"bob@example.com", :work=>"robert@example.com"}

pp h
# {:email_addresses=>{:home=>"bob@example.com", :work=>"robert@example.com"},
#  :nickname=>"Bob",
#  :name=>"Robert",
#  :age=>43}
```

Discussion

There are a number of ways of printing hash contents. The solution you choose
depends on the complexity of the hash you're trying to print, where you're trying to
print the hash, and your personal preferences. The best general-purpose solution is
the pp library.

When a given hash element is too big to fit on one line, pp knows to put it on multiple lines. Not only that, but (as with Hash#inspect), the output is valid Ruby syntax
for creating the hash: you can copy and paste it directly into a Ruby program to recreate the hash.

The pp library can also pretty-print to I/O streams besides standard output, and can
print to shorter lines (the default line length is 79). This example prints the hash to
$stderr and wraps at column 50:

```
PP::pp(h, $stderr, 50)
# {:nickname=>"Bob",
#  :email_addresses=>
#   {:home=>"bob@example.com",
#    :work=>"robert@example.com"},
#  :age=>43,
#  :name=>"Robert"}
# => #<IO:0x2c8cc>
```

You can also print hashes by converting them into YAML with the yaml library.
YAML is a human-readable markup language for describing data structures:

```
require 'yaml'
puts h.to_yaml
# ---
# :nickname: Bob
# :age: 43
# :name: Robert
# :email_addresses:
#   :home: bob@example.com
#   :work: robert@example.com
```

If none of these is suitable, you can print the hash out yourself by using Hash#each_pair to iterate over the hash elements:

```
h[:email_addresses].each_pair do |key, val|
  puts "#{key} => #{val}"
end
# home => bob@example.com
# work => robert@example.com
```

See Also

- Recipe 8.10, "Getting a Human-Readable Printout of Any Object," covers the general case of this problem
- Recipe 13.1, "Serializing Data with YAML"

5.10 Inverting a Hash

Problem

Given a hash, you want to switch the keys and values. That is, you want to create a new hash whose keys are the values of the old hash, and whose values are the keys of the old hash. If the old hash mapped "human" to "wolf;" you want the new hash to map "wolf" to "human."

Solution

The simplest technique is to use the Hash#invert method:

```
phone_directory = {  'Alice' => '555-1212',
                     'Bob' => '555-1313',
                     'Mallory' => '111-1111' }
phone_directory.invert
# => {"111-1111"=>"Mallory", "555-1212"=>"Alice", "555-1313"=>"Bob"}
```

Discussion

Hash#invert probably won't do what you want if your hash maps more than one key to the same value. Only one of the keys for that value will show up as a value in the inverted hash:

```
phone_directory = {  'Alice' => '555-1212',
                     'Bob' => '555-1313',
                     'Carol' => '555-1313',
                     'Mallory' => '111-1111',
                     'Ted' => '555-1212' }
phone_directory.invert
# => {"111-1111"=>"Mallory", "555-1212"=>"Ted", "555-1313"=>"Bob"}
```

To preserve all the data from the original hash, borrow the idea behind Recipe 5.6, and write a version of invert that keeps an array of values for each key. The following is based on code by Tilo Sloboda:

```
class Hash
  def safe_invert
    new_hash = {}
    self.each do |k,v|
      if v.is_a? Array
        v.each { |x| new_hash.add_or_append(x, k) }
      else
        new_hash.add_or_append(v, k)
      end
    end
    return new_hash
  end
```

The add_or_append method a lot like the method MultivaluedHash#[]= defined in Recipe 5.6:

```
  def add_or_append(key, value)
    if has_key?(key)
      self[key] = [value, self[key]].flatten
    else
      self[key] = value
    end
  end
end
```

Here's safe_invert in action:

```
phone_directory.safe_invert
# => {"111-1111"=>"Mallory", "555-1212"=>["Ted", "Alice"],
#     "555-1313"=>["Bob", "Carol"]}

phone_directory.safe_invert.safe_invert
# => {"Alice"=>"555-1212", "Mallory"=>"111-1111", "Ted"=>"555-1212",
# =>   "Carol"=>"555-1313", "Bob"=>"555-1313"}
```

Ideally, if you called an inversion method twice you'd always get the same data you started with. The safe_invert method does better than invert on this score, but it's not perfect. If your original hash used arrays as hash keys, safe_invert will act as if you'd individually mapped each element in the array to the same value. Call safe_invert twice, and the arrays will be gone.

See Also

- Recipe 5.5, "Using an Array or Other Modifiable Object as a Hash Key"
- "True Inversion of a Hash in Ruby," by Tilo Sloboda (*http://www.unixgods.org/~tilo/Ruby/invert_hash.html*)
- The Facets library defines a Hash#inverse method much like safe_invert

5.11 Choosing Randomly from a Weighted List

Problem

You want to pick a random element from a collection, where each element in the collection has a different probability of being chosen.

Solution

Store the elements in a hash, mapped to their relative probabilities. The following code will work with a hash whose keys are mapped to relative integer probabilities:

```
def choose_weighted(weighted)
  sum = weighted.inject(0) do |sum, item_and_weight|
    sum += item_and_weight[1]
  end
  target = rand(sum)
  weighted.each do |item, weight|
    return item if target <= weight
    target -= weight
  end
end
```

For instance, if all the keys in the hash map to 1, the keys will be chosen with equal probability. If all the keys map to 1, except for one which maps to 10, that key will be picked 10 times more often than any single other key. This algorithm lets you simulate those probability problems that begin like, "You have a box containing 51 black marbles and 17 white marbles...":

```
marbles = { :black => 51, :white => 17 }
3.times { puts choose_weighted(marbles) }
# black
# white
# black
```

I'll use it to simulate a lottery in which the results have different probabilities of showing up:

```
lottery_probabilities = { "You've wasted your money!" => 1000,
                          "You've won back the cost of your ticket!" => 50,
                          "You've won two shiny zorkmids!" => 20,
                          "You've won five zorkmids!" => 10,
                          "You've won ten zorkmids!" => 5,
                          "You've won a hundred zorkmids!" => 1 }

# Let's buy some lottery tickets.
5.times { puts choose_weighted(lottery_probabilities) }
# You've wasted your money!
# You've wasted your money!
# You've wasted your money!
# You've wasted your money!
# You've won five zorkmids!
```

Discussion

An extremely naive solution would put the elements in a list and choose one at random. This doesn't solve the problem because it ignores weights altogether: low-weight elements will show up exactly as often as high-weight ones. A less naive solution would be to repeat each element in the list a number of times proportional to its weight. Under this implementation, our simulation of the marble box would contain :black 51 times and :white 17 times, just like a real marble box. This is a common quick-and-dirty solution, but it's hard to maintain, and it uses lots of memory.

The algorithm given above actually works the same way as the less naive solution: the numeric weights stand in for multiple copies of the same object. Instead of picking one of the 68 marbles, we pick a number between 0 and 67 inclusive. Since we know there are 51 black marbles, we simply decide that the numbers from 0 to 50 will represent black marbles.

For the implementation given above to work, all the weights in the hash must be integers. This isn't a big problem the first time you create a hash, but suppose that after the lottery has been running for a while, you decide to add a new jackpot that's 10 times less common than the 100-zorkmid jackpot. You'd like to give this new possibility a weight of 0.1, but that won't work with the choose_weighted implementation. You'll need to give it a weight of 1, and multiply all the existing weights by 10.

There is an alternative, though: normalize the weights so that they add up to 1. You can then generate a random floating-point number between 0 and 1, and use a similar algorithm to the one above. This approach lets you weight the hash keys using any numeric objects you like, since normalization turns them all into small floating-point numbers anyway.

```
def normalize!(weighted)
  sum = weighted.inject(0) do |sum, item_and_weight|
    sum += item_and_weight[1]
  end
  sum = sum.to_f
  weighted.each { |item, weight| weighted[item] = weight/sum }
end

lottery_probabilities["You've won five hundred zorkmids!"] = 0.1
normalize!(lottery_probabilities)
# => { "You've wasted your money!" => 0.920725531718995,
#      "You've won back the cost of your ticket!" => 0.0460362765859497,
#      "You've won two shiny zorkmids!" => 0.0184145106343799,
#      "You've won five zorkmids!" => 0.00920725531718995,
#      "You've won ten zorkmids!" => 0.00460362765859497,
#      "You've won a hundred zorkmids!" => 0.000920725531718995,
#      "You've won five hundred zorkmids!" => 9.20725531718995e-05 }
```

Once the weights have been normalized, we know that they sum to one (within the limits of floating-point arithmetic). This simplifies the code that picks an element at random, since we don't have to sum up the weights every time:

```
def choose_weighted_assuming_unity(weighted)
  target = rand
  weighted.each do |item, weight|
    return item if target <= weight
    target -= weight
  end
end

5.times { puts choose_weighted_assuming_unity(lottery_probabilities) }
# You've wasted your money!
# You've wasted your money!
# You've wasted your money!
# You've wasted your money!
# You've won back the cost of your ticket!
```

See Also

- Recipe 2.5, "Generating Random Numbers"
- Recipe 6.9, "Picking a Random Line from a File"

5.12   Building a Histogram

Problem

You have an array that contains a lot of references to relatively few objects. You want to create a histogram, or frequency map: something you can use to see how often a given object shows up in the array.

Solution

Build the histogram in a hash, mapping each object found to the number of times it appears.

```
module Enumerable
  def to_histogram
    inject(Hash.new(0)) { |h, x| h[x] += 1; h}
  end
end

[1, 2, 2, 2, 3, 3].to_histogram
# => {1=>1, 2=>3, 3=>2}

["a", "b", nil, "c", "b", nil, "a"].to_histogram
# => {"a"=>2, "b"=>2, "c"=>1, nil=>2}

"Aye\nNay\nNay\nAbstaining\nAye\nNay\nNot Present\n".to_histogram
# => {"Abstaining\n"=>1, "Nay\n"=>3, "Not Present\n"=>1, "Aye\n"=>2}

survey_results = { "Alice" => :red, "Bob" => :green, "Carol" => :green,
                   "Mallory" => :blue }
survey_results.values.to_histogram
# => {:red=>1, :green=>2, :blue=>1}
```

Discussion

Making a histogram is an easy and fast (linear-time) way to summarize a dataset. Histograms expose the relative popularity of the items in a dataset, so they're useful for visualizing optimization problems and dividing the "head" from the "long tail."

Once you have a histogram, you can find the most or least common elements in the list, sort the list by frequency of appearance, or see whether the distribution of items matches your expectations. Many of the other recipes in this book build a histogram as a first step towards a more complex algorithm.

Here's a quick way of visualizing a histogram as an ASCII chart. First, we convert the histogram keys to their string representations so they can be sorted and printed. We also store the histogram value for the key, since we can't do a histogram lookup later based on the string value we'll be using.

```ruby
def draw_graph(histogram, char="#")
  pairs = histogram.keys.collect { |x| [x.to_s, histogram[x]] }.sort
```

Then we find the key with the longest string representation. We'll pad the rest of the histogram rows to this length, so that the graph bars will line up correctly.

```ruby
largest_key_size = pairs.max { |x,y| x[0].size <=> y[0].size }[0].size
```

Then we print each key-value pair, padding with spaces as necessary.

```ruby
pairs.inject("") do |s,kv|
  s << "#{kv[0].ljust(largest_key_size)} |#{char*kv[1]}\n"
end
end
```

Here's a histogram of the color survey results from the Solution:

```ruby
puts draw_graph(survey_results.values.to_histogram)
# blue  |#
# green |##
# red   |#
```

This code generates a bunch of random numbers, then graphs the random distribution:

```ruby
random = []
100.times { random << rand(10) }
puts draw_graph(random.to_histogram)
# 0 |###########
# 1 |########
# 2 |#######
# 3 |#########
# 4 |##########
# 5 |#############
# 6 |###############
# 7 |########
# 8 |#######
# 9 |##########
```

See Also

- Recipe 2.8, "Finding Mean, Median, and Mode"
- Recipe 4.9, "Sorting an Array by Frequency of Appearance"

5.13   Remapping the Keys and Values of a Hash

Problem

You have two hashes with common keys but differing values. You want to create a new hash that maps the values of one hash to the values of another.

Solution

```
class Hash
  def tied_with(hash)
    remap do |h,key,value|
      h[hash[key]] = value
    end.delete_if { |key,value| key.nil? || value.nil? }
  end
```

Here is the Hash#remap method:

```
  def remap(hash={})
    each { |k,v| yield hash, k, v }
    hash
  end
end
```

Here's how to use Hash#tied_with to merge two hashes:

```
a = {1 => 2, 3 => 4}
b = {1 => 'foo', 3 => 'bar'}
a.tied_with(b)                    # => {"foo"=>2, "bar"=>4}
b.tied_with(a)                    # => {2=>"foo", 4=>"bar"}
```

Discussion

This remap method can be handy when you want to make a similar change to every item in a hash. It is also a good example of using the yield method.

Hash#remap is conceptually similar to Hash#collect, but Hash#collect builds up a nested array of key-value pairs, not a new hash.

See Also

- The Facets library defines methods Hash#update_each and Hash#replace_each! for remapping the keys and values of a hash

5.14 Extracting Portions of Hashes

Problem

You have a hash that contains a lot of values, but only a few of them are interesting. You want to select the interesting values and ignore the rest.

Solution

You can use the Hash#select method to extract part of a hash that follows a certain rule. Suppose you had a hash where the keys were Time objects representing a certain date, and the values were the number of web site clicks for that given day. We'll simulate such as hash with random data:

```
require 'time'
click_counts = {}
1.upto(30) { |i| click_counts[Time.parse("2006-09-#{i}")] = 400 + rand(700) }
p click_counts
# {Sat Sep 23 00:00:00 EDT 2006=>803, Tue Sep 12 00:00:00 EDT 2006=>829,
#  Fri Sep 01 00:00:00 EDT 2006=>995, Mon Sep 25 00:00:00 EDT 2006=>587,
#  ...
```

You might want to know the days when your click counts were low, to see if you could spot a trend. Hash#select can do that for you:

```
low_click_days = click_counts.select {|key, value| value < 450 }
# [[Thu Sep 14 00:00:00 EDT 2006, 449], [Mon Sep 11 00:00:00 EDT 2006, 406],
#  [Sat Sep 02 00:00:00 EDT 2006, 440], [Mon Sep 04 00:00:00 EDT 2006, 431],
#  ...
```

Discussion

The array returned by Hash#select contains a number of key-value pairs as two-element arrays. The first element of one of these inner arrays is a key into the hash, and the second element is the corresponding value. This is similar to how Hash#each yields a succession of two-element arrays.

If you want another hash instead of an array of key-value pairs, you can use Hash#inject instead of Hash#select. In the code below, kv is a two-element array containing a key-value pair. kv[0] is a key from click_counts, and kv[1] is the corresponding value.

```
low_click_days_hash = click_counts.inject({}) do |h, kv|
  k, v = kv
  h[k] = v if v < 450
  h
end
# => {Mon Sep 25 00:00:00 EDT 2006=>403,
#     Wed Sep 06 00:00:00 EDT 2006=>443,
#     Thu Sep 28 00:00:00 EDT 2006=>419}
```

You can also use the Hash.[] constructor to create a hash from the array result of Hash#select:

```
low_click_days_hash = Hash[*low_click_days.flatten]
# => {Thu Sep 14 00:00:00 EDT 2006=>449, Mon Sep 11 00:00:00 EDT 2006=>406,
#     Sat Sep 02 00:00:00 EDT 2006=>440, Mon Sep 04 00:00:00 EDT 2006=>431,
#     ...
```

See Also

- Recipe 4.13, "Extracting Portions of Arrays"

5.15 Searching a Hash with Regular Expressions

Credit: Ben Giddings

Problem

You want to grep a hash: that is, find all keys and/or values in the hash that match a regular expression.

Solution

The fastest way to grep the keys of a hash is to get the keys as an array, and grep that:

```
h = { "apple tree" => "plant", "ficus" => "plant",
      "shrew" => "animal", "plesiosaur" => "animal" }
h.keys.grep /p/
# => ["apple tree", "plesiosaur"]
```

The solution for grepping the values of a hash is similar (substitute Hash#values for Hash#keys), unless you need to map the values back to the keys of the hash. If that's what you need, the fastest way is to use Hash#each to get key-value pairs, and match the regular expression against each value.

```
h.inject([]) { |res, kv| res << kv if kv[1] =~ /p/; res }
# => [["ficus", "plant"], ["apple tree", "plant"]]
```

The code is similar if you need to find key-value pairs where either the key or the value matches a regular expression:

```
class Hash
  def grep(pattern)
    inject([]) do |res, kv|
      res << kv if kv[0] =~ pattern or kv[1] =~ pattern
      res
    end
  end
end

h.grep(/pl/)
# => [["ficus", "plant"], ["apple tree", "plant"], ["plesiosaur", "animal"]]
h.grep(/plant/)      # => [["ficus", "plant"], ["apple tree", "plant"]]
h.grep(/i.*u/)       # => [["ficus", "plant"], ["plesiosaur", "animal"]]
```

Discussion

Hash defines its own grep method, but it will never give you any results. Hash#grep is inherited from Enumerable#grep, which tries to match the output of each against the given regular expression. Hash#each returns a series of two-item arrays containing key-value pairs, and an array will never match a regular expression. The Hash#grep implementation above is more useful.

Hash#keys.grep and Hash#values.grep are more efficient than matching a regular expression against each key or value in a Hash, but those methods create a new array containing all the keys in the Hash. If memory usage is your primary concern, iterate over each_key or each_value instead:

```
res = []
h.each_key { |k| res << k if k =~ /p/ }
res                 # => ["apple tree", "plesiosaur"]
```

## CHAPTER 6

Files and Directories

As programming languages increase in power, we programmers get further and further from the details of the underlying machine language. When it comes to the operating system, though, even the most modern programming languages live on a level of abstraction that looks a lot like the C and Unix libraries that have been around for decades.

We covered this kind of situation in Chapter 3 with Ruby's Time objects, but the issue really shows up when you start to work with files. Ruby provides an elegant object-oriented interface that lets you do basic file access, but the more advanced file libraries tend to look like the C libraries they're based on. To lock a file, change its Unix permissions, or read its metadata, you'll need to remember method names like mtime, and the meaning of obscure constants like File::LOCK_EX and 0644. This chapter will show you how to use the simple interfaces, and how to make the more obscure interfaces easier to use.

Looking at Ruby's support for file and directory operations, you'll see four distinct tiers of support. The most common operations tend to show up on the lower-numbered tiers:

1. File objects to read and write the contents of files, and Dir objects to list the contents of directories. For examples, see Recipes 6.5, 6.7, and 6.17. Also see Recipe 6.13 for a Ruby-idiomatic approach.

2. Class methods of File to manipulate files without opening them. For instance, to delete a file, examine its metadata, or change its permissions. For examples, see Recipes 6.1, 6.3, and 6.4.

3. Standard libraries, such as find to walk directory trees, and fileutils to perform common filesystem operations like copying files and creating directories. For examples, see Recipes 6.8, 6.12, and 6.20.

4. Gems like file-tail, lockfile, and rubyzip, which fill in the gaps left by the standard library. Most of the file-related gems covered in this book deal with specific file formats, and are covered in Chapter 12.

Kernel#open is the simplest way to open a file. It returns a File object that you can read from or write to, depending on the "mode" constant you pass in. I'll introduce read mode and write mode here; there are several others, but I'll talk about most of those as they come up in recipes.

To write data to a file, pass a mode of 'w' to open. You can then write lines to the file with File#puts, just like printing to standard output with Kernel#puts. For more possibilities, see Recipe 6.7.

```
open('beans.txt', "w") do |file|
  file.puts('lima beans')
  file.puts('pinto beans')
  file.puts('human beans')
end
```

To read data from a file, open it for read access by specifying a mode of 'r', or just omitting the mode. You can slurp the entire contents into a string with File#read, or process the file line-by-line with File#each. For more details, see Recipe 6.6.

```
open('beans.txt') do |file|
  file.each { |l| puts "A line from the file: #{l}" }
end
# A line from the file: lima beans
# A line from the file: pinto beans
# A line from the file: human beans
```

As seen in the examples above, the best way to use the open method is with a code block. The open method creates a new File object, passes it to your code block, and closes the file automatically after your code block runs—even if your code throws an exception. This saves you from having to remember to close the file after you're done with it. You could rely on the Ruby interpreter's garbage collection to close the file once it's no longer being used, but Ruby makes it easy to do things the right way.

To find a file in the first place, you need to specify its disk path. You may specify an absolute path, or one relative to the current directory of your Ruby process (see Recipe 6.21). Relative paths are usually better, because they're more portable across platforms. Relative paths like "beans.txt" or "subdir/beans.txt" will work on any platform, but absolute Unix paths look different from absolute Windows paths:

```
# A stereotypical Unix path.
open('/etc/passwd')

# A stereotypical Windows path; note the drive letter.
open('c:/windows/Documents and Settings/User1/My Documents/ruby.doc')
```

Windows paths in Ruby use forward slashes to separate the parts of a path, even though Windows itself uses backslashes. Ruby will also accept backslashes in a Windows path, so long as you escape them:

```
open('c:\\windows\\Documents and Settings\\User1\\My Documents\\ruby.doc')
```

Although this chapter focuses mainly on disk files, most of the methods of File are actually methods of its superclass, IO. You'll encounter many other classes that are also subclasses of IO, or just respond to the same methods. This means that most of the tricks described in this chapter are applicable to classes like the Socket class for Internet sockets and the infinitely useful StringIO (see Recipe 6.15).

Your Ruby program's standard input, output, and error ($stdin, $stdout, and $stderr) are also IO objects, which means you can treat them like files. This one-line program echoes its input to its output:

```
$stdin.each { |l| puts l }
```

The Kernel#puts command just calls $stdout.puts, so that one-liner is equivalent to this one:

```
$stdin.each { |l| $stdout.puts l }
```

Not all file-like objects support all the methods of IO. See Recipe 6.11 for ways to get around the most common problem with unsupported methods. Also see Recipe 6.16 for more on the default IO objects.

Several of the recipes in this chapter (such as Recipes 6.12 and 6.20) create specific directory structures to demonstrate different concepts. Rather than bore you by filling up recipes with the Ruby code to create a certain directory structure, I've written a method that takes a short description of a directory structure, and creates the appropriate files and subdirectories:

```
# create_tree.rb
def create_tree(directories, parent=".")
  directories.each_pair do |dir, files|
    path = File.join(parent, dir)
    Dir.mkdir path unless File.exists? path
    files.each do |filename, contents|
      if filename.respond_to? :each_pair    # It's a subdirectory
        create_tree filename, path
      else                                  # It's a file
        open(File.join(path, filename), 'w') { |f| f << contents || "" }
      end
    end
  end
end
```

Now I can present the directory structure as a data structure and you can create it with a single method call:

```
require 'create_tree'
create_tree 'test' =>
  [ 'An empty file',
    ['A file with contents', 'Contents of file'],
    { 'Subdirectory' => ['Empty file in subdirectory',
                         ['File in subdirectory', 'Contents of file'] ] },
    { 'Empty subdirectory' => [] }
  ]
```

```
require 'find'
Find.find('test') { |f| puts f }
# test
# test/Empty subdirectory
# test/Subdirectory
# test/Subdirectory/File in subdirectory
# test/Subdirectory/Empty file in subdirectory
# test/A file with contents
# test/An empty file

File.read('test/Subdirectory/File in subdirectory')
# => "Contents of file"
```

6.1 Checking to See If a File Exists

Problem

Given a filename, you want to see whether the corresponding file exists and is the right kind for your purposes.

Solution

Most of the time you'll use the File.file? predicate, which returns true only if the file is an existing regular file (that is, not a directory, a socket, or some other special file).

```
filename = 'a_file.txt'
File.file? filename                     # => false

require 'fileutils'
FileUtils.touch(filename)
File.file? filename                     # => true
```

Use the File.exists? predicate instead if the file might legitimately be a directory or other special file, or if you plan to create a file by that name if it doesn't exist. File.exists? will return true if a file of the given name exists, no matter what kind of file it is.

```
directory_name = 'a_directory'
FileUtils.mkdir(directory_name)
File.file? directory_name               # => false
File.exists? directory_name             # => true
```

Discussion

A true response from File.exists? means that the file is present on the filesystem, but says nothing about what type of file it is. If you open up a directory thinking it's a regular file, you're in for an unpleasant surprise. This is why File.file? is usually more useful than File.exists?.

Ruby provides several other predicates for checking the type of a file: the other commonly useful one is File.directory?:

```
File.directory? directory_name                    # => true
File.directory? filename                           # => false
```

The rest of the predicates are designed to work on Unix systems. `File.blockdev?` tests for block-device files (such as hard-drive partitions), `File.chardev?` tests for character-device files (such as TTYs), `File.socket?` tests for socket files, and `File.pipe?` tests for named pipes,

```
File.blockdev? '/dev/hda1'                         # => true
File.chardev? '/dev/tty1'                          # => true
File.socket? '/var/run/mysqld/mysqld.sock'         # => true
system('mkfifo named_pipe')
File.pipe? 'named_pipe'                             # => true
```

`File.symlink?` tests whether a file is a symbolic link to another file, but you only need to use it when you want to treat symlinks differently from other files. A symlink to a regular file will satisfy `File.file?`, and can be opened and used just like a regular file. In most cases, you don't even have to know it's a symlink. The same goes for symlinks to directories and to other types of files.

```
new_filename = "#{filename}2"
File.symlink(filename, new_filename)

File.symlink? new_filename                         # => true
File.file? new_filename                            # => true
```

All of Ruby's file predicates return false if the file doesn't exist at all. This means you can test "exists and is a directory" by just testing `directory?`; it's the same for the other predicates.

See Also

• Recipe 6.8, "Writing to a Temporary File," and Recipe 6.14, "Backing Up to Versioned Filenames," deal with writing to files that don't currently exist

6.2 Checking Your Access to a File

Problem

You want to see what you can do with a file: whether you have read, write, or (on Unix systems) execute permission on it.

Solution

Use the class methods `File.readable?`, `File.writeable?`, and `File.executable?`.

```
File.readable?('/bin/ls')                          # => true
File.readable?('/etc/passwd-')                     # => false

filename = 'test_file'
File.open(filename, 'w') {}
```

```
File.writable?(filename)                   # => true
File.writable?('/bin/ls')                  # => false

File.executable?('/bin/ls')                # => true
File.executable?(filename)                 # => false
```

Discussion

Ruby's file permission tests are Unix-centric, but readable? and writable? work on any platform; the rest fail gracefully when the OS doesn't support them. For instance, Windows doesn't have the Unix notion of execute permission, so File.executable? always returns true on Windows.

The return value of a Unix permission test depends in part on whether your user owns the file in question, or whether you belong to the Unix group that owns it. Ruby provides convenience tests File.owned? and File.grpowned? to check this.

```
File.owned? 'test_file'                    # => true
File.grpowned? 'test_file'                 # => true
File.owned? '/bin/ls'                      # => false
```

On Windows, File.owned? always returns true (even for a file that belongs to another user) and File.grpowned? always returns false.

The File methods described above should be enough to answer most permission questions about a file, but you can also see a file's Unix permissions in their native form by looking at the file's *mode*. The mode is a number, each bit of which has a different meaning within the Unix permission system.[*] You can view a file's mode with File::Lstat#mode.

The result of mode contains some extra bits describing things like the type of a file. You probably want to strip that information out by masking those bits. This example demonstrates that the file originally created in the solution has a Unix permission mask of 0644:

```
File.lstat('test_file').mode & 0777        # Keep only the permission bits.
# => 420                                   # That is, 0644 octal.
```

Setuid and setgid scripts

readable?, writable?, and executable? return answers that depend on the effective user and group ID you are using to run the Ruby interpreter. This may not be your actual user or group ID: the Ruby interpreter might be running setuid or setgid, or you might have changed their effective ID with Process.euid= or Process.egid=.

Each of the permission checks has a corresponding method that returns answers from the perspective of the process's real user and real group IDs: executable_real?,

---

[*] If you're not familiar with this, Recipe 6.3 describes the significance of the permission bits in a file's mode.

readable_real?, and writable_real?. If you're running the Ruby interpreter setuid, then readable_real? (for instance) will give different answers from readable?. You can use this to disallow users from reading or modifying certain files unless they actually are the root user, not just taking on the root users' privileges through setuid.

For instance, consider the following code, which prints our real and effective user and group IDs, then checks to see what it can do to a system file:

```ruby
def what_can_i_do?
  sys = Process::Sys
  puts "UID=#{sys.getuid}, GID=#{sys.getgid}"
  puts "Effective UID=#{sys.geteuid}, Effective GID=#{sys.getegid}"

  file = '/bin/ls'
  can_do = [:readable?, :writable?, :executable?].inject([]) do |arr, method|
    arr << method if File.send(method, file); arr
  end
  puts "To you, #{file} is: #{can_do.join(', ')}"
end
```

If you run this code as root, you can call this method and get one set of answers, then take on the guise of a less privileged user and get another set of answers:

```ruby
what_can_i_do?
# UID=0, GID=0
# Effective UID=0, Effective GID=0
# To you, /bin/ls is: readable?, writable?, executable?

Process.uid = 1000
what_can_i_do?
# UID=0, GID=0
# Effective UID=1000, Effective GID=0
# To you, /bin/ls is: readable?, executable?
```

See Also

- Recipe 6.3, "Changing the Permissions on a File"
- Recipe 23.3, "Running Code as Another User," has more on setting the effective user ID

6.3   Changing the Permissions on a File

Problem

You want to control access to a file by modifying its Unix permissions. For instance, you want to make it so that everyone on your system can read a file, but only you can write to it.

Solution

Unless you've got a lot of Unix experience, it's hard to remember the numeric codes for the nine Unix permission bits. Probably the first thing you should do is define constants for them. Here's one constant for every one of the permission bits. If these names are too concise for you, you can name them USER_READ, GROUP_WRITE, OTHER_ EXECUTE, and so on.

```
class File
  U_R = 0400
  U_W = 0200
  U_X = 0100
  G_R = 0040
  G_W = 0020
  G_X = 0010
  O_R = 0004
  O_W = 0002
  O_X = 0001
end
```

You might also want to define these three special constants, which you can use to set the user, group, and world permissions all at once:

```
class File
  A_R = 0444
  A_W = 0222
  A_X = 0111
end
```

Now you're ready to actually change a file's permissions. Every Unix file has a permission bitmap, or *mode*, which you can change (assuming you have the permissions!) by calling File.chmod. You can manipulate the constants defined above to get a new mode, then pass it in along with the filename to File.chmod.

The following three chmod calls are equivalent: for the file my_file, they give read-write access to to the user who owns the file, and restrict everyone else to read-only access. This is equivalent to the permission bitmap 11001001, the octal number 0644, or the decimal number 420.

```
open("my_file", "w") {}

File.chmod(File::U_R | File::U_W | File::G_R | File::O_R, "my_file")
File.chmod(File::A_R | File::U_W, "my_file")
File.chmod(0644, "my_file")                    # Bitmap: 110001001

File::U_R | File::U_W | File::G_R | File::O_R   # => 420
File::A_R | File::U_W                           # => 420
0644                                            # => 420
File.lstat("my_file").mode & 0777               # => 420
```

Note how I build a full permission bitmap by combining the permission constants with the OR operator (|).

Discussion

A Unix file has nine associated permission bits that are consulted whenever anyone tries to access the file. They're divided into three sets of three bits. There's one set for the user who owns the file, one set is for the user group who owns the file, and one set is for everyone else.

Each set contains one bit for each of the three basic things you might do to a file in Unix: read it, write it, or execute it as a program. If the appropriate bit is set for you, you can carry out the operation; if not, you're denied access.

When you put these nine bits side by side into a bitmap, they form a number that you can pass into File.chmod. These numbers are difficult to construct and read without a lot of practice, which is why I recommend you use the constants defined above. It'll make your code less buggy and more readable.*

File.chmod completely overwrites the file's current permission bitmap with a new one. Usually you just want to change one or two permissions: make sure the file isn't world-writable, for instance. The simplest way to do this is to use File.lstat#mode to get the file's current permission bitmap, then modify it with bit operators to add or remove permissions. You can pass the result into File.chmod.

Use the XOR operator (^) to remove permissions from a bitmap, and the OR operator, as seen above, to add permissions:

```
# Take away the world's read access.
new_permission = File.lstat("my_file").mode ^ File::O_R
File.chmod(new_permission, "my_file")

File.lstat("my_file").mode & 0777           # => 416    # 0640 octal

# Give everyone access to everything
new_permission = File.lstat("my_file").mode | File::A_R | File::A_W | File::A_X
File.chmod(new_permission, "my_file")

File.lstat("my_file").mode & 0777           # => 511    # 0777 octal

# Take away the world's write and execute access
new_permission = File.lstat("my_file").mode ^ (File::O_W | File::O_X)
File.chmod(new_permission, "my_file")

File.lstat("my_file").mode & 0777           # => 508    # 0774 octal
```

If doing bitwise math with the permission constants is also too complicated for you, you can use code like this to parse a permission string like the one accepted by the Unix chmod command:

```
class File
  def File.fancy_chmod(permission_string, file)
```

---

* It's true that it's more macho to use the numbers, but if you really wanted to be macho you'd be writing a shell script, not a Ruby program.

```
    mode = File.lstat(file).mode
    permission_string.scan(/[ugoa][+-=][rwx]+/) do |setting|
      who = setting[0..0]
      setting[2..setting.size].each_byte do |perm|
        perm = perm.chr.upcase
        mask = eval("File::#{who.upcase}_#{perm}")
      (setting[1] == ?+) ? mode |= mask : mode ^= mask
      end
    end
    File.chmod(mode, file)
  end
end


# Give the owning user write access
File.fancy_chmod("u+w", "my_file")

File.lstat("my_file").mode & 0777            # => 508    # 0774 octal

# Take away the owning group's execute access
File.fancy_chmod("g-x", "my_file")

File.lstat("my_file").mode & 0777            # => 500    # 0764 octal

# Give everyone access to everything
File.fancy_chmod("a+rwx", "my_file")

File.lstat("my_file").mode & 0777            # => 511    # 0777 octal

# Give the owning user access to everything. Then take away the
# execute access for users who aren't the owning user and aren't in
# the owning group.
File.fancy_chmod("u+rwxo-x", "my_file")
File.lstat("my_file").mode & 0777            # => 510    # 0774 octal
```

Unix-like systems such as Linux and Mac OS X support the full range of Unix permissions. On Windows systems, the only one of these operations that makes sense is adding or subtracting the U_W bit of a file—making a file read-only or not. You can use File.chmod on Windows, but the only bit you'll be able to change is the user write bit.

See Also

- Recipe 6.2, "Checking Your Access to a File"
- Recipe 23.9, "Normalizing Ownership and Permissions in User Directories"

6.4   Seeing When a File Was Last Used

Problem

You want to see when a file was last accessed or modified.

Solution

The result of File.stat contains a treasure trove of metadata about a file. Perhaps the most useful of its methods are the two time methods mtime (the last time anyone wrote to the file), and atime (the last time anyone read from the file).

```
open("output", "w") { |f| f << "Here's some output.\n" }
stat = File.stat("output")
stat.mtime                              # => Thu Mar 23 12:23:54 EST 2006
stat.atime                              # => Thu Mar 23 12:23:54 EST 2006

sleep(2)
open("output", "a") { |f| f << "Here's some more output.\n" }
stat = File.stat("output")
stat.mtime                              # => Thu Mar 23 12:23:56 EST 2006
stat.atime                              # => Thu Mar 23 12:23:54 EST 2006

sleep(2)
open("output") { |f| contents = f.read }
stat = File.stat("output")
stat.mtime                              # => Thu Mar 23 12:23:56 EST 2006
stat.atime                              # => Thu Mar 23 12:23:58 EST 2006
```

Discussion

A file's atime changes whenever data is read from the file, and its mtime changes whenever data is written to the file.

There's also a ctime method, but it's not as useful as the other two. Contrary to semi-popular belief, ctime does not track the creation time of the file (there's no way to track this in Unix). A file's ctime is basically a more inclusive version of its mtime. The ctime changes not only when someone modifies the contents of a file, but when someone changes its permissions or its other metadata.

All three methods are useful for separating the files that actually get used from the ones that just sit there on disk. They can also be used in sanity checks.

Here's code for the part of a game that saves and loads the game state to a file. As a deterrent against cheating, when the game loads a save file it performs a simple check against the file's modification time. If it differs from the timestamp recorded inside the file, the game refuses to load the save file.

The save_game method is responsible for recording the timestamp:

```
def save_game(file)
  score = 1000
  open(file, "w") do |f|
    f.puts(score)
    f.puts(Time.new.to_i)
  end
end
```

The load_game method is responsible for comparing the timestamp within the file to the time the filesystem has associated with the file:

```
def load_game(file)
  open(file) do |f|
    score = f.readline.to_i
    time = Time.at(f.readline.to_i)
    difference = (File.stat(file).mtime - time).abs
    raise "I suspect you of cheating." if difference > 1
    "Your saved score is #{score}."
  end
end
```

This mechanism can detect simple forms of cheating:

```
save_game("game.sav")
sleep(2)
load_game("game.sav")
# => "Your saved score is 1000."

# Now let's cheat by increasing our score to 9000

open("game.sav", "r+b") { |f| f.write("9") }

load_game("game.sav")
# RuntimeError: I suspect you of cheating.
```

Since it's possible to modify a file's times with tools like the Unix touch command, you shouldn't depend on these methods to defend you against a skilled attacker actively trying to fool your program.

See Also

- An example in Recipe 3.12, "Running a Code Block Periodically," monitors a file for changes by checking its mtime periodically
- Recipe 6.20, "Finding the Files You Want," shows examples of filesystem searches that make comparisons between the file times

6.5   Listing a Directory

Problem

You want to list or process the files or subdirectories within a directory.

Solution

If you're starting from a directory name, you can use Dir.entries to get an array of the items in the directory, or Dir.foreach to iterate over the items. Here's an example of each run on a sample directory:

```
# See the chapter intro to get the create_tree library
require 'create_tree'
```

```
create_tree 'mydir' =>
  [ {'subdirectory' => [['file_in_subdirectory', 'Just a simple file.']] },
    '.hidden_file', 'ruby_script.rb', 'text_file' ]

Dir.entries('mydir')

# => [".", "..", ".hidden_file", "ruby_script.rb", "subdirectory",
#    "text_file"]

Dir.foreach('mydir') { |x| puts x if x != "." && x != ".."}
# .hidden_file
# ruby_script.rb
# subdirectory
# text_file
```

You can also use Dir[] to pick up all files matching a certain pattern, using a format similar to the bash shell's glob format (and somewhat less similar to the wildcard format used by the Windows command-line shell):

```
# Find all the "regular" files and subdirectories in mydir. This excludes
# hidden files, and the special directories . and ..
Dir["mydir/*"]
# => ["mydir/ruby_script.rb", "mydir/subdirectory", "mydir/text_file"]

# Find all the .rb files in mydir
Dir["mydir/*.rb"]                    # => ["mydir/ruby_script.rb"]
```

You can also open a directory handle with Dir#open, and treat it like any other Enumerable. Methods like each, each_with_index, grep, and reject will all work (but see below if you want to call them more than once). As with File#open, you should do your directory processing in a code block so that the directory handle will get closed once you're done with it.

```
Dir.open('mydir') { |d| d.grep /file/ }
# => [".hidden_file", "text_file"]

Dir.open('mydir') { |d| d.each { |x| puts x } }
# .
# ..
# .hidden_file
# ruby_script.rb
# subdirectory
# text_file
```

Discussion

Reading entries from a Dir object is more like reading data from a file than iterating over an array. If you call one of the Dir instance methods and then want to call another one on the same Dir object, you'll need to call Dir#rewind first to go back to the beginning of the directory listing:

```
#Get all contents other than ".", "..", and hidden files.

d = Dir.open('mydir')
d.reject { |f| f[0] == '.' }
# => ["subdirectory", "ruby_script.rb", "text_file"]
```

```
#Now the Dir object is useless until we call Dir#rewind.
d.entries.size                                    # => 0
d.rewind
d.entries.size                                    # => 6

#Get the names of all files in the directory.
d.rewind
d.reject { |f| !File.file? File.join(d.path, f) }
# => [".hidden_file", "ruby_script.rb", "text_file"]

d.close
```

Methods for listing directories and looking for files return string pathnames instead of File and Dir objects. This is partly for efficiency, and partly because creating a File or Dir actually opens up a filehandle on that file or directory.

Even so, it's annoying to have to take the output of these methods and patch together real File or Dir objects on which you can operate. Here's a simple method that will build a File or Dir, given a filename and the name or Dir of the parent directory:

```
def File.from_dir(dir, name)
  dir = dir.path if dir.is_a? Dir
  path = File.join(dir, name)
  (File.directory?(path) ? Dir : File).open(path) { |f| yield f }
end
```

As with File#open and Dir#open, the actual processing happens within a code block:

```
File.from_dir("mydir", "subdirectory") do |subdir|
  File.from_dir(subdir, "file_in_subdirectory") do |file|
    puts %{My path is #{file.path} and my contents are "#{file.read}".}
  end
end
# My path is mydir/subdirectory/file_in_subdirectory and my contents are
# "Just a simple file".
```

Globs make excellent shortcuts for finding files in a directory or a directory tree. Especially useful is the ** glob, which matches any number of directories. A glob is the easiest and fastest way to recursively process every file in a directory tree, although it loads all the filenames into an array in memory. For a less memory-intensive solution, see the find library, described in Recipe 6.12.

```
Dir["mydir/**/*"]
# => ["mydir/ruby_script.rb", "mydir/subdirectory", "mydir/text_file",
#      "mydir/subdirectory/file_in_subdirectory"]

Dir["mydir/**/*file*"]
# => ["mydir/text_file", "mydir/subdirectory/file_in_subdirectory"]
```

A brief tour of the other features of globs:

```
#Regex-style character classes
Dir["mydir/[rs]*"]    # => ["mydir/ruby_script.rb", "mydir/subdirectory"]
Dir["mydir/[^s]*"]    # => ["mydir/ruby_script.rb", "mydir/text_file"]
```

```
# Match any of the given strings
Dir["mydir/{text,ruby}*"]  # => ["mydir/text_file", "mydir/ruby_script.rb"]

# Single-character wildcards
Dir["mydir/?ub*"]     # => ["mydir/ruby_script.rb", "mydir/subdirectory"]
```

Globs will not pick up files or directories whose names start with periods, unless you match them explicitly:

```
Dir["mydir/.*"]       # => ["mydir/.", "mydir/..", "mydir/.hidden_file"]
```

See Also

- Recipe 6.12, "Walking a Directory Tree"
- Recipe 6.20, "Finding the Files You Want"

6.6   Reading the Contents of a File

Problem

You want to read some or all of a file into memory.

Solution

Open the file with Kernel#open, and pass in a code block that does the actual reading. To read the entire file into a single string, use IO#read:

```
#Put some stuff into a file.
open('sample_file', 'w') do |f|
  f.write("This is line one.\nThis is line two.")
end

# Then read it back out.
open('sample_file') { |f| f.read }
# => "This is line one.\nThis is line two."
```

To read the file as an array of lines, use IO#readlines:

```
open('sample_file') { |f| f.readlines }
# => ["This is line one.\n", "This is line two."]
```

To iterate over each line in the file, use IO#each. This technique loads only one line into memory at a time:

```
open('sample_file').each { |x| p x }
# "This is line one.\n"
# "This is line two."
```

Discussion

How much of the file do you want to read into memory at once? Reading the entire file in one gulp uses memory equal to the size of the file, but you end up with a string, and you can use any of Ruby's string processing techniques on it.

The alternative is to process the file one chunk at a time. This uses only the memory needed to store one chunk, but it can be more difficult to work with, because any given chunk may be incomplete. To process a chunk, you may end up reading the next chunk, and the next. This code reads the first 50-byte chunk from a file, but it turns out not to be enough:

```
puts open('conclusion') { |f| f.read(50) }
# "I know who killed Mr. Lambert," said Joe. "It was
```

If a certain string always marks the end of a chunk, you can pass that string into IO#each to get one chunk at a time, as a series of strings. This lets you process each full chunk as a string, and it uses less memory than reading the entire file.

```
# Create a file...
open('end_separated_records', 'w') do |f|
  f << %{This is record one.
It spans multiple lines.ENDThis is record two.END}
end

# And read it back in.
open('end_separated_records') { |f| f.each('END') { |record| p record } }
# "This is record one.\nIt spans multiple lines.END"
# "This is record two.END"
```

You can also pass a delimiter string into IO#readlines to get the entire file split into an array by the delimiter string:

```
# Create a file...
open('pipe_separated_records', 'w') do |f|
  f << "This is record one.|This is record two.|This is record three."
end

# And read it back in.
open('pipe_separated_records') { |f| f.readlines('|') }
# => ["This is record one.|", "This is record two.|",
#     "This is record three."]
```

The newline character usually makes a good delimiter (many scripts process a file one line at a time), so by default, IO#each and IO#readlines split the file by line:

```
open('newline_separated_records', 'w') do |f|
  f.puts 'This is record one. It cannot span multiple lines.'
  f.puts 'This is record two.'
end

open('newline_separated_records') { |f| f.each { |x| p x } }
# "This is record one. It cannot span multiple lines.\n"
# "This is record two.\n"
```

The trouble with newlines is that different operating systems have different newline formats. Unix newlines look like "\n", while Windows newlines look like "\r\n", and the newlines for old (pre-OS X) Macintosh files look like "\r". A file uploaded to a web application might come from any of those systems, but IO#each and

IO#readlines split files into lines depending on the newline character of the OS that's running the Ruby script (this is kept in the special variable $/). What to do?

By passing "\n" into IO#each or IO#readlines, you can handle the newlines of files created on any recent operating system. If you need to handle all three types of newlines, the easiest way is to read the entire file at once and then split it up with a regular expression.

```
open('file_from_unknown_os') { |f| f.read.split(/\r?\n|\r(?!\n)/) }
```

IO#each and IO#readlines don't strip the delimiter strings from the end of the lines. Assuming the delimiter strings aren't useful to you, you'll have to strip them manually.

To strip delimiter characters from the end of a line, use the String#chomp or String#chomp! methods. By default, these methods will remove the last character or set of characters that can be construed as a newline. However, they can be made to strip any other delimiter string from the end of a line.

```
"This line has a Unix/Mac OS X newline.\n".chomp
# => "This line has a Unix/Mac OS X newline."

"This line has a Windows newline.\r\n".chomp
# => "This line has a Windows newline."

"This line has an old-style Macintosh newline.\r".chomp
# => "This line has an old-style Macintosh newline."

"This string contains two newlines.\n\n".chomp
# "This string contains two newlines.\n"

'This is record two.END'.chomp('END')
# => "This is record two."

'This string contains no newline.'.chomp
# => "This string contains no newline."
```

You can chomp the delimiters as IO#each yields each record, or you can chomp each line returned by IO#readlines:

```
open('pipe_separated_records') do |f|
  f.each('|') { |l| puts l.chomp('|') }
end
# This is record one.
# This is record two.
# This is record three.

lines = open('pipe_separated_records') { |f| f.readlines('|') }
# => ["This is record one.|", "This is record two.|",
#      "This is record three."]
lines.each { |l| l.chomp!('|') }
# => ["This is record one.", "This is record two.", "This is record three."]
```

You've got a problem if a file is too big to fit into memory, and there are no known delimiters, or if the records between the delimiters are themselves too big to fit in memory. You've got no choice but to read from the file in chunks of a certain number of bytes. This is also the best way to read binary files; see Recipe 6.17 for more.

Use IO#read to read a certain number of bytes, or IO#each_byte to iterate over the File one byte at a time. The following code uses IO#read to continuously read uniformly sized chunks until it reaches end-of-file:

```
class File
  def each_chunk(chunk_size=1024)
    yield read(chunk_size) until eof?
  end
end

open("pipe_separated_records") do |f|
  f.each_chunk(15) { |chunk| puts chunk }
end
# This is record
# one.|This is re
# cord two.|This
# is record three
# .
```

All of these methods are made available by the IO class, the superclass of File. You can use the same methods on Socket objects. You can also use each and each_byte on String objects, which in some cases can save you from having to create a StringIO object (see Recipe 6.15 for more on those beasts).

See Also

- Recipe 6.11, "Performing Random Access on "Read-Once" Input Streams"
- Recipe 6.17, "Processing a Binary File," goes into more depth about reading files as chunks of bytes
- Recipe 6.15, "Pretending a String Is a File"

6.7 Writing to a File

Problem

You want to write some text or Ruby data structures to a file. The file might or might not exist. If it does exist, you might want to overwrite the old contents, or just append new data to the end of the file.

Solution

Open the file in write mode ('w'). The file will be created if it doesn't exist, and truncated to zero bytes if it does exist. You can then use IO#write or the << operator to write strings to the file, as though the file itself were a string and you were appending to it.

You can also use IO#puts or IO#p to write lines to the file, the same way you can use Kernel#puts or Kernel#p to write lines to standard output.

Both of the following chunks of code destroy the previous contents of the file output, then write a new string to the file:

```
open('output', 'w') { |f| f << "This file contains great truths.\n" }
open('output', 'w') do |f|
   f.puts 'The great truths have been overwritten with an advertisement.'
end

open('output') { |f| f.read }
# => "The great truths have been overwritten with an advertisement.\n"
```

To append to a file without overwriting its old contents, open the file in append mode ('a') instead of write mode:

```
open('output', "a") { |f| f.puts 'Buy Ruby(TM) brand soy sauce!' }

open('output') { |f| puts f.read }
# The great truths have been overwritten with an advertisement.
# Buy Ruby(TM) brand soy sauce!
```

Discussion

Sometimes you'll only need to write a single (possibly very large) string to a file. Usually, though, you'll be getting your strings one at a time from a data structure or some other source, and you'll call puts or the append operator within some kind of loop:

```
open('output', 'w') do |f|
   [1,2,3].each { |i| f << i << ' and a ' }
end

open('output') { |f| f.read }                # => "1 and a 2 and a 3 and a "
```

Since the << operator returns the filehandle it wrote to, you can chain calls to it. As seen above, this feature lets you write multiple strings to a file in a single line of Ruby code.

Because opening a file in write mode destroys the file's existing contents, you should only use it when you don't care about the old contents, or after you've read them into memory for later use. Append mode is nondestructive, making it useful for files like log files, which need to be updated periodically without destroying their old contents.

Buffered I/O

There's no guarantee that data will be written to your file as soon as you call << or puts. Since disk writes are expensive, Ruby lets changes to a file pile up in a buffer. It occasionally flushes the buffer, sending the data to the operating system so it can be written to disk.

You can manually flush Ruby's buffer for a particular file by calling its IO#flush method. You can turn off Ruby's buffering altogether by setting IO.sync to false. However, your operating system probably does some disk buffering of its own, so doing these things won't neccessarily write your changes directly to disk.

```
open('output', 'w') do |f|
  f << 'This is going into the Ruby buffer.'
  f.flush          # Now it's going into the OS buffer.
end

IO.sync = false
open('output', 'w') { |f| f << 'This is going straight into the OS buffer.' }
```

See Also

- Recipe 1.1, "Building a String from Parts"
- Recipe 6.6, "Reading the Contents of a File"
- Recipe 6.19, "Truncating a File"

6.8 Writing to a Temporary File

Problem

You want to write data to a secure temporary file with a unique name.

Solution

Create a Tempfile object. It has all the methods of a File object, and it will be in a location on disk guaranteed to be unique.

```
require 'tempfile'
out = Tempfile.new("tempfile")
out.path                        # => "/tmp/tempfile23786.0"
```

A Tempfile object is opened for read-write access (mode w+), so you can write to it and then read from it without having to close and reopen it:

```
out << "Some text."
out.rewind
out.read                        # => "Some text."
out.close
```

Note that you can't pass a code block into the Tempfile constructor: you have to assign the temp file to an object, and call Tempfile#close when you're done.

Discussion

To avoid security problems, use the Tempfile class to generate temp file names, instead of writing the code yourself. The Tempfile class creates a file on disk guaranteed not to be in use by any other thread or process, and sets that file's permissions so that only you can read or write to it. This eliminates any possibility that a hostile process might inject fake data into the temp file, or read what you write.[*]

The name of a temporary file incorporates the string you pass into the `Tempfile` constructor, the process ID of the current process (`$$`, or `$PID` if you've done an `include English`), and a unique number. By default, temporary files are created in `Dir::tmpdir` (usually /tmp), but you can pass in a different directory name:

```
out = Tempfile.new("myhome_tempfile", "/home/leonardr/temp/")
```

No matter where you create your temporary files, when your process exits, all of its temporary files are automatically destroyed. If you want the data you wrote to temporary files to live longer than your process, you should copy or move the temporary files to "real" files:

```
require 'fileutils'
FileUtils.mv(out.path, "/home/leonardr/old_tempfile")
```

The `tempfile` assumes that the operating system can atomically open a file and get an exclusive lock on it. This doesn't work on all filesystems. Ara Howard's `lockfile` library (available as a gem of the same name) uses linking, which is atomic everywhere.

6.9   Picking a Random Line from a File

Problem

You want to choose a random line from a file, without loading the entire file into memory.

Solution

Iterate over the file, giving each line a chance to be the randomly selected one:

```
module Enumerable
  def random_line
    selected = nil
    each_with_index { |line, lineno| selected = line if rand < 1.0/lineno }
    return selected.chomp if selected
  end
end

#Create a file with 1000 lines
open('random_line_test', 'w') do |f|
  1000.times { |i| f.puts "Line #{i}" }
end

#Pick random lines from the file.
f = open('random_line_test')
```

---

[*] Unless the hostile process is running as you or as the root user, but then you've got bigger problems.

```
f.random_line                                    # => "Line 520"
f.random_line                                    # => nil
f.rewind
f.random_line                                    # => "Line 727"
```

Discussion

The obvious solution reads the entire file into memory:

```
File.open('random_line_test') do |f|
  l = f.readlines
  l[rand(l.size)].chomp
end
# => "Line 708"
```

The recommended solution is just as fast, and only reads one line at a time into memory. However, once it's done, the file pointer has been set to the end of the file and you can't access the file anymore without calling File#rewind. If you want to pick a lot of random lines from a file, reading the entire file into memory might be preferable to iterating over it multiple times.

This recipe makes for a good command-line tool. The following code uses the special variable $., which holds the number of the line most recently read from a file:

```
$ ruby -e 'rand < 1.0/$. and line = $_ while gets; puts line.chomp if line'
```

The algorithm works because, although lines that come earlier in the file have a better chance of being selected initially, they also have more chances to be replaced by a later line. A proof by induction demonstrates that the algorithm gives equal weight to each line in the file.

The base case is a file of a single line, where it will obviously work: any value of Kernel#rand will be less than 1, so the first line will always be chosen.

Now for the inductive step. Assume that the algorithm works for a file of n lines: that is, each of the first n lines has a $1/n$ chance of being chosen. Then, add another line to the file and process the new line. The chance that line $n+1$ will become the randomly chosen line is $1/(n+1)$. The remaining probability, $n/n+1$, is the chance that one of the other n lines is the randomly chosen one.

Our inductive assumption was that each of the n original lines had an equal chance of being chosen, so this remaining $n/n+1$ probability must be distributed evenly across the n original lines. Given a line in the first n, what's it's chance of being the chosen one? It's just $n/n+1$ divided by n, or $1/n+1$. Line $n+1$ and all earlier lines have a $1/n+1$ chance of being chosen, so the choice is truly random.

See Also

- Recipe 2.5, "Generating Random Numbers"
- Recipe 4.10, "Shuffling an Array"
- Recipe 5.11, "Choosing Randomly from a Weighted List"

6.10 Comparing Two Files

Problem

You want to see if two files contain the same data. If they differ, you might want to represent the differences between them as a string: a patch from one to the other.

Solution

If two files differ, it's likely that their sizes also differ, so you can often solve the problem quickly by comparing sizes. If both files are regular files with the same size, you'll need to look at their contents.

This code does the cheap checks first:

1. If one file exists and the other does not, they're not the same.
2. If neither file exists, say they're the same.
3. If the files are the same file, they're the same.
4. If the files are of different types or sizes, they're not the same.

```
class File
  def File.same_contents(p1, p2)
    return false if File.exists?(p1) != File.exists?(p2)
    return true if !File.exists?(p1)
    return true if File.expand_path(p1) == File.expand_path(p2)
    return false if File.ftype(p1) != File.ftype(p2) ||
      File.size(p1) != File.size(p2)
```

Otherwise, it compares the files contents, a block at a time:

```
    open(p1) do |f1|
      open(p2) do |f2|
        blocksize = f1.lstat.blksize
        same = true
        while same && !f1.eof? && !f2.eof?
          same = f1.read(blocksize) == f2.read(blocksize)
        end
        return same
      end
    end
  end
end
```

To illustrate, I'll create two identical files and compare them. I'll then make them slightly different, and compare them again.

```
1.upto(2) do |i|
  open("output#{i}", 'w') { |f| f << 'x' * 10000 }
end
File.same_contents('output1', 'output2')              # => true
```

```
open("output1", 'a') { |f| f << 'x' }
open("output2", 'a') { |f| f << 'y' }
File.same_contents('output1', 'output2')              # => false

File.same_contents('nosuchfile', 'output1')           # => false
File.same_contents('nosuchfile1', 'nosuchfile2')      # => true
```

Discussion

The code in the Solution works well if you only need to determine whether two files are identical. If you need to see the differences between two files, the most useful tool is is Austin Ziegler's Diff::LCS library, available as the diff-lcs gem. It implements a sophisticated diff algorithm that can find the differences between any two enumerable objects, not just strings. You can use its LCS module to represent the differences between two nested arrays, or other complex data structures.

The downside of such flexibility is a poor interface when you just want to diff two files or strings. A diff is represented by an array of Change objects, and though you can traverse this array in helpful ways, there's no simple way to just turn it into a string representation of the sort you might get by running the Unix command diff.

Fortunately, the lcs-diff gem comes with command-line diff programs ldiff and htmldiff. If you need to perform a textual diff from within Ruby code, you can do one of the following:

1. Call out to one of those programs: assuming the gem is installed, this is more portable than relying on the Unix diff command.

2. Import the program's underlying library, and fake a command-line call to it. You'll have to modify your own program's ARGV, at least temporarily.

3. Write Ruby code that copies one of the underlying implementations to do what you want.

Here's some code, adapted from the ldiff command-line program, which builds a string representation of the differences between two strings. The result is something you might see by running ldiff, or the Unix command diff. The most common diff formats are :unified and :context.

```
require 'rubygems'
require 'diff/lcs/hunk'

def diff_as_string(data_old, data_new, format=:unified, context_lines=3)
```

First we massage the data into shape for the diff algorithm:

```
data_old = data_old.split(/\n/).map! { |e| e.chomp }
data_new = data_new.split(/\n/).map! { |e| e.chomp }
```

Then we perform the diff, and transform each "hunk" of it into a string:

```
output = ""
diffs = Diff::LCS.diff(data_old, data_new)
```

```
      return output if diffs.empty?
      oldhunk = hunk = nil
      file_length_difference = 0
      diffs.each do |piece|
        begin
          hunk = Diff::LCS::Hunk.new(data_old, data_new, piece, context_lines,
                              file_length_difference)
          file_length_difference = hunk.file_length_difference
          next unless oldhunk

          # Hunks may overlap, which is why we need to be careful when our
          # diff includes lines of context. Otherwise, we might print
          # redundant lines.
          if (context_lines > 0) and hunk.overlaps?(oldhunk)
            hunk.unshift(oldhunk)
          else
            output << oldhunk.diff(format)
          end
        ensure
          oldhunk = hunk
          output << "\n"
        end
      end

      #Handle the last remaining hunk
      output << oldhunk.diff(format) << "\n"
    end
```

Here it is in action:

```
s1 = "This is line one.\nThis is line two.\nThis is line three.\n"
s2 = "This is line 1.\nThis is line two.\nThis is line three.\n" +
     "This is line 4.\n"
puts diff_as_string(s1, s2)
# @@ -1,4 +1,5 @@
# -This is line one.
# +This is line 1.
#  This is line two.
#  This is line three.
# +This is line 4.
```

With all that code, on a Unix system you could be forgiven for just calling out to the Unix diff program:

```
open('old_file', 'w') { |f| f << s1 }
open('new_file', 'w') { |f| f << s2 }

puts %x{diff old_file new_file}
# 1c1
# < This is line one.
# ---
# > This is line 1.
# 3a4
# > This is line 4.
```

See Also

- The `algorithm-diff` gem is another implementation of a general diff algorithm; its API is a little simpler than `diff-lcs`, but it has the same basic structure; both gems are descended from Perl's `Algorithm::Diff` module

- It's not available as a gem, but the `diff.rb` package is a little easier to script from Ruby if you need to create a textual diff of two files; look at how the `unixdiff.rb` program creates a `Diff` object and manipulates it (*http://users.cybercity.dk/ ~dsl8950/ruby/diff.html*)

- The MD5 checksum is often used in file comparisons: I didn't use it in this recipe because when you're only comparing two files, it's faster to compare their contents; in Recipe 23.7, "Finding Duplicate Files," though, the MD5 checksum is used as a convenient shorthand for the contents of many files

6.11 Performing Random Access on "Read-Once" Input Streams

Problem

You have an IO object, probably a socket, that doesn't support random-access methods like seek, pos=, and rewind. You want to treat this object like a file on disk, where you can jump around and reread parts of the file.

Solution

The simplest solution is to read the entire contents of the socket (or as much as you're going to need) and put it into a StringIO object. You can then treat the StringIO object exactly like a file:

```
require 'socket'
require 'stringio'

sock = TCPSocket.open("www.example.com", 80)
sock.write("GET /\n")

file = StringIO.new(sock.read)
file.read(10)                            # => "<HTML>\r\n<H"
file.rewind
file.read(10)                            # => "<HTML>\r\n<H"
file.pos = 90
file.read(15)                            # => " this web page "
```

Discussion

A socket is supposed to work just like a file, but sometimes the illusion breaks down. Since the data is coming from another computer over which you have no control, you can't just go back and reread data you've already read. That data has already been sent over the pipe, and the server doesn't care if you lost it or need to process it again.

If you have enough memory to read the entire contents of a socket, it's easy to put the results into a form that more closely simulates a file on disk. But you might not want to read the entire socket, or the socket may be one that keeps sending data until you close it. In that case you'll need to buffer the data as you read it. Instead of using memory for the entire contents of the socket (which may be infinite), you'll only use memory for the data you've actually read.

This code defines a `BufferedIO` class that adds data to an internal `StringIO` as it's read from its source:

```ruby
class BufferedIO
  def initialize(io)
    @buff = StringIO.new
    @source = io
    @pos = 0
  end

  def read(x=nil)
    to_read = x ? to_read = x+@buff.pos-@buff.size : nil
    _append(@source.read(to_read)) if !to_read or to_read > 0
    @buff.read(x)
  end

  def pos=(x)
   read(x-@buff.pos) if x > @buff.size
    @buff.pos = x
  end

  def seek(x, whence=IO::SEEK_SET)
    case whence
      when IO::SEEK_SET then self.pos=(x)
      when IO::SEEK_CUR then self.pos=(@buff.pos+x)
      when IO::SEEK_END then read; self.pos=(@buff.size-x)
      # Note: SEEK_END reads all the socket data.
    end
    pos
  end

  # Some methods can simply be delegated to the buffer.
  ["pos", "rewind", "tell"].each do |m|
    module_eval "def #{m}\n@buff.#{m}\nend"
  end

  private

  def _append(s)
  @buff << s
    @buff.pos -= s.size
  end
end
```

Now you can seek, rewind, and generally move around in an input socket as if it were a disk file. You only have to read as much data as you need:

```
sock = TCPSocket.open("www.example.com", 80)
sock.write("GET /\n")
file = BufferedIO.new(sock)

file.read(10)                               # => "<HTML>\r\n<H"
file.rewind                                 # => 0
file.read(10)                               # => "<HTML>\r\n<H"
file.pos = 90                               # => 90
file.read(15)                               # => " this web page "
file.seek(-10, IO::SEEK_CUR)                # => 95
file.read(10)                               # => " web page "
```

BufferedIO doesn't implement all the methods of IO, only the ones not implemented by socket-type IO objects. If you need the other methods, you should be able to implement the ones you need using the existing methods as guidelines. For instance, you could implement readline like this:

```
class BufferedIO
  def readline
    oldpos = @buff.pos
    line = @buff.readline unless @buff.eof?
    if !line or line[-1] != ?\n
      _append(@source.readline) # Finish the line
      @buff.pos = oldpos         # Go back to where we were
      line = @buff.readline      # Read the line again
    end
    line
  end
end

file.readline              # => "by typing &quot;example.com&quot;,\r\n"
```

See Also

- Recipe 6.17, "Processing a Binary File," for more information on IO#seek

6.12 Walking a Directory Tree

Problem

You want to recursively process every subdirectory and file within a certain directory.

Solution

Suppose that the directory tree you want to walk looks like this (see this chapter's introduction section for the create_tree library that can build this directory tree automatically):

```
require 'create_tree'
create_tree './' =>
  [ 'file1',
    'file2',
        { 'subdir1/' => [ 'file1' ] },
        { 'subdir2/' => [ 'file1',
                          'file2',
                          { 'subsubdir/' => [ 'file1' ] }
                        ]
        }
  ]
```

The simplest solution is to load all the files and directories into memory with a big recursive file glob, and iterate over the resulting array. This uses a lot of memory because all the filenames are loaded into memory at once:

```
Dir['**/**']
# => ["file1", "file2", "subdir1", "subdir2", "subdir1/file1",
#      "subdir2/file1", "subdir2/file2", "subdir2/subsubdir",
#      "subdir2/subsubdir/file1"]
```

A more elegant solution is to use the `find` method in the `Find` module. It performs a depth-first traversal of a directory tree, and calls the given code block on each directory and file. The code block should take as an argument the full path to a directory or file.

This snippet calls `Find.find` with a code block that simply prints out each path it receives. This demonstrates how Ruby performs the traversal:

```
require 'find'
Find.find('./') { |path| puts path }
# ./
# ./subdir2
# ./subdir2/subsubdir
# ./subdir2/subsubdir/file1
# ./subdir2/file2
# ./subdir2/file1
# ./subdir1
# ./subdir1/file1
# ./file2
# ./file1
```

Discussion

Even if you're not a system administrator, the demands of keeping your own files organized will frequently call for you to process every file in a directory tree. You may want to backup, modify, or delete each file in the directory structure, or you may just want to see what's there.

Normally you'll want to at least look at every file in the tree, but sometimes you'll want to skip certain directories. For instance, you might know that a certain directory is full of a lot of large files you don't want to process. When your block is passed a path to a directory, you can prevent `Find.find` from recursing into a directory by calling Find.prune. In this example, I'll prevent Find.find from processing the files in the subdir2 directory.

```
Find.find('./') do |path|
  Find.prune if File.basename(path) == 'subdir2'
  puts path
end
# ./
# ./subdir1
# ./subdir1/file1
# ./file2
# ./file1
```

Calling Find.prune when your block has been passed a file will only prevent Find. find from processing that one file. It won't halt the processing of the rest of the files in that directory:

```
Find.find('./') do |path|
  if File.basename(path) =~ /file2$/
    puts "PRUNED #{path}"
    Find.prune
  end
  puts path
end
# ./
# ./subdir2
# ./subdir2/subsubdir
# ./subdir2/subsubdir/file1
# PRUNED ./subdir2/file2
# ./subdir2/file1
# ./subdir1
# ./subdir1/file1
# PRUNED ./file2
# ./file1
```

Find.find works by keeping a queue of files to process. When it finds a directory, it inserts that directory's files at the beginning of the queue. This gives it the characteristics of a depth-first traversal. Note how all the files in the top-level directory are processed after the subdirectories. The alternative would be a breadth-first traversal, which would process the files in a directory before even touching the subdirectories.

If you want to do a breadth-first traversal instead of a depth-first one, the simplest solution is to use a glob and sort the resulting array. Pathnames sort naturally in a way that simulates a breadth-first traversal:

```
Dir["**/**"].sort.each { |x| puts x }
# file1
# file2
# subdir1
# subdir1/file1
# subdir2
# subdir2/file1
# subdir2/file2
# subdir2/subsubdir
# subdir2/subsubdir/file1
```

See Also

- Recipe 6.20, "Finding the Files You Want"
- Recipe 23.7, "Finding Duplicate Files"

6.13   Locking a File

Problem

You want to prevent other threads or processes from modifying a file that you're working on.

Solution

Open the file, then lock it with File#flock. There are two kinds of lock; pass in the File constant for the kind you want.

- File::LOCK_EX gives you an exclusive lock, or write lock. If your thread has an exclusive lock on a file, no other thread or process can get a lock on that file. Use this when you want to write to a file without anyone else being able to write to it.
- File::LOCK_SH will give you a shared lock, or read lock. Other threads and processes can get their own shared locks on the file, but no one can get an exclusive lock. Use this when you want to read a file and know that it won't change while you're reading it.

Once you're done using the file, you need to unlock it. Call File#flock again, and pass in File::LOCK_UN as the lock type. You can skip this step if you're running on Windows.

The best way to handle all this is to enclose the locking and unlocking in a method that takes a block, the way open does:

```
def flock(file, mode)
  success = file.flock(mode)
  if success
    begin
      yield file
    ensure
      file.flock(File::LOCK_UN)
    end
  end
  return success
end
```

This makes it possible to lock a file without having to worry about unlocking it later. Even if your block raises an exception, the file will be unlocked and another thread can use it.

```
open('output', 'w') do |f|
  flock(f, File::LOCK_EX) do |f|
```

```
      f << "Kiss me, I've got a write lock on a file!"
    end
  end
```

Discussion

Different operating systems support different ways of locking files. Ruby's `flock` implementation tries to hide the differences behind a common interface that looks like Unix's file locking interface. In general, you can use `flock` as though you were on Unix, and your scripts will work across platforms.

On Unix, both exclusive and shared locks work only if all threads and processes play by the rules. If one thread has an exclusive lock on a file, another thread can still open the file without locking it and wreak havoc by overwriting its contents. That's why it's important to get a lock on any file that might conceivably be used by another thread or another process on the system.

Ruby's block-oriented coding style makes it easy to do the right thing with locking. The following shortcut method works with the `flock` method previously defined. It takes care of opening, locking, unlocking, and closing a file, letting you focus on whatever you want to do with the file's contents.

```
def open_lock(filename, openmode="r", lockmode=nil)
  if openmode == 'r' || openmode == 'rb'
    lockmode ||= File::LOCK_SH
  else
    lockmode ||= File::LOCK_EX
  end
  value = nil
  open(filename, openmode) do |f|
    flock(f, lockmode) do
      begin
        value = yield f
      ensure
        f.flock(File::LOCK_UN) # Comment this line out on Windows.
      end
    end
    return value
  end
end
```

This code creates two threads, each of which want to access the same file. Thanks to locks, we can guarantee that only one thread is accessing the file at a time (see Chapter 20 if you're not comfortable with threads).

```
t1 = Thread.new do
  puts 'Thread 1 is requesting a lock.'
  open_lock('output', 'w') do |f|
    puts 'Thread 1 has acquired a lock.'
    f << "At last we're alone!"
    sleep(5)
  end
```

```
      puts 'Thread 1 has released its lock.'
    end

    t2 = Thread.new do
      puts 'Thread 2 is requesting a lock.'
      open_lock('output', 'r') do |f|
        puts 'Thread 2 has acquired a lock.'
        puts "File contents: #{f.read}"
      end
      puts 'Thread 2 has released its lock.'
    end
    t1.join
    t2.join
    # Thread 1 is requesting a lock.
    # Thread 1 has acquired a lock.
    # Thread 2 is requesting a lock.
    # Thread 1 has released its lock.
    # Thread 2 has acquired a lock.
    # File contents: At last we're alone!
    # Thread 2 has released its lock.
```

Nonblocking locks

If you try to get an exclusive or shared lock on a file, your thread will block until
Ruby can lock the file. But you might be left waiting a long time, perhaps forever.
The code that has the file locked may be buggy and in an infinite loop; or it may
itself be blocking, waiting to lock a file that *you* have locked.

You can avoid deadlock and similar problems by asking for a nonblocking lock.
When you do, if Ruby can't lock the file for you, File#flock returns false, rather than
waiting (possibly forever) for another thread or process to release its lock. If you
don't get a lock, you can wait a while and try again, or you can raise an exception
and let the user deal with it.

To make a lock into a nonblocking lock, use the OR operator (|) to combine File::
LOCK_NB with either File::LOCK_EX or File::LOCK_SH.

The following code will print "I've got a lock!" if it can get an exclusive lock on the
file "output"; otherwise it will print "I couldn't get a lock." and continue:

```
    def try_lock
      puts "I couldn't get a lock." unless
        open_lock('contested', 'w', File::LOCK_EX | File::LOCK_NB) do
        puts "I've got a lock!"
        true
      end
    end

    try_lock
    # I've got a lock!

    open('contested', 'w').flock(File::LOCK_EX) # Get a lock, hold it forever.
```

```
try_lock
# I couldn't get a lock.
```

See Also

- Chapter 20, especially Recipe 20.11, "Avoiding Deadlock," which covers other types of deadlock problems in a multithreaded environment

6.14   Backing Up to Versioned Filenames

Problem

You want to copy a file to a numbered backup before overwriting the original file. More generally: rather than overwriting an existing file, you want to use a new file whose name is based on the original filename.

Solution

Use String#succ to generate versioned suffixes for a filename until you find one that doesn't already exist:

```
class File
  def File.versioned_filename(base, first_suffix='.0')
    suffix = nil
    filename = base
    while File.exists?(filename)
      suffix = (suffix ? suffix.succ : first_suffix)
      filename = base + suffix
    end
    return filename
  end
end

5.times do |i|
  name = File.versioned_filename('filename.txt')
  open(name, 'w') { |f| f << "Contents for run #{i}" }
  puts "Created #{name}"
end
# Created filename.txt
# Created filename.txt.0
# Created filename.txt.1
# Created filename.txt.2
# Created filename.txt.3
```

If you want to copy or move the original file to the versioned filename as a prelude to writing to the original file, include the ftools library to add the class methods File. copy and File.move. Then call versioned_filename and use File.copy or File.move to put the old file in its new place:

```
require 'ftools'
class File
```

```
def File.to_backup(filename, move=false)
  new_filename = nil
  if File.exists? filename
    new_filename = File.versioned_filename(filename)
    File.send(move ? :move : :copy, filename, new_filename)
  end
  return new_filename
end
```

Let's back up filename.txt a couple of times. Recall from earlier that the files filename.txt.[0-3] already exist.

```
File.to_backup('filename.txt')                # => "filename.txt.4"
File.to_backup('filename.txt')                # => "filename.txt.5"
```

Now let's do a destructive backup:

```
File.to_backup('filename.txt', true)          # => "filename.txt.6"
File.exists? 'filename.txt'                    # => false
```

You can't back up what doesn't exist:

```
File.to_backup('filename.txt')                # => nil
```

Discussion

If you anticipate more than 10 versions of a file, you should add additional zeroes to the initial suffix. Otherwise, filename.txt.10 will sort before filename.txt.2 in a directory listing. A commonly used suffix is ".000".

```
200.times do |i|
  name = File.versioned_filename('many_versions.txt', '.000')
  open(name, 'w') { |f| f << "Contents for run #{i}" }
  puts "Created #{name}"
end
# Created many_versions.txt
# Created many_versions.txt.000
# Created many_versions.txt.001
# ...
# Created many_versions.txt.197
# Created many_versions.txt.198
```

The result of versioned_filename won't be trustworthy if other threads or processes on your machine might be trying to write the same file. If this is a concern for you, you shouldn't be satisfied with a negative result from File.exists?. In the time it takes to open that file, some other process or thread might open it before you. Once you find a file that doesn't exist, you must get an exclusive lock on the file before you can be totally certain it's okay to use.

Here's how such an implementation might look on a Unix system. The versioned_filename methods return the name of a file, but this implementation needs to return the actual file, opened and locked. This is the only way to avoid a race condition between the time the method returns a filename, and the time you open and lock the file.

```
class File
  def File.versioned_file(base, first_suffix='.0', access_mode='w')
    suffix = file = locked = nil
    filename = base
    begin
      suffix = (suffix ? suffix.succ : first_suffix)
      filename = base + suffix
      unless File.exists? filename
        file = open(filename, access_mode)
        locked = file.flock(File::LOCK_EX | File::LOCK_NB)
        file.close unless locked
      end
    end until locked
    return file
  end
end

File.versioned_file('contested_file')  # => #<File:contested_file.0>
File.versioned_file('contested_file')  # => #<File:contested_file.1>
File.versioned_file('contested_file')  # => #<File:contested_file.2>
```

The construct begin...end until locked creates a loop that runs at least once, and
continues to run until the variable locked becomes true, indicating that a file has
been opened and successfully locked.

See Also

- Recipe 6.13, "Locking a File"

6.15 Pretending a String Is a File

Problem

You want to call code that expects to read from an open file object, but your source
is a string in memory. Alternatively, you want to call code that writes its output to a
file, but have it actually write to a string.

Solution

The StringIO class wraps a string in the interface of the IO class. You can treat it like
a file, then get everything that's been "written" to it by calling its string method.

Here's a StringIO used as an input source:

```
require 'stringio'
s = StringIO.new %{I am the very model of a modern major general.
I've information vegetable, animal, and mineral.}

s.pos                                # => 0
s.each_line { |x| puts x }
# I am the very model of a modern major general.
# I've information vegetable, animal, and mineral.
```

```
s.eof?                              # => true
s.pos                               # => 95
s.rewind
s.pos                               # => 0
s.grep /general/
# => ["I am the very model of a modern major general.\n"]
```

Here are StringIO objects used as output sinks:

```
s = StringIO.new
s.write('Treat it like a file.')
s.rewind
s.write("Act like it's")
s.string                            # => "Act like it's a file."

require 'yaml'
s = StringIO.new
YAML.dump(['A list of', 3, :items], s)
puts s.string
# ---
# - A list of
# - 3
# - :items
```

Discussion

The Adapter is a common design pattern: to make an object acceptable as input to a method, it's wrapped in another object that presents the appropriate interface. The StringIO class is an Adapter between String and File (or IO), designed for use with methods that work on File or IO instances. With a StringIO, you can disguise a string as a file and use those methods without them ever knowing they haven't really been given a file.

For instance, if you want to write unit tests for a library that reads from a file, the simplest way is to pass in predefined StringIO objects that simulate files with various contents. If you need to modify the output of a method that writes to a file, a StringIO can capture the output, making it easy to modify and send on to its final destination.

StringIO-type functionality is less necessary in Ruby than in languages like Python, because in Ruby, strings and files implement a lot of the same methods to begin with. Often you can get away with simply using these common methods. For instance, if all you're doing is writing to an output sink, you don't need a StringIO object, because String#<< and File#<< work the same way:

```
def make_more_interesting(io)
  io << "... OF DOOM!"
end

make_more_interesting("Cherry pie")       # => "Cherry pie... OF DOOM!"

open('interesting_things', 'w') do |f|
```

```
    f.write("Nightstand")
    make_more_interesting(f)
end
open('interesting_things') { |f| f.read }    # => "Nightstand... OF DOOM!"
```

Similarly, `File` and `String` both include the `Enumerable` mixin, so in a lot of cases you can read from an object without caring what type it is. This is a good example of Ruby's duck typing.

Here's a string:

```
poem = %{The boy stood on the burning deck
Whence all but he had fled
He'd stayed above to wash his neck
Before he went to bed}
```

and a file containing that string:

```
output = open("poem", "w")
output.write(poem)
output.close
input = open("poem")
```

will give the same result when you call an `Enumerable` method:

```
poem.grep /ed$/
# => ["Whence all but he had fled\n", "Before he went to bed"]
input.grep /ed$/
# => ["Whence all but he had fled\n", "Before he went to bed"]
```

Just remember that, unlike a string, you can't iterate over a file multiple times without calling rewind:

```
input.grep /ed$/                            # => []
input.rewind
input.grep /ed$/
# => ["Whence all but he had fled\n", "Before he went to bed"]
```

`StringIO` comes in when the `Enumerable` methods and `<<` aren't enough. If a method you're writing needs to use methods specific to `IO`, you can accept a string as input and wrap it in a `StringIO`. The class also comes in handy when you need to call a method someone else wrote, not anticipating that anyone would ever need to call it with anything other than a file:

```
def fifth_byte(file)
  file.seek(5)
  file.read(1)
end

fifth_byte("123456")
# NoMethodError: undefined method `seek' for "123456":String
fifth_byte(StringIO.new("123456"))          # => "6"
```

When you write a method that accepts a file as an argument, you can silently accommodate callers who pass in strings by wrapping in a `StringIO` any string that gets passed in:

```
def file_operation(io)
  io = StringIO(io) if io.respond_to? :to_str && !io.is_a? StringIO
  #Do the file operation...
end
```

A StringIO object is always open for both reading and writing:

```
s = StringIO.new
s << "A string"
s.read                              # => ""
s << ", and more."
s.rewind
s.read                              # => "A string, and more."
```

Memory access is faster than disk access, but for large amounts of data (more than about 10 kilobytes), StringIO objects are slower than disk files. If speed is your aim, your best bet is to write to and read from temp files using the tempfile module. Or you can do what the open-uri library does: start off by writing to a StringIO and, if it gets too big, switch to using a temp file.

See Also

- Recipe 6.8, "Writing to a Temporary File"
- Recipe 6.11, "Performing Random Access on "Read-Once" Input Streams"

6.16 Redirecting Standard Input or Output

Problem

You don't want the standard input, output, or error of your process to go to the default IO objects set up by the Ruby interpreter. You want them to go to other file-type objects of your own choosing.

Solution

You can assign any IO object (a File, a Socket, or what have you) to the global variables $stdin, $stdout, or $stderr. You can then read from or write to those objects as though they were the originals.

This short Ruby program demonstrates how to redirect the Kernel methods that print to standard output. To avoid confusion, I'm presenting it as a standalone Ruby program rather than an interactive irb session.[*]

```
#!/usr/bin/ruby -w
# ./redirect_stdout.rb
require 'stringio'
new_stdout = StringIO.new
```

_____

[*] irb prints the result of each Ruby expression to $stdout, which tends to clutter the results in this case.

```
$stdout = new_stdout
puts "Hello, hello."
puts "I'm writing to standard output."

$stderr.puts "#{new_stdout.size} bytes written to standard ouput so far."
$stderr.puts "You haven't seen anything on the screen yet, but you soon will:"
$stderr.puts new_stdout.string
```

Run this program and you'll see the following:

```
$ ruby redirect_stdout.rb
46 bytes written to standard output so far.
You haven't seen anything on the screen yet, but you soon will:
Hello, hello.
I'm writing to standard output.
```

Discussion

If you have any Unix experience, you know that when you run a Ruby script from the command line, you can make the shell redirect its standard input, output, and error streams to files or other programs. This technique lets you do the same thing from within a Ruby script.

You can use this as a quick and dirty way to write errors to a file, write output to a StringIO object (as seen above), or even read input from a socket. Within a script, you can programatically decide where to send your output, or receive standard input from multiple sources. These things are generally not possible from the command line without a lot of fancy shell scripting.

The redirection technique is especially useful when you've written or inherited a script that prints text to standard output, and you need to make it capable of printing to any file-like object. Rather than changing almost every line of your code, you can just set $stdout at the start of your program, and let it run as is. This isn't a perfect solution, but it's often good enough.

The original input and output streams for a process are always available as the constants STDIN, STDOUT, and STDERR. If you want to temporarily swap one IO stream for another, change back to the "standard" standard output by setting $stdin = STDIN. Keep in mind that since the $std objects are global variables, even a temporary change affects all threads in your script.

See Also

- Recipe 6.15, "Pretending a String Is a File," has much more information on StringIO

6.17 Processing a Binary File

Problem

You want to read binary data from a file, or write it to one.

Solution

Since Ruby strings make no distinction between binary and text data, processing a binary file needn't be any different than processing a text file. Just make sure you add "b" to your file mode when you open a binary file on Windows.

This code writes 10 bytes of binary data to a file, then reads it back:

```
open('binary', 'wb') do |f|
  (0..100).step(10) { |b| f << b.chr }
end

s = open('binary', 'rb') { |f| f.read }
# => "\000\n\024\036(2<FPZd"
```

If you want to process a binary file one byte at a time, you'll probably enjoy the way each_byte returns each byte of the file as a number, rather than as single-character strings:

```
open('binary', 'rb') { |f| f.each_byte { |b| puts b } }
# 0
# 10
# 20
# ...
# 90
# 100
```

Discussion

The methods introduced earlier to deal with text files work just as well for binary files, assuming that your binary files are supposed to be processed from beginning to end, the way text files typically are. If you want random access to the contents of a binary file, you can manipulate your file object's "cursor."

Think of the cursor as a pointer to the first unread byte in the open file. The current position of the cursor is accessed by the method IO#pos. When you open the file, it's set to zero, just before the first byte. You can then use IO#read to read a number of bytes starting from the current position of the cursor, incrementing the cursor as a side effect.

```
f = open('binary')
f.pos                             # => 0
f.read(1)                         # => "\000"
f.pos                             # => 1
```

You can also just set pos to jump to a specific byte in the file:

```
f.pos = 4                                      # => 4
f.read(2)                                      # => "(2"
f.pos                                          # => 6
```

You can use IO#seek to move the cursor forward or backward relative to its current position (with File::SEEK_CUR), or to move to a certain distance from the *end* of a file (with File::SEEK_END). Unlike the iterator methods, which go through the entire file once, you can use seek or set pos to jump anywhere in the file, even to a byte you've already read.

```
f.seek(8)
f.pos                                          # => 8

f.seek(-4, File::SEEK_CUR)
f.pos                                          # => 4
f.seek(2, File::SEEK_CUR)
f.pos                                          # => 6

# Move to the second-to-last byte of the file.
f.seek(-2, File::SEEK_END)
f.pos                                          # => 9
```

Attempting to read more bytes than there are in the file returns the rest of the bytes, and set your file's eof? flag to true:

```
f.read(500)                                    # => "Zd"
f.pos                                          # => 11
f.eof?                                         # => true
f.close
```

Often you need to read from and write to a binary file simultaneously. You can open any file for simultaneous reading and writing using the "r+" mode (or, in this case, "rb+"):

```
f = open('binary', 'rb+')
f.read                                         # => "\000\n\024\036(2<FPZd"
f.pos = 2
f.write('Hello.')
f.rewind
f.read                                         # => "\000\nHello.PZd"
f << 'Goodbye.'
f.rewind
f.read                                         # => "\000\nHello.PZdGoodbye."

f.close
```

You can append new data to the end of a file you've opened for read-write access, and you can overwrite existing data byte for byte, but you can't insert new data into the middle of a file. This makes the read-write technique useful for binary files, where exact byte offsets are often important, and less useful for text files, where it might make sense to add an extra line in the middle.

Why do you need to append "b" to the file mode when opening a binary file on Windows? Because otherwise Windows will mangle any newline characters that show up in your binary file. The "b" tells Windows to leave the newlines alone, because they're not really newlines: they're binary data. Since it doesn't hurt anything on Unix to put "b" in the file mode, you can make your code cross-platform by appending "b" to the mode whenever you open a file you plan to treat as binary. Note that "b" by itself is not a valid file mode: you probably want "rb".

An MP3 example

Because every binary format is different, probably the best I can do to help you beyond this point is show you an example. Consider MP3 music files. Many MP3 files have a 128-byte data structure at the end called an *ID3 tag*. These 128 bytes are literally packed with information about the song: its name, the artist, which album it's from, and so on. You can parse this data structure by opening an MP3 file and doing a series of reads from a pos near the end of the file.

According to the ID3 standard, if you start from the 128th-to-last byte of an MP3 file and read three bytes, you should get the string "TAG". If you don't, there's no ID3 tag for this MP3 file, and nothing to do. If there is an ID3 tag present, then the 30 bytes after "TAG" contain the name of the song, the 30 bytes after that contain the name of the artist, and so on. Here's some code that parses a file's ID3 tag and puts the results into a hash:

```
def parse_id3(mp3_file)
  fields_and_sizes = [[:track_name, 30], [:artist_name, 30],
                      [:album_name, 30], [:year, 4], [:comment, 30],
                      [:genre, 1]]
  tag = {}
  open(mp3_file) do |f|
    f.seek(-128, File::SEEK_END)
    if f.read(3) == 'TAG' # An ID3 tag is present
      fields_and_sizes.each do |field, size|
        # Read the field and strip off anything after the first null
        # character.
        data = f.read(size).gsub(/\000.*/, '')
        # Convert the genre string to a number.
        data = data[0] if field == :genre
        tag[field] = data
      end
    end
  end
  return tag
end

parse_id3('ID3.mp3')
# => {:year=>"2005", :artist_name=>"The ID Three",
#     :album_name=>"Binary Brain Death",
```

```
#      :comment=>"http://www.example.com/id3/", :genre=>22,
#      :track_name=>"ID 3"}

parse_id3('Too Indie For ID3 Tags.mp3')          # => {}
```

Rather than specifying the genre of the music as a string, the :genre element of the hash is a single byte, an entry into a lookup table shared by all applications that use ID3. In this table, genre number 22 is "Death metal".

It's less code to specify the byte offsets for a binary file is in the format recognized by String#unpack, which can parse the bytes of a string according to a given format. It returns an array containing the results of the parsing.

```
#Returns [track, artist, album, year, comment, genre]
def parse_id3(mp3_file)
  format = 'Z30Z30Z30Z4Z30C'
  open(mp3_file) do |f|
    f.seek(-128, File::SEEK_END)
    if f.read(3) == "TAG" # An ID3 tag is present
      return f.read(125).unpack(format)
    end
  end
  return nil
end

parse_id3('ID3.mp3')
# => ["ID 3", "The ID Three", "Binary Brain Death", "2005", "http://www.example.com/
id3/", 22]
```

As you can see, the unpack format is obscure but very concise. The string "Z30Z30Z30Z4Z30C" passed into String#unpack completely describes the elements of the ID3 format after the "TAG":

- Three strings of 30 bytes, with null characters stripped ("Z30Z30Z30")
- A string of 4 bytes, with null characters stripped ("Z4")
- One more string of 30 bytes, with null characters stripped ("Z30")
- A single character, represented as an unsigned integer ("C")

It doesn't describe what those elements are supposed to be used for, though.

When writing binary data to a file, you can use Array#pack, the opposite of String#unpack:

```
id3 = ["ID 3", "The ID Three", "Binary Brain Death", "2005",
       "http://www.example.com/id3/", 22]
id3.pack 'Z30Z30Z30Z4Z30C'
# => "ID 3\000\000\000\000\000...http://www.example.com/id3/\000\000\000\026"
```

See Also

- The ID3 standard, described at *http://en.wikipedia.org/wiki/ID3* along with the table of genres; the code in this recipe parses the original ID3v1 standard, which is much simpler than ID3v2
- ri String#unpack and ri Array#pack

6.18 Deleting a File

Problem

You want to delete a single file, or a whole directory tree.

Solution

Removing a file is simple, with File.delete:

```
import 'fileutils'
FileUtils.touch "doomed_file"
File.exists? "doomed_file"                    # => true
File.delete "doomed_file"
File.exists? "doomed_file"                    # => false
```

Removing a directory tree is also fairly simple. The most confusing thing about it is the number of different methods Ruby provides to do it. The method you want is probably FileUtils.remove_dir, which recursively deletes the contents of a directory:

```
Dir.mkdir "doomed_directory"
File.exists? "doomed_directory"               # => true
FileUtils.remove_dir "doomed_directory"
File.exists? "doomed_directory"               # => false
```

Discussion

Ruby provides several methods for removing directories, but you really only need remove_dir. Dir.delete and FileUtils.rmdir will only work if the directory is already empty. The rm_r and rm_rf defined in FileUtils are similar to remove_dir, but if you're a Unix user you may find their names more mneumonic.

You should also know about the :secure option to rm_rf, because the remove_dir method and all its variants are vulnerable to a race condition when you remove a world-writable directory. The risk is that a process owned by another user might create a symlink in that directory while you're deleting it. This would make you delete the symlinked file along with the files you actually meant to delete.

Passing in the :secure option to rm_rf slows down deletions significantly (it has to change the permissions on the directory before deleting it), but it avoids the race condition. If you're running Ruby 1.8, you'll also need to hack the FileUtils module a little bit to work around a bug (the bug is fixed in Ruby 1.9):

```ruby
# A hack to make a method used by rm_rf actually available
module FileUtils
  module_function :fu_world_writable?
end

Dir.mkdir "/tmp/doomed_directory"
FileUtils.rm_rf("/tmp/doomed_directory", :secure=>true)
File.exists? "/tmp/doomed_directory"                # => false
```

Why isn't the :secure option the default for rm_rf? Because secure deletion isn't thread-safe: it actually changes the current working directory of the process. You need to choose between thread safety and a possible security hole.

6.19   Truncating a File

Problem

You want to truncate a file to a certain length, probably zero bytes.

Solution

Usually, you want to destroy the old contents of a file and start over. Opening a file for write access will automatically truncate it to zero bytes, and let you write new contents to the file:

```ruby
filename = 'truncate.txt'
open(filename, 'w') { |f| f << "All of this will be truncated." }
File.size(filename)                          # => 30

f = open(filename, 'w') {}
File.size(filename)                          # => 0
```

If you just need to truncate the file to zero bytes, and not write any new contents to it, you can open it with an access mode of File::TRUNC.

```ruby
open(filename, 'w') { |f| f << "Here are some new contents." }

File.size(filename)                          # => 27

f = open(filename, File::TRUNC) {}
File.size(filename)                          # => 0
```

You can't actually do anything with a FILE whose access mode is File::TRUNC:

```ruby
open(filename, File::TRUNC) do |f|
  f << "At last, an empty file to write to!"
end
# IOError: not opened for writing
```

Discussion

Transient files are the most likely candidates for truncation. Log files are often truncated, automatically or by hand, before they grow too large.

The most common type of truncation is truncating a file to zero bytes, but the File.truncate method can truncate a file to any number of bytes, not just zero. You can also use the instance method, File#truncate, to truncate a file you've opened for writing:

```
f = open(filename, 'w') do |f|
  f << 'These words will remain intact after the file is truncated.'
end
File.size(filename)   # => 59

File.truncate(filename, 30)
File.size(filename)                    # => 30
open(filename) { |f| f.read }          # => "These words will remain intact"
```

These methods don't always make a file smaller. If the file starts out smaller than the size you give, they append zero-bytes (\000) to the end of file until the file reaches the specified size.

```
f = open(filename, "w") { |f| f << "Brevity is the soul of wit." }
File.size(filename)                    # => 27
File.truncate(filename, 30)
File.size(filename)                    # => 30
open(filename) { |f| f.read }
# => "Brevity is the soul of wit.\000\000\000"
```

File.truncate and File#truncate act like the bed of Procrustes: they force a file to be a certain number of bytes long, whether that means stretching it or chopping off the end.

6.20 Finding the Files You Want

Problem

You want to locate all the files in a directory hierarchy that match some criteria. For instance, you might want to find all the empty files, all the MP3 files, or all the files named "README."

Solution

Use the Find.find method to walk the directory structure and accumulate a list of matching files.

Pass in a block to the following method and it'll walk a directory tree, testing each file against the code block you provide. It returns an array of all files for which the value of the block is true.

```
require 'find'
module Find
  def match(*paths)
    matched = []
    find(*paths) { |path| matched << path if yield path }
    return matched
  end
  module_function :match
end
```

Here's what Find.match might return if you used it on a typical disorganized home directory:

```
Find.match("./") { |p| File.lstat(p).size == 0 }
# => ["./Music/cancelled_download.MP3", "./tmp/empty2", "./tmp/empty1"]

Find.match("./") { |p| ext = p[-4...p.size]; ext && ext.downcase == ".mp3" }
# => ["./Music/The Snails - Red Rocket.mp3",
# =>  "./Music/The Snails - Moonfall.mp3", "./Music/cancelled_download.MP3"]

Find.match("./") { |p| File.split(p)[1] == "README" }
# => ["./rubyprog-0.1/README", "./tmp/README"]
```

Discussion

This is an especially useful chunk of code for system administration tasks. It gives you functionality at least as powerful as the Unix find command, but you can write your search criteria in Ruby and you won't have to remember the arcane syntax of find.

As with Find.walk itself, you can stop Find.match from processing a directory by calling Find.prune:

```
Find.match("./") do |p|
  Find.prune if p == "./tmp"
  File.split(p)[1] == "README"
end
# => ["./rubyprog-0.1/README"]
```

You can even look inside each file to see whether you want it:

```
# Find all files that start with a particular phrase.
must_start_with = "This Ruby program"
Find.match("./") do |p|
  if File.file? p
    open(p) { |f| f.read(must_start_with.size) == must_start_with }
  else
    false
  end
end
# => ["./rubyprog-0.1/README"]
```

A few other useful things to search for using this function:

```
# Finds files that were probably left behind by emacs sessions.
def emacs_droppings(*paths)
  Find.match(*paths) do |p|
    (p[-1] == ?~ and p[0] != ?~) or (p[0] == ?# and p[-1] == ?#)
  end
end

# Finds all files that are larger than a certain threshold. Use this to find
# the files hogging space on your filesystem.
def bigger_than(bytes, *paths)
  Find.match(*paths) { |p| File.lstat(p).size > bytes }
end

# Finds all files modified more recently than a certain number of seconds ago.
def modified_recently(seconds, *paths)
  time = Time.now - seconds
  Find.match(*paths) { |p| File.lstat(p).mtime > time }
end

# Finds all files that haven't been accessed since they were last modified.
def possibly_abandoned(*paths)
  Find.match(*paths) { |p| f = File.lstat(p); f.mtime == f.atime }
end
```

See Also

- Recipe 6.12, "Walking a Directory Tree"

6.21 Finding and Changing the Current Working Directory

Problem

You want to see which directory the Ruby process considers its current working directory, or change that directory.

Solution

To find the current working directory, use `Dir.getwd`:

```
Dir.getwd                        # => "/home/leonardr"
```

To change the current working directory, use `Dir.chdir`:

```
Dir.chdir("/bin")
Dir.getwd                        # => "/bin"
File.exists? "ls"                # => true
```

Discussion

The current working directory of a Ruby process starts out as the directory you were in when you started the Ruby interpreter. When you refer to a file without providing an absolute pathname, Ruby assumes you want a file by that name in the current working directory. Ruby also checks the current working directory when you require a library that can't be found anywhere else.

The current working directory is a useful default. If you're writing a Ruby script that operates on a directory tree, you might start from the current working directory if the user doesn't specify one.

However, you shouldn't rely on the current working directory being set to any particular value: this makes scripts brittle, and prone to break when run from a different directory. If your Ruby script comes bundled with libraries, or needs to load additional files from subdirectories of the script directory, you should set the working directory in code.

You can change the working directory as often as necessary, but it's more reliable to use absolute pathnames, even though this can make your code less portable. This is especially true if you're writing multithreaded code.

The current working directory is global to a process. If multiple threads are running code that changes the working directory to different values, you'll never know for sure what the working directory is at any given moment.

See Also

- Recipe 6.18, "Deleting a File," shows some problems created by a process-global working directory

CHAPTER 7

Code Blocks and Iteration

In Ruby, a code block (or just "block") is an object that contains some Ruby code, and the context neccesary to execute it. Code blocks are the most visually distinctive aspect of Ruby, and also one of the most confusing to newcomers from other languages. Essentially, a Ruby code block is a method that has no name.

Most other languages have something like a Ruby code block: C's function pointers, C++'s function objects, Python's lambdas and list comprehensions, Perl's anonymous functions, Java's anonymous inner classes. These features live mostly in the corners of those languages, shunned by novice programmers. Ruby can't be written without code blocks. Of the major languages, only Lisp is more block-oriented.

Unlike most other languages, Ruby makes code blocks easy to create and imposes few restrictions on them. In every other chapter of this book, you'll see blocks passed into methods like it's no big deal (which it isn't):

```
[1,2,3].each { |i| puts i}
# 1
# 2
# 3
```

In this chapter, we'll show you how to write that kind of method, the kinds of method that are useful to write that way, and when and how to treat blocks as first-class objects.

Ruby provides two syntaxes for creating code blocks. When the entire block will fit on one line, it's most readable when enclosed in curly braces:

```
[1,2,3].each { |i| puts i }
# 1
# 2
# 3
```

When the block is longer than one line, it's more readable to begin it with the do keyword and end it with the end keyword:

```
[1,2,3].each do |i|
  if i % 2 == 0
```

```
    puts "#{i} is even."
  else
    puts "#{i} is odd."
  end
end
# 1 is odd.
# 2 is even.
# 3 is odd.
```

Some people use the bracket syntax when they're interested in the return value of the block, and the do...end syntax when they're interested in the block's side effects.

Keep in mind that the bracket syntax has a higher precedence than the do..end syntax. Consider the following two snippets of code:

```
1.upto 3 do |x|
  puts x
end
# 1
# 2
# 3

1.upto 3 { |x| puts x }
# SyntaxError: compile error
```

In the second example, the code block binds to the number 3, not to the function call 1.upto 3. A standalone variable can't take a code block, so you get a compile error. When in doubt, use parentheses.

```
1.upto(3) { |x| puts x }
# 1
# 2
# 3
```

Usually the code blocks passed into methods are anonymous objects, created on the spot. But you can instantiate a code block as a Proc object by calling lambda. See Recipe 7.1 for more details.

```
hello = lambda { "Hello" }
hello.call
# => "Hello"

log = lambda { |str| puts "[LOG] #{str}" }
log.call("A test log message.")
# [LOG] A test log message.
```

Like any method, a block can accept arguments. A block's arguments are defined in a comma-separated list at the beginning of the block, enclosed in pipe characters:

```
{1=>2, 2=>4}.each { |k,v| puts "Key #{k}, value #{v}" }
# Key 1, value 2
# Key 2, value 4
```

Arguments to blocks look almost like arguments to methods, but there are a few restrictions: you can't set default values for block arguments, you can't expand hashes or arrays inline, and a block cannot itself take a block argument.*

Since `Proc` objects are created like other objects, you can create factory methods whose return values are customized pieces of executable Ruby code. Here's a simple factory method for code blocks that do multiplication:

```
def times_n(n)
  lambda { |x| x * n }
end
```

The following code uses the factory to create and use two customized methods:

```
times_ten = times_n(10)
times_ten.call(5)                              # => 50
times_ten.call(1.25)                           # => 12.5

circumference = times_n(2*Math::PI)
circumference.call(10)        # => 62.8318530717959
circumference.call(3)                          # => 18.8495559215388
[1, 2, 3].collect(&circumference)
# => [6.28318530717959, 12.5663706143592, 18.8495559215388]
```

You may have heard people talking about Ruby's "closures." What is a closure, and how is it different from a block? In Ruby, there is no difference between closures and blocks. Every Ruby block is also a closure.†

So what makes a Ruby block a closure? Basically, a Ruby block carries around the context in which it was defined. A block can reference the variables that were in scope when it was defined, even if those variables later go out of scope. Here's a simple example; see Recipe 7.4 for more.

```
ceiling = 50
# Which of these numbers are less than the target?
[1, 10, 49, 50.1, 200].select { |x| x < ceiling }
# => [1, 10, 49]
```

The variable ceiling is within scope when the block is defined, but it goes out of scope when the flow of execution enters the select method. Nonetheless, the block can access ceiling from within select, because it carries its context around with it. That's what makes it a closure.

We suspect that a lot of people who say "closures" when talking about Ruby blocks just do it to sound smart. Since we've already ruined any chance we might have had

---

* In Ruby 1.9, a block can itself take a block argument: |arg1, arg2, &block|. This makes methods like Module#define_method more useful. In Ruby 2.0, you'll be able to give default values to block arguments.

† Someone could argue that a block isn't *really* a closure if it never actually uses any of the context it carries around: you could have done the same job with a "dumb" block, assuming Ruby supported those. For simplicity's sake, we do not argue this.

at sounding smart, we've decided refer to Ruby closures as just plain "blocks" throughout this book. The only exceptions are in the rare places where we must discuss the context that makes Ruby's code blocks real closures, rather than "dumb" blocks.

7.1   Creating and Invoking a Block

Problem

You want to put some Ruby code into an object so you can pass it around and call it later.

Solution

By this time, you should familiar with a block as some Ruby code enclosed in curly brackets. You might think it possible to define a block object as follows:

```
aBlock = { |x| puts x }              # WRONG

# SyntaxError: compile error
```

That doesn't work because a block is only valid Ruby syntax when it's an argument to a method call. There are several equivalent methods that take a block and return it as an object. The most favored method is Kernel#lambda:*

```
aBlock = lambda { |x| puts x }        # RIGHT
```

To call the block, use the call method:

```
aBlock.call "Hello World!"
# Hello World!
```

Discussion

The ability to assign a bit of Ruby code to a variable is very powerful. It lets you write general frameworks and plug in specific pieces of code at the crucial points.

As you'll find out in Recipe 7.2, you can accept a block as an argument to a method by prepending & to the argument name. This way, you can write your own trivial version of the lambda method:

```
def my_lambda(&aBlock)
  aBlock
end

b = my_lambda { puts "Hello World My Way!" }
b.call
# Hello World My Way!
```

---

* The name lambda comes from the lambda calculus (a mathematical formal system) via Lisp.

A newly defined block is actually a Proc object.

```
b.class                              # => Proc
```

You can also initialize blocks with the Proc constructor or the method Kernel#proc. The methods Kernel#lambda, Kernel#proc, and Proc.new all do basically the same thing. These three lines of code are nearly equivalent:

```
aBlock = Proc.new { |x| puts x }
aBlock = proc { |x| puts x }
aBlock = lambda { |x| puts x }
```

What's the difference? Kernel#lambda is the preferred way of creating block objects, because it gives you block objects that act more like Ruby methods. Consider what happens when you call a block with the wrong number of arguments:

```
add_lambda = lambda { |x,y| x + y }

add_lambda.call(4)
# ArgumentError: wrong number of arguments (1 for 2)

add_lambda.call(4,5,6)
# ArgumentError: wrong number of arguments (3 for 2)
```

A block created with lambda acts like a Ruby method. If you don't specify the right number of arguments, you can't call the block. But a block created with Proc.new acts like the anonymous code block you pass into a method like Enumerable#each:

```
add_procnew = Proc.new { |x,y| x + y }

add_procnew.call(4)
# TypeError: nil can't be coerced into Fixnum

add_procnew.call(4,5,6)                          # => 9
```

If you don't specify enough arguments when you call the block, the rest of the arguments are given nil. If you specify too many arguments, the extra arguments are ignored. Unless you want this kind of behavior, use lambda.

In Ruby 1.8, Kernel#proc acts like Kernel#lambda. In Ruby 1.9, Kernel#proc acts like Proc.new, as better befits its name.

See Also

- Recipe 7.2, "Writing a Method That Accepts a Block"
- Recipe 10.4, "Getting a Reference to a Method"

7.2 Writing a Method That Accepts a Block

Problem

You want to write a method that can accept and call an attached code block: a method that works like Array#each, Fixnum#upto, and other built-in Ruby methods.

Solution

You don't need to do anything special to make your method capable of accepting a block. Any method can use a block if the caller passes one in. At any time in your method, you can call the block with yield:

```ruby
def call_twice
  puts "I'm about to call your block."
  yield
  puts "I'm about to call your block again."
  yield
end

call_twice { puts "Hi, I'm a talking code block." }
# I'm about to call your block.
# Hi, I'm a talking code block.
# I'm about to call your block again.
# Hi, I'm a talking code block.
```

Another example:

```ruby
def repeat(n)
  if block_given?
    n.times { yield }
  else
    raise ArgumentError.new("I can't repeat a block you don't give me!")
  end
end

repeat(4) { puts "Hello." }
# Hello.
# Hello.
# Hello.
# Hello.

repeat(4)
# ArgumentError: I can't repeat a block you don't give me!
```

Discussion

Since Ruby focuses so heavily on iterator methods and other methods that accept code blocks, it's important to know how to use code blocks in your own methods.

You don't have to do anything special to make your method capable of taking a code block. A caller can pass a code block into *any* Ruby method; it's just that there's no point in doing that if the method never invokes yield.

```ruby
puts("Print this message.") { puts "And also run this code block!" }
# Print this message.
```

The yield keyword acts like a special method, a stand-in for whatever code block was passed in. When you call it, it's exactly as the code block were a Proc object and you had invoked its call method.

This may seem mysterious if you're unfamiliar with the practice of passing blocks around, but it is usually the preferred method of calling blocks in Ruby. If you feel more comfortable receiving a code block as a "real" argument to your method, see Recipe 7.3.

You can pass in arguments to `yield` (they'll be passed to the block) and you can do things with the value of the `yield` statement (this is the value of the last statement in the block).

Here's a method that passes arguments into its code block, and uses the value of the block:

```
def call_twice
  puts "Calling your block."
  ret1 = yield("very first")
  puts "The value of your block: #{ret1}"

  puts "Calling your block again."
  ret2 = yield("second")
  puts "The value of your block: #{ret2}"
end

call_twice do |which_time|
  puts "I'm a code block, called for the #{which_time} time."
  which_time == "very first" ? 1 : 2
end
# Calling your block.
# I'm a code block, called for the very first time.
# The value of your block: 1
# Calling your block again.
# I'm a code block, called for the second time.
# The value of your block: 2
```

Here's a more realistic example. The method `Hash#find` takes a code block, passes each of a hash's key-value pairs into the code block, and returns the first key-value pair for which the code block evaluates to true.

```
squares = {0=>0, 1=>1, 2=>4, 3=>9}
squares.find { |key, value| key > 1 }          # => [2, 4]
```

Suppose we want a method that works like `Hash#find`, but returns a new hash containing *all* the key-value pairs for which the code block evaluates to true. We can do this by passing arguments into the `yield` statement and using its result:

```
class Hash
  def find_all
    new_hash = Hash.new
    each { |k,v| new_hash[k] = v if yield(k, v) }
    new_hash
  end
end

squares.find_all { |key, value| key > 1 }          # => {2=>4, 3=>9}
```

As it turns out, the Hash#delete_if method already does the inverse of what we want. By negating the result of our code block, we can make Hash#delete_if do the job of Hash#find_all. We just need to work off of a duplicate of our hash, because delete_if is a destructive method:

```
squares.dup.delete_if { |key, value| key > 1 }   # => {0=>0, 1=>1}
squares.dup.delete_if { |key, value| key <= 1 }  # => {2=>4, 3=>9}
```

Hash#find_all turns out to be unnecessary, but it made for a good example.

You can write a method that takes an *optional* code block by calling Kernel#block_given? from within your method. That method returns true only if the caller of your method passed in a code block. If it returns false, you can raise an exception, or you can fall back to behavior that doesn't need a block and never uses the yield keyword.

If your method calls yield and the caller didn't pass in a code block, Ruby will throw an exception:

```
[1, 2, 3].each
# LocalJumpError: no block given
```

See Also

- Recipe 7.3, "Binding a Block Argument to a Variable"

7.3   Binding a Block Argument to a Variable

Problem

You've written a method that takes a code block, but it's not enough for you to simply call the block with yield. You need to somehow bind the code block to a variable, so you can manipulate the block directly. Most likely, you need to pass it as the code block to another method.

Solution

Put the name of the block variable at the end of the list of your method's arguments. Prefix it with an ampersand so that Ruby knows it's a block argument, not a regular argument.

An incoming code block will be converted into a Proc object and bound to the block variable. You can pass it around to other methods, call it directly using call, or yield to it as though you'd never bound it to a variable at all. All three of the following methods do exactly the same thing:

```
def repeat(n)
  n.times { yield } if block_given?
end
repeat(2) { puts "Hello." }
# Hello.
# Hello.
```

```
def repeat(n, &block)
  n.times { block.call } if block
end
repeat(2) { puts "Hello." }
# Hello.
# Hello.

def repeat(n, &block)
  n.times { yield } if block
end
repeat(2) { puts "Hello." }
# Hello.
# Hello.
```

Discussion

If &foo is the name of a method's last argument, it means that the method accepts an optional block named foo. If the caller chooses to pass in a block, it will be made available as a Proc object bound to the variable foo. Since it is an optional argument, foo will be nil if no block is actually passed in. This frees you from having to call Kernel#block_given? to see whether or not you got a block.

When you call a method, you can pass in any Proc object as the code block by prefixing the appropriate variable name with an ampersand. You can even do this on a Proc object that was originally passed in as a code block to your method.

Many methods for collections, like each, select, and detect, accept code blocks. It's easy to wrap such methods when your own methods can bind a block to a variable. Here, a method called biggest finds the largest element of a collection that gives a true result for the given block:

```
def biggest(collection, &block)
  block ? collection.select(&block).max : collection.max
end

array = [1, 2, 3, 4, 5]
biggest(array) {|i| i < 3}          # => 2
biggest(array) {|i| i != 5 }        # => 4
biggest(array)                      # => 5
```

This is also very useful when you need to write a frontend to a method that takes a block. Your wrapper method can bind an incoming code block to a variable, then pass it as a code block to the other method.

This code calls a code block limit times, each time passing in a random number between min and max:

```
def pick_random_numbers(min, max, limit)
  limit.times { yield min+rand(max+1) }
end
```

This code is a wrapper method for `pick_random_numbers`. It calls a code block 6 times, each time with a random number from 1 to 49:

```
def lottery_style_numbers(&block)
  pick_random_numbers(1, 49, 6, &block)
end

lottery_style_numbers { |n| puts "Lucky number: #{n}" }
# Lucky number: 20
# Lucky number: 39
# Lucky number: 41
# Lucky number: 10
# Lucky number: 41
# Lucky number: 32
```

The code block argument must always be the very last argument defined for a method. This means that if your method takes a variable number of arguments, the code block argument goes *after* the container for the variable arguments:

```
def invoke_on_each(*args, &block)
  args.each { |arg| yield arg }
end

invoke_on_each(1, 2, 3, 4) { |x| puts x ** 2 }
# 1
# 4
# 9
# 16
```

See Also

- Recipe 8.11, "Accepting or Passing a Variable Number of Arguments"
- Recall from the chapter introduction that in Ruby 1.8, a code block cannot itself take a block argument; this is fixed in Ruby 1.9

7.4 Blocks as Closures: Using Outside Variables Within a Code Block

Problem

You want to share variables between a method, and a code block defined within it.

Solution

Just reference the variables, and Ruby will do the right thing. Here's a method that adds a certain number to every element of an array:

```
def add_to_all(array, number)
  array.collect { |x| x + number }
end

add_to_all([1, 2, 3], 10)                # => [11, 12, 13]
```

Enumerable#collect can't access number directly, but it's passed a block that can access it, since number was in scope when the block was defined.

Discussion

A Ruby block is a *closure*: it carries around the context in which it was defined. This is useful because it lets you define a block as though it were part of your normal code, then tear it off and send it to a predefined piece of code for processing.

A Ruby block contains references to the variable bindings, not copies of the values. If the variable changes later, the block will have access to the new value:

```
tax_percent = 6
position = lambda do
  "I have always supported a #{tax_percent}% tax on imported limes."
end
position.call
# => "I have always supported a 6% tax on imported limes."

tax_percent = 7.25
position.call
# => "I have always supported a 7.25% tax on imported limes."
```

This works both ways: you can rebind or modify a variable from within a block.

```
counter = 0
4.times { counter += 1; puts "Counter now #{counter}"}
# Counter now 1
# Counter now 2
# Counter now 3
# Counter now 4
counter                                          # => 4
```

This is especially useful when you want to simulate inject or collect in conjunction with a strange iterator. You can create a storage object outside the block, and add things to it from within the block. This code simulates Enumerable#collect, but it collects the elements of an array in reverse order:

```
accumulator = []
[1, 2, 3].reverse_each { |x| accumulator << x + 1 }

accumulator              # => [4, 3, 2]
```

The accumulator variable is not within the scope of Array#reverse_each, but it is within the scope of the block.

7.5   Writing an Iterator Over a Data Structure

Problem

You've created a custom data structure, and you want to implement an each method for it, or you want to implement an unusual way of iterating over an existing data structure.

Solution

Complex data structures are usually constructed out of the basic data structures: hashes, arrays, and so on. All of the basic data structures have defined the each method. If your data structure is composed entirely of scalar values and these simple data structures, you can write a new each method in terms of the each methods of its components.

Here's a simple tree data structure. A tree contains a single value, and a list of children (each of which is a smaller tree).

```
class Tree
  attr_reader :value
  def initialize(value)
    @value = value
    @children = []
  end

  def <<(value)
    subtree = Tree.new(value)
    @children << subtree
    return subtree
  end
end
```

Here's code to create a specific Tree (Figure 7-1):

```
t = Tree.new("Parent")
child1 = t << "Child 1"
child1 << "Grandchild 1.1"
child1 << "Grandchild 1.2"
child2 = t << "Child 2"
child2 << "Grandchild 2.1"
```

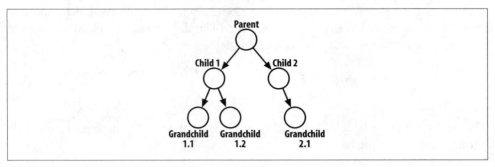

Figure 7-1. A simple tree

How can we iterate over this data structure? Since a tree is defined recursively, it makes sense to iterate over it recursively. This implementation of Tree#each yields the value stored in the tree, then iterates over its children (the children are stored in an array, which already supports each) and recursively calls Tree#each on every child tree.

```ruby
class Tree
  def each
    yield value
    @children.each do |child_node|
      child_node.each { |e| yield e }
    end
  end
end
```

The each method traverses the tree in a way that looks right:

```ruby
t.each { |x| puts x }
# Parent
# Child 1
# Grandchild 1.1
# Grandchild 1.2
# Child 2
# Grandchild 2.1
```

Discussion

The simplest way to build an iterator is recursively: to use smaller iterators until you've covered every element in your data structure. But what if those iterators aren't there? More likely, what if they're there but they give you elements in the wrong order? You'll need to go down a level and write some loops.

Loops are somewhat declassé in Ruby because iterators are more idiomatic, but when you're *writing* an iterator you may have no choice but to use a loop. Here's a reprint of an iterator from Recipe 4.1, which illustrates how to use a while loop to iterate over an array from both sides:

```ruby
class Array
  def each_from_both_sides()
    front_index = 0
    back_index = self.length-1
    while front_index <= back_index
      yield self[front_index]
      front_index += 1
      if front_index <= back_index
        yield self[back_index]
        back_index -= 1
      end
    end
  end
end

%w{Curses! been again! foiled I've}.each_from_both_sides { |x| puts x }
# Curses!
# I've
# been
# foiled
# again!
```

Here are two more simple iterators. The first one yields each element multiple times in a row:

```
module Enumerable
  def each_n_times(n)
    each { |e| n.times { yield e } }
  end
end

%w{Hello Echo}.each_n_times(3) { |x| puts x }
# Hello
# Hello
# Hello
# Echo
# Echo
# Echo
```

The next one returns the elements of an Enumerable in random order; see Recipe 4.10 for a more efficient way to do the shuffling.

```
module Enumerable
  def each_randomly
    (sort_by { rand }).each { |e| yield e }
  end
end
%w{Eat at Joe's}.each_randomly { |x| puts x }
# Eat
# Joe's
# at
```

See Also

- Recipe 4.1, "Iterating Over an Array"
- Recipe 4.10, "Shuffling an Array"
- Recipe 5.7, "Iterating Over a Hash"
- Recipe 7.6, "Changing the Way an Object Iterates"
- Recipe 7.8, "Stopping an Iteration"
- Recipe 7.9, "Looping Through Multiple Iterables in Parallel"

7.6 Changing the Way an Object Iterates

Problem

You want to use a data structure as an Enumerable, but the object's implementation of #each doesn't iterate the way you want. Since all of Enumerable's methods are based on each, this makes them all useless to you.

Discussion

Here's a concrete example: a simple array.

```
array = %w{bob loves alice}
array.collect { |x| x.capitalize }
# => ["Bob", "Loves", "Alice"]
```

Suppose we want to call collect on this array, but we don't want collect to use each: we want it to use reverse_each. Something like this hypothetical collect_reverse method:

```
array.collect_reverse { |x| x.capitalize }
# => ["Alice", "Loves", "Bob"]
```

Actually defining a collect_reverse method would add significant new code and only solve part of the problem. We could overwrite the array's each implementation with a singleton method that calls reverse_each, but that's hacky and it would surely have undesired side effects.

Fortunately, there's an elegant solution with no side effects: wrap the object in an Enumerator. This gives you a new object that acts like the old object would if you'd swapped out its each method:

```
require 'enumerator'
reversed_array = array.to_enum(:reverse_each)
reversed_array.collect { |x| x.capitalize }
# => ["Alice", "Loves", "Bob"]

reversed_array.each_with_index do |x, i|
  puts %{#{i}=>"#{x}"}
end
# 0=>"alice"
# 1=>"loves"
# 2=>"bob"
```

Note that you can't use the Enumerator for our array as though it were the actual array. Only the methods of Enumerable are supported:

```
reversed_array[0]
# NoMethodError: undefined method `[]' for #<Enumerable::Enumerator:0xb7c2cc8c>
```

Discussion

Whenever you're tempted to reimplement one of the methods of Enumerable, try using an Enumerator instead. It's like modifying an object's each method, but it doesn't affect the original object.

This can save you a lot of work. Suppose you have a tree data structure that provides three different iteration styles: each_prefix, each_postfix, and each_infix. Rather than implementing the methods of Enumerable for all three iteration styles, you can let each_prefix be the default implementation of each, and call tree.to_enum(:each_postfix) or tree.to_enum(:each_infix) if you need an Enumerable that acts differently.

A single underlying object can have multiple `Enumerable` objects. Here's a second `Enumerable` for our simple array, in which each acts like `each_with_index` does for the original array:

```
array_with_index = array.enum_with_index
array_with_index.each do |x, i|
  puts %{#{i}=>"#{x}"}
end
# 0=>"bob"
# 1=>"loves"
# 2=>"alice"

array_with_index.each_with_index do |x, i|
  puts %{#{i}=>#{x.inspect}}
end
# 0=>["bob", 0]
# 1=>["loves", 1]
# 2=>["alice", 2]
```

When you require `'enumerator'`, `Enumerable` sprouts two extra enumeration methods, `each_cons` and `each_slice`. These make it easy to iterate over a data structure in chunks. An example is the best way to show what they do:

```
sentence = %w{Well, now I've seen everything!}

two_word_window = sentence.to_enum(:each_cons, 2)
two_word_window.each { |x| puts x.inspect }
# ["Well,", "now"]
# ["now", "I've"]
# ["I've", "seen"]
# ["seen", "everything!"]

two_words_at_a_time = sentence.to_enum(:each_slice, 2)
two_words_at_a_time.each { |x| puts x.inspect }
# ["Well,", "now"]
# ["I've", "seen"]
# ["everything!"]
```

Note how any arguments passed into `to_enum` are passed along as arguments to the iteration method itself.

In Ruby 1.9, the `Enumerable::Enumerator` class is part of the Ruby core; you don't need the require statement. Also, `each_cons` and `each_slice` are built-in methods of `Enumerable`.

See Also

- Recipe 7.9, "Looping Through Multiple Iterables in Parallel"
- Recipe 20.6, "Running a Code Block on Many Objects Simultaneously"

7.7   Writing Block Methods That Classify or Collect

Problem

The basic block methods that come with the Ruby standard library aren't enough for you. You want to define your own method that classifies the elements in an enumeration (like Enumerable#detect and Enumerable#find_all), or that does a transformation on each element in an enumeration (like Enumerable#collect).

Solution

You can usually use inject to write a method that searches or classifies an enumeration of objects. With inject you can write your own versions of methods such as detect and find_all:

```
module Enumerable
  def find_no_more_than(limit)
    inject([]) do |a,e|
      a << e if yield e
      return a if a.size >= limit
      a
    end
  end
end
```

This code finds at most three of the even numbers in a list:

```
a = [1, 2, 3, 4, 5, 6, 7, 8, 9, 10]
a.find_no_more_than(3) { |x| x % 2 == 0 }          # => [2, 4, 6]
```

If you find yourself needing to write a method like collect, it's probably because, for your purposes, collect itself yields elements in the wrong order. You can't use inject, because that yields elements in the same order as collect.

You need to find or write an iterator that yields elements in the order you want. Once you've done that, you have two options: you can write a collect equivalent on top of the iterator method, or you can use the iterator method to build an Enumerable object, and call its collect method (as seen in Recipe 7.6).

Discussion

We discussed these block methods in more detail in Chapter 4, because arrays are the simplest and most common enumerable data type, and the most common. But almost any data structure can be enumerated, and a more complex data structure can be enumerated in more different ways.

As you'll see in Recipe 9.4, the Enumerable methods, like detect and inject, are actually implemented in terms of each. The detect and inject methods yield to the code block every element that comes out of each. The value of the yield statement is used to determine whether the element matches some criteria.

In a method like detect, the iteration may stop once it finds an element that matches. In a method like find_all, the iteration goes through all elements, collecting the ones that match.

Methods like collect work the same way, but instead of returning a subset of elements based on what the code block says, they collect the values returned by the code block in a new data structure, and return the data structure once the iteration is completed.

If you're using a particular object and you wish its collect method used a different iterator, then you should turn the object into an Enumerator and call its collect method. But if you're writing a class and you want to expose a new collect-like method, you'll have to define a new method.* In that case, the best solution is probably to expose a method that returns a custom Enumerator: that way, your users can use all the methods of Enumerable, not just collect.

See Also

- Recipe 4.5, "Sorting an Array"
- Recipe 4.11, "Getting the N Smallest Items of an Array"
- Recipe 4.15, "Partitioning or Classifying a Set"
- Recipe 7.6, "Changing the Way an Object Iterates"
- If all you want is to make your custom data structure support the methods of Enumerable, see Recipe 9.4, "Implementing Enumerable: Write One Method, Get 22 Free"

7.8   Stopping an Iteration

Problem

You want to interrupt an iteration from within the code block you passed into it.

Solution

The simplest way to interrupt execution is to use break. A break statement will jump out of the closest enclosing loop defined in the current method:

```
1.upto(10) do |x|
  puts x
  break if x == 3
end
# 1
# 2
# 3
```

---

* Of course, behind the scenes, your method could just create an appropriate Enumerator and call its collect implemenation.

Discussion

The break statement is simple but it has several limitations. You can't use break within a code block defined with Proc.new or (in Ruby 1.9 and up) Kernel#proc. If this is a problem for you, use lambda instead:

```
aBlock = Proc.new do |x|
  puts x
  break if x == 3
  puts x + 2
end

aBlock.call(5)
# 5
# 7

aBlock.call(3)
# 3
# LocalJumpError: break from proc-closure
```

More seriously, you can't use break to jump out of multiple loops at once. Once a loop has run, there's no way to know whether it completed normally or by using break.

The simplest way around this problem is to enclose the code you want to skip within a catch block with a descriptive symbolic name. You can then throw the corresponding symbol when you want to jump to the end of the catch block. This lets you skip out of any number of nested loops and method calls.

The throw/catch syntax isn't exception handling—exceptions use a raise/rescue syntax. This is a special flow control construct designed to replace the use of exceptions for flow control (as sometimes happens in Java programs). It's a bit like an old-style global GOTO, capable of suddenly moving execution to a faraway part of your program. It keeps your code more readable than a GOTO, though, because it's restricted: a throw can only jump to the end of a corresponding catch block.

The best example of the catch..throw syntax is the Find.find function described in Recipe 6.12. When you pass a code block into Find.find, it yields up every directory and file in a certain directory tree. When your code block is given a directory, it can stop find from recursing into that directory by calling Find.prune, which throws a :prune symbol. Using break would stop the find operation altogether; throwing a symbol lets Find.prune know to just skip one directory.

Here's a simplified view of the Find.find and Find.prune code:

```
def find(*paths)
  paths.each do |p|
    catch(:prune) do
      # Process p as a file or directory...
    end
    # When you call Find.prune you'll end up here.
```

```
    end
  end

  def prune
    throw :prune
  end
```

When you call `Find.prune`, execution jumps to immediately after the `catch(:prune)` block. `Find.find` then starts processing the next file or directory.

See Also

- Recipe 6.12, "Walking a Directory Tree"
- `ri Find`

7.9   Looping Through Multiple Iterables in Parallel

Problem

You want to traverse multiple iteration methods simultaneously, probably to match up the corresponding elements in several different arrays.

Solution

The `SyncEnumerator` class, defined in the generator library, makes it easy to iterate over a bunch of arrays or other `Enumerable` objects in parallel. Its each method yields a series of arrays, each array containing one item from each underlying `Enumerable` object:

```
require 'generator'

enumerator = SyncEnumerator.new(%w{Four seven}, %w{score years},
                                %w{and ago})
enumerator.each do |row|
  row.each { |word| puts word }
  puts '---'
end
# Four
# score
# and
# ---
# seven
# years
# ago
# ---

enumerator = SyncEnumerator.new(%w{Four and}, %w{score seven years ago})
enumerator.each do |row|
  row.each { |word| puts word }
  puts '---'
end
# Four
```

```
# score
# ---
# and
# seven
# ---
# nil
# years
# ---
# nil
# ago
# ---
```

You can reproduce the workings of a SyncEnumerator by wrapping each of your Enumerable objects in a Generator object. This code acts like SyncEnumerator#each, only it yields each individual item instead of arrays containing one item from each Enumerable:

```ruby
def interosculate(*enumerables)
  generators = enumerables.collect { |x| Generator.new(x) }
  done = false
  until done
    done = true
    generators.each do |g|
      if g.next?
        yield g.next
        done = false
      end
    end
  end
end

interosculate(%w{Four and}, %w{score seven years ago}) do |x|
  puts x
end
# Four
# score
# and
# seven
# years
# ago
```

Discussion

Any object that implements the each method can be wrapped in a Generator object. If you've used Java, think of a Generator as being like a Java Iterator object. It keeps track of where you are in a particular iteration over a data structure.

Normally, when you pass a block into an iterator method like each, that block gets called for every element in the iterator without interruption. No code outside the block will run until the iterator is done iterating. You can stop the iteration by writing a break statement inside the code block, but you can't restart a broken iteration later from the same place—unless you use a Generator.

Think of an iterator method like each as a candy dispenser that pours out all its candy in a steady stream once you push the button. The Generator class lets you turn that candy dispenser into one which dispenses only one piece of candy every time you push its button. You can carry this new dispenser around and ration your candy more easily.

In Ruby 1.8, the Generator class uses continuations to achieve this trick. It sets bookmarks for jumping out of an iteration and then back in. When you call Generator#next the generator "pumps" the iterator once (yielding a single element), sets a bookmark, and returns control back to your code. The next time you call Generator#next, the generator jumps back to its previously set bookmark and "pumps" the iterator once more.

Ruby 1.9 uses a more efficient implementation based on threads. This implementation calls each Enumerable object's each method (triggering the neverending stream of candy), but it does it in a separate thread for each object. After each piece of candy comes out, Ruby freezes time (pauses the thread) until the next time you call Generator#next.

It's simple to wrap an array in a generator, but if that's all there were to generators, you wouldn't need to mess around with Generators or even SyncEnumerables. It's easy to simulate the behavior of SyncEnumerable for arrays by starting an index into each array and incrementing it whenever you want to get another item from a particular array. Generator methods are truly useful in their ability to turn *any* type of iteration into a single-item candy dispenser.

Suppose that you want to use the functionality of a generator to iterate over an array, but you have an unusual type of iteration in mind. For instance, consider an array that looks like this:

```
l = ["junk1", 1, "junk2", 2, "junk3", "junk4", 3, "junk5"]
```

Let's say you'd like to iterate over the list but skip the "junk" entries. Wrapping the list in a generator object doesn't work; it gives you all the entries:

```
g = Generator.new(l)
g.next                         # => "junk1"
g.next                         # => 1
g.next                         # => "junk2"
```

It's not difficult to write an iterator method that skips the junk. Now, we don't want an iterator method—we want a Generator object—but the iterator method is a good starting point. At least it proves that the iteration we want can be implemented in Ruby.

```
def l.my_iterator
  each { |e| yield e unless e =~ /^junk/ }
end

l.my_iterator { |x| puts x }
```

```
# 1
# 2
# 3
```

Here's the twist: when you wrap an array in a `Generator` or a `SyncEnumerable` object, you're actually wrapping the array's each method. The `Generator` doesn't just happen to yield elements in the same order as each: it's actually calling each, but using continuation (or thread) trickery to pause the iteration after each call to `Generator#next`.

By defining an appropriate code block and passing it into the `Generator` constructor, you can make a generation object of out of any piece of iteration code—not only the each method. The generator will know to call and interrupt that block of code, just as it knows to call and interrupt each when you pass an array into the constructor. Here's a generator that iterates over our array the way we want:

```
g = Generator.new { |g| l.each { |e| g.yield e unless e =~ /^junk/ } }
g.next                                       # => 1
g.next                                       # => 2
g.next                                       # => 3
```

The `Generator` constructor can take a code block that accepts the generator object itself as an argument. This code block performs the iteration that you'd like to have wrapped in a generator. Note the basic similarity of the code block to the body of the `l#my_iterator` method. The only difference is that instead of the `yield` keyword we call the `Generator#yield` function, which handles some of the work involved with setting up and jumping to the continuations (`Generator#next` handles the rest of the continuation work).

Once you see how this works, you can eliminate some duplicate code by wrapping the `l#my_iterator` method itself in a `Generator`:

```
g = Generator.new { |g| l.my_iterator { |e| g.yield e } }
g.next                                       # => 1
g.next                                       # => 2
g.next                                       # => 3
```

Here's a version of the `interosculate` method that can wrap methods as well as arrays. It accepts any combination of `Enumerable` objects and `Method` objects, turns each one into a `Generator` object, and loops through all the `Generator` objects, getting one element at a time from each:

```
def interosculate(*iterables)
  generators = iterables.collect do |x|
    if x.is_a? Method
      Generator.new { |g| x.call { |e| g.yield e } }
    else
      Generator.new(x)
    end
  end
  done = false
  until done
```

```
      done = true
      generators.each do |g|
        if g.next?
          yield g.next
          done = false
        end
      end
    end
  end
```

Here, we pass interosculate an array and a Method object, so that we can iterate through two arrays in opposite directions:

```
words1 = %w{Four and years}
words2 = %w{ago seven score}
interosculate(words1, words2.method(:reverse_each)) { |x| puts x }
# Four
# score
# and
# seven
# years
# ago
```

See Also

- Recipe 7.5, "Writing an Iterator Over a Data Structure"
- Recipe 7.6, "Changing the Way an Object Iterates"

7.10   Hiding Setup and Cleanup in a Block Method

Problem

You have a setup method that always needs to run before custom code, or a cleanup method that needs to run afterwards. You don't trust the person writing the code (possibly yourself) to remember to call the setup and cleanup methods.

Solution

Create a method that runs the setup code, yields to a code block (which contains the custom code), then runs the cleanup code. To make sure the cleanup code always runs, even if the custom code throws an exception, use a begin/finally block.

```
def between_setup_and_cleanup
  setup
  begin
    yield
  finally
    cleanup
  end
end
```

Here's a concrete example. It adds a DOCTYPE and an HTML tag to the beginning of an HTML document. At the end, it closes the HTML tag it opened earlier. This saves you a little bit of work when you're generating HTML files.

```
def write_html(out, doctype=nil)
  doctype ||= %{<!DOCTYPE HTML PUBLIC "-//W3C//DTD HTML 4.01 Transitional//EN"
          "http://www.w3.org/TR/html4/loose.dtd">}
  out.puts doctype
  out.puts '<html>'
  begin
    yield out
  ensure
    out.puts '</html>'
  end
end

write_html($stdout) do |out|
  out.puts '<h1>Sorry, the Web is closed.</h1>'
end
# <!DOCTYPE HTML PUBLIC "-//W3C//DTD HTML 4.01 Transitional//EN"
#      "http://www.w3.org/TR/html4/loose.dtd">
# <html>
# <h1>Sorry, the Web is closed.</h1>
# </html>
```

Discussion

This useful technique shows up most often when there are scarce resources (such as file handles or database connections) that *must* be closed when you're done with them, lest they all get used up. A language that makes the programmer remember these resources tends to leak those resources, because programmers are lazy. Ruby makes it easy to be lazy and still do the right thing.

You've probably used this technique already, with the the Kernel#open and File#open methods for opening files on disk. These methods accept a code block that manipulates an already open file. They open the file, call your code block, and close the file once you're done:

```
open('output.txt', 'w') do |out|
  out.puts 'Sorry, the filesystem is also closed.'
end
```

Ruby's standard cgi module takes the write_html example to its logical conclusion.[*] You can construct an entire HTML document by nesting blocks inside each other. Here's a small Ruby CGI that outputs much the same document as the write_html example above.

```
#!/usr/bin/ruby

# closed_cgi.rb
```

---

[*] But your code will be more maintainable if you do HTML with templates instead of writing it in Ruby code.

```
require 'cgi'
c = CGI.new("html4")

c.out do
  c.html do
    c.h1 { 'Sorry, the Web is closed.' }
  end
end
```

Note the multiple levels of blocks: the block passed into CGI#out simply calls CGI#html to generate the DOCTYPE and the <html> tags. The <html> tags contain the result of a call to CGI#h1, which encloses some plain text in <h1> tags. The program produces this output:

```
Content-Type: text/html
Content-Length: 137

<!DOCTYPE HTML PUBLIC "-//W3C//DTD HTML 4.01//EN"
  "http://www.w3.org/TR/html4/strict.dtd">
<HTML><H1>Sorry, the Web is closed.</H1></HTML>
```

The XmlMarkup class in Ruby's builder gem works the same way: you can write Ruby code that resembles the structure of the document it creates:

```
require 'rubygems'
require 'builder'
xml = Builder::XmlMarkup.new.message('type' => 'apology') do |b|
  b.content('Sorry, Web Services are closed.')
end
puts xml
# <message type="apology">
#  <content>Sorry, Web Services are closed.</content>
# </message>
```

See Also

- Recipe 6.13, "Locking a File," uses this technique to create a method that locks a file, and automatically unlocks it when you're done using it
- Recipe 11.9, "Creating and Modifying XML Documents"
- Recipe 20.11, "Avoiding Deadlock," uses this technique to have your thread lock multiple resources in the right order, and unlock them when you're done using them

7.11 Coupling Systems Loosely with Callbacks

Problem

You want to combine different types of objects without hardcoding them full of references to each other.

Solution

Use a callback system, in which objects register code blocks with each other to be executed as needed. An object can call out to its registered callbacks when it needs something, or it can send notification to the callbacks when it does something.

To implement a callback system, write a "register" or "subscribe" method that accepts a code block. Store the registered code blocks as Proc objects in a data structure: probably an array (if you only have one type of callback) or a hash (if you have multiple types). When you need to call the callbacks, iterate over the data structure and call each of the registered code blocks.

Here's a mixin module that gives each instance of a class its own hash of "listener" callback blocks. An outside object can listen for a particular event by calling subscribe with the name of the event and a code block. The dispatcher itself is responsible for calling notify with an appropriate event name at the appropriate time, and the outside object is responsible for passing in the name of the event it wants to "listen" for.

```
module EventDispatcher
  def setup_listeners
    @event_dispatcher_listeners = {}
  end

  def subscribe(event, &callback)
    (@event_dispatcher_listeners[event] ||= []) << callback
  end

  protected
  def notify(event, *args)
    if @event_dispatcher_listeners[event]
      @event_dispatcher_listeners[event].each do |m|
        m.call(*args) if m.respond_to? :call
      end
    end
    return nil
  end
end
```

Here's a Factory class that keeps a set of listeners. An outside object can choose to be notified every time a Factory object is created, or every time a Factory object produces a widget:

```
class Factory
  include EventDispatcher

  def initialize
    setup_listeners
  end

  def produce_widget(color)
    #Widget creation code goes here...
```

```
      notify(:new_widget, color)
    end
  end
```

Here's a listener class that's interested in what happens with Factory objects:

```
class WidgetCounter
  def initialize(factory)
    @counts = Hash.new(0)
    factory.subscribe(:new_widget) do |color|
      @counts[color] += 1
      puts "#{@counts[color]} #{color} widget(s) created since I started watching."
    end
  end
end
```

Finally, here's the listener in action:

```
f1 = Factory.new
WidgetCounter.new(f1)
f1.produce_widget("red")
# 1 red widget(s) created since I started watching.

f1.produce_widget("green")
# 1 green widget(s) created since I started watching.

f1.produce_widget("red")
# 2 red widget(s) created since I started watching.

# This won't produce any output, since our listener is listening to
# another Factory.
Factory.new.produce_widget("blue")
```

Discussion

Callbacks are an essential technique for making your code extensible. This technique has many names (callbacks, hook methods, plugins, publish/subscribe, etc.) but no matter what terminology is used, it's always the same. One object asks another to call a piece of code (the callback) when some condition is met. This technique works even when the two objects know almost nothing about each other. This makes it ideal for refactoring big, tightly integrated systems into smaller, loosely coupled systems.

In a pure listener system (like the one given in the Solution), the callbacks set up lines of communication that always move from the event dispatcher to the listeners. This is useful when you have a master object (like the Factory), from which numerous lackey objects (like the WidgetCounter) take all their cues.

But in many loosely coupled systems, information moves both ways: the dispatcher calls the callbacks and then uses the return results. Consider the stereotypical web portal: a customizable homepage full of HTML boxes containing sports scores, weather predictions, and so on. Since new boxes are always being added to the system, the core portal software shouldn't have to know anything about a specific box. The boxes should also know as little about the core software as possible, so that changing the core doesn't require a change to all the boxes.

A simple change to the `EventDispatcher` class makes it possible for the dispatcher to use the return values of the registered callbacks. The original implementation of `EventDispatcher#notify` called the registered code blocks, but ignored their return value. This version of `EventDispatcher#notify` yields the return values to a block passed in to `notify`:

```ruby
module EventDispatcher
  def notify(event, *args)
    if @event_dispatcher_listeners[event]
      @event_dispatcher_listeners[event].each do |m|
        yield(m.call(*args)) if m.respond_to? :call
      end
    end
    return nil
  end
end
```

Here's an insultingly simple portal rendering engine. It lets boxes register to be rendered inside an HTML table, on one of two rows on the portal page:

```ruby
class Portal
  include EventDispatcher

  def initialize
    setup_listeners
  end

  def render
    puts '<table>'
    render_block = Proc.new { |box| puts "  <td>#{box}</td>" }
    [:row1, :row2].each do |row|
      puts ' <tr>'
      notify(row, &render_block)
      puts ' </tr>'
    end
    puts '</table>'
  end
end
```

Here's the rendering engine rendering a specific user's portal layout. This user likes to see a stock ticker and a weather report on the left, and a news box on the right. Note that there aren't even any classes for these boxes; they're so simple they can be implemented as anonymous code blocks:

```ruby
portal = Portal.new
portal.subscribe(:row1) { 'Stock Ticker' }
portal.subscribe(:row1) { 'Weather' }
portal.subscribe(:row2) { 'Pointless, Trivial News' }
```

```
portal.render
# <table>
#   <tr>
#     <td>Stock Ticker</td>
#     <td>Weather</td>
#   </tr>
#   <tr>
#     <td>Pointless, Trivial News</td>
#   </tr>
# </table>
```

If you want the registered listeners to be shared across all instances of a class, you can make `listeners` a class variable, and make `subscribe` a module method. This is most useful when you want listeners to be notified whenever a new instance of the class is created.

## CHAPTER 8

Objects and Classes

Ruby is an object-oriented programming language; this chapter will show you what that really means. Like all modern languages, Ruby supports object-oriented notions like classes, inheiritance, and polymorphism. But Ruby goes further than other languages you may have used. Some languages are strict and some are permissive; Ruby is one of the most permissive languages around.

Strict languages enforce strong typing, usually at compile type: a variable defined as an array can't be used as another data type. If a method takes an array as an argument, you can't pass in an array-like object unless that object happens to be a subclass of the array class or can be converted into an array.

Ruby enforces dynamic typing, or *duck typing* ("if it quacks like a duck, it is a duck"). A strongly typed language enforces its typing everywhere, even when it's not needed. Ruby enforces its duck typing relative to a particular task. If a variable quacks like a duck, it is one—assuming you wanted to hear it quack. When you want "swims like a duck" instead, duck typing will enforce the swimming, and not the quacking.

Here's an example. Consider the following three classes, Duck, Goose, and DuckRecording:

```ruby
class Duck
  def quack
    'Quack!'
  end

  def swim
    'Paddle paddle paddle...'
  end
end

class Goose
  def honk
    'Honk!'
  end
```

```
    def swim
      'Splash splash splash...'
    end
  end

  class DuckRecording
    def quack
      play
    end

    def play
      'Quack!'
    end
  end
```

If Ruby was a strongly typed language, a method that told a Duck to quack would fail when given a DuckRecording. The following code is written in the hypothetical language Strongly-Typed Ruby; it won't work in real Ruby.

```
  def make_it_quack(Duck duck)
    duck.quack
  end

  make_it_quack(Duck.new)                  # => "Quack!"
  make_it_quack(DuckRecording.new)
  # TypeException: object not of type Duck
```

If you were expecting a Duck, you wouldn't be able to tell a Goose to swim:

```
  def make_it_swim(Duck duck)
    duck.swim
  end

  make_it_swim(Duck.new)                   # => "Paddle paddle paddle..."
  make_it_swim(Goose.new)
  # TypeException: object not of type Goose
```

Since real Ruby uses duck typing, you can get a recording to quack or a goose to swim:

```
  def make_it_quack(duck)
    duck.quack
  end
  make_it_quack(Duck.new)                  # => "Quack!"
  make_it_quack(DuckRecording.new)         # => "Quack!"

  def make_it_swim(duck)
    duck.swim
  end
  make_it_swim(Duck.new)                   # => "Paddle paddle paddle..."
  make_it_swim(Goose.new)                  # => "Splash splash splash..."
```

But you can't make a recording swim or a goose quack:

```
  make_it_quack(Goose.new)
  # NoMethodError: undefined method `quack' for #<Goose:0x2bb8a8>
```

```
make_it_swim(DuckRecording.new)
# NoMethodError: undefined method `swim' for #<DuckRecording:0x2b97d8>
```

Over time, strict languages develop workarounds for their strong typing (have you ever done a cast when retrieving something from an Java collection?), and then workarounds for the workarounds (have you ever created a parameterized Java collection using generics?). Ruby just doesn't bother with any of it. If an object supports the method you're trying to use, Ruby gets out of its way and lets it work.

Ruby's permissiveness is more a matter of attitude than a technical advancement. Python lets you reopen a class after its original definition and modify it after the fact, but the language syntax doesn't make many allowances for it. It's sort of a dirty little secret of the language. In Ruby, this behavior is not only allowed, it's encouraged. Some parts of the standard library add functionality to built-in classes when imported, just to make it easier for the programmer to write code. The Facets Core library adds dozens of convenience methods to Ruby's standard classes. Ruby is proud of this capability, and urges programmers to exploit it if it makes their lives easier.

Strict languages end up needing code generation tools that hide the restrictions and complexities of the language. Ruby has code generation tools built right into the language, saving you work while leaving complete control in your hands (see Chapter 10).

Is this chaotic? It can be. Does it matter? *Only when it actually interferes with you getting work done.* In this chapter and the next two, we'll show you how to follow common conventions, and how to impose order on the chaos when you need it. With Ruby you can impose the *right kind* of order on your objects, tailored for your situation, not a one-size-fits all that makes you jump through hoops most of the time.

These recipes are probably less relevant to the problems you're trying to solve than the other ones in this book, but they're not less important. This chapter and the next two provide a general-purpose toolbox for doing the dirty work of actual programming, whatever your underlying purpose or algorithm. These are the chapters you should turn to when you find yourself stymied by the Ruby language itself, or grinding through tedious makework that Ruby's labor-saving techniques can eliminate. Every other chapter in this book uses the ideas behind these recipes.

8.1 Managing Instance Data

Problem

You want to associate a variable with an object. You may also want the variable to be readable or writable from outside the object.

Solution

Within the code for the object's class, define a variable and prefix its name with an at sign (@). When an object runs the code, a variable by that name will be stored within the object.

An instance of the Frog class defined below might eventually have two instance variables stored within it, @name and @speaks_english:

```ruby
class Frog
  def initialize(name)
    @name = name
  end

  def speak
    # It's a well-known fact that only frogs with long names start out
    # speaking English.
    @speaks_english ||= @name.size > 6
    @speaks_english ? "Hi. I'm #{@name}, the talking frog." : 'Ribbit.'
  end
end

Frog.new('Leonard').speak      # => "Hi. I'm Leonard, the talking frog."

lucas = Frog.new('Lucas')
lucas.speak                    # => "Ribbit."
```

If you want to make an instance variable readable from outside the object, call the attr_reader method on its symbol:

```ruby
lucas.name
# NoMethodError: undefined method `name' for #<Frog:0xb7d0327c @speaks_english=true,
@name="Lucas">

class Frog
  attr_reader :name
end
lucas.name                     # => "Lucas"
```

Similarly, to make an instance variable readable *and writable* from outside the object, call the attr_accessor method on its symbol:

```ruby
lucas.speaks_english = false
# => NoMethodError: undefined method `speaks_english=' for #<Frog:0xb7d0327c @speaks_
#    english=false, @name="Lucas">

class Frog
  attr_accessor :speaks_english
end
lucas.speaks_english = true
lucas.speak                    # => "Hi. I'm Lucas, the talking frog."
```

Discussion

Some programming languages have complex rules about when one object can directly access to another object's instance variables. Ruby has one simple rule: it's never allowed. To get or set the value of an instance variable from outside the object that owns it, you need to call an explicitly defined getter or setter method.

Basic getter and setter methods look like this:

```
class Frog
  def speaks_english
    @speaks_english
  end

  def speaks_english=(value)
    @speaks_english = value
  end
end
```

But it's boring and error-prone to write that yourself, so Ruby provides built-in *decorator* methods like Module#attr_reader and Module#attr_accessor. These methods use metaprogramming to generate custom getter and setter methods for your class. Calling attr_reader :speaks_english generates the getter method speaks_english and attaches it to your class. Calling attr_accessor :instance_variable generates both the getter method speaks_english and the setter method speaks_english=.

There's also an attr_writer decorator method, which only generates a setter method, but you won't use it very often. It doesn't usually make sense for an instance variable to be writable from the outside, but not readable. You'll probably use it only when you plan to write your own custom getter method instead of generating one.

Another slight difference between Ruby and some other programming languages: in Ruby, instance variables (just like other variables) don't exist until they're defined. Below, note how the @speaks_english variable isn't defined until the Frog#speak method gets called:

```
michael = Frog.new("Michael")
# => #<Frog:0xb7cf14c8 @name="Michael">
michael.speak               # => "Hi. I'm Michael, the talking frog."
michael
# => #<Frog:0xb7cf14c8 @name="Michael", @speaks_english=true>
```

It's possible that one Frog object would have the @speaks_english instance variable set while another one would not. If you call a getter method for an instance variable that's not defined, you'll get nil. If this behavior is a problem, write an initialize that initializes all your instance variables.

Given the symbol for an instance variable, you can retrieve the value with Object#instance_variable_get, and set it with Object#instance_variable_set.

Because this method ignores encapsulation, you should only use it in within the class itself: say, within a call to Module#define_method.

This use of instance_variable_get violates encapsulation, since we're calling it from outside the Frog class:

```
michael.instance_variable_get("@name")          # => "Michael"
michael.instance_variable_set("@name", 'Bob')
michael.name                                      # => "Bob"
```

This use doesn't violate encapsulation (though there's no real need to call define_method here):

```
class Frog
  define_method(:scientific_name) do
    species = 'vulgaris'
    species = 'loquacious' if instance_variable_get('@speaks_english')
    "Rana #{species}"
  end
end
michael.scientific_name                           # => "Rana loquacious"
```

See Also

- Recipe 10.10, "Avoiding Boilerplate Code with Metaprogramming"

8.2   Managing Class Data

Problem

Instead of storing a bit of data along with every instance of a class, you want to store a bit of data along with the class itself.

Solution

Instance variables are prefixed by a single at sign; class variables are prefixed by two at signs. This class contains both an instance variable and a class variable:

```
class Warning
  @@translations = { :en => 'Wet Floor',
                     :es => 'Piso Mojado' }

  def initialize(language=:en)
    @language = language
  end

  def warn
    @@translations[@language]
  end
end

Warning.new.warn                      # => "Wet Floor"
Warning.new(:es).warn                 # => "Piso Mojado"
```

Discussion

Class variables store information that's applicable to the class itself, or applicable to every instance of the class. They're often used to control, prevent, or react to the instantiation of the class. A class variable in Ruby acts like a static variable in Java.

Here's an example that uses a class constant and a class variable to control when and how a class can be instantiated:

```ruby
class Fate
  NAMES = ['Klotho', 'Atropos', 'Lachesis'].freeze
  @@number_instantiated = 0

  def initialize
    if @@number_instantiated >= NAMES.size
      raise ArgumentError, 'Sorry, there are only three Fates.'
    end
    @name = NAMES[@@number_instantiated]
    @@number_instantiated += 1
    puts "I give you... #{@name}!"
  end
end

Fate.new
# I give you... Klotho!
# => #<Fate:0xb7d2c348 @name="Klotho">

Fate.new
# I give you... Atropos!
# => #<Fate:0xb7d28400 @name="Atropos">

Fate.new
# I give you... Lachesis!
# => #<Fate:0xb7d22168 @name="Lachesis">

Fate.new
# ArgumentError: Sorry, there are only three Fates.
```

It's not considered good form to write setter or getter methods for class variables. You won't usually need to expose any class-wide information apart from helpful constants, and those you can expose with class constants such as NAMES above.

If you do want to write setter or getter methods for class variables, you can use the following class-level equivalents of Module#attr_reader and Module#attr_writer. They use metaprogramming to define new accessor methods:[*]

```ruby
class Module
  def class_attr_reader(*symbols)
    symbols.each do |symbol|
```

---

[*] In Ruby 1.9, Object#send can't be used to call private methods. You'll need to replace the calls to send with calls to Object#funcall.

```
      self.class.send(:define_method, symbol) do
        class_variable_get("@@#{symbol}")
      end
    end
  end

  def class_attr_writer(*symbols)
    symbols.each do |symbol|
      self.class.send(:define_method, "#{symbol}=") do |value|
        class_variable_set("@@#{symbol}", value)
      end
    end
  end

  def class_attr_accessor(*symbols)
    class_attr_reader(*symbols)
    class_attr_writer(*symbols)
  end
end
```

Here is Module#class_attr_reader being used to give the Fate class an accessor for its class variable:

```
Fate.number_instantiated
# NoMethodError: undefined method `number_instantiated' for Fate:Class

class Fate
  class_attr_reader :number_instantiated
end
Fate.number_instantiated          # => 3
```

You can have both a class variable foo and an instance variable foo, but this will only end up confusing you. For instance, the accessor method foo must retrieve one or the other. If you call attr_accessor :foo and then class_attr_accessor :foo, the class version will silently overwrite the instance version.

As with instance variables, you can bypass encapsulation and use class variables directly with class_variable_get and class_variable_set. Also as with instance variables, you should only do this from *inside* the class, usually within a define_method call.

See Also

- If you want to create a singleton, don't mess around with class variables; instead, use the singleton library from Ruby's standard library
- Recipe 8.18, "Implementing Class and Singleton Methods"
- Recipe 10.10, "Avoiding Boilerplate Code with Metaprogramming"

8.3 Checking Class or Module Membership

Problem

You want to see if an object is of the right type for your purposes.

Solution

If you plan to call a specific method on the object, just check to see whether the object reponds to that method:

```
def send_as_package(obj)
  if obj.respond_to? :package
    packaged = obj.package
  else
    $stderr.puts "Not sure how to package a #{obj.class}."
    $stderr.puts 'Trying generic packager.'
    package = Package.new(obj)
  end
  send(package)
end
```

If you really can only accept objects of one specific class, or objects that include one specific module, use the is_a? predicate:

```
def multiply_precisely(a, b)
  if a.is_a? Float or b.is_a? Float
    raise ArgumentError, "I can't do precise multiplication with floats."
  end
  a * b
end

multiply_precisely(4, 5)                              # => 20
multiply_precisely(4.0, 5)
# ArgumentError: I can't do precise multiplication with floats.
```

Discussion

Whenever possible, you should use duck typing (Object#respond_to?) in preference to class typing (Object#is_a?). Duck typing is one of the great strengths of Ruby, but it only works if everyone uses it. If you write a method that only accepts strings, instead of accepting anything that supports to_str, then you've broken the duck typing illusion for everyone who uses your code.

Sometimes you can't use duck typing, though, or sometimes you need to combine it with class typing. Sometimes two different classes define the same method (especially one of the operators) in completely different ways. Duck typing makes it possible to silently do the right thing, but if you know that duck typing would silently do the *wrong* thing, a little class typing won't hurt.

Here's a method that uses duck typing to see whether an operation is supported, and class typing to cut short a possible problem before it occurs:

```ruby
def append_to_self(x)
  unless x.respond_to? :<<
    raise ArgumentError, "This object doesn't support the left-shift operator."
  end
  if x.is_a? Numeric
    raise ArgumentError,
     "The left-shift operator for this object doesn't do an append."
  end
  x << x
end

append_to_self('abc')                             # => "abcabc"
append_to_self([1, 2, 3])                         # => [1, 2, 3, [...]]

append_to_self({1 => 2})
# ArgumentError: This object doesn't support the left-shift operator.

append_to_self(5)
# ArgumentError: The left-shift operator for this object doesn't do an append.
5 << 5                                            # => 160
# That is, 5 * (2 ** 5)
```

An alternative solution approximates the functionality of Java's interfaces. You can create a dummy module for a given capability, have all appropriate classes include it, and use is_a? to check for inclusion of the module. This requires that each participating class signal its ability to perform a certain task, but it doesn't tie you to any particular class hierarchy, and it saves you from calling the wrong method just because it has the right name.

```ruby
module ShiftMeansAppend
  def <<(x)
  end
end

class String
  include ShiftMeansAppend
end

class Array
  include ShiftMeansAppend
end

def append_to_self(x)
  unless x.is_a? ShiftMeansAppend
    raise ArgumentError, "I can't trust this object's left-shift operator."
  end
  x << x
end
```

```
append_to_self 4
# ArgumentError: I can't trust this object's left-shift operator.

append_to_self '4'                          # => "44"
```

See Also

- Recipe 1.12, "Testing Whether an Object Is String-Like"

8.4   Writing an Inherited Class

Problem

You want to create a new class that extends or modifies the behavior of an existing class.

Solution

If you're writing a new method that conceptually belongs in the original class, you can reopen the class and append your method to the class definition. You should only do this if your method is generally useful, and you're sure it won't conflict with a method defined by some library you include in the future.

This code adds a scramble method to Ruby's built-in String class (see Recipe 4.10 for a faster way to sort randomly):

```
class String
  def scramble
    split(//).sort_by { rand }.join
  end
end

"I once was a normal string.".scramble
# => "i arg cn lnws.Ioateosma n r"
```

If your method isn't generally useful, or you don't want to take the risk of modifying a class after its initial creation, create a subclass of the original class. The subclass can override its parent's methods, or add new ones. This is safer because the original class, and any code that depended on it, is unaffected. This subclass of String adds one new method and overrides one existing one:

```
class UnpredictableString < String
  def scramble
    split (//).sort_by { rand }.join
  end

  def inspect
    scramble.inspect
  end
end
```

```
str = UnpredictableString.new("It was a dark and stormy night.")
# => " hsar gsIo atr tkd  naaniwdt.ym"
str
# => "ts dtnwIktsr oydnhgi   .mara aa"
```

Discussion

All of Ruby's classes can be subclassed, though a few of them can't be *usefully* sub-classed (see Recipe 8.18 for information on how to deal with the holdouts).

Ruby programmers use subclassing less frequently than they would in other languages, because it's often acceptable to simply reopen an existing class (even a built-in class) and attach a new method. We do this throughout this book, adding useful new methods to built-in classes rather than defining them in Kernel, or putting them in subclasses or utility classes. Libraries like Rails and Facets Core do the same.

This improves the organization of your code. But the risk is that a library you include (or a library included by one you include) will define the same method in the same built-in class. Either the library will override your method (breaking your code), or you'll override its method (breaking its code, which will break your code). There is no general solution to this problem short of adopting naming conventions, or always subclassing and never modifying preexisting classes.

You should certainly subclass if you're writing a method that isn't generally useful, or that only applies to certain instances of a class. For instance, here's a method Array#sum that adds up the elements of an array:

```
class Array
  def sum(start_at=0)
    inject(start_at) { |sum, x| sum + x }
  end
end
```

This works for arrays that contain only numbers (or that contain only strings), but it will fail for other kinds of arrays.

```
[79, 14, 2].sum                    # => 95
['so', 'fa'].sum('')               # => "sofa"
[79, 'so'].sum
# TypeError: String can't be coerced into Fixnum
```

Maybe you should signal this by putting it in a subclass called NumericArray or SummableArray:

```
class NumericArray < Array
  def sum
    inject(0) { |sum, x| sum + x }
  end
end
```

The NumericArray class doesn't actually do type checking to make sure it only contains numeric objects, but since it's a different class, you and other programmers are less likely to use sum where it's not appropriate.[*]

You should also subclass if you want to override a method's behavior. In the UnpredictableString example, I overrode the inspect method in my subclass. If I'd just modified String#inspect, the rest of my program would have been thrown into confusion. Rarely is it acceptable to override a method in place: one example would be if you've written a drop-in implementation that's more efficient.

See Also

- Recipe 8.18, "Implementing Class and Singleton Methods," shows you how to extend the behavior of a particular *object* after it's been created
- *http://www.rubygarden.org/ruby?TheOpenNatureOfRuby*

8.5   Overloading Methods

Problem

You want to create two different versions of a method with the same name: two methods that differ in the arguments they take.

Solution

A Ruby class can have only one method with a given name. Within that single method, though, you can put logic that branches depending on how many and what kinds of objects were passed in as arguments.

Here's a Rectangle class that represents a rectangular shape on a grid. You can instantiate a Rectangle in one of two ways: by passing in the coordinates of its top-left and bottom-left corners, or by passing in its top-left corner along with its length and width. There's only one initialize method, but you can act as though there were two.

```
# The Rectangle constructor accepts arguments in either of the following forms:
#  Rectangle.new([x_top, y_left], length, width)
#  Rectangle.new([x_top, y_left], [x_bottom, y_right])
class Rectangle
  def initialize(*args)
    case args.size
    when 2
      @top_left, @bottom_right = args
```

---

[*] This isn't a hard and fast rule. Array#sort won't work on arrays whose elements can't be mutually compared, but it would be a big inconvenience to put sort in a subclass of Array or leave it out of the Ruby standard library. You might feel the same way about sum; but then, you're not the Ruby standard library.

```
      when 3
        @top_left, length, width = args
        @bottom_right = [@top_left[0] + length, @top_left[1] - width]
      else
        raise ArgumentError, "This method takes either 2 or 3 arguments."
      end

      # Perform additional type/error checking on @top_left and
      # @bottom_right...
    end
  end
```

Here's the Rectangle constructor in action:

```
Rectangle.new([10, 23], [14, 13])
# => #<Rectangle:0xb7d15828 @bottom_right=[14, 13], @top_left=[10, 23]>

Rectangle.new([10, 23], 4, 10)
# => #<Rectangle:0xb7d0da4c @bottom_right=[14, 13], @top_left=[10, 23]>

Rectangle.new
# => ArgumentError: This method takes either 2 or 3 arguments.
```

Discussion

In strongly typed languages like C++ and Java, you must often create multiple versions of the same method with different arguments. For instance, Java's StringBuffer class implements over 10 variants of its append method: one that takes a boolean, one that takes a string, and so on.

Ruby's equivalent of StringBuffer is StringIO, and its equivalent of the append method is StringIO#<<. In Ruby, that method can only be defined once, but it can take an object of any type. There's no need to write different versions of the method for taking different kinds of object. If you need to do type checking (such as making sure the object has a string representation), you put it in the method body rather than in the method definition.

Ruby's loose typing eliminates most of the need for method overloading. Its default arguments, variable-length argument lists, and (simulated) keyword arguments eliminate most of the remaining cases. What's left? Mainly methods that can take two completely different sets of arguments, like the Rectangle constructor given in the Solution.

To handle these, write a method that takes a variable number of arguments, and give it some extra code at the front that figures out which set of arguments was passed. Rectangle#initialize rejects argument lists that are of the wrong length. Additional code could enforce duck typing to make sure that the arguments passed in are of the right type. See Recipe 10.16 for simple ways to do argument validation.

See Also

- Recipe 8.11, "Accepting or Passing a Variable Number of Arguments"
- Recipe 8.12, "Simulating Keyword Arguments"
- Recipe 10.16, "Enforcing Software Contracts"

8.6   Validating and Modifying Attribute Values

Problem

You want to let outside code set your objects' instance variables, but you also want to impose some control over the values your variables are set to. You might want a chance to validate new values before accepting them. Or you might want to accept values in a form convenient to the caller, but transform them into a different form for internal storage.

Solution

Define your own setter method for each instance variable you want to control. The setter method for an instance variable `quantity` would be called `quantity=`. When a user issues a statement like `object.quantity = 10`, the method `object#quantity=` is called with the argument 10.

It's up to the `quantity=` method to decide whether the instance variable `quantity` should actually take the value 10. A setter method is free to raise an `ArgumentException` if it's passed an invalid value. It may also modify the provided value, massaging it into the canonical form used by the class. If it can get an acceptable value, its last act should be to modify the instance variable.

I'll define a class that keeps track of peoples' first and last names. It uses setter methods to enforce two somewhat parochial rules: everyone must have both a first and a last name, and everyone's first name must begin with a capital letter:

```
class Name

  # Define default getter methods, but not setter methods.
  attr_reader :first, :last

  # When someone tries to set a first name, enforce rules about it.
  def first=(first)
    if first == nil or first.size == 0
      raise ArgumentError.new('Everyone must have a first name.')
    end
    first = first.dup
    first[0] = first[0].chr.capitalize
    @first = first
  end
```

```
      # When someone tries to set a last name, enforce rules about it.
      def last=(last)
        if last == nil or last.size == 0
          raise ArgumentError.new('Everyone must have a last name.')
        end
        @last = last
      end

      def full_name
        "#{@first} #{@last}"
      end

      # Delegate to the setter methods instead of setting the instance
      # variables directly.
      def initialize(first, last)
        self.first = first
        self.last = last
      end
    end
```

I've written the Name class so that the rules are enforced both in the constructor and after the object has been created:

```
jacob = Name.new('Jacob', 'Berendes')
jacob.first = 'Mary Sue'
jacob.full_name                              # => "Mary Sue Berendes"

john = Name.new('john', 'von Neumann')
john.full_name                               # => "John von Neumann"
john.first = 'john'
john.first                                   # => "John"
john.first = nil
# ArgumentError: Everyone must have a first name.

Name.new('Kero, international football star and performance artist', nil)
# ArgumentError: Everyone must have a last name.
```

Discussion

Ruby never lets one object access another object's instance variables. All you can do is call methods. Ruby *simulates* instance variable access by making it easy to define getter and setter methods whose names are based on the names of instance variables. When you access object.my_var, you're actually calling a method called my_var, which (by default) just happens to return a reference to the instance variable my_var.

Similarly, when you set a new value for object.my_var, you're actually passing that value into a setter method called my_var=. That method might go ahead and stick your new value into the instance variable my_var. It might accept your value, but silently clean it up, convert it to another format, or otherwise modify it. It might be picky and reject your value altogether by raising an ArgumentError.

When you're defining a class, you can have Ruby generate a setter method for one of your instance variables by calling Module#attr_writer or Module#attr_accessor on the symbol for that variable. This saves you from having to write code, but the default setter method lets anyone set the instance variable to any value at all:

```
class SimpleContainer
  attr_accessor :value
end

c = SimpleContainer.new

c.respond_to? "value="                    # => true

c.value = 10; c.value                      # => 10

c.value = "some random value"; c.value     # => "some random value"

c.value = [nil, nil, nil]; c.value         # => [nil, nil, nil]
```

A lot of the time, this kind of informality is just fine. But sometimes you don't trust the data coming in through the setter methods. That's when you can define your own methods to stop bad data before it infects your objects.

Within a class, you have direct access to the instance variables. You can simply assign to an instance variable and the setter method won't be triggered. If you do want to trigger the setter method, you'll have to call it explicitly. Note how, in the Name#initialize method above, I call the first= and last= methods instead of assigning to @first and @last. This makes sure the validation code gets run for the initial values of every Name object. I can't just say first = first, because first is a variable name in that method.

See Also

- Recipe 8.1, "Managing Instance Data"
- Recipe 13.14, "Validating Data with ActiveRecord"

8.7   Defining a Virtual Attribute

Problem

You want to create accessor methods for an attribute that isn't directly backed by any instance variable: it's a calculated value derived from one or more different instance variables.

Solution

Define accessor methods for the attribute in terms of the instance variables that are actually used. There need not be any relationship between the names of the accessor methods and the names of the instance variables.

The following class exposes four accessor methods: degrees, degrees=, radians, and radians=. But it only stores one instance variable: @radians.

```
class Arc
  attr_accessor :radians

  def degrees
    @radians * 180 / Math::PI
  end

  def degrees=(degrees)
    @radians = degrees * Math::PI / 180
  end
end

arc = Arc.new
arc.degrees = 180
arc.radians                          # => 3.14159265358979
arc.radians = Math::PI / 2
arc.degrees                          # => 90.0
```

Discussion

Ruby accessor methods usually correspond to the names of the instance variables they access, but this is nothing more than a convention. Outside code has no way of knowing what your instance variables are called, or whether you have any at all, so you can create accessors for virtual attributes with no risk of outside code thinking they're backed by real instance variables.

See Also

- Recipe 2.9, "Converting Between Degrees and Radians"

8.8 Delegating Method Calls to Another Object

Problem

You'd like to delegate some of an object's method calls to a different object, or make one object capable of "impersonating" another.

Solution

If you want to completely impersonate another object, or delegate most of one object's calls to another, use the delegate library. It generates custom classes whose instances can impersonate objects of any other class. These custom classes respond to all methods of the class they shadow, but they don't do any work of their own apart from calling the same method on some instance of the "real" class.

Here's some code that uses delegate to generate CardinalNumber, a class that acts almost like a Fixnum. CardinalNumber defines the same methods as Fixnum does, and it takes a genuine Fixnum as an argument to its constructor. It stores this object as a member, and when you call any of Fixnum's methods on a CardinalNumber object, it delegates that method call to the stored Fixnum. The only major exception is the to_s method, which I've decided to override.

```ruby
require 'delegate'

# An integer represented as an ordinal number (1st, 2nd, 3rd...), as
# opposed to an ordinal number (1, 2, 3...) Generated by the
# DelegateClass to have all the methods of the Fixnum class.
class OrdinalNumber < DelegateClass(Fixnum)
  def to_s
    delegate_s = __getobj__.to_s
    check = abs
    if to_check == 11 or to_check == 12
      suffix = "th"
    else
      case check % 10
        when 1 then suffix = "st"
        when 2 then suffix = "nd"
        else suffix = "th"
      end
    end
    return delegate_s + suffix
  end
end

4.to_s                                      # => "4"
OrdinalNumber.new(4).to_s                   # => "4th"

OrdinalNumber.new(102).to_s                 # => "102nd"
OrdinalNumber.new(11).to_s                  # => "11th"
OrdinalNumber.new(-21).to_s                 # => "-21st"

OrdinalNumber.new(5).succ                   # => 6
OrdinalNumber.new(5) + 6                    # => 11
OrdinalNumber.new(5) + OrdinalNumber.new(6) # => 11
```

Discussion

The delegate library is useful when you want to extend the behavior of objects you don't have much control over. Usually these are objects you're not in charge of instantiating—they're instantiated by factory methods, or by Ruby itself. With delegate, you can create a class that wraps an already existing object of another class and modifies its behavior. You can do all of this without changing the original class. This is especially useful if the original class has been frozen.

There are a few methods that delegate won't delegate: most of the ones in Kernel. public_instance_methods. The most important one is is_a?. Code that explicitly checks the type of your object will be able to see that it's not a real instance of the object it's impersonating. Using is_a? instead of respond_to? is often bad Ruby practice, but it happens pretty often, so you should be aware of it.

The Forwardable module is a little more precise and a little less discerning: it lets you delegate any of an object's methods to another object. A class that extends Forwardable can use the def_delegator decorator method, which takes as arguments an object symbol and a method symbol. It defines a new method that delegates to the method of the same name in the given object. There's also a def_delegators method, which takes multiple method symbols as arguments and defines a delegator method for each one. By calling def_delegator multiple times, you can have a single Forwardable delegate different methods to different subobjects.

Here I'll use Forwardable to define a simple class that works like an array, but supports none of Array's methods except the append operator, <<. Note how the << method defined by def_delegator is passed through to modify the underlying array.

```
class AppendOnlyArray
  extend Forwardable
  def initialize
    @array = []
  end

  def_delegator :@array, :<<
end

a = AppendOnlyArray
a << 4
a << 5
a.size
# => undefined method `size' for #<AppendOnlyArray:0xb7d23c5c @array=[4, 5]>
```

AppendOnlyArray is pretty useless, but the same principle makes Forwardable useful if you want to expose only a portion of a class' interface. For instance, suppose you want to create a data structure that works like a Hash, but only supports random access. You don't want to support keys, each, or any of the other ways of getting information out of a hash without providing a key.

You could subclass Hash, then redefine or delete all the methods that you don't want to support. Then you could worry a lot about having missed some of those methods. Or you could define a subclass of Forwardable and define only the methods of Hash that you *do* want to support.

```
class RandomAccessHash
  extend Forwardable
```

```
    def initialize
      @delegate_to = {}
    end

    def_delegators :@delegate_to, :[], "[]="
  end

  balances_by_account_number = RandomAccessHash.new

  # Load balances from a database or something.
  balances_by_account_number["101240A"] = 412.60
  balances_by_account_number["104918J"] = 10339.94
  balances_by_account_number["108826N"] = 293.01
```

Random access works if you know the key, but anything else is forbidden:

```
  balances_by_account_number["104918J"]          # => 10339.94
  balances_by_account_number.each do |number, balance|
    puts "I now know the balance for account #{number}: it's #{balance}"
  end
  # => NoMethodError: undefined method `each' for #<RandomAccessHash:0xb7d49078>
```

See Also

- An alternative to using `SimpleDelegator` to write delegator methods is to skip out on the methods altogether, and instead implement a `method_missing` which does the delegating. Recipe 2.13, "Simulating a Subclass of Fixnum," uses this technique. You might especially find this recipe interesting if you'd like to make arithmetic on `CardinalNumber` objects yield new `CardinalNumber` objects instead of `Fixnum` objects.

8.9 Converting and Coercing Objects to Different Types

Problem

You have an object of one type and you want to use it as though it were of another type.

Solution

You might not have to do anything at all. Ruby doesn't enforce type safety unless the programmer has explicitly written it in. If your original class defines the same methods as the class you were thinking of converting it to, you might be able to use your object as is.

If you do have to convert from one class to another, Ruby provides conversion methods for most common paths:

```
  "4".to_i                                  # => 4
  4.to_s                                    # => "4"
```

```
Time.now.to_f                              # => 1143572140.90932
{ "key1" => "value1", "key2" => "value2" }.to_a
# => [["key1", "value1"], ["key2", "value2"]]
```

If all else fails, you might be able to manually create an instance of the new class, and set its instance variables using the old data.

Discussion

Some programming languages have a "cast" operator that forces the compiler to treat an object of one type like an object of another type. A cast is usually a programmer's assertion that he knows more about the types of objects than the compiler. Ruby has no cast operator. From Ruby's perspective, type checking is just an extra hoop you have to jump through. A cast operator would make it easier to jump through that hoop, but Ruby omits the hoop altogether.

Wherever you're tempted to cast an object to another type, you should be able to just do nothing. If your object can be used as the other type, there's no problem: if not, then casting it to that type wouldn't have helped anyway.

Here's a concrete example. You probably don't need to convert a hash into an array just so you can pass it into an iteration method that expects an array. If that method only calls each on its argument, it doesn't really "expect an array:" it expects a reasonable implementation of each. Ruby hashes provide that implementation just as well as arrays.

```
def print_each(array)
  array.each { |x| puts x.inspect }
end

hash = { "pickled peppers" => "peck of",
         "sick sheep"      => "sixth" }
print_each(hash.to_a)
# ["sick sheep", "sixth"]
# ["pickled peppers", "peck of"]

print_each(hash)
# ["sick sheep", "sixth"]
# ["pickled peppers", "peck of"]
```

Ruby does provide methods for *converting* one data type into another. These methods follow the naming convention to_[other type], and they usually create a brand new object of the new type, but containing the old data. They are generally used when you want to use some method of the new data type, or display or store the data in another format.

In the case of print_each, not converting the hash to an array gives the same results as converting, and the code is shorter and faster when it doesn't do the conversion. But converting a hash into an array of key-value pairs does let you call methods defined by Array but not by Hash. If what you really want is an array—something ordered, something you can modify with push and pop—there's no reason not to convert to an array and stop using the hash.

```
array = hash.to_a
# => [["sick sheep", "sixth"], ["pickled peppers", "peck of"]]

# Print out a tongue-twisting invoice.
until array.empty?
  item, quantity = array.pop
  puts "#{quantity} #{item}"
end
# peck of pickled peppers
# sixth sick sheep
```

Some methods convert one data type to another as a side effect: for instance, sorting a hash implicitly converts it into an array, since hashes have no notion of ordering.

```
hash.sort
# => [["pickled peppers", "peck of"], ["sick sheep", "sixth"]]
```

Number conversion and coercion

Most of the commonly used conversion methods in stock Ruby are in the number classes. This makes sense because arithmetic operations can give different results depending on the numeric types of the inputs. This is one place where Ruby's conversion methods *are* used as a substitute for casting. Here, to_f is used to force Ruby to perform floating-point division instead of integer division:

```
3/4                                            # => 0
3/4.to_f                                        # => 0.75
```

Integers and floating-point numbers have to_i and to_f methods to convert back and forth between each other. BigDecimal or Rational objects define the same methods; they also define some brand new conversion methods: to_d to convert a number to BigDecimal, and to_r to convert a number to Rational. To convert to or from Rational objects you just have to require 'rational'. To convert to or from BigDecimal objects you must require 'bigdecimal' and also require 'bigdecimal/utils'.

```
require 'rational'
Rational(1, 3).to_f                             # => 0.333333333333333
Rational(11, 5).to_i                            # => 2
2.to_r                                          # => Rational(2, 1)
```

Here's a table that shows how to convert between Ruby's basic numeric types.

	Integer	Floating-point	BigDecimal	Rational
Integer	to_i(identity)	to_f	to_r.to_d	to_r
Float	to_i(decimal discard)	to_f (new)	to_d	to_d.to_r (include bigdecimal/util)
BigDecimal	to_i	to_f	to_d (new)	to_r (include bigdecimal/util)
Rational	to_i(dec discard)	to_f (approx)	to_d (include bigdecimal/util)	to_r (identity)

Two cases deserve special mention. You can't convert a floating-point number directly into rational number, but you can do it through BigDecimal. The result will be imprecise, because floating-point numbers are imprecise.

```
require 'bigdecimal'
require 'bigdecimal/util'

one_third = 1/3.0           # => 0.333333333333333
one_third.to_r
# NoMethodError: undefined method `to_r' for 0.333333333333333:Float
one_third.to_d.to_r        # => Rational(333333333333333, 1000000000000000)
```

Similarly, the best way to convert an Integer to a BigDecimal is to convert it to a rational number first.

```
20.to_d
# NoMethodError: undefined method `to_d' for 20:Fixnum
20.to_r.to_d              # => #<BigDecimal:b7bfd214,'0.2E2',4(48)>
```

When it needs to perform arithmetic operations on two numbers of different types, Ruby uses a method called coerce. Every numeric type implements a coerce method that takes a single number as its argument. It returns an array of two numbers: the object itself and the argument passed into coerce. Either or both numbers might undergo a conversion, but whatever happens, both the numbers in the return array must be of the same type. The arithmetic operation is performed on these two numbers, coerced into the same type.

This way, the authors of numeric classes don't have to make their arithmetic operations support operations on objects of different types. If they implement coerce, they know that their arithmetic operations will only be passed in another object of the same type.

This is easiest to see for the Complex class. Below, every input to coerce is transformed into an equivalent complex number so that it can be used in arithmetic operations along with the complex number *i*:

```
require 'complex'
i = Complex(0, 1)                     # => Complex(0, 1)
i.coerce(3)                           # => [Complex(3, 0), Complex(0, 1)]
i.coerce(2.5)                         # => [Complex(2.5, 0), Complex(0, 1)]
```

This, incidentally, is why 3/4 uses integer division but 3/4.to_f uses floating-point division. 3.coerce(4) returns two integer objects, so the arithmetic methods of Fixnum are used. 3.coerce(4.0) returns two floating-point numbers, so the arithmetic methods of Float are used.

Other conversion methods

All Ruby objects define conversion methods to_s and inspect, which give a string representation of the object. Usually inspect is the more readable of the two formats.

```
[1, 2, 3].to_s                        # => "123"
[1, 2, 3].inspect                     # => "[1, 2, 3]"
```

Here's a grab bag of other notable conversion methods found within the Ruby standard library. This should give you a picture of what Ruby conversion methods typically do.

- MatchData#to_a creates an array containing the match groups of a regular expression match.
- Matrix#to_a converts a mathematical matrix into a nested array.
- Enumerable#to_a iterates over any enumerable object and collects the results in an array.
- Net::HTTPHeader#to_hash returns a hash mapping the names of HTTP headers to their values.
- String#to_f and String#to_i parse strings into numeric objects. Including the bigdecimal/util library will define String#to_d, which parses a string into a BigDecimal object.
- Including the yaml library will define to_yaml methods for all of Ruby's built-in classes: Array#to_yaml, String#to_yaml, and so on.

See Also

- Recipe 1.12, "Testing Whether an Object Is String-Like"
- Recipe 2.1, "Parsing a Number from a String"
- Recipe 8.10, "Getting a Human-Readable Printout of Any Object"

8.10 Getting a Human-Readable Printout of Any Object

Problem

You want to look at a natural-looking rendition of a given object.

Solution

Use Object#inspect. Nearly all the time, this method will give you something more readable than simply printing out the object or converting it into a string.

```
a = [1,2,3]
puts a
# 1
# 2
# 3

puts a.to_s
# 123

puts a.inspect
# [1, 2, 3]
```

```
puts /foo/
# (?-mix:foo)
puts /foo/.inspect
# /foo/
f = File.open('foo', 'a')
puts f
# #<File:0xb7c31c30>
puts f.inspect
# #<File:foo>
```

Discussion

Even very complex data structures can be inspected and come out looking just like they would in Ruby code to define that data structure. In some cases, you can even run the output of inspect through eval to recreate the object.

```
periodic_table = [{ :symbol => "H", :name => "hydrogen", :weight => 1.007 },
                  { :symbol => "Rg", :name => "roentgenium", :weight => 272 }]
puts periodic_table.inspect
# [{:symbol=>"H", :name=>"hydrogen", :weight=>1.007},
#  {:symbol=>"Rg", :name=>"roentgenium", :weight=>272}]

eval(periodic_table.inspect)[0]
# => {:symbol=>"H", :name=>"hydrogen", :weight=>1.007}
```

By default, an object's inspect method works the same way as its to_s method.[*] Unless your classes override inspect, inspecting one of your objects will yield a boring and not terribly helpful string, containing only the object's class name, object_id, and instance variables:

```
class Dog
  def initialize(name, age)
    @name = name
    @age = age * 7 #Compensate for dog years
  end
end

spot = Dog.new("Spot", 2.1)
spot.inspect
# => "#<Dog:0xb7c16bec @name="Spot", @age=14.7>"
```

That's why you'll help out your future self by defining useful inspect methods that give relevant information about the objects you'll be instantiating.

```
class Dog
  def inspect
    "<A Dog named #{@name} who's #{@age} in dog years.>"
  end
```

---

[*] Contrary to what ri Object#inspect says, Object#inspect does *not* delegate to the Object#to_s method: it just happens to work a lot like Object#to_s. If you only override to_s, inspect won't be affected.

```
  def to_s
    inspect
  end
end
spot.inspect
# => "<A Dog named Spot who's 14.7 in dog years.>"
```

Or, if you believe in being able to eval the output of inspect:

```
class Dog
  def inspect
    %{Dog.new("#{@name}", #{@age/7})}
  end
end
spot.inspect
# => "Dog.new("Spot", 2.1)"
eval(spot.inspect).inspect
# => "Dog.new("Spot", 2.1)"
```

Just don't *automatically* eval the output of inspect, because, as always, that's dangerous:

```
strange_dog_name = %{Spot", 0); puts "Executing arbitrary Ruby..."; puts("}
spot = Dog.new(strange_dog_name, 0)
puts spot.inspect
# Dog.new("Spot", 0); puts "Executing arbitrary Ruby..."; puts("", 0)
eval(spot.inspect)
# Executing arbitrary Ruby...
#
# 0
```

8.11 Accepting or Passing a Variable Number of Arguments

Problem

You want to write a method that can accept any number of arguments. Or maybe you want to pass the contents of an array as arguments into such a method, rather than passing in the array itself as a single argument.

Solution

To accept any number of arguments to your method, prefix the last argument name with an asterisk. When the method is called, all the "extra" arguments will be collected in a list and passed in as that argument:

```
def sum(*numbers)
  puts "I'm about to sum the array #{numbers.inspect}"
  numbers.inject(0) { |sum, x| sum += x }
end

sum(1, 2, 10)
# I'm about to sum the array [1, 2, 10]
# => 13
```

```
sum(2, -2, 2, -2, 2, -2, 2, -2, 2)
# I'm about to sum the array [2, -2, 2, -2, 2, -2, 2, -2, 2]
# => 2

sum
# I'm about to sum the array []
# => 0
```

To pass an array of arguments into a method, use the asterisk signifier before the array you want to be turned into "extra" arguments:

```
to_sum = []
1.upto(10) { |x| to_sum << x }
sum(*to_sum)
# I'm about to sum the array [1, 2, 3, 4, 5, 6, 7, 8, 9, 10]
# => 55
```

Bad things happen if you forget the asterisk: your entire array is treated as a single "extra" argument:

```
sum(to_sum)
# I'm about to sum the array [[1, 2, 3, 4, 5, 6, 7, 8, 9, 10]]
# TypeError: Array can't be coerced into Fixnum
```

Discussion

Why make a method take a variable number of arguments, instead of just having it take a single array? It's basically for the convenience of the user. Consider the Kernel#printf method, which takes one fixed argument (a format string), and then a variable number of inputs to the format string:

```
printf('%s | %s', 'left', 'right')
# left | right
```

It's very rare that the caller of printf already has her inputs lying around in an array. Fortunately, Ruby is happy to create the array on the user's behalf. If the caller does already have an array of inputs, it's easy to pass the contents of that array as "extra" arguments by sticking the asterisk onto the appropriate variable name:

```
inputs = ['left', 'right']
printf('%s | %s', *inputs)
# left | right
```

As you can see, a method can take a fixed number of "normal" arguments and then a variable number of "extra" arguments. When defining such a method, just make sure that the last argument is the one you prefix with the asterisk:

```
def format_list(header, footer='', *data)
  puts header
  puts (line = '-' * header.size)
  puts data.join("\n")
  puts line
  puts footer
end
```

```
cozies = 21
gaskets = 10
format_list("Yesterday's productivity numbers:", 'Congratulations!',
            "#{cozies} slime mold cozies", "#{gaskets} Sierpinski gaskets")
# Yesterday's productivity numbers:
# --------------------------------
# 21 slime mold cozies
# 10 Sierpinski gaskets
# --------------------------------
# Congratulations!
```

You can use the asterisk trick to call methods that don't take a variable number of arguments. You just need to make sure that the array you're using has enough elements to provide values for all of the method's required arguments.

You'll find this especially useful for constructors that take many arguments. The following code initializes four Range objects from four arrays of constructor arguments:

```
ranges = [[1, 10], [1, 6, true], [25, 100, false], [6, 9]]
ranges.collect { |l| Range.new(*l) }
# => [1..10, 1...6, 25..100, 6..9]
```

8.12 Simulating Keyword Arguments

Problem

A function or method can accept many optional arguments. You want to let callers pass in only the arguments they have values for, but Ruby doesn't support keyword arguments as Python and Lisp do.

Solution

Write your function to accept as its final argument a map of symbols to values. Consult the map as necessary to see what arguments were passed in.

```
def fun_with_text(text, args={})
  text = text.upcase if args[:upcase]
  text = text.downcase if args[:downcase]
  if args[:find] and args[:replace]
    text = text.gsub(args[:find], args[:replace])
  end
  text = text.slice(0, args[:truncate_at]) if args[:truncate_at]
  return text
end
```

Ruby has syntactic sugar that lets you define a hash inside a function call without putting it in curly brackets. This makes the code look more natural:

```
fun_with_text("Foobar", {:upcase => true, :truncate_at => 5})
# => "FOOBA"
fun_with_text("Foobar", :upcase => true, :truncate_at => 5)
# => "FOOBA"
```

```
fun_with_text("Foobar", :find => /(o+)/, :replace => '\1d', :downcase => true)
# => "foodbar"
```

Discussion

This simple code works well in most cases, but it has a couple of shortcomings compared to "real" keyword arguments. These simulated keyword arguments don't work like regular arguments because they're hidden inside a hash. You can't reject an argument that's not part of the "signature," and you can't force a caller to provide a particular keyword argument.

Each of these problems is easy to work around (for instance, does a required argument really need to be a keyword argument?), but it's best to define the workaround code in a mixin so you only have to do it once. The following code is based on a KeywordProcessor module by Gavin Sinclair:

```
###
# This mix-in module lets methods match a caller's hash of keyword
# parameters against a hash the method keeps, mapping keyword
# arguments to default parameter values.
#
# If the caller leaves out a keyword parameter whose default value is
# :MANDATORY (a constant in this module), then an error is raised.
#
# If the caller provides keyword parameters which have no
# corresponding keyword arguments, an error is raised.
#
module KeywordProcessor
  MANDATORY = :MANDATORY

  def process_params(params, defaults)
    # Reject params not present in defaults.
    params.keys.each do |key|
      unless defaults.has_key? key
        raise ArgumentError, "No such keyword argument: #{key}"
      end
    end
    result = defaults.dup.update(params)

    # Ensure mandatory params are given.
    unfilled = result.select { |k,v| v == MANDATORY }.map { |k,v| k.inspect }
    unless unfilled.empty?
      msg = "Mandatory keyword parameter(s) not given: #{unfilled.join(', ')}"
      raise ArgumentError, msg
    end

    return result
  end
end
```

Here's KeywordProcessor in action. Note how I set a default other than nil for a keyword argument, by defining it in the default value of args:

```
class TextCanvas
  include KeywordProcessor

  def render(text, args={}.freeze)
    args = process_params(args, {:font => 'New Reykjavik Solemn', :size => 36,
                                :bold => false, :x => :MANDATORY,
                                :y => :MANDATORY }.freeze)
    # ...
    puts "DEBUG: Found font #{args[:font]} in catalog."
    # ...
  end
end

canvas = TextCanvas.new

canvas.render('Hello', :x => 4, :y => 100)
# DEBUG: Found font New Reykjavik Solemn in catalog.

canvas.render('Hello', :x => 4, :y => 100, :font => 'Lacherlich')
# DEBUG: Found font Lacherlich in catalog.

canvas.render('Hello', :font => "Lacherlich")
# ArgumentError: Mandatory keyword parameter(s) not given: :x, :y

canvas.render('Hello', :x => 4, :y => 100, :italic => true)
# ArgumentError: No such keyword argument: italic
```

Ruby 2.0 will, hopefully, have full support for keyword arguments.

See Also

- Recipe 8.8, "Delegating Method Calls to Another Object"
- The KeywordProcessor module is based on the one in "Emulating Keyword Arguments in Ruby"; I modified it to be less oriented around the initialize method (*http://www.rubygarden.org/ruby?KeywordArguments*)

8.13 Calling a Superclass's Method

Problem

When overriding a class's method in a subclass, you want to extend or decorate the behavior of the superclass, rather than totally replacing it.

Solution

Use the super keyword to call the superclass implementation of the current method.

When you call super with no arguments, the arguments to your method are passed to the superclass method exactly as they were recieved by the subclass. Here's a Recipe class that defines (among other things) a cook method.

```
class Recipe
  # ... The rest of the Recipe implementation goes here.
  def cook(stove, cooking_time)
    dish = prepare_ingredients
    stove << dish
    wait_for(cooking_time)
    return dish
  end
end
```

Here's a subclass of `Recipe` that tacks some extra behavior onto the recipe. It passes all of its arguments directly into super:

```
class RecipeWithExtraGarlic < Recipe
  def cook(stove, cooking_time)

    5.times { add_ingredient(Garlic.new.chop) }
    super
  end
end
```

A subclass implementation can also choose to pass arguments into super. This way, a subclass can accept different arguments from its superclass implementation:

```
class BakingRecipe < Recipe
  def cook(cooking_time, oven_temperature=350)
    oven = Oven.new(oven_temperature)
    super(oven, cooking_time)
  end
end
```

Discussion

You can call super at any time in the body of a method—before, during, or after calling other code. This is in contrast to languages like Java, where you must call super in the method's first statement or never call it at all. If you need to, you can even call super multiple times within a single method.

Often you want to create a subclass method that exposes exactly the same interface as its parent. You can use the *args constructor to make the subclass method accept any arguments at all, then call super with no arguments to pass all those arguments (as well as any attached code block) into the superclass implementation. Let the superclass deal with any problems with the arguments.

The `String#gsub` method exposes a fairly complicated interface, but the `String` subclass defined here doesn't need to know anything about it:

```
class MyString < String
  def gsub(*args)
    return "#{super} -- This string modified by MyString#gsub (TM)"
  end
end
```

```
str = MyString.new("Here's my string")
str.gsub("my", "a")
# => "Here's a string -- This string modified by MyString#gsub (TM)"

str.gsub(/m| s/) { |match| match.strip.capitalize }
# => "Here's MyString -- This string modified by MyString#gsub (TM)"
```

If the subclass method takes arguments but the superclass method takes none, be sure to invoke super with an empty pair of parentheses. Usually you don't have to do this in Ruby, but super is not a real method call. If you invoke super without parentheses, it will pass all the subclass arguments into the superclass implementation, which won't be able to handle them.

In the example below, calling just super would result in an `ArgumentError`: it would pass a numeric argument into `String#succ!`, which takes no arguments:

```
class MyString
  def succ!(skip=1)
    skip.times { super() }
    self
  end
end

str = MyString.new('a')
str.succ!(3)                        # => "d"
```

Invoking super works for class methods as well as instance methods:

```
class MyFile < File
  def MyFile.ftype(*args)
    return "The type is #{super}."
  end
end

File.ftype("/bin")                    # => "directory"
MyFile.ftype("/bin")                  # => "The type is directory."
```

8.14 Creating an Abstract Method

Problem

You want to define a method of a class, but leave it for subclasses to fill in the actual implementations.

Solution

Define the method normally, but have it do nothing except raise a `NotImplementedError`:

```
class Shape2D
  def area
    raise NotImplementedError.
```

```
        new("#{self.class.name}#area is an abstract method.")
    end
  end

  Shape2D.new.area
  # NotImplementedError: Shape2D#area is an abstract method.
```

A subclass can redefine the method with a concrete implementation:

```
  class Square < Shape2D
    def initialize(length)
      @length = length
    end

    def area
      @length ** 2
    end
  end

  Square.new(10).area                    # => 100
```

Discussion

Ruby doesn't have a built-in notion of an abstract method or class, and though it has many built-in classes that might be considered "abstract," it doesn't enforce this abstractness the way C++ and Java do. For instance, you can instantiate an instance of Object or Numeric, even though those classes don't do anything by themselves.

In general, this is in the spirit of Ruby. But it's sometimes useful to define a super-class method that every subclass is expected to implement. The NotImplementedError error is the standard way of conveying that a method is not there, whether it's abstract or just an unimplemented stub.

Unlike other programming languages, Ruby will let you instantiate a class that defines an abstract method. You won't have any problems until you actually call the abstract method; even then, you can catch the NotImplementedError and recover. If you want, you can make an entire class abstract by making its initialize method raise a NotImplementedError. Then no one will be able to create instances of your class:[*]

```
  class Shape2D
    def initialize
     raise NotImplementedError.
      new("#{self.class.name} is an abstract class.")
    end
  end

  Shape2D.new
  # NotImplementedError: Shape2D is an abstract class.
```

---

[*] Of course, unless you freeze the class afterwards, someone else can reopen your class, define an empty initialize, and *then* create instances of your class.

We can do the same thing in less code by defining a decorator method of `Class` that creates an abstract method by the given name.

```ruby
class Class
  def abstract(*args)
    args.each do |method_name|

      define_method(method_name) do |*args|
        if method_name == :initialize
          msg = "#{self.class.name} is an abstract class."
        else
          msg = "#{self.class.name}##{method_name} is an abstract method."
        end
        raise NotImplementedError.new(msg)

      end
    end
  end
end
```

Here's an abstract class that defines an abstract method `move`:

```ruby
class Animal
  abstract :initialize, :move
end

Animal.new
# NotImplementedError: Animal is an abstract class.
```

Here's a concrete subclass that doesn't bother to define an implementation for the abstract method:

```ruby
class Sponge < Animal
  def initialize
    @type = :Sponge
  end
end

sponge = Sponge.new
sponge.move
# NotImplementedError: Sponge#move is an abstract method.
```

Here's a concrete subclass that implements the abstract method:

```ruby
class Cheetah < Animal
  def initialize
    @type = :Cheetah
  end

  def move
    "Running!"
  end
end

Cheetah.new.move
# => "Running!"
```

Abstract methods declared in a class are, by convention, eventually defined in the subclasses of that class. But Ruby doesn't enforce this either. An abstract method has a definition; it just happens to be one that always throws an error.

Since Ruby lets you reopen classes and redefine methods later, the definition of a concrete method can happen later in time instead of further down the inheritance tree. The Sponge class defined above didn't have a move method, but we can add one now:

```ruby
class Sponge
  def move
    "Floating on ocean currents!"
  end
end
sponge.move
# => "Floating on ocean currents!"
```

You can create an abstract singleton method, but there's not much point unless you intend to fill it in later. Unlike instance methods, singleton methods aren't inherited by subclasses. If you were to define Superclass.foo abstract, then define it for real as Subclass.foo, you would have accomplished little: Superclass.foo would still exist separately and would still be abstract.

8.15 Freezing an Object to Prevent Changes

Problem

You want to prevent any further changes to the state of an object.

Solution

Freeze the object with Object#freeze:

```ruby
frozen_string = 'Brrrr!'
frozen_string.freeze
frozen_string.gsub('r', 'a')                    # => "Baaaa!"
frozen_string.gsub!('r', 'a')
# TypeError: can't modify frozen string
```

Discussion

When an object is frozen, its instance variables are permanently bound to their current values. The values themselves are not frozen: *their* instance variables can still be modified, to the extent they were modifiable before:

```ruby
sequences = [[1,2,3], [1,2,4], [1,4,9]].freeze
sequences << [2,3,5]
# TypeError: can't modify frozen array
sequences[2] << 16                              # => [1, 4, 9, 16]
```

A frozen object cannot be unfrozen, and if cloned, the clone will also be frozen. Calling Object#dup (as opposed to Object#clone) on a frozen object yields an unfrozen object with the same instance variables.

```
frozen_string.clone.frozen?                    # => true
frozen_string.dup.frozen?                      # => false
```

Freezing an object does not prevent reassignment of any variables bound to that object.

```
frozen_string = 'A new string.'
frozen_string.frozen?                          # => false
```

To prevent objects from changing in ways confusing to the user or to the Ruby interpreter, Ruby sometimes copies objects and freezes the copies. When you use a string as a hash key, Ruby actually copies the string, freezes the copy, and uses the copy as the hash key: that way, if the original string changes later on, the hash key isn't affected.

Constant objects are often frozen as a second line of defense against the object being modified in place. You can freeze an object whenever you need a permanent reference to an object; this is most commonly seen with strings:

```
API_KEY = "100f7vo4gg".freeze

API_KEY[0] = 4
# TypeError: can't modify frozen string

API_KEY = "400f7vo4gg"
# warning: already initialized constant API_KEY
```

Frozen objects are also useful in multithreaded code. For instance, Ruby's internal file operations work from a frozen copy of a filename instead of using the filename directly. If another thread modifies the original filename in the middle of an operation that's supposed to be atomic, there's no problem: Ruby wasn't relying on the original filename anyway. You can adopt this copy-and-freeze pattern in multithreaded code to prevent a data structure you're working on from being changed by another thread.

Another common programmer-level use of this feature is to freeze a class in order to prevent future modifications to it (by yourself, other code running in the same environment, or other people who use your code as a library). This is not quite the same as the final construct in C# and Java, because you can still subclass a frozen class, and override methods in the subclass. Calling freeze only stops the in-place modification of a class. The simplest way to do it is to call freeze as the last statement in the class definition:

```
class MyClass
  def my_method
    puts "This is the only method allowed in MyClass."
  end
```

```
    freeze
end

class MyClass
  def my_method
    "I like this implementation of my_method better."
  end
end
# TypeError: can't modify frozen class

class MyClass
  def my_other_method
    "Oops, I forgot to implement this method."
  end
end
# TypeError: can't modify frozen class

class MySubclass < MyClass
  def my_method
    "This is only one of the methods available in MySubclass."
  end

  def my_other_method
    "This is the other one."
  end
end

MySubclass.new.my_method
# => "This is only one of the methods available in MySubclass."
```

See Also

- Recipe 4.7, "Making Sure a Sorted Array Stays Sorted," defines a convenience method for making a frozen copy of an object
- Recipe 5.5, "Using an Array or Other Modifiable Object as a Hash Key"
- Recipe 8.16, "Making a Copy of an Object"
- Recipe 8.17, "Declaring Constants"

8.16   Making a Copy of an Object

Problem

You want to make a copy of an existing object: a new object that can be modified separately from the original.

Solution

Ruby provides two ways of doing this. If you only want to have to remember one way, remember Object#clone:

```
s1 = 'foo'                                # => "foo"
s2 = s1.clone                             # => "foo"
s1[0] = 'b'
[s1, s2]                                  # => ["boo", "foo"]
```

Discussion

Ruby has two object-copy methods: a quick one and a thorough one. The quick one,
Object#dup, creates a new instance of an object's class, then sets all of the new
object's instance variables so that they reference the same objects as the original
does. Finally, it makes the new object tainted if the old object was tainted.

The downside of dup is that it creates a new instance of the object's *original* class. If
you open up a specific object and give it a singleton method, you implicitly create a
metaclass, an anonymous subclass of the original class. Calling dup on the object will
yield a copy that lacks the singleton methods. The other object-copy method,
Object#clone, makes a copy of the metaclass and instantiates the copy, instead of
instantiating the object's original class.

```
material = 'cotton'
class << material
  def definition
      puts 'The better half of velour.'
  end
end

material.definition
# The better half of velour.

'cotton'.definition
# NoMethodError: undefined method `definition' for "cotton":String

material.clone.definition
# The better half of velour.

material.dup.definition
# NoMethodError: undefined method `definition' for "cotton":String
```

Object#clone is also more strict about propagating Ruby's internal flags: it will prop-
agate both an object's "tainted?" flag and its "frozen?" flag. If you want to make an
unfrozen copy of a frozen object, you must use Object#dup.

Object#clone and Object#dup both perform shallow copies: they make copies of an
object without also copying its instance variables. You'll end up with two objects
whose instance variables point to the same objects. Modifications to one object's
instance variables will be visible in the other object. This can cause problems if
you're not expecting it:

```
class StringHolder
  attr_reader :string
  def initialize(string)
    @string = string
```

```
      end
    end

    s1 = StringHolder.new('string')
    s2 = s1.dup
    s3 = s1.clone

    s1.string[1] = 'p'
    s2.string                                   # => "spring"
    s3.string                                   # => "spring"
```

If you want to do a deep copy, an easy (though not particularly quick) way is to serialize the object to a binary string with `Marshal`, then load a new object from the
string:

```
    class Object
      def deep_copy
        Marshal.load(Marshal.dump(self))
      end
    end

    s1 = StringHolder.new('string')
    s2 = s1.deep_copy
    s1.string[1] = 'p'
    s1.string                                   # => "spring"
    s2.string                                   # => "string"
```

Note that this will only work on an object that has no singleton methods:

```
    class << s1
      def definition
        puts "We hold strings so you don't have to."
      end
    end
    s1.deep_copy
    # TypeError: singleton can't be dumped
```

When an object is cloned or duplicated, Ruby creates a new instance of its class or
superclass, but without calling the `initialize` method. If you want to define some
code to run when an object is cloned or duplicated, define an `initialize_copy` method.
This is a hook method that gives you a chance to modify the copy before Ruby passes it
back to whoever called `clone` or `dup`. If you want to simulate a deep copy without using
`Marshal`, this is your chance to modify the copy's instance variables:

```
    class StringHolder
      def initialize_copy(from)
        @string = from.string.dup
      end
    end

    s1 = StringHolder.new('string')
    s2 = s1.dup
    s3 = s1.clone
```

```
s1.string[1] = "p"
s2.string                                  # => "string"
s3.string                                  # => "string"
```

This table summarizes the differences between clone, dup, and the deep-copy technique that uses Marshal.

	Object#clone	Object#dup	Deep copy with Marshal
Same instance variables?	New references to the same objects	New references to the same objects	New objects
Same metaclass?	Yes	No	Yes[a]
Same singleton methods?	Yes	No	N/A[a]
Same frozen state?	Yes	No	No
Same tainted state?	Yes	Yes	Yes

[a] Marshal can't serialize an object whose metaclass is different from its original class.

See Also

• Recipe 13.2, "Serializing Data with Marshal"

8.17 Declaring Constants

Problem

You want to prevent a variable from being assigned a different value after its initial definition.

Solution

Declare the variable as a constant. You can't absolutely prohibit the variable from being assigned a different value, but you can make Ruby generate a warning whenever that happens.

```
not_a_constant = 3
not_a_constant = 10

A_CONSTANT = 3
A_CONSTANT = 10
# warning: already initialized constant A_CONSTANT
```

Discussion

A constant variable is one whose name starts with a capital letter. By tradition, Ruby constant names consist entirely of capital letters, numbers, and underscores. Constants don't mesh well with Ruby's philosophy of unlimited changability: there's no way to absolutely prevent someone from changing your constant. However, they are a useful signal to the programmers who come after you, letting them know not to redefine a constant without a very good reason.

Constants can occur anywhere in code. If they appear within a class or module, you can access them from outside the class or module with the double-colon operator (::). The name of the class or module qualifies the name of the constant, preventing confusion with other constants that may have the same name but be defined in different scopes.

```
CONST = 4

module ConstModule
  CONST = 6
end

class ConstHolder
  CONST = 8

  def my_const
    return CONST
  end
end

CONST                          # => 4
ConstModule::CONST             # => 6
ConstHolder::CONST             # => 8
ConstHolder.new.my_const       # => 8
```

The thing that's constant about a constant is its reference to an object. If you change the reference to point to a different object, you'll get a warning. Unfortunately, there's no way to tell Ruby to treat the redeclaration of a constant as an error.

```
E = 2.718281828               # => 2.718281828
E = 6                         # warning: already initialized constant E
E                             # => 6
```

However, you can use Module#remove_const as a sneaky way to "undeclare" a constant. You can then declare the constant again, without even triggering a warning. Clearly, this is potent and potentially dangerous stuff:

```
# This should make things a lot simpler.
module Math
 remove_const(:PI)
 PI = 3
end
Math::PI                       # => 3
```

If a constant points to a mutable object like an array or a string, the object itself can change without triggering the constant warning. You can prevent this by freezing the object to which the constant points:

```
RGB_COLORS = [:red, :green, :blue]   # => [:red, :green, :blue]
RGB_COLORS << :purple                # => [:red, :green, :blue, :purple]
```

```
RGB_COLORS = [:red, :green, :blue]
# warning: already initialized constant RGB_GOLORS
RGB_COLORS                              # => [:red, :green, :blue]

RGB_COLORS.freeze
RGB_COLORS << :purple
# TypeError: can't modify frozen array
```

Freezing operates on the object, not the reference. It does nothing to prevent a constant reference from being assigned to another object.

```
HOURS_PER_DAY = 24
HOURS_PER_DAY.freeze # This does nothing since Fixnums are already immutable.

HOURS_PER_DAY = 26
# warning: already initialized constant HOURS_PER_DAY
HOURS_PER_DAY                           # => 26
```

See Also

- Recipe 8.15, "Freezing an Object to Prevent Changes"

8.18   Implementing Class and Singleton Methods

Problem

You want to associate a new method with a class (as opposed to the instances of that class), or with a particular object (as opposed to other instances of the same class).

Solution

To define a class method, prefix the method name with the class name in the method definition. You can do this inside or outside of the class definition.

The Regexp.is_valid? method, defined below, checks whether a string can be compiled into a regular expression. It doesn't make sense to call it on an already instantiated Regexp, but it's clearly related functionality, so it belongs in the Regexp class (assuming you don't mind adding a method to a core Ruby class).

```
class Regexp
  def Regexp.is_valid?(str)
    begin
      compile(str)
      valid = true
    rescue RegexpError
      valid = false
    end
  end
end
Regexp.is_valid? "The horror!"          # => true
Regexp.is_valid? "The)horror!"          # => false
```

Here's a `Fixnum.random` method that generates a random number in a specified range:

```
def Fixnum.random(min, max)
  raise ArgumentError, "min > max" if min > max
  return min + rand(max-min+1)
end
Fixnum.random(10, 20)                          # => 13
Fixnum.random(-5, 0)                           # => -5
Fixnum.random(10, 10)                          # => 10
Fixnum.random(20, 10)
# ArgumentError: min > max
```

To define a method on one particular other object, prefix the method name with the variable name when you define the method:

```
company_name = 'Homegrown Software'
def company_name.legalese
  return "#{self} is a registered trademark of ConglomCo International."
end

company_name.legalese
# => "Homegrown Software is a registered trademark of ConglomCo International."
'Some Other Company'.legalese
# NoMethodError: undefined method `legalese' for "Some Other Company":String
```

Discussion

In Ruby, a singleton method is a method defined on one specific object, and not available to other instances of the same class. This is kind of analogous to the Singleton pattern, in which all access to a certain class goes through a single instance, but the name is more confusing than helpful.

Class methods are actually a special case of singleton methods. The object on which you define a new method is the Class object itself.

Some common types of class methods are listed here, along with illustrative examples taken from Ruby's standard library:

- Methods that instantiate objects, and methods for retrieving an object that implements the Singleton pattern. Examples: `Regexp.compile`, `Date.parse`, `Dir.open`, and `Marshal.load` (which can instantiate objects of many different types). Ruby's standard constructor, the `new` method, is another example.

- Utility or helper methods that use logic associated with a class, but don't require an instance of that class to operate. Examples: `Regexp.escape`, `Dir.entries`, `File.basename`.

- Accessors for class-level or Singleton data structures. Examples: `Thread.current`, `Struct.members`, `Dir.pwd`.

- Methods that implicitly operate on an object that implements the Singleton pattern. Examples: `Dir.chdir`, `GC.disable` and `GC.enable`, and all the methods of `Process`.

When you define a singleton method on an object other than a class, it's usually to redefine an existing method for a particular object, rather than to define a brand new method. This behavior is common in frameworks, such as GUIs, where each individual object has customized behavior. Singleton method definition is a cheap substitute for subclassing when you only need to customize the behavior of a single object:

```
class Button
  #A stub method to be overridden by subclasses or individual Button objects
  def pushed
  end
end

button_a = Button.new
def button_a.pushed
  puts "You pushed me! I'm offended!"
end

button_b = Button.new
def button_b.pushed
  puts "You pushed me; that's okay."
end

Button.new.pushed
#

button_a.pushed
# You pushed me! I'm offended!

button_b.pushed
# You pushed me; that's okay.
```

When you define a method on a particular object, Ruby acts behind the scenes to transform the object into an anonymous subclass of its former class. This new class is the one that actually defines the new method or overrides the methods of its superclass.

8.19 Controlling Access by Making Methods Private

Problem

You've refactored your code (or written it for the first time) and ended up a method that should be marked for internal use only. You want to prevent outside objects from calling such methods.

Solution

Use private as a statement before a method definition, and the method will not be callable from outside the class that defined it. This class defines an initializer, a public method, and a private method:

```
class SecretNumber
  def initialize
    @secret = rand(20)
  end
```

```
  def hint
    puts "The number is #{"not " if secret <= 10}greater than 10."
  end

  private
  def secret
    @secret
  end
end

s = SecretNumber.new
s.secret
# NoMethodError: private method `secret' called for
#   #<SecretNumber:0xb7c2e83c @secret=19>

s.hint
# The number is greater than 10.
```

Unlike in many other programming languages, a private method in Ruby *is* accessible to subclasses of the class that defines it:

```
class LessSecretNumber < SecretNumber
  def hint
    lower = secret-rand(10)-1
    upper = secret+rand(10)+1
    "The number is somewhere between #{lower} and #{upper}."
  end
end

ls = LessSecretNumber.new
ls.hint
# => "The number is somewhere between -3 and 16."
ls.hint
# => "The number is somewhere between -1 and 15."
ls.hint
# => "The number is somewhere between -2 and 16."
```

Discussion

Like many parts of Ruby that look like special language features, Ruby's privacy keywords are actually methods. In this case, they're methods of Module. When you call private, protected, or public, the current module (remember that a class is just a special kind of module) changes the rules it applies to newly defined methods from that point on.

Most languages that support method privacy make you put a keyword before every method saying whether it's public, private, or protected. In Ruby, the special privacy methods act as toggles. When you call the private keyword, all methods you define after that point are declared as private, until the module definition ends or you call a different privacy method. This makes it easy to group methods of the same privacy level—a good, general programming practice:

```
class MyClass
  def public_method1
  end

  def public_method2
  end

  protected

  def protected_method1
  end

  private

  def private_method1
  end

  def private_method2
  end
end
```

Private and protected methods work a little differently in Ruby than in most other programming languages. Suppose you have a class called Foo and a subclass SubFoo. In languages like Java, SubFoo has no access to any private methods defined by Foo. As seen in the Solution, Ruby provides no way to hide a class's methods from its subclasses. In this way, Ruby's private works like Java's protected.

Suppose further that you have two instances of the Foo class, A and B. In languages like Java, A and B can call each other's private methods. In Ruby, you need to use a protected method for that. This is the main difference between private and protected methods in Ruby.

In the example below, I try to add another type of hint to the LessSecretNumber class, one that lets you compare the relative magnitudes of two secret numbers. It doesn't work because one LessSecretNumber can't call the private methods of another LessSecretNumber:

```
class LessSecretNumber
  def compare(other)
    if secret == other.secret
    comparison = "equal to"
    else
      comparison = secret > other.secret ? "greater than" : "less than"
    end
    "This secret number is #{comparison} the secret number you passed in."
  end
end

a = LessSecretNumber.new
b = LessSecretNumber.new
a.hint
# => "The number is somewhere between 17 and 22."
```

```
b.hint
# => "The number is somewhere between 0 and 12."
a.compare(b)
# NoMethodError: private method `secret' called for
# #<LessSecretNumber:0xb7bfe13c @secret=6>
```

But if I make make the secret method protected instead of private, the compare
method starts working. You can change the privacy of a method after the fact by
passing its symbol into one of the privacy methods:

```
class SecretNumber
  protected :secret
end
a.compare(b)
# => "This secret number is greater than the secret number you passed in."
b.compare(a)
# => "This secret number is less than the secret number you passed in."
```

Instance variables are always private: accessible by subclasses, but not from other
objects, even other objects of the same class. If you want to make an instance variable accessible to the outside, you should define a getter method with the same name
as the variable. This method can be either protected or public.

You can trick a class into calling a private method from outside by passing the
method's symbol into Object#send (in Ruby 1.8) or Object#funcall (in Ruby 1.9).
You'd better have a really good reason for doing this.

```
s.send(:secret)                                      # => 19
```

See Also

• Recipe 8.2, "Managing Class Data," has a pretty good reason for using the
  Object#send trick

## CHAPTER 9

Modules and Namespaces

A Ruby module is nothing more than a grouping of objects under a single name. The objects may be constants, methods, classes, or other modules.

Modules have two uses. You can use a module as a convenient way to bundle objects together, or you can incorporate its contents into a class with Ruby's include statement.

When a module is used as a container for objects, it's called a *namespace*. Ruby's Math module is a good example of a namespace: it provides an overarching structure for constants like Math::PI and methods like Math::log, which would otherwise clutter up the main Kernel namespace. We cover this most basic use of modules in Recipes 9.5 and 9.7.

Modules are also used to package functionality for inclusion in classes. The Enumerable module isn't supposed to be used on its own: it adds functionality to a class like Array or Hash. We cover the use of modules as packaged functionality for existing classes in Recipes 9.1 and 9.4.

Module is actually the superclass of Class, so every Ruby class is also a module. Throughout this book we talk about using methods of Module from within classes. The same methods will work exactly the same way within modules. The only thing you can't do with a module is instantiate an object from it:

```
Class.superclass                        # => Module
Math.class                              # => Module
Math.new
# NoMethodError: undefined method `new' for Math:Module
```

9.1 Simulating Multiple Inheritance with Mixins

Problem

You want to create a class that derives from two or more sources, but Ruby doesn't support multiple inheritance.

Solution

Suppose you created a class called Taggable that lets you associate tags (short strings of informative metadata) with objects. Every class whose objects should be taggable could derive from Taggable.

This would work if you made Taggable the top-level class in your class structure, but that won't work in every situation. Eventually you might want to do something like make a string taggable. One class can't subclass both Taggable and String, so you'd have a problem.

Furthermore, it makes little sense to instantiate and use a Taggable object by itself—there is nothing there to tag! Taggability is more of a feature of a class than a full-fledged class of its own. The Taggable functionality only works in conjunction with some other data structure.

This makes it an ideal candidate for implementation as a Ruby module instead of a class. Once it's in a module, any class can include it and use the methods it defines.

```
require 'set' # Deals with a collection of unordered values with no duplicates

# Include this module to make your class taggable. The names of the
# instance variable and the setup method are prefixed with "taggable_"
# to reduce the risk of namespace collision. You must call
# taggable_setup before you can use any of this module's methods.
module Taggable
  attr_accessor :tags

  def taggable_setup
    @tags = Set.new
  end

  def add_tag(tag)
    @tags << tag
  end

  def remove_tag(tag)
    @tags.delete(tag)
  end
end
```

Here's a taggable string class: it subclasses String, but it also includes the functionality of Taggable.

```
class TaggableString < String
  include Taggable
  def initialize(*args)
    super
    taggable_setup
  end
end
```

```
s = TaggableString.new('It was the best of times, it was the worst of times.')
s.add_tag 'dickens'
s.add_tag 'quotation'
s.tags                              # => #<Set: {"dickens", "quotation"}>
```

Discussion

A Ruby class can only have one superclass, but it can include any number of modules. These modules are called *mixins*. If you write a chunk of code that can add functionality to classes in general, it should go into a mixin module instead of a class.

The only objects that need to be defined as classes are the ones that get instantiated and used on their own (modules can't be instantiated).

If you come from Java, you might think of a module as being the combination of an interface and its implementation. By including a module, your class implements certain methods, and announces that since it implements those methods it can be treated a certain way.

When a class includes a module with the include keyword, all of the module's methods and constants are made available from within that class. They're not copied, the way a method is when you alias it. Rather, the class becomes aware of the methods of the module. If a module's methods are changed later (even during runtime), so are the methods of all the classes that include that module.

Module and class definitions have an almost identical syntax. If you find out after implementing a class that you should have done it as a module, it's not difficult to translate the class into a module. The main problem areas will be methods defined both by your module and the classes that include it: especially methods like initialize.

Your module can define an initialize method, and it will be called by a class whose constructor includes a super call (see Recipe 9.8 for an example), but sometimes that doesn't work. For instance, Taggable defines a taggable_setup method that takes no arguments. The String class, the superclass of TaggableString, takes one and only one argument. TaggableString can call super within its constructor to trigger both String#initialize and a hypothetical Taggable#initialize, but there's no way a single super call can pass one argument to one method and zero arguments to another.

That's why Taggable doesn't define an initialize method.[*] Instead, it defines a taggable_setup method and (in the module documentation) asks everyone who includes the module to call taggable_setup within their initialize method. Your module can define a <module name>_setup method instead of initialize, but you need to document it, or your users will be very confused.

---

[*] An alternative is to define Taggable#initialize to take a variable number of arguments, and then just ignore all the arguments. This only works because Taggable can initialize itself without any outside information.

It's okay to expect that any class that includes your module will implement some methods you can't implement yourself. For instance, all of the methods in the Enumerable module are defined in terms of a method called each, but Enumerable never actually defines each. Every class that includes Enumerable must define what each means within that class before it can use the Enumerable methods.

If you have such undefined methods, it will cut down on confusion if you provide a default implementation that raises a helpful exception:

```ruby
module Complaint
  def gripe
    voice('In all my years I have never encountered such behavior...')
  end

  def faint_praise
    voice('I am pleased to notice some improvement, however slight...')
  end

  def voice(complaint_text)
    raise NotImplementedError,
    "#{self.class} included the Complaint module but didn't define voice!"
  end
end

class MyComplaint
  include Complaint
end

MyComplaint.new.gripe
# NotImplementedError: MyComplaint included the Complaint module
# but didn't define voice!
```

If two modules define methods with the same name, and a single class includes both modules, the class will have only one implementation of that method: the one from the module that was included last. The method of the same name from the other module will simply not be available. Here are two modules that define the same method:

```ruby
module Ayto
  def potato
    'Pohtayto'
  end
end

module Ahto
  def potato
    'Pohtahto'
  end
end
```

One class can mix in both modules:

```ruby
class Potato
  include Ayto
  include Ahto
end
```

But there can be only one potato method for a given class or module.*

```
Potato.new.potato                              # => "Pohtahto"
```

This rule sidesteps the fundamental problem of multiple inheritance by letting the programmer explicitly choose which ancestor they would like to inherit a particular method from. Nevertheless, it's good programming practice to give distinctive names to the methods in your modules. This reduces the risk of namespace collisions when a class mixes in more than one module. Collisions can occur, and the later module's method will take precedence, even if one or both methods are protected or private.

See Also

- If you want a real-life implementation of a Taggable-like mixin, see Recipe 13.18, "Adding Taggability with a Database Mixin"

9.2   Extending Specific Objects with Modules

Credit: Phil Tomson

Problem

You want to add instance methods from a module (or modules) to specific objects. You don't want to mix the module into the object's class, because you want certain objects to have special abilities.

Solution

Use the Object#extend method.

For example, let's say we have a mild-mannered Person class:

```
class Person
  attr_reader :name, :age, :occupation

  def initialize(name, age, occupation)
    @name, @age, @occupation = name, age, occupation
  end

  def mild_mannered?
    true
  end
end
```

Now let's create a couple of instances of this class.

```
jimmy = Person.new('Jimmy Olsen', 21, 'cub reporter')
clark = Person.new('Clark Kent', 35, 'reporter')
```

---

* You could get both methods by aliasing Potato#potato to another method after mixing in Ayto but before mixing in Ahto. There would still only be one Potato#potato method, and it would still be Ahto#potato, but the implementation of Ayto#potato would survive under a different name.

```
jimmy.mild_mannered?                                      # => true
clark.mild_mannered?                                      # => true
```

But it happens that some Person objects are not as mild-mannered as they might appear. Some of them have super powers.

```
module SuperPowers
  def fly
    'Flying!'
  end

  def leap(what)
    "Leaping #{what} in a single bound!"
  end

  def mild_mannered?
    false
  end

  def superhero_name
    'Superman'
  end
end
```

If we use include to mix the SuperPowers module into the Person class, it will give every person super powers. Some people are bound to misuse such power. Instead, we'll use extend to give super powers only to certain people:

```
clark.extend(SuperPowers)
clark.superhero_name                                     # => "Superman"
clark.fly                                                # => "Flying!"
clark.mild_mannered?                                     # => false
jimmy.mild_mannered?                                     # => true
```

Discussion

The extend method is used to mix a module's methods into an object, while include is used to mix a module's methods into a class.

The astute reader might point out that classes are actually objects in Ruby. Let us see what happens when we use extend in a class definition:

```
class Person
  extend SuperPowers
end

#which is equivalent to:
Person.extend(SuperPowers)
```

What exactly are we extending here? Within the class definition, extend is being called on the Person class itself: we could have also written self. extend(SuperPowers). We're extending the Person class with the methods defined in

SuperPowers. This means that the methods defined in the SuperPowers module have now become class methods of Person:

```
Person.superhero_name          # => "Superman"
Person.fly                     # => "Flying!"
```

This is not what we intended in this case. However, sometimes you do want to mix methods into a class, and Class#extend is an easy and powerful way to do it.

See Also

- Recipe 9.3, "Mixing in Class Methods," shows how to mix in class methods with include

9.3   Mixing in Class Methods

Credit: Phil Tomson

Problem

You want to mix class methods into a class, instead of mixing in instance methods.

Solution

The simplest way to accomplish this is to call extend on the class object, as seen in the Discussion of Recipe 9.2. Just as you can use extend to add singleton methods to an object, you can use it to add class methods to a class. But that's not always the best option. Your users may not know that your module provides or even requires some class methods, so they might not extend their class when they should. How can you make an include statement mix in class methods as well?

To begin, within your module, define a submodule called ClassMethods,* which contains the methods you want to mix into the class:

```
module MyLib
  module ClassMethods
    def class_method
      puts "This method was first defined in MyLib::ClassMethods"
    end
  end
end
```

To make this code work, we must also define the included callback method within the MyLib module. This method is called every time a module is included in the class, and it's passed the class object in which our module is being included. Within the

---

* The name ClassMethods has no special meaning within Ruby: technically, you can call your submodule whatever you want. But the Ruby community has standardized on ClassMethods as the name of this submodule, and it's used in many Ruby libraries, so you should use it too.

callback method, we extend that class object with our `ClassMethods` module, making all of its instance methods into class methods. Continuing the example:

```
module MyLib
  def self.included(receiver)
    puts "MyLib is being included in #{receiver}!"
    receiver.extend(ClassMethods)
  end
end
```

Now we can include our `MyLib` module in a class, and get the contents of `ClassMethods` mixed in as genuine class methods:

```
class MyClass
  include MyLib
end
# MyLib is being included in MyClass!

MyClass.class_method
# This method was first defined in MyLib::ClassMethods
```

Discussion

`Module#included` is a callback method that is automatically called during the inclusion of a module into a class. The default `included` implementation is an empty method. In the example, `MyLib` overrides it to extend the class that's including the `MyLib` module with the contents of the `MyLib::ClassMethods` submodule.

The `Object#extend` method takes a `Module` object as a parameter. It mixes all the methods defined in the module into the receiving object. Since classes are themselves objects, and the singleton methods of a `Class` object are just its class methods, calling extend on a class object fills it up with new class methods.

See Also

- Recipe 7.11, "Coupling Systems Loosely with Callbacks," covers callbacks in general and shows how to write your own
- Recipe 10.6, "Listening for Changes to a Class," covers Ruby's other class and module callback methods

9.4 Implementing Enumerable: Write One Method, Get 22 Free

Problem

You want to give a class all the useful iterator and iteration-related features of Ruby's arrays (sort, detect, inject, and so on), but your class can't be a subclass of `Array`. You don't want to define all those methods yourself.

Solution

Implement an each method, then include the Enumerable module. It defines 22 of the most useful iteration methods in terms of the each implementation you provide.

Here's a class that keeps multiple arrays under the covers. By defining each, it can expose a large interface that lets the user treat it like a single array:

```
class MultiArray
  include Enumerable

  def initialize(*arrays)
    @arrays = arrays
  end

  def each
    @arrays.each { |a| a.each { |x| yield x } }
  end
end

ma = MultiArray.new([1, 2], [3], [4])
ma.collect                                    # => [1, 2, 3, 4]
ma.detect { |x| x > 3 }                       # => 4
ma.map { |x| x ** 2 }                         # => [1, 4, 9, 16]
ma.each_with_index { |x, i| puts "Element #{i} is #{x}" }
# Element 0 is 1
# Element 1 is 2
# Element 2 is 3
# Element 3 is 4
```

Discussion

The Enumerable module is the most common mixin module. It lets you add a lot of behavior to your class for a little investment. Since Ruby relies so heavily on iterator methods, and almost every data structure can be iterated over in some way, it's no wonder that so many of the classes in Ruby's standard library include Enumerable: Dir, Hash, Range, and String, just to name a few.

Here's the complete list of methods you can get by including Enumerable. Many of them are described elsewhere in this book, especially in Chapter 4. Perhaps the most useful are collect, inject, find_all, and sort_by.

```
Enumerable.instance_methods.sort
# => ["all?", "any?", "collect", "detect", "each_with_index", "entries",
# =>  "find", "find_all", "grep", "include?", "inject", "map", "max",
# =>  "member?", "min", "partition", "reject", "select", "sort", "sort_by",
# =>  "to_a", "zip"]
```

Although you can get all these methods simply by implementing an each method, some of the methods won't work unless your each implementation returns objects that can be compared to each other. For example, a data structure that contains both numbers and strings can't be sorted, since it makes no sense to compare a number to a string:

```
ma.sort                              # => [1, 2, 3, 4]
mixed_type_ma = MultiArray.new([1, 2, 3], ["a", "b", "c"])
mixed_type_ma.sort
# ArgumentError: comparison of Fixnum with String failed
```

The methods subject to this restriction are max, min, sort, and sort_by. Since you probably don't have complete control over the types of the data stored in your data structure, the best strategy is probably to just let a method fail if the data is incompatible. This is what Array does:

```
[1, 2, 3, "a", "b", "c"].sort
# ArgumentError: comparison of Fixnum with String failed
```

One more example: in this one, I'll make Module itself include Enumerable. My each implementation will iterate over the instance methods defined by a class or module. This makes it easy to find methods of a class that meet certain criteria.

```
class Module
  include Enumerable
  def each
    instance_methods.each { |x| yield x }
  end
end

# Find all instance methods of String that modify the string in place.
String.find_all { |method_name| method_name[-1] == ?! }
# => ["sub!", "upcase!", "delete!", "lstrip!", "succ!", "gsub!",
# =>  "squeeze!", "downcase!", "rstrip!", "slice!", "chop!", "capitalize!",
# =>  "tr!", "chomp!", "next!", "swapcase!", "reverse!", "tr_s!", "strip!"]

# Find all instance methods of Fixnum that take 2 arguments.
sample = 0
sample.class.find_all { |method_name| sample.method(method_name).arity == 2 }
# => ["instance_variable_set", "between?"]
```

See Also

- Many of the recipes in Chapter 4 actually cover methods of Enumerable; see especially Recipe 4.12, "Building Up a Hash Using Injection"
- Recipe 9.1, "Simulating Multiple Inheritance with Mixins"

9.5   Avoiding Naming Collisions with Namespaces

Problem

You want to define a class or module whose name conflicts with an existing class or module, or you want to prevent someone else from coming along later and defining a class whose name conflicts with yours.

Solution

A Ruby module can contain classes and other modules, which means you can use it as a namespace.

Here's some code from a physics library that defines a class called String within the StringTheory module. The real name of this class is its fully-qualified name: StringTheory::String. It's a totally different class from Ruby's built-in String class.

```ruby
module StringTheory
  class String
    def initialize(length=10**-33)
      @length = length
    end
  end
end

String.new                                       # => ""

StringTheory::String.new
# => #<StringTheory::String:0xb7c343b8 @length=1.0e-33>
```

Discussion

If you've read Recipe 8.17, you've already seen namespaces in action. The constants defined in a module are qualified with the module's name. This lets Math::PI have a different value from Greek::PI.

You can qualify the name of any Ruby object this way: a variable, a class, or even another module. Namespaces let you organize your libraries, and make it possible for them to coexist alongside others.

Ruby's standard library uses namespaces heavily as an organizing principle. An excellent example is REXML, the standard XML library. It defines a REXML namespace that includes lots of XML-related classes like REXML::Comment and REXML::Instruction. Naming those classes Comment and Instruction would be a disaster: they'd get overwritten by other librarys' Comment and Instruction classes. Since nothing about the generic-sounding names relates them to the REXML library, you might look at someone else's code for a long time before realizing that the Comment objects have to do with XML.

Namespaces can be nested: see for instance rexml's REXML::Parsers module, which contains classes like REXML::Parsers::StreamParser. Namespaces group similar classes in one place so you can find what you're looking for; nested namespaces do the same for namespaces.

In Ruby, you should name your top-level module after your software project (SAX), or after the task it performs (XML::Parser). If you're writing Yet Another implementation of something that already exists, you should make sure your namespace includes your project name (XML::Parser::SAX). This is in contrast to Java's namespaces: they exist in its package structure, which follows a naming convention that includes a domain name, like org.xml.sax.

All code within a module is implicitly qualified with the name of the module. This can cause problems for a module like StringTheory, if it needs to use Ruby's built-in String class for something. This should be fixed in Ruby 2.0, but you can also fix it by setting the built-in String class to a variable before defining your StringTheory::String class. Here's a version of the StringTheory module that can use Ruby's built-in String class:

```
module StringTheory2
  RubyString = String
  class String
    def initialize(length=10**-33)
      @length = length
    end
  end

  RubyString.new("This is a built-in string, not a StringTheory2::String")
end
# => "This is a built-in string, not a StringTheory2::String"
```

See Also

- Recipe 8.17, "Declaring Constants"
- Recipe 9.7, "Including Namespaces"

9.6 Automatically Loading Libraries as Needed

Problem

You've written a big library with multiple components. You'd like to split it up so that users don't have to load the entire library into memory just to use part of it. But you don't want to make your users explicitly require each part of the library they plan to use.

Solution

Split the big library into multiple files, and set up autoloading for the individual files by calling Kernel#autoload. The individual files will be loaded as they're referenced.

Suppose you have a library, functions.rb, that provides two very large modules:

```
# functions.rb
module Decidable
  # ... Many, many methods go here.
end

module Semidecidable
  # ... Many, many methods go here.
end
```

You can provide the same interface, but possibly save your users some memory, by splitting `functions.rb` into three files. The `functions.rb` file itself becomes a stub full of autoload calls:

```
# functions.rb
autoload :Decidable, "decidable.rb"
autoload :Semidecidable, "semidecidable.rb"
```

The modules themselves go into the files mentioned in the new `functions.rb`:

```
# decidable.rb
module Decidable
  # ... Many, many methods go here.
end
# semidecidable.rb
module Semidecidable
  # ... Many, many methods go here.
end
```

The following code will work if all the modules are in `functions.rb`, but it will also work if `functions.rb` only contains calls to autoload:

```
require 'functions'
Decidable.class                          # => Module
# More use of the Decidable module follows...
```

When `Decidable` and `Semidecidable` have been split into autoloaded modules, that code only loads the `Decidable` module. Memory is saved that would otherwise be used to contain the unsed `Semidecidable` module.

Discussion

Refactoring a library to consist of autoloadable components takes a little extra planning, but it's often worth it to improve performance for the people who use your library.

Each call to `Kernel#autoload` binds a symbol to the path of the Ruby file that's supposed to define that symbol. If the symbol is referenced, that file is loaded exactly as though it had been passed as an argument into `require`. If the symbol is never referenced, the user saves some memory.

Since you can use autoload wherever you might use `require`, you can autoload built-in libraries when the user triggers some code that needs them. For instance, here's some code that loads Ruby's built-in set library as needed:

```
autoload :Set, "set.rb"

def random_set(size)
  max = size * 10
  set = Set.new
  set << rand(max) until set.size == size
  return set
end

# More code goes here...
```

If random_set is never called, the set library will never be loaded, and memory will be saved. As soon as random_set gets called, the set library is autoloaded, and the code works even though we never explicitly require 'set':

```
random_set(10)
# => #<Set: {39, 83, 73, 40, 90, 25, 91, 31, 76, 54}>

require 'set'                                        # => false
```

9.7   Including Namespaces

Problem

You want to use the objects within a module without constantly qualifying the object names with the name of their module.

Solution

Use include to copy a module's objects into the current namespace. You can then use them from the current namespace, without qualifying their names.

Instead of this:

```
require 'rexml/document'

REXML::Document.new(xml)
```

You might write this:

```
require 'rexml/document'
include REXML

Document.new(xml)
```

Discussion

This is the exact same include statement you use to incorporate a mixin module into a class you're writing. It does the same thing here as when it includes a mixin: it copies the contents of a module into the current namespace.

Here, though, the point isn't to add new functionality to a class or module: it's to save you from having to do so much typing. This technique is especially useful with large library modules like Curses and the Rails libraries.

This use of include comes with the same caveats as any other: if you already have variables with the same names as the objects being included, the included objects will be copied in over them and clobber them.

You can, of course, import a namespace that's nested within a namespace of its own. Instead of this:

```
require 'rexml/parsers/pullparser'

REXML::Parsers::PullParser.new("Some XML")
```

You might write this:

```
require 'rexml/parsers/pullparser'
include REXML::Parsers

PullParser.new("Some XML")
```

See Also

- Recipe 11.3, "Extracting Data While Parsing a Document"

9.8 Initializing Instance Variables Defined by a Module

Credit: Phil Tomson

Problem

You have a mixin module that defines some instance variables. Given a class that mixes in the module, you want to initialize the instance variables whenever an instance of the class is created.

Solution

Define an `initialize` method in the module, and call super in your class's constructor. Here's a `Timeable` module that tracks when objects are created and how old they are:

```
module Timeable
  attr_reader :time_created

  def initialize
    @time_created = Time.now
  end

  def age      #in seconds
    Time.now - @time_created
  end
end
```

`Timeable` has an instance variable `time_created`, and an `initialize` method that assigns `Time.now` (the current time) to the instance variable. Now let's mix `Timeable` into another class that also defines an `initialize` method:

```
class Character
  include Timeable
  attr_reader :name
  def initialize( name )
    @name = name
    super( ) #calls Timeable's initialize
  end
end
```

```
c = Character.new "Fred"

c.time_created
# => Mon Mar 27 18:34:31 EST 2006
```

Discussion

You can define and access instance variables within a module's instance methods, but you can't actually instantiate a module. A module's instance variables only exist within objects of a class that includes the module. However, classes don't usually need to know about the instance variables defined by the modules they include. That sort of information should be initialized and maintained by the module itself.

The Character#initialize method overrides the Timeable#initialize method, but you can use super to call the Timeable constructor from within the Character constructor. When a module is included in a class, that module becomes an *ancestor* of the class. We can test this in the context of the example above by calling the Module#ancestors on the Character class:

```
Character.ancestors          # => [Character, Timeable, Object, Kernel]
```

When you call super from within a method (such as initialize), Ruby finds every ancestor that defines a method with the same name, and calls it too.

See Also

- Recipe 8.13, "Calling a Superclass's Method"
- Sometimes an initialize method won't work; see Recipe 9.3, "Mixing in Class Methods," for when it won't work, and how to manage without one
- Recipe 9.9, "Automatically Initializing Mixed-In Modules," covers an even more complex case, when you want a module to perform some initialization, without making the class that includes do anything at all beyond the initial include

9.9   Automatically Initializing Mixed-In Modules

Credit: Phil Tomson

Problem

You've written a module that gets mixed into classes. Your module has some initialization code that needs to run whenever the mixed-into class is initialized. You do not want users of your module to have to call super in their initialize methods.

Solution

First, we need a way for classes to keep track of which modules they've included. We also need to redefine Class#new to call a module-level initialize method for each included module. Fortunately, Ruby's flexibility lets us makes changes to the built-in Class class (though this should never be done lightly):

```
class Class
  def included_modules
    @included_modules ||= []
  end

  alias_method :old_new, :new
  def new(*args, &block)
    obj = old_new(*args, &block)
    self.included_modules.each do |mod|
      mod.initialize if mod.respond_to?(:initialize)
    end
    obj
  end
end
```

Now every class has a list of included modules, accessible from the included_modules class method. We've also redefined the Class#new method so that it iterates through all the modules in included_modules, and calls the module-level initialize method of each.

All that's missing is a way to add included modules to included_modules. We'll put this code into an Initializable module. A module that wants to be initializable can mix this module into itself and define an initialize method:

```
module Initializable

  def self.included(mod)
    mod.extend ClassMethods
  end

  module ClassMethods
    def included(mod)
      if mod.class != Module  #in case Initializeable is mixed-into a class
        puts "Adding #{self} to #{mod}'s included_modules" if $DEBUG
        mod.included_modules << self
      end
    end
  end
end
```

The included callback method is called whenever this module is included in another module. We're using the pattern shown in Recipe 9.3 to add an included callback method into the receiving module. If we didn't do this, you'd have to use that pattern yourself for every module you wanted to be Initializable.

Discussion

That's a lot of code, but here's the payoff. Let's define a couple of modules which include Initializeable and define initialize module methods:

```
module A
  include Initializable
  def self.initialize
    puts "A's initialized."
  end
end

module B
  include Initializable
  def self.initialize
    puts "B's initialized."
  end
end
```

We can now define a class that mixes in both modules. Instantiating the class instantiates the modules, with not a single super call in sight!

```
class BothAAndB
  include A
  include B
end

both = BothAAndB.new
# A's initialized.
# B's initialized.
```

The goal of this recipe is very similar to Recipe 9.8. In that recipe, you call super in a class's initialize method to call a mixed-in module's initialize method. That recipe is a lot simpler than this one and doesn't require any changes to built-in classes, so it's often preferable to this one.

Consider a case like the BothAAndB class above. Using the techniques from Recipe 9.8, you'd need to make sure that both A and B had calls to super in their initialize methods, so that each module would get initialized. This solution moves all of that work into the Initializable module and the built-in Class class. The other drawback of the previous technique is that the user of your module needs to know to call super somewhere in their initialize method. Here, everything happens automatically.

This technique is not without its pitfalls. Anytime you redefine critical built-in methods like Class#new, you need to be careful: someone else may have already redefined it elsewhere in your program. Also, you won't be able to define your own included method callback in a module which includes Initializeable: doing so will override the callback defined by Initializable itself.

See Also

- Recipe 9.3, "Mixing in Class Methods"
- Recipe 9.8, "Initializing Instance Variables Defined by a Module"

## CHAPTER 10

Reflection and Metaprogramming

In a dynamic language like Ruby, few pieces are static. Classes can grow new methods and lose the ones they had before. Methods can be defined manually, or automatically with well-written code.

Probably the most interesting aspect of the Ruby programming philosophy is its use of reflection and metaprogramming to save the programmer from having to write repetitive code. In this chapter, we will teach you the ways and the joys of these techniques.

Reflection lets you treat classes and methods as objects. With reflection you can see which methods you can call on an object (Recipes 10.2 and 10.3). You can grab one of its methods as an object (Recipe 10.4), and call it or pass it in to another method as a code block. You can get references to the class an object implements and the modules it includes, and print out its inheritance structure (Recipe 10.1). Reflection is especially useful when you're interactively examining an unfamiliar object or class structure.

Metaprogramming is to programming as programming is to doing a task by hand. If you need to sort a file of a hundred lines, you don't open it up in a text editor and start shuffling the lines: you write a program to do the sort. By the same token, if you need to give a Ruby class a hundred similar methods, you shouldn't just start writing the methods one at a time. You should write Ruby code that defines the methods for you (Recipe 10.10). Or you should make your class capable of intercepting calls to those methods: this way, you can implement the methods without ever defining them at all (Recipe 10.8).

Methods you've seen already, like attr_reader, use metaprogramming to define custom methods according to your specifications. Recipe 8.2 created a few more of these "decorator" methods; Recipe 10.16 in this chapter shows a more complex example of the same principle.

You can metaprogram in Ruby either by writing normal Ruby code that uses a lot of reflection, or by generating a string that contains Ruby code, and evaluating the string. Writing normal Ruby code with reflection is generally safer, but sometimes the reflection just gets to be too much and you need to evaluate a string. We provide a demonstration recipe for each technique (Recipes 10.10 and 10.11).

10.1 Finding an Object's Class and Superclass

Problem

Given a class, you want an object corresponding to its class, or to the parent of its class.

Solution

Use the Object#class method to get the class of an object as a Class object. Use Class#superclass to get the parent Class of a Class object:

```
'a string'.class                      # => String
'a string'.class.name                 # => "String"
'a string'.class.superclass           # => Object
String.superclass                     # => Object
String.class                          # => Class
String.class.superclass               # => Module
'a string'.class.new                  # => ""
```

Discussion

Class objects in Ruby are first-class objects that can be assigned to variables, passed as arguments to methods, and modified dynamically. Many of the recipes in this chapter and Chapter 8 discuss things you can do with a Class object once you have it.

The superclass of the Object class is nil. This makes it easy to iterate up an inheritance hierarchy:

```
class Class
  def hierarchy
    (superclass ? superclass.hierarchy : []) << self
  end
end

Array.hierarchy                         # => [Object, Array]

class MyArray < Array
end
MyArray.hierarchy                       # => [Object, Array, MyArray]
```

While Ruby does not support multiple inheritance, the language allows mixin Modules that simulate it (see Recipe 9.1). The Modules included by a given Class (or another Module) are accessible from the Module#ancestors method.

A class can have only one superclass, but it may have any number of ancestors. The list returned by Module#ancestors contains the entire inheritance hierarchy (including the class itself), any modules the class includes, and the ever-present Kernel module, whose methods are accessible from anywhere because Object itself mixes it in.

```
String.superclass        # => Object
String.ancestors         # => [String, Enumerable, Comparable, Object, Kernel]
Array.ancestors          # => [Array, Enumerable, Object, Kernel]
MyArray.ancestors        # => [MyArray, Array, Enumerable, Object, Kernel]

Object.ancestors         # => [Object, Kernel]

class MyClass
end
MyClass.ancestors        # => [MyClass, Object, Kernel]
```

See Also

- Most of Chapter 8
- Recipe 9.1, "Simulating Multiple Inheritance with Mixins"

10.2 Listing an Object's Methods

Problem

Given an unfamiliar object, you want to see what methods are available to call.

Solution

All Ruby objects implement the Object#methods method. It returns an array containing the names of the object's public instance methods:

```
Object.methods
# => ["name", "private_class_method", "object_id", "new",
#     "singleton_methods", "method_defined?", "equal?", ... ]
```

To get a list of the singleton methods of some object (usually, but not always, a class), use Object#singleton_methods:

```
Object.singleton_methods    # => []
Fixnum.singleton_methods    # => ["induced_from"]

class MyClass
  def MyClass.my_singleton_method
  end

  def my_instance_method
  end
end
MyClass.singleton_methods    # => ["my_singleton_method"]
```

To list the instance methods of a class, call instance_methods on the object. This lets you list the instance methods of a class without instantiating the class:

```
''.methods == String.instance_methods        # => true
```

The output of these methods are most useful when sorted:

```
Object.methods.sort
# => ["<", "<=", "<=>", "==", "===", "=~", ">", ">=",
#     "__id__", "__send__", "allocate", "ancestors", ... ]
```

Ruby also defines some elementary predicates along the same lines. To see whether a class defines a certain instance method, call method_defined? on the class or respond_to? on an instance of the class. To see whether a class defines a certain class method, call respond_to? on the class:

```
MyClass.method_defined? :my_instance_method   # => true
MyClass.new.respond_to? :my_instance_method   # => true
MyClass.respond_to? :my_instance_method       # => false

MyClass.respond_to? :my_singleton_method      # => true
```

Discussion

It often happens that while you're in an interactive Ruby session, you need to look up which methods an object supports, or what a particular method is called. Looking directly at the object is faster than looking its class up in a book. If you're using a library like Rails or Facets, or your code has been adding methods to the built-in classes, it's also more reliable.

Noninteractive code can also benefit from knowing whether a given object implements a certain method. You can use this to enforce an interface, allowing any object to be passed into a method so long as the argument implements certain methods (see Recipe 10.16).

If you find yourself using respond_to? a lot in an interactive Ruby session, you're a good customer for irb's autocomplete feature. Put the following line in your .irbrc file or equivalent:

```
require 'irb/completion'
#Depending on your system, you may also have to add the following line:
IRB.conf[:use_readline] = true
```

Then you can type (for instance) "[1,2,3].", hit the Tab key, and see a list of all the methods you can call on the array [1, 2, 3].

methods, instance_methods, and singleton_methods will only return public methods, and method_defined? will only return true if you give it the name of a public method. Ruby provides analogous methods for discovering protected and private methods, though these are less useful. All the relevant methods are presented in Table 10-1.

Table 10-1. Discovering protected and private methods

Goal	Public	Protected	Private
List the methods of an object	methods or public_methods	protected_methods	private_methods
List the instance methods defined by a class	instance_methods or public_instance_methods	protected_instance_methods	private_instance_methods

Table 10-1. Discovering protected and private methods (continued)

Goal	Public	Protected	Private
List the singleton methods defined by a class	`singleton_methods`	N/A	N/A
Does this class define such-and-such an instance method?	`method_defined?` or `public_method_defined?`	`protected_method_defined?`	`private_method_defined?`
Will this object respond to such-and-such an instance method?	`respond_to?`	N/A	N/A

Just because you can see the names of protected or private methods in a list doesn't mean you can call the methods, or that `respond_to?` will find them:

```
String.private_instance_methods.sort
# => ["Array", "Float", "Integer", "String", "`", "abort", "at_exit",
#     "autoload","autoload?", "binding", "block_given?", "callcc", ... ]
String.new.respond_to? :autoload?                        # => false

String.new.autoload?
# NoMethodError: private method `autoload?' called for "":String
```

See Also

- To strip away irrelevant methods, see Recipe 10.3, "Listing Methods Unique to an Object"
- Recipe 10.4, "Getting a Reference to a Method," shows how to assign a `Method` object to a variable, given its name; among other things, this lets you find out how many arguments a method takes
- See Recipe 10.6, "Listening for Changes to a Class," to set up a hook to be called whenever a new method or singleton method is defined for a class
- Recipe 10.16, "Enforcing Software Contracts"

10.3 Listing Methods Unique to an Object

Problem

When you list the methods available to an object, the list is cluttered with extraneous methods defined in the object's superclasses and mixed-in modules. You want to see a list of only the methods defined by that object's direct class.

Solution

Subtract the instance methods defined by the object's superclass. You'll be left with only the methods defined by the object's direct class (plus any methods defined on the object after its creation). The `my_methods_only` method defined below gives this capability to every Ruby object:

```ruby
class Object
  def my_methods_only
    my_super = self.class.superclass
    return my_super ? methods - my_super.instance_methods : methods
  end
end

s = ''
s.methods.size                              # => 143
Object.instance_methods.size                # =>  41
s.my_methods_only.size                      # => 102
(s.methods - Object.instance_methods).size  # => 102

def s.singleton_method()
end
s.methods.size                              # => 144
s.my_methods_only.size                      # => 103

class Object
  def new_object_method
  end
end
s.methods.size                              # => 145
s.my_methods_only.size                      # => 103

class MyString < String
  def my_string_method
  end
end
MyString.new.my_methods_only                # => ["my_string_method"]
```

Discussion

The `my_methods_only` technique removes methods defined in the superclass, the parent classes of the superclass, and in any mixin modules included by those classes. For instance, it removes the 40 methods defined by the Object class when it mixed in the Kernel module. It will not remove methods defined by mixin modules included by the class itself.

Usually these methods aren't clutter, but there can be a lot of them (for instance, Enumerable defines 22 methods). To remove them, you can start out with my_methods_only, then iterate over the ancestors of the class in question and subtract out all the methods defined in modules:

```ruby
class Object
  def my_methods_only_no_mixins
    self.class.ancestors.inject(methods) do |mlist, ancestor|
      mlist = mlist - ancestor.instance_methods unless ancestor.is_a? Class
      mlist
```

```
    end
end

[].methods.size                            # => 121
[].my_methods_only.size                    # => 78
[].my_methods_only_no_mixins.size          # => 57
```

See Also

- Recipe 10.1, "Finding an Object's Class and Superclass," explores ancestors in more detail

10.4 Getting a Reference to a Method

Problem

You want to the name of a method into a reference to the method itself.

Solution

Use the eponymous Object#method method:

```
s = 'A string'
length_method = s.method(:length)   # => #<Method: String#length>
length_method.arity                 # => 0
length_method.call                  # => 8
```

Discussion

The Object#methods introspection method returns an array of strings, each containing the name of one of the methods available to that object. You can pass any of these names into an object's method method and get a Method object corresponding to that method of that object.

A Method object is bound to the particular object whose method method you called. Invoke the method's Method#call method, and it's just like calling the object's method directly:

```
1.succ                     # => 2
1.method(:succ).call       # => 2
```

The Method#arity method indicates how many arguments the method takes. Arguments, including block arguments, are passed to call just as they would be to the original method:

```
5.method('+').call(10)             # => 15

[1,2,3].method(:each).call { |x| puts x }
# 1
# 2
# 3
```

A Method object can be stored in a variable and passed as an argument to other methods. This is useful for passing preexisting methods into callbacks and listeners:

```
class EventSpawner

  def initialize
    @listeners = []
    @state = 0
  end

  def subscribe(&listener)
    @listeners << listener
  end

  def change_state(new_state)
    @listeners.each { |l| l.call(@state, new_state) }
    @state = new_state
  end
end

class EventListener
  def hear(old_state, new_state)
    puts "Method triggered: state changed from #{old_state} " +
      "to #{new_state}."
  end
end

spawner = EventSpawner.new
spawner.subscribe do |old_state, new_state|
 puts "Block triggered: state changed from #{old_state} to #{new_state}."
end

spawner.subscribe &EventListener.new.method(:hear)
spawner.change_state(4)
# Block triggered: state changed from 0 to 4.
# Method triggered: state changed from 0 to 4.
```

A Method can also be used as a block:

```
s = "sample string"
replacements = { "a" => "i", "tring" => "ubstitution" }

replacements.collect(&s.method(:gsub))
# => ["simple string", "sample substitution"]
```

You can't obtain a reference to a method that's not bound to a specific object, because the behavior of call would be undefined. You *can* get a reference to a class method by calling method on the class. When you do this, the bound object is the class itself: an instance of the Class class. Here's an example showing how to obtain references to an instance and a class method of the same class:

```
class Welcomer
 def Welcomer.a_class_method
   return "Greetings from the Welcomer class."
 end
```

```
  def an_instance_method
    return "Salutations from a Welcomer object."
  end
end

Welcomer.method("an_instance_method")
# NameError: undefined method `an_instance_method' for class `Class'
Welcomer.new.method("an_instance_method").call
# => "Salutations from a Welcomer object."
Welcomer.method("a_class_method").call
# => "Greetings from the Welcomer class."
```

See Also

- Recipe 7.11, "Coupling Systems Loosely with Callbacks," contains a more complex listener example

10.5   Fixing Bugs in Someone Else's Class

Problem

You're using a class that's got a bug in one of its methods. You know where the bug is and how to fix it, but you can't or don't want to change the source file itself.

Solutions

Extend the class from within your program and overwrite the buggy method with an implementation that fixes the bug. Create an alias for the buggy version of the method, so you can still access it if necessary.

Suppose you're trying to use the buggy method in the `Multiplier` class defined below:

```
class Multiplier
  def double_your_pleasure(pleasure)
    return pleasure * 3 # FIXME: Actually triples your pleasure.
  end
end

m = Multiplier.new
m.double_your_pleasure(6)                                 # => 18
```

Reopen the class, alias the buggy method to another name, then redefine it with a correct implementation:

```
class Multiplier
  alias :double_your_pleasure_BUGGY :double_your_pleasure
  def double_your_pleasure(pleasure)
    return pleasure * 2
  end
end
```

```
m.double_your_pleasure(6)                              # => 12

m.double_your_pleasure_BUGGY(6)                        # => 18
```

Discussion

In many programming languages a class, function, or method can't be modified after its initial definition. In other languages, this behavior is possible but not encouraged. For Ruby programmers, the ability to reprogram classes on the fly is just another technique for the toolbox, to be used when necessary. It's most commonly used to add new code to a class, but it can also be used to deploy a drop-in replacement for buggy or slow implementation of a method.

Since Ruby is (at least right now) a purely interpreted language, you should be able to find the source code of any Ruby class used by your program. If a method in one of those classes has a bug, you should be able to copy and paste the original Ruby implementation into your code and fix the bug in the new copy.* This is not an elegant technique, but it's often better than distributing a slightly modified version of the entire class or library (that is, copying and pasting a whole file).

When you fix the buggy behavior, you should also send your fix to the maintainer of the software that contains the bug. The sooner you can get the fix out of your code, the better. If the software package is abandoned, you should at least post the fix online so others can find it.

If a method isn't buggy, but simply doesn't do what you'd like it to do, add a new method to the class (or create a subclass) instead of redefining the old one. Methods you don't know about may use the behavior of the method as it is. Of course, there could be methods that rely on the buggy behavior of a buggy method, but that's less likely.

See Also

- Throughout this book we use techniques like this to work around bugs and performance problems in the Ruby standard library (although most of the bugs have been fixed in Ruby 1.9); see, for instance, Recipe 2.7, "Taking Logarithms," Recipe 2.16, "Generating Prime Numbers," and Recipe 6.18, "Deleting a File"
- Recipe 10.14, "Aliasing Methods"

---

* Bugs in Ruby C extensions are much more difficult to patch. You might be able to write equivalent Ruby code, but there's probably a reason why the original code was written in C. Since C doesn't share Ruby's attitude towards redefining functions on the fly, you'll need to fix the bug in the original C code and recompile the extension.

10.6   Listening for Changes to a Class

Credit: Phil Tomson

Problem

You want to be notified when the definition of a class changes. You might want to keep track of new methods added to the class, or existing methods that get removed or undefined. Being notified when a module is mixed into a class can also be useful.

Solution

Define the class methods method_added, method_removed, and/or method_undefined. Whenever the class gets a method added, removed, or undefined, Ruby will pass its symbol into the appropriate callback method.

The following example prints a message whenever a method is added, removed, or undefined. If the method "important" is removed, undefined, or redefined, it throws an exception.

```
class Tracker
  def important
    "This is an important method!"
  end

  def self.method_added(sym)
    if sym == :important
      raise 'The "important" method has been redefined!'
    else
      puts %{Method "#{sym}" was (re)defined.}
    end
  end

  def self.method_removed(sym)
    if sym == :important
      raise 'The "important" method has been removed!'
    else
      puts %{Method "#{sym}" was removed.}
    end
  end

  def self.method_undefined(sym)
    if sym == :important
      raise 'The "important" method has been undefined!'
    else
      puts %{Method "#{sym}" was removed.}
    end
  end
end
```

If someone adds a method to the class, a message will be printed:

```
class Tracker
  def new_method
```

```
      'This is a new method.'
    end
  end
  # Method "new_method" was (re)defined.
```

Short of freezing the class, you can't prevent the important method from being removed, undefined, or redefined, but you can raise a stink (more precisely, an exception) if someone changes it:

```
class Tracker
  undef :important
end
# RuntimeError: The "important" method has been undefined!
```

Discussion

The class methods we've defined in the Tracker class (method_added, method_removed, and method_undefined) are hook methods. Some other piece of code (in this case, the Ruby interpreter) knows to call any methods by that name when certain conditions are met. The Module class defines these methods with empty bodies: by default, nothing special happens when a method is added, removed, or undefined.

Given the code above, we will not be notified if our Tracker class later mixes in a module. We won't hear about the module itself, nor about the new methods that are available because of the module inclusion.

```
class Tracker
  include Enumerable
end

# Nothing!
```

Detecting module inclusion is trickier. Ruby provides a hook method Module#included, which is called on a module whenever it's mixed into a class. But we want the opposite: a hook method that's called on a particular *class* whenever it includes a *module*. Since Ruby doesn't provide a hook method for module inclusion, we must define our own. To do this, we'll need to change Module#include itself.

```
class Module
 alias_method :include_no_hook, :include
 def include(*modules)
   # Run the old implementation.
   include_no_hook(*modules)

   # Then run the hook.
   modules.each do |mod|
     self.include_hook mod
   end
 end

 def include_hook
   # Do nothing by default, just like Module#method_added et al.
   # This method must be overridden in a subclass to do something useful.
```

```
    end
  end
```

Now when a module is included into a class, Ruby will call that class's `include_hook` method. If we define a `Tracker#include_hook` method, we can have Ruby notify us of inclusions:

```
class Tracker
  def self.include_hook(mod)
    puts %{"#{mod}" was included in #{self}.}
  end
end

class Tracker
  include Enumerable
end
# "Enumerable" was included in Tracker.
```

See Also

- Recipe 9.3, "Mixing in Class Methods," for more on the `Module#included` method
- Recipe 10.13, "Undefining a Method," for the difference between removing and undefining a method

10.7 Checking Whether an Object Has Necessary Attributes

Problem

You're writing a class or module that delegates the creation of some of its instance variables to a hook method. You want to be make sure that the hook method actually created those instance variables.

Solution

Use the `Object#instance_variables` method to get a list of the instance variables. Check them over to make sure all the necessary instance variables have been defined. This `Object#must_have_instance_variables` method can be called at any time:

```
class Object
  def must_have_instance_variables(*args)
    vars = instance_variables.inject({}) { |h,var| h[var] = true; h }
    args.each do |var|
      unless vars[var]
        raise ArgumentError, %{Instance variable "@#{var} not defined"}
      end
    end
  end
end
```

The best place to call this method is in initialize or some other setup method of a module. Alternatively, you could accept values for the instance variables as arguments to the setup method:

```
module LightEmitting
  def LightEmitting_setup
    must_have_instance_variables :light_color, :light_intensity
    @on = false
  end

  # Methods that use @light_color and @light_intensity follow...
end
```

You can call this method from a class that defines a virtual setup method, to make sure that subclasses actually use the setup method correctly:

```
class Request
  def initialize
    gather_parameters # This is a virtual method defined by subclasses
    must_have_instance_variables :action, :user, :authentication
  end

  # Methods that use @action, @user, and @authentication follow...
end
```

Discussion

Although Object#must_have_instance_variables is defined and called like any other method, it's conceptually a "decorator" method similar to attr_accessor and private. That's why I didn't use parentheses above, even though I called it with multiple arguments. The lack of parentheses acts as a visual indicator that you're calling a decorator method, one that alters or inspects a class or object.

Here's a similar method that you can use from outside the object. It basically implements a batch form of duck typing: instead of checking an object's instance variables (which are only available inside the object), it checks whether the object supports all of the methods you need to call on it. It's useful for checking from the outside whether an object is the "shape" you expect.

```
class Object
  def must_support(*args)
    args.each do |method|
      unless respond_to? method
        raise ArgumentError, %{Must support "#{method}"}
      end
    end
  end
end

obj = "a string"
obj.must_support :to_s, :size, "+".to_sym
obj.must_support "+".to_sym, "-".to_sym
# ArgumentError: Must support "-"
```

See Also

- Recipe 10.16, "Enforcing Software Contracts"

10.8 Responding to Calls to Undefined Methods

Problem

Rather than having Ruby raise a `NoMethodError` when someone calls an undefined method on an instance of your class, you want to intercept the method call and do something else with it.

Or you are faced with having to explicitly define a large (possibly infinite) number of methods for a class. You would rather define a single method that can respond to an infinite number of method names.

Solution

Define a `method_missing` method for your class. Whenever anyone calls a method that would otherwise result in a `NoMethodError`, the `method_missing` method is called instead. It is passed the symbol of the nonexistent method, and any arguments that were passed in.

Here's a class that modifies the default error handling for a missing method:

```
class MyClass
  def defined_method
    'This method is defined.'
  end

  def method_missing(m, *args)
    "Sorry, I don't know about any #{m} method."
  end
end

o = MyClass.new
o.defined_method                        # => "This method is defined."
o.undefined_method
# => "Sorry, I don't know about any undefined_method method."
```

In the second example, I'll define an infinitude of new methods on `Fixnum` by giving it a `method_missing` implementation. Once I'm done, `Fixnum` will answer to any method that looks like "plus_#" and takes no arguments.

```
class Fixnum
  def method_missing(m, *args)
    if args.size > 0
      raise ArgumentError.new("wrong number of arguments (#{args.size} for 0)")
    end
```

```
      match = /^plus_([0-9]+)$/.match(m.to_s)
      if match
        self + match.captures[0].to_i
      else
        raise NoMethodError.
    new("undefined method `#{m}' for #{inspect}:#{self.class}")
      end
    end
end

4.plus_5                                       # => 9
10.plus_0                                      # => 10
-1.plus_2                                      # => 1
100.plus_10000                                 # => 10100
20.send(:plus_25)                              # => 45

100.minus_3
# NoMethodError: undefined method `minus_3' for 100:Fixnum
100.plus_5(105)
# ArgumentError: wrong number of arguments (1 for 0)
```

Discussion

The method_missing technique is frequently found in delegation scenarios, when one object needs to implement all of the methods of another object. Rather than defining each method, a class implements method_missing as a catch-all, and uses send to delegate the "missing" method calls to other objects. The built-in delegate library makes this easy (see Recipe 8.8), but for the sake of illustration, here's a class that delegates almost all its methods to a string. Note that this class doesn't itself subclass String.

```
class BackwardsString
  def initialize(s)
   @s = s
  end

  def method_missing(m, *args, &block)
    result = @s.send(m, *args, &block)
    result.respond_to?(:to_str) ? BackwardsString.new(result) : result
  end

  def to_s
   @s.reverse
  end

  def inspect
    to_s
  end
end
```

The interesting thing here is the call to Object#send. This method takes the name of another method, and calls that method with the given arguments. We can delegate any missing method call to the underlying string without even looking at the method name.

```
s = BackwardsString.new("I'm backwards.")        # => .sdrawkcab m'I
s.size                                           # => 14
s.upcase                                         # => .SDRAWKCAB M'I
s.reverse                                        # => I'm backwards.
s.no_such_method
# NoMethodError: undefined method `no_such_method' for "I'm backwards.":String
```

The method_missing technique is also useful for adding syntactic sugar to a class. If one method of your class is frequently called with a string argument, you can make object.string a shortcut for object.method("string"). Consider the Library class below, and its simple query interface:

```
class Library < Array

  def add_book(author, title)
    self << [author, title]
  end

  def search_by_author(key)
    reject { |b| !match(b, 0, key) }
  end

  def search_by_author_or_title(key)
    reject { |b| !match(b, 0, key) && !match(b, 1, key) }
  end

  :private

  def match(b, index, key)
    b[index].index(key) != nil
  end
end

l = Library.new
l.add_book("James Joyce", "Ulysses")
l.add_book("James Joyce", "Finnegans Wake")
l.add_book("John le Carre", "The Little Drummer Boy")
l.add_book("John Rawls", "A Theory of Justice")

l.search_by_author("John")
# => [["John le Carre", "The Little Drummer Boy"],
#     ["John Rawls", "A Theory of Justice"]]

l.search_by_author_or_title("oy")
# => [["James Joyce", "Ulysses"], ["James Joyce", "Finnegans Wake"],
#     ["John le Carre", "The Little Drummer Boy"]]
```

We can make certain queries a little easier to write by adding some syntactic sugar. It's as simple as defining a wrapper method; its power comes from the fact that Ruby directs all unrecognized method calls to this wrapper method.

```
class Library
  def method_missing(m, *args)
    search_by_author_or_title(m.to_s)
  end
end

l.oy
# => [["James Joyce", "Ulysses"], ["James Joyce", "Finnegans Wake"],
#      ["John le Carre", "The Little Drummer Boy"]]

l.Fin
# => [["James Joyce", "Finnegans Wake"]]

l.Jo
# => [["James Joyce", "Ulysses"], ["James Joyce", "Finnegans Wake"],
#      ["John le Carre", "The Little Drummer Boy"],
#      ["John Rawls", "A Theory of Justice"]]
```

You can also define a method_missing method on a class. This is useful for adding syntactic sugar to factory classes. Here's a simple factory class that makes it easy to create strings (as though this weren't already easy):

```
class StringFactory
  def StringFactory.method_missing(m, *args)
    return String.new(m.to_s, *args)
  end
end

StringFactory.a_string                    # => "a_string"
StringFactory.another_string              # => "another_string"
```

As before, an attempt to call an explicitly defined method will not trigger method_missing:

```
StringFactory.superclass                  # => Object
```

The method_missing method intercepts all calls to undefined methods, including the mistyped names of calls to "real" methods. This is a common source of bugs. If you run into trouble using your class, the first thing you should do is add debug statements to method_missing, or comment it out altogether.

If you're using method_missing to implicitly define methods, you should also be aware that Object.respond_to? returns false when called with the names of those methods. After all, they're not defined!

```
25.respond_to? :plus_20                   # => false
```

You can override respond_to? to fool outside objects into thinking you've got explicit definitions for methods you've actually defined implicitly in method_missing. Be very careful, though; this is another common source of bugs.

```
class Fixnum
  def respond_to?(m)
    super or (m.to_s =~ /^plus_([0-9]+)$/) != nil
```

```
    end
  end

  25.respond_to? :plus_20              # => true
  25.respond_to? :succ                 # => true
  25.respond_to? :minus_20             # => false
```

See Also

- Recipe 2.13, "Simulating a Subclass of Fixnum"
- Recipe 8.8, "Delegating Method Calls to Another Object," for an alternate implementation of delegation that's usually easier to use

10.9 Automatically Initializing Instance Variables

Problem

You're writing a class constructor that takes a lot of arguments, each of which is simply assigned to an instance variable.

```
class RGBColor(red=0, green=0, blue=0)
  @red = red
  @green = green
  @blue = blue
end
```

You'd like to avoid all the typing necessary to do those variable assignments.

Solution

Here's a method that initializes the instance variables for you. It takes as an argument the list of variables passed into the initialize method, and the binding of the
variables to values.

```
class Object
  private
  def set_instance_variables(binding, *variables)
    variables.each do |var|
      instance_variable_set("@#{var}", eval(var, binding))
    end
  end
end
```

Using this method, you can eliminate the tedious variable assignments:

```
class RGBColor
  def initialize(red=0, green=0, blue=0)
    set_instance_variables(binding, *local_variables)
  end
end

RGBColor.new(10, 200, 300)
# => #<RGBColor:0xb7c22fc8 @red=10, @blue=300, @green=200>
```

Discussion

Our set_instance_variables takes a list of argument names to turn into instance variables, and a Binding containing the values of those arguments as of the method call. For each argument name, an eval statement binds the corresponding instance variable to the corresponding value in the Binding. Since you control the names of your own variables, this eval is about as safe as it gets.

The names of a method's arguments aren't accessible from Ruby code, so how do we get that list? Through trickery. When a method is called, any arguments passed in are immediately bound to local variables. At the very beginning of the method, these are the *only* local variables defined. This means that calling Kernel#local_variables at the beginning of a method will get a list of all the argument names.

If your method accepts arguments that you *don't* want to set as instance variables, simply remove their names from the result of Kernel#local_variables before passing the list into set_instance_variables:

```ruby
class RGBColor
  def initialize(red=0, green=0, blue=0, debug=false)
    set_instance_variables(binding, *local_variables-['debug'])
    puts "Color: #{red}/#{green}/#{blue}" if debug
  end
end

RGBColor.new(10, 200, 255, true)
# Color: 10/200/255
# => #<RGBColor:0xb7d309fc @blue=255, @green=200, @red=10>
```

10.10 Avoiding Boilerplate Code with Metaprogramming

Problem

You've got to type in a lot of repetitive code that a trained monkey could write. You're resentful at having to do this yourself, and angry that the repetitive code will clutter up your class listings.

Solution

Ruby is happy to be the trained monkey that writes your repetitive code. You can define methods algorithmically with Module#define_method.

Usually the repetitive code is a bunch of similar methods. Suppose you need to write code like this:

```ruby
class Fetcher
  def fetch(how_many)
    puts "Fetching #{how_many ? how_many : "all"}."
  end
```

```
    def fetch_one
      fetch(1)
    end

    def fetch_ten
      fetch(10)
    end

    def fetch_all
      fetch(nil)
    end
  end
```

You can define this exact same code without having to write it all out. Create a data structure that contains the differences between the methods, and iterate over that structure, defining a method each time with define_method.

```
class GeneratedFetcher
  def fetch(how_many)
    puts "Fetching #{how_many ? how_many : "all"}."
  end

  [["one", 1], ["ten", 10], ["all", nil]].each do |name, number|
    define_method("fetch_#{name}") do
      fetch(number)
    end
  end
end

GeneratedFetcher.instance_methods - Object.instance_methods
# => ["fetch_one", "fetch", "fetch_ten", "fetch_all"]

GeneratedFetcher.new.fetch_one
# Fetching 1.

GeneratedFetcher.new.fetch_all
# Fetching all.
```

This is less to type, less monkeyish, and it takes up less space in your class listing. If you need to define more of these methods, you can add to the data structure instead of writing out more boilerplate.

Discussion

Programmers have always preferred writing new code to cranking out variations on old code. From lex and yacc to modern programs like Hibernate and Cog, we've always used tools to generate code that would be tedious to write out manually.

Instead of generating code with an external tool, Ruby programmers do it from within Ruby.* There are two officially sanctioned techniques. The nicer technique is

---

* This would make a good bumper sticker: "Ruby programmers do it from within Ruby."

to use define_method to create a method whose implementation can use the local variables available at the time it was defined.

The built-in decorator methods we've already seen use metaprogramming. The attr_reader method takes a string as an argument, and defines a method whose name and implementation is based on that string. The code that's the same for every reader method is factored out into attr_reader; all you have to provide is the tiny bit that's different every time.

Methods whose code you generated are indistinguishable from methods that you wrote out longhand. They will show up in method lists and in generated RDoc documentation (if you're metaprogramming with string evaluations, as seen in the next recipe, you can even generate the RDoc documentation and put it at the beginning of a generated method).

Usually you'll use metaprogramming the way attr_reader does: to attach new methods to a class or module. For this you should use define_method, if possible. However, the block you pass into define_method needs to itself be valid Ruby code, and this can be cumbersome. Consider the following generated methods:

```ruby
class Numeric
  [["add", "+"], ["subtract", "-"], ["multiply", "*",],
   ["divide", "/"]].each do |method, operator|
    define_method("#{method}_2") do
      method(operator).call(2)
    end
  end
end

4.add_2                                         # => 6
10.divide_2                                     # => 5
```

Within the block passed into define_method, we have to jump through some reflection hoops to get a reference to the operator we want to use. You can't just write self operator 2, because operator isn't an operator: it's a variable containing an operator name. See the next recipe for another metaprogramming technique that uses string substitution instead of reflection.

Another of define_method's shortcomings is that in Ruby 1.8, you can't use it to define a method that takes a block. The following code will work in Ruby 1.9 but not in Ruby 1.8:

```ruby
define_method "call_with_args" do |*args, &block|
  block.call(*args)
end

call_with_args(1, 2) { |n1, n2| n1 + n2 }        # => 3
call_with_args "mammoth" { |x| x.upcase }        # => "MAMMOTH"
```

See Also

- Metaprogramming is used throughout this book to generate a bunch of methods at once, or to make it easy to define certain kinds of methods; see, for instance, Recipe 4.7, "Making Sure a Sorted Array Stays Sorted"
- Because `define_method` is a private method, you can only use it within a class definition; Recipe 8.2, "Managing Class Data," shows a case where it needs to be called outside of a class definition
- The next recipe, Recipe 10.11, "Metaprogramming with String Evaluations"
- Metaprogramming is a staple of Ruby libraries; it's used throughout Rails, and in smaller libraries like `delegate`

10.11 Metaprogramming with String Evaluations

Problem

You're trying to write some metaprogramming code using `define_method`, but there's too much reflection going on for your code to be readable. It gets confusing and is almost as frustrating as having to write out the code in longhand.

Solution

You can define new methods by generating the definitions as strings and running them as Ruby code with one of the `eval` methods.

Here's a reprint of the metaprogramming example from the previous recipe, which uses `define_method`:

```
class Numeric
  [['add', '+'], ['subtract', '-'],
   ['multiply', '*',], ['divide', '/']].each do |method, operator|
    define_method("#{method}_2") do
      method(operator).call(2)
    end
  end
end
```

The important line of code, `method(operator).call(2)`, isn't something you'd write in normal programming. You'd write something like `self + 2` or `self / 2`, depending on which operator you wanted to apply. By writing your method definitions as strings, you can do metaprogramming that looks more like regular programming:

```
class Numeric
  [['add', '+'], ['subtract', '-'],
   ['multiply', '*',], ['divide', '/']].each do |method, operator|
    module_eval %{ def #{method}_2
                     self.#{operator}(2)
                   end }
```

```
    end
  end

  4.add_2                               # => 6
  10.divide_2                           # => 5
```

Discussion

You can do all of your metaprogramming with define_method, but the code doesn't look a lot like the code you'd write in normal programming. You can't set an instance variable with @foo = 4; you have to call instance_variable_set('foo', 4).

The alternative is to generate a method definition as a string and execute the string as Ruby code. Most interpreted languages have a way of parsing and executing arbitrary strings as code, but it's usually regarded as a toy or a hazard, and not given much attention. Ruby breaks this taboo.

The most common evalutation method used for metaprogramming is Module#module_eval. This method executes a string as Ruby code, within the context of a class or module. Any methods or class variables you define within the string will be attached to the class or module, just as if you'd typed the string within the class or module definition. Thanks to the variable substitutions, the generated string looks exactly like the code you'd type in manually.

The following four pieces of code all define a new method String#last:

```
class String
  def last(n)
    self[-n, n]
  end
end
"Here's a string.".last(7)             # => "string."

class String
  define_method('last') do |n|
    self[-n, n]
  end
end
"Here's a string.".last(7)             # => "string."

class String
  module_eval %{def last(n)
                  self[-n, n]
                end}
end
"Here's a string.".last(7)             # => "string."

String.module_eval %{def last(n)
                       self[-n, n]
                     end}

"Here's a string.".last(7)             # => "string."
```

The `instance_eval` method is less popular than `module_eval`. It works just like `module_eval`, but it runs inside an instance of a class rather than the class itself. You can use it to define singleton methods on a particular object, or to set instance variables. Of course, you can also call `define_method` on a specific object.

The other evaluation method is just plain `eval`. This method executes a string exactly as though you had written it as Ruby code in the same spot:

```
class String
  eval %{def last(n)
           self[-n, n]
         end}
end
"Here's a string.".last(7)              # => "string."
```

You must be very careful when you use the eval methods, lest the end-user of a program trick you into running arbitrary Ruby code. When you're metaprogramming, though, it's not usually a problem: the only strings that get evaluated are ones you constructed yourself from hardcoded data, and by the time your class is loaded and ready to use, the eval calls have already run. You should be safe unless your eval statement contains strings obtained from untrusted sources. This might happen if you're creating a custom class, or modifying a class in response to user input.

10.12 Evaluating Code in an Earlier Context

Problem

You've written a method that evaluates a string as Ruby code. But whenever anyone calls the method, the objects referenced by your string go out of scope. Your string can't be evaluated within a method.

For instance, here's a method that takes a variable name and tries to print out the value of the variable.

```
def broken_print_variable(var_name)
  eval %{puts "The value of #{var_name} is " + #{var_name}.to_s}
end
```

The eval code only works when it's run in the same context as the variable definition. It doesn't work as a method, because your local variables go out of scope when you call a method.

```
tin_snips = 5

broken_print_variable('tin_snips')
# NameError: undefined local variable or method `tin_snips' for main:Object

var_name = 'tin_snips'
eval %{puts "The value of #{var_name} is " + #{var_name}.to_s}
# The value of tin_snips is 5
```

Solution

The eval method can execute a string of Ruby code as though you had written in some other part of your application. This magic is made possible by Binding objects. You can get a Binding at any time by calling Kernel#binding, and pass it in to eval to recreate your original environment where it wouldn't otherwise be available. Here's a version of the above method that takes a Binding:

```ruby
def print_variable(var_name, binding)
  eval %{puts "The value of #{var_name} is " + #{var_name}.to_s}, binding
end

vice_grips = 10
print_variable('vice_grips', binding)
# The value of vice_grips is 10
```

Discussion

A Binding object is a bookmark of the Ruby interpreter's state. It tracks the values of any local variables you have defined, whether you are inside a class or method definition, and so on.

Once you have a Binding object, you can pass it into eval to run code in the same context as when you created the Binding. All the local variables you had back then will be available. If you called Kernel#binding within a class definition, you'll also be able to define new methods of that class, and set class and instance variables.

Since a Binding object contains references to all the objects that were in scope when it was created, those objects can't be garbage-collected until both they and the Binding object have gone out of scope.

See Also

- This trick is used in several places throughout this book; see, for example, Recipe 1.3, "Substituting Variables into an Existing String," and Recipe 10.9, "Automatically Initializing Instance Variables"

10.13 Undefining a Method

Problem

You want to remove an already defined method from a class or module.

Solution

From within a class or module, you can use Module#remove_method to remove a method's implementation, forcing Ruby to delegate to the superclass or a module included by a class.

In the code below, I subclass Array and override the << and [] methods to add some randomness. Then I decide that overriding [] wasn't such a good idea, so I undefine that method and get the inherited Array behavior back. The override of << stays in place.

```
class RandomizingArray < Array
  def <<(e)
    insert(rand(size), e)
  end

  def [](i)
    super(rand(size))
  end
end

a = RandomizingArray.new
a << 1 << 2 << 3 << 4 << 5 << 6          # => [6, 3, 4, 5, 2, 1]

# That was fun; now let's get some of those entries back.
a[0]                                     # => 1
a[0]                                     # => 2
a[0]                                     # => 5
#No, seriously, a[0].
a[0]                                     # => 4
#It's a madhouse! A madhouse!
a[0]                                     # => 3
#That does it!

class RandomizingArray
  remove_method('[]')
end

a[0]                                     # => 6
a[0]                                     # => 6
a[0]                                     # => 6

# But the overridden << operator still works randomly:
a << 7                                   # => [6, 3, 4, 7, 5, 2, 1]
```

Discussion

Usually you'll override a method by redefining it to implement your own desired behavior. However, sometimes a class will override an inherited method to do something you don't like, and you just want the "old" implementation back.

You can only use remove_method to remove a method from a class or module that explicitly defines it. You'll get an error if you try to remove a method from a class that merely inherits that method. To make a subclass stop responding to an inherited method, you should *undefine* the method with undef_method.

Using undef_method on a class prevents the appropriate method signals from reaching objects of that class, but it has no effect on the parent class.

```
class RandomizingArray
  remove_method(:length)
end
# NameError: method `length' not defined in RandomizingArray

class RandomizingArray
  undef_method(:length)
end

RandomizingArray.new.length
# NoMethodError: undefined method `length' for []:RandomizingArray
Array.new.length                                    # => 0
```

As you can see, it's generally safer to use undef_method on the class you actually want to change than to use remove_method on its parent or a module it includes.

You can use remove_method to remove singleton methods once you're done with them. Since remove_method is private, using it to remove a singleton method requires some unorthodox syntax:

```
my_array = Array.new
def my_array.random_dump(number)
  number.times { self << rand(100) }
end

my_array.random_dump(3)
my_array.random_dump(2)
my_array                               # => [6, 45, 12, 49, 66]

# That's enough of that.
class << my_array
  remove_method(:random_dump)
end
my_array.random_dump(4)
# NoMethodError: undefined method `random_dump' for [6, 45, 12, 49, 66]:Array
```

When you define a singleton method on an object, Ruby silently defines an anonymous subclass used only for that one object. In the example above, my_array is actually an anonymous subclass of Array that implements a method random_dump. Since the subclass has no name (my_array is a variable name, not a class name), there's no way of using the class <ClassName> syntax. We must "append" onto the definition of the my_array object.

Class methods are just a special case of singleton methods, so you can also use remove_method to remove class methods. Ruby also provides a couple of related methods for removing things besides methods. Module#remove_constant undefines a constant so that it can be redefined with a different value, as seen in Recipe 8.17. Object#remove_instance_variable removes an instance variable from a single instance of a class:

```
class OneTimeContainer
  def initialize(value)
```

```
        @use_just_once_then_destroy = value
    end

    def get_value
      remove_instance_variable(:@use_just_once_then_destroy)
    end
end

object_1 = OneTimeContainer.new(6)
object_1.get_value
# => 6
object_1.get_value
# NameError: instance variable @use_just_once_then_destroy not defined

object_2 = OneTimeContainer.new('ephemeron')
object_2.get_value
# => "ephemeron"
```

You can't remove a particular instance variable from all instances by modifying the class because the class is its own object, one which probably never defined that instance variable in the first place:

```
class MyClass
  remove_instance_variable(:@use_just_once_then_destroy)
end
# NameError: instance variable @use_just_once_then_destroy not defined
```

You should definitely not use these methods to remove methods or constants in system classes or modules: that might make arbitrary parts of the Ruby standard library crash or act unreliably. As with all metaprogramming, it's easy to abuse the power to remove and undefine methods at will.

See Also

- Recipe 8.17, "Declaring Constants"
- Recipe 10.5, "Fixing Bugs in Someone Else's Class"

10.14 Aliasing Methods

Problem

You (or your users) frequently misremember the name of a method. To reduce the confusion, you want to make the same method accessible under multiple names.

Alternatively, you're about to redefine a method and you'd like to keep the old version available.

Solution

You can create alias methods manually, but in most cases, you should let the `alias` command do it for you. In this example, I define an `InventoryItem` class that includes a `price` method to calculate the price of an item in quantity. Since it's likely that someone might misremember the name of the `price` method as `cost`, I'll create an alias:

```
class InventoryItem
  attr_accessor :name, :unit_price

  def initialize(name, unit_price)
    @name, @unit_price = name, unit_price
  end

  def price(quantity=1)
    @unit_price * quantity
  end

  #Make InventoryItem#cost an alias for InventoryItem#price
  alias :cost :price

  #The attr_accessor decorator created two methods called "unit_price" and
  #"unit_price=". I'll create aliases for those methods as well.
  alias :unit_cost :unit_price
  alias :unit_cost= :unit_price=
end

bacon = InventoryItem.new("Chunky Bacon", 3.95)
bacon.price(100)                              # => 395.0
bacon.cost(100)                               # => 395.0

bacon.unit_price                              # => 3.95
bacon.unit_cost                               # => 3.95
bacon.unit_cost = 3.99
bacon.cost(100)                               # => 399.0
```

Discussion

It's difficult to pick the perfect name for a method: you must find the word or short phrase that best conveys an operation on a data structure, possibly an abstract operation that has different "meanings" depending on context.

Sometimes there will be no good name for a method and you'll just have to pick one; sometimes there will be *too many* good names for a method and you'll just have to pick one. In either case, your users may have difficulty remembering the "right" name of the method. You can help them out by creating aliases.

Ruby itself uses aliases in its standard library: for instance, for the method of `Array` that returns the number of items in the array. The terminology used in area varies widely. Some languages use `length` or `len` to find the length of a list, and some use `size`.*

---

* Java uses both: `length` is a member of a Java array, and `size` is a method that returns the size of a collection.

Ruby compromises by calling its method `Array#length`, but also creating an alias called `Array#size`.* You can use either `Array#length` or `Array#size` because they do the same thing based on the same code. If you come to Ruby from Python, you can make yourself a little more comfortable by creating yet another alias for `length`:

```
class Array
  alias :len :length
end

[1, 2, 3, 4].len                              # => 4
```

The `alias` command doesn't make a single method respond to two names, or create a shell method that delegates to the "real" method. It makes an entirely separate copy of the old method under the new name. If you then modify the original method, the alias will not be affected.

This may seem wasteful, but it's frequently useful to Ruby programmers, who love to redefine methods that aren't working the way they'd like. When you redefine a method, it's good practice to first `alias` the old method to a different name, usually the original name with an _old suffix. This way, the old functionality isn't lost.

This code (very unwisely) redefines `Array#length`, creating a copy of the original method with an alias:

```
class Array
  alias :length_old :length
  def length
    return length_old / 2
  end
end
```

Note that the alias `Array#size` still works as it did before:

```
array = [1, 2, 3, 4]
array.length                                  # => 2
array.size                                    # => 4
array.length_old                              # => 4
```

Since the old implementation is still available, it can be aliased back to its original name once the overridden implementation is no longer needed.

```
class Array
  alias :length :length_old
end

array.length                                  # => 4
```

If you find this behavior confusing, your best alternative is to avoid `alias` altogether. Instead, define a method with the new name that simply delegates to the "real"

---

* Throughout this book, we use `Array#size` instead of `Array#length`. We do this mainly because it makes the lines of code a little shorter and easier to fit on the page. This is probably not a concern for you, so use whichever one you're comfortable with.

method. Here I'll modify the InventoryItem class so that cost delegates to price, rather than having alias create a copy of price and calling the copy cost.

```
class InventoryItem
  def cost(*args)
    price(*args)
  end
end
```

If I then decide to modify price to tack on sales tax, cost will not have to be modified or realiased.

```
bacon.cost(100)                              # => 399.0

require 'bigdecimal'
require 'bigdecimal/util'
class InventoryItem
  def price(quantity=1, sales_tax=BigDecimal.new("0.0725"))
    base_price = (unit_price * quantity).to_d
    price = (base_price + (base_price * sales_tax).round(2)).to_f
  end
end

bacon.price(100)                             # => 427.93
bacon.cost(100)                              # => 427.93
```

We don't even need to change the signature of the cost method to match that of price, since we used the *args construction to accept and delegate any arguments at all:

```
bacon.cost(100, BigDecimal.new("0.05"))      # => 418.95
```

See Also

- Recipe 2.9, "Converting Between Degrees and Radians"
- Recipe 4.7, "Making Sure a Sorted Array Stays Sorted"
- Recipe 17.14, "Running Multiple Analysis Tools at Once"

10.15 Doing Aspect-Oriented Programming

Problem

You want to "wrap" a method with new code, so that calling the method triggers some new feature in addition to the original code.

Solution

You can arrange for code to be called before and after a method invocation by using method aliasing and metaprogramming, but it's simpler to use the glue gem or the

AspectR third-party library. The latter lets you define "aspect" classes whose methods are called before and after other methods.

Here's a simple example that traces calls to specific methods as they're made:

```ruby
require 'aspectr'
class Verbose < AspectR::Aspect

  def describe(method_sym, object, *args)
    "#{object.inspect}.#{method_sym}(#{args.join(",")})"
  end

  def before(method_sym, object, return_value, *args)
    puts "About to call #{describe(method_sym, object, *args)}."
  end

  def after(method_sym, object, return_value, *args)
    puts "#{describe(method_sym, object, *args)} has returned " +
      return_value.inspect + '.'
  end
end
```

Here, I'll wrap the push and pop methods of an array. Every time I call those methods, the aspect code will run and some diagnostics will be printed.

```ruby
verbose = Verbose.new
stack = []
verbose.wrap(stack, :before, :after, :push, :pop)

stack.push(10)
# About to call [].push(10).
# [10].push(10) has returned [[10]].

stack.push(4)
# About to call [10].push(4).
# [10, 4].push(4) has returned [[10, 4]].

stack.pop
# About to call [10, 4].pop().
# [10].pop() has returned [4].
```

Discussion

There's a pattern that shows up again and again in Ruby (we cover it in Recipe 7.10). You write a method that performs some task-specific setup (like initializing a timer), runs a code block, then performs task-specific cleanup (like stopping the timer and printing out timing results). By passing in a code block to one of these methods you give it a new *aspect*: the same code runs as if you'd just called Proc#call on the code block, but now it's got something extra: the code gets timed, or logged, or won't run without authentication, or it automatically performs some locking.

Aspect-oriented programming lets you permanently add these aspects to previously defined methods, without having to change any of the code that calls them. It's a good way to modularize your code, and to modify existing code without having to do a lot of metaprogramming yourself. Though less mature, the AspectR library has the same basic features of Java's AspectJ.

The Aspect#wrap method modifies the methods of some other object or class. In the example above, the push and pop methods of the stack are modified: you could also modify the Array#push and Array#pop methods themselves, by passing in Array instead of stack.

Aspect#wrap aliases the old implementations to new names, and defines the method anew to include calls to a "pre" method (@Verbose#before in the example) and/or a "post" method (@Verbose#after in the example).

You can wrap the same method with different aspects at the same time:

```
class EvenMoreVerbose < AspectR::Aspect
  def useless(method_sym, object, return_value, *args)
    puts "More useless verbosity."
  end
end

more_verbose = EvenMoreVerbose.new
more_verbose.wrap(stack, :useless, nil, :push)
stack.push(60)
# About to call [10].push(60).
# More useless verbosity.
# [10, 60].push(60) has returned [[10, 60]].
```

You can also undo the effects of a wrap call with Aspect#unwrap.

```
verbose.unwrap(stack, :before, :after, :push, :pop)
more_verbose.unwrap(stack, :useless, nil, :push)
stack.push(100)                          # => [10, 60, 100]
```

Because they use aliasing under the covers, you can't use AspectR or glue to attach aspects to operator methods like <<. If you do, AspectR (for instance) will try to define a method called __aop__singleton_<<, which isn't a valid method name. You'll need to do the alias yourself, using a method name like "old_lshift", and define a new << method that makes the pre- and post-calls.

See Also

- The AspectR home page is at *http://aspectr.sourceforge.net/*
- Recipe 7.10, "Hiding Setup and Cleanup in a Block Method"
- Recipe 10.14, "Aliasing Methods"
- Recipe 20.4, "Synchronizing Access to an Object"

10.16 Enforcing Software Contracts

Credit: Maurice Codik

Problem

You want your methods to to validate their arguments, using techniques like duck typing and range validation, without filling your code with tons of conditions to test arguments.

Solution

Here's a Contracts module that you can mix in to your classes. Your methods can then define and enforce contracts.

```ruby
module Contracts
  def valid_contract(input)
    if @user_defined and @user_defined[input]
      @user_defined[input]
    else
      case input
      when :number
        lambda { |x| x.is_a? Numeric }
      when :string
        lambda { |x| x.respond_to? :to_str }
      when :anything
        lambda { |x| true }
      else
        lambda { |x| false }
      end
    end
  end

  class ContractViolation < StandardError
  end

  def define_data(inputs={}.freeze)
    @user_defined ||= {}
    inputs.each do |name, contract|
      @user_defined[name] = contract if contract.respond_to? :call
    end
  end

  def contract(method, *inputs)
    @contracts ||= {}
    @contracts[method] = inputs
    method_added(method)
  end

  def setup_contract(method, inputs)
    @contracts[method] = nil
    method_renamed = "__#{method}".intern
```

```
      conditions = ""
      inputs.flatten.each_with_index do |input, i|
        conditions << %{
          if not self.class.valid_contract(#{input.inspect}).call(args[#{i}])
            raise ContractViolation, "argument #{i+1} of method '#{method}' must" +
                  "satisfy the '#{input}' contract", caller
          end
        }
      end

      class_eval %{
        alias_method #{method_renamed.inspect}, #{method.inspect}
        def #{method}(*args)
          #{conditions}
          return #{method_renamed}(*args)
        end
      }
    end

    def method_added(method)
      inputs = @contracts[method]
      setup_contract(method, inputs) if inputs
    end
  end
```

You can call the define_data method to define contracts, and call the contract method to apply these contracts to your methods. Here's an example:

```
class TestContracts
  def hello(n, s, f)
    n.times { f.write "hello #{s}!\n" }
  end
```

The hello method takes as its arguments a positive number, a string, and a file-type object that can be written to. The Contracts module defines a :string contract for making sure an item is stringlike. We can define additional contracts as code blocks; these contracts make sure an object is a positive number, or an open object that supports the write method:

```
  extend Contracts

  writable_and_open = lambda do |x|
    x.respond_to?('write') and x.respond_to?('closed?') and not x.closed?
  end

  define_data(:writable => writable_and_open,
              :positive => lambda {|x| x >= 0 })
```

Now we can call the contract method to create a contract for the three arguments of the hello method:

```
  contract :hello, [:positive, :string, :writable]
end
```

Here it is in action:

```
tc = TestContracts.new
tc.hello(2, 'world', $stdout)
# hello world!
# hello world!

tc.hello(-1, 'world', $stdout)
# Contracts::ContractViolation: argument 1 of method 'hello' must satisfy the
# 'positive' contract

tc.hello(2, 3001, $stdout)
# test-contracts.rb:22: argument 2 of method 'hello' must satisfy the
# 'string' contract (Contracts::ContractViolation)

closed_file = open('file.txt', 'w') { }
tc.hello(2, 'world', closed_file)
# Contracts::ContractViolation: argument 3 of method 'hello' must satisfy the
# 'writable' contract
```

Discussion

The Contracts module uses many of Ruby's metaprogramming features to make these runtime checks possible. The line of code that triggers it all is this one:

```
contract :hello, [:positive, :string, :writable]
```

That line of code replaces the old implementation of hello with one that looks like this:

```
def hello(n,s,f)
  if not (n >= 0)
    raise ContractViolation,
    "argument 1 of method 'hello' must satisfy the 'positive' contract", caller
  end
  if not (s.respond_to? String)
    raise ContractViolation,
    "argument 2 of method 'hello' must satisfy the 'string' contract",
    caller
  end
  if not (f.respond_to?('write') and f.respond_to?('closed?')
        and not f.closed?)
    raise ContractViolation,
    "argument 3 of method 'hello' must satisfy the 'writable' contract",
    caller
  end
  return __hello(n,s,f)
end

def __hello(n,s,f)
  n.times { f.write "hello #{s}!\n" }
end
```

The body of define_data is simple: it takes a hash that maps contract names to Proc objects, and adds each new contract definition to the user_defined hash of custom contracts for this class.

The contract method takes a method symbol and an array naming the contracts to impose on that method's arguments. It registers a new set of contracts by sending them to the method symbol in the @contracts hash. When Ruby adds a method definition to the class, it automatically calls the Contracts::method_added hook, passing in the name of the method name as the argument. Contracts::method_added checks whether or not the newly added method has a contract defined for it. If it finds one, it calls setup_contract.

All of the heavy lifting is done in setup_contract. This is how it works, step by step:

- Remove the method's information in @contracts. This prevents an infinite loop when we redefine the method using alias_method later.
- Generate the new name for the method. In this example, we simply append two underscores to the front.
- Create all of the code to test the types of the arguments. We loop through the arguments using Enumerable#each_with_index, and build up a string in the conditions variable that contains the code we need. The condition code uses the valid_contract method to translate a contract name (such as :number), to a Proc object that checks whether or not its argument satisfies that contract.
- Use class_eval to insert our code into the class that called extend Contracts. The code in the eval statment does the following:
  - Call alias_method to rename the newly added method to our generated name.
  - Define a new method with the original's name that checks all of our conditions and then calls the renamed function to get the original functionality.

See Also

- Recipe 13.14, "Validating Data with ActiveRecord"
- Ruby also has an Eiffel-style Design by Contract library, which lets you define invariants on classes, and pre- and post-conditions on methods; it's available as the dbc gem

## CHAPTER 11

XML and HTML

XML and HTML are the most popular markup languages (textual ways of describing structured data). HTML is used to describe textual documents, like you see on the Web. XML is used for just about everything else: data storage, messaging, configuration files, you name it. Just about every software buzzword forged over the past few years involves XML.

Java and C++ programmers tend to regard XML as a lightweight, agile technology, and are happy to use it all over the place. XML *is* a lightweight technology, but only compared to Java or C++. Ruby programmers see XML from the other end of the spectrum, and from there it looks pretty heavy. Simpler formats like YAML and JSON usually work just as well (see Recipe 13.1 or Recipe 13.2), and are easier to manipulate. But to shun XML altogether would be to cut Ruby off from the rest of the world, and nobody wants that. This chapter covers the most useful ways of parsing, manipulating, slicing, and dicing XML and HTML documents.

There are two standard APIs for manipulating XML: DOM and SAX. Both are over-kill for most everyday uses, and neither is a good fit for Ruby's code-block–heavy style. Ruby's solution is to offer a pair of APIs that capture the style of DOM and SAX while staying true to the Ruby programming philosophy.[*] Both APIs are in the standard library's REXML package, written by Sean Russell.

Like DOM, the Document class parses an XML document into a nested tree of objects. You can navigate the tree with Ruby accessors (Recipe 11.2) or with XPath queries (Recipe 11.4). You can modify the tree by creating your own Element and Text objects (Recipe 11.9). If even Document is too heavyweight for you, you can use the XmlSimple library to transform an XML file into a nested Ruby hash (Recipe 11.6).

With a DOM-style API like Document, you have to parse the entire XML file before you can do anything. The XML document becomes a large number of Ruby objects

---

[*] REXML also provides the SAX2Parser and SAX2Listener classes, which implement the basic SAX2 API.

nested under a Document object, all sitting around taking up memory. With a SAX-style parser like the StreamParser class, you can process a document as it's parsed, creating only the objects you want. The StreamParser API is covered in Recipe 11.3.

The main problem with the REXML APIs is that they're very picky. They'll only parse a document that's valid XML, or close enough to be have an unambiguous representation. This makes them nearly useless for parsing HTML documents off the World Wide Web, since the average web page is not valid XML. Recipe 11.5 shows how to use the third-party tools Rubyful Soup and SGMLParser; they give a DOM- or SAX-style interface that handles even invalid XML.

- *http://www.germane-software.com/software/rexml/*
- *http://www.germane-software.com/software/rexml/docs/tutorial.html*

11.1 Checking XML Well-Formedness

Credit: Rod Gaither

Problem

You want to check that an XML document is well-formed before processing it.

Solution

The best way to see whether a document is well-formed is to try to parse it. The REXML library raises an exception when it can't parse an XML document, so just try parsing it and rescue any exception.

The valid_xml? method below returns nil unless it's given a valid XML document. If the document is valid, it returns a parsed Document object, so you don't have to parse it again:

```
require 'rexml/document'
def valid_xml?(xml)
 begin
   REXML::Document.new(xml)
 rescue REXML::ParseException
   # Return nil if an exception is thrown
 end
end
```

Discussion

To be useful, an XML document must be structured correctly or "well-formed." For instance, an opening tag must either be self-closing or be paired with an appropriate closing tag.

As a file and messaging format, XML is often used in situations where you don't have control over the input, so you can't assume that it will always be well-formed. Rather than just letting REXML throw an exception, you'll need to handle ill-formed XML gracefully, providing options to retry or continue on a different path.

This bit of XML is not well-formed: it's missing ending tags for both the `pending` and `done` elements:

```
bad_xml = %{
<tasks>
 <pending>
   <entry>Grocery Shopping</entry>
 <done>
   <entry>Dry Cleaning</entry>
</tasks>}

valid_xml?(bad_xml)                          # => nil
```

This bit of XML is well-formed, so `valid_xml?` returns the parsed `Document` object.

```
good_xml = %{
<groceries>
 <bread>Wheat</bread>
 <bread>Quadrotriticale</bread>
</groceries>}

doc = valid_xml?(good_xml)
doc.root.elements[1]                         # => <bread> ... </>
```

When your program is responsible for writing XML documents, you'll want to write unit tests that make sure you generate valid XML. You can use a feature of the Test::Unit library to simplify the checking. Since invalid XML makes REXML throw an exception, your unit test can use the `assert_nothing_thrown` method to make sure your XML is valid:

```
doc = nil
assert_nothing_thrown {doc = REXML::Document.new(source_xml)}
```

This is a simple, clean test to verify XML when using a unit test.

Note that `valid_xml?` doesn't work perfectly: some invalid XML is unambiguous, which means REXML can parse it. Consider this truncated version of the valid XML example. It's missing its closing tags, but there's no ambiguity about which closing tag should come first, so REXML can parse the file and provide the closing tags:

```
invalid_xml = %{
<groceries>
 <bread>Wheat
}

(valid_xml? invalid_xml) == nil              # => false # That is, it is "valid"
REXML::Document.new(invalid_xml).write
# <groceries>
#    <bread>Wheat
# </bread></groceries>
```

See Also

- Official information on XML can be found at *http://www.w3.org/XML/*
- The Wikipedia has a good description of the difference between Well-Formed and Valid XML documents at *http://en.wikipedia.org/wiki/Xml#Correctness_in_an_XML_document*
- Recipe 11.5, "Parsing Invalid Markup"
- Recipe 17.3, "Handling an Exception"

11.2 Extracting Data from a Document's Tree Structure

Credit: Rod Gaither

Problem

You want to parse an XML file into a Ruby data structure, to traverse it or extract data from it.

Solution

Pass an XML document into the REXML::Document constructor to load and parse the XML. A Document object contains a tree of subobjects (of class Element and Text) representing the tree structure of the underlying document. The methods of Document and Element give you access to the XML tree data. The most useful of these methods is #each_element.

Here's some sample XML and the load process. The document describes a set of orders, each of which contains a set of items. This particular document contains a single order for two items.

```
orders_xml = %{
<orders>
  <order>
    <number>105</number>
    <date>02/10/2006</date>
    <customer>Corner Store</customer>
    <items>
      <item upc="404100" desc="Red Roses" qty="240" />
      <item upc="412002" desc="Candy Hearts" qty="160" />
    </items>
  </order>
</orders>}

require 'rexml/document'
orders = REXML::Document.new(orders_xml)
```

To process each order in this document, we can use `Document#root` to get the document's root element (<orders>) and then call `Element#each_element` to iterate over the children of the root element (the <order> elements). This code repeatedly calls each to move down the document tree and print the details of each order in the document:

```
orders.root.each_element do |order|      # each <order> in <orders>
  order.each_element do |node|           # <customer>, <items>, etc. in <order>
    if node.has_elements?
      node.each_element do |child|       # each <item> in <items>
        puts "#{child.name}: #{child.attributes['desc']}"
      end
    else
      # the contents of <number>, <date>, etc.
      puts "#{node.name}: #{node.text}"
    end
  end
end
# number: 105
# date: 02/10/2006
# customer: Corner Store
# item: Red Roses
# item: Candy Hearts
```

Discussion

Parsing an XML file into a `Document` gives you a tree-like data structure that you can treat kind of like an array of arrays. Starting at the document root, you can move down the tree until you find the data that interests you. In the example above, note how the structure of the Ruby code mirrors the structure of the original document. Every call to each_element moves the focus of the code down a level: from <orders> to <order> to <items> to <item>.

There are many other methods of `Element` you can use to navigate the tree structure of an XML document. Not only can you iterate over the child elements, you can reference a specific child by indexing the parent as though it were an array. You can navigate through siblings with `Element.next_element` and `Element.previous_element`. You can move up the document tree with `Element.parent`:

```
my_order = orders.root.elements[1]
first_node = my_order.elements[1]
first_node.name                           # => "number"
first_node.next_element.name              # => "date"
first_node.parent.name                    # => "order"
```

This only scratches the surface; there are many other ways to interact with the data loaded from an XML source. For example, explore the convenience methods `Element.each_element_with_attribute` and `Element.each_element_with_text`, which let you select elements based on features of the elements themselves.

See Also

- The RDoc documentation for the REXML::Document and REXML::Element classes
- The section "Tree Parsing XML and Accessing Elements" in the REXML Tutorial (*http://www.germane-software.com/software/rexml/docs/tutorial.html#id2247335*)
- If you want to start navigating the document at some point other than the root, an XPath statement is probably the simplest way to get where you want; see Recipe 11.4, "Navigating a Document with XPath"

11.3   Extracting Data While Parsing a Document

Credit: Rod Gaither

Problem

You want to process a large XML file without loading it all into memory.

Solution

The method REXML::Document.parse_stream gives you a fast and flexible way to scan a large XML file and process the parts that interest you.

Consider this XML document, the output of a hypothetical program that runs automated tasks. We want to parse the document and find the tasks that failed (that is, returned an error code other than zero).

```
event_xml = %{
<events>
  <clean system="dev" start="01:35" end="01:55" area="build" error="1" />
  <backup system="prod" start="02:00" end="02:35" size="2300134" error="0" />
  <backup system="dev" start="02:00" end="02:01" size="0" error="2" />
  <backup system="test" start="02:00" end="02:47" size="327450" error="0" />
</events>}
```

We can process the document as it's being parsed by writing a REXML:: StreamListener subclass that responds to parsing events such as tag_start and tag_ end. Here's a subclass that listens for tags with a nonzero value for their error attribute. It prints a message for every failed event it finds.

```
require 'rexml/document'
require 'rexml/streamlistener'

class ErrorListener
  include REXML::StreamListener
  def tag_start(name, attrs)
    if attrs["error"] != nil and attrs["error"] != "0"
      puts %{Event "#{name}" failed for system "#{attrs["system"]}" } +
    %{with code #{attrs["error"]}}
    end
  end
end
```

To actually parse the XML data, pass it along with the `StreamListener` into the method `REXML::Document.parse_stream`:

```
REXML::Document.parse_stream(event_xml, ErrorListener.new)
# Event "clean" failed for system "dev" with code 1
# Event "backup" failed for system "dev" with code 2
```

Discussion

We could find the failed events in less code by loading the XML into a `Document` and running an XPath query. That approach would work fine for this example, since the document only contains four events. It wouldn't work as well if the document were a file on disk containing a billion events. Building a `Document` means building an elaborate in-memory data structure representing the entire XML document. If you only care about part of a document (in this case, the failed events), it's faster and less memory-intensive to process the document as it's being parsed. Once the parser reaches the end of the document, you're done.

The stream-oriented approach to parsing XML can be as simple as shown in this recipe, but it can also handle much more complex scenarios. Your `StreamListener` subclass can keep arbitrary state in instance variables, letting you track complex combinations of elements and attributes.

See Also

- The RDoc documentation for the `REXML::StreamParser` class
- The "Stream Parsing" section of the REXML Tutorial (*http://www.germane-software.com/software/rexml/docs/tutorial.html#id2248457*)
- Recipe 11.2, "Extracting Data from a Document's Tree Structure"

11.4 Navigating a Document with XPath

Problem

You want to find or address sections of an XML document in a standard, programming-language–independent way.

Solution

The XPath language defines a way of referring to almost any element or set of elements in an XML document, and the REXML library comes with a complete XPath implementation. `REXML::XPath` provides three class methods for locating `Element` objects within parsed documents: `first`, `each`, and `match`.

Take as an example the following XML description of an aquarium. The aquarium contains some fish and a gaudy castle decoration full of algae. Due to an aquarium stocking mishap, some of the smaller fish have been eaten by larger fish, just like in those cartoon food chain diagrams. (Figure 11-1 shows the aquarium.)

```
xml = %{
<aquarium>
 <fish color="blue" size="small" />

 <fish color="orange" size="large">
   <fish color="green" size="small">
    <fish color="red" size="tiny" />
   </fish>
 </fish>

 <decoration type="castle" style="gaudy">
  <algae color="green" />
 </decoration>
</aquarium>}

require 'rexml/document'
doc = REXML::Document.new xml
```

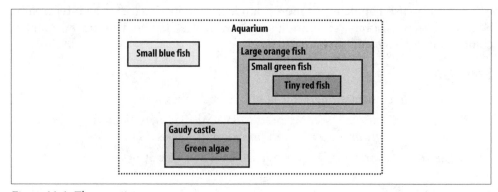

Figure 11-1. The aquarium

We can use REXML::Xpath.first to get the Element object corresponding to the first <fish> tag in the document:

```
REXML::XPath.first(doc, '//fish')
# => <fish size='small' color='blue'/>
```

We can use match to get an array containing all the elements that are green:

```
REXML::XPath.match(doc, '//[@color="green"]')
# => [<fish size='small' color='green'> ... </>, <algae color='green'/>]
```

We can use each with a code block to iterate over all the fish that are inside other fish:

```
def describe(fish)
  "#{fish.attribute('size')} #{fish.attribute('color')} fish"
end
```

```
REXML::XPath.each(doc, '//fish/fish') do |fish|
  puts "The #{describe(fish.parent)} has eaten the #{describe(fish)}."
end
# The large orange fish has eaten the small green fish.
# The small green fish has eaten the tiny red fish.
```

Discussion

Every element in a Document has an xpath method that returns the canonical XPath path to that element. This path can be considered the element's "address" within the document. In this example, a complex bit of Ruby code is replaced by a simple XPath expression:

```
red_fish = doc.children[0].children[3].children[1].children[1]
# => <fish size='tiny' color='red'/>

red_fish.xpath
# => "/aquarium/fish[2]/fish/fish"

REXML::XPath.first(doc, red_fish.xpath)
# => <fish size='tiny' color='red'/>
```

Even a brief overview of XPath is beyond the scope of this recipe, but here are some more examples to give you ideas:

```
# Find the second green element.
REXML::XPath.match(doc, '//[@color="green"]')[1]
# => <algae color='green'/>

# Find the color attributes of all small fish.
REXML::XPath.match(doc, '//fish[@size="small"]/@color')
# => [color='blue', color='green']

# Count how many fish are inside the first large fish.
REXML::XPath.first(doc, "count(//fish[@size='large'][1]//*fish)")
# => 2
```

The Elements class acts kind of like an array that supports XPath addressing. You can make your code more concise by passing an XPath expression to Elements#each, or using it as an array index.

```
doc.elements.each('//fish') { |f| puts f.attribute('color') }
# blue
# orange
# green
# red

doc.elements['//fish']
# => <fish size='small' color='blue'/>
```

Within an XPath expression, the first element in a list has an index of 1, not 0. The XPath expression //fish[size='large'][1] matches the first large fish, not the second large fish, the way `large_fish[1]` would in Ruby code. Pass a number as an array index to an `Elements` object, and you get the same behavior as XPath:

```
doc.elements[1]
# => <aquarium> ... </>
doc.children[0]
# => <aquarium> ... </>
```

See Also

- The XPath standard, at *http://www.w3.org/TR/xpath*, has more XPath examples
- *XPath and XPointer* by John E. Simpson (O'Reilly)

11.5   Parsing Invalid Markup

Problem

You need to extract data from a document that's supposed to be HTML or XML, but that contains some invalid markup.

Solution

For a quick solution, use Rubyful Soup, written by Leonard Richardson and found in the `rubyful_soup` gem. It can build a document model even out of invalid XML or HTML, and it offers an idiomatic Ruby interface for searching the document model. It's good for quick screen-scraping tasks or HTML cleanup.

```
require 'rubygems'
require 'rubyful_soup'

invalid_html = 'A lot of <b class=1>tags are <i class=2>never closed.'
soup = BeautifulSoup.new(invalid_html)
puts soup.prettify
# A lot of
#  <b class="1">tags are
#   <i class="2">never closed.
#   </i>
#  </b>

soup.b.i                                   # => <i class="2">never closed.</i>
soup.i                                     # => <i class="2">never closed.</i>
soup.find(nil, :attrs=>{'class' => '2'})   # => <i class="2">never closed.</i>
soup.find_all('i')                         # => [<i class="2">never closed.</i>]

soup.b['class']                            # => "1"

soup.find_text(/closed/)                   # => "never closed."
```

If you need better performance, do what Rubyful Soup does and write a custom parser on top of the event-based parser `SGMLParser` (found in the `htmltools` gem). It works a lot like REXML's `StreamListener` interface.

Discussion

Sometimes it seems like the authors of markup parsers do their coding atop an ivory tower. Most parsers simply refuse to parse bad markup, but this cuts off an enormous source of interesting data. Most of the pages on the World Wide Web are invalid HTML, so if your application uses other peoples' web pages as input, you need a forgiving parser. Invalid XML is less common but by no means rare.

The SGMLParser class in the htmltools gem uses regular expressions to parse an XML-like data stream. When it finds an opening or closing tag, some data, or some other part of an XML-like document, it calls a hook method that you're supposed to define in a subclass. SGMLParser doesn't build a document model or keep track of the document state: it just generates events. If closing tags don't match up or if the markup has other problems, it won't even notice.

Rubyful Soup's parser classes define SGMLParser hook methods that build a document model out of an ambiguous document. Its BeautifulSoup class is intended for HTML documents: it uses heuristics like a web browser's to figure out what an ambiguous document "really" means. These heuristics are specific to HTML; to parse XML documents, you should use the BeautifulStoneSoup class. You can also subclass BeautifulStoneSoup and implement your own heuristics.

Rubyful Soup builds a densely linked model of the entire document, which uses a lot of memory. If you only need to process certain parts of the document, you can implement the SGMLParser hooks yourself and get a faster parser that uses less memory.

Here's a SGMLParser subclass that extracts URLs from a web page. It checks every A tag for an href attribute, and keeps the results in a set. Note the similarity to the LinkGrabber class defined in Recipe 11.13.

```
require 'rubygems'
require 'html/sgml-parser'
require 'set'

html = %{<a name="anchor"><a href="http://www.oreilly.com">O'Reilly</a>
        <b>irrelevant</b><a href="http://www.ruby-lang.org/">Ruby</a>}

class LinkGrabber < HTML::SGMLParser
  attr_reader :urls

  def initialize
    @urls = Set.new
    super
  end

  def do_a(attrs)
    url = attrs.find { |attr| attr[0] == 'href' }
    @urls << url[1] if url
  end
end
```

```
extractor = LinkGrabber.new
extractor.feed(html)
extractor.urls
# => #<Set: {"http://www.ruby-lang.org/", "http://www.oreilly.com"}>
```

The equivalent Rubyful Soup program is quicker to write and easier to understand, but it runs more slowly and uses more memory:

```
require 'rubyful_soup'

urls = Set.new
BeautifulStoneSoup.new(html).find_all('a').each do |tag|
  urls << tag['href'] if tag['href']
end
```

You can improve performance by telling Rubyful Soup's parser to ignore everything except A tags and their contents:

```
puts BeautifulStoneSoup.new(html, :parse_only_these => 'a')
# <a name="anchor"></a>
# <a href="http://www.oreilly.com">O'Reilly</a>
# <a href="http://www.ruby-lang.org/">Ruby</a>
```

But the fastest implementation will always be a custom SGMLParser subclass. If your parser is part of a full application (rather than a one-off script), you'll need to find the best tradeoff between performance and code legibility.

See Also

- Recipe 11.13, "Extracting All the URLs from an HTML Document"
- The Rubyful Soup documentation (*http://www.crummy.com/software/RubyfulSoup/documentation.html*)
- The htree library defines a forgiving HTML/XML parser that can convert a parsed document into a REXML Document object (*http://cvs.m17n.org/~akr/htree/*)
- The HTML TIDY library can fix up most invalid HTML so that it can be parsed by a standard parser; it's a C library with Ruby bindings; see *http://tidy.sourceforge.net/* for the library, and *http://rubyforge.org/projects/tidy* for the bindings

11.6 Converting an XML Document into a Hash

Problem

When you parse an XML document with Document.new, you get a representation of the document as a complex data structure. You'd like to represent an XML document using simple, built-in Ruby data structures.

Solution

Use the XmlSimple library, found in the xml-simple gem. It parses an XML document into a hash.

Consider an XML document like this one:

```
xml = %{
<freezer temp="-12" scale="celcius">
 <food>Phyllo dough</food>
 <food>Ice cream</food>
 <icecubetray>
  <cube1 />
  <cube2 />
 </icecubetray>
</freezer>}
```

Here's how you parse it with XMLSimple:

```
require 'rubygems'
require 'xmlsimple'

doc = XmlSimple.xml_in xml
```

And here's what it looks like:

```
require 'pp'
pp doc
# {"icecubetray"=>[{"cube2"=>[{}], "cube1"=>[{}]}],
#  "food"=>["Phyllo dough", "Ice cream"],
#  "scale"=>"celcius",
#  "temp"=>"-12"}
```

Discussion

XmlSimple is a lightweight alternative to the Document class. Instead of exposing a tree of Element objects, it exposes a nested structure of Ruby hashes and arrays. There's no performance savings (XmlSimple actually builds a Document class behind the scenes and iterates over it, so it's about half as fast as Document), but the resulting object is easy to use. XmlSimple also provides several tricks that can make a document more concise and navigable.

The most useful trick is the KeyAttr one. Suppose you had a better-organized freezer than the one above, a freezer in which everything had its own name attribute:[*]

```
xml = %{
<freezer temp="-12" scale="celcius">
 <item name="Phyllo dough" type="food" />
 <item name="Ice cream" type="food" />
 <item name="Ice cube tray" type="container">
  <item name="Ice cube" type="food" />
```

---

[*] Okay, it's not really better organized. In fact, it's exactly the same. But it sure looks cooler!

```
      <item name="Ice cube" type="food" />
    </item>
</freezer>}
```

You could parse this data with just a call to XmlSimple.xml_in, but you get a more concise representation by specifing the name attribute as a KeyAttr argument. Compare:

```
parsed1 = XmlSimple.xml_in xml
pp parsed1
# {"scale"=>"celcius",
#  "item"=>
#   [{"name"=>"Phyllo dough", "type"=>"food"},
#    {"name"=>"Ice cream", "type"=>"food"},
# {"name"=>"Ice cube tray",
#      "type"=>"container",
#      "item"=>
#       [{"name"=>"Ice cube", "type"=>"food"},
#         {"name"=>"Ice cube", "type"=>"food"}]}],
#  "temp"=>"-12"}

parsed2 = XmlSimple.xml_in(xml, 'KeyAttr' => 'name')
pp parsed2
# {"scale"=>"celcius",
#  "item"=>
#   {"Phyllo dough"=>{"type"=>"food"},
#    "Ice cube tray"=>
#     {"type"=>"container",
#      "item"=>{"Ice cube"=>{"type"=>"food"}}},
#    "Ice cream"=>{"type"=>"food"}},
# "temp"=>"-12"}
```

The second parsing is also easier to navigate:

```
parsed1["item"].detect { |i| i['name'] == 'Phyllo dough' }['type']
# => "food"
parsed2["item"]["Phyllo dough"]["type"]
# => "food"
```

But notice that the second parsing represents the ice cube tray as containing only one ice cube. This is because both ice cubes have the same name. When two tags at the same level have the same KeyAttr, one overwrites the other in the hash.

You can modify the data structure with normal Ruby hash and array methods, then write it back out to XML with XMLSimple.xml_out:

```
parsed1["item"] << {"name"=>"Curry leaves", "type"=>"spice"}
parsed1["item"].delete_if { |i| i["name"] == "Ice cube tray" }

puts XmlSimple.xml_out(parsed1, "RootName"=>"freezer")
# <freezer scale="celcius" temp="-12">
#   <item name="Phyllo dough" type="food" />
#   <item name="Ice cream" type="food" />
#   <item name="Curry leaves" type="spice" />
# </freezer>
```

Be sure to specify a RootName argument when you call xml_out. When it parses a file, XmlSimple removes one level of indirection by throwing away the name of your document's root element. You can prevent this by using the KeepRoot argument in your original call to xml_in. You'll need an extra hash lookup to navigate the resulting data structure, but you'll retain the name of your root element.

```
parsed3 = XmlSimple.xml_in(xml, 'KeepRoot'=>true)
# Now there's no need to add an extra root element when writing back to XML.
XmlSimple.xml_out(parsed3, 'RootName'=>nil)
```

One disadvantage of XmlSimple is that, since it puts elements into a hash, it replaces the order of the original document with the random-looking order of a Ruby hash. This is fine for a document listing the contents of a freezer—where order doesn't matter—but it would give interesting results if you tried to use it on a web page.

Another disadvantage is that, since an element's attributes and children are put into the same hash, you have no reliable way of telling one from the other. Indeed, attributes and subelements may even end up in a list together, as in this example:

```
pp XmlSimple.xml_in(%{
<freezer temp="-12" scale="celcius">
 <temp>Body of temporary worker who knew too much</temp>
</freezer>})
# {"scale"=>"celcius",
#  "temp"=>["-12", "Body of temp worker who knew too much"]}
```

See Also

- The XmlSimple home page at *http://www.maik-schmidt.de/xml-simple.html* has much more information about the options you can pass to XmlSimple.xml_in

11.7 Validating an XML Document

Credit: Mauro Cicio

Problem

You want to check whether an XML document conforms to a certain schema or DTD.

Solution

Unfortunately, as of this writing there are no stable, pure Ruby libraries that do XML validation. You'll need to install a Ruby binding to a C library. The easiest one to use is the Ruby binding to the GNOME libxml2 toolkit. (There are actually two Ruby bindings to libxml2, so don't get confused: we're referring to the one you get when you install the libxml-ruby gem.)

To validate a document against a DTD, create a a Dtd object and pass it into Document#validate. To validate against an XML Schema, pass in a Schema object instead.

Consider the following DTD, for a cookbook like this one:

```
require 'rubygems'
require 'libxml'

dtd = XML::Dtd.new(%{<!ELEMENT rubycookbook (recipe+)>
<!ELEMENT recipe (title?, problem, solution, discussion, seealso?)+>
<!ELEMENT title (#PCDATA)>
<!ELEMENT problem (#PCDATA)>
<!ELEMENT solution (#PCDATA)>
<!ELEMENT discussion (#PCDATA)>
<!ELEMENT seealso (#PCDATA)>})
```

Here's an XML document that looks like it conforms to the DTD:

```
open('cookbook.xml', 'w') do |f|
  f.write %{<?xml version="1.0"?>
<rubycookbook>
 <recipe>
   <title>A recipe</title>
   <problem>A difficult/common problem</problem>
   <solution>A smart solution</solution>
   <discussion>A deep solution</discussion>
   <seealso>Pointers</seealso>
 </recipe>
</rubycookbook>
}
end
```

But does it really? We can tell for sure with Document#validate:

```
document = XML::Document.file('cookbook.xml')
document.validate(dtd)                          # => true
```

Here's a Schema definition for the same document. We can validate the document against the schema by making it into a Schema object and passing *that* into Document#validate:

```
schema = XML::Schema.from_string %{<?xml version="1.0"?>

<xsd:schema xmlns:xsd="http://www.w3.org/2001/XMLSchema">
  <xsd:element name="recipe" type="recipeType"/>

  <xsd:element name="rubycookbook" type="rubycookbookType"/>

  <xsd:element name="title"      type="xsd:string"/>
  <xsd:element name="problem"    type="xsd:string"/>
  <xsd:element name="solution"   type="xsd:string"/>
  <xsd:element name="discussion" type="xsd:string"/>
  <xsd:element name="seealso"    type="xsd:string"/>

  <xsd:complexType name="rubycookbookType">
   <xsd:sequence>
      <xsd:element ref="recipe"/>
    </xsd:sequence>
  </xsd:complexType>
```

```
    <xsd:complexType name="recipeType">
      <xsd:sequence>
        <xsd:element ref="title"/>
        <xsd:element ref="problem"/>
        <xsd:element ref="solution"/>
        <xsd:element ref="discussion"/>
        <xsd:element ref="seealso"/>
      </xsd:sequence>
    </xsd:complexType>

  </xsd:schema>
  }

  document.validate(schema)                          # => true
```

Discussion

Programs that use XML validation are more robust and less complicated than non-validating versions. Before starting work on a document, you can check whether or not it's in the format you expect. Most services that accept XML as input don't have forgiving parsers, so you *must* validate your document before submitting it or it might fail without you even noticing.

One of the most popular and complete XML libraries around is the GNOME Libxml2 library. Despite its name, it works fine outside the GNOME platform, and has been ported to many different OSes. The Ruby project libxml (*http://libxml. rubyforge.org*) is a Ruby wrapper around the GNOME Libxml2 library. The project is not yet in a mature state, but it's very active and the validation features are definitively usable. Not only does libxml support validation and a complete range of XML manipolation techniques, it can also improve your program's speed by an order of magnitude, since it's written in C instead of REXML's pure Ruby.

Don't confuse the libxml *project* with the libxml *library*. The latter is part of the XML::Tools project. It binds against the GNOME Libxml2 library, but it doesn't expose that library's validation features. If you try the example code above but can't find the XML::Dtd or the XML::Schema classes, then you've got the wrong binding. If you installed the libxml-ruby package on Debian GNU/Linux, you've got the wrong one. You need the one you get by installing the libxml-ruby gem. Of course, you'll need to have the actual GNOME libxml library installed as well.

See Also

- The Ruby libxml project page (*http://www.rubyforge.org/projects/libxml*)
- The *other* Ruby libxml binding (the one that doesn't do validation) is part of the XML::Tools project (*http://rubyforge.org/projects/xml-tools/*); don't confuse the two!
- The GNOME libxml project homepage (*http://xmlsoft.org/*)
- Refer to *http://www.w3.org/XML* for the difference between a DTD and a Schema

11.8 Substituting XML Entities

Problem

You've parsed a document that contains internal XML entities. You want to substitute the entities in the document for their values.

Solution

To perform entity substitution on a specific text element, call its value method. If it's the first text element of its parent, you can call text on the parent instead.

Here's a simple document that defines and uses two entities in a single text node. We can substitute those entities for their values without changing the document itself:

```
require 'rexml/document'

str = %{<?xml version="1.0"?>
<!DOCTYPE doc [
 <!ENTITY product 'Stargaze'>
 <!ENTITY version '2.3'>
]>
<doc>
 &product; v&version; is the most advanced astronomy product on the market.
</doc>}
doc = REXML::Document.new str

doc.root.children[0].value
# => "\n Stargaze v2.3 is the most advanced astronomy product on the market.\n"
doc.root.text
# => "\n Stargaze v2.3 is the most advanced astronomy product on the market.\n"

doc.root.children[0].to_s
# => "\n &product; v&version; is the most advanced astronomy product on the market.\n"
doc.root.write
# <doc>
#  &product; v&version; is the most advanced astronomy program on the market.
# </doc>
```

Discussion

Internal XML entities are often used to factor out data that changes a lot, like dates or version numbers. But REXML only provides a convenient way to perform substitution on a single text node. What if you want to perform substitutions throughout the entire document?

When you call Document#write to send a document to some IO object, it ends up calling Text#to_s on each text node. As seen in the Solution, this method presents a "normalized" view of the data, one where entities are displayed instead of having their values substituted in.

We could write our own version of Document#write that presents an "unnormalized" view of the document, one with entity values substituted in, but that would be a lot of work. We could hack Text#to_s to work more like Text#value, or hack Text#write to call the value method instead of to_s. But it's less intrusive to do the entity replacement outside of the write method altogether. Here's a class that wraps any IO object and performs entity replacement on all the text that comes through it:

```
require 'delegate'
require 'rexml/text'
class EntitySubstituter < DelegateClass(IO)
  def initialize(io, document, filter=nil)
    @document = document
    @filter = filter
    super(io)
  end

  def <<(s)
    super(REXML::Text::unnormalize(s, @document.doctype, @filter))
  end
end

output = EntitySubstituter.new($stdout, doc)
doc.write(output)
# <?xml version='1.0'?><!DOCTYPE doc [
# <!ENTITY product "Stargaze">
# <!ENTITY version "2.3">
# ]>
# <doc>
#  Stargaze v2.3 is the most advanced astronomy product on the market.
# </doc>
```

Because it processes the entire output of Document#write, this code will replace *all* entity references in the document. This includes any references found in attribute values, which may or may not be what you want.

If you create a Text object manually, or set the value of an existing object, REXML assumes that you're giving it unnormalized text, and normalizes it. This can be problematic if your text contains strings that happen to be the values of entities:

```
text_node = doc.root.children[0]
text_node.value = "&product; v&version; has a catalogue of 2.3 " +
                  "million celestial objects."

doc.write
# <?xml version='1.0'?><!DOCTYPE doc [
# <!ENTITY product "Stargaze">
# <!ENTITY version "2.3">
# ]>
# <doc>&product; v&version; has a catalogue of &version; million celestial objects.
  </doc>
```

To avoid this, you can create a "raw" text node:

```
text_node.raw = true
doc.write
# <?xml version='1.0'?><!DOCTYPE doc [
# <!ENTITY product "Stargaze">
# <!ENTITY version "2.3">
# ]>
# <doc>&product; v&version; has a catalogue of 2.3 million celestial objects.</doc>

text_node.value
# => "Stargaze v2.3 has a catalogue of 2.3 million celestial objects."
text_node.to_s
# => "&product; v&version; has a catalogue of 2.3 million celestial objects."
```

In addition to entities you define, REXML automatically processes five named character entities: the ones for left and right angle brackets, single and double quotes, and the ampersand. Each is replaced with the corresponding ASCII character.

```
str = %{
  <!DOCTYPE doc [ <!ENTITY year '2006'> ]>
  <doc>&#169; &year; Komodo Dragon &amp; Bob Productions</doc>
}

doc = REXML::Document.new str
text_node = doc.root.children[0]

text_node.value
# => "&copy; 2006 Komodo Dragon & Bob Productions"
text_node.to_s
# => "&copy; &year; Komodo Dragon &amp; Bob Productions"
```

"©" is an HTML character entity representing the copyright symbol, but REXML doesn't know that. It only knows about the five XML character entities. Also, REXML only knows about internal entities: ones whose values are defined within the same document that uses them. It won't resolve external entities.

See Also

- The section "Text Nodes" of the REXML tutorial (*http://www.germane-software. com/software/rexml/docs/tutorial.html#id2248004*)

11.9   Creating and Modifying XML Documents

Problem

You want to modify an XML document, or create a new one from scratch.

Solution

To create an XML document from scratch, just start with an empty Document object.

```
require 'rexml/document'
require
doc = REXML::Document.new
```

To add a new element to an existing document, pass its name and any attributes into its parent's add_element method. You don't have to create the Element objects yourself.

```
meeting = doc.add_element 'meeting'
meeting_start = Time.local(2006, 10, 31, 13)
meeting.add_element('time', { 'from' => meeting_start,
                              'to' => meeting_start + 3600 })

doc.children[0]                              # => <meeting> ... </>
doc.children[0].children[0]
# => "<time from='Tue Oct 31 13:00:00 EST 2006'
#       to='Tue Oct 31 14:00:00 EST 2006'/>"

doc.write($stdout, 1)
# <meeting>
#  <time from='Tue Oct 31 13:00:00 EST 2006'
#        to='Tue Oct 31 14:00:00 EST 2006'/>
# </meeting>
doc.children[0]                              # => <?xml ... ?>
doc.children[1]                              # => <meeting> ... </>
```

To append a text node to the contents of an element, use the add_text method. This code adds an <agenda> element to the <meeting> element, and gives it two different text nodes:

```
agenda = meeting.add_element 'agenda'
doc.children[1].children[1]                  # => <agenda/>

agenda.add_text "Nothing of importance will be decided."
agenda.add_text " The same tired ideas will be rehashed yet again."

doc.children[1].children[1]                  # => <agenda> ... </>

doc.write($stdout, 1)
# <meeting>
#  <time from='Tue Oct 31 13:00:00 EST 2006'
#        to='Tue Oct 31 14:00:00 EST 2006'/>
#  <agenda>
#   Nothing of importance will be decided. The same tired ideas will be
#   rehashed yet again.
#  </agenda>
# </meeting>
```

Element#text= is a nice shortcut for giving an element a single text node. You can also use to overwrite a document's initial text nodes:

```
item1 = agenda.add_element 'item'
doc.children[1].children[1].children[1]      # => <item/>
item1.text = 'Weekly status meetings: improving attendance'
doc.children[1].children[1].children[1]      # => <item> ... </>
```

```
doc.write($stdout, 1)
# <meeting>
#  <time from='Tue Oct 31 13:00:00 EST 2006'
#        to='Tue Oct 31 14:00:00 EST 2006'/>
#  <agenda>
#    Nothing of importance will be decided. The same tired ideas will be
#    rehashed yet again.
#    <item>Weekly status meetings: improving attendance</item>
#  </agenda>
# </meeting>
```

Discussion

If you can access an element or text node (numerically or with XPath), you can modify or delete it. You can modify an element's name with name=, and modify one of its
attributes by assigning to an index of attributes. This code uses these methods to
make major changes to a document:

```
doc = REXML::Document.new %{<?xml version='1.0'?>
<girl size="little">
 <foods>
  <sugar />
  <spice />
 </foods>
 <set of="nice things" cardinality="all" />
</girl>
}

root = doc[1]                          # => <girl size='little'> ... </>
root.name = 'boy'

root.elements['//sugar'].name = 'snails'
root.delete_element('//spice')

set = root.elements['//set']
set.attributes["of"] = "snips"
set.attributes["cardinality"] = 'some'

root.add_element('set', {'of' => 'puppy dog tails', 'cardinality' => 'some' })
doc.write
# <?xml version='1.0'?>
# <boy size='little'>
#  <foods>
#    <snails/>
#
#  </foods>
#  <set of='snips' cardinality='some'/>
# <set of='puppy dog tails' cardinality='some'/></boy>
```

You can delete an attribute with Element#delete_attribute, or by assigning nil to it:

```
root.attributes['size'] = nil
doc.write($stdout, 0)
# <?xml version='1.0'?>
```

```
# <boy>
#   <foods>
#   ...
# </boy>
```

You can use methods like `replace_with` to swap out one node for another:

```
doc.elements["//snails"].replace_with(REXML::Element.new("escargot"))
```

All these methods are convenient, but `add_element` in particular is not very idiomatic. The `cgi` library lets you structure method calls and code blocks so that your Ruby code has the same nesting structure as the HTML it generates. Why shouldn't you be able to do the same for XML? Here's a new method for `Element` that makes it possible:

```
class REXML::Element
  def with_element(*args)
    e = add_element(*args)
    yield e if block_given?
  end
end
```

Now you can structure your Ruby code the same way you structure your XML:

```
doc = REXML::Document.new
doc.with_element('girl', {'size' => 'little'}) do |girl|
  girl.with_element('foods') do |foods|
    foods.add_element('sugar')
    foods.add_element('spice')
  end
  girl.add_element('set', {'of' => 'nice things', 'cardinality' => 'all'})
end

doc.write($stdout, 0)
# <girl size='little'>
#   <foods>
#     <sugar/>
#     <spice/>
#   </foods>
#   <set of='nice things' cardinality='all'/>
# </girl>
```

The builder gem also lets you build XML this way.

See Also

- Recipe 7.10, "Hiding Setup and Cleanup in a Block Method," has an example of using the `XmlMarkup` class in the builder gem.

11.10 Compressing Whitespace in an XML Document

Problem

When REXML parses a document, it respects the original whitespace of the document's text nodes. You want to make the document smaller by compressing extra whitespace.

Solution

Parse the document by creating a REXML::Document out of it. Within the Document constructor, tell the parser to compress all runs of whitespace characters:

```
require 'rexml/document'

text = %{<doc><a>Some        whitespace</a>     <b>Some    more</b></doc>}

REXML::Document.new(text, { :compress_whitespace => :all }).to_s
# => "<doc><a>Some whitespace</a> <b>Some more</b></doc>"
```

Discussion

Sometimes whitespace within a document is significant, but usually (as with HTML) it can be compressed without changing the meaning of the document. The resulting document takes up less space on the disk and requires less bandwidth to transmit.

Whitespace compression doesn't have to be all-or-nothing. REXML gives two ways to configure it. Instead of passing :all as a value for :compress_whitespace, you can pass in a list of tag names. Whitespace will only be compressed in those tags:

```
REXML::Document.new(text, { :compress_whitespace => %w{a} }).to_s
# => "<doc><a>Some whitespace</a>     <b>Some    more</b></doc>"
```

You can also switch it around: pass in :respect_whitespace and a list of tag names whose whitespace you *don't* want to be compressed. This is useful if you know that whitespace is significant within certain parts of your document.

```
REXML::Document.new(text, { :respect_whitespace => %w{a} }).to_s
# => "<doc><a>Some        whitespace</a> <b>Some more</b></doc>"
```

What about text nodes containing *only* whitespace? These are often inserted by XML pretty-printers, and they can usually be totally discarded without altering the meaning of a document. If you add :ignore_whitespace_nodes => :all to the parser configuration, REXML will simply decline to create text nodes that contain nothing but whitespace characters. Here's a comparison of :compress_whitespace alone, and in conjunction with :ignore_whitespace_nodes:

```
text = %{<doc><a>Some    text</a>\n  <b>Some    more</b>\n\n}
REXML::Document.new(text, { :compress_whitespace => :all }).to_s
# => "<doc><a>Some text</a>\n <b>Some more</b>\n</doc>"
```

```
REXML::Document.new(text, { :compress_whitespace => :all,
                            :ignore_whitespace_nodes => :all }).to_s
# => "<doc><a>Some text</a><b>Some more</b></doc>"
```

By itself, :compress_whitespace shouldn't make a document less human-readable, but :ignore_whitespace_nodes almost certainly will.

See Also

- Recipe 1.11, "Managing Whitespace"

11.11 Guessing a Document's Encoding

Credit: Mauro Cicio

Problem

You want to know the character encoding of a document that doesn't declare it explicitly.

Solution

Use the Ruby bindings to the libcharguess library. Once it's installed, using libcharguess is very simple.

Here's an XML document written in Italian, with no explicit encoding:

```
doc = %{<?xml version="1.0"?>
    <menu tipo="specialità" giorno="venerdì">
    <primo_piatto>spaghetti al ragù</primo_piatto>
        <bevanda>frappè</bevanda>
    </menu>}
```

Let's find its encoding:

```
require 'charguess'

CharGuess::guess doc
# => "windows-1252"
```

This is a pretty good guess: the XML is written in the ISO-8859-1 encoding, and many web browsers treat ISO-8859-1 as Windows-1252.

Discussion

In XML, the character-encoding indication is optional, and may be provided as an attribute of the XML declaration in the first line of the document:

```
<xml version="1.0" encoding="utf-8"?>
```

If this is missing, you must guess the document encoding to process the document. You can assume the lowest common denominator for your community (usually this means assuming that everything is either UTF-8 or ISO-8859-1), or you can use a library that examines the document and uses heuristics to guess the encoding.

As of the time of writing, there are no pure Ruby libraries for guessing the encoding of a document. Fortunately, there is a small Ruby wrapper around the Charguess library. This library can guess with 95% accuracy the encoding of any text whose charset is one of the following: BIG5, HZ, JIS, SJIS, EUC-JP, EUC-KR, EUC-TW, GB2312, Bulgarian, Cyrillic, Greek, Hungarian, Thai, Latin1, and UTF8.

Note that Charguess is not XML- or HTML-specific. In fact, it can guess the encoding of an arbitrary string:

```
CharGuess::guess("\xA4\xCF")                    # => "EUC-JP"
```

It's fairly easy to install libcharguess, since the library is written in portable C++. Unfortunately, it doesn't take care to put its header files in a standard location. This makes it a little tricky to compile the Ruby bindings, which depend on the charguess.h header. When you run extconf.rb to prepare the bindings, you must explicitly tell the script where to find libcharguess's headers. Here's how you might compile the Ruby bindings to libcharguess:

```
$ ruby extconf.rb --with-charguess-include=/location/of/charguess.h
$ make
$ make install
```

See Also

- To find your way through the jungle of character encodings, the Wikipedia entry on character encodings makes a good reference (*http://en.wikipedia.org/wiki/Character_encoding*)
- A good source for sample texts in various charsets is *http://vancouver-webpages. com/multilingual/*
- The XML specification has a section on character encoding autodetection (*http:// www.w3.org/TR/REC-xml/#sec-guessing*)
- The Charguess library is at *http://libcharguess.sourceforge.net*; its Ruby bindings are available from *http://raa.ruby-lang.org/project/charguess*

11.12 Converting from One Encoding to Another

Credit: Mauro Cicio

Problem

You want to convert a document to a given charset encoding (probably UTF-8).

Solution

If you don't know the document's current encoding, you can guess at it using the Charguess library described in the previous recipe. Once you know the current encoding, you can convert the document to another encoding using Ruby's standard iconv library.

Here's an XML document written in Italian, with no explicit encoding:

```
doc = %{<?xml version="1.0"?>
    <menu tipo="specialità" giorno="venerdì">
    <primo_piatto>spaghetti al ragù</primo_piatto>
      <bevanda>frappè</bevanda>
    </menu>}
```

Let's figure out its encoding and convert it to UTF-8:

```
require 'iconv'
require 'charguess' # not necessary if input encoding is known

input_encoding = CharGuess::guess doc              # => "windows-1252"
output_encoding = 'utf-8'

converted_doc = Iconv.new(output_encoding, input_encoding).iconv(doc)

CharGuess::guess(converted_doc)                    # => "UTF-8"
```

Discussion

The heart of the iconv library is the Iconv class, a wrapper for the Unix 95 iconv( ) family of functions. These functions translate strings between various encoding systems. Since iconv is part of the Ruby standard library, it should be already available on your system.

Iconv works well in conjunction with Charguess: even if Charguess guesses the encoding a little bit wrong (such as guessing Windows-1252 for an ISO-8859-1 document), it always makes a good enough guess that iconv can convert the document to another encoding.

Like Charguess, the Iconv library is not XML- or HTML-specific. You can use libcharguess and iconv together to convert an arbitrary string to a given encoding.

See Also

- Recipe 11.11, "Guessing a Document's Encoding"
- The iconv library is documented at *http://www.ruby-doc.org/stdlib/libdoc/iconv/rdoc/classes/Iconv.html*; you can find pointers to *The Open Group* Unix library specifications

11.13 Extracting All the URLs from an HTML Document

Problem

You want to find all the URLs on a web page.

Solution

Do you only want to find links (that is, URLs mentioned in the HREF attribute of an A tag)? Do you also want to find the URLs of embedded objects like images and applets? Or do you want to find *all* URLs, including ones mentioned in the text of the page?

The last case is the simplest. You can use URI.extract to get all the URLs found in a string, or to get only the URLs with certain schemes. Here we'll extract URLs from some HTML, whether or not they're inside A tags:

```
require 'uri'

text = %{"My homepage is at
<a href="http://www.example.com/">http://www.example.com/</a>, and be sure
to check out my weblog at http://www.example.com/blog/. Email me at <a
href="mailto:bob@example.com">bob@example.com</a>.}

URI.extract(text)
# => ["http://www.example.com/", "http://www.example.com/",
#      "http://www.example.com/blog/.", "mailto:bob@example.com"]

# Get HTTP(S) links only.
URI.extract(text, ['http', 'https'])
# => ["http://www.example.com/", "http://www.example.com/"
#      "http://www.example.com/blog/."]
```

If you only want URLs that show up inside certain tags, you need to parse the HTML. Assuming the document is valid, you can do this with any of the parsers in the rexml library. Here's an efficient implementation using REXML's stream parser. It retrieves URLs found in the HREF attributes of A tags and the SRC attributes of IMG tags, but you can customize this behavior by passing a different map to the constructor.

```
require 'rexml/document'
require 'rexml/streamlistener'
require 'set'

class LinkGrabber
  include REXML::StreamListener
  attr_reader :links

  def initialize(interesting_tags = {'a' => %w{href}, 'img' => %w{src}}.freeze)
    @tags = interesting_tags
    @links = Set.new
  end
```

```
    def tag_start(name, attrs)
      @tags[name].each do |uri_attr|
        @links << attrs[uri_attr] if attrs[uri_attr]
      end if @tags[name]
    end

    def parse(text)
      REXML::Document.parse_stream(text, self)
    end
  end

  grabber = LinkGrabber.new
  grabber.parse(text)
  grabber.links
  # => #<Set: {"http://www.example.com/", "mailto:bob@example.com"}>
```

Discussion

The `URI.extract` solution uses regular expressions to find everything that looks like a URL. This is faster and easier to write than a REXML parser, but it will find *every* absolute URL in the document, including any mentioned in the text and any in the document's initial DOCTYPE. It will *not* find relative URLs hidden within HREF attributes, since those don't start with an access scheme like "http://".

`URI.extract` treats the period at the end of the first sentence ("check out my weblog at…") as though it were part of the URL. URLs contained within English text are often ambiguous in this way. "*http://www.example.com/blog/.*" is a perfectly valid URL and might be correct, but that period is probably just punctuation. Accessing the URL is the only sure way to know for sure, but it's almost always safe to strip those characters:

```
END_CHARS = %{.,'?!:;}
URI.extract(text, ['http']).collect { |u| END_CHARS.index(u[-1]) ? u.chop : u }
# => ["http://www.example.com/", "http://www.example.com/",
#     "http://www.example.com/blog/"]
```

The parser solution defines a listener that hears about every tag present in its `interesting_tags` map. It checks each tag for attributes that tend to contain URLs: "href" for `<a>` tags and "src" for `<img>` tags, for instance. Every URL it finds goes into a set.

The use of a set here guarantees that the result contains no duplicate URLs. If you want to gather (possibly duplicate) URLs in the order they were found in the document, use a list, the way `URI.extract` does.

The `LinkGrabber` solution will not find URLs in the text portions of the document, but it will find relative URLs. Of course, you still need to know how to turn relative URLs into absolute URLs. If the document has a `<base>` tag, you can use that. Otherwise, the base depends on the original URL of the document.

Here's a subclass of `LinkGrabber` that changes relative links to absolute links if possible. Since it uses `URI.join`, which returns a URI object, your set will end up containing URI objects instead of strings:

```
class AbsoluteLinkGrabber < LinkGrabber
  include REXML::StreamListener
  attr_reader :links

  def initialize(original_url = nil,
              interesting_tags = {'a' => %w{href}, 'img' => %w{src}}.freeze)
    super(interesting_tags)
    @base = original_url
  end

  def tag_start(name, attrs)
    if name == 'base'
      @base = attrs['href']
    end
    super
  end

  def parse(text)
    super
    # If we know of a base URL by the end of the document, use it to
    # change all relative URLs to absolute URLs.
    @links.collect! { |l| URI.join(@base, l) } if @base
  end
end
```

If you want to use the parsing solution, but the web page has invalid HTML that chokes the REXML parsers (which is quite likely), try the techniques mentioned in Recipe 11.5.

Almost 20 HTML tags can have URLs in one or more of their attributes. If you want to collect *every* URL mentioned in an appropriate part of a web page, here's a big map you can pass in to the constructor of `LinkGrabber` or `AbsoluteLinkGrabber`:

```
URL_LOCATIONS = { 'a' => %w{href},
  'area' => %w{href},
  'applet' => %w{classid},
  'base' => %w{href},
  'blockquote' => %w{cite},
  'body' => %w{background},
  'codebase' => %w{classid},
  'del' => %w{cite},
  'form' => %w{action},
  'frame' => %w{src longdesc},
  'iframe' => %w{src longdesc},
  'input' => %w{src usemap},
  'img' => %w{src longdesc usemap},
  'ins' => %w{cite},
  'link' => %w{href},
  'object' => %w{usemap archive codebase data},
```

```
      'profile' => %w{head},
      'q' => %w{cite},
      'script' => %w{src}}.freeze
```

See Also

- Recipe 11.4, "Navigating a Document with XPath"
- Recipe 11.5, "Parsing Invalid Markup"
- I compiled that big map of URI attributes from the W3C's Index of Attributes for HTML 4.0; look for the attributes of type %URI; (*http://www.w3.org/TR/REC-html40/index/attributes.html*)

11.14 Transforming Plain Text to HTML

Problem

You want to add simple markup to plaintext and turn it into HTML.

Solution

Use RedCloth, written by "why the lucky stiff" and available as the RedCloth gem. It extends Ruby's string class to support Textile markup: its to_html method converts Textile markup to HTML.

Here's a simple document:

```
require 'rubygems'
require 'redcloth'

text = RedCloth.new %{Who would ever write "HTML":http://www.w3.org/MarkUp/
markup directly?

I mean, _who has the time_? Nobody, that's who:

|_. Person |_. Has the time?        |
|   Jake   |      No                |
|   Alice  |      No                |
|   Rodney | Not since the accident |
}

puts text.to_html
# <p>Who would ever write
# <a href="http://www.w3.org/MarkUp/"><span class="caps">HTML</span></a>
# markup directly?</p>
#
# <p>I mean, <em>who has the time</em>? Nobody, that&#8217;s who:</p>
#
# <table>
#  <tr>
#   <th>Person </th>
#   <th>Has the time?        </th>
```

```
#    </tr>
#    ...
```

The Textile version is more readable and easier to edit.

Discussion

The Textile markup language lets you produce HTML without having to write any HTML. You just add punctuation to plain text, to convey what markup you'd like. Paragraph breaks are represented by blank lines, italics by underscores, tables by ASCII-art drawings of tables.

A text-based markup that converts to HTML is very useful in weblog and wiki software, where the markup will be edited many times. It's also useful for hiding the complexity of HTML from new computer users. We wrote this entire book using a Textile-like markup, though it was converted to Docbook instead of HTML.

See Also

- The RedCloth homepage (*http://www.whytheluckystiff.net/ruby/redcloth/*)
- A comprehensive Textile reference (*http://hobix.com/textile/*) and a quick reference (*http://hobix.com/textile/quick.html*)
- You can experiment with Textile markup at the language's homepage (*http://www.textism.com/tools/textile/*)
- Markdown (*http://daringfireball.net/projects/markdown/*) is another popular simple markup language for plain text; you can turn Markdown text to XHTML with the BlueCloth gem (project page: *http://www.deveiate.org/projects/BlueCloth*); because BlueCloth and RedCloth both define String#to_html, it's not easy to use them both in the same program

11.15 Converting HTML Documents from the Web into Text

Problem

You want to get a text summary of a web site.

Solution

The open-uri library is the easiest way to grab the content of a web page; it lets you open a URL as though it were a file:

```
require 'open-uri'

example = open('http://www.example.com/')
# => #<StringIO:0xb7bb601c>

html = example.read
```

As with a file, the read method returns a string. You can do a series of sub and gsub methods to clean the code into a more readable format.

```
plain_text = html.sub(%r{<body.*?>(.*?)</body>}mi, '\1').gsub(/<.*?>/m, ' ').
    gsub(%r{(\n\s*){2}}, "\n\n")
```

Finally, you can use the standard CGI library to unescape HTML entities like < into their ASCII equivalents (<):

```
require 'cgi'
plain_text = CGI.unescapeHTML(plain_text)
```

The final product:

```
puts plain_text
# Example Web Page
#
# You have reached this web page by typing "example.com",
# "example.net",
# or "example.org" into your web browser.
# These domain names are reserved for use in documentation and are not available
# for registration. See  RFC
# 2606 , Section 3.
```

Discussion

The open-uri library extends the open method so that you can access the contents of web pages and FTP sites with the same interface used for local files.

The simple regular expression substitutions above do nothing but remove HTML tags and clean up excess whitespace. They work well for well-formatted HTML, but the web is full of mean and ugly HTML, so you may consider taking a more involved approach. Let's define a HTMLSanitizer class to do our dirty business.

An HTMLSanitizer will start off with some HTML, and through a series of search-and-replace operations transform it into plain text. Different HTML tags will be handled differently. The contents of some HTML tags should simply be removed in a plain-text rendering. For example, you probably don't want to see the contents of <head> and <script> tags. Other tags affect what the rendition should look like, for instance, a <p> tag should be represented as a blank line:

```
require 'open-uri'
require 'cgi'

class HTMLSanitizer
  attr_accessor :html

  @@ignore_tags = ['head', 'script', 'frameset' ]
  @@inline_tags = ['span', 'strong', 'i', 'u'   ]
  @@block_tags  = ['p', 'div', 'ul', 'ol'       ]
```

The next two methods define the skeleton of our HTML sanitizer:

```
def initialize(source='')
  begin
    @html = open(source).read
```

```
    rescue Errno::ENOENT
      # If it's not a file, assume it's an HTML string
      @html = source
    end
  end

  def plain_text
    # remove pre-existing blank spaces between tags since we will
    # be adding spaces on our own
    @plain_text = @html.gsub(/\s*(<.*?>)/m, '\1')

    handle_ignore_tags
    handle_inline_tags
    handle_block_tags
    handle_all_other_tags

    return CGI.unescapeHTML(@plain_text)
  end
```

Now we need to fill in the handle_ methods defined by HTMLSanitizer#plain_text.
These methods perform search-and-replace operations on the @plain_text instance
variable, gradually transforming it from HTML into plain text. Because we are modifying @plain_text in place, we will need to use String#gsub! instead of String#gsub.

```
  private

  def tag_regex(tag)
    %r{<#{tag}.*?>(.*?)</#{tag}>}mi
  end

  def handle_ignore_tags
    @@ignore_tags.each { |tag| @plain_text.gsub!(tag_regex(tag), '') }
  end
  def handle_inline_tags
    @@inline_tags.each { |tag| @plain_text.gsub!(tag_regex(tag), '\1 ') }
  end
  def handle_block_tags
    @@block_tags.each { |tag| @plain_text.gsub!(tag_regex(tag), "\n\\1\n") }
  end

  def handle_all_other_tags
    @plain_text.gsub!(/&#x00A;/mi, "\n")
    @plain_text.gsub!(/<.*?>/m, ' ')
    @plain_text.gsub!(/(\n\s*){2}/, "\n\n")
  end
end
```

To use this class, simply initialize it with a URL and call the plain_text method:

```
puts HTMLSanitizer.new('http://slashdot.org/').plain_text
# Stories
# Slash Boxes
# Comments
#
```

```
# Slashdot
#
# News for nerds, stuff that matters
#
# Login
#
# Why Login?    Why Subscribe?
# ...
```

See Also

- Recipe 14.1, "Grabbing the Contents of a Web Page"
- For a more sophisticated text renderer, parse the HTML document with the techniques described in Recipe 11.2, "Extracting Data from a Document's Tree Structure," or Recipe 11.5, "Parsing Invalid Markup"

11.16 A Simple Feed Aggregator

Credit: Rod Gaither

XML is the basis for many specialized langages. One of the most popular is RSS, an XML format often used to store lists of articles from web pages. With a tool called an aggregator, you can collect weblog entries and articles from several web sites' RSS feeds, and read all those web sites at once without having to skip from one to the other. Here, we'll create a simple aggregator in Ruby.

Before aggregating RSS feeds, let's start by reading a single one. Fortunately we have several options for parsing RSS feeds into Ruby data structures. The Ruby standard library has built-in support for the three major versions of the RSS format (0.9, 1.0, and 2.0). This example uses the standard rss library to parse an RSS 2.0 feed and print out the titles of the items in the feed:

```
require 'rss/2.0'
require 'open-uri'

url = 'http://www.oreillynet.com/pub/feed/1?format=rss2'
feed = RSS::Parser.parse(open(url).read, false)
puts "=== Channel: #{feed.channel.title} ==="
feed.items.each do |item|
  puts item.title
  puts " (#{item.link})"
  puts
  puts item.description
end
# === Channel: O'Reilly Network Articles ===
# How to Make Your Sound Sing with Vocoders
# (http://digitalmedia.oreilly.com/2006/03/29/vocoder-tutorial-and-tips.html)
# ...
```

Unfortunately, the standard rss library is a little out of date. There's a newer syndication format called Atom, which serves the same purpose as RSS, and the rss library doesn't support it. Any serious aggregator must support all the major syndication formats.

So instead, our aggregator will use Lucas Carlson's Simple RSS library, available as the simple-rss gem. This library supports the three main versions of RSS, plus Atom, and it does so in a relaxed way so that ill-formed feeds have a better chance of being read.

Here's the example above, rewritten to use Simple RSS. As you can see, only the name of the class is different:

```
require 'rubygems'
require 'simple-rss'
url = 'http://www.oreillynet.com/pub/feed/1?format=rss2'
feed = RSS::Parser.parse(open(url), false)
puts "=== Channel: #{feed.channel.title} ==="
feed.items.each do |item|
  puts item.title
  puts " (#{item.link})"
  puts
  puts item.description
end
```

Now we have a general method of reading a single RSS or Atom feed. Time to work on some aggregation!

Although the aggregator will be a simple Ruby script, there's no reason not to use Ruby's object-oriented features. Our approach will be to create a class to encapsulate the aggregator's data and behavior, and then write a sample program to use the class.

The RSSAggregator class that follows is a bare-bones aggregator that reads from multiple syndication feeds when instantiated. It uses a few simple methods to expose the data it has read.

```
#!/usr/bin/ruby
# rss-aggregator.rb - Simple RSS and Atom Feed Aggregator

require 'rubygems'
require 'simple-rss'
require 'open-uri'

class RSSAggregator
  def initialize(feed_urls)
    @feed_urls = feed_urls
    @feeds = []
    read_feeds
  end

  protected
  def read_feeds
    @feed_urls.each { |url| @feeds.push(SimpleRSS.new(open(url).read)) }
  end
```

```ruby
  public
  def refresh
    @feeds.clear
    read_feeds
  end

  def channel_counts
    @feeds.each_with_index do |feed, index|
      channel = "Channel(#{index.to_s}): #{feed.channel.title}"
      articles = "Articles: #{feed.items.size.to_s}"
      puts channel + ', ' + articles
    end
  end

  def list_articles(id)
    puts "=== Channel(#{id.to_s}): #{@feeds[id].channel.title} ==="
    @feeds[id].items.each { |item| puts ' ' + item.title }
  end

  def list_all
    @feeds.each_with_index { |f, i| list_articles(i) }
  end
end
```

Now we just need a few more lines of code to instantiate and use an RSSAggregator object:

```ruby
test = RSSAggregator.new(ARGV)
test.channel_counts
puts "\n"
test.list_all
```

Here's the output from a run of the test program against a few feed URLs:

```
$ ruby rss-aggregator.rb http://www.rubyriver.org/rss.xml \
  http://rss.slashdot.org/Slashdot/slashdot \
  http://www.oreillynet.com/pub/feed/1 \
  http://safari.oreilly.com/rss/
Channel(0): RubyRiver, Articles: 20
Channel(1): Slashdot, Articles: 10
Channel(2): O'Reilly Network Articles, Articles: 15
Channel(3): O'Reilly Network Safari Bookshelf, Articles: 10
=== Channel(0): RubyRiver ===
 Mantis style isn't eas...
 It's wonderful when tw...
 Red tailed hawk
 37signals
 ...
```

While a long way from a fully functional RSS aggregator, this program illustrates the basic requirements of any real aggregator. From this starting point, you can expand and refine the features of RSSAggregator.

One very important feature missing from the aggregator is support for the If-Modified-Since HTTP request header. When you call RSSAggregator#refresh, your aggregator downloads the specified feeds, even if it just grabbed the same feeds and none of them have changed since then. This wastes bandwidth.

Polite aggregators keep track of when they last grabbed a certain feed, and when they request it again they do a conditional request by supplying an HTTP request header called If-Modified Since. The details are a little beyond our scope, but basically the web server serves the reuqested feed only if it has changed since the last time the RSSAggregator downloaded it.

Another important feature our RSSAggregator is missing is the ability to store the articles it fetches. A real aggregator would store articles on disk or in a database to keep track of which stories are new since the last fetch, and to keep articles available even after they become old news and drop out of the feed.

Our simple aggregator counts the articles and lists their titles for review, but it doesn't actually provide access to the article detail. As seen in the first example, the SimpleRSS.item has a link attribute containing the URL for the article, and a description attribute containing the (possibly HTML) body of the article. A real aggregator might generate a list of articles in HTML format for use in a browser, or convert the body of each article to text for output to a terminal.

See Also

- Recipe 14.1, "Grabbing the Contents of a Web Page"
- Recipe 14.3, "Customizing HTTP Request Headers"
- Recipe 11.15, "Converting HTML Documents from the Web into Text"
- A good comparison of the RSS and Atom formats (*http://www.intertwingly.net/wiki/pie/Rss20AndAtom10Compared*)
- Details on the Simple RSS project (*http://simple-rss.rubyforge.org/*)
- The FeedTools project has a more sophisticated aggregator library that supports caching and If-Modified-Since; see *http://sporkmonger.com/projects/feedtools/* for details
- "HTTP Conditional Get for RSS Hackers" is a readable introduction to If-Modified-Since (*http://fishbowl.pastiche.org/2002/10/21/http_conditional_get_for_rss_hackers*)

Graphics and Other File Formats

Hundreds of standards exist for storing structured data in text or binary files. Some of these are so popular that we've devoted entire chapters to them (Chapters 11 and 13). Some are so simple that you can process them with the ad hoc techniques listed in Chapters 1 and 6. This chapter is a grab bag that tries to cover the rest of the field.

We focus especially on graphics, probably the most common binary files. Ruby lacks a mature image manipulation library like the Python Imaging Library, but it does have bindings to ImageMagick and GraphicsMagick, popular and stable C libraries. The RMagick library provides the same interface against ImageMagick and Graphics-Magick, so it doesn't matter which one you use.

You can get RMagick by installing the `RMagick` or `Rmagick-win32` gem. Unfortunately, the C libraries themselves are difficult to install: they have a lot of dependencies, especially if you want to process image formats like GIF and PostScript. The installation FAQ can help (*http://rmagick.rubyforge.org/install-faq.html*). On Debian GNU/Linux, you can just install the `imagemagick` package and then the `RMagick` gem.

The first recipes in this chapter show how to use RMagick to manipulate and convert images (on the question of *finding* images, see Recipe 16.2). Then it gets miscellaneous: we cover encryption, archive formats, Excel spreadsheets, and music files. We don't have space to cover every popular file format, but this chapter should give you an idea of what's out there. If this chapter lacks a recipe on your file format of choice, you may be able to find a Ruby library for it on the RAA, or by doing a web search for ruby [*file format name*].

12.1 Thumbnailing Images

Credit: Antonio Cangiano

Problem

Given an image, you want to create a smaller image to serve as a thumbnail.

Solution

Use RMagick, available from the `rmagick` or `rmagick-win32` gems. Its Magick module gives you a simple but versatile way to manipulate images. The class `Magick::Image` lets you resize images four different ways: with `resize`, `scale`, `sample`, or `thumbnail`.

All four methods accept a pair integer values, corresponding to the width and height in pixels of the thumbnail you want. Here's an example that uses `resize`: it takes the file `myimage.jpg` and makes a thumbnail of it 100 pixels wide by 100 pixels tall:

```
require 'rubygems'
require 'RMagick'

img = Magick::Image.read('myimage.jpg').first
width, height = 100, 100
thumb = img.resize(width, height)
thumb.write('mythumbnail.jpg')
```

Discussion

The class method `Image.read`, used in the Solution, receives an image filename as an argument and returns an array of `Image` objects.[*] You obtain the first (and, usually, only) element through `Array#first`.

The code given in the Solution produces a thumbnail that is 100 pixels by 100, no matter what dimensions the original image had. If the original image was a square, its proportions will be maintained. But if the initial image was a rectangle, squishing it into a 100×100 box will distort it.

If all your thumbnails need to be the same size, you might be willing to live with this distortion. But to maintain the proportions between the longest and shortest dimensions, you should define your thumbnail's width and height in terms of the original image's aspect ratio. You can get the image's original width and height by using its accessor methods, `Magick::Image#columns` and `Magick::Image#rows`.

A simpler solution is to pass `resize` a floating-point number as a scaling factor. This changes the image's size without altering the aspect ratio. Here's how to generate an image that is 15% the size of the original:

```
scale_factor = 0.15
thumb = img.resize(scale_factor)
thumb.write("mythumbnail.jpg")
```

To impose a maximum size on an image without altering its aspect ratio, use `change_ geometry`:

```
def thumb_no_bigger_than(img, width, height)
  img.change_geometry("#{width}x#{height}") do |cols, rows, img|
```

---

[*] Why an array? Because you can pass in an animated GIF or a multilayered image file to `Image.read`. If you do, the array will contain an `Image` object for each image in the animated GIF, or for each layer in the multi-layered file.

```
        img.resize(cols, rows)
    end
end

img.rows                                    # => 470
img.columns                                 # => 892
thumb = thumb_no_bigger_than(img, 100, 100)
thumb.rows                                  # => 53
thumb.columns                               # => 100
```

There are other ways of getting a thumbnail besides using resize. All of the following lines give you some kind of thumbnail. The methods used below also have equivalent methods (like scale!) that modify an Image object in place:

```
thumb = img.scale(width, height)
thumb = img.scale(scale_factor)
thumb = img.sample(width, height)
thumb = img.sample(scale_factor)
thumb = img.thumbnail(width, height)
thumb = img.thumbnail(scale_factor)
```

You might also want to generate a thumbnail by cropping an image, rather than resizing it. The following code extracts an 80×100 pixel rectangle taken from the center of the image:

```
thumb = img.crop(Magick::CenterGravity, 80, 100)
```

Which of these methods should you use? Magick::Image#resize is the most advanced method, because it accepts two optional arguments: filter and blur. When you specify a filter, you alter the resizing algorithm's tradeoff between speed and quality. Refer to the RMagick guide for a complete list of available filters.

The second optional argument, blur, is a floating-point number that can be used to blur (values greater than 1) or sharpen (values less than 1) your image as it's resized. Blurring an image is a way to hide visual artifacts created by the thumbnailing process.

The scale method is simpler than resize, because it accepts only a width and height pair, or a scale factor. When you want to generate a thumbnail that's 10% the size of your original image or smaller, thumbnail is faster than resize.

Finally, sample scales images with pixel sampling. Unlike the other methods, it doesn't introduce any new colors through interpolation.

The best advice is to try these methods out with your images. Through trial and error, you can determine what works best for your application.

Using crop means approaching the problem in a different way. crop only includes a portion of the original image in the thumbnail. crop has several signatures, each of which requires the output image's width and height:

```
# With an x, y offset relative to the upper-left corner:
thumb = img.crop(x, y, width, height)
```

```
# With a GravityType and the x, y offset:
thumb = img.crop(Magick::WestGravity, x, y, width, height)

# With a GravityType:
thumb = img.crop(Magick::EastGravity, width, height)
```

GravityType is a constant that lets you specify the position of the region that needs to be cropped. The available options are quite self-explanatory.

Be aware that the x and y offset passed to the method crop(gravity, x, y, width, height) are not always calculated from the upper-left corner, but that they depend on the GravityType being used. Refer to the crop documentation for specific details.

You may also want to enforce rules on your list of images so that they all match. For example, you may require all your thumbnails to be smaller than 80 × 100 pixels, or you might want them to all have an equal width of 120 pixels. You may even decide that all images smaller than a certain limit should not be resized at all. For details on techniques for this, see the RMagick documentation of the Image#change_geometry method.

See Also

- This chapter's introduction discusses installing RMagick

12.2   Adding Text to an Image

Credit: Antonio Cangiano

Problem

You want to add some text to an image—perhaps a caption or a copyright statement.

Solution

Create an RMagick Draw object and call its annotate method, passing in your image and the text.

The following code adds the copyright string '© NPS' to the bottom-right corner of the canyon.png image. It also specifies the font, the text color and size, and other features of the text:

```
require 'rubygems'
require 'RMagick'

img = Magick::Image.read('canyon.png').first
my_text = "\251 NPS"

copyright = Magick::Draw.new
copyright.annotate(img, 0, 0, 3, 18, my_text) do
 self.font = 'Helvetica'
 self.pointsize = 12
```

```
  self.font_weight = Magick::BoldWeight
  self.fill = 'white'
  self.gravity = Magick::SouthEastGravity
end
img.write('canyoncopyrighted.png')
```

The resulting image looks like Figure 12-1.

Figure 12-1. With a copyright message in the bottom-right corner

Discussion

The annotate method takes a code block that sets properties on the `Magick::Draw` object, describing how the annotation should be done. You can also set the properties on the `Draw` object before calling annotate. This code works the same as the code given in the Solution:

```
require 'rubygems'
require 'RMagick'

img = Magick::Image.read("canyon.png").first
my_text = '\251 NPS'

copyright = Magick::Draw.new
copyright.font = 'Helvetica'
copyright.pointsize = 12
copyright.font_weight = Magick::BoldWeight
copyright.fill = 'white'
copyright.gravity = Magick::SouthEastGravity
copyright.annotate(img, 0, 0, 3, 18, my_text)
img.write('canyoncopyrighted.png')
```

What do these attributes do?

- The font attribute selects the font type from among those installed on your system. You can also specify the path to a specific font that is in a nonstandard location (e.g., "/home/antonio/Arial.ttf").

- pointsize is the font size in points (the default is 12). By default, there is one pixel per point, so you can just specify the font size in pixels.

- font_weight accepts a WeightType constant. This can be a number (100, 200, 300, ... 900), BoldWeight (equivalent to 700), or the default of NormalWeight (equivalent to 400).

- If you need your text to be italicized, you can set the font_style attribute to Magick::ItalicStyle.

- fill defines the text color. The default is "black". You can use X or SVG color names (such as "white", "red", "gray85", and "salmon"), or you can express the color in terms of RGB values (such as "#fff" or "#ffffff"—two of the most common formats)

- gravity controls which part of the image will contain the annotated text, subject to the arguments passed in to annotate. SouthEastGravity means that offsets will be calculated from the bottom-right corner of the image.

Draw#annotate itself takes six arguments:

- The Image object, or else an ImageList containing the images you want to annotate.

- The width and height of the rectangle in which the text is to be positioned.

- The x and y offsets of the text, relative to that rectangle and to the gravity of the Draw object.

- The text to be written.

In the Solution I wrote:

```
copyright.annotate(img, 0, 0, 3, 15, my_text)
```

The width and height are zeros, which indicates that annotate should use the whole image as its annotation rectangle. Earlier I gave the Draw object a gravity attribute of SouthEastGravity. This means that annotate will position the text at the bottom-right corner of the rectangle: that is, at the bottom-right corner of the image itself. The offsets of 3 and 18 indicate that the text should start vertically 18 pixels from the bottom of the box, and end horizontally 3 pixels from the right border of the box.

To position the text in the center of the image, I just change the gravity:

```
copyright.gravity = Magick::CenterGravity
copyright.annotate(img, 0, 0, 0, 0, my_text)
```

Note that I didn't have to specify any offsets: CenterGravity orients the text to be is in the exact center of the image (Figure 12-2). Specifying offsets would only move the text off-center.

The Magick library does substitutions for various special characters: for instance, the string "%t" will be replaced with the filename of the image. For more information about special characters, GravityType constants, and other annotate attributes that can let you fully customize the text appearance, refer to the RMagick documentation.

Figure 12-2. With a copyright message in the center of the image

See Also

- RMagick Documentation (*http://studio.imagemagick.org/RMagick/doc/*)
- On converting points to pixels (*http://redux.imagemagick.org/RMagick/doc/draw. html#get_type_metrics*)
- SVG color keywords list (*http://www.w3.org/TR/SVG/types.html#ColorKeywords*)
- This chapter's introduction gives instructions on installing RMagick

12.3 Converting One Image Format to Another

Credit: Antonio Cangiano

Problem

You want to convert an image to a different format.

Solution

With RMagick, you can just read in the file and write it out with a different extension. This code converts a PNG file to JPEG format:

```
require 'rubygems'
require 'RMagick'

img = Magick::Image.read('myimage.png').first
img.write('myimage.jpg')
```

Discussion

As seen in the previous two recipes, Magick::Image.read receives the PNG image and returns an array of Image objects, from which we select the first and only image.

RMagick lets us convert the file into a JPEG by simply changing the filename's extension when we call the `write` method.

The underlying C library, ImageMagick or GraphicsMagick, has three ways of determining the format of image files:

- Checking an explicitly specified format prefix: for example, "GIF:myimage.jpg" indicates that the file myimage contains a GIF image, even though the file extension says otherwise.

- Looking inside the file for a "magic number", a set of bytes that indicates the format.

- Checking the file extension: for example, "myphoto.gif" is presumably a GIF file.

Although the format prefix takes precedence over the magic number, RMagick won't be fooled by an incorrect prefix. Eventually it will have to parse the image file, and the format mismatch will be revealed:

```
Magick::Image.read("JPG:myimage.png")
# Magick::ImageMagickError: Not a JPEG file: starts with 0x89 0x50 `myimage.png':
```

When you write an image to an output file, you can choose the output format by specifying a file extension or a prefix.

```
img = Magick::Image.read("myimage.png").first
img.write("myimage.jpg")           # Writes a JPEG
img.write("myimage.gif")           # Writes a GIF
img.write("JPG:myimage")           # Writes a JPEG
img.write("JPG:myimage.gif")       # Writes a JPEG
```

You can also get or set the file format of an image by calling the `Image#format` or `Image#format=` methods:

```
img.format                         # => "PNG"
img.format = "GIF"
img.format                         # => "GIF"
```

Of course, RMagick can't read to and write from every graphical file format in existence. How can you tell whether your version of RMagick knows how to write a particular file format?

You can query RMagick's capabilities by calling `Magick.formats`. This method returns a hash that maps an image format to a four-character code:

```
Magick.formats["GIF"]              # => "*rw+"
Magick.formats["JPG"]              # => "*rw-"
Magick.formats["AVI"]              # => "*r--"
Magick.formats["PS"]               # => " rw+"
```

The code represents the things that RMagick can do with that file format:

- The first character is an asterisk if RMagick has native blob support for that format. If not, the first character is a space. RMagick can convert most image formats into a generic string format (with Image#to_blob) that can be stored in the database as a BLOB and converted back into an Image object with Image.from_blob.

- The second character is "r" if RMagick knows how to read files in that format. Otherwise, it's a minus sign.
- The third character is "w" if RMagick knows how to write files in that format. Otherwise, it's a minus sign.
- The final character is "+" if RMagick knows how to cram multiple images into a single file (as in an animated GIF).

Here's a little bit of metaprogramming that adds four predicate methods to Magick, one for each element of the four-character code. You can use these methods instead of parsing the code string:

```
module Magick
  [["native_blob?", ?*], ["readable?", ?r],
   ["writable?", ?w], ["multi_image?", ?+]].each_with_index do |m, i|
    define_method(m[0]) do |format|
      code = formats[format]
      return code && code[i] == m[1]
    end
    module_function(m[0])
  end
end
```

This code demonstrates that the GIF file format supports multi-image files, but the JPG format doesn't:

```
Magick.multi_image? 'GIF'                         # => true
Magick.multi_image? 'JPG'                         # => false
```

ImageMagick and GraphicsMagick support the most common image formats (over 90 in total). However, they delegate support for many of these formats to external libraries or programs, which you may need to install separately. For instance, to read or write Postscript files, you'll need to have the Ghostscript program installed.

See Also

- RMagick Documentation (*http://studio.imagemagick.org/RMagick/doc/*)
- List of supported ImageMagick formats (*http://www.imagemagick.org/script/formats.php*)

12.4 Graphing Data

Problem

You want to convert a bunch of data into a graph; usually a line chart, bar chart, or pie chart.

Solution

Use the Gruff library, written by Geoffrey Grosenbach. Install the gruff gem and build a Gruff object corresponding to the type of graph you want (for instance, Gruff::Line, Gruff::Bar, or Gruff::Pie). Add a dataset to the graph by passing data a label and an array of data points.

Here's code to create a graph that compares the running times of different sorts of algorithms:

```ruby
require 'rubygems'
require 'gruff'

g = Gruff::Line.new(600)        # The graph will be 600 pixels wide.
g.title = 'Algorithm running times'
g.theme_37signals               # The best-looking theme, in my opinion.

range = (1..101)
g.data('Constant', range.collect { 1 })
g.data('O(log n)', range.collect { |x| Math::log(x) / Math::log(2) })
g.data('O(n)', range.collect { |x| x })
g.data('O(n log n)', range.collect { |x| x * Math::log(x) / Math::log(2) })

g.labels = {10 => 'n=10', 50 => 'n=50', 100 => 'n=100' }
g.write('algorithms.png')
```

Figure 12-3 shows the graph it produces.

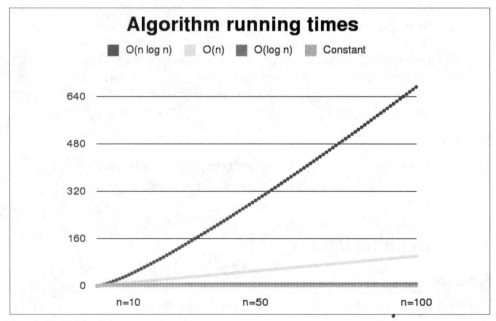

Figure 12-3. A line chart

Here's code to create a pie chart (shown in Figure 12-4). Note that the numbers given for the datasets don't have to add up to 100. Gruff automatically scales the the pie chart to display the right proportions.

```
p = Gruff::Pie.new
p.theme_monochrome
p.title = "Survey: the value of pi"
p.data('"About three"', [3])
p.data('3.14', [8])
p.data('3.1415', [11])
p.data('22/7', [8])

p.write('pipie.png')
```

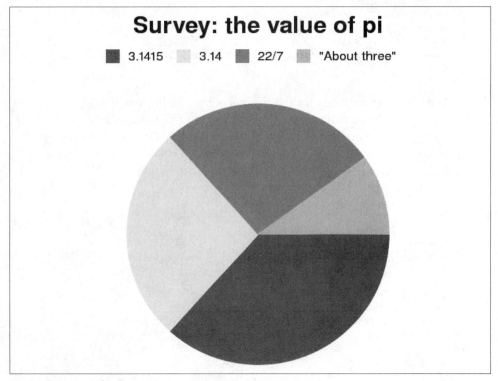

Figure 12-4. A pi chart

Discussion

Most of the time, programmers who need a graphing library need a *simple* graphing library: one that lets them easily produce a quick pie, line, or bar graph. Gruff works well for graphing simple datasets, but it doesn't have the functionality of a full-fledged math program.

Gruff's interface for customizing the display of datasets also leaves something to be desired. Instead of letting you tweak the colors individually, it provides a number of themes that package together a background image, a text color, and a number of colors used in the graphs. Unfortunately, most of the provided themes are ugly (theme_37signals is pretty nice, though).

Here's a custom theme that makes monochrome graphs whose "colors" can be fairly easily distinguished. It takes advantage of the fact that it's easy to distinguish dark shades of gray from light shades, and that lighter shades are more easily distinguishable from one another. The graphs in this recipe were actually created with this theme_monochrome, so that the "colors" would be more easily distinguishable in a printed book.

```
class Gruff::Base
  def theme_monochrome
    reset_themes
    @colors = "6E9C7ADB".scan(/./).collect { |c| "##{c * 6}"}
    @marker_color = 'black'
    @base_image = render_gradiated_background('white', 'white')
  end
end
```

This code adds writer methods for the various colors, letting you modify the current theme on an ad hoc basis. colors sets the colors used to differentiate datasets from each other. marker_color method sets the color of the title and axis labels. background sets the background to a solid color, or to a gradient between two colors.

```
class Gruff::Base
  def colors=(colors)
    @colors = colors
  end

  def marker_color=(color)
    @marker_color = color
  end

  def background=(color1, color2=nil)
    color2 ||= color1
    @base_image = render_gradiated_background(color1, color2)
  end
end
```

See Also

- The Gruff homepage (*http://nubyonrails.topfunky.com/pages/gruff*)
- A couple of other Ruby graphing libraries deserve mention:
  - MRPlot is useful for plotting mathematical functions; its default implementation works on top of RMagick (*http://harderware.bleedingmind.com/index.php?l=en&p=mrplot*)
  - The SVG::Graph library doesn't need any external libraries and produces beautiful SVG graphs; unfortunately, not many programs have support for

SVG graphics, although newer versions of Firefox do (*http://www.germane-software.com/software/SVG/SVG::Graph/*)

12.5 Adding Graphical Context with Sparklines

Problem

You want to display a small bit of statistical context—a trend or a set of percentages—in the middle of a piece of text, without breaking up the flow of the text.

Solution

Install the sparklines gem (written by Geoffrey Grosenbach) and create a sparkline: a tiny embedded graphic that can go next to a piece of text without being too intrusive. If you're creating an HTML page, the image doesn't even need to have its own file: it can be embedded directly in the HTML.

This code creates a sparkline for a company's stock price, and embeds it in HTML after the company's stock symbol:

```
require 'rubygems'
require 'sparklines'
require 'base64'

def embedded_sparkline
  %{<img src="data:image/png;base64,#{Base64.encode64(yield)}">}
end

# This method scales data so that the smallest item becomes 0 and the
# largest becomes 100.
def scale(data)
  min, max = data.min, data.max
  data.collect { |x| (x - min) / (max - min) * 100}
end

# Randomly generate closing prices for the past month.
prices = [rand(10)]
30.times { prices << prices.last + (rand - 0.5) }

# Generate HTML containing a stock graph as an embedded sparkline.
sparkline = embedded_sparkline { Sparklines.plot(scale(prices)) }
open('stock.html', 'w') do |f|
  f << "Is EvilCorp (NASDAQ:EVIL #{sparkline}) poised for a comeback?"
end
```

This code generates HTML that renders as shown in Figure 12-5.

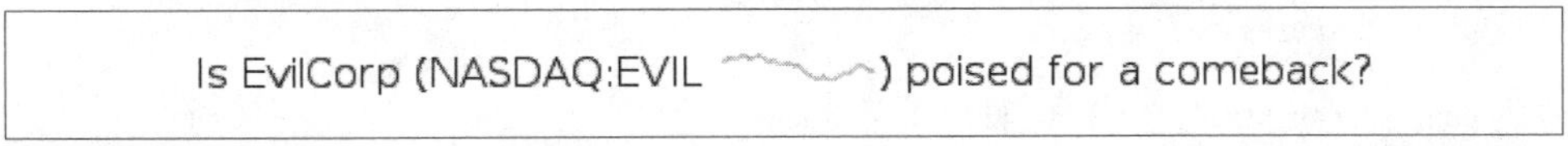

Is EvilCorp (NASDAQ:EVIL ⎯⎯⌒⎯⎯) poised for a comeback?

Figure 12-5. A stock price history sparkline

Since it has no labels, the meaning of the sparkline must be determined from context. In this case, the graphic follows a stock symbol, so you can guess that it graphs the stock price. In a different context, the sparkline for EvilCorp might be the company's reported earnings over time, or the results of a poll that tracks public opinion of the company.

Embedded sparklines won't show up in Internet Explorer, but if you're using Rails you can use the sparklines_generator gem to put cross-browser sparklines in your views.

Discussion

Sparklines are a way of graphically conveying information that would take lots of text to explain. They were invented by interface expert Edward Tufte, who describes them as "intense, simple, word-sized graphics." As implemented in the Ruby Sparklines library, a sparkline displays a small graph that shows a set of related numbers or a single percentage.

Sparklines are especially useful for annotating text with statistical summaries. We humans are visual creatures: when we read a text with sparklines, we come away with a better feel for the underlying numbers because we can visualize them as we read.

Sparklines are good at showing trends and making anomalies obvious. With sparklines, you can distinguish a winning sports team from a losing one at a glance, or notice an abnormally large expense report. Since neither the sparklines nor their axes are labelled, sparklines are not so good at displaying multifaceted information or absolute quantities.

Because sparklines show trends better than absolute values, it's often useful to scale your data so that it takes up the entire width of the sparkline (as in the stock price examples). But if you want to compare two sparklines to each other (for instance, to compare the stock prices of two companies), you shouldn't scale the data.

The Sparklines library can create several types of graph. Here's some code that annotates a politician's stump speech with small pie charts representing polling data. Only two colors are allowed in a sparklines pie chart: we'll choose a dark color to represent the percentage of people who agree with a statement, and a light color to represent the percentage who disagree. At a glance, the politician can see which parts of the speech are working and which need to be retooled.

```
agree_percentages = [ 55, 71, 44, 55, 81, 68 ]

speech = %{This country faces a crisis and a crossroads. %s Our taxes
are too high %s and our poodles are too well-groomed. %s Our children
learn less in school %s and listen to louder music at home. %s The
Internet scares me. %s}

open('speech.html', 'w') do |f|
  sparklines = agree_percentages.collect do |p|
```

```
      embedded_sparkline do
        Sparklines.plot([p], :type => 'pie', :remain_color => 'pink',
                             :share_color=>'blue',
                             :background_color=>'transparent')
      end
    end
    f << speech % sparklines
  end
```

The resulting HTML file renders as shown in Figure 12-6.

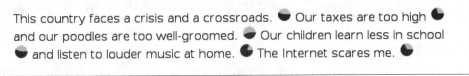

Figure 12-6. A speech, annotated with poll result sparklines

The result of Sparklines.plot is a binary string containing an image in PNG format. The string can be written to a PNG file on disk, or it can be encoded with the Base64 library and embedded into a web page. The total size of speech.html, with six embedded sparklines, is about six kilobytes. Unfortunately, the Internet Explorer browser doesn't support the trick that lets you embed small images into a web page.

Sparklines in Rails Views

If you're using Rails, you can install the sparklines_generator gem on top of sparklines. This gem provides a controller and a helper that let you incorporate sparklines into your views, without having to worry about encoding the files or being incompatible with IE.

To add sparklines to your application, run this command to give yourself a sparklines controller:

```
$ ./script/generate sparklines
      create  app/controllers/sparklines_controller.rb
      create  app/helpers/sparklines_helper.rb
```

Add a require 'sparklines' statement to your config/environment.rb file, and call helper :sparklines from any controllers in which you want to use sparklines. You can then call the sparkline_tag method from within your views.

A view that renders part of an annotated speech might look like this:

```
This country faces a crisis and a crossroads.

<%= sparkline_tag [55, 10, 10, 20, 30], :type => "pie", :remain_color=>"pink",
:share_color => "blue", :background_color => "transparent" %>
```

That view generates HTML that looks like this:

```
This country faces a crisis and a crossroads.

<img
src="/sparklines?share_color=blue&remain_color=pink&results=55&type=pie&background_
color=transparent"
class="sparkline" alt="Sparkline Graph" />
```

Instead of embedding the sparkline within the HTML page (which won't work in IE), we call out to the sparklines controller, whose only purpose is to generate image files of sparklines on demand. This image is displayed like any other external image fetched through HTTP.

See Also

- The home page for the Sparklines library, which includes a tutorial on installation and use within Rails (*http://nubyonrails.com/articles/2005/07/28/sparklines-graph-library-for-ruby*)
- The sparklines gem requires RMagick; a pure Ruby implementation with fewer features is available (*http://redhanded.hobix.com/inspect/sparklinesForMinimalists.html*)
- Sparklines are described in Edward Tufte's book, *Beautiful Evidence* (Graphics Pr); you can see a version of the sparklines chapter from that book online (*http://www.edwardtufte.com/bboard/q-and-a-fetch-msg?msg_id=0001OR&topic_id=1*)

12.6 Strongly Encrypting Data

Problem

You want to encrypt some data: to keep it private, or to keep it safe when sent through an insecure medium like email.

Solution

There are at least two good symmetric-key cryptography libraries for Ruby: Pelle Braendgaard's EzCrypto (available as the ezcrypto gem) and Richard Kernahan's Crypt (a third-party download).

EzCrypto is a user-friendly Ruby wrapper around the OpenSSL library, which you may need to install separately. Here's how to encrypt and decrypt a string with EzCrypto:

```
require 'rubygems'
require 'ezcrypto'

plaintext = '24.9195N 17.821E'

ezcrypto_key = EzCrypto::Key.with_password 'My secret key', 'salt string'
ezcrypto_ciphertext = ezcrypto_key.encrypt(plaintext)
# => "F\262\260\273\217\tR\351\362-\021-a\336\324Qc..."
```

```
ezcrypto_key.decrypt(ezcrypto_ciphertext)
# => "24.9195N 17.821E"
```

The Crypt library gives each encryption algorithm its own class, so you need to decide which you want to use. I'll use the AES/Rijndael algorithm: all the other algorithms have the same interface.[*]

```
require 'crypt/rijndael'

aes_key = Crypt::Rijndael.new('My secret key')
aes_cyphertext = aes_key.encrypt_string(plaintext)
# => "\e\003\203\030]\203\t\346..."

aes_key.decrypt_string(aes_cyphertext)
# => "24.9195N 17.821E"
```

Discussion

EzCrypto is available as a gem (ezcrypto), and it's fast because the actual encryption and decryption happens in the C OpenSSL libraries. Crypt is a pure Ruby implementation, so it's slower, but you don't have to worry about OpenSSL being installed.

EzCrypto and Crypt both implement several symmetric key algorithms. With EzCrypto, you can also specify the algorithm to use when you create an EzCrypto key. With Crypt, you need to instantiate the appropriate algorithm's class:

```
# EzCrypto example
blowfish_key = EzCrypto::Key.with_password('My secret password', 'salt string',
                                           :algorithm=>'blowfish')
# Crypt example
require 'crypt/blowfish'
blowfish_key = Crypt::Blowfish.new('My secret password')
```

The Crypt classes provide some convenience methods for encrypting and decrypting files and streams. The encrypt_file method takes two filenames: it reads from one file, encrypts the data, and writes ciphertext to the other. The encrypt_stream method is a little more general: it reads plaintext from one IO object and writes ciphertext to the other.

All the algorithms supported by Crypt and EzCrypto are symmetric-key algorithms: you must use the same key to encrypt and decrypt the data. This is simple when you're only encrypting data so that you can decrypt it later, but it's not so simple when you're sending encrypted data to someone else. You need to securely share the key with the other person ahead of time, or you need to use public-key algorithms like the ones provided by the Ruby PKCS implementation.

---

[*] The Crypt::IDEA class works a little differently, but that algorithm is patented, so you shouldn't use it anyway.

There was some controversy about whether this recipe should even be included in this Cookbook. A little knowledge is a dangerous thing, and a little is all we can impart in the space we have for a recipe. Simply using an encryption algorithm won't automatically make your data secure. It won't be secure if you use a lousy password (like, say, "My secret password", as in the examples above).

Further, your data won't be secure if you store your keys on disk the wrong way. It won't be secure if your computer doesn't have a reliable enough source of random numbers. When you prompt the user for their password, the operating system might pick that moment to swap to disk the chunk of memory that contains the password, where an attacker could find it. Even experts frequently make mistakes when they're writing cryptography code.

That said, a strong encryption algorithm is better than a weak one, and trying to write your own algorithm is just about the worst mistake you can make. All we ask that you be careful. Instead of worrying about writing an algorithm to encrypt your data, get a book on security and focus your efforts on making sure you use the existing algorithms correctly.

See Also

- Download the Crypt library from *http://crypt.rubyforge.org/*, and install it by running ruby install.rb
- The EzCrypto documentation (*http://ezcrypto.rubyforge.org/*)
- The Ruby OpenSSL project (*http://www.nongnu.org/rubypki/*)
- The Ruby PKCS project homepage (*http://dev.ctor.org/pkcs1*)

12.7 Parsing Comma-Separated Data

Problem

You have a plain-text string in a comma-delimited format. You need to parse this string, either to build a data structure or to perform some operation on the data and write it back out.

Solution

The built-in csv library can parse most common character-delimited formats. The FasterCSV library, available as the fastercsv gem, improves on csv's performance and interface. I'll show you both, but I recommend fastercsv unless you can't use any software at all outside the standard library.

CSV::Reader.parse and FasterCSV.parse work the same way: they accept a string or an open file as an argument, and yield each parsed row of the comma-delimited file

as an array. The csv yields a Row object that acts like an array full of Column objects.
FasterCSV just yields an array of strings.

```
require 'csv'
primary_colors = "red,green,blue\nred,yellow,blue"

CSV::Reader.parse(primary_colors) { |row| row.each { |cell| puts cell }}
# red
# green
# blue
# red
# yellow
# blue

require 'rubygems'
require 'faster_csv'
shakespeare = %{Sweet are the uses of adversity,As You Like It
"We few, we happy few",Henry V
"Seems, madam! nay it is; I know not ""seems.""",Hamlet}

FasterCSV.parse(shakespeare) { |row| puts "'#{row[0]}' -- #{row[1]}"}
# 'Sweet are the uses of adversity' -- As You Like It
# 'We few, we happy few' -- Henry V
# 'Seems, madam! nay it is; I know not "seems."' -- Hamlet
```

Discussion

Comma-delimited formats are among the most basic portable file formats. Unfortunately, they're also among the least standardized. There are many different formats, and some are internally inconsistent.

FasterCSV and the csv library can't parse every comma-delimited format, but they will parse common formats like the one used by Microsoft Excel, and they're your best tool for making sense of the myriad.

FasterCSV and csv both model a comma-delimited file as a nested array of strings. The csv library's CSV class uses Row objects and Column objects instead of arrays and strings, but it's the same idea. The terminology is from the spreadsheet world—understandably, since a CSV file is a common way of portably storing spreadsheet data.

The complications begin when the spreadsheet cells themselves contain commas or newlines. The standard way to handle this when exporting to comma-delimited format is to surround those cells with double quotes. Then the question becomes what to do with cells that contain double-quote characters. Both Ruby CSV libraries assume that double-quote characters are escaped by doubling, turning each " into "", as in the Hamlet quotation:

```
%{"Seems, madam! nay it is; I know not ""seems.""",Hamlet}
```

If you're certain that there are no commas or newlines embedded in your data, and thus no need for quote handling, you can use String#split to parse delimited records more quickly than csv. To output to this format, you can use Array#join:

```ruby
def parse_delimited_naive(input, fieldsep=',', rowsep="\n")
  input.split(rowsep).inject([]) do |arr, line|
    arr << line.split(fieldsep)
  end
end

def join_delimited_naive(structure, fieldsep=',', rowsep="\n")
  rows = structure.inject([]) do |arr, parsed_line|
    arr << parsed_line.join(fieldsep)
  end
  rows.join(rowsep)
end

parse_delimited_naive("1,2,3,4\n5,6,7,8")
# => [["1", "2", "3", "4"], ["5", "6", "7", "8"]]

join_delimited_naive(parse_delimited_naive("1,2,3,4\n5,6,7,8"))
# => "1,2,3,4\n5,6,7,8"

parse_delimited_naive('1;2;3;4|5;6;7;8', ';', '|')
# => [["1", "2", "3", "4"], ["5", "6", "7", "8"]]

parse_delimited_naive('1,"2,3",4')
# => [["1", ""2", "3"", "4"]]
```

This is not recommended unless you wrote all the relevant code yourself, or can manually inspect the code as well as the dataset. Just because you haven't seen any quoted cells yet doesn't mean there won't be any in the future. When in doubt, use csv or fastercsv. Handwritten CSV generators and parsers are a leading cause of bad data.

To create a comma-delimited file, open an output file with CSV.open or FasterCSV. open, and append a series of arrays to the resulting file-like object. Every array you append will be converted to a comma-delimited row in the destination file.

```ruby
data = [[1,2,3],['A','B','C'],['do','re','mi']]

writer = FasterCSV.open('first3.csv', 'w')
data.each { |x| writer << x }
writer.close
puts open('first3.csv').read()
# 1,2,3
# A,B,C
# do,re,mi

data = []
FasterCSV.foreach('first3.csv') { |row| data << row }
data
# => [["1", "2", "3"], ["A", "B", "C"], ["do", "re", "mi"]]
```

See Also

- The FasterCSV documentation (*http://fastercsv.rubyforge.org/*)
- Chapter 11

12.8 Parsing Not-Quite-Comma-Separated Data

Problem

You need to parse a plain-text string or file that's in a format similar to comma-delimited format, but its delimiters are some strings other than commas and newlines.

Solution

When you call a CSV::Reader method, you can specify strings to act as a row separator (the string between each Row) and a field separator (the string between each Column). You can do the same with simulated keyword arguments passed into FasterCSV.parse. This should let you parse most formats similar to the comma-delimited format:

```
require 'csv'

pipe_separated="1|2ENDa|bEND"

CSV::Reader.parse(pipe_separated, '|', 'END') { |r| r.each { |c| puts c } }
# 1
# 2
# a
# b

require 'rubygems'
require 'faster_csv'
FasterCSV.parse(pipe_separated, :col_sep=>'|', :row_sep=>'END') do |r|
  r.each { |c| puts c }
end
# 1
# 2
# a
# b
```

Discussion

Value-delimited formats tend to differ along three axes:

- The field separator (usually a single comma)
- The row separator (usually a single newline)
- The quote character (usually a double quote)

Like Reader methods, Writer methods accept custom values for the field and row separators.

```
data = [[1,2,3],['A','B','C'],['do','re','mi']]

open('first3.csv', 'w') do |output|
  CSV::Writer.generate(output, ':', '-END-') do |writer|
    data.each { |x| writer << x }
  end
end
open('first3.csv') { |input| input.read( ) }
# => "1:2:3-END-A:B:C-END-do:re:mi-END-"

FasterCSV.open('first3.csv', 'w', :col_sep=>':', :row_sep=>'-END-') do |output|
  data.each { |x| output << x }
end
open('first3.csv') { |input| input.read( ) }
# => "1:2:3-END-A:B:C-END-do:re:mi-END-"
```

It's rare that you'll need to override the quote character, and neither csv nor fastercsv will let you do it. Both libraries' quote characters are hardcoded to the double-quote character. If you need to parse a format that has different quote character, the simplest thing to do is subclass FasterCSV and override its init_parsers method.

Change the regular expression assigned to @parsers[:csv_row], replacing all double quotes with the quote character you want. The most common alternate quote character is the single quote: to get that, you'd have an init_parsers method like this:

```
class MyFasterCSV < FasterCSV
  def init_parsers(options)
    super
    @parsers[:csv_row] =
        / \G(?:^|#{Regexp.escape(@col_sep)})    # anchor the match
          (?: '((?>[^']*)(?>''[^']*)*)'         # find quoted fields
          |                                     # ... or ...
          ([^'#{Regexp.escape(@col_sep)}]*)     # unquoted fields
          )/x
  end
end
MyFasterCSV.parse("1,'2,3',4") { |r| puts r }
# 1
# 2,3
# 4
```

Some value-delimited files are simply corrupt: they were generated by programs that didn't think to escape quote marks or to quote cells with embedded delimiters. Neither csv nor fastercsv can parse these files, because they're ambiguous or invalid.

```
missing_quotes=%{20051002, Alice says, "I saw that!"}
CSV::Reader.parse(missing_quotes) { |r| r.each { |c| puts c } }
# CSV::IllegalFormatError: CSV::IllegalFormatError

unescaped_quotes=%{20051002, "Alice says, "I saw that!""}
FasterCSV.parse(unescaped_quotes) { |r| r.each { |c| puts c } }
# FasterCSV::MalformedCSVError: Unclosed quoted field.
```

Your best strategy for dealing with this kind of file is to use regular expressions to massage the data into a form that fastercsv can parse, or to parse it with String#split and deal with any quoting problems afterwards. In either case, your code will have to work with the particular quirks of the data you're trying to parse.

See Also

- Recipe 12.7, "Parsing Comma-Separated Data"

12.9 Generating and Parsing Excel Spreadsheets

Problem

Your program needs to parse data from Excel spreadsheets, or generate new Excel spreadsheets.

Solution

To generate Excel files, use the spreadsheet library, available as a third-party gem (see the See Also section below for where to get it). With it you can create simple Excel spreadsheets. As of this writing, spreadsheet does not support formulas or large spreadsheets (seven megabytes is the limit).

This code creates an Excel spreadsheet containing some random numbers with a total, and saves it to disk:

```
require 'rubygems'
require 'spreadsheet/excel'

SUM_SPREADSHEET = 'sum.xls'
workbook = Spreadsheet::Excel.new(SUM_SPREADSHEET)
worksheet = workbook.add_worksheet('Random numbers and their sum.')
sum = 0
random_numbers = (0..9).collect { rand(100) }
worksheet.write_column(0, 0, random_numbers)

format = workbook.add_format(:bold => true)
worksheet.write(10, 0, "Sum:", format)
worksheet.write(10, 1, random_numbers.inject(0) { |sum, x| sum + x })
workbook.close
```

To parse an Excel file, use the parseexcel library, also available as a third-party download. It can parse simple data out of the Excel file format. This code parses the Excel file generated by the previous code:

```
require 'parseexcel/parser'
workbook = Spreadsheet::ParseExcel::Parser.new.parse(SUM_SPREADSHEET)

worksheet = workbook.worksheet(0)
sum = (0..9).inject(0) do |sum, row|
```

```
    sum + worksheet.cell(row, 0).value.to_i
  end

  worksheet.cell(10, 0).value                                  # => "Sum:"
  worksheet.cell(10, 1).value                                  # => 602.0
  sum                                                          # => 602
```

Like spreadsheet, parseexcel doesn't recognize spreadsheet formulas.

Discussion

The comma-separated file is the *lingua franca* for spreadsheet data, but sometimes you must deal with real spreadsheet files. You can save other people's time by accepting their Excel spreadsheets as input, instead of insisting they convert everything to CSV for you. And nothing impresses manager types like an automatically generated spreadsheet file they can poke at.

The spreadsheet and parseexcel libraries are only suitable for creating or parsing simple spreadsheets: more or less the ones that export well to comma-delimited format. If you want to handle more complex Excel files from Ruby, you have a couple options. The POI Java library can write various Microsoft Office files, and it has Ruby bindings. If you're running on a Windows computer that has Excel installed, you can use Ruby's built-in win32ole library to communicate with the Excel installation.

Hopefully this will be fixed by the time you read this, but just in case: spreadsheets generated with spreadsheet may show up as black-on-black in some spreadsheet programs (Gnumeric is one). This is because spreadsheet generates workbooks with a default format that specifies no background color. So each spreadsheet program uses *its* default color, and some of them make unfortunate choices. Here's a subclass of Workbook that specifies default text and background colors, so that you don't end up with a black-on-black spreadsheet:

```
  class ExcelWithBackground < Spreadsheet::Excel
    def initialize(*args)
      super(*args)
      @format = Format.new(:bg_color => 'white', :fg_color => 'black')
    end
  end

  workbook = ExcelWithBackground.new(SUM_SPREADSHEET)
  # ...
```

See Also

- You can download parseexcel from *http://download.ywesee.com/parseexcel/*
- The spreadsheet homepage is at *http://rubyspreadsheet.sourceforge.net/*; it's available as a gem (*http://prdownloads.sourceforge.net/rubyspreadsheet/*), but since it's not hosted on RubyForge, you can't just install it with gem install spreadsheet-excel: you must download the gem and run gem install on the local gem file

- POI (*http://jakarta.apache.org/poi/index.html*) and its Ruby bindings (*http://jakarta.apache.org/poi/poi-ruby.html*)
- Information on scripting Excel in Ruby (*http://www.rubygarden.org/ruby?ScriptingExcel*)
- The "Ruby and Microsoft Windows" chapter in the Pickaxe Book—*Programming Ruby* by Dave Thomas, with Chad Fowler and Andy Hunt (Pragmatic Bookshelf)

12.10 Compressing and Archiving Files with Gzip and Tar

Problem

You want to write compressed data to a file to save space, or uncompress the contents of a compressed file. If you're compressing data, you might want to compress multiple files into a single archive file.

Solution

The most common compression format on Unix systems is gzip. Ruby's zlib library lets you read to and write from gzipped I/O streams as though they were normal files. The most useful classes in this library are GzipWriter and GzipReader.*

Here's GzipWriter being used to create a compressed file, and GzipReader decompressing the same file:

```
require 'zlib'

file = 'compressed.gz'
Zlib::GzipWriter.open(file) do |gzip|
  gzip << "For my next trick, I'll be written to a compressed file."
  gzip.close
end

open(file, 'rb') { |f| f.read(10) }
# => "\037\213\010\000\201\2766D\000\003"

Zlib::GzipReader.open(file) { |gzip| gzip.read }
# => "For my next trick, I'll be written to a compressed file."
```

---

* The compressed strings in these examples are actually larger than the originals. This is because I used very short strings to save space in the book, and short strings don't compress well. Any compression technique introduces some overhead; with gzip, you don't actually save any space by compressing a text string of less than about 100 bytes.

Discussion

`GzipWriter` and `GzipReader` are most commonly used to write to files on disk, but you can wrap any file-like object in the appropriate class and automatically compress everything you write to it, or decompress everything you read from it.

The following code works the same way as the compression code in the Solution, but it's more flexible: the `File` object that's passed into the `Zlib::GzipWriter` constructor could just as easily be a `Socket` or other file-like object.

```
open('compressed.gz', 'wb') do |file|
  gzip = Zlib::GzipWriter.new(file)
  gzip << "For my next trick, I'll be written to a compressed file."
  gzip.close
end
```

If you need to compress or decompress a string, use the `Zlib::Deflate` or `Zlib::Inflate` classes rather than constructing a `StringIO` object:

```
deflated = Zlib::Deflate.deflate("I'm a compressed string.")
# => "x\234\363T\317UHTH..."
Zlib::Inflate.inflate(deflated)
# => "I'm a compressed string."
```

Tar files

Gzip compresses a single file. What if you want to smash multiple files together into a single archive file? The standard archive format for Unix is tar, and tar files are sometimes called tarballs. A tarball might also be compressed with gzip to save space, but on Unix the archiving and the compression are separate steps (unlike on Windows, where a ZIP file both archives multiple files and compresses them).

The Minitar library is the simplest way to create tarballs in pure Ruby. It's available as the `archive-tar-minitar` gem.[*]

Here's some code that creates a tarball containing two files and a directory. Note the Unix permission modes (0644, 0755, and 0600). These are the permissions the files will have when they're extracted, perhaps by the Unix tar command.

```
require 'rubygems'
require 'archive/tar/minitar'

open('tarball.tar', 'wb') do |f|
  Archive::Tar::Minitar::Writer.open(f) do |w|
```

---

[*] The RubyGems package defines the `Gem::Package::TarWriter` and `Gem::Package::TarReader` classes, which expose an interface similar to Minitar's. You can use these classes if you're fanatical about minimizing your dependencies, but I don't recommend it. These classes only implement the bare-bones functionality necessary to pack and unpack gem-like tarballs, and they also make your code look like it has something to do with RubyGems.

```
    w.add_file('file1', :mode => 0644, :mtime => Time.now) do |stream, io|
        stream.write('This is file 1.')
      end

    w.mkdir('subdirectory', :mode => 0755, :mtime => Time.now)

    w.add_file('subdirectory/file2', :mode => 0600,
                 :mtime => Time.now) do |stream, io|
        stream.write('This is file 2.')
      end
    end
  end
```

Here's a method that reads a tarball and print out its contents:

```
def browse_tarball(filename)
  open(filename, 'rb') do |f|
    Archive::Tar::Minitar::Reader.open(f).each do |entry|
      puts %{I see a file "#{entry.name}" that's #{entry.size} bytes long.}
    end
  end
end

browse_tarball('tarball.tar')
# I see a file "file1" that's 15 bytes long.
# I see a file "subdirectory" that's 0 bytes long.
# I see a file "subdirectory/file2" that's 15 bytes long.
```

And here's a simple method for archiving a number of disk files into a compressed tarball. Note how the Minitar Writer is wrapped within a GzipWriter, which automatically compresses the data as it's written. Minitar doesn't have to know about the GzipWriter, because all file-like objects look more or less the same.

```
def make_tarball(destination, *paths)
  Zlib::GzipWriter.open(destination) do |gzip|
    out = Archive::Tar::Minitar::Output.new(gzip)
    paths.each do |file|
      puts "Packing #{file}"
      Archive::Tar::Minitar.pack_file(file, out)
    end
    out.close
  end
end
```

This code creates some files and tars them up:

```
Dir.mkdir('colors')
paths = ['colors/burgundy', 'colors/beige', 'colors/clear']
paths.each do |path|
  open(path, 'w') do |f|
    f.puts %{This is a dummy file.}
  end
end

make_tarball('new_tarball.tgz', *paths)
```

```
# Packing colors/burgundy
# Packing colors/beige
# Packing colors/clear
# => #<File:new_tarball.tgz (closed)>
```

See Also

- On Windows, both compression and archiving are usually handled with ZIP files; see the next recipe, Recipe 12.11, "Reading and Writing ZIP Files," for details
- Recipe 14.3, "Customizing HTTP Request Headers," uses zlib to decompress the gzipped body of a response from a web server

12.11 Reading and Writing ZIP Files

Problem

You want to create or examine a ZIP archive from within Ruby code.

Solution

Use the rubyzip gem. Its Zip module gives you several ways of putting files into ZIP archives, and taking them out again. The simplest interface is the Zip:: ZipFileSystem, which duplicates most of the File and Dir operations within the context of a ZIP file. You can use this to create ZIP files:

```
require 'rubygems'
require 'zip/zipfilesystem'

Zip::ZipFile.open('zipfile.zip', Zip::ZipFile::CREATE) do |zip|
  zip.file.open('file1', 'w') { |f1| f1 << 'This is file 1.' }
  zip.dir.mkdir('subdirectory')
  zip.file.open('subdirectory/file2', 'w') { |f1| f1 << 'This is file 2.' }
end
```

You can use the same interface to read a ZIP file. Here's a method that uses the equivalent of Dir#foreach to recursively print out the contents of a ZIP file:

```
def process_zipfile(zip, path='')
  if zip.file.file? path
    puts %{#{path}: "#{zip.read(path)}"}
  else
    unless path.empty?
      path += '/'
      puts path
    end
    zip.dir.foreach(path) do |filename|
      process_zipfile(zip, path + filename)
    end
  end
end
```

And here it is running against the ZIP file I just created:

```
Zip::ZipFile.open('zipfile.zip') do |zip|
  process_zipfile(zip)
end
# subdirectory/
# subdirectory/file2: "This is file 2."
# file1: "This is file 1."
```

Discussion

ZIP, or PKZip, is the most popular compression format on Windows. As seen in the previous recipe, Unix separates the tasks of stuffing several files into a single archive (*tar*), and compressing the resulting file (*gzip*). On Windows, ZIP files perform both tasks. If you want to compress a single file, you need to put it into a ZIP file all by itself.

The rubyzip library provides several interfaces for creating and reading ZIP files. Zip::ZipFileSystem is the easiest for most programmers: in the example above, zip.file has about the same interface as the File class, and zip.dir is similar to the Dir class. The analogy holds because a ZIP file actually contains a tiny filesystem inside it.[*]

If you're porting Java code, or you're already familiar with Java's java.util.zip library, you might prefer the Zip::ZipFile class. It more or less duplicates Java's ZipFile class in a Ruby idiom. Here it is being used to create the same ZIP file I created in the Solution:

```
Zip::ZipFile.open('zipfile2.zip', Zip::ZipFile::CREATE) do |zip|
  zip.get_output_stream('file1') { |f| f << 'This is file 1.' }
  zip.mkdir('subdirectory')
  zip.get_output_stream('subdirectory/file2') { |f| f << 'This is file 2.' }
end
```

See Also

- The RDoc for the rubyzip gem (*http://rubyzip.sourceforge.net/*)

12.12 Reading and Writing Configuration Files

Problem

You want to store your application's configuration on disk, in a format parseable by Ruby but easily editable by someone with a text editor.

---

[*] This is how Windows XP's Explorer can let you browse a ZIP file as though it were a directory tree.

Solution

Put your configuration into a data structure, and write the data structure to disk as YAML. So long as you only use built-in Ruby data types (strings, numbers, arrays, hashes, and so on), the YAML file will be human-readable and -editable.

```
require 'yaml'
configuration = { 'color' => 'blue',
                  'font' => 'Septimus',
                  'font-size'  => 7 }
open('text.cfg', 'w') { |f| YAML.dump(configuration, f) }

open('text.cfg') { |f| puts f.read }
# ---
# font-size: 7
# color: blue
# font: Septimus

open('text.cfg') { |f| YAML.load(f) }
# => {"font-size"=>7, "color"=>"blue", "font"=>"Septimus"}
```

It's easy for a user to edit this: it's just a colon-separated, line-delimited set of key names and values. Not a problem, even for a relatively unsophisticated user.

Discussion

YAML is a serialization format, designed to store data structures to disk and read them back later. But there's no reason why the data structures can't be modified by other programs while they're on disk. Since simple YAML files are human-editable, they make good configuration files.

A YAML file typically contains a single data structure. The most common structures for configuration data are a hash (seen in the Solution) and an array of hashes.

```
configuration = [ { 'name' => 'Alice', 'donation' => 50 },
                  { 'name' => 'Bob', 'donation' => 15, 'currency' => "EUR" } ]
open('donors.cfg', 'w') { |f| YAML.dump(configuration, f) }
open('donors.cfg') { |f| puts f.read }
# ---
# - name: Alice
#   donation: 50
# - name: Bob
#   donation: 15
#   currency: EUR
```

In Recipe 5.1 we advise saving memory by using symbols as hash keys instead of strings. If your hash is going to be converted into human-editable YAML, you should always use strings. Otherwise, people editing the YAML may become confused. Compare the following two bits of YAML:

```
puts { 'measurements' => 'metric' }.to_yaml
# ---
# measurements: metric
```

```
puts { :measurements => :metric }.to_yaml
# ---
# :measurements: :metric
```

Outside the context of a Ruby program, the symbol `:measurements` is too easy to confuse with the string ":measurements".

See Also

- Recipe 13.1, "Serializing Data with YAML"

12.13 Generating PDF Files

Problem

You want to create a text or graphical document as a PDF, where you have complete control over the layout.

Solution

Use Austin Zeigler's `PDF::Writer` library, available as the `pdf-writer` gem. Its API gives you fine-grained control over the placement of text, images, and shapes.

This code uses `PDF::Writer` to produce a simple flyer with an image and a border (Figure 12-7). It assumes you've got a graphic called `sue.png` to insert into the document:

Figure 12-7. The flyer

```
require 'rubygems'
require 'pdf/writer'                                    # => false

# Putting "false" on the next line suppresses a huge output dump when
# you run this code in irb.
pdf = PDF::Writer.new; false

pdf.text("LOST\nDINOSAUR", :justification => :center, :font_size => 42,
         :left => 50, :right => 50)
pdf.image("sue.png", :left=> 100, :justification => :center, :resize => 0.75)
pdf.text(%{Three-year-old <i>Tyrannosaurus rex</i>\nSpayed\nResponds to "Sue"},
         :left => 80, :font_size => 20, :justification => :left)
pdf.text("(555) 010-7829", :justification => :center, :font_size => 36)

pdf.rectangle(pdf.left_margin + 25, pdf.y-25,
              pdf.margin_width-50, pdf.margin_height-pdf.y+50).stroke; false

pdf.save_as('flyer.pdf')
```

Discussion

So long as you're only calling `Writer#text` and `Writer#image`, PDF generation is easy. PDF automatically adds new text and images to the bottom of the current text, creating new pages as needed.

It gets tricky when you want to do something more complex, like draw shapes. Then you need to specify the placement and dimensions in coordinates.

Take as an example the `Writer#rectangle` call in the Solution:

```
pdf.rectangle(pdf.left_margin, pdf.y-25,
              pdf.margin_width, pdf.margin_height-pdf.y+25).stroke
```

The first two arguments are coordinates: the left edge of the rectangle and the bottom edge of the rectangle. The second two arguments are the width and height of the rectangle.

The width is simple enough: my box starts at the left margin and its width is `pdf.margin_width` *user space units*.[*] That is, my box takes up the entire width of the page except for the margin. The height is a little more tricky, because I do my own margins (25 user space units above and below the text), and because PDF coordinates start from the bottom-left of the page, not the top-left. Think of a Cartesian plane: the point (0,0) is below the point (0,1) and left of the point (1,0). That's how it is on a PDF page.

`Writer#y` gives you the current position of the `PDF::Writer` "cursor:" the y-coordinate of the space directly under the most recently added text or image. I use this to place the bottom of the box just under the text.

---

[*] A PDF user space unit is 1/72 of an inch.

If you want to generate many PDF documents from a template, you don't need to generate the whole document from scratch each time. You can create a PDF::Writer containing the skeleton of a document (say, just the corporate letterhead), then use Marshal.dump to save it to a binary string. You can then use Marshal.load as many times as necessary to get new documents, and fill in the blanks separately for each document.[*]

Here's a Ruby class that generates personalized certificates of achievement. We generate the PDF ahead of time with generate_pdf, leaving a blank space for the name. We can then fill in names by calling award_to. Instead of rerunning the PDF generation code every time, award_to copies the predefined PDF over and over again by loading it from its marshalled format.

```ruby
require 'rubygems'
require 'pdf/writer'

class Certificate

  def initialize(achievement)
    @without_name = Marshal.dump(generate_pdf(achievement))
  end

  def award_to(name)
    pdf = Marshal.load(@without_name)
    pdf.move_pointer(-225)
    pdf.text("<i>#{name}</i>", :font_size => 64,
             :justification => :center)
    return pdf
  end

  private
  def generate_pdf(achievement)
    pdf = PDF::Writer.new( :orientation => :landscape )
    pdf.info.title = "Certificate of Achievement"
    draw_border(pdf, 10, 12, 16, 18)
    draw_text(pdf, achievement)
    return pdf
  end

  def draw_border(pdf, *px_pos)
    px_pos.each do |px|
      pdf.rectangle(px, px, pdf.page_width - (px * 2),
                    pdf.page_height - (px * 2)).stroke
    end
  end

  def draw_text(pdf, achievement)
    pdf.select_font "Times-Roman"
```

---

[*] Yes, this is kind of hacky. The best we can say is that the author of PDF::Writer himself recommends it (see "Creating Printable Documents with Ruby," cited in the following See Also section).

```
pdf.text("\n", :font_size => 52)
pdf.text("Certificate of Achievement\n", :justification => :center)
pdf.text("\n", :font_size => 18)
pdf.text("hereby granted to\n", :justification => :center)
pdf.text("\n\n", :font_size => 64)
pdf.text("in recognition of achieving the status of",
          :font_size => 18, :justification => :center)
pdf.text(achievement, :font_size => 64, :justification => :center)
  end
end
```

Now we can create a certificate and award it to many different people:

```
certificate = Certificate.new('Ruby Hacker'); false
['Tricia Ball', 'Marty Wise', 'Dung Nguyen'].each do |name|
  certificate.award_to(name).save_as("#{name}.pdf")
end
```

Figure 12-8 shows what Tricia Ball.pdf looks like.

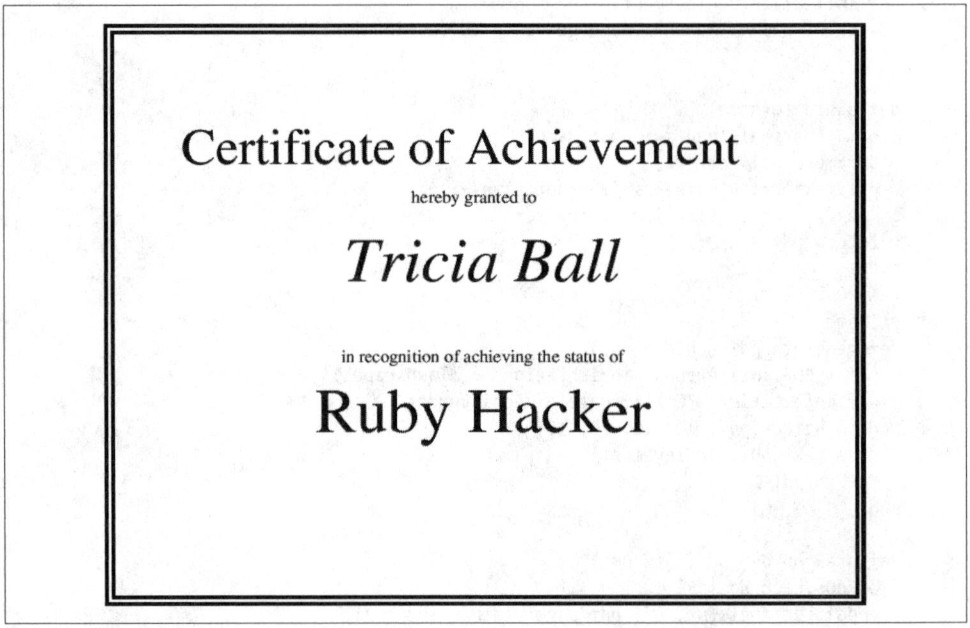

Certificate of Achievement

hereby granted to

Tricia Ball

in recognition of achieving the status of

Ruby Hacker

Figure 12-8. Congratulations!

This recipe only scratches the surface of what you can do with the PDF::Writer library. Fortunately, there's an excellent manual and RDoc documentation. Although the library provides a lot of classes, most of the methods you want will be in PDF::Writer and the mixin PDF::Writer::Graphics.

See Also

- The PDF::Writer homepage (*http://ruby-pdf.rubyforge.org/pdf-writer/*)
- Generated RDoc (*http://ruby-pdf.rubyforge.org/pdf-writer/doc/index.html*)
- "Creating Printable Documents with Ruby," published in artima's *Ruby Code & Style*, provides a helpful overview of the library as well as many links to PDF releated resources (*http://www.artima.com/rubycs/articles/pdf_writerP.html*)
- The pdf-writer gem includes the source for the manual (manual.pwd) and a script (bin/techbook) that turns it into PDF format; the manual is also available online (*http://ruby-pdf.rubyforge.org/pdf-writer/manual/index.html*)
- If you want to *read* a PDF file and extract its text, try Hannes Wyss's rpdf2txt library (*http://raa.ruby-lang.org/project/rpdf2txt/*)
- Recipe 8.16 for more about the Marshal technique for copying an object
- The Certificate class is used again in Recipe 14.19, "Running Servlets with WEBrick"

12.14 Representing Data as MIDI Music

Problem

You want to represent a series of data points as a musical piece, or just create music algorithmically.

Solution

Jim Menard's midilib library makes it easy to generate MIDI music files from Ruby. It's available as the midilib gem.

Here's a simple method for visualizing a list of numbers as a piano piece. The largest number in the list is mapped to the highest note on the piano keyboard (MIDI note 108), and the smallest number to the lowest note (MIDI note 21).

```
require 'rubygems'
require 'midilib'                          # => false

class Array
  def to_midi(file, note_length='eighth')

    midi_max = 108.0
    midi_min = 21.0

    low, high = min, max
    song = MIDI::Sequence.new

    # Create a new track to hold the melody, running at 120 beats per minute.
    song.tracks << (melody = MIDI::Track.new(song))
```

```
      melody.events << MIDI::Tempo.new(MIDI::Tempo.bpm_to_mpq(120))

      # Tell channel zero to use the "piano" sound.
      melody.events << MIDI::ProgramChange.new(0, 0)

      # Create a series of note events that play on channel zero.
      each do |number|
        midi_note = (midi_min + ((number-midi_min) * (midi_max-low)/high)).to_i
        melody.events << MIDI::NoteOnEvent.new(0, midi_note, 127, 0)
        melody.events << MIDI::NoteOffEvent.new(0, midi_note, 127,
                                                song.note_to_delta(note_length))
      end

      open(file, 'w') { |f| song.write(f) }
    end
  end
```

Now you can get an audible representation of any list of numbers:

```
((1..100).collect { |x| x ** 2 }).to_midi('squares.mid')
```

Discussion

The midilib library provides a set of classes for modeling a MIDI file: you can parse a MIDI file, modify it with Ruby code, and write it back to disk.

A MIDI file is modeled by a Sequence object, which contains Track objects. A track is a mainly a series of Event objects: for instance, each note in the piece has a NoteOnEvent and a NoteOffEvent.

Array#to_midi works by transforming each number in the array into a corresponding MIDI note. A standard piano keyboard can produce notes ranging from MIDI note 21 to MIDI note 108, with middle C being at MIDI note 60. Array#to_midi scales the values of the array to fit into this range as closely as possible, using the same formula you'd use to convert between two temperature scales.

Working directly with the MIDI classes is difficult, especially if you want to compose music instead of just transfering a data stream into MIDI note events. Here's a subclass of MIDI::Track that provides some simplifying assumptions and some higher-level musical functions, making it easy to compose simple multitrack tunes. Each TimedTrack uses its own MIDI channel and makes sounds from only one instrument. A TimedTrack can sound chords (this is very difficult with stock midilib), and instead of having to remember the MIDI note range, you can refer to notes in terms of half-steps away from middle C.

```
class TimedTrack < MIDI::Track
  MIDDLE_C = 60
  @@channel_counter=0

  def initialize(number, song)
    super(number)
    @sequence = song
```

```ruby
    @time = 0
    @channel = @@channel_counter
    @@channel_counter += 1
  end

  # Tell this track's channel to use the given instrument, and
  # also set the track's instrument display name.
  def instrument=(instrument)
    @events << MIDI::ProgramChange.new(@channel, instrument)
    super(MIDI::GM_PATCH_NAMES[instrument])
  end

  # Add one or more notes to sound simultaneously. Increments the per-track
  # timer so that subsequent notes will sound after this one finishes.
  def add_notes(offsets, velocity=127, duration='quarter')
    offsets = [offsets] unless offsets.respond_to? :each
    offsets.each do |offset|
      event(MIDI::NoteOnEvent.new(@channel, MIDDLE_C + offset, velocity))
    end
    @time += @sequence.note_to_delta(duration)
    offsets.each do |offset|
      event(MIDI::NoteOffEvent.new(@channel, MIDDLE_C + offset, velocity))
    end
    recalc_delta_from_times
  end

  # Uses add_notes to sound a chord (a major triad in root position), using the
  # given note as the low note. Like add_notes, increments the per-track timer.
  def add_major_triad(low_note, velocity=127, duration='quarter')
    add_notes([0, 4, 7].collect { |x| x + low_note }, velocity, duration)
  end

  private

  def event(event)
    @events << event
    event.time_from_start = @time
  end
end
```

Here's a script to write a randomly generated composition with two tracks. The melody track (a trumpet) takes a random walk around the musical scale, and the harmony track (an organ) plays a matching chord at the beginning of each measure.

```ruby
song = MIDI::Sequence.new
song.tracks << (melody = TimedTrack.new(0, song))
song.tracks << (background = TimedTrack.new(1, song))

melody.instrument = 56            # Trumpet
background.instrument = 19        # Church organ

melody.events << MIDI::Tempo.new(MIDI::Tempo.bpm_to_mpq(120))
melody.events << MIDI::MetaEvent.new(MIDI::META_SEQ_NAME,
                                     'A random Ruby composition')
```

```ruby
# Some musically pleasing intervals: thirds and fifths.
intervals = [-5, -1, 0, 4, 7]

# Start at middle C.
note = 0
# Create 8 measures of music in 4/4 time
(8*4).times do |i|
  note += intervals[rand(intervals.size)]

  #Reset to middle C if we go out of the MIDI range
  note = 0 if note < -39 or note > 48

  # Add a quarter note on every beat.
  melody.add_notes(note, 127, 'quarter')

  # Add a chord of whole notes at the beginning of each measure.
  background.add_major_triad(note, 50, 'whole') if i % 4 == 0
end

open('random.mid', 'w') { |f| song.write(f) }
```

See Also

- midilib has a comprehensive set of RDoc, available online at *http://midilib.rubyforge.org/*
- The library's examples/ directory has several good programs that demonstrate how to create and "play" MIDI files
- The TimedTrack class presented takes several ideas from Emanuel Borsboom's Midi Scripter application; the Midi Scripter generates MIDI files from Ruby code that incorporates musical notation—it's not really designed for use as a library, but it would make a good one (*http://www.epiphyte.ca/downloads/midi_scripter/README.html*)
- The names of the standard MIDI instrument and drum sounds are kept in the arrays MIDI::GM_PATCH_NAMES and MIDI::GM_DRUM_NOTE_NAMES; this isn't as useful as it could be, because you'll usually end up referring to instruments by their numeric IDs; the Wikipedia has a good mapping of numbers to names (*http://en.wikipedia.org/wiki/General_MIDI#Program_change_events*)

Databases and Persistence

We all want to leave behind something that will outlast us, and Ruby processes are no exception. Every program you write leaves some record of its activity, even if it's just data written to standard output. Most larger programs take this one step further: they store data from one run in a structured file, so that on another run they can pick up where they left off. There are a number of ways to persist data, from simple to insanely complex.

Simple persistence mechanisms like YAML let you write Ruby data structures to disk and load them back later. This is great for simple programs that don't handle much data. Your program can store its entire state in a disk file, and load the file on its next invocation to pick up where it left off. If you never keep more data than can fit into memory, the simplest way to make it permanent is to store it with YAML, Marshal, or Madeleine, and reload it later (see Recipes 13.1, 13.2, and 13.3). Madeleine also lets you revisit the *prior* states of your data.

If your dataset won't fit in memory, you need a database: a way of storing data on disk (usually in an indexed binary format) and retrieving parts of it quickly. The Berkeley database is the simplest database we cover: it operates like a hash, albeit a hash potentially much bigger than any you could keep in memory (Recipe 13.6).

But when most people think of a "database" they think of a relational database: MySQL, Postgres, Oracle, SQLite, or the like. A persistence mechanism stores data as Ruby data structures, and a Berkeley DB stores data as a hash of strings. But relational databases store data in the form of structured records with typed fields.

Because the tables of a relational database can have a complex structure and contain gigabytes of data, their contents are not accessed like normal Ruby data structures. Instead they're queried with SQL, a special programming language based on relational algebra. Most of the development time that goes into Ruby database libraries is spent trying to hide this fact. Several libraries hide the details of communication between a Ruby program and a SQL database; the balance of this chapter is devoted to showing how to use them.

Every relational database exposes a C API, and Ruby bindings to each API are available. We show you how to use the two most popular open source databases: MySQL (Recipe 13.9) and Postgres (Recipe 13.10).* But every database has different bindings, and speaks a slightly different variant of SQL. Fortunately, there are other libraries that hide these differences behind a layer of abstraction. Once you install the bindings, you can install abstraction layers atop them and rely on the abstraction layer to keep track of the differences between databases.

Ruby's simplest database abstraction library is DBI (it's modeled after Perl's DBI module). It does nothing more than provide a uniform interface to the different database bindings. You still have to write all the SQL yourself (and if you're serious about database neutrality, you must use the lowest common denominator of SQL), but you only have to learn a single binding API.

The more popular database abstraction libraries are ActiveRecord (the library of choice for Rails applications) and Og. Not only do these libraries hide the differences between databases, they hide most of the actual SQL. The database tables are represented as Ruby classes, the rows in the database tables as instances of those classes. You can find, create, and modify database rows by manipulating normal-looking Ruby objects. Neither Og nor ActiveRecord can do everything that raw SQL can, so you may also need to use DBI or one of the database-specific bindings.

One standard argument for database abstraction layers is that they make it easy to switch an application's underlying database without having to rewrite all the code. They certainly do make this easier, but it almost never happens.† The real advantage is that with abstraction layers, you don't have to learn all the different database bindings. Even if you never change databases for any given project, throughout your career you'll find yourself using different databases on different projects. Learning how to use a database abstraction layer can save you from having to learn multiple database-specific bindings.

Whether you use ActiveRecord, Og, DBI, or database-specific bindings, you'll need an actual database for your code to connect to. The recipes in this chapter assume you've got a database called cookbook and that you connect to it with the username "cookbook_user" and the password "password".

Here's how to set up cookbook as a MySQL database:

```
$ mysql -u root
Welcome to the MySQL monitor.  Commands end with ; or \g.
```

---

* SQLite deserves an honorable mention because, unlike other relational databases, it doesn't require a server to run. The client code can directly query the database file. This makes things a lot easier to set up. Note that SQLite has two incompatible file formats (version 2 and version 3), and a gem exists for each version. You probably want the sqlite3-ruby gem.

† What does happen is that you may write a product designed to work with whatever database the user has installed. You can't always require that your users run a specific database.

```
Your MySQL connection id is 6 to server version: 4.0.24_Debian-10-log

Type 'help;' or '\h' for help. Type '\c' to clear the buffer.

mysql> create database cookbook;
Query OK, 1 row affected (0.00 sec)

mysql> grant all privileges on cookbook.* to 'cookbook_user'@'localhost' identified
by 'password';
Query OK, 0 rows affected (0.00 sec)
```

Here's how to set cookbook up as a Postgres database (you'll probably need to run these commands as the postgres user):

```
$ createuser
Enter name of user to add: cookbook_user
Enter password for new user: password
Enter it again: password
Shall the new user be allowed to create databases? (y/n) y
Shall the new user be allowed to create more new users? (y/n) n
CREATE USER

$ createdb cookbook
CREATE DATABASE
```

To avoid showing you the database connection code in every single recipe, we've factored it out into a library. If you want to run the code in this chapter's recipes, you should put the following code in a file called cookbook_dbconnect.rb. Keep it in the directory where you keep the recipe code, or somewhere in your library include path, so that require 'cookbook_dbconnect' will work.

This file defines database connection functions for DBI, ActiveRecord, and Og:

```
# cookbook_dbconnect.rb
require 'rubygems'
require 'dbi'
require 'active_record'
require 'og'
```

The with_db method gets a database connection through DBI and runs a code block in the context of that connection:

```
def with_db
  DBI.connect("dbi:Mysql:cookbook:localhost",
              "cookbook_user", "password") do |c|
    yield c
  end
end
```

The activerecord_connect method only needs to be called once at the beginning of a program: after that, ActiveRecord will acquire database connections as needed.

```
def activerecord_connect
  ActiveRecord::Base.establish_connection(:adapter => "mysql",
                                          :host => "localhost",
```

```
                          :username => "cookbook_user",
                          :password => "password",
                          :database => "cookbook")
     end
```

For your reference, this table presents the ActiveRecord adapter names for various kinds of databases.

Database	Adapter name
MySQL	mysql
PostgreSQL	postgresql
Oracle	oci
Microsoft SQL Server	sqlserver
SQLite 2	sqlite
SQLite 3	sqlite3
DB2	db2

The og_connect also needs to be called only once. One caveat: you must call it *after* you've defined the classes for your Og data model.

```
     def og_connect
       Og.setup( { :destroy => false,
                   :store => :mysql,
                   :user => "cookbook_user",
                   :password => "password",
                   :name => "cookbook" } )
     end
```

This version of cookbook_dbconnect assumes you're running against a MySQL database. For a different database, you just need to change the database name so that DBI, ActiveRecord, and Og know which adapter they should use.

Here are some resources for more information about databases in Ruby:

- *http://ruby-dbi.rubyforge.org/*
- *http://www.rubyonrails.org/show/ActiveRecord*
- *http://www.rubygarden.com/index.cgi/Libraries/og_tutorial.rdoc*

13.1 Serializing Data with YAML

Problem

You want to serialize a data structure and use it later. You may want to send the data structure to a file, then load it into a program written in a different programming language.

Solution

The simplest way is to use the built-in yaml library. When you require yaml, all Ruby objects sprout to_yaml methods that convert them to the YAML serialization format. A YAML string is human-readable, and it intuitively corresponds to the object from which it was derived:

```
require 'yaml'

10.to_yaml                    # => "--- 10\n"
'ten'.to_yaml                 # => "--- ten\n"
'10'.to_yaml                  # => "--- \"10\"\n"
```

Arrays are represented as bulleted lists:

```
puts %w{Brush up your Shakespeare}.to_yaml
# ---
# - Brush
# - up
# - your
# - Shakespeare
```

Hashes are represented as colon-separated key-value pairs:

```
puts ({ 'star' => 'hydrogen', 'gold bar' => 'gold' }).to_yaml
# ---
# star: hydrogen
# gold bar: gold
```

More complex Ruby objects are represented in terms of their classes and member variables:

```
require 'set'
puts Set.new([1, 2, 3]).to_yaml
# --- !ruby/object:Set
# hash:
#   1: true
#   2: true
#   3: true
```

You can dump a data structure to a file with YAML.dump, and load it back with YAML.load:

```
users = [{:name => 'Bob', :permissions => ['Read']},
         {:name => 'Alice', :permissions => ['Read', 'Write']}]

# Serialize
open('users', 'w') { |f| YAML.dump(users, f) }

# And deserialize
users2 = open("users") { |f| YAML.load(f) }
# => [{:permissions=>["Read"], :name=>"Bob"},
#     {:permissions=>["Read", "Write"], :name=>"Alice"}]
```

YAML implementations are available for Perl, Python, Java, PHP, JavaScript, and OCaml, so if you stick to the "standard" data types (strings, arrays, and so on), the serialized file will be portable across programming languages.

Discussion

If you've ever used Python's `pickle` module or serialized a Java object, you know how convenient it is to be able to dump an object to disk and load it back later. You don't have to define a custom data format or write an XML generator: you just shove the object into a file or a database, and read it back later. The only downside is that the serialized file is usually a binary mess that can only be understood by the serialization library.

YAML is a human-readable and somewhat cross-language serialization standard. Its format describes the simple data structures common to all modern programming languages. YAML can serialize and deserialize any combination of strings, booleans, numbers, dates and times, arrays (possibly nested arrays), and hashes (again, possibly nested ones).

You can also use YAML to serialize Ruby-specific objects: symbols, ranges, and regular expressions. Indeed, you can use YAML to serialize instances of custom classes: YAML serializes the class of the object and the values of its instance variables. There's no guarantee, though, that other programming languages will understand what you mean.[*]

Not only is YAML human-readable, it's human-writable. You can write YAML files in a text editor and load them into Ruby as objects. If you're having trouble with the YAML representation of a particular data structure, your best bet is to define a simple version of that data structure in an irb session, dump it to YAML, and work from there.

```
quiz_question = ['What color is Raedon?', ['Blue', 'Albino', '*Yellow']]
puts quiz_question.to_yaml
# ---
# - What color is Raedon?
# - - Blue
#   - Albino
#   - "*Yellow"
```

Before you get drunk with power, you should know that YAML shares the limitations of other serialization schemes. Most obviously, you can only deserialize objects in an environment like the one in which you serialized them. Suppose you convert a Set object to YAML in one Ruby session:

```
require 'yaml'
require 'set'
```

---

[*] Ruby can also read YAML descriptions of Perl's regular expressions.

```
set = Set.new([1, 2, 3])
open("set", "w") { |f| YAML.dump(set, f) }
```

In another Ruby session, you might try to convert the YAML back into a Set, without first requiring the set library:

```
# Bad code -- don't try this!
require 'yaml'
set = open("set") { |f| YAML.load(f) }
# => #<YAML::Object:0xb7bd8620 @ivars={"hash"=>{1=>true, 2=>true, 3=>true}},
#       @class="Set">
```

Instead of a Set, you've got an unresolved object of class YAML::Object. The set has been loaded from the file and deserialized, but Ruby can't resolve its class name.

YAML can only serialize data; it can't serialize Ruby code or system resources (such as filehandles or open sockets). This means some objects can't be fully converted to YAML. The following code successfully serializes and deserializes a File object, but the deserialized File isn't open and doesn't point to anything in particular:

```
handle = open('a_file', 'w')
handle.path
# => "a_file"

handle2 = YAML.load(YAML.dump(handle))
# => #<File:0xb7bd9a58>
handle2.path
# IOError: uninitialized stream
```

The essence of the File object—its handle to a file on disk, granted by the operating system—has been lost.

Objects that contain Ruby code will lose their code when dumped to YAML. This means that Proc and Binding objects will turn up empty. Objects with singleton methods will be dumped without them. Classes can't be dumped to YAML at all.

But these are all edge cases. Most data structures, even complex ones, can be serialized to YAML and stay readable to boot.

See Also

- Ruby standard library documentation for the yaml library
- The YAML web page (*http://www.yaml.org/*)
- Recipe 12.12, "Reading and Writing Configuration Files"
- An episode of the Ruby Quiz focused on creating a serializable Proc object (*http://www.rubyquiz.com/quiz38.html*)

13.2   Serializing Data with Marshal

Problem

You want to serialize a data structure to disk faster than YAML can do it. You don't care about the readability of the serialized data structure, or portability to other programming languages.

Solution

Use the Marshal module, built into Ruby. It works more or less like YAML, but it's much faster. The Marshal.dump method transforms a data structure into a binary string, which you can write to a file and reconstitute later with Marshal.load.

```
Marshal.dump(10)                          # => "\004\010i\017"
Marshal.dump('ten')                       # => "\004\010\"\010ten"
Marshal.dump('10')                        # => "\004\010\"\a10"

Marshal.load(Marshal.dump(%w{Brush up your Shakespeare}))
# => ["Brush", "up", "your", "Shakespeare"]

require 'set'
Marshal.load(Marshal.dump(Set.new([1, 2, 3])))
# => #<Set: {1, 2, 3}>
```

Discussion

Marshal is what most programmers coming from other languages expect from a serializer. It's fast (much faster than yaml), and it produces unreadable blobs of binary data. It can serialize almost anything that yaml can (see Recipe 13.1 for examples), and it can also handle a few cases that yaml can't. For instance, you can use Marshal to serialize a reference to a class:

```
Marshal.dump(Set)                    # =>"\004\010c\010Set"
```

Note that the serialized version of Set is little more than a reference to the class. Like YAML, Marshal depends on the presence of the original classes, and you can't deserialize a reference to a class you don't have.* With YAML, you'll get an unresolved YAML::Object; with Marshal, you get an ArgumentError:

```
#!/usr/bin/ruby -w

Marshal.load("\004\010c\010Set")
# ArgumentError: undefined class/module Set
```

Like YAML, Marshal only serializes data structures. It can't serialize Ruby code (like Proc objects), or resources allocated by other processes (like filehandles or database

---

* This also means that if you add methods to a class, then serialize the class, your methods don't get saved.

connections). However, the two libraries differ in their error handling. YAML tends to serialize as much as it can: it can serialize a `File` object, but when you deserialize it, you get an object that doesn't point to any actual file. Marshal just gives you an error when you try to serialize a file:

```
open('output', 'w') { |f| Marshal.dump(f) }
# TypeError: can't dump File
```

See Also

• Recipe 13.1, "Serializing Data with YAML," has more on serialization in general

13.3 Persisting Objects with Madeleine

Problem

You want to store objects in RAM and persist them between independent executions of the program. This will let your program recall its state indefinitely and access it very quickly.

Solution

Use the Madeleine library available as the `madeleine` gem. It transparently persists any Ruby object that can be serialized with `Marshal`. Unlike a conventional database persistence layer, Madeleine keeps all of its objects in RAM at all times.

To use Madeleine, you have to decide which objects in your system need to be serialized, and which ones you might have saved to a database traditionally. Here's a simple Madeleine-backed program for conducting yes/no polls, in which agreement adds one to a total and disagreement subtracts one:

```
#!/usr/bin/ruby -w
# poll.rb
require 'rubygems'
require 'madeleine'

class Poll
  attr_accessor :name
  attr_reader :total

  def initialize(name)
    @name = name
    @total = 0
  end

  def agree
    @total += 1
  end
end
```

```
    def disagree
      @total -= 1
    end
end
```

So far there's been no Madeleine code, just a normal class with instance variables and accessors. But how will we store the state of the poll between invocations of the polling program? Since instances of the `Poll` class can be serialized with `Marshall`, we can wrap a `Poll` object in a `MadeleineSnapshot`, and keep it in a file:

```
poll = SnapshotMadeleine.new('poll_data') do
  Poll.new('Is Ruby great?')
end
```

The system accessor retrieves the object wrapped by `MadeleineSnapshot`:

```
if ARGV[0] == 'agree'
  poll.system.agree
elsif ARGV[0] == 'disagree'
  poll.system.disagree
end

puts "Name: #{poll.system.name}"
puts "Total: #{poll.system.total}"
```

You can save the current state of the object with `take_snapshot`:

```
poll.take_snapshot
```

Here are a few sample runs of the `poll.rb` program:

```
$ ruby poll.rb agree
Name: Is Ruby great?
Total: 1

$ ruby poll.rb agree
Name: Is Ruby great?
Total: 2

$ ruby poll.rb disagree
Name: Is Ruby great?
Total: 1
```

Discussion

Recall this piece of code:

```
poll = SnapshotMadeleine.new('poll_data') do
  Poll.new('Is Ruby great?')
end
```

The first time that code is run, Madeleine creates a directory called `poll_data`. Then it runs the code block. The result of the code block is the object whose state will be tracked in the `poll_data` directory.

On subsequent runs, the poll_data directory already exists, and Madeleine loads the current state of the Poll object from the latest snapshot in the directory. It doesn't run the code block.

Here are the contents of poll_data after we run the program three times:

```
$ ls poll_data
000000000000000000001.snapshot
000000000000000000002.snapshot
000000000000000000003.snapshot
```

Every time we call poll.take_snapshot, Madeleine serializes the Poll object to a snapshot file in poll_data. If the data ever gets corrupted, you can remove the corrupted snapshot files and revert to a previous version of the data.

A clever trick for programs like our poll application is to use Kernel#at_exit to automatically save the state of an object when the program ends. This way, even if your program is killed by a Unix signal, or throws an exception, your data will be saved.*

```
at_exit { poll.take_snapshot }
```

In applications where a process runs indefinitely, you can save snapshots at regular intervals by spawning a separate thread:

```
def save_recurring_snapshots(madeleine_object, time_interval)
  loop do
    madeleine_object.take_snapshot
    sleep time_interval
  end
end

Thread.new { save_recurring_snapshots(poll, 24*60*60) }
```

See Also

- Recipe 3.12, "Running a Code Block Periodically"
- Recipe 13.2, "Serializing Data with Marshal"
- The Madeleine design rules document lays out the conditions your code must meet if you want to snapshot it with Madeleine (*http://madeleine.sourceforge.net/docs/designRules.html*)
- The RDoc documentation for Madeleine (*http://madeleine.sourceforge.net/docs/api/*)
- For more on the technique of object prevalence, see the web site for the Prevayler Java project, especially the "Articles" section (*http://www.prevayler.org/wiki.jsp*)

---

* Of course, these things might happen when your data is in an inconsistent state and you don't *want* it to be saved.

13.4 Indexing Unstructured Text with SimpleSearch

Problem

You want to index a number of texts and do quick keyword searches on them.

Solution

Use the SimpleSearch library, available in the SimpleSearch gem.

Here's how to create and save an index:

```
require 'rubygems'
require 'search/simple'

contents = Search::Simple::Contents.new
contents << Search::Simple::Content.
              new('In the beginning God created the heavens...',
                  'Genesis.txt', Time.now)
contents << Search::Simple::Content.new('Call me Ishmael...',
                                        'MobyDick.txt', Time.now)
contents << Search::Simple::Content.new('Marley was dead to begin with...',
                                        'AChristmasCarol.txt', Time.now)

searcher = Search::Simple::Searcher.load(contents, 'index_file')
```

Here's how to load and search an existing index:

```
require 'rubygems'
require 'search/simple'

searcher = nil
open('index_file') do |f|
  searcher = Search::Simple::Searcher.new(Marshal.load(f), Marshal.load(f),
                                          'index_file')
end

searcher.find_words(['begin']).results.collect { |result| result.name }
# => ["AChristmasCarol.txt", "Genesis.txt"]
```

Discussion

SimpleSearch is a library that makes it easy to do fast keyword searching on unstructured text documents. The index itself is represented by a Searcher object, and each document you feed it is a Content object.

To create an index, you must first construct a number of Content objects and a Contents object to contain them. A Content object contains a piece of text, a unique identifier for that text (often a filename, though it could also be a database ID or a URL), and the time at which the text was last modified. Searcher.load transforms a Contents object into a searchable index that gets serialized to disk with Marshal.

The indexer analyzes the text you gives it, removes stop words (like "a"), truncates words to their roots (so "beginning" becomes "begin"), and puts every word of the text into binary data structures. Given a set of words to find and a set of words to exclude, SimpleSearch uses these structures to quickly find a set of documents.

Here's how to add some new documents to an existing index:

```
class Search::Simple::Searcher
  def add_contents(contents)
    Search::Simple::Searcher.create_indices(contents, @dict,
                                             @document_vectors)
    dump                                  # Re-serialize the file
  end
end

contents = Search::Simple::Contents.new
contents << Search::Simple::Content.new('A spectre is haunting Europe...',
                                        'TheCommunistManifesto.txt', Time.now)
searcher.add_contents(contents)
searcher.find_words(['spectre']).results[0].name
# => "TheCommunistManifesto.txt"
```

SimpleSearch doesn't support incremental indexing. If you update or delete a document, you must recreate the entire index from scratch.

See Also

- The SimpleSearch home page (*http://www.chadfowler.com/SimpleSearch/*)
- The sample application within the SimpleSearch gem: search-simple.rb
- Recipe 13.2, "Serializing Data with Marshal"
- For a more sophisticated indexer, see Recipe 13.5, "Indexing Structured Text with Ferret"

13.5 Indexing Structured Text with Ferret

Problem

You want to perform searches on structured text. For instance, you might want to search just the headline of a news story, or just the body.

Discussion

The Ferret library can tokenize and search structured data. It's a pure Ruby port of Java's Lucene library, and it's available as the ferret gem.

Here's how to create and populate an index with Ferret. I'll create a searchable index of useful Ruby packages, stored as a set of binary files in the ruby_packages/ directory.

```
require 'rubygems'
require 'ferret'
```

```
PACKAGE_INDEX_DIR = 'ruby_packages/'
Dir.mkdir(PACKAGE_INDEX_DIR) unless File.directory? PACKAGE_INDEX_DIR
index = Ferret::Index::Index.new(:path => PACKAGE_INDEX_DIR,
                                 :default_search_field => 'name|description')
index << { :name => 'SimpleSearch',
           :description => 'A simple indexing library.',
           :supports_structured_data => false,
           :complexity => 2 }
index << { :name => 'Ferret',
           :description => 'A Ruby port of the Lucene library.
                           More powerful than SimpleSearch',
           :supports_structured_data => true,
           :complexity => 5 }
```

By default, queries against this index will search the "name" and "description" fields, but you can search against any field:

```
index.search_each('library') do |doc_id, score|
  puts index.doc(doc_id).field('name').data
end
# SimpleSearch
# Ferret

index.search_each('description:powerful AND supports_structured_data:true') do
|doc_id, score|
  puts index.doc(doc_id).field("name").data
end
# Ferret

index.search_each("complexity:<5") do |doc_id, score|
  puts index.doc(doc_id).field("name").data
end
# SimpleSearch
```

Discussion

When should you use Ferret instead of SimpleText? SimpleText is good for unstructured data like plain text. Ferret excels at searching structured data, the kind you find in databases.

Relational databases are good at finding exact field matches, but not very good at locating keywords within large strings. Ferret works best when you need full text search but you want to keep some of the document structure. I've also had great success using Ferret[*] to bring together data from disparate sources (some in databases, some not) into one structured, searchable index.

There are two things you can do with Ferret: add text to the index, and query the index. Ferret offers you a lot of control over both activities. I'll briefly cover the most interesting features.

---

[*] Actually, I was using Lucene. Same idea.

You can feed an index by passing in a hash of field names to values, or you can feed it fully formed Ferret::Document objects. This gives you more control over which fields you'd like to index. Here, I'll create an index of news stories taken from a hypothetical database:

```
# This include will cut down on the length of the Field:: constants below.
include Ferret::Document

def index_story(index, db_id, headline, story)
  doc = Document.new
  doc << Field.new("db_id", db_id, Field::Store::YES, Field::Index::NO)
  doc << Field.new("headline", headline, Field::Store::YES, Field::Index::TOKENIZED)
  doc << Field.new("story", story, Field::Store::NO, Field::Index::TOKENIZED)
  index << doc
end

STORY_INDEX_DIR = 'news_stories/'
Dir.mkdir(STORY_INDEX_DIR) unless File.directory? STORY_INDEX_DIR
index = Ferret::Index::Index.new(:path => STORY_INDEX_DIR)

index_story(index, 1, "Lizardoids Control the Media, Sources Say",
            "Don't count on reading this story in your local paper anytime
             soon, because ...")

index_story(index, 2, "Where Are My Pants? An Editorial",
            "This is an outrage. The lizardoids have gone too far! ...")
```

In this case, I'm storing the database ID in the Document, but I'm not indexing it. I don't want anyone to search on it, but I need some way of tying a Document in the index to a record in the database. That way, when someone does a search, I can print out the headline and provide a link to the original story.

I treat the body of the story exactly the opposite way: the words get indexed, but the original text is not stored and can't be recovered from the Document object. I'm not going to be displaying the text of the story along with my search results, and the text is already in the database, so why store it again in the index?

The simplest way to search a Ferret index is with Index#search_each, as demonstrated in the Solution. This takes a query and a code block. For each document that matched the search query, it yields the document ID and a number between 0 and 1, representing the quality of the match.

You can get more information about the search results by calling search instead of search_each. This gives you a Ferret::Search::TopDocs object that contains the search results, as well as useful information like how many documents were matched. Call each on a TopDocs object and it'll act just as if you'd called search_each.

Here's some code that does a search and prints the results:

```
def search_news(index, query)
  results = index.search(query)
  puts "#{results.size} article(s) matched:"
```

```
    results.each do |doc_id, score|
      story = index.doc(doc_id)
      puts " #{story.field("headline").data} (score: #{score})"
      puts " http://www.example.com/news/#{story.field("db_id").data}"
      puts
    end
  end

search_news(index, "pants editorial")
# 1 article(s) matched:
#  Where Are My Pants? An Editorial (score: 0.0908329636861293)
# http://www.example.com/news/2
```

You can weight the fields differently to fine-tune the results. This query makes a match in the headline count twice as much as a match in the story:

```
search_news(index, "headline:lizardoids^1 OR story:lizardoids^0.5")
# 2 article(s) matched:
#  Lizardoids Control the Media, Sources Say (score: 0.195655948031232)
#  http://www.example.com/news/1
#
#  Where Are My Pants? An Editorial (score: 0.0838525491562421)
#  http://www.example.com/news/2
```

Queries can be strings or Ferret::Search::Query objects. Pass in a string, and it just gets parsed and turned into a Query. The main advantage of creating your own Query objects is that you can put a user-friendly interface on your search functionality, instead of making people always construct Ferret queries by hand. The weighted_ query method defined below takes a single keyword and creates a Query object equivalent to the rather complicated weighted query given above:

```
def weighted_query(term)
  query = Ferret::Search::BooleanQuery.new
  query << term_clause("headline", term, 1)
  query << term_clause("story", term, 0.5)
end

def term_clause(field, term, weight)
  t = Ferret::Search::TermQuery.new(Ferret::Index::Term.new(field, term))
  t.boost = weight
  return Ferret::Search::BooleanClause.new(t)
end
```

Ferret can be clumsy to use. It's got a lot of features to learn, and sometimes it seems like you spend all your time composing small objects into bigger objects (as in weighted_query above, which creates instances of four different classes). This is partly because Ferret is so flexible, and partly because the API comes mainly from Java. But nothing else works as well for searching structured text.

See Also

- The Ferret homepage (*http://ferret.davebalmain.com/*)

- The Ferret Query Language, described in the RDoc for the QueryParser class (*http://ferret.davebalmain.com/api/classes/Ferret/QueryParser.html*)
- Apache Lucene, the basis for Ferret, lives at *http://lucene.apache.org/java/*

13.6 Using Berkeley DB Databases

Problem

You want a simple, fast database that doesn't need a server to run.

Solution

Ruby's standard dbm library lets you store a database in a set of standalone binary files. It's not a SQL database: it's more like a fast disk-based hash that only stores strings.

```
require 'dbm'

DBM.new('random_thoughts') do |db|
  db['tape measure'] =
    "What if there was a tape measure you could use as a yo-yo?"
  db[23] = "Fnord."
end

DBM.open('random_thoughts') do |db|
  puts db['tape measure']
  puts db['23']
end
# What if there was a tape measure you could use as a yo-yo?
# Fnord.

DBM.open('random_thoughts') { |db| db[23] }
# TypeError: can't convert Fixnum into String

Dir['random_thoughts.*']
# => ["random_thoughts.pag", "random_thoughts.dir"]
```

Discussion

The venerable Berkeley DB format lets you store enormous associative datasets on disk and quickly access them by key. It dates from before programming languages had built-in hash structures, so it's not as useful as it used to be. In fact, if your hash is small enough to fit in memory, it's faster to simply use a Ruby hash that you serialize to disk with Marshal.

If you do need to use a DBM object, you can treat it almost exactly like a Ruby hash: it supports most of the same methods.

There are many, many implementations of the Berkeley DB, and the file formats differ widely between versions, so DBM files are not very portable. If you're creating your own databases, you should use the generic dbm library. It provides a uniform interface to all the DBM implementations, using the best library you have installed on your computer.*

Ruby also provides gdbm and sdbm libraries, interfaces to specific database formats, but you should only need these if you're trying to load a Berkeley DB file produced by some other program.

There's also the SleepyCat library, a more ambitious implementation of the Berkeley DB that implements features of traditional databases like transactions and locking. Its Ruby bindings are available as a third-party download. It's still much closer to a disk-based data structure than to a relational database, and the basic interface is similar to that of dbm, though less Ruby-idiomatic:

```ruby
require 'bdb'

db = BDB::Hash.create('random_thoughts2.db', nil, BDB::CREATE)
db['Why do we park on a driveway but'] = 'it never rains but it pours.'
db.close

db = BDB::Hash.open('random_thoughts2.db', nil, 'r')
db['Why do we park on a driveway but']
# => "it never rains but it pours."
db.close
```

The SleepyCat library provides several different hashlike data structures. If you want a hash whose keys stay sorted alphabetically, you can create a BDB::Btree instead of a BDB::Hash:

```ruby
db = BDB::Btree.create('element_reviews.db', nil, BDB::CREATE)
db['earth'] = 'My personal favorite element.'
db['water'] = 'An oldie but a goodie.'
db['air'] = 'A good weekend element when you're bored with other elements.'
db['fire'] = 'Perhaps the most overrated element.'

db.each { |k,v| puts k }
# air
# earth
# fire
# water

db['water']                          # => "An oldie but a goodie."
db.close
```

See Also

- On Debian GNU/Linux, the DBM extensions to Ruby come in separate packages from Ruby itself: libdbm-ruby, libgdbm-ruby, and libsdbm-ruby
- You can get the Ruby binding to the Sleepycat library at *http://moulon.inra.fr/ruby/bdb.html*

---

* Actually, it uses the best DBM library you had installed when you installed the dbm Ruby extension.

- Confused by all the different, mutually incompatible implementations of the Berkeley DB idea? Try reading "Unix Incompatibility Notes: DBM Hash Libraries" (*http://www.unixpapa.com/incnote/dbm.html*)
- If you need a *relational* database that doesn't require a server to run, try SQLite: it keeps its databases in standalone files, and you can use it with ActiveRecord or DBI; its Ruby binding is packaged as the `sqlite3-ruby` gem, and its home page is at *http://www.sqlite.org/*

13.7 Controlling MySQL on Unix

Problem

The standard Ruby database interfaces assume you're connecting to a preexisting database, and that you already have access to this database. You want to create and administer MySQL databases from within Ruby.

Solution

Sam Ruby came up with an elegant solution to this problem. The `mysql` method defined below opens up a pipe to a MySQL client program and sends SQL input to it:

```
def mysql(opts, stream)
  IO.popen("mysql #{opts}", 'w') { |io| io.puts stream }
end
```

You can use this technique to create, delete, and administer MySQL databases:

```
mysql '-u root -p[password]', <<-end
  drop database if exists website_db;
  create database website_db;
  grant all on website_db.* to #{`id -un`.strip}@localhost;
end
```

Discussion

This solution looks so elegant because of the `<<-end` declaration, which allows you to end the string the same way you end a code block.

One shortcoming of this solution is that the `IO.popen` call opens up a one-way communication with the MySQL client. This makes it difficult to call SQL commands and get the results back. If that's what you need, you can use `IO.popen` interactively; see Recipe 23.1.

See Also

- Recipe 23.1, "Scripting an External Program"

13.8 Finding the Number of Rows Returned by a Query

Problem

Writing a DBI program, you want an efficient way to see how many rows were returned by a query.

Solution

A do command returns the number of rows affected by the command, so that one's easy. To demonstrate, I'll create a database table that keeps track of my prized collection of lowercase letters:

```
require 'cookbook_dbconnect'

with_db do |c|

  c.do %{drop table if exists letters}

  c.do %{create table letters(id INT NOT NULL PRIMARY KEY AUTO_INCREMENT,
                              letter CHAR(1) NOT NULL)}
  letter_sql = ('a'..'z').collect.join('"),("')

  c.do %{insert into letters(letter) values ("#{letter_sql}")}
end
# => 26
```

When you execute a query, you get back a StatementHandle object representing the request. If you're using a MySQL database, you can call rows on this object to get the number of rows in the result set:

```
vowel_query = %{select id from letters where letter in ("a","e","i","o","u")}
with_db do |c|
  h = c.execute vowel_query
  "My collection contains #{h.rows} vowels."
end
# => "My collection contains 5 vowels."
```

If you're not using MySQL, things are a bit trickier. The simplest thing to do is simply retrieve all the rows as an array, then use the array's size as the number of rows:

```
with_db do |c|
  vowels = c.select_all(vowel_query)
  "My collection still contains #{vowels.size} vowels."
end
# => "My collection still contains 5 vowels."
```

But this can be disastrously inefficient; see below for details.

Discussion

When you select some items out of a Ruby array, say with `Array#grep`, Ruby gives you the results in a brand new array. Once the array has been created, there's no cost to checking its size by calling `Array#size`.

A database query acts differently. Your query might have matched millions of rows, and each result might contain kilobytes of data. This is why normally you iterate over a result set instead of using `select_all` to get it as an array. Getting the whole result set at once might use a huge amount of memory, which is why using `select_all` can be disastrous.

You've got two other options. If you're going to be iterating over the entire dataset anyway, *and* you don't need the count until you're all done, you can count the rows as you go. This will save memory over the `fetch_all` approach:

```
with_db do |c|
  rows = 0

  c.execute(vowel_query).each do |row|
    rows += 1
    # Process the row...
  end
  "Yup, all #{rows} vowels are still there."
end
# => "Yup, all 5 vowels are still there."
```

Otherwise, your only choice is to run *two* queries: the actual query, and a slightly modified version of the query that uses SELECT COUNT instead of SELECT. A method like this will work for simple cases (cases that don't contain GROUP BY statements). It uses a regular expression to turn a SELECT query into a SELECT COUNT query, runs both queries, and returns both the count and the query handle.

```
module DBI
  class DatabaseHandle
    def execute_with_count(query, *args)
      re = /^\s*select .* from/i
      count_query = query.sub(re, 'select count(*) from')
      count = select_one(count_query)
      [count, execute(query)]
    end
  end
end

with_db do |c|
  count, handle = c.execute_with_count(vowel_query)
  puts "I can't believe none of the #{count} vowels " +
    "have been stolen from my collection!"

  puts 'Here they are in the database:'
  handle.each do |r|
    puts "Row #{r['id']}"
```

```
    end
end
# I can't believe none of the 5 vowels have been stolen from my collection!
# Here they are in the database:
# Row 1
# Row 5
# Row 9
# Row 15
# Row 21
```

See Also

- The Ruby DBI tutorial describes the MySQL rows trick but says not to depend on it; we figure as long as you know about the alternatives, you're not dependent on the database-specific shortcut (*http://www.kitebird.com/articles/ruby-dbi.html*)

13.9 Talking Directly to a MySQL Database

Problem

You want to send SQL queries and commands directly to a MySQL database.

Solution

Do you really need to do this? Almost all the time, it's better to use the generic DBI library. The biggest exception is when you're writing a a Rails application, and you need to run a SQL command that you can't express with ActiveRecord.*

If you really want to communicate directly with MySQL, use the Ruby bindings to the MySQL client library (found in the mysql gem). It provides an interface that's pretty similar to DBI's.

Here's a MySQL-specific version of the method with_db, defined in this chapter's introduction. It returns a Mysql object, which you can use to run queries or get server information.

```
require 'rubygems'
require 'mysql'

def with_db
  dbh = Mysql.real_connect('localhost', 'cookbook_user', 'password',
                           'cookbook')
  begin
    yield dbh
  ensure
    dbh.close
  end
end
```

---

* You could use DBI with ActiveRecord, but most Rails programmers go straight to the database.

The `Mysql#query` method runs any SQL statement, whether it's a SELECT query or something else. When it runs a query, the return value is a result-set object (a `MysqlRes`); otherwise, it's `nil`. Here it is running some SQL commands:

```
with_db do |db|
  db.query('drop table if exists secrets')
  db.query('create table secrets( id INT NOT NULL PRIMARY KEY AUTO_INCREMENT,
                                  secret LONGTEXT )'·)
  db.query(%{insert into secrets(secret) values
    ("Oh, MySQL, you're the only one who really understands me.")})
end
```

And here's a query:

```
with_db do |db|
  res = db.query('select * from secrets')
  res.each { |row| puts "#{row[0]}: #{row[1]}" }
  res.free
end
# 1: Oh, MySQL, you're the only one who really understands me.
```

Discussion

Like the database connection itself, the result set you get from query wants to be closed when you're done with it. This calls for yet another instance of the pattern seen in `with_db`, in which setup and cleanup are delegated to a method that takes a code block. Here's some code that alters query to take a code block:

```
class Mysql
  alias :query_no_block :query
  def query(sql)
    res = query_no_block(sql)
    return res unless block_given?
    begin
      yield res
    ensure
      res.free if res
    end
  end
end
```

Now we can write more concise query code, and not have to worry about freeing the result set:

```
with_db do |db|
  db.query('select * from secrets') do |res|
    res.each { |row| puts "#{row[0]}: #{row[1]}" }
  end
end
# 1: Oh, MySQL, you're the only one who really understands me.
```

The method `MysqlRes#each` yields you the rows of a result set as arrays. `MysqlRes#each_hash` also gives you one row at a time, but in hash form: you can access a row's fields by name instead of position. `MysqlRes#num_rows` gives you the number of rows matched by a query.

```
with_db do |db|
  db.query('select * from secrets') do |res|
    puts "#{res.num_rows} row(s) matched:"
    res.each_hash do |hash|
      hash.each { |k,v| puts "  #{k} = #{v}" }
    end
  end
end
# 1 row(s) matched:
#  id = 1
#  secret = Oh, MySQL, you're the only one who really understands me.
```

The MySQL interface provides no protection against SQL injection attacks. If you're sending SQL containing the values of possibly tainted variables, you'll need to quote those values yourself.

See Also

- Recipe 13.15, "Preventing SQL Injection Attacks," for more on SQL injection
- "Using the Ruby MySQL Module" (*http://www.kitebird.com/articles/ruby-mysql.html*)
- MySQL bindings (*http://www.tmtm.org/en/mysql/ruby/*)

13.10 Talking Directly to a PostgreSQL Database

Problem

You want to send SQL queries and commands directly to a PostgreSQL database.

Solution

As with the MySQL recipe preceding this one, ask: do you really need to do this? The generic DBI library usually works just fine. As before, the main exception is when you need to make low-level SQL calls from within a Rails application.

There are two APIs for communicating with a PostgreSQL database, and both are available as gems. The `postgres` gem provides a Ruby binding to the C client library, and the `postgres-pr` gem provides a pure Ruby interface.

Here's a Postgres-specific version of the method `with_db`, defined in the chapter intro. It returns a `PGconn` object, which you can use to run queries or get server information. This code assumes you're accessing the database through TCP/IP on port 5432 of your local machine.

```
require 'rubygems'
require 'postgres'
```

```
def with_db
  db = PGconn.connect('localhost', 5432, '', '', 'cookbook',
                      'cookbook_user', 'password')
  begin
    yield db
  ensure
    db.close
  end
end
```

The `PGconn#exec` method runs any SQL statement, whether it's a SELECT query or something else. When it runs a query, the return value is a result-set object (a `PGresult`); otherwise, it's `nil`. Here it is running some SQL commands:

```
with_db do |db|
  begin
    db.exec('drop table secrets')
  rescue PGError
    # Unlike MySQL, Postgres does not have a "drop table unless exists"
    # command. We can simulate it by issuing a "drop table" command and
    # ignoring any error due to the table not existing in the first place.
    # This is essentialy what MySQL's "drop table unless exists" does.
  end

  db.exec('create table secrets( id SERIAL PRIMARY KEY,
                                 secret TEXT )')
  db.exec(%{insert into secrets(secret) values
           ('Oh, Postgres, you\\'re the only one who really understands me.')})
end
```

Here's a query:

```
with_db do |db|
  res = db.query('select * from secrets')
  res.each { |row| puts "#{row[0]}: #{row[1]}" }
end
# 1: Oh, Postgres, you're the only one who really understands me.
```

Discussion

Note the slight differences between the Postgres implementation of SQL and the MySQL implementation. The "drop table if exists" syntax is MySQL-specific. Postgres names the data types differently, and expects string values to be single-quoted.

Like the database connection itself, the result set you get from exec wants to be closed when you're done with it. As we did with query in the MySQL binding, we can alter exec to take an optional code block and do the cleanup for us:

```
class PGconn
  alias :exec_no_block :exec
  def exec(sql)
    res = exec_no_block(sql)
    return res unless block_given?
    begin
```

```
      yield res
    ensure
      res.clear if res
    end
  end
end
```

Now we can write more concise query code, and not have to worry about freeing the
result set:

```
with_db do |db|
  db.exec('select * from secrets') do |res|
    res.each { |row| puts "#{row[0]}: #{row[1]}" }
  end
end
# 1: Oh, Postgres, you're the only one who really understands me.
```

The method PGresult#each yields you the rows of a result set as arrays, and
PGresult#num_tuples gives you the number of rows matched by a query. The Postgres database binding has no equivalent of the MySQL binding's each_hash, but you
can write one pretty easily:

```
class PGresult
  def each_hash
    f = fields
    each do |array|
      hash = {}
      fields.each_with_index do |field, i|
        hash[field] = array[i]
      end
      yield hash
    end
  end
end
```

Here it is in action:

```
with_db do |db|
  db.exec("select * from secrets") do |res|
    puts "#{res.num_tuples} row(s) matched:"
    res.each_hash do |hash|
      hash.each { |k,v| puts " #{k} = #{v}" }
    end
  end
end
# 1 row(s) matched:
#  id = 1
#  secret = Oh, Postgres, you're the only one who really understands me.
```

See Also

- The Postgres reference (*http://www.postgresql.org/docs/manuals/*)
- The reference for the Ruby Postgres binding (*http://ruby.scripting.ca/postgres/*)

- If you can't get the native Postgres binding installed, try the postgres-pr gem; it implements a pure Ruby client to the Postgres server, with more or less the same interface as the native binding
- The PGconn.quote method helps you defend against SQL injection attacks; see Recipe 13.15, "Preventing SQL Injection Attacks," for more

13.11 Using Object Relational Mapping with ActiveRecord

Problem

You want to store data in a database without having to use SQL to access it.

Solution

Use the ActiveRecord library, available as the activerecord gem. It automatically defines Ruby classes that access the contents of database tables.

As an example, let's create two tables in the MySQL database cookbook (see the chapter introduction for more on creating the database itself). The blog_posts table, defined below in SQL, models a simple weblog containing a number of posts. Each blog post can have a number of comments, so we also define a comments table.

```
use cookbook;

DROP TABLE IF EXISTS blog_posts;
CREATE TABLE blog_posts (
  id INT(11) NOT NULL AUTO_INCREMENT,
  title VARCHAR(200),
  content TEXT,
  PRIMARY KEY (id)
) ENGINE=InnoDB;

DROP TABLE IF EXISTS comments;
CREATE TABLE comments (
  id INT(11) NOT NULL AUTO_INCREMENT,
  blog_post_id INT(11),
  author VARCHAR(200),
  content TEXT,
  PRIMARY KEY (id)
) ENGINE=InnoDB;
```

Here are two Ruby classes to represent those tables, and the relationship between them:

```
require 'cookbook_dbconnect'
activerecord_connect                    # See chapter introduction

class BlogPost < ActiveRecord::Base
  has_many :comments
end
```

```
class Comment < ActiveRecord::Base
  belongs_to :blog_post
end
```

Now you can create entries in the tables without writing any SQL:

```
post = BlogPost.create(:title => 'First post',
                       :content => "Here are some pictures of our iguana.")

comment = Comment.create(:blog_post => post, :author => 'Alice',
                         :content => "That's one cute iguana!")

post.comments.create(:author => 'Bob', :content => 'Thank you, Alice!')
```

You can also query the tables, relate blog posts to their comments, and relate comments back to their blog posts:

```
blog_post = BlogPost.find(:first)

puts %{#{blog_post.comments.size} comments for "#{blog_post.title}"}
# 2 comments for "First post"

blog_post.comments.each do |comment|
  puts "Comment author: #{comment.author}"
  puts "Comment: #{comment.content}"
end
# Comment author: Alice
# Comment: That's one cute iguana!
# Comment author: Bob
# Comment: Thank you, Alice!

first_comment = Comment.find(:first)
puts %{The first comment was made on "#{first_comment.blog_post.title}"}
# The first comment was made on "First post"
```

Discussion

ActiveRecord uses naming conventions, database introspection, and metaprogramming to hide much of the work involved in defining a Ruby class that corresponds to a database table. All you have to do is define the classes (BlogPost and Comment, in our example) and the relationships between them (BlogPost has_many :comments, Comment belongs_to :blog_post).

Our tables are designed to fit ActiveRecord's conventions about table and field names. The table names are lowercase, pluralized noun phrases, with underscores separating the words. The table names blog_posts and comments correspond to the Ruby classes BlogPost and Comment.

Also notice that each table has an autoincremented id field named id. This is a convention defined by ActiveRecord. Foreign key references are also named by convention: blog_post_id refers to the id field of the blog_posts table. It's possible to change ActiveRecord's assumptions about naming, but it's simpler to just design your tables to fit the default assumptions.

For "normal" columns, the ones that don't participate in relationships with other tables, you don't need to do anything special. ActiveRecord examines the database tables themselves to find out which columns are available. This is how we were able to use accessor methods for blog_posts.title without explicitly defining them: we defined them in the database, and ActiveRecord picked them up.

Relationships between tables are defined within Ruby code, using decorator methods. Again, naming conventions simplify the work. The call to the has_many decorator in the BlogPost definition creates a one-to-many relationship between blog posts and comments. You can then call BlogPost#comments to get an array full of comments for a particular post. The call to belongs_to in the Comment definition creates the same relationship in reverse.

There are two more decorator methods that describe relationships between tables. One of them is the has_one association, which is rarely used: if there's a one-to-one relationship between the rows in two tables, then you should probably just merge the tables.

The other decorator is has_and_belongs_to_many, which lets you join two different tables with an intermediate join table. This lets you create many-to-many relationships, common in (to take one example) permissioning systems.

For an example of has_and_belongs_to_many, let's make our blog a collaborative effort. We'll add an users table to contain the posts' authors' names, and fix it so that each blog post can have multiple authors. Of course, each author can also contribute to multiple posts, so we've got a many-to-many relationship between users and blog posts.

```
use cookbook;

DROP TABLE IF EXISTS users;
CREATE TABLE users (
  id INT(11) NOT NULL AUTO_INCREMENT,
  name VARCHAR(200),
  PRIMARY KEY (id)
) ENGINE=InnoDB;
```

Because a blog post can have multiple authors, we can't just add an author_id field to the blog_posts table. That would only give us space for a single author per blog post. Instead, we create a join table that maps authors to blog posts.

```
use cookbook;

DROP TABLE IF EXISTS blog_posts_users;
CREATE TABLE blog_posts_users (
  blog_post_id INT(11),
  user_id INT(11)
) ENGINE=InnoDB;
```

Here's another naming convention. ActiveRecord expects you to name a join table with the names of the tables that it joins, concatenated together with underscores. It expects the table names to be in alphabetical order (in this case, the blog_posts table comes before the users table).

Now we can create a User class that mirrors the users table, and modify the BlogPost class to reflect its new relationship with users:

```
class User < ActiveRecord::Base
  has_and_belongs_to_many :blog_posts
end

class BlogPost < ActiveRecord::Base
  has_and_belongs_to_many :authors, :class_name => 'User'
  has_many :comments, :dependent => true
end
```

The has_and_belongs_to_many decorator method defines methods that navigate the join table. We specify the :class_name argument because otherwise ActiveRecord has no idea which ActiveRecord class corresponds to an "authors" relationship. Without :class_name, it would look for a nonexistent Author class.

With the relationships in place, it's easy to find blog posts for an author, and authors for a blog post:

```
# Retroactively make Bob and Carol the collaborative authors of our
# first blog post.
User.create(:name => 'Bob', :blog_posts => [post])
User.create(:name => 'Carol', :blog_posts => [post])

author = User.find(:first)
puts "#{author.name} has made #{author.blog_posts.size} blog post(s)."
# Bob has made 1 blog post(s).

puts %{The blog post "#{post.title}" has #{post.authors.size} author(s).}
# The blog post "First post" has 2 author(s).
```

As with the has_many or belongs_to relationships, the has_and_belongs_to_many relationship gives you a create method that lets you create new items and their relationships to other items:

```
author.blog_posts.create(:title => 'Second post',
                         :content => 'We have some cats as well.')
```

And since the blog_posts method returns an array-like object, you can iterate over it to find all the blog posts to which a given user contributed:

```
author.blog_posts.each do |post|
  puts %{#{author.name}'s blog post "#{post.title}" } +
       "has #{post.comments.size} comments."
end
# Bob's blog post "First post" has 2 comments.
# Bob's blog post "Second post" has 0 comments.
```

If you want to delete an item from the database, you can use the destroy method available to all ActiveRecord objects:

```
BlogPost.find(:first).destroy
```

However, deleting a blog post does not automatically remove all the comments associated with that blog post. You must tell ActiveRecord that comments cannot exist independently of a blog post, like so:

```
class BlogPost < ActiveRecord::Base
  has_many :comments, :dependent => destroy
end
```

Why doesn't ActiveRecord do this automatically? Because it's not always a good idea. Think about authors: unlike comments, authors *can* exist independently of a blog post. Deleting a blog post shouldn't automatically delete all of its authors. ActiveRecord depends on you to make this kind of judgment, using your knowledge about your application.

See Also

- *http://rails.rubyonrails.com/classes/ActiveRecord/Associations/ClassMethods.html*
- Recipe 15.7, "Understanding Pluralization Rules," for more on the connection between the table name and the ActiveRecord class name

13.12 Using Object Relational Mapping with Og

Credit: Mauro Cicio

Problem

You want to store data in a database, without having to use SQL to create or access the database.

Solution

Use the Og (ObjectGraph) library, available as the og gem. Where ActiveRecord has a database-centric approach to object-relational mapping, Og is Ruby-centric. With ActiveRecord, you define the database schema ahead of time and have the library figure out what the Ruby objects should look like. With Og, you define the Ruby objects and let the library take care of creating the database schema.

The only restriction Og imposes on your class definitions is that you must use special versions of the decorator methods for adding attribute accessors. For instance, instead of calling attribute to define accessor methods, you call property.

Here we define a basic schema for a weblog program, like that defined in Recipe 13.11:

```
require 'cookbook_dbconnect'
require 'og'

class BlogPost
  property :title, :content, String
end
```

```
class Comment
  property :author, :content, String
  belongs_to :blog_post, BlogPost
end

# Now that Comment's been defined, add a reference to it in BlogPost.
class BlogPost
  has_many :comments, Comment
end
```

After defining the schema, we call the og_connect method defined in the chapter introduction. Og automatically creates any necessary database tables:

```
og_connect
# Og uses the Mysql store.
# Created table 'ogcomment'.
# Created table 'ogblogpost'.
```

Now we can create a blog post and some comments:

```
post = BlogPost.new
post.title = "First post"
post.content = "Here are some pictures of our iguana."
post.save!

[["Alice", "That's one cute iguana!"],
 ["Bob", "Thank you, Alice!"]].each do |author, content|
  comment = Comment.new
  comment.blog_post = post
  comment.author = author
  comment.content = content
  comment.save!
end
```

As with ActiveRecord, we can query the tables, relate blog posts to their comments, and relate comments back to their blog posts:

```
post = BlogPost.first
puts %{#{post.comments.size} comments for "#{post.title}"}
# 2 comments for "First post"

post.comments.each do |comment|
  puts "Comment author: #{comment.author}"
  puts "Comment: #{comment.content}"
end
# Comment author: Alice
# Comment: That's one cute iguana!
# Comment author: Bob
# Comment: Thank you, Alice!

puts %{The first comment was made on "#{Comment.first.blog_post.title}"}
# The first comment was made on "First post"
```

Discussion

Like the ActiveRecord library, Og implements Martin Fowler's Active Record Pattern. While ActiveRecord does this by making all classes derive from the base class `ActiveRecord::Base`, Og does it by using custom attribute accessors instead of the traditional Ruby accessors. In this example, `Comment` and `BlogPost` are POR (Plain Old Ruby) classes, with accessor methods like `author` and `author=`, but those methods were defined with Og decorators instead of the standard Ruby decorators. This table shows the mapping between the two sets of decorators.

Standard Ruby accessors	Og accessors
attribute	property
attr_accessor	prop_accessor
attr_reader	prop_reader
attr_writer	prop_writer

Each of the Og decorator methods takes a Ruby class as its last argument: `String`, `Integer`, or the like. Og uses this to define the type of the corresponding database row. You can also specify `Object` as a field type, and Og will transparently store YAML representations of arbitrary Ruby objects in the corresponding database field.

ActiveRecord defines all kinds of conventions about how you're supposed to name your database tables and fields. Og doesn't care: it names database tables and fields that correspond to the names you use in your Ruby code.

Just as with ActiveRecord, relationships between Og tables are defined within Ruby code, using decorator methods. The API is almost exactly the same as ActiveRecord's. In the Solution section, we saw how to create a one-to-many relationship between blog posts and comments: by calling `belongs_to` in `Comment` and `has_many` in `BlogPost`. This relationship makes it possible to simply call `BlogPost#comments` and get an array of comments on a post.

Og defines two more decorator methods for describing relationships between tables. One of them is the `has_one` association, which is rarely used: if there's a one-to-one relationship between the rows in two tables, then you should probably just merge the tables.

The other decorator is `many_to_many`, which lets you to join two different tables with an intermediate join table. This lets you create many-to-many relationships, common in (to take one example) permissioning systems.

For an example of `many_to_many`, let's make our blog a collaborative effort. We'll add a `User` class that holds the posts' authors' names, and fix it so that each blog post can have multiple authors. Of course, each author can also contribute to multiple posts, so we've got a many-to-many relationship between users and blog posts. Og needs to know the class definition in order to create the necessary database tables, so the following code snippet should appear before the og_connect invocation in your program:

```
class Person
  property :name, String
  many_to_many :posts, BlogPost
end
```

The many_to_many decorator tells Og to create a table to store the people, and a join table to map authors to their blog posts. It also defines methods that navigate the join table, as we'll see in a moment.

Of course, the many-to-many relationship goes both ways: BlogPost has a many-to-many relationship to Person. So add a many_to_many call to the definition of BlogPost (this, too, must show up before your og_connect call):

```
class BlogPost
  many_to_many :authors, Person
end
```

With these relationships in place, it's easy to find blog posts for an author, and authors for a blog post:

```
og_connect

# Retroactively make Bob and Carol the collaborative authors of our
# first blog post.
['Bob', 'Carol'].each do |name|
  p = Person.new
  p.name = name
  p.save
end
Person.find_by_name('Bob').add_post(post)
Person.find_by_name('Carol').add_post(post)

author = Person.first
puts "#{author.name} has made #{author.posts.size} blog post(s)."
# Bob has made 1 blog post(s).

puts %{The blog post "#{post.title}" has #{post.authors.size} author(s).}
# The blog post "First post" has 2 author(s).
```

To add an anonymous BlogPost on the fly, use the add_post method as follows:

```
author.add_post(BlogPost.create_with({
    :title => 'Second post',
    :content => 'We have some cats as well.'
  } ))
```

Since Person posts returns an array-like object, you can iterate over it to find all the blog posts to which a given user contributed:

```
author.posts.each do |post|
  puts %{#{author.name}'s blog post "#{post.title}" has #{post.comments.size}
comments.}
end
```

```
# Bob's blog post "First post" has 2 comments.
# Bob's blog post "Second post" has 0 comments.
```

If you want to delete an object from the database, you can use the delete method available to all Og database objects:

```
BlogPost.first.delete
```

Deleting a blog post will automatically remove all the comments associated with that blog post. This automatic deletion (i.e., cascade deletion) is not always a good idea. For instance, we *don't* want the authors of a blog post to be deleted when the post itself is deleted! We can avoid the cascade deletion by passing false in as an argument to the delete method:

```
BlogPost.first.delete(false)
```

If you want some associated objects (like comments) to get cascade-deleted, and other objects (like authors) to be left alone, the best strategy is to implement the cascade yourself, in post-delete hooks.

See Also

- The Active Record pattern is described in *Patterns of Enterprise Application Architecture* by Martin Fowler (Addison-Wesley)

13.13 Building Queries Programmatically

Problem

You have to write fragments of SQL to pass parameters into an ActiveRecord query. You'd like to dispense with SQL altogether, and represent the query paramaters as a Ruby data structure.

Solution

Here's a simple solution. The method ActiveRecord::Base.find_by_map defined below picks up where find leaves off. Normally a query is represented by a SQL fragment, passed in as the :conditions argument. Here, the :conditions argument contains a mapping of database field names to the desired values:

```
require 'cookbook_dbconnect'

class ActiveRecord::Base
  def self.find_by_map(id, args={}.freeze)
    sql = []
    values = []
    args[:conditions].each do |field, value|
      sql << "#{field} = ?"
      values << value
    end if args[:conditions]
    args[:conditions] = [sql.join(' AND '), values]
```

```
    find(id, args)
  end
end
```

Here's `find_by_map` in action, using the `BlogPost` class first seen in Recipe 13.11:

```
activerecord_connect

class BlogPost < ActiveRecord::Base
end

BlogPost.create(:title => 'Game Review: Foosball Carnage',
                :content => 'Four stars!')
BlogPost.create(:title => 'Movie Review: Foosball Carnage: The Movie',
                :content => 'Zero stars!')

BlogPost.find_by_map(:first,
                     :conditions => {:title =>
                                      'Game Review: Foosball Carnage' }
                    ).content
# => "Four stars!"
```

Discussion

ActiveRecord saves you from having to write a lot of SQL, but you still have to write out the equivalent of a SQL WHERE clause every time you call `ActiveRecord::Base#find`. The `find_by_map` method lets you define those queries as Ruby hashes.

But `find_by_map` only lets you run one type of query: the kind where you're restricting fields of the database to specific values. What if you want to do a query that matches a field with the LIKE construct, or combine multiple clauses into a single query with AND or OR?

A hash can only represent a very simple SQL query, but the `Criteria` object, below, can represent almost any WHERE clause. The implementation is more complex but the idea is the same. We define a data structure that can represent the WHERE clause of a SQL query, and a way of converting the data structure into a real WHERE clause.

Here's the basic class. A `Criteria` acts like a hash, except it maps a field name to a value *and* a SQL operator. Instead of mapping `:title` to `'Game Review: Foosball Carnage'`, you can map it to `['%Foosball%', 'LIKE']`. Each `Criteria` object can be chained to other objects as part of an AND or OR clause.

```
class Criteria < Hash
  def initialize(values)
    values.each { |k,v| add(k, *v) }
    @or_criteria = nil
    @and_criteria = nil
  end

  :private
  attr_accessor :or_criteria, :and_criteria
```

```
:public
def add(field, value, operation='=')
  self[field] = [value, operation]
end

def or(criteria)
  c = self
  while c.or_criteria != nil
    break if c == criteria
    c = c.or_criteria
  end

  c.or_criteria = criteria
  return self
end

def and(criteria)
  c = self
  while c.and_criteria != nil
    break if c == criteria
    c = c.and_criteria
  end

  c.and_criteria = criteria
  return self
end
```

This method turns a Criteria object, and any other objects to which it's chained, into a SQL string with substitutions, and an array of values to use in the substitutions:

```
class Criteria
  def to_where_clause
    sql = []
    values = []
    each do |field, value|
      if value.respond_to? :to_str
        value, operation = value, '='
      else
        value, operation = value[0..1]
      end
      sql << "#{field} #{operation} ?"
      values << value
    end
    sql = '(' + sql.join(' AND ') + ')'

    if or_criteria
      or_where = or_criteria.to_where_clause
      sql = "(#{sql} OR #{or_where.shift})"
      values += or_where
    end

    if and_criteria
      and_where = and_criteria.to_where_clause
      sql = "(#{sql} AND #{and_where.shift})"
```

```
        values += and_where
    end
    return values.unshift(sql)
  end
end
```

Now it's simple to write a version of find that accepts a Criteria:

```
class ActiveRecord::Base
  def self.find_by_criteria(id, criteria, args={}.freeze)
    args = args.dup
    args[:conditions] = criteria.to_where_clause
    find(id, args)
  end
end
```

Here's Criteria used to express a complex SQL WHERE clause with a little bit of Ruby code. This query searches the blog_post table for reviews of bad movies and good games. The movies and the games must not be about the game of cricket.

```
review = Criteria.new(:title => ['%Review%', 'LIKE'])
bad_movie = Criteria.new(:title => ["%Movie%", 'LIKE'],
                         :content => 'Zero stars!')
good_game = Criteria.new(:title => ['%Game%', 'LIKE'],
                         :content => 'Four stars!')
no_cricket = Criteria.new(:title => ['%Cricket%', 'NOT LIKE'])

review.and(bad_movie.or(good_game)).and(no_cricket)
review.to_where_clause
# => ["((title LIKE ?) AND
#      (((content = ? AND title LIKE ?) OR (content = ? AND title LIKE ?))
#      AND (title NOT LIKE ?)))",
#    "%Review%", "Zero stars!", "%Movie%", "Four stars!", "%Game%",
#    "%Cricket%"]

BlogPost.find_by_criteria(:all, review).each { |post| puts post.title }
# Game Review: Foosball Carnage
# Movie Review: Foosball Carnage: The Movie
```

The technique is a general one. It's easier for a human to construct Ruby data structures than to write valid SQL clauses, so write code to convert the one into the other. You can use this technique wherever any library expects you to write SQL.

For instance, the find method expects SQL fragments representing a query's ORDER BY or GROUP BY clause. You could represent each as an array of fields, and generate the SQL as needed.

```
# Just an idea...
order_by = [[:title, 'ASC']]
```

See Also

- The Criteria class is inspired by the one in the Torque ORM library for Java (*http://db.apache.org/torque/*)

13.14 Validating Data with ActiveRecord

Problem

You want to prevent bad data from getting into your ActiveRecord data objects, whether the source of the data is clueless users or buggy code.

Solution

The simplest way is to use the methods defined by the ActiveRecord::Validations module. Each of these methods (validates_length_of, validates_presence_of, and so on) performs one kind of validation. You can use them to declare restrictions on the data in your object's fields.

Let's add some validation code to the Comment class for the weblog application first seen in Recipe 13.11. Recall that a Comment object has two main fields: the name of the author, and the text of the comment. We'll reject any comment that leaves either field blank. We'll also reject comments that are too long, and comments whose body contains any string from a customizable list of profane words.

```
require 'cookbook_dbconnect'
activerecord_connect

class Comment < ActiveRecord::Base
  @@profanity = %w{trot krip}
  @@no_profanity_re = Regexp.new('^(?!.*(' + @@profanity.join('|') + '))')

  validates_presence_of %w{author}
  validates_length_of :content, :in => 1..200
  validates_format_of :content, :with => @@no_profanity_re,
                      :message => 'contains profanity'
end
```

Comment objects that don't fit these criteria won't be saved to the database.

```
comment = Comment.create
comment.errors.on 'author'                  # => "can't be blank"
comment.errors['content']
# => "is too short (minimum is 1 characters)"
comment.save                                # => false

comment = Comment.create(:content => 'x' * 1000)
comment.errors['content']
# => "is too long (maximum is 200 characters)"

comment = Comment.create(:author => 'Alice',
  :content => "About what I'd expect from a trotting krip such as yourself!")
comment.errors.count                        # => 1
comment.errors.each_full { |msg| puts msg }
# Content contains profanity

comment = Comment.create(:author => 'Alice', :content => 'I disagree!')
comment.save                                # => true
```

Discussion

Every ActiveRecord record has an associated `ActiveRecord::Errors` object, which starts out empty. Before the record is saved to the database, all the predefined restrictions for that class of object are checked. Every problem encountered while applying the restrictions adds an entry to the `Errors` object.

If, at the end of this trial by ordeal, the `Errors` object is still empty, ActiveRecord presumes the data is valid, and saves the object to the database.

ActiveRecord's `Validations` module provides many methods that implement validation rules. Apart from the examples given above, the `validates_numericality_of` method requires an integer value (or a floating-point value if you specify `:integer =>` `false`). The `requires_inclusion_of` method will reject any value not found in a predefined list of acceptable values.

If the predefined validation rules aren't enough for you, you can also write a custom validation rule using `validate_each`. For instance, you might validate URL fields by fetching the URLs and making sure they're valid.

The method `Errors#each_full` prepends each error message with the corresponding field name. This is why the actual error messages look like "is empty" and "contains profanity": so each_full will yield "Author is empty" and "Content contains profanity".

ActiveRecord assumes you named your fields so that these messages will be readable. You can customize the messages by passing in keyword arguments like `:message`, but then you'll need to access the messages with `Errors#each` instead of `Errors#each_` `full`. Here's an alternate implementation of the `Comment` validation rules that customizes the messages:

```
require 'cookbook_dbconnect'
activerecord_connect

class Comment < ActiveRecord::Base
  @@profanity = %w{trot krip}
  @@no_profanity_re = Regexp.new('^(?!.*(' + @@profanity.join('|') + '))')

  validates_presence_of %w{author}, :message => 'Please enter your name.'
  validates_length_of :content, :in => 1..200,
              :too_short => 'Please enter a comment.',
                    :too_long => 'Comments are limited to 200 characters.'
  validates_format_of :content, :with => @@no_profanity_re,
                    :message => 'Try to express yourself without profanity.'
end
```

The declarative validation style should be flexible enough for you, but you can do custom validation by defining a `validate` method. Your implementation is responsible for checking the current state of an object, and populating the `Errors` object with any appropriate error messages.

Sometimes new objects have different validation rules from existing objects. You can selectively apply a validation rule by passing it the :on option. Pass in :on => :create, and the validation rule will only be triggered the first time an object is saved to the database. Pass in :on => :update, and the validation rule will be triggered every time *except* the first. You can also define the custom validation methods validate_on_add and validate_on_update as well as just plain validate.

See Also

- Recipe 1.19, "Validating an Email Address"
- Recipe 8.6, "Validating and Modifying Attribute Values"
- The built-in validation methods (*http://rubyonrails.org/api/classes/ActiveRecord/ Validations/ClassMethods.html*)
- Some sample validate implementations (*http://rubyonrails.org/api/classes/ ActiveRecord/Validations.html*)
- The Errors class defines a few helper methods for doing validation in a validate implementation (*http://rubyonrails.org/api/classes/ActiveRecord/Errors.html*)
- Og defines some declarative validation methods, similar to ActiveRecord's (*http:// www.nitrohq.com/view/Validation/Og*)

13.15 Preventing SQL Injection Attacks

Problem

You want to harden your code against SQL injection attacks, whether in DBI or ActiveRecord code.

Solution

With both ActiveRecord and DBI applications, you should create your SQL with question marks where variable interpolations should go. Pass in the variables along with the SQL to DatabaseHandle#execute, and the database will make sure the values are properly quoted.

Let's work against a simple database table tracking people's names:

```
use cookbook;

DROP TABLE IF EXISTS names;
CREATE TABLE names (
  first VARCHAR(200),
  last VARCHAR(200)
) ENGINE=InnoDB;

INSERT INTO names values ('Leonard', 'Richardson'),
                         ('Lucas', 'Carlson'),
                         ('Michael', 'Loukides');
```

Here's a simple script that searches against that table. It's been hardened against SQL injection attacks with three techniques:

```ruby
#!/usr/bin/ruby
# no_sql_injection.rb

require 'cookbook_dbconnect'
activerecord_connect
class Name < ActiveRecord::Base; end

print 'Enter a last name to search for: '
search_for = readline.chomp

# Technique 1: use ActiveRecord question marks
conditions = ["last = ?", search_for]

Name.find(:all, :conditions => conditions).each do |r|
  puts %{Matched "#{r.first} #{r.last} with ActiveRecord question marks"}
end

# Technique 2: use ActiveRecord named variables
conditions = ["last = :last", {:last => search_for}]

Name.find(:all, :conditions => conditions).each do |r|
  puts %{Matched "#{r.first} #{r.last}" with ActiveRecord named variables}
end

# Technique 3: use DBI question marks
with_db do |db|
  sql = 'SELECT first, last FROM names WHERE last = ?'

  db.execute(sql, [search_for]).fetch_hash do |r|
    puts %{Matched "#{r['first']} #{r['last']}" with DBI question marks}
  end
end

puts "Done"
```

Here's how this script looks in use:

```
$ ruby no_sql_injection.rb
Enter a last name to search for: Richardson
Matched "Leonard Richardson" with ActiveRecord question marks
Matched "Leonard Richardson" with ActiveRecord named variables
Matched "Leonard Richardson" with DBI question marks
Done

# See the Discussion if you're not sure how this attack is supposed to work.
$ ruby no_sql_injection.rb
Enter a last name to search for: " or 1=1
Done
```

Discussion

SQL is a programming lanuage, and running SQL is like calling eval on a string of Ruby code. Unless you have complete control over the entire SQL string and all the variables interpolated into it, you need to be very careful. Just one mistake can leave you open to information leakage or database corruption.

Here's a naive version of `sql_injection.rb` that's vulnerable to an injection attack. If you habitually write code like this, you may be in trouble:

```ruby
#!/usr/bin/ruby
# sql_injection.rb
require 'cookbook_dbconnect'

print "Enter a last name to search for: "
search_for = readline.chomp
query = %{select first, last from names where last="#{search_for}"}
puts query if $DEBUG
with_db do |db|
  db.execute(query).fetch_hash do |r|
    puts %{Matched "#{r['first']} #{r['last']}"}
  end
end
```

Looks fine, right?

```
$ ruby -d sql_injection.rb
Enter a last name to search for: Richardson
select first_name, last_name from people where last_name="Richardson"
Matched "Leonard Richardson"
```

Not necessarily. Whatever I type is simply being stuck into a SQL statement. What if I typed as my "query" part of a SQL WHERE clause? One that, when combined with the original WHERE clause, matched anything and everything?

```
$ ruby -d sql_injection.rb
Enter a last name to search for: " or 1=1
select first_name, last_name from people where last_name="" or 1=1
Matched "Leonard Richardson"
Matched "Lucas Carlson"
Matched "Michael Loukides"
```

I can see every name in the table.

This is just one example. SQL injection attacks can also alter or delete data from a database.

The correct version of this program, the one described in the Solution, quotes my attempt at a SQL injection attack. My attack is executed as a normal query: the program looks for people (or robots, I guess) whose last name is the string " or 1=1. Quoting the data makes the application do what you want it to do every time, no matter what kind of weird data a user can come up with.

DBI will not run two SQL commands in a single do or execute call, so certain types of SQL injection attacks are impossible with DBI. You can hijack a SELECT statement to make it select something else, but unlike with some other systems, you can't make a SELECT also do an UPDATE or DELETE. An attacker can't use SQL injection to drop database tables unless your application already runs a DROP TABLE command somewhere.

You don't usually write full-blown SQL statements with ActiveRecord, but you do write conditions: snippets of SQL that get turned into to the WHERE clauses of SELECT or UPDATE statements. Whenever you write SQL, you must take these precautions.

See Also

- "Securing your Rails application" in the Ruby on Rails manual (*http://manuals.rubyonrails.com/read/chapter/43*)
- The RDoc for the ActiveRecord::Base class
- "SQL Injection Attacks by Example" is a readable introduction to this topic (*http://www.unixwiz.net/techtips/sql-injection.html*)
- "Using the Ruby DBI Module" has a section on quoting (*http://www.kitebird.com/articles/ruby-dbi.html#TOC_8*)

13.16 Using Transactions in ActiveRecord

Problem

You want to perform database operations as a group: if one of the operations fails, it should be as though none of them had ever happened.

Solution

Include active_record/transactions, and you'll give each ActiveRecord class a transaction method. This method starts a database transaction, runs a code block, then commits the transaction. If the code block throws an exception, the database transaction is rolled back.

Here's some simple initialization code to give ActiveRecord access to the database tables for the weblog system first seen in Recipe 13.11:

```
require 'cookbook_dbconnect'
activerecord_connect # See chapter introduction

class User < ActiveRecord::Base
  has_and_belongs_to_many :blog_posts
end

class BlogPost < ActiveRecord::Base
  has_and_belongs_to_many :authors, :class_name => 'User'
end
```

The create_from_new_author method below creates a new entry in the users table, then associates it with a new entry in the blog_posts table. But there's a 50% chance that an exception will be thrown right after the new author is created. If that happens, the author creation is rolled back: in effect, it never happened.

```
require 'active_record/transactions'

class BlogPost
  def BlogPost.create_from_new_author(author_name, title, content)
    transaction do
      author = User.create(:name => author_name)
      raise 'Random failure!' if rand(2) == 0
      create(:authors => [author], :title => title, :content => content)
    end
  end
end
```

Since the whole operation is enclosed within a transaction block, an exception won't leave the database in a state where the author has been created but the blog entry hasn't:

```
BlogPost.create_from_new_author('Carol', 'The End Is Near',
                                'A few more facts of doom...')
# => #<BlogPost:0xb78b7c7c ... >

# The method succeeded; Carol's in the database:
User.find(:first, :conditions=>"name='Carol'")
# => #<User:0xb7888ae4 @attributes={"name"=>"Carol", ... }>

# Let's do another one...
BlogPost.create_from_new_author('David', 'The End: A Rebuttal',
                                'The end is actually quite far away...')
# RuntimeError: Random failure!

# The method failed; David's not in the database:
User.find(:first, :conditions=>"name='David'")
# => nil
```

Discussion

You should use database transactions whenever one database operation puts the database into an inconsistent state, and a second operation brings the database back into consistency. All kinds of things can go wrong between the first and second operation. The database server might crash or your application might throw an exception. The Ruby interpreter might decide to stop running your thread for an arbitrarily long time, giving other threads a chance to marvel at the inconsistent state of the database. An inconsistent database can cause problems that are very difficult to debug and fix.

ActiveRecord's transactions piggyback on top of database transactions, so they'll only work if your database supports transactions. Most databases do these days;

chances are you won't have trouble unless you're using a MySQL database and not using InnoDB tables. However, most of the open source databases don't support *nested* transactions, so you're limited to one transaction at a time with a given database connection.

In addition to a code block, the transaction method can take a number of ActiveRecord objects. These are the objects that participate in the transaction. If the transaction fails, then not only will the database be restored to its previous state, so will the member variables of the objects.

This is useful if you're defining a method that modifies ActiveRecord objects themselves, not just the database representations of those objects. For instance, a shopping cart object might keep a running total that's consulted by the application, but not stored in the database.

See Also

- *http://wiki.rubyonrails.com/rails/pages/HowToUseTransactions*
- *http://rubyonrails.org/api/classes/ActiveRecord/Transactions/ClassMethods.html*

13.17 Adding Hooks to Table Events

Problem

You want to run some code whenever a database row is added, updated, or deleted. For instance, you might want to send out email whenever a new blog post is created.

Solution

For Og, use the aspect-oriented features of Glue::Aspect. You can use its before and after methods to register code blocks that run before or after any Og method. The methods you're most likely to wrap are og_insert, og_update, and og_delete.

In the following code, I take the BlogPost class first defined in Recipe 13.12, and give its og_insert method an aspect that sends out email:

```
require 'cookbook_dbconnect'
require 'og'
require 'glue/aspects'

class BlogPost
  property :title, :content, String
  after :on => :og_insert do |post|
    puts %{Sending email notification of new post "#{post.title}"}
    # Actually send the email here...
  end
end

og_connect
```

```
post = BlogPost.new
post.title = 'Robots are taking over'
post.content = 'Think about it! When was the last time you saw another human?'
post.save!
# Sending email notification of new post "Robots are taking over"
```

This technique works with ActiveRecord as well (since aspect-oriented programming is a generic technique), but ActiveRecord defines two different approaches: callbacks and the ActiveRecord::Observer class.

Any ActiveRecord::Base subclass can define a number of callback methods: before_find, after_save, and so on. These methods run before or after the corresponding ActiveRecord methods. Here's an callback-based ActiveRecord implementation of the Og example, running against the blog_post table first defined in Recipe 13.11. *If you ran the previous example in a session, quit it now and start a new session.*

```
require 'cookbook_dbconnect'
activerecord_connect

class BlogPost < ActiveRecord::Base
  def after_create
    puts %{Sending email notification of new blog post "#{title}"}
    # Actually send the email here...
  end
end

post = BlogPost.create(:title => 'Robots: Gentle Yet Misunderstood',
                       :content => 'Popular misconceptions about robERROR 40')
# Sending email notification of new blog post "Robots: Gentle Yet Misunderstood
```

Discussion

ActiveRecord's callback interface is simple, but it's got a big disadvantage compared to Og's. You can attach multiple aspects to a single method, but you can only define a callback method once.

This makes little difference when you only want the callback method to do one thing. But suppose that in addition to sending email whenever a blog post is created, you also want to notify people of new posts through an instant messenger client, and to regenerate static syndication feeds to reflect the new post.

If you used a callback, you'd have to lump all of that code together in after_create. With aspects, each piece of functionality can go into a separate aspect. It's easy to add more, or to disable a single one without affecting the others. Aspects keep auxilliary code from cluttering up your core data classes.

Fortunately, ActiveRecord provides a strategy other than the callback methods. You can define a subclass of ActiveRecord::Observer, which implements any of the callback methods, and use the observe decorator to attach it to the classes you want to watch. Multiple Observers can watch a single class, so you can split up the work.

Here's a third example of the email notification code. *Again, start a new session if you're following this recipe in* irb.

```
require 'cookbook_dbconnect'
activerecord_connect

class BlogPost < ActiveRecord::Base
end

class MailObserver < ActiveRecord::Observer
  observe BlogPost
  def after_create(post)
    puts %{Sending email notification of new blog post "#{post.title}"}
    # Actually send the email here.
  end
end
ActiveRecord::Base.observers = MailObserver

post = BlogPost.new(:title => "ERROR 40",
                    :content => "ERROR ERROR ERROR ERROR ERROR")
post.save
# Sending email notification of new blog post "ERROR 40"
```

Note the call to ActiveRecord::Base.observers=. Calling this method starts the observer running. You can call ActiveRecord::Base.observers= whenever you need to add one or more Observers. Despite the implication of the method name, calling it twice won't overwrite one set of observers with another.

In a Rails application, observers are traditionally started by putting code like the following in the environment.rb file:

```
# environment.rb
config.active_record.observers = MailObserver
```

When working with ActiveRecord, if you want to attach an Observer to a specific ActiveRecord class, you can name it after that class: for instance, BlogPostObserver will automatically observe the BlogPost class. Obviously, this only works for a single Observer.

See Also

- Recipe 10.15
- ActiveRecord callbacks documentation (*http://rubyonrails.org/api/classes/Active-Record/Callbacks.html*)
- ActiveRecord Observer documentation (*http://rails.rubyonrails.com/classes/Active-Record/Observer.html*)
- Og used to define a class called Og::Observer that worked like ActiveRecord's ActiveRecord::Observer, but it's been deprecated in favor of aspects; some of the documentation for Og::Observer is still online, so be careful not to get confused

13.18 Adding Taggability with a Database Mixin

Problem

Without writing a lot of code, you want to make one of your database tables "taggable"—make it possible to add short strings describing a particular item in the table.

Solution

Og comes complete with a tagging mixin. Just call is Taggable on every class you want to be taggable. Og will create all the necessary tables.

Here's the BlogPost class from Recipe 13.12, only this time it's Taggable. Og automatically creates a Tag class and the necessary database tables:

```
require 'cookbook_dbconnect'
require 'og'
require 'glue/taggable'

class BlogPost
  is Taggable
  property :title, :content, String
end
og_connect

# Now we can play around with tags.
post = BlogPost.new
post.title = 'Some more facts about video games'
post.tag(['editorial', 'games'])

BlogPost.find_with_tags('games').each { |puts| puts post.title }
# Some more facts about video games

Tag.find_by_name('editorial').blog_posts.each { |post| puts post.title }
# Some more facts about video games
```

To get this feature in ActiveRecord, you'll need to install the acts_as_taggable gem, and you must create the database tables yourself. Here are the tables necessary to add tags to the ActiveRecord BlogPost class (first described in Recipe 13.11): a generic tags table and a join table connecting it to blog_posts.

```
DROP TABLE IF EXISTS tags;
CREATE TABLE tags (
  id INT(11) NOT NULL AUTO_INCREMENT,
  name VARCHAR(32),
  PRIMARY KEY (id)
) ENGINE=InnoDB;

DROP TABLE IF EXISTS tags_blog_posts;
CREATE TABLE tags_blog_posts (
    tag_id INT(11),
```

```
    blog_post_id INT(11)
) ENGINE=InnoDB;
```

Note that the join table violates the normal ActiveRecord naming rule. It's called tags_blog_posts, even though alphabetical ordering of its component tables would make it blog_posts_tags. ActiveRecord does this so all of your application's tags_ join tables will show up together in a sorted list. If you want to call the table blog_ posts_tags instead, you'll need to pass the name as the :join_table parameter when you call the acts_as_taggable decorator below.

Here's the ActiveRecord code that makes BlogPost taggable. *If you ran the previous example, run this one in a new* irb *session so that you can define a new* BlogPost *class.*

```
require 'cookbook_dbconnect'
require 'taggable'
activerecord_connect

class Tag < ActiveRecord::Base
end

class BlogPost < ActiveRecord::Base
  acts_as_taggable
end

# Now we can play around with tags.
post = BlogPost.create(:title => 'Some more facts about inflation.')
post.tag(['editorial', 'economics'])

BlogPost.find_tagged_with(:any=>'editorial').each { |post| puts post.title }
# Some more facts about inflation.
```

Discussion

A mixin class like Enumerable is an easy way to add a lot of functionality to an existing class without writing much code. Database mixins work the same way: you can add new objects and relationships to your data model without having to write a lot of database code. Of course, you'll still need to decide how to incorporate tags into your user interface.

The Og and ActiveRecord tagging mixins work the same way, although the Og mixin hides the details. In addition to your original database table (the one you want to tag), you need a table that contains tags, and a join table connecting the tags to the tagged. Whether you use Og or ActiveRecord, the database schema looks something like Figure 13-1.

Figure 13-1. BlogPosts are associated with Tags through a join table

The tagging mixin saves you from having to write code for managing the tag table, and the original table's relationship with it.

But there are two ways to tag something, and we've only covered one. You add tags to BlogPost if you want one set of tags for each blog post, probably set by the author of the post. The tags act as canonical categories. What if you want to create a tag system where everyone has their own set of tags for blog posts? Instead of a single system imposed by the authors, every user gets to define a categorization system that makes sense to them.

When you do this, the application doesn't tag a blog post itself. It tags *one person's relationship* to a blog post. The schema looks something like Figure 13-2.

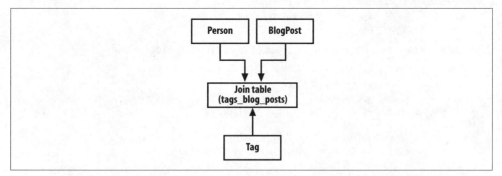

Figure 13-2. When tags are per-user, the join table associates BlogPosts, Tags, and People

Let's implement per-user tagging in ActiveRecord. Instead of making the tags_blog_posts table connect a blog post directly to a tag, we'll have it connect a tag, a blog post, *and* a person.

```
DROP TABLE IF EXISTS tags_blog_posts;
CREATE TABLE tags_blog_posts (
    tag_id INT(11),
    blog_post_id INT(11),
    created_by_id INT(11)
) ENGINE=InnoDB;
```

Here's the Ruby code. First, some setup we've seen before:

```
require 'cookbook_dbconnect'
require 'taggable'
activerecord_connect

class Tag < ActiveRecord::Base
end

class Person < ActiveRecord::Base
end
```

When each blog post had one set of tags, we called acts_as_taggable with no arguments, and the BlogPost class was associated directly with the Tag class. This time, we tell acts_as_taggable that BlogPost objects are associated with Tag through the TagBlogPost class:

```
# ActiveRecord will automatically define the TagBlogPost class when
# we reference it.
class BlogPost < ActiveRecord::Base
  acts_as_taggable :join_class_name => 'TagBlogPost'
end
```

Now we tell TagBlogPost that it's associated with the Person class: every TagBlogPost represents one person's opinions about a single blog post:

```
# Specify that a TagBlogPost is associated with a specific user.
class TagBlogPost
  belongs_to :created_by, :class_name => 'Person',
             :foreign_key => 'created_by_id'
end
```

Now each Person can have their own set of tags on each BlogPost:

```
post = BlogPost.create(:title => 'My visit to the steel mill.')
alice = Person.create(:name=>"Alice")
post.tag(['travelogue', 'metal', 'interesting'],
         :attributes => { :created_by => alice })

alices_interests = BlogPost.find_tagged_with(:all => 'interesting',
      :condition => "tags_people.created_by_id = #{alice.id}")
alices_interests.each { |article| puts article.title }
# My visit to the steel mill.
```

Og and ActiveRecord each come with several common mixins. For instance, you can use a mixin to model parent-child relationships between tables (Og is Hierarchical, ActiveRecord acts_as_tree and acts_as_nested_set), or to treat the rows of a table as an ordered lists (Og is Orderable, ActiveRecord acts_as_list). These can save you a lot of time.

See Also

- The built-in ActiveRecord mixins are all in the ActiveRecord::Acts module; see the generated documentation at *http://rubyonrails.org/api/*
- The taggable reference for ActiveRecord (*http://taggable.rubyforge.org/*)

Internet Services

Network programming is hard. The C socket library is the standard way of writing Internet clients and servers. It's like the file API descibed in Chapter 6, with its special flags and meager abstraction, only much more complicated. It's a shame because networked applications are the coolest kind of application. Only computer nerds like you and me care about XML or the best way to sort a list, but everyone uses Internet applications.

Fortunately, network programming is easy. Ruby provides bindings to the C socket library (in socket), but you'll probably never need to use them. Existing Ruby libraries (some in the standard distribution) can speak every popular high-level Internet protocol.

The most popular Internet service is, of course, the Web, and Ruby's most popular Internet library (or any kind of library, actually) is the Rails framework. We've devoted the entire next chapter to Rails (Chapter 15) so that we can cover other technologies here.

Apart from Rails, most of the interesting stuff you can do with Ruby happens on the client end. We start with a set of recipes for requesting web pages (Recipes 14.1, 14.2, and 14.3), which are brought together at the end of the chapter with Recipe 14.20. Combine these recipes with one from Chapter 11 (probably Recipe 11.5), and you can make your own spider or web browser.

Then we present Ruby clients for the most popular Internet protocols. Ruby can do just about everything you do online: send and receive email, perform nameserver queries, even transfer files with FTP, SCP, or BitTorrent. With the Ruby interfaces, you can write custom clients for these protocols, or integrate them into larger programs.

It's less likely that you'll be writing your own server in Ruby. A server only exists to service clients, so there's not much you can do but faithfully implement the appropriate protocol. If you do write a server, it'll probably be for a custom protocol, one for which no other server exists.

Ruby provides two basic servers that you can use as a starting point. The gserver library described in Recipe 14.14 provides a generic framework for almost any kind of Internet server. Here you do have to do some socket programming, but only the easy parts. gserver takes care of all the socket-specific details, and you can just treat the sockets like read-write IO objects. You can use the techniques described in Chapter 6 to communicate with your clients.

The other basic server is WEBrick, a simple but powerful web server that's used as the basis for Rails and the Ruby SOAP server. If you've built a protocol on top of HTTP, WEBrick makes a good starting point for a server. Recipe 14.19 shows how to use WEBrick to hook pieces of Ruby code up to the Web.

Apart from Rails, web services are the major network-related topic not covered in this chapter. As with Rails, this is because they have their own chapter: Chapter 16.

14.1 Grabbing the Contents of a Web Page

Problem

You want to display or process a specific web page.

Solution

The simplest solution is to use the open-uri library. It lets you open a web page as though it were a file. This code fetches the oreilly.com homepage and prints out the first part of it:

```
require 'open-uri'
puts open('http://www.oreilly.com/').read(200)
# <!DOCTYPE html PUBLIC "-//W3C//DTD XHTML 1.0 Transitional//EN"
#         "http://www.w3.org/TR/xhtml1/DTD/xhtml1-transitional.dtd">
# <html xmlns="http://www.w3.org/1999/xhtml" xml:lang="en" lang="en">
```

For more complex applications, you'll need to use the net/http library. Use Net::HTTP.get_response to make an HTTP request and get the response as a Net::HTTPResponse object containing the response code, headers, and body.

```
require 'net/http'
response = Net::HTTP.get_response('www.oreilly.com', '/about/')
response.code                                # => "200"
response.body.size                           # => 21835
response['Content-type']
# => "text/html; charset=ISO-8859-1"
puts response.body[0,200]
# <!DOCTYPE html PUBLIC "-//W3C//DTD XHTML 1.0 Transitional//EN"
#     "http://www.w3.org/TR/xhtml1/DTD/xhtml1-transitional.dtd">
#
#
# <html>
# <head>
# <meta http-equiv="content-type" content="text/html; c
```

Rather than passing in the hostname, port, and path as separate arguments, it's usually easier to create URI objects from URL strings and pass those into the Net::HTTP methods.

```
require 'uri'
Net::HTTP.get(URI.parse("http://www.oreilly.com"))
Net::HTTP.get_response(URI.parse("http://www.oreilly.com/about/"))
```

Discussion

If you just want the text of the page, use get. If you also want the response code or the values of the HTTP response headers, use get_reponse.

The get_response method returns some HTTPResponse subclass of Net:HTTPResponse, which contains all information about an HTTP response. There's one subclass for every response code defined in the HTTP standard; for instance, HTTPOK for the 200 response code, HTTPMovedPermanently for the 301 response code, and HTTPNotFound for the 404 response code. There's also an HTTPUnknown subclass for any response codes not defined in HTTP.

The only difference between these subclasses is the class name and the code member. You can check the response code of an HTTP response by comparing specific classes with is_a?, or by checking the result of HTTPResponse#code, which returns a String:

```
puts "Success!" if response.is_a? Net::HTTPOK
# Success!

puts case response.code[0] # Check the first byte of the response code.
  when ?1 then "Status code indicates an HTTP informational response."
  when ?2 then "Status code indicates success."
  when ?3 then "Status code indicates redirection."
  when ?4 then "Status code indicates client error."
  when ?5 then "Status code indicates server error."
  else "Non-standard status code."
end
# Status code indicates success.
```

You can get the value of an HTTP response header by treating HTTPResponse as a hash, passing the header name into HTTPResponse#[]. The only difference from a real Hash is that the names of the headers are case-insensitive. Like a hash, HTTPResponse supports the iteration methods #each, #each_key, and #each_value:

```
response['Server']
# => "Apache/1.3.34 (Unix) PHP/4.3.11 mod_perl/1.29"
response['SERVER']
# => "Apache/1.3.34 (Unix) PHP/4.3.11 mod_perl/1.29"

response.each_key { |key| puts key }
# x-cache
# p3p
# content-type
# date
```

```
# server
# transfer-encoding
```

If you do a request by calling NET::HTTP.get_response with no code block, Ruby will read the body of the web page into a string, which you can fetch with the HTTPResponse::body method. If you like, you can process the body as you read it, one segment at a time, by passing a code block to HTTPResponse::read_body:

```
Net::HTTP.get_response('www.oreilly.com', '/about/') do |response|
  response.read_body do |segment|
    puts "Received segment of #{segment.size} byte(s)!"
  end
end
# Received segment of 614 byte(s)!
# Received segment of 1024 byte(s)!
# Received segment of 848 byte(s)!
# Received segment of 1024 byte(s)!
# ...
```

Note that you can only call read_body once per request. Also, there are no guarantees that a segment won't end in the middle of an HTML tag name or some other inconvenient place, so this is best for applications where you're not handing the web page as structured data: for instance, when you're simply piping it to some other source.

See Also

- Recipe 14.2, "Making an HTTPS Web Request"
- Recipe 14.3, "Customizing HTTP Request Headers"
- Recipe 14.20, "A Real-World HTTP Client," covers a lot of edge cases you'll need to handle if you want to write a general-purpose client
- Most HTML you'll find on the web is invalid, so to parse it you'll need the tricks described in Recipe 11.5, "Parsing Invalid Markup"

14.2   Making an HTTPS Web Request

Problem

You want to connect to an HTTPS web site, one whose traffic is encrypted using SSL.

Solution

You need the OpenSSL extension to Ruby. You'll know if it's installed if you can require the net/https library without getting a LoadError.

```
require 'net/https'                          # => true
```

You can't make HTTPS requests with the convenience methods described in Recipe 14.1, but you can use the Net::HTTP::Get and Net::HTTP::Post class described in

Recipe 14.3. To make an HTTPS request, just instantiate a Net::HTTP object and set its use_ssl member to true.

In this example, I try to download a page from a web server that only accepts HTTPS connections. Instead of listening on port 80 like a normal web server, this server listens on port 443 and expects an encrypted request. I can only connect with a Net::HTTP instance that has the use_ssl flag set.

```
require 'net/http'
uri = URI.parse("https://www.donotcall.gov/")

request = Net::HTTP.new(uri.host, uri.port)
response = request.get("/")
# Errno::ECONNRESET: Connection reset by peer

require 'net/https'
request.use_ssl = true
request.verify_mode = OpenSSL::SSL::VERIFY_NONE
response = request.get("/")
# => #<Net::HTTPOK 200 OK readbody=true>
response.body.size                      # => 6537
```

Discussion

The default Ruby installation for Windows includes the OpenSSL extension, but if you're on a Unix system, you might have to install it yourself. On Debian GNU/ Linux, the package name is libopenssl-ruby[Ruby version]: for instance, libopenssl-ruby1.8. You might need to download the extension from the Ruby PKI homepage (see below), and compile and install it with Make.

Setting verify_mode to OpenSSL:SSL::VERIFY_NONE suppresses some warnings, but the warnings are kind of serious: they mean that OpenSSL won't verify the server's certificate or proof of identity. Your conversation with the server will be confidential, but you won't be able to definitively authenticate the server: it might be an imposter.

You can have OpenSSL verify server certificates if you keep a few trusted certificates on your computer. You don't need a certificate for every server you might possibly access. You just need certificates for a few "certificate authorities:" the organizations that actually sign most other certificates. Since web browsers need these certificates too, you probably already have a bunch of them installed, although maybe not in a format that Ruby can use (if you don't have them, see below).

On Debian GNU/Linux, the ca-certificates package installs a set of trusted server certificates into the directory /etc/ssl/certs. I can set my request object's ca_path to that directory, and set its verify_mode to OpenSSL::SSL::VERIFY_PEER. Now OpenSSL can verify that I'm actually talking to the web server at donotcall.gov, and not an imposter.

```
request = Net::HTTP.new(uri.host, uri.port)
request.use_ssl = true
```

```
request.ca_path = "/etc/ssl/certs/"
request.verify_mode = OpenSSL::SSL::VERIFY_PEER
response = request.get("/")
# => #<Net::HTTPOK 200 OK readbody=true>
```

The SSL certificate for www.donotcall.gov (*http://www.donotcall.gov*) happens to be signed by Network Solutions. I already have Network Solutions' certificate installed on my computer, so I can verify the signature. If I trust Network Solutions, I can trust donotcall.gov.

See Also

- Recipe 14.1, "Grabbing the Contents of a Web Page"
- HTTPS is just one more thing a robust web client needs to support; Recipe 14.20, "A Real-World HTTP Client," shows how to integrate it into a general framework
- The Ruby OpenSSL project homepage (*http://www.nongnu.org/rubypki/*)
- The (unofficial) Mozilla Certificate FAQ provides a good introduction to SSL certificates (*http://www.hecker.org/mozilla/ca-certificate-faq/background-info*)
- If you don't have any certs on your system or they're not in a format you can give to Ruby, you can download a bundle of all the certs recognized by the Mozilla web browser; instead of setting ca_path to a directory, you'll set ca_file to the location of the file you download (*http://curl.haxx.se/docs/caextract.html*)
- You can create your own server certificates with the QuickCert program; your certificates won't be recognized by any certificate authority, but if you control the clients as well as the server, you can manually install the server certificate on every client (*http://segment7.net/projects/ruby/QuickCert/*)

14.3 Customizing HTTP Request Headers

Problem

When you make an HTTP request, you want to specify custom HTTP headers like "User-Agent" or "Accept-Language".

Solution

Pass in a Hash of header values to Net::HTTP#get or Net::HTTP#post:

```
require 'net/http'
require 'uri'

#A simple wrapper method that accepts either strings or URI objects
#and performs an HTTP GET.
module Net
  class HTTP
    def HTTP.get_with_headers(uri, headers=nil)
      uri = URI.parse(uri) if uri.respond_to? :to_str
```

```
        start(uri.host, uri.port) do |http|
          return http.get(uri.path, headers)
        end
      end
    end
end

#Let's get a web page in German.
res = Net::HTTP.get_with_headers('http://www.google.com/',
                                 {'Accept-Language' => 'de'})

#Check a bit of the body to make sure it's really in German.
s = res.body.size
res.body[s-200..s-140]
# => "ngebote</a> - <a href=/intl/de/about.html>Alles \374ber Google</"
```

Discussion

Usually you can retrieve the web pages you want without specifying any custom HTTP headers. As you start performing more complicated interactions with web servers, you'll find yourself customizing the headers more.

For instance, if you write a web spider or client, you'll want it to send a "User-Agent" header on every request, identifying itself to the web server. Unlike the HTTP client libraries for other programming languages, the net/http library doesn't send a "User-Agent" header by default; it's your reponsibility to send one.

```
Net::HTTP.get_with_headers(url, {'User-Agent' => 'Ruby Web Browser v1.0'})
```

You can often save bandwidth (at the expense of computer time) by sending an "Accept-Encoding" header, requesting that a web server compress data before sending it to you. Gzip compression is the most common way a server compresses HTTP response data; you can reverse it with Ruby's zlib library:

```
uncompressed = Net::HTTP.get_with_headers('http://www.cnn.com/')
uncompressed.body.size
# => 65150

gzipped = Net::HTTP.get_with_headers('http://www.cnn.com/',
                                     {'Accept-Encoding' => 'gzip'})
gzipped['Content-Encoding']
# => "gzip"
gzipped.body.size
# => 14600

require 'zlib'
require 'stringio'
body_io = StringIO.new(gzipped.body)
unzipped_body = Zlib::GzipReader.new(body_io).read()
unzipped_body.size
# => 65150
```

If you want to build up a HTTP request with multiple values for the same HTTP header, you can construct a `Net::HTTP::Get` (or `Net::HTTP::Post`) object and call the `add_field` method multiple times. The example in the Solution used the "Accept-Language" header to request a document in a specific language. The following code fetches the same URL, but its "Accept-Language" header indicates that it will accept a document written in any of four different dialects:

```
uri = URI.parse('http://www.google.com/')

request = Net::HTTP::Get.new(uri.path)
['en_us', 'en', 'en_gb', 'ja'].each do |language|
  request.add_field('Accept-Language', language)
end
request['Accept-Language']
# => "en_us, en, en_gb, ja"

Net::HTTP.start(uri.host, uri.port) do |http|
  response = http.request(request)
  # ... process the HTTPResponse object here
end
```

See Also

- Recipe 12.10, "Compressing and Archiving Files with Gzip and Tar," for more about the zlib library
- Recipe 14.1, "Grabbing the Contents of a Web Page"
- Recipe 14.20, "A Real-World HTTP Client," covers a lot of edge cases you'll need to handle if you want to write a general-purpose client
- REST web services often use the value of the "Accept" header to provide multiple representations of the same resource; Joe Gregorio's article "Should you use Content Negotiation in your Web Services?" explains why it's a better idea to provide a different URL for each representation (*http://bitworking.org/news/ WebServicesAndContentNegotiation*)
- Recipe 16.1 for more on REST web services

14.4 Performing DNS Queries

Problem

You want to find the IP address corresponding to a domain name, or see whether a domain provides a certain service (such as an email server).

Solution

Use the `Resolv::DNS` class in the standard resolv library to perform DNS lookups. The most commonly used method is `DNS#each_address`, which iterates over the IP addresses assigned to a domain name.

```
require 'resolv'
Resolv::DNS.new.each_address("oreilly.com") { |addr| puts addr }
# 208.201.239.36
# 208.201.239.37
```

Discussion

If you need to check the existence of a particular type of DNS record (such as a MX record for a mail server), use `DNS#getresources` or the iterator `DNS#each_resource`. Both methods take a domain name and a class denoting a type of DNS record. They perform a DNS lookup and, for each matching DNS record, return an instance of the given class.

These are the three most common classes:

`DNS::Resource::IN::A`
Indicates a DNS record pointing to an IP address for the domain.

`DNS::RESOURCE::IN::NS`
Indicates a DNS record pointing to a DNS nameserver.

`DNS::Resource::IN::MX`
Indicates a DNS record pointing to a mail server.

This code finds the mail servers and name servers responsible for oreilly.com:

```
dns = Resolv::DNS.new
domain = "oreilly.com"
dns.each_resource(domain, Resolv::DNS::Resource::IN::MX) do |mail_server|
  puts mail_server.exchange
end
# smtp1.oreilly.com
# smtp2.oreilly.com

dns.each_resource(domain, Resolv::DNS::Resource::IN::NS) do |nameserver|
  puts nameserver.name
end
# a.auth-ns.sonic.net
# b.auth-ns.sonic.net
# c.auth-ns.sonic.net
# ns.oreilly.com
```

If your application needs to do a lot of DNS lookups, you can greatly speed things up by creating a separate thread for each lookup. Most of the time spent doing a DNS lookup is spent connecting to the network, so doing all the lookups in parallel can save a lot of time. If you do this, you should include the resolv-replace library along with resolv, to make sure your DNS lookups are thread-safe.

Here's some code that sees which one-letter *.com* domains (*a.com*, *b.com*, etc.) are mapped to IP addresses. It runs all 26 DNS queries at once, in 26 threads, and summarizes the results.

```ruby
require 'resolv-replace'
def multiple_lookup(*names)
  dns = Resolv::DNS.new
  results = {}
  threads = []
  names.each do |name|
    threads << Thread.new(name) do |name|
      begin
        dns.each_address(name) { |a| (results[name] ||= []) << a }
      rescue Resolv::ResolvError
        results[name] = nil
      end
    end
  end
  threads.each { |t| t.join }
  return results
end

domains = ("a".."z").collect { |l| l + '.com' }
multiple_lookup(*domains).each do |name, addresses|
  if addresses
    puts "#{name}: #{addresses.size} address#{addresses.size == 1 ? "" : "es"}"
  end
end
# x.com: 4 addresses
# z.com: 1 address
# q.com: 1 address
```

See Also

- Chapter 20 uses a DNS lookup of an MX record to check whether the domain of an email address is valid
- A DNS lookup is the classic example of a high-latency operation; much of Chapter 20 deals with ways of making high-latency operations run more quickly: see especially Recipe 20.3, "Doing Two Things at Once with Threads," and Recipe 20.6, "Running a Code Block on Many Objects Simultaneously"

14.5 Sending Mail

Problem

You want to send an email message, either an autogenerated one or one entered in by an end user.

Solution

First you need to turn the parts of the email message into a single string, representing the whole message complete with headers and/or attachments. You can construct the string manually or use a number of libraries, including RubyMail, TMail, and ActionMailer. Since ActionMailer is one of the dependencies of Rails, I'll use it throughout this recipe. ActionMailer uses TMail under the covers, and it's provided by the actionmailer gem.

Here, I use ActionMailer to construct a simple, single-part email message:

```
require 'rubygems'
require 'action_mailer'

class SimpleMailer < ActionMailer::Base
  def simple_message(recipient)
    from 'leonardr@example.org'
    recipients recipient
    subject 'A single-part message for you'
    body 'This message has a plain text body.'
  end
end
```

ActionMailer then makes two new methods available for generating this kind of email message: SimpleMailer.create_simple_message, which returns the email message as a data structure, and SimpleMailer.deliver_simple_message, which actually sends the message.

```
puts SimpleMailer.create_simple_message('lucas@example.com')
# From: leonardr@example.org
# To: lucas@example.com
# Subject: A single-part message for you
# Content-Type: text/plain; charset=utf-8
#
# This message has a plain text body.
```

To deliver the message, call deliver_simple_message instead of create_simple_message. First, though, you'll need to tell ActionMailer about your SMTP server. If you're sending mail from example.org and you've got an SMTP server on the local machine, you might send a message this way:

```
ActionMailer::Base.server_settings = { :address => 'localhost',
                                        :port => 25, # 25 is the default
                                        :domain => 'example.org' }

SimpleMailer.deliver_simple_message('lucas@example.com')
```

If you're using your ISP's SMTP server, you'll probably need to send authentication information so the server knows you're not a spammer. Your ActionMailer setup will probably look like this:

```
ActionMailer::Base.server_settings = { :address => 'smtp.example.org',
                                        :port => 25,
                                        :domain => 'example.org',
```

```
                             :user_name => 'leonardr@example.org',
                             :password => 'my_password',
                             :authentication => :login }

    SimpleMailer.deliver_simple_message('lucas@example.com')
```

Discussion

Unless you're writing a general-purpose mail client, you probably won't be letting
your users compose emails from scratch. More likely, you'll define a template for
every *type* of email your application might send, and fill it in with custom data every
time you send a message.*

This is what ActionMailer is designed for. The `simple_message` method defined above
is actually a hook method that makes ActionMailer respond to two other methods:
`create_simple_message` and `deliver_simple_message`. The hook method defines the
headers and body of a message template, the `create_` method instantiates the template with specific values, and the `deliver_` method actually delivers the email. You
never call `simple_message` directly.

Within your hook method, you can set most of the standard email headers by calling a method of the same name (`subject`, `cc`, and so on). You can also set custom
headers by modifying the `@headers` instance variable:

```
    class SimpleMailer
      def headerful_message
        @headers['A custom header'] = 'Its value'
        body 'Body'
      end
    end

    puts SimpleMailer.create_headerful_message
    # Content-Type: text/plain; charset=utf-8
    # A custom header: Its value
    #
    # Body
```

You can create a multipart message with attachments by passing the MIME type of
the attachment into the `attachment` method.

Here's a method that creates a message containing a dump of the files in a directory
(perhaps a bunch of logfiles). It uses the `mime-types` gem to determine the probable
MIME type of a file, based on its filename:

```
    require 'mime/types'

    class SimpleMailer
      def directory_dump_message(recipient, directory)
```

---

* You can use ActionMailer even if you are writing a general-purpose mail client (just write a single hook
  method called `custom_messge` that takes a whole lot of arguments), but you might prefer to drop down a level
  and use TMail or RubyMail.

```
      from 'directory-dump@example.org'
      recipients recipient
      subject "Dump of #{directory}"
      body %{Here are the files currently in "#{directory}":}

    Dir.new(directory).each do |f|
      path = File.join(directory, f)
      if File.file? path
        mime_type = MIME::Types.of(f).first
        content_type = (mime_type ? mime_type.content_type :
                         'application/binary')
        attachment(content_type) do |a|
          a.body = File.read(path)
          a.filename = f
          a.transfer_encoding = 'quoted-printable' if content_type =~ /^text\//
        end
      end
    end
  end
end

SimpleMailer.create_directory_dump_message('lucas@example.com',
                                           'email_test')
```

Here it is in action:

```
Dir.mkdir('email_test')
open('email_test/image.jpg', 'wb') { |f| f << "\377\330\377\340\000\020JFIF" }
open('email_test/text.txt', 'w') { |f| f << "Here's some text." }

puts SimpleMailer.create_directory_dump_message('lucas@example.com',
                                                'email_test')
# From: directory-dump@example.org
# To: lucas@example.com
# Subject: Dump of email_test
# Mime-Version: 1.0
# Content-Type: multipart/mixed; boundary=mimepart_443d73ecc651_3ae1..fdbeb1ba4328
#
#
# --mimepart_443d73ecc651_3ae1..fdbeb1ba4328
# Content-Type: text/plain; charset=utf-8
# Content-Disposition: inline
#
# Here are the files currently in "email_test":
# --mimepart_443d73ecc651_3ae1..fdbeb1ba4328
# Content-Type: image/jpeg; name=image.jpg
# Content-Transfer-Encoding: Base64
# Content-Disposition: attachment; filename=image.jpg
#
# /9j/4AAQSkZJRg==
#
# --mimepart_443d73ecc651_3ae1..fdbeb1ba4328
# Content-Type: text/plain; name=text.txt
# Content-Transfer-Encoding: Quoted-printable
```

```
# Content-Disposition: attachment; filename=text.txt
#
# Here's some text.=
#
# --mimepart_443d73ecc651_3ae1..fdbeb1ba4328--
```

If you're a minimalist, you can use the net/smtp library to send email without install-ing any gems. There's nothing in the Ruby standard library to help you with creating the email string, though; you'll have to build it manually. Once you've got the string, you can send it as an email message with code like this:

```
require 'net/smtp'
Net::SMTP.start('smtp.example.org', 25, 'example.org',
                'leonardr@example.org', 'my_password', :login) do |smtp|
  smtp.send_message(message_string, from_address, to_address)
end
```

Whether you use Net::SMTP or ActionMailer to deliver your mail, the possible SMTP authentication schemes are represented with symbols (:login, :plain, and :cram_md5). Any given SMTP server may support any or all of these schemes. Try them one at a time, or ask your system administrator or ISP which one to use.

See Also

- Recipe 15.19, "Sending Mail with Rails," if you're using Rails
- The ActionMailer documentation (*http://www.lickey.com/rubymail/rubymail/doc/*)
- The standard for email messages (RFC 2822)
- More ActionMailer examples (*http://am.rubyonrails.com/classes/ActionMailer/Base.html*)

14.6   Reading Mail with IMAP

Credit: John Wells

Problem

You want to connect to an IMAP server in order to read and manipulate the mes-sages stored there.

Solution

The net/imap.rb package, written by Shugo Maeda, is part of Ruby's standard library, and provides a very capable base on which to build an IMAP-oriented email application. In the following sections, I'll walk you through various ways of using this API to interact with an IMAP server.

For this recipe, let's assume you have access to an IMAP server running at *mail. myhost.com* on the standard IMAP port 143. Your username is, conveniently, "username", and your password is "password".

To make the initial connection to the server, it's as simple as:

```
require 'net/imap'

conn = Net::IMAP.new('mail.myhost.com', 143)
conn.login('username', 'password')
```

Assuming no error messages were received, you now have a connection to the IMAP server. The `Net::IMAP` object puts all the capabilities of IMAP at your fingertips.

Before doing anything, though, you must tell the server which mailbox you're interested in working with. On most IMAP servers, your default mailbox is called "INBOX". You can change mailboxes with `Net::IMAP#examine`:

```
conn.examine('INBOX')
# Use Net::IMAP#select instead for read-only access
```

A search provides a good example of how a `Net::IMAP` object lets you interact with the server. To search for all messages in the selected mailbox from a particular address, you can use this code:

```
conn.search(['FROM', 'jabba@huttfoundation.org']).each do |sequence|
    fetch_result = conn.fetch(sequence, 'ENVELOPE')
    envelope = fetch_result[0].attr['ENVELOPE']
    printf("%s - From: %s - To: %s - Subject: %s\n", envelope.date,
        envelope.from[0].name, envelope.to[0].name, envelope.subject)
end
# Wed Feb 08 14:07:21 EST 2006 - From: The Hutt Foundation - To: You - Subject: Bwah!
# Wed Feb 08 11:21:19 EST 2006 - From: The Hutt Foundation - To: You - Subject: Go to
# do wa IMAP
```

Discussion

The details of the IMAP protocol are a bit esoteric, and to really understand it you'll need to read the RFC. That said, the code in the solution shouldn't be too hard to understand: it uses the IMAP `SEARCH` command to find all messages with the `FROM` field set to "*jabba@huttfoundation.org*".

The call to `Net::IMAP#search` returns an array of message sequence IDs: a key to a message within the IMAP server. We iterate over these keys and send each one back to the server, using IMAP's `FETCH` command to ask for the envelope (the headers) of each message. Note that the Ruby method for an IMAP instruction often shares the instruction's name, only in lowercase to keep with the Ruby way.

The `ENVELOPE` parameter we pass to `Net::IMAP#fetch` tells the server to give us summary information about the message by parsing the RFC2822 message headers. This way we don't have to download the entire body of the message just to look at the headers.

You'll also notice that Net::IMAP#fetch returns an array, and that we access its first element to get the information we're after. This is because Net::IMAP#fetch lets you to pass an array of sequence numbers instead of just one. It returns an array of Net::IMAP::FetchData objects with an element corresponding to each number passed in. You get an array even if you only pass in one sequence number.

There are also other cool things you can do.

Check for new mail

You can see how many new messages have arrived by examining the responses sent by the server when you select a mailbox. These are stored in a hash: the responses member of your connection object. Per the IMAP spec, the value of RECENT is the number of new messages unseen by any client. EXISTS tells how many total messages are in the box. Once a client connects and opens the mailbox, the RECENT response will be unset, so you'll only see a new message count the first time you run the command:

```
puts "#{conn.responses["RECENT"]} new messages, #{conn.responses["EXISTS"]} total"
# 10 new messages, 1022 total
```

Retrieve a UID for a particular message

The sequence number is part of a relative sequential numbering of all the messages in the current mailbox. Sequence numbers get reassigned upon message deletion and other operations, so they're not reliable over the long term. The UID is more like a primary key for the message: it is assigned when a message arrives and is guaranteed not to be reassigned or reused for the life of the mailbox. This makes it a more reliable way of making sure you've got the right message:

```
uids = conn.search(["FROM", "jabba@huttfoundation.org"]).collect do |sequence|
  fetch_result = conn.fetch(sequence, "UID")
  puts "UID: #{fetch_result[0].attr["UID"]}"
end
# UID: 203
# UID: 206
```

Why are message UIDs useful? Consider the following scenario. We've just retrieved message information for messages between January 2000 and January 2006. While viewing the output, we saw a message that looked interesting, and noted the UID was 203.

To view the message body, we use code like this:

```
puts conn.uid_fetch(203, 'BODY[TEXT]')[0].attr['BODY[TEXT]']
```

Reading headers made easy

In our first example in this recipe, we accessed message headers through use of the IMAP ENVELOPE parameter. Because displaying envelope information is such a common task, I prefer to take advantage of Ruby's open classes and add this functionality directly to `Net::IMAP`:

```ruby
class Net::IMAP
  def get_msg_info(msg_sequence_num)
    # code we used above
    fetch_result = fetch(msg_sequence_num, '(UID ENVELOPE)')
    envelope = fetch_result[0].attr['ENVELOPE']
    uid = fetch_result[0].attr['UID']
    info = {'UID'     => uid,
            'Date'    => envelope.date,
            'From'    => envelope.from[0].name,
            'To'      => envelope.to[0].name,
            'Subject' => envelope.subject}
  end
end
```

Now, we can make use of this code wherever it's convenient. For example, in this search for all messages received in a certain date range:

```ruby
conn.search(['BEFORE', '01-Jan-2006',
             'SINCE', '01-Jan-2000']).each do |sequence|
    conn.get_msg_info(sequence).each {|key, val| puts "#{key}: #{val}" }
end
```

Forwarding mail to a cell phone

As a final, somewhat practical example, let's say you're waiting for a very important email from someone at huttfoundation.org. Let's also assume you have an SMTP server at the same host as your IMAP server, running on port 25.

You'd like to have a program that could check your email every five minutes. If a new message from anyone at *huttfoundation.org* is found, you'd like to forward that message to your cell phone via SMS. The email address of your cell phone is *5555555555@mycellphoneprovider.com*.

```ruby
#!/usr/bin/ruby -w
# forward_important_messages.rb

require 'net/imap'
require 'net/smtp'

address = 'huttfoundation.org'
from = 'myhomeemail@my.mailhost.com'
to = '5555555555@mycellphoneprovider.com'
smtp_server = 'my.mailhost.com'
imap_server = 'my.mailhost.com'
username = 'username'
password = 'password'

while true do
  conn = imap = Net::IMAP.new(imap_server, 143)
  conn.login(username, password)
```

```
conn.select('INBOX')
uids = conn.search(['FROM', address, 'UNSEEN']).each do |sequence|
    fetch_result = conn.fetch(sequence, 'BODY[TEXT]')
  text = fetch_result[0].attr['BODY[TEXT]']
      count = 1
  while(text.size > 0) do
      # SMS messages limited to 160 characters
    msg = text.slice!(0, 159)
    full_msg = "From: #{from}\n"
    full_msg += "To: #{to}\n"
    full_msg += "Subject: Found message from #{address} (#{count})!\n"
    full_msg += "Date: #{Time.now}\n"
    full_msg += msg + "\n"
    Net::SMTP.start(smtp_server, 25) do |smtp|
        smtp.send_message full_msg, from, to
    end
    count += 1
  end
  # set Seen flag, so our search won't find the message again
  conn.store(sequence, '+FLAGS', [:Seen])
end
conn.disconnect
# Sleep for 5 minutes.
sleep (60*60*5)
end
```

This recipe should give you a hint of the power you have when you access IMAP mailboxes. Please note that to really understand IMAP, you need to read the IMAP RFC, as well as RFC2822, which describes the Internet Message Format. Multipart messages and MIME types are beyond of the scope of this recipe, but are both something you'll deal with regularly when accessing mailboxes.

See Also

- ri Net::IMAP
- The IMAP RFC (RFC3501) (*http://www.faqs.org/rfcs/rfc3501.html*)
- The Internet Message Format RFC (RFC2822) (*http://www.faqs.org/rfcs/rfc2822. html*)
- Recipe 3.12, "Running a Code Block Periodically"
- Recipe 14.5, "Sending Mail"

14.7 Reading Mail with POP3

Credit: John Wells

Problem

You want to connect to an POP server in order to read and download the messages stored there.

Solution

The net/pop.rb package, written by Minero Aoki, is part of Ruby's standard library, and provides a foundation on which to build a POP (Post Office Protocol)-oriented email application. As with the previous recipe on IMAP, we'll walk through some common ways of accessing a mail server with the POP API.

For this recipe, we assume you have access to a POP3 server running at mail.myhost. com on the standard POP3 port 110. Just as in the previous IMAP example, your username is "username", and password is (yep) "password".

To make the initial connection to the server, it's as simple as:

```
require 'net/pop'

conn = Net::POP3.new('mail.myhost.com')
conn.start('username', 'password')
```

If you receive no errors, you've got an open session to your POP3 server, and can use the conn object to communicate with the server.

The following code acts like a typical POP3 client: having connected to the server, it downloads all the new messages, and then deletes them from the server. The deletion is commented out so you don't lose mail accidentally while testing this code:

```
require 'net/pop'

conn = Net::POP3.new('mail.myhost.com')
conn.start('username', 'password')

conn.mails.each do |msg|
    File.open(msg.uidl, 'w') { |f| f.write msg.pop }
    # msg.delete
end

conn.finish
```

Discussion

POP3 is a much simpler protocol than IMAP, and arguably a less powerful one. It doesn't support the concept of folders, so there's no need to start off by selecting a particular folder (like we did in the IMAP recipe). Once you start a session, you have immediate access to all messages currently retained on the server.

IMAP stores your folders and your messages on the server itself. This way you can access the same messages and the same folders from different clients on different machines. For example, you might go to work and access an IMAP folder with Mozilla Thunderbird, then go home and access the same folder with a web-based mail client.

With POP3, there are no server-side folders. You're supposed to archive your messages on the client side. If you use a POP3 client to download messages at work, when you get home you won't be able to access those messages. They're on your work computer, not on the POP3 server.

IMAP assigns a unique, unchanging ID to each message in the mailbox. By contrast, when you start a POP3 session, POP3 gives each message a "sequence number" reflecting its position in the mailbox at that time. The next time you connect to the POP3 server, the same message may have a different sequence number, as new, incoming messages can affect the sequencing. This is why POP3 clients typically download messages immediately and delete them from the server.

If we want to go outside this basic pattern, and leave the messages on the server, how can we keep track of messages from one connection to another? POP3 does provide a unique string ID for each message: a *Unique Identification Listing,* or UIDL. You can use a UIDL (which persists across POP3 sessions) to get a sequence number (which doesn't) and retrieve a message across separate connections.

This code finds the IDs of email messages from a particular source:

```
conn = Net::POP3.new('mail.myhost.com')
conn.start('username', 'password')
ids = conn.mails.collect {|msg| msg.uidl if msg.pop.match('jabba')}
conn.finish
# => ["UID2-1141260595", "UID3-1141260595"]
```

Now we have unique identifiers for each of our matching messages. Given these, we can start a new POP3 session and use these UIDLs to retrieve each message individually:

```
conn2 = Net::POP3.new('mail.myhost.com')
conn.start('username', 'password')

conn.each_mail {|msg| puts msg.pop if msg.uidl=='UID3-1141260595'}

conn.finish
# Return-Path: <jabba@huttfoundation.org>
# X-Original-To: username@my.mailhost.com
# Delivered-To: username@localhost
# ...
```

Here we call the method Net::POP3#each_mail to iterate over all the messages in the mailbox. Each message is passed into the code block as a Net::POPMail message. We look at each message's UIDL and, when we find the message we want, we call Net::POPMail#pop to print it out.

Forwarding mail to a cell phone

Let's revisit our example from the IMAP recipe. You're waiting for a very important email, and you want to have it forwarded to your cell phone as soon as it comes in. You're able to send mail through a SMTP server hosted on port 25 of the same machine as your POP3 server. The email address of your cell phone is *5555555555@mycellphoneprovider.com.*

This program checks your POP3 server for new email every five minutes. If a new message from anyone at huttfoundation.org is found, it forwards the message to your cell phone via SMS.

```ruby
#!/usr/bin/env ruby
# forward_important_messages.rb

require 'net/pop'
require 'net/smtp'

$address = 'huttfoundation.org'
$from = 'myhomeemail@my.mailhost.com'
$to = '5555555555@mycellphoneprovider.com'
smtp_server = 'my.mailhost.com'
pop_server = 'my.mailhost.com'
username = 'username'
password = 'password'

$found = Hash.new

def send_msg (text)
  count = 1
  while(text.size > 0) do
    # SMS messages limited to 160 characters
    msg = text.slice!(0, 159)
    full_msg = "From: #{$from}\n"
    full_msg += "To: #{$to}\n"
    full_msg += "Subject: Found message from #{$address} (#{count})!\n"
    full_msg += "Date: #{Time.now}\n"
    full_msg += msg + "\n"
    Net::SMTP.start(smtp_server, 25) do |smtp|
      smtp.send_message full_msg, $from, $to
    end
    count += 1
  end
end

loop do
  conn = Net::POP3.new(pop_server)
  conn.start('username', 'password')

  uidls = conn.mails.collect do |msg|
    msg.uidl if msg.pop.match(/#{$address}/)
  end

  uidls.each do |one_id|
    if ! $found.has_key? one_id
      $found[one_id] = true
      conn.each_mail do |msg|
        send_msg(msg.uidl) if msg.uidl==one_id
      end
    end
  end
```

```
  conn.finish
  # Sleep for 5 minutes.
  sleep (60*60*5)
end
```

See Also

- Recipe 14.6, "Reading Mail with IMAP"
- RFC1939 describes the POP3 protocol

14.8 Being an FTP Client

Problem

You want to automatically connect to an FTP server, and upload or download files.

Solution

Use the Net::FTP class. It provides a filesystem-like interface to an FTP server. In this example, I log anonymously into a popular FTP site, browse one of its directories, and download two of its files:

```
require 'net/ftp'
ftp = Net::FTP.open('ftp.ibiblio.org') do |ftp|
  ftp.login
  ftp.chdir('pub/linux/')
  ftp.list('*Linux*') { |file| puts file }
  puts

  puts 'Saving a text file to disk while processing it.'
  ftp.gettextfile('How-do-I-get-Linux') { |line| puts "! #{line}" }
  puts "Saved #{File.size 'How-do-I-get-Linux'} bytes."
  puts

  puts 'Saving a binary file to disk.'
  ftp.getbinaryfile('INDEX.whole.gz')
 puts "Saved #{File.size 'INDEX.whole.gz'} bytes."
end
# -rw-r--r--   1 (?)       users      16979001 Jan  1 11:31 00-find.Linux.gz
# -rw-rw-r--   1 (?)       admin            73 Mar  9 2001 How-do-I-get-Linux

# Saving a text file to disk while processing it.
# !
# !   Browse to http://metalab.unc.edu/linux/HOWTO/Installation-HOWTO.html
# !
# Saved 73 bytes.

# Saving a binary file to disk.
# Saved 213507 bytes.
```

Discussion

Once the preferred way of storing and serving files through the Internet, FTP is being largely superceded by SCP for copying files, the web for distributing files, and Bit-Torrent for distributing very large files. There are still many anonymous FTP servers, though, and many web hosting companies still expect you to upload your web pages through FTP.

The `login` method logs in to the server. Calling it without arguments logs you in anonymously, which traditionally limits you to download privileges. Calling it with a username and password logs you in to the server:

```
ftp.login('leonardr', 'mypass')
```

The methods `chdir` and `list` let you navigate the FTP server's directory structure. They work more or less like the Unix cd and ls commands (in fact, `list` is aliased to `ls` and `dir`).

There are also two "get" methods and two "put" methods. The "get" methods are `getbinaryfile` and `gettextfile`. They retrieve the named file from the FTP server and write it to disk. The `gettextfile` method converts between platform-specific newline formats as it downloads. This way you can download a text file from a Unix server to your Windows machine, and have the Unix newlines automatically converted into Windows newlines. On the other hand, if you use `gettextfile` on a binary file, you'll probably corrupt the file as you download it.

You can specify a local name for the file and a block to process the data as it comes in. A block passed into `gettextfile` will be called for each line of a downloaded file; a block passed into `getbinaryfile` will be passed for each downloaded chunk.

A file you download with one of the "get" methods will be written to disk even if you pass in a block to process it. If you want to process a file *without* writing it to disk, just define some methods like these:

```
class Net::FTP
  def processtextfile(remotefile)
    retrlines('RETR ' + remotefile) { |line| yield line }
  end

  def processbinaryfile(remotefile, blocksize=DEFAULT_BLOCKSIZE)
    retrbinary('RETR ' + remotefile, blocksize) { |data| yield data }
  end
end
```

The two "put" methods are (you guessed it) `puttextfile` and `putbinaryfile`. They are the exact opposites of their get counterparts: they take the path to a local file, and write it to a file on the FTP server. They, too, can take a code block that processes each line or chunk of the file as it's read. This example automatically uploads the *index.html* file to my ISP's hosted web space.

```
require 'net/ftp'
Net::FTP.open('myisp.example.com') do |ftp|
  ftp.login('leonardr', 'mypass')
  ftp.chdir('public_html')
  ftp.puttextfile('index.html')
end
```

In general, you can't use the "put" methods if you're logged in as an anonymous user. Some FTP servers do have special *incoming/* directories to which anonymous users can upload their submissions.

See Also

• ri Net::FTP

14.9   Being a Telnet Client

Problem

You want to connect to a telnet service or use telnet to get low-level access to some other kind of server.

Solution

Use the Net::Telnet module in the Ruby standard library.

The following code uses a Telnet object to simulate an HTTP client. It sends a raw HTTP request to the web server at *http://www.oreilly.com*. Every chunk of data received from the web server is passed into a code block, and its size is added to a tally. Eventually the web server stops sending data, and the telnet session times out.

```
require 'net/telnet'

webserver = Net::Telnet::new('Host' => 'www.oreilly.com',
                             'Port' => 80,
                             'Telnetmode' => false)
size = 0
webserver.cmd("GET / HTTP/1.1\nHost: www.oreilly.com\n") do |c|
  size += c.size
  puts "Read #{c.size} bytes; total #{size}"
end
# Read 1431 bytes; total 1431
# Read 1434 bytes; total 2865
# Read 1441 bytes; total 4306
# Read 1436 bytes; total 5742
# ...
# Read 1430 bytes; total 39901
# Read 2856 bytes; total 42757
# /usr/lib/ruby/1.8/net/telnet.rb:551:in `waitfor':
#   timed out while waiting for more data (Timeout::Error)
```

Discussion

Telnet is a lightweight protocol devised for connecting to a generic service running on another computer. For a long time, the most commonly exposed service was a Unix shell: you would "telnet in" to a machine on the network, log in, and run shell commands on the other machine as though it were local.

Because telnet is an insecure protocol, it's very rare now to use it for remote login. Everyone uses SSH for that instead (see the next recipe). Telnet is still useful for two things:

1. As a diagnostic tool (as seen in the Solution). Telnet is very close to being a generic TCP protocol. If you know, say, HTTP, you can connect to an HTTP server with telnet, send it a raw HTTP request, and view the raw HTTP response.

2. As a client to text-based services other than remote shells: mainly old-school entertainments like BBSes and MUDs.

Telnet objects implement a simple loop between you and some TCP server:

1. You send a string to the server.

2. You read data from the server a chunk at a time and process each chunk with a code block. The continues until a chunk of data contains text that matches a regular expression known as a *prompt*.

3. In response to the prompt, you send another string to the server. The loop restarts.

In this example, I script a Telnet object to log me in to a telnet-accessible BBS. I wait for the BBS to send me strings that match certain prompts ("What is your name?" and "password:"), and I send back strings of my own in response to the prompts.

```
require 'net/telnet'

bbs = Net::Telnet::new('Host' => 'bbs.example.com')

puts bbs.waitfor(/What is your name\?/)
# The Retro Telnet BBS
# Where it's been 1986 since 1993.
# Dr. Phineas Goodbody, proprietor
#
# What is your name? (NEW for new user)

bbs.cmd('String'=>'leonardr', 'Match'=>/password:/) { |c| puts c }
# Hello, leonardr. Please enter your password:

bbs.cmd('my_password') { |c| puts c }
# Welcome to the Retro Telnet BBS, leonardr.
# Choose from the menu below:
# ...
```

The problem with this code is the "prompt" concept was designed for use with remote shells. A Unix shell shows you a prompt after every command you run. The prompt always ends in a dollar sign or some other character: it's easy for telnet to pick out a shell prompt in the data stream. But no one uses telnet for remote shells anymore, so this is not very useful. The BBS software defines a different prompt for every interaction: one prompt for the name and a different one for the password. The web page grabber in the Solution doesn't define a prompt at all, because there's no such thing in HTTP. For the type of problem we still solve with telnet, prompts are a pain.

What's the alternative? Instead of having cmd wait for a prompt, you can just have it wait for the server to go silent. Here's an implementation of the web page grabber from the Solution, which stops reading from the server if it ever goes more than a tenth of a second without receiving any data:

```
require 'net/telnet'

webserver = Net::Telnet::new('Host' => 'www.oreilly.com',
                             'Port' => 80,
                             'Waittime' => 0.1,
                             'Prompt' => /.*/,
                             'Telnetmode' => false)
size = 0
webserver.cmd("GET / HTTP/1.1\nHost: www.oreilly.com\n") do |c|
  size += c.size
  puts "Read #{c.size} bytes; total #{size}"
end
```

Here, the prompt matches any string at all. The end of every data chunk is potentially the "prompt" for the next command! But Telnet only acts on this if the server sends no more data in the next tenth of a second.

When you have Telnet communicate with a server this way, you never know for sure if you really got all the data. It's possible that the server just got really slow all of a sudden. If that happens, you may lose data or it may end up read by your next call to cmd. The best you can do is try to make your Waittime large enough so that this doesn't happen.

In this example, I use Telnet to script a bit of a text adventure game that's been made available over the net. This example uses the same trick (a Prompt that matches anything) as the previous one, but I've bumped up the Waittime because this server is slower than the oreilly.com web server:

```
require 'net/telnet'
adventure = Net::Telnet::new('Host' => 'games.example.com',
                             'Port' => 23266,
                             'Waittime' => 2.0,
                             'Prompt' => /.*/)

commands = ['no', 'enter building', 'get lamp'] # And so on...
commands.each do |command|
  adventure.cmd(command) { |c| print c }
end
```

```
# Welcome to Adventure!!  Would you like instructions?
# no
#
# You are standing at the end of a road before a small brick building.
# Around you is a forest.  A small stream flows out of the building and
# down a gully.
# enter building
#
# You are inside a building, a well house for a large spring.
# There are some keys on the ground here.
# There is a shiny brass lamp nearby.
# There is food here.
# There is a bottle of water here.
#
# get lamp
# OK
```

See Also

- The Ruby documentation for the net/telnet standard library
- Recipe 14.10, "Being an SSH Client"
- The telnet text adventure is based on the version of Colossal Cave hosted at forkexec.com; the site has lots of other games you can play via telnet (*http://games.forkexec.com/*)

14.10 Being an SSH Client

Problem

You want to securely send data or commands back and forth between your computer, and another computer on which you have a shell account.

Solution

Use the Net::SSH module, which implements the SSH2 protocol. It's found in the net-ssh gem, although some operating systems package it themselves.[*] It lets you implement Ruby applications that work like the familiar ssh and scp.

You can start an SSH session by passing a hostname to Net::SSH::start, along with your shell username and password on that host. If you have an SSH public/private key pair set up between your computer and the remote host, you can omit the username and password:

```
require 'rubygems'
require 'net/ssh'
```

---

[*] For instance, it's available on Debian GNU/Linux as the package libnet-ssh-ruby1.8.

```
Net::SSH.start('example.com', :username=>'leonardr',
               :password=>'mypass') do |session|
  # Manipulate your Net::SSH::Session object here...
end
```

Net::SSH::start takes a code block, to which it passes a Net::SSH::Session object. You use the session object to send encrypted data between the machines, or to spawn processes on the remote machine. When the code block ends, the SSH session is automatically terminated.

Discussion

It seems strange now, but until the late 1990s, people routinely used unsecured protocols like telnet to get shell access to remote machines. Remote access was so useful that we were willing to jeopardize our electronic safety by sending our shell passwords (not to mention all the data we looked at) unencrypted across the network. Fortunately, we don't have to make that trade-off anymore. The SSH protocol makes it easy to send encrypted traffic between machines, and the client tools ssh and scp have almost completely replaced tools like RSH and nonanonymous FTP.

The Net::SSH library provides a low-level interface to the SSH2 protocol, but most of the time you won't need it. Instead, you'll use one of the abstractions that make it easy to spawn and control processes on a remote machine. The simplest abstraction is the popen3 method, which works like the local popen3 method in Ruby's open3 library. It's covered in more detail in Recipe 20.10, but here's a simple example:

```
Net::SSH.start('example.com', :username=>'leonardr',
               :password=>'mypass') do |session|
  cmd = 'ls -l /home/leonardr/test_dir'
  session.process.popen3(cmd) do |stdin, stdout, stderr|
    puts stdout.read
  end
end
# -rw-rw-r--   1 leonardr leonardr      33 Dec 29 20:40 file1
# -rw-rw-r--   1 leonardr leonardr     102 Dec 29 20:40 file2
```

You can run a sequence of commands in a single user shell by calling session.shell. sync:

```
Net::SSH.start('example.com', :username=>'leonardr',
               :password=>'mypass') do |session|
  shell = session.shell.sync
  puts "Original working directory: #{shell.pwd.stdout}"
  shell.cd 'test_dir'
  puts "Working directory now: #{shell.pwd.stdout}"
  puts 'Directory contents:'
  puts shell.ls("-l").stdout
  shell.exit
end
# Original working directory: /home/leonardr
# Working directory now: /home/leonardr/test_dir
# Directory contents:
```

```
# -rw-rw-r--    1 leonardr leonardr     33 Dec 29 20:40 file1
# -rw-rw-r--    1 leonardr leonardr    102 Dec 29 20:40 file2
```

The main downside of a synchronized shell is that you usually can't pass standard input data into the commands you run. There's no way to close the standard input stream, so the process will hang forever waiting for more standard input.* To pass standard input into a remote process, you should use popen3. With a little trickery, you can control multiple processes simultaneously through your SSH connection; see Recipe 14.11 for details.

If your public/private key pair for a host is protected by a passphrase, you will be prompted for the passphrase Net::SSH tries to make a connection to that host. This makes your key more secure, but it will foil your plans to use Net::SSH in an automated script.

You can also use Net::SSH to do TCP/IP port forwarding. As of this writing, you can't use it to do X11 forwarding.

See Also

- Recipe 20.10, "Controlling a Process on Another Machine," covers Net:SSH's implementation of popen3 in more detail. Recipe 14.11 shows how to implement an scp-like service on top of the Net:SSH API, but these three recipes together only scratch the surface of what's possible with Net:SSH. The library manual (*http://net-ssh.rubyforge.org/*) is comprehensive and easy to read; it covers many topics not touched upon here, like low-level SSH2 operations, callback methods other than on_success, port forwarding, and nonsynchonized user shells

- Recipe 14.2, "Making an HTTPS Web Request," has information on installing the OpenSSL extension

- Learn more about public/private keys in the article "OpenSSH key management, Part 1" (*http://www-128.ibm.com/developerworks/library/l-keyc.html*)

14.11 Copying a File to Another Machine

Problem

You want to programatically send files to another computer, the way the Unix scp command does.

---

* The exception is a command like bc, which terminates itself if it sees the line "quit\n" in its standard input. Commands like cat always look for more standard input.

Solution

Use the Net:SSH library to get a secure shell connection to the other machine. Start a cat process on the other machine, and write the file you want to copy to its standard input.

```
require 'rubygems'
require 'net/ssh'

def copy_file(session, source_path, destination_path=nil)
  destination_path ||= source_path
  cmd = %{cat > "#{destination_path.gsub('"', '\"')}"}
  session.process.popen3(cmd) do |i, o, e|
    puts "Copying #{source_path} to #{destination_path}... "
    open(source_path) { |f| i.write(f.read) }
    puts 'Done.'
  end
end

Net::SSH.start('example.com', :username=>'leonardr',
               :password=>'mypass') do |session|
  copy_file(session, '/home/leonardr/scripts/test.rb')
  copy_file(session, '/home/leonardr/scripts/"test".rb')
end
# Copying /home/leonardr/scripts/test.rb to /home/leonardr/scripts/test.rb...
# Done.
# Copying /home/leonardr/scripts/"test".rb to /home/leonardr/scripts/"test".rb...
# Done.
```

Discussion

The scp command basically implements the old rcp protocol over a secured connection. This code uses a shortcut to achieve the same result: it uses the high-level SSH interface to spawn a process on the remote host which writes data to a file.

Since you can run multiple processes at once over your SSH session, you can copy multiple files simultaneously. For every file you want to copy, you need to spawn a cat process:

```
def do_copy(session, source_path, destination_path=nil)
  destination_path ||= source_path
  cmd = %{cat > "#{destination_path.gsub('"', '\"')}"}
  cat_process = session.process.open(cmd)

  cat_process.on_success do |p|
    p.write(open(source_path) { |f| f.read })
    p.close
    puts "Copied #{source_path} to #{destination_path}."
  end
end
```

The call to session.process.open creates a process-like object that runs a cat command on the remote system. The call to on_success registers a callback code block with the process. That code block will run once the cat command has been set up and is accepting standard input. Once that happens, it's safe to start writing data to the file on the remote system.

Once you've set up all your copy operations, you should call session.loop to perform all the copy operations simultaneously. The processes won't actually be initialized until you call session.loop.

```
Net::SSH.start('example.com', :username=>'leonardr',
               :password=>'mypass') do |session|
  do_copy(session, '/home/leonardr/scripts/test.rb')
  do_copy(session, '/home/leonardr/new_index.html',
               '/home/leonardr/public_html/index.html')
  session.loop
end
# Copied /home/leonardr/scripts/test.rb to /home/leonardr/scripts/test.rb
# Copied /home/leonardr/new_index.html to /home/leonardr/public_html/index.html
```

14.12 Being a BitTorrent Client

Problem

You want to write a Ruby script that downloads or shares large files with BitTorrent.

Solution

The third-party RubyTorrent library implements the BitTorrent protocol; you can use it to write BitTorrent clients. The RubyTorrent package has no setup.rb file, so you'll need to manually copy the files into your Ruby classpath or package them with your application.

The BitTorrent class acts as a BitTorrent client, so to download a torrent, all you have to do is give it the path or URL to a *.torrent* file. This code will download the classic B-movie *Night of the Living Dead* to the current working directory:

```
require 'rubytorrent'
file = 'http://publicdomaintorrents.com/bt/btdownload.php?type=torrent' +
       '&file=Night_of_the_Living_Dead.avi.torrent'
client = RubyTorrent::BitTorrent.new(file)
```

Run this in irb, keep your session open, and in a few hours (or days), you'll have your movie!*

---

* That is, assuming the torrent is still active when you read this. Incidentally, *Night of the Living Dead* is in the public domain because of a mishap regarding the copyright notice.

Discussion

BitTorrent is the most efficient way yet devised for sharing large files between lots of people. As you download the file you're also sharing what you've downloaded with others: the more people are trying to download the file, the faster it is for everyone.

RubyTorrent is a simple client library to the BitTorrent protocol. In its simplest form, you simply construct a BitTorrent object with the URL or path to a torrent information file, and wait for the download to complete. However, there's a lot more you can do to provide a better user interface.

The BitTorrent object has several methods that let you keep track of the progress of the download:

```
client.num_active_peers                    # => 9
# That is, 9 other people are downloading this file along with me.

client.ulrate                              # => 517.638825414351
client.dlrate                              # => 17532.608916979
# That is, about 3 kb/sec uploading and 17 kb/sec downloading.

client.percent_completed                   # => 0.25
```

You can also register code blocks to be run at certain points in the client's lifecycle. Here's a more advanced BitTorrent client that registers code blocks to let the user know about new and dropped peer connections. It also uses a thread to occasionally report on the progress of the download. The user can specify which port to use when uploading data to peers, and a maximum upload rate in kilobytes.

```ruby
#!/usr/bin/ruby
# btclient.rb
require 'rubytorrent'

def download(torrent, destination=nil, local_port=6881, max_ul=40)
  client = RubyTorrent::BitTorrent.new(torrent, destination,
                                       :port => local_port,
                                       :ulratelim => max_ul * 1024)

  thread = Thread.new do
    until client.complete?
      if client.tracker
        puts '%s: %dk of %dk (%.2f%% complete)' % [Time.now,
          client.bytes_completed / 1024, client.total_bytes / 1024,
          client.percent_completed]
        sleep(60)
      else
        sleep(5)
      end
    end
  end

  client.on_event(self, :tracker_connected) do |src, url|
    puts "[Connected to tracker at #{url}]"
```

```
    end
    client.on_event(self, :added_peer) do |src, peer|
      puts "[Connected to #{peer}.]"
    end
    client.on_event(self, :removed_peer) do |src, peer|
      puts "[Lost connection to #{peer.name}.]"
    end
    client.on_event(self, :complete) do
      puts 'Download complete.'
      thread.kill
      client.shutdown
    end

    thread.join
  end

  download(*ARGV)
```

See Also

- Get RubyTorrent at *http://rubytorrent.rubyforge.org/*; see especially the API reference at *http://rubytorrent.rubyforge.org/api.txt*
- The `btpeer.rb` and `rtpeer-ncurses.rb` files in the RubyTorrent package provide more in-depth client examples
- A few sources for interesting BitTorrent files:
  - *http://www.publicdomaintorrents.com/*
  - *http://torrent.ibiblio.org/*

14.13 Pinging a Machine

Problem

You want to check whether a particular machine or domain name can be reached from your computer.

Solution

Use Ruby's standard ping library. Its single method, `Ping.pingecho`, tries to get some machine on the network to respond to its entreaties. It takes either a domain name or an IP address, and returns true if it gets a response.

```
require 'ping'

Ping.pingecho('oreilly.com')                           # => true

# timeout of 10 seconds instead of the default 5 seconds
Ping.pingecho('127.0.0.1', 10)                         # => true
```

```
# ping port 80 instead of the default echo port
Ping.pingecho('slashdot.org', 5, 80)                    # => true

Ping.pingecho('no.such.domain')                         # => false
Ping.pingecho('222.222.222.222')                        # => false
```

Discussion

`Ping.pingecho` performs a TCP echo: it tries to make a TCP connection to the given machine, and if the machine responds (even if to refuse the connection) it means the machine was reachable.

This is not the ICMP echo of the Unix `ping` command, but the difference almost never matters. If you absolutely need an ICMP echo, you can invoke `ping` with a system call and check the return value:

```
system('ping -c1 www.oreilly.com')
# 64 bytes from 208.201.239.36: icmp_seq=0 ttl=42 time=27.2 ms
#
# --- www.oreilly.com ping statistics ---
# 1 packets transmitted, 1 packets received, 0% packet loss
# round-trip min/avg/max = 27.2/27.2/27.2 ms
# => true
```

If the domain has a DNS entry but can't be reached, `Ping::pingecho` may raise a `Timeout::Error` instead of returning false.

Some very popular or very paranoid domains, such as microsoft.com, don't respond to incoming ping requests. However, you can usually access the web server or some other service on the domain. You can see whether such a domain is reachable by using one of Ruby's other libraries:

```
Ping.pingecho('microsoft.com')                          # => false

require 'net/http'
Net::HTTP.start('microsoft.com') { 'success!' }         # => "success!"
Net::HTTP.start('no.such.domain') { "success!" }
# SocketError: getaddrinfo: Name or service not known
```

14.14 Writing an Internet Server

Problem

You want to run a server for a TCP/IP application-level protocol, but no one has written a Ruby server for the protocol yet. This may be because it's a protocol you've made up.

Solution

Use the gserver library in Ruby's standard library. It implements a generic TCP/IP server suitable for small to medium-sized tasks.

Here's a very simple chat server written with gserver. It has no end-user features to speak of. People connect to the server with a telnet client, and are identified to each other only by hostname. But it's a fully functional, multithreaded, logging server written in about 30 lines of Ruby.

```
#!/usr/bin/ruby -w
# chat.rb
require 'gserver'

class ChatServer < GServer

  def initialize(port=20606, host=GServer::DEFAULT_HOST)
    @clients = []
    super(port, host, Float::MAX, $stderr, true)
  end

  def serve(sock)
    begin
      @clients << sock
      hostname = sock.peeraddr[2] || sock.peeraddr[3]
      @clients.each do |c|
        c.puts "#{hostname} has joined the chat." unless c == sock
      end
      until sock.eof? do
        message = sock.gets.chomp
        break if message == "/quit"
        @clients.each { |c| c.puts "#{hostname}: #{message}" unless c == sock }
      end
    ensure
      @clients.delete(sock)
      @clients.each { |c| c.puts "#{hostname} has left the chat." }
    end
  end
end

server = ChatServer.new(*ARGV[0..2] || 20606)
server.start(-1)
server.join
```

Start the server in a Ruby session, and then use several instances of the telnet program to connect to port 20606 (from several different hosts, if you can). Your telnet sessions will be able to communicate with each other through the server. Your Ruby session will see a log of the connections and disconnections.

Discussion

The GServer class wraps Ruby's underlying TCPServer class in a loop that continually receives TCP connections and spawns new threads to process them. Each new thread passes its TCP connection (a TCPSocket object) into the GServer#serve method, which your subclass is responsible for providing.

The TCPSocket works like a bidirectional file. Writing to it pushes data to the client, and reading from it reads data from the client. A server like the sample chat server reads one line at a time from the client; a web server would read the entire request before sending back any data.

In the chat server example, the server echoes one client's input to all the others. In most applications, the client sockets won't even know about each other (think a web or FTP server).

The GServer constructor deserves a closer look. Here's its signature, from gserver.rb:

```
def initialize(port, host = DEFAULT_HOST, maxConnections = 4,
    stdlog = $stderr, audit = false, debug = false)
```

The port and host should be familiar to you from other types of server. maxConnections controls the maximum number of clients that can connect to the server at once. Because a chat server is very high-latency, I set the number effectively to infinity in ChatServer.

stdlog is an IO object to be used as a log. You can write a timestamped entry to the log by calling GServer#log. Setting audit to true turns on some default log messages: these are displayed, for instance, whenever a client connects to or disconnects from the server. Finally, setting debug to true means that, if your code throws an exception, the exception object will be passed into GServer#error. You can override this method to do your own error handling.

Gserver is easy to use, but not as efficient as a Ruby Internet server could be. For high-performance servers, you'll want to use IO.select and TCPServer objects, programming to the C sockets API.

See Also

• ri GServer

14.15 Parsing URLs

Problem

You want to parse a string representation of a URL into a data structure that articulates the parts of the URL.

Solution

URI.parse transforms a string describing a URL into a URI object.* The parts of the URL can be determined by interrogating the URI object.

---

* The class name is URI, but I use both "URI" and "URL" because they are more or less interchangeable.

534 | Chapter 14: Internet Services

```
require 'uri'

URI.parse('https://www.example.com').scheme         # => "https"
URI.parse('http://www.example.com/').host           # => "www.example.com"
URI.parse('http://www.example.com:6060/').port      # => 6060
URI.parse('http://example.com/a/file.html').path    # => "/a/file.html"
```

URI.split transforms a string into an array of URL parts. This is more efficient than URI.parse, but you have to know which parts correspond to which slots in the array:

```
URI.split('http://example.com/a/file.html')
# => ["http", nil, "example.com", nil, nil, "/a/file.html", nil, nil, nil]
```

Discussion

The URI module contains classes for five of the most popular URI schemas. Each one can store in a structured format the data that makes up a URI for that schema. URI.parse creates an instance of the appropriate class for a particular URL's scheme.

Every URI can be decomposed into a set of *components*, joined by constant strings. For example: the components for a HTTP URI are the scheme ("http"), the hostname ("www.example.com (*http://www.example.com*)"), and so on. Each URI schema has its own components, and each of Ruby's URI classes stores the names of its components in an ordered array of symbols, called component:

```
URI::HTTP.component
# => [:scheme, :userinfo, :host, :port, :path, :query, :fragment]

URI::MailTo.component
# => [:scheme, :to, :headers]
```

Each of the components of a URI class has a corresponding accessor method, which you can call to get one component of a URI. You can also instantiate a URI class directly (rather than going through URI.parse) by passing in the appropriate component symbols as a map of keyword arguments.

```
URI::HTTP.build(:host => 'example.com', :path => '/a/file.html',
                :fragment => 'section_3').to_s
# => "http://example.com/a/file.html#section_3"
```

The following debugging method iterates over the components handled by the scheme of a given URI object, and prints the corresponding values:

```
class URI::Generic
  def dump
    component.each do |m|
      puts "#{m}: #{send(m).inspect}"
    end
  end
end
```

URI::HTTP and URI::HTTPS are the most commonly encountered subclasses of URI, since most URIs are the URLs to web pages. Both classes provide the same interface.

```
url = 'http://leonardr:pw@www.subdomain.example.com:6060' +
    '/cgi-bin/mycgi.cgi?key1=val1#anchor'
URI.parse(url).dump
# scheme: "http"
# userinfo: "leonardr:pw"
# host: "www.subdomain.example.com"
# port: 6060
# path: "/cgi-bin/mycgi.cgi"
# query: "key1=val1"
# fragment: "anchor"
```

A URI::FTP object represents an FTP server, or a path to a file on an FTP server. The typecode component indicates whether the file in question is text, binary, or a directory; it typically won't be known unless you create a URI::FTP object and specify one.

```
URI::parse('ftp://leonardr:password@ftp.example.com/a/file.txt').dump
# scheme: "ftp"
# userinfo: "leonardr:password"
# host: "ftp.example.com"
# port: 21
# path: "/a/file.txt"
# typecode: nil
```

A URI::Mailto represents an email address, or even an entire message to be sent to that address. In addition to its component array, this class provides a method (to_mailtext) that formats the URI as an email message.

```
uri = URI::parse('mailto:leonardr@example.com?Subject=Hello&body=Hi!')
uri.dump
# scheme: "mailto"
# to: "leonardr@example.com"
# headers: [["Subject", "Hello"], ["body", "Hi!"]]

puts uri.to_mailtext
# To: leonardr@example.com
# Subject: Hello
#
# Hi!
```

A URI::LDAP object contains a path to an LDAP server or a query against one:

```
URI::parse("ldap://ldap.example.com").dump
# scheme: "ldap"
# host: "ldap.example.com"
# port: 389
# dn: nil
# attributes: nil
# scope: nil
# filter: nil
# extensions: nil

URI::parse('ldap://ldap.example.com/o=Alice%20Exeter,c=US?extension').dump
# scheme: "ldap"
# host: "ldap.example.com"
```

```
# port: 389
# dn: "o=Alice%20Exeter,c=US"
# attributes: "extension"
# scope: nil
# filter: nil
# extensions: nil
```

The `URI::Generic` class, superclass of all of the above, is a catch-all class that holds URIs with other schemes, or with no scheme at all. It holds much the same components as `URI::HTTP`, although there's no guarantee that any of them will be non-nil for a given `URI::Generic` object.

`URI::Generic` also exposes two other components not used by any of its built-in subclasses. The first is opaque, which is the portion of a URL that couldn't be parsed (that is, everything after the scheme):

```
uri = URI.parse('tag:example.com,2006,my-tag')
uri.scheme                                    # => "tag"
uri.opaque                                    # => "example.com,2006,my-tag"
```

The second is registry, which is only used for URI schemes whose naming authority is registry-based instead of server-based. It's likely that you'll never need to use registry, since almost all URI schemes are server-based (for instance, HTTP, FTP, and LDAP all use the DNS system to designate a host).

To combine the components of a URI object into a string, simply call to_s:

```
uri = URI.parse('http://www.example.com/#anchor')
uri.port = 8080
uri.to_s                          # => "http://www.example.com:8080/#anchor"
```

See Also

- Recipe 11.13, "Extracting All the URLs from an HTML Document"
- `ri URI`

14.16 Writing a CGI Script

Credit: Chetan Patil

Problem

You want to expose Ruby code through an existing web server, without having to do any special configuration.

Solution

Most web servers are set up to run CGI scripts, and it's easy to write CGI scripts in Ruby. Here's a simple CGI script that calls the Unix command ps, parses its results, and outputs the list of running processes as an HTML document.[*] Anyone with access to the web server can then look at the processes running on the system.

```ruby
#!/usr/bin/ruby
# ps.cgi

processes = %x{ps aux}.collect do |proc|
  '<tr><td>' + proc.split(/\s+/, 11).join('</td><td>') + '</td></tr>'
end

puts 'Content-Type: text/html'
# Output other HTTP headers here...
puts "\n"

title = %{Processes running on #{ENV['SERVER_NAME'] || `hostname`.strip}}
puts <<-end
  <HTML>
   <HEAD><TITLE>#{title}</TITLE></HEAD>
   <BODY>
   <H1>#{title}</H1>
   <TABLE>
    #{processes.join("\n")}
   </TABLE>
   </BODY>
   </HTML>
end

exit 0
```

Discussion

CGI was the first major technology to add dynamic elements to the previously static Web. A CGI resource is requested like any static HTML document, but behind the scenes the web server executes an external program (in this case, a Ruby script) instead of serving a file. The output of the program—text, HTML, or binary data—is sent as part of the HTTP response to the browser.

CGI has a very simple interface, based on environment variables and standard input and output; one that should be very familiar to writers of command-line programs. This simplicity is CGI's weakness: it leaves too many things undefined. But when a Rails application would be overkill, a CGI script might be the right size.

CGI programs typically reside in a special directory of the web server's web space (often the /cgi-bin directory). On Unix systems, CGI files must be made executable by the web server, and the first line of the script must point to the system's Ruby interpreter (usually /usr/bin/ruby or /usr/local/bin/ruby).

---

[*] On Windows, you could do this example by running some other command such as dir, listing the running Windows services as seen in Recipe 23.2, or just printing a static message.

A CGI script gets most of its input from environment variables like QUERY_STRING and PATH_INFO, which are set by the web server. The web server also uses environment variables to tell the script where and how it's being run: note how the sample script uses ENV['SERVER_NAME'] to find the machine's hostname for display.

There are only a few restrictions on the output of a CGI script. Before the "real" output, you need to send some HTTP headers. The only required header is Content-Type, which tells the browser what MIME type to expect from the document the CGI is going to output. This is also your chance to set other HTTP headers, such as Content-length, Expires, Location, Pragma, and Status.

The headers are separated from the content by a blank line. If the blank line is missing, the server may incorrectly interpret the entire data stream as a HTTP header—a leading cause of errors. Other possible problems include:

- The first line of the file contains the wrong path to the Ruby executable.
- The permissions on the CGI script don't allow the web server to access or execute it.
- You used binary mode FTP to upload the script to your server from another platform, and the server doesn't understand that platform's line endings: use text mode FTP instead.
- The web server is not configured to run Ruby scripts as CGI, or to run CGI scripts at all.
- The script contains a compile error. Try running it manually from the command line.

If you get the dreaded error "premature end of script headers" from your web server, these issues are the first things to check.

Newer versions of Ruby include the CGI support library cgi. Except for extremely simple CGIs, it's better to use this library than to simply write HTML to standard output. The CGI class makes it easy to retrieve HTTP request parameters and to manage cookies. It also provides custom methods for generating HTML, using Ruby code that has the same structure as the eventual output.

Here's the code from ps.cgi, rewritten to use the CGI class. Instead of writing HTML, we make the CGI class do it. CGI also takes care of the content type, since we're using the default (text/html).

```
#!/usr/bin/ruby
# ps2.cgi

require 'cgi'

# New CGI object
cgi = CGI.new('html3')
```

```
processes = `ps aux`.collect { |proc| proc.split(/\s+/, 11) }

title = %{Processes running on #{ENV['SERVER_NAME'] || %x{hostname}.strip}}

cgi.out do
  cgi.html do
    cgi.head { cgi.title { title } } + cgi.body do
      cgi.table do
        (processes.collect do |fields|
          cgi.tr { fields.collect { |field| cgi.td { field } }.join " " }
        end).join "\n"
      end
    end
  end
end

exit 0
```

Since CGI allows any user to execute an external CGI program on your web server, security is of paramount importance. Popular CGI hacks include corrupting the program's input by inserting special characters in the QUERY_STRING, stealing confidential user data by modifying the parameters posted to the CGI program, and launching denial-of-service attacks to render the web server inoperable. CGI programs need to be carefully inspected for possible bugs and exploits. A few simple techniques will improve your security: call taint on external data, set your $SAFE variable to 1 or higher, and don't use methods like eval, system, or popen unless you have to.

See Also

- The CGI documentation (*http://hoohoo.ncsa.uiuc.edu/cgi/*), especially the list of environment variables (*http://hoohoo.ncsa.uiuc.edu/cgi/env.html*)
- Recipe 14.17, "Setting Cookies and Other HTTP Response Headers"
- Recipe 14.18, "Handling File Uploads via CGI"
- Chapter 15

14.17 Setting Cookies and Other HTTP Response Headers

Credit: Mauro Cicio

Problem

You're writing a CGI program and you want to customize the HTTP headers you send in response to a request. For instance, you may want to set a client-side cookie so that you can track state between HTTP requests.

Solution

Pass a hash of headers into the CGI#out method that creates the HTTP response. Each key of the hash is the name of a header to set, or a special value (like cookie), which the CGI class knows how to interpret.

Here's a CGI script that demonstrates how to set some response headers, including a cookie and a custom HTTP header called "Recipe Name".

First we process any incoming cookie. Every time you hit this CGI, the value stored in your cookie will be incremented, and the date of your last visit will be reset.

```ruby
#!/usr/bin/ruby
# headers.cgi

require "cgi"
cgi = CGI.new("html3")

# Retrieve or create the "rubycookbook" cookie
cookie = cgi.cookies['rubycookbook']
cookie = CGI::Cookie.new('rubycookbook', 'hits=0',
                          "last=#{Time.now}") if cookie.empty?

# Read the values in the cookie for future use
hits = cookie.value[0].split('=')[1]
last = cookie.value[1].split('=')[1]

# Set new values in the cookie
cookie.value[0] = "hits=#{hits.succ}"
cookie.value[1] = "last=#{Time.now}"
```

Next, we build a hash of HTTP headers, and send the headers by passing the hash into CGI#out. We then generate the output document. Since the end user doesn't usually see the HTTP headers they're served, we'll make them visible by repeating them in the output document (Figure 14-1):

```ruby
# Create a hash of HTTP response headers.
header = { 'status'      => 'OK',
           'cookie'      => [cookie],
           'Refresh'     => 2,
           'Recipe Name' => 'Setting HTTP Response Headers',
           'server'      => ENV['SERVER_SOFTWARE']   }

cgi.out(header) do
  cgi.html('PRETTY' => '  ') do
    cgi.head { cgi.title { 'Setting HTTP Response Headers' } } +
    cgi.body do
      cgi.p('Your headers:') +
      cgi.pre{ cgi.header(header) } +
      cgi.pre do
        "Number of times your browser hit this cgi: #{hits}\n"+
        "Last connected: #{last}"
      end
```

```
          end
       end
     end
```

```
Your headers:

     Status: 200 OK
     Server: Apache/2.0.49 (Unix) mod_ssl/2.0.49 OpenSSL/0.9.7a DAV/2 PHP/4.3.9 mo(
     Content-Type: text/html
     Set-Cookie: rubycookbook=hits%3D60&last%3DWed+Mar+08+11%3A46%3A33+PST+2006; p;
     Recipe Name: Setting HTTP Response Headers
     Refresh: 2




Number of times your browser hit this cgi: 59
Last connected: Wed Mar 08 11:46:31 PST 2006
```

Figure 14-1. This CGI lets you see the response headers, including the cookie

The Refresh header makes your web browser refresh the page every two seconds. You can visit this CGI once and watch the number of hits (stored in the client-side cookie) start to mount up.

Discussion

An HTTP Response consists of two sections (a header section and a body section) separated by a blank line. The body contains the document to be rendered by the browser (usually an HTML page) and the header carries metadata: information about the connection, the response, and the document itself. The CGI#out method takes a hash representing the HTTP headers, and a code block that generates the body.

CGI#out recognizes a few special values that make it easier to set custom headers. For instance, the header hash in the example above maps the key "cookie" to a CGI::Cookie object. CGI#out knows enough to turn cookie into the standard HTTP header Set-Cookie, and to transform the CGI::Cookie object into a string rendition.

If CGI#out doesn't know about a certain key, it simply sends it as an HTTP header, as-is. CGI#out has no special knowledge of our "Refresh" and "Recipe Name" headers, so it writes them verbatim to the HTTP response. "Refresh" is a standard HTTP response header recognized by most web browsers; "Recipe Name" is a header I made up for this recipe, and web browsers should ignore it.

See Also

- The CGI documentation (*http://www.ruby-doc.org/core/classes/CGI.html*), especially the list of recognized header keys and status codes

14.18 Handling File Uploads via CGI

Credit: Mauro Cicio

Problem

You want to let a visitor to your web site upload a file to the web server, either for storage or processing.

Solution

The CGI class provides a simple interface for accessing data sent through HTTP file upload. You can access an uploaded file through CGI#params as though it were any other CGI form variable.

If the uploaded file size is smaller than 10 kilobytes, its contents are made available as a StringIO object. Otherwise, the file is put into a Tempfile on disk: you can read the file from disk and process it, or move it to a permanent location.

Here's a CGI that accepts file uploads and saves the files to a special directory on disk:

```
#!/usr/bin/ruby
# upload.rb

# Save uploaded files to this directory
UPLOAD_DIR = "/usr/local/www/uploads"

require 'cgi'
require 'stringio'
```

The CGI has two main parts: a method that prints a file upload form and a method that processes the results of the form. The method that prints the form is very simple:

```
def display_form(cgi)
  action = env['script_name']
  return <<EOF
<form action="#{action}" method="post" enctype="multipart/form-data">
  File to Upload: <input type="file" name="file_name"><br>
  Your email address: <input type="text" name="email_address"
                      value="guest@example.com"><br>
  <input type="submit" name="Submit" value="Submit Form">
  </form>
EOF
end
```

The method that processes the form is a little more complex:

```
def process_form(cgi)
  email = cgi.params['email_address'][0]
  fileObj = cgi.params['file_name'][0]

  str = '<h1>Upload report</h1>' +
    "<p>Thanks for your upload, #{email.read}</p>"
  if fileObj
    path = fileObj.original_filename
    str += "Original Filename : #{path}" + cgi.br
    dest = File.join(UPLOAD_DIR, sanitize_filename(path))

    str += "Destination : #{dest} <br>"
    File.open(dest.untaint, 'wb') { |f| f << fileObj.read }

    # Delete the temporary file if one was created
    local_temp_file = fileObj.local_path( )
    File.unlink(local_temp_file) if local_temp_file
  end
  return str
end
```

The process_form method calls a method sanitize_filename to pick a new filename based on the original. The new filename is stripped of characters in the upload file's name that aren't valid on the server's filesystem. This is important for security reasons. It's also important to pick a new name because Internet Explorer on Windows submits filenames like "c:\hot\fondue.txt" where other browsers would submit "fondue.txt". We'll define that method now:

```
def sanitize_filename(path)
  if RUBY_PLATFORM =~ %r{unix|linux|solaris|freebsd}
    # Not required for unix platforms since all characters
    # are allowed (except for /, which is stripped out below).
  elsif RUBY_PLATFORM =~ %r{win32}
    # Replace illegal characters for NTFS with _
    path.gsub!(/[\x00-\x1f\/|?*]/,'_')
  else
    # Assume a very restrictive OS such as MSDOS
    path.gsub!(/[\/|\?*+\]\[ \x00-\x1fa-z]/,'_')
  end

  # For files uploaded by Windows users, strip off the beginning path.
  return path.gsub(/^.*[\\\/]/, '')
end
```

Finally we have the CGI code itself, which calls the appropriate method and prints out the results in an HTML page:

```
cgi = CGI.new('html3')
if cgi.request_method !~ %r{POST}
  buf = display_form(cgi)
else
  buf = process_form(cgi)
end
```

```
cgi.out( ) do
  cgi.html( ) do
    cgi.head{ cgi.title{'Upload Form'} } + cgi.body( ) { buf }
  end
end

exit 0
```

Discussion

This CGI script presents the user with a form that lets them choose a file from their local system to upload. When the form is POSTed, CGI accepts the uploaded file data and stores it as a CGI parameters. As with any other CGI parameter (like email_ address), the uploaded file is keyed off of the name of the HTML form element: in this case, file_name.

If the file is larger than 10 kilobytes, it will be written to a temporary file and the contents of CGI[:file_name] will be a Tempfile object. If the file is small, it will be kept directly in memory as a StringIO object. Either way, the object will have a few methods not found in normal Tempfile or StringIO objects. The most useful of these are original_filename, content_type, and read.

The original_filename method returns the name of the file, as seen on the computer of the user who uploaded it. The content_type method returns the MIME type of the uploaded file, again as estimated by the computer that did the upload. You can use this to restrict the types of file you'll accept as uploads (note, however, that a custom client can lie about the content type):

```
# Limit uploads to BMP files.
raise 'Wrong type!' unless fileObj.content_type =~ %r{image/bmp}
```

Every StringIO object supports a read method that simply returns the contents of the underlying string. For the sake of a uniform interface, a Tempfile object created by file upload also has a read method that returns the contents of a file. For most applications, you don't need to check whether you've got a StringIO or a Tempfile: you can just call read and get the data. However, a Tempfile can be quite large—there's a reason it was written to disk in the first place—so don't do this unless you trust your users or have a lot of memory. Otherwise, check the size of a Tempfile with File.size and read it a block at a time.

To see where a Tempfile is located on disk, call its local_path method. If you plan to write the uploaded file to disk, it's more efficient to move a Tempfile with FileUtils.mv than to read it into memory and immediately write it back to another location.

Temporary files are deleted when the Ruby interpreter exits, but some web frameworks keep a single Ruby interpreter around indefinitely. If you're not careful, a long-running application can fill up your disk or partition with old temporary files. Within a CGI script, you should explicitly delete temporary files when you're done with them—except, of course, the ones you move to permanent positions elsewhere on the filesystem.

See Also

- RFC1867 describes HTTP file upload
- For more on the StringIO and Tempfile classes used to store uploaded files, see Recipe 6.8, "Writing to a Temporary File," and Recipe 6.15, "Pretending a String Is a File"
- *http://wiki.rubyonrails.com/rails/pages/HowtoUploadFiles*

14.19 Running Servlets with WEBrick

Credit: John-Mason Shackelford

Problem

You want to embed a server in your Ruby application. Your project is not a traditional web application, or else it's too small to justify the use of a framework like Rails or Nitro.

Solution

Write a custom servlet for WEBrick, a web server implemented in Ruby and included in the standard library.*

Configure WEBrick by creating a new HTTPServer instance and mouting servlets. The default FileHandler acts like a "normal" web server: it serves a URL-space corresponding to a directory on disk. It delegates requests for *.cgi files to the CGIHandler, renders *.rhtml files with ERb using the ERBHandler servlet, and serves other files (such as static HTML files) as they are.

This server mounts three servlets on a server running on port 8000 on your local machine. Each servlet serves documents, CGI scripts, and .rhtml templates from a different directory on disk:

```
#!/usr/bin/ruby
# simple_servlet_server.rb
require 'webrick'
include WEBrick

s = HTTPServer.new(:Port => 8000)
```

---

* Don't confuse WEBrick servlets with Java servlets. The concepts are similar, but they don't implement the same API.

```
# Add a mime type for *.rhtml files
HTTPUtils::DefaultMimeTypes.store('rhtml', 'text/html')

# Required for CGI on Windows; unnecessary on Unix/Linux
s.config.store( :CGIInterpreter, "#{HTTPServlet::CGIHandler::Ruby}")

# Mount servlets
s.mount('/',       HTTPServlet::FileHandler, '/var/www/html')
s.mount('/bruce',  HTTPServlet::FileHandler, '/home/dibbbr/htdoc')
s.mount('/marty',  HTTPServlet::FileHandler, '/home/wisema/htdoc')

# Trap signals so as to shutdown cleanly.
['TERM', 'INT'].each do |signal|
  trap(signal){ s.shutdown }
end

# Start the server and block on input.
s.start
```

Discussion

WEBrick is robust, mature, and easy to extend. Beyond serving static HTML pages, WEBrick supports traditional CGI scripts, ERb-based templating like PHP or JSP, and custom servlet classes. While most of WEBrick's API is oriented toward responding to HTTP requests, you can also use it to implement servers that speak another protocol. (For more on this capability, see the Daytime server example on the WEBrick home page.)

The first two arguments to HTTPServer#mount (the mount directory and servlet class) are used by the mount method itself; any additional arguments are simply passed along to the servlet. This way, you can configure a servlet while you mount it; the FileHandler servlet requires an argument telling it which directory on disk contains the web content.

When a client requests a URL, WEBrick tries to match it against the entries in its mounting table. The mounting order is irrelevant. Where multiple mount locations might apply to a single directory, WEBrick picks the longest match.

When the request is for a directory (like *http://localhost/bruce/*), the server looks for the files *index.html*, *index.htm*, *index.cgi*, or *index.rhtml*. This is configurable via the :DirectoryIndex configuration parameter. The snippet below adds another file to the list of directory index files:

```
s.config.store(:DirectoryIndex,
               s.config[:DirectoryIndex] << "default.htm")
```

When the standard handlers provided by WEBrick won't work for you, write a custom servlet. Rubyists have written custom WEBrick servlets to handle SOAP and XML-RPC services, implement a WebDAV server, process eruby templates instead of ERb templates, and fork processes to distribute load on machines with multiple CPUs.

To write your own WEBrick servlet, simply subclass HTTPServlet::AbstractServlet and write do_ methods corresponding to the HTTP methods you wish to handle. Then mount your servlet class as shown in the Solution. The following example handles HTTP GET requests via the do_GET method, and POSTs via an alias. HEAD and OPTIONS requests are implemented in the AbstractServlet itself.

```ruby
#!/usr/bin/ruby
# custom_servlet_server.rb
require 'webrick'
include WEBrick

class CustomServlet < HTTPServlet::AbstractServlet
  def do_GET(request, response)
    response.status = 200 # Success
    response.body = "Hello World"
    response['Content-Type'] = 'text/plain'
  end

  # Respond with an HTTP POST just as we do for the HTTP GET.
  alias :do_POST :do_GET
end

# Mount servlets.
s = HTTPServer.new(:Port => 8001 )
s.mount('/tricia', CustomServlet )

# Trap signals so as to shutdown cleanly.
['TERM', 'INT'].each do |signal|
  trap(signal){ s.shutdown }
end

# Start the server and block on input.
s.start
```

Start that server, visit *http://localhost:8001/tricia/*, and you'll see the string "Hello World".

Beyond defining handlers for arbitrary HTTP methods and configuring custom servlets with mount options, we can also control how often servlet instances are initialized. Ordinarily, a new servlet instance is instantiated for every request. Since each request has its own instance of the servlet class, you are free to write custom servlets without worrying about the servlet's state and thread safety (unless, of course, you share resources between servlet instances).

But you can get faster request handling—at the expense of a slower startup time—by moving some work out of the do_ methods and into the sevlet's initialize method. Instead of creating a new servlet instance with every request, you can override the class method HTTPServlet::AbstractServlet.get_instance and manage a pool of servlet instances. This works especially well when your request handling methods are reentrant, so that you can avoid cost costly thread synchronization.

The following example uses code from Recipe 12.13 to serve up a certificate of completion to the individual named by the HTTP request. We use the templating approach discussed in the PDF recipe to prepare most of the certificate ahead of time. During request handling, we do nothing but fill in the recipient's name.

The PooledServlet class below does the work of pooling the servlet handlers:

```ruby
#!/usr/bin/ruby
# certificate_server.rb
require 'webrick'
require 'thread'
require 'cgi'

include WEBrick

class PooledServlet < HTTPServlet::AbstractServlet

  INIT_MUTEX   = Mutex.new
  SERVLET_POOL = []

  @@pool_size = 2

  # Create a single instance of the servlet  to avoid repeating the costly
  # initialization.
  def self.get_instance(config, *options)
    unless SERVLET_POOL.size == @@pool_size
      INIT_MUTEX.synchronize do
        SERVLET_POOL.clear
        @@pool_size.times{ SERVLET_POOL << new( config, *options ) }
      end
    end
    s = SERVLET_POOL.find{|s| ! s.busy?} while s.nil?
    return s
  end

  def self.pool_size( size )
    @@pool_size = size
  end

  def busy?
    @busy
  end

  def service(req, res)
    @busy = true
    super
    @busy = false
  end
end
```

Note that by placing the synchronize block within the unless block, we expose ourselves to the possibility that, when the server first starts up, the servlet pool may be initialized more than once. But it's not really a problem if that does happen, and if we put the synchronize block there we don't have to synchronize on every single request.

You've heard it before: "Avoid premature optimization." Assumptions about the impact of the servlet pool size on memory consumption and performance often prove to be wrong, given the complexities introduced by garbage collection and the variation in the efficiency of various operations on different platforms. Code first, tune later.

Here's the application-specific code. The file certificate_pdf.rb should contain the Certificate class defined in the Discussion of Recipe 12.13.

When the servlet is initialized, we generate the PDF certificate, leaving the name blank:

```ruby
require 'certificate_pdf'

class PDFCertificateServlet < PooledServlet

  pool_size 10

  def initialize(server, *options)
    super
    @certificate = Certificate.new(options.first)
  end
```

When the client makes a request, we load the certificate, fill in the name, and send it as the body of the HTTP response:

```ruby
  def do_GET(request, response)
    if name = request.query['name']
      filled_in = @certificate.award_to(CGI.unescape(name))

      response.body             = filled_in.render
      response.status           = 200                     # Success
      response['Content-Type'] = 'application/pdf'
      response['Size']          = response.body.size
    else
      raise HTTPStatus::Forbidden.new("missing attribute: 'name'")
    end
  end
```

The rest of the code should look familiar by now:

```ruby
  # Respond with an HTTP POST just as we do for the HTTP GET
  alias :do_POST :do_GET
end

# Mount servlets
s = HTTPServer.new(:Port => 8002)
s.mount('/', PDFCertificateServlet, 'Ruby Hacker')

# Trap signals so as to shutdown cleanly.
['TERM', 'INT'].each do |signal|
  trap(signal){ s.shutdown }
end
```

```
# Start the server and block on input.
s.start
```

Start this server, and you can visit *http://localhost:8002/?name=My+Name* to get a customized PDF certificate.

The code above illustrates many other basic features of WEBrick: access to request parameters, servlet configuration at mount time, use of a servlet pool to handle expensive operations up front, and error pages.

Besides `HTTPStatus::Forbidden`, demonstrated above, WEBrick provides exceptions for each of the HTTP 1.1 status codes. The classes are not listed in the RDoc, but you can infer them from `HTTPStatus::StatusMessage` table. The class names correspond to the names given in the WC3 reference listed below.

See Also

- Recipe 12.13, "Generating PDF Files," for the `CertificatePDF` class used by the certificate server
- WEBrick's web site (*http://webrick.org/*) offers a number of examples as well as links to related libraries
- Mongrel is an up-and-coming Ruby web server that might be the next WEBrick (*http://mongrel.rubyforge.org/*)
- The RDoc is available online at *http://www.ruby-doc.org/stdlib/libdoc/webrick/rdoc/index.html*
- *Gnome's Guide to WEBrick* at *http://microjet.ath.cx/webrickguide/html/html_webrick.html* provides the most comprehensive coverage of WEBrick beyond the RDoc and the source itself; the *Guide* is available in both html and PDF formats
- Eric Hodel has written a couple of short articles on WEBrick servlets and working with HTTP cookies (*http://segment7.net/projects/ruby/WEBrick/index.html*)
- An article on the *Linux Journal* web site, "At the Forge—Getting Started with Ruby," provides a basic introduction to Ruby CGI and WEBrick servlets (*http://www.linuxjournal.com/article/8356*)
- For a complete list of HTTP 1.1 status codes and explanations as to what they mean, see *http://www.w.org/Protocols/rfc2616/rfc2616-sec10.html*

14.20 A Real-World HTTP Client

The first three recipes in this chapter cover different ways of fetching web pages. The techniques they describe work well if you just need to fetch one specific web page, but in the interests of simplicity they omit some details you'll need to consider when writing a web spider, a web browser, or any other serious HTTP client. This recipe creates a library that deals with the details.

Mixed HTTP and HTTPS

Any general client will have to be able to make both HTTP and HTTPS requests. But the simple Net:HTTP methods that work in Recipe 14.1 can't be used to make HTTPS requests. Our library will use use HTTPRequest objects for everything. If the user requests a URL that uses the "https" scheme, we'll flip the request object's use_ssl switch, as seen in Recipe 14.2.

Redirects

Lots of things can go wrong with an HTTP request: the page might have moved, it might require authentication, or it might simply be gone. Most HTTP errors call for higher-level handling or human intervention, but when a page has moved, a smart client can automatically follow it to its new location.

Our library will automatically follow redirects that provide "Location" fields in their responses. It'll prevent infinite redirect loops by refusing to visit a URL it's already visited. It'll prevent infinite redirect chains by limiting the number of redirects. After all the redirects are followed, it'll make the final URI available as a member of the response object.

Proxies

Users use HTTP proxies to make high-latency connections work faster, surf anonymously, and evade censorship. Each individual client program needs to be programmed to use a proxy, and it's an easy feature to overlook if you don't use a proxy yourself. Fortunately, it's easy to support proxies in Ruby: the Proxy class will create a custom Net::HTTP subclass that works through a certain proxy.

This library defines a single new method: Net::HTTP.fetch, an all-singing, all-dancing factory for HTTPRequest objects. It silently handles HTTPS URLs (assuming you have net/https installed) and HTTP redirects, and it transparently handles proxies. This might go into a file called http_fetch.rb:

```ruby
require 'net/http'
require 'set'

class Net::HTTPResponse
  attr_accessor :final_uri
end

module Net
  begin
    require 'net/https'
    HTTPS_SUPPORTED = true
  rescue LoadError
    HTTPS_SUPPORTED = false
  end

  class HTTP
    # Makes an HTTP request and returns the HTTPResponse object.
    # Args: :proxy_host, :proxy_port, :action (:get, :post, etc.),
    #       :data (for :post action), :max_redirects.
```

```
def HTTP.fetch(uri, args={}.freeze, &before_fetching)
  # Process the arguments with default values
  uri = URI.parse(uri) unless uri.is_a? URI
  proxy_host = args[:proxy_host]
  proxy_port = args[:proxy_port] || 80
  action = args[:action] || :get
  data = args[:data]
  max_redirects = args[:max_redirects] || 10
```

We will always work on a Proxy object, even if no proxy is specified. A Proxy with no proxy_host makes direct HTTP connections. This way, the code works the same way whether we're actually using an HTTP proxy or not:

```
# Use a proxy class to create the request object
proxy_class = Proxy(proxy_host, proxy_port)
request = proxy_class.new(uri.host, uri.port)
```

We will use SSL to handle URLs of the "https" scheme. Note that we do not set any certificate paths here, or do any other SSL configuration. If you want to do that, you'll need to pass an appropriate code block into fetch (see below for an example):

```
request.use_ssl = true if HTTPS_SUPPORTED and uri.scheme == 'https'
yield request if block_given?
```

Now we activate the request and get an HTTPResponse object back:

```
response = request.send(action, uri.path, data)
```

Our HTTPResponse object might be a document, it might be an error, or it might be a redirect. If it's a redirect, we can make things easier for the caller of this method by following the redirect. This piece of the method finds the redirected URL and sends it into a recursive fetch call, after making sure that we aren't stuck in an infinite loop or an endless chain of redirects:

```
urls_seen = args[:_urls_seen] || Set.new
if response.is_a?(Net::HTTPRedirection)          # Redirect
  if urls_seen.size < max_redirects && response['Location']
    urls_seen << uri
    new_uri = URI.parse(response['Location'])
    break if urls_seen.member? new_uri           # Infinite redirect loop

    # Request the new location just as we did the old one.
    new_args = args.dup
    puts "Redirecting to #{new_uri}" if $DEBUG
    new_args[:_urls_seen] = urls_seen
    response = HTTP.fetch(new_uri, new_args, &before_fetching)
  end
else                          # No redirect
  response.final_uri = uri
end
return response
  end
 end
end
```

That's pretty dense code, but it ties a lot of functionality into a single method with a relatively simple API. Here's a simple example, in which `Net::HTTP.fetch` silently follows an HTTP redirect. Note the `final_uri` is different from the original URI.

```
response = Net::HTTP.fetch("http://google.com/")
puts "#{response.final_uri} body is #{response.body.size} bytes."
# http://www.google.com/ body is 2444 bytes.
```

With `fetch`, redirects work even through proxies. This example accesses the Google homepage through a public HTTP proxy in Singapore. When it requests "*http://google.com/*", it's redirected to "*http://www.google.com/*", as in the previous example. But when Google notices that the IP address is coming from Singapore, it sends *another* redirect:

```
response = Net::HTTP.fetch("http://google.com/",
                           :proxy_host => "164.78.252.199")
puts "#{response.final_uri} body is #{response.body.size} bytes."
# http://www.google.com.sg/ body is 2853 bytes.
```

There are HTTPS proxies as well. This code uses an HTTPS proxy in the U.S. to make a secure connection to "*https://paypal.com/*". It's redirected to "*https://paypal.com/us/*". The second request is secured in the same way as the one that caused the redirect. Note that this code will only work if you have the Ruby SSL library installed.

```
response = Net::HTTP.fetch("https://paypal.com/",
                           :proxy_host => "209.40.194.8") do |request|
  request.ca_path = "/etc/ssl/certs/"
  request.verify_mode = OpenSSL::SSL::VERIFY_PEER
end
puts "#{response.final_uri} body is #{response.body.size} bytes."
# https://paypal.com/us/ body is 16978 bytes.
```

How does this work? The code block is actually called twice: once before requesting "*https://paypal.com/*" and once before requesting "*https://paypal.com/us/*". This is what `fetch`'s code block is for: it's run on the `HTTPRequest` object before the request is actually made. If the code block were only called once, then the second request wouldn't have access to any certificates.

`Net::HTTP.fetch` will follow redirects served by the web server, but it won't follow redirects contained in the META tags of an HTML document. To follow those redirects, you'll have to parse the document as HTML.

See Also

- Recipe 14.1, "Grabbing the Contents of a Web Page"
- Recipe 14.2, "Making an HTTPS Web Request"
- Recipe 14.3, "Customizing HTTP Request Headers"
- Several web sites have lists of public HTTP and HTTPS proxies (for instance, *http://www.samair.ru/proxy/* and *http://tools.rosinstrument.com/proxy/*); if you want to set up a proxy on your local network, Squid is a good choice (*http://www.squid-cache.org/*)

Web Development: Ruby on Rails

Ruby on Rails is unquestionably Ruby's killer app. It can take a lot of credit for lifting Ruby from obscurity outside its native Japan. No other programming language can boast a simple web application framework that also has almost all of that language's developer mindshare.* This chapter demonstrates the principles underlying basic Rails usage (in recipes like Recipe 15.6), gives Rails implementations of common web application patterns (Recipes 15.4 and 15.8) and shows how to use standard Ruby tools from within Rails (Recipes 15.22 and 15.23).

Despite its quality and popularity, Rails does not bring anything new to web development. Its foundations are in standard programming patterns like ActiveRecord and Model-View-Controller. It reuses many preexisting Ruby libraries (like Rake and ERb). The power of Rails is in combining these standard techniques with a ruthless dedication to automating menial tasks, and to asserting resonable default behaviors.

If Rails has a secret, it's the power of naming conventions. The vast majority of web applications are CRUD applications: create, read, update, and delete information from a database. In these types of applications, Rails shines. You start with a database schema and with almost no code, but Rails ties together many pieces with naming conventions and shortcuts. This lets you put meat on your application very quickly.

Because so many settings and names can be sensibly derived from other pieces of information, Rails has much less "paperwork" than other frameworks. Data that's implicit in the code or the database schema doesn't need to be specified anywhere else. An essential part of this system is the ActiveSupport system for pluralizing nouns (Recipe 15.7).

---

* Python, for instance, has several excellent web application frameworks, but that's just the problem. It has *several*, and a powerful community is fractured on the issue of which to use. Ruby has no major web application frameworks apart from Rails. In a sense, Ruby's former obscurity is what made the dominance of Rails possible.

Where naming conventions can't do the job, Rails uses decorator methods to declare relationships between objects. This happens within the Ruby classes affected by those relationships, not in a bloated XML configuration file. The result is a smaller, simpler to understand, and more flexible application.

As mentioned above, Rails is built on top of common Ruby libraries, and many of them are also covered elsewhere in this book. These libraries include ActiveRecord (much of Chapter 13, but especially Recipe 13.11), ActionMailer (Recipe 14.5), ERb (Recipe 1.3), Rake (Chapter 19), and Test::Unit (Recipe 17.7). Some of these predate Rails, and some were written for Rails but can be used outside of it. The opposite is also true: since a Rails application can be used for many purposes, nearly every recipe in this book is useful within a Rails program.

Rails is available as the `rails` gem, which contains libraries and the `rails` command-line program. This is the program you run to create a Rails application. When you invoke this program (for instance, with `rails mywebapp`), Rails generates a directory structure for your web application, complete with a WEBrick testing server and unit testing framework. When you use the `script/generate` script to jumpstart the creation of your application, Rails will populate this directory structure with more files. The code generated by these scripts is minimal and equivalent to the code generated by most IDEs when starting a project.

The architecture of Rails is the popular Model-View-Controller architecture. This divides the web application into three predictably named parts. We'll cover them in detail throughout this chapter, but here's an introductory reference.

The *model* is a representation of the dataset used by the application. This is usually a set of Ruby classes, subclasses of `ActiveRecord::Base`, each corresponding to a table in the application database. The first serious model in this chapter shows up in Recipe 15.6. To generate a model for a certain database table, invoke `script/generate model` with the name of the table, like so:

```
$ script/generate model users
```

This creates a file called *app/models/users.rb*, which defines a `User` ActiveRecord class as well as the basic structure to unit test that model. It does not create the actual database table.

The *controller* is a Ruby class (a subclass of `ActionController::Base`) whose methods define operations on the model. Each operation is defined as a method of the controller.

To generate a controller, invoke `script/generate controller` with the name of the controller, and the actions you want to expose:

```
$ script/generate controller user add delete login logout
```

This command creates a file `app/controllers/user_controller.rb`, which defines a class `UserController`. The class defines four stub methods: `add`, `delete`, `login`, and `logout`, each corresponding to an action the end user can perform on the objects of the underlying User model. It also creates the template for functionally unit testing your controller.

The controller shows up in the very first recipe of this chapter (Recipe 15.1).

The *view* is the user interface for the application. It's contained in a set of ERb templates, stored in *.rhtml* files. Most importantly, there is usually one *.rhtml* file for each action of each controller: this is the web interface for that particular action. The same command that created the UserController class above also created four files in *app/views/user/*: *add.rhtml*, *delete.rhtml*, *login.rhtml*, and *logout.rhtml*. As with the UserController class, these start out as stub files; your job is to customize them to present an interface to your application.

Like the controller, the view shows up in the first recipe of this chapter, Recipe 15.1. Recipes like 15.3, 15.5, and 15.14 show how to customize your views.

This division is not arbitrary. If you restrict code that changes the database to the model, it's easy to unit test that code and audit it for security problems. By moving all of your processing code into the controller, you separate the display of the user interface from its internal workings. The most obvious benefit of this is that you can have a UI designer modify your view templates without making them work around a lot of Ruby code.

The best recipes for learning how Model-View-Controller works are Recipe 15.2, which explores the relationship between the controller and the view; and Recipe 15.16, which combines all three.

Here are some more resources for getting started with Rails:

- This book's sister publication, *Rails Cookbook* by Rob Orsini (O'Reilly), covers Rails problems in more detail, as does *Rails Recipes* by Chad Fowler (Pragmatic Programmers)

- *Agile Web Development with Rails* by Dave Thomas, David Hansson, Leon Breedt, Mike Clark, Thomas Fuchs, and Andrea Schwarz (Pragmatic Programmers) is the standard reference for Rails programmers

- The Ruby on Rails web site at *http://www.rubyonrails.com/*, especially the RDoc documentation (*http://api.rubyonrails.org/*) and wiki (*http://wiki.rubyonrails.com/*)

15.1 Writing a Simple Rails Application to Show System Status

Problem

You would like to get started with Rails by building a very simple application.

Solution

This example displays the running processes on a Unix system. If you're developing on Windows, you can substitute some other command (such as the output of a `dir`) or just have your application print a static message.

First, make sure you have the `rails` gem installed.

To create a Rails application, run the `rails` command and pass in the name of your application. Our application will be called "status".

```
$ rails status
      create
      create   app/controllers
      create   app/helpers
      create   app/models
      create   app/views/layouts
      create   config/environments
  ...
```

A Rails application needs at least two parts: a *controller* and a *view*. Our controller will get information about the system, and our view will display it.

You can generate a controller and the corresponding view with the generate script. The following invocation defines a controller and view that implement a single action called index. This will be the main (and only) screen of our application.

```
$ cd status
$ ./script/generate controller status index
      exists   app/controllers/
      exists   app/helpers/
      create   app/views/status
      exists   test/functional/
      create   app/controllers/status_controller.rb
      create   test/functional/status_controller_test.rb
      create   app/helpers/status_helper.rb
      create   app/views/status/index.rhtml
```

The generated controller is in the Ruby source file `app/controllers/status_controller.rb`. That file defines a class `StatusController` that implements the index action as an empty method called index. Fill out the index method so that it exposes the objects you want to use in the view:

```ruby
class StatusController < ApplicationController
  def index
    # This variable won't be accessible to the view, since it is local
    # to this method
    time = Time.now

    # These variables will be accessible in the view, since they are
    # instance variables of the StatusController.
    @time = time
    @ps = `ps aux`
  end
end
```

The generated view is in app/views/status/index.rhtml. It starts out as a static HTML snippet. Change it to an ERb template that uses the instance variables set in StatusController#index:

```
<h1>Processes running at <%= @time %></h1>
<pre><%= @ps %></pre>
```

Now our application is complete. To run it, start up the Rails server with the following command:

```
$ ./script/server
=> Booting WEBrick...
=> Rails application started on http://0.0.0.0:3000
=> Ctrl-C to shutdown server; call with --help for options
...
```

You can see the application by visiting *http://localhost:3000/status/*.

Of course, you wouldn't expose this application to the outside world because it might give an attacker information about your system.

Discussion

The first thing you should notice about a Rails application is that you do not create separate code files for every URL. Rails uses an architecture in which the controller (a Ruby source file) and a view (an ERb template in an .rhtml file) team up to serve a number of *actions*. Each action handles some of the URLs on your site.

Consider a URL like *http://www.example.com/hello/world*. To serve that URL in your Rails application, you'd create a hello controller and give it an action called world.

```
$ ./script/generate controller hello world
```

Your controller class would have a world method, and your *views/hello* directory would have a *world.rhtml* file containing the view.

```
class HelloController < ApplicationController
  def world
  end
end
```

Visiting *http://www.example.com/hello/world* would invoke the HelloController#world method, interpret the *world.rhtml* template to obtain some HTML output, and serve that output to the client.

The default action for a controller is index, just as the default page in a directory of a static web server is *index.html*. So visiting *http://www.example.com/hello/* is the same as visiting *http://www.example.com/hello/index/*.

As mentioned above, a view file is only the main snippet of the final page served by Rails. It's not a full HTML page, and you should never put <html> or <body> tags inside it (see Recipe 15.3). Since a view file is an ERB template, you should also never call puts or print inside a view. ERB was introduced in Recipe 1.3, but it's worth exploring here within the context of a Rails application.

To insert the value of a Ruby expression into an ERB template, use the `<%= %>` directive. Here's a possible *world.rhtml* view for our `hello` action:

```
<p>Several increasingly silly ways of displaying "Hello world!":</p>

<p><%= "Hello world!" %></p>
<p><%= "Hello" + "world!" %></p>
<p><%= w = "world"
       "Hello #{w}!" %></p>
<p><%= 'H' + ?e.chr + ('l' * 2) %><%=('o word!').gsub('d', 'ld')%></p>
```

The last example is excessive, but it proves a point. You shouldn't have to put so much Ruby code in your view template (it should probably go into your controller, or you'll end up with sloppy PHP-like code), but it's possible if you need to do it.

The equals sign in the ERb directive means that the output is to be printed. If you want to execute a command without output, omit the equals sign and use the `<% %>` directive.

```
<% hello = "Hello" %>
<% world = "world!" %>
<%= hello %> <%= world %>
```

A view and a controller may be based on nothing more than some data obtained from within Ruby code (like the current time and the output of ps aux). But most real-world views and controllers are based on a *model*: a set of database tables containing data that the view displays and the controller manipulates. This is the famous "Model-View-Controller" architecture, and it's by no means unique to Rails.

See Also

- Recipe 1.3, "Substituting Variables into an Existing String," has more on ERB
- Recipe 15.3, "Creating a Layout for Your Header and Footer"

15.2 Passing Data from the Controller to the View

Problem

You want to pass data between a controller and its views.

Solution

The view is an ERB template that is interpreted within the context of its controller object. A view cannot call any of the controller's methods, but it can access the controller's instance variables. To pass data to the view, set an instance variable of the controller.

Here's a `NovelController` class, to be put into app/controllers/novel_controller.rb. You can generate stubs for it by running `script/generate controller novel index`.

```
class NovelController < ApplicationController
  def index
    @title = 'Shattered View: A Novel on Rails'
    one_plus_one = 1 + 1
    increment_counter one_plus_one
  end

  def helper_method
    @help_message = "I see you've come to me for help."
  end

  private

  def increment_counter(by)
    @counter ||= 0
    @counter += by
  end
end
```

Since this is the `Novel` controller and the `index` action, the corresponding view is in app/views/novel/index.rhtml.

```
<h1><%= @title %></h1>

<p>I looked up, but saw only the number <%= @counter %>.</p>

<p>"What are you doing here?" I asked sharply. "Was it <%=
@counter.succ %> who sent you?"</p>
```

The view is interpreted after `NovelController#index` is run. Here's what the view can and can't access:

- It can access the instance variables `@title` and `@counter`, because they've been defined on the `NovelController` object by the time `NovelController#index` finishes running.
- It can call instance methods of the instance variables `@title` and `@counter`.
- It cannot access the instance variable `@help_message`, because that variable is defined by the method `helper_method`, which never gets called.
- It cannot access the variable `one_plus_one`, because that's not an instance variable: it's local to the `index` method.
- Even though it runs in the context of `NovelController`, it cannot call any method of `NovelController`—neither `helper_method` nor `set_another_variable`. Nor can it call `index` again.

Discussion

The action method of a controller is responsible for creating and storing (in instance variables) all the objects the view will need to do its job. These variables might be as simple as strings, or they might be complex helper classes. Either way, most of your application's logic should be in the controller. It's okay to do things in the view like iterate over data structures, but most of the work should happen in the controller or in one of the objects it exposes through an instance variable.

Rails instantiates a new `NovelController` object for every request. This means you can't persist data between requests by putting it in controller instance variables. No matter how many times you reload the page, the `@counter` variable will never be more than two. Every time `increment_counter` is called, it's called on a brand new `NovelController` object.

Like any Ruby class, a Rails controller can define class variables and constants, but they will not be available to the view. Consider a `NovelController` that looks like this:

```
class NovelController < ApplicationController
  @@numbers = [1, 2, 3]
  TITLE = 'Revenge of the Counting Numbers'
end
```

Neither `@@numbers` nor `TITLE` are accessible from within any of this controller's views. They can only be used by the controller methods.

However, contants defined outside of the context of a controller are accessible to every view. This is useful if you want to declare the web site's name in one easy-to-change location. The `config/environment.rb` file is a good place to define these constants:

```
# config/environment.rb
AUTHOR = 'Lucas Carlson'
...
```

It is almost always a bad idea to use global variables in object-oriented programming. But Ruby does have them, and a global variable will be available to any view once it's been defined. They will be universally available whether they were defined within the scope of the action, the controller, or outside of any scope.

```
$one = 1
class NovelController < ApplicationController
  $two = 2
  def sequel
    $three = 3
  end
end
```

Here's a view, `sequel.rhtml`, that uses those three global variables:

```
Here they come, the counting numbers, <%= $one %>, <%= $two %>, <%= $three %>.
```

15.3 Creating a Layout for Your Header and Footer

Problem

You want to create a header and footer for every page on your web application. Certain pages should have special headers and footers, and you may want to dynamically determine which header and footer to use for a given request.

Solution

Many web applications let you define header and footer files, and automatically include those files at the top and bottom of every page. Rails inverts this pattern. A single file called contains both the header and footer, and the contents of each particular page are inserted into this file.

To apply a layout to every page in your web application, create a file called *app/views/layouts/application.rhtml*. It should look something like this:

```
<html>
  <head>
    <title>My Website</title>
  </head>
  <body>
    <%= @content_for_layout %>
  </body>
</html>
```

The key piece of information in any layout file is the directive `<%= content_for_layout %>`. This is replaced by the content of each individual page.

You can make customized layouts for each controller independently by creating files in the *app/views/layouts* folder. For example, *app/views/layouts/status.rhtml* is the layout for the `status` controller, `StatusController`. The layout file for `PriceController` would be *price.rhtml*.

Customized layouts override the site-wide layout; they don't add to it.

Discussion

Just like your main view templates, your layout templates have access to all the instance variables set by the action. Anything you can do in a view, you can do in a layout template. This means you can do things like set the page title dynamically in the action, and then use it in the layout:

```
class StatusController < ActionController:Base
  def index
    @title = "System Status"
  end
end
```

Now the application.rhtml file can access @title like this:

```
<html>
  <head>
    <title>My Website - <%= @title %></title>
  </head>
  <body>
    <%= @content_for_layout %>
  </body>
</html>
```

application.rhtml doesn't just happen to be the default layout template for a Rails application's controllers. It happens this way because every controller inherits from ApplicationController. By default, a layout's name is derived from the name of the controller's class. So ApplicationController turns into application.rhtml. If you had a controller named MyFunkyController, the default filename for the layout would be app/views/layouts/my_funky.rhtml. If that file didn't exist, Rails would look for a layout corresponding to the superclass of MyFunkyController, and find it in app/views/layouts/application.rhtml.

To change a controller's layout file, call its layout method:

```
class FooController < ActionController:Base
  # Force the layout for /foo to be app/views/layouts/bar.rhtml,
  # not app/view/layouts/foo.rhtml.
  layout 'bar'
end
```

If you're using the render method in one of your actions (see Recipe 15.5), you can pass in a :layout argument to render and give that action a different layout from the rest of the controller. In this example, most actions of the FooController use bar.rhtml for their layout, but the count action uses count.rhtml:

```
class FooController < ActionController:Base
  layout 'bar'

  def count
    @data = [1,2,3]
    render :layout => 'count'
  end
end
```

You can even have an action without a layout. This code gives all of FooController's actions a layout of bar.html, except for the count action, which has no layout at all: it's responsible for all of its own HTML.

```
class FooController < ActionController:Base
  layout 'bar', :except => 'count'
end
```

If you need to calculate the layout file dynamically, pass a method symbol into the layout method. This tells layout to call a method on each request; the return value of this method defines the layout file. The method can call `action_name` to determine the action name of the current request.

```
class FooController < ActionController:Base
  layout :figure_out_layout

  private

  def figure_out_layout
    if action_name =~ /pretty/
      'pretty'          # use pretty.rhtml for the layout
    else
      'standard'        # use standard.rhtml
    end
  end
end
```

Finally, `layout` accepts a lambda function as an argument. This lets you dynamically decide on a layout with less code:

```
class FooController < ActionController:Base
  layout lambda { |controller| controller.logged_in? ? 'user' : 'guest' }
end
```

It's freeing for both the programmer and the designer to use a layout file instead of separate headers and footers: it's easier to see the whole picture. But if you need to use explicit headers and footers, you can. Create files called app/views/layouts/_header.rhtml and app/views/layouts/_footer.rhtml. The underscores indicate that they are "partials" (see Recipe 15.14). To use them, set your actions up to use no layout at all, and write the following code in your view files:

```
<%= render :partial => 'layouts/header' %>
... your view's content goes here ...
<%= render :partial => 'layouts/footer' %>
```

See Also

- Recipe 15.5, "Displaying Templates with Render"
- Recipe 15.14, "Refactoring the View into Partial Snippets of Views"

15.4   Redirecting to a Different Location

Problem

You want to redirect your user to another of your application's actions, or to an external URL.

Solution

The class `ActionController::Base` (superclass of `ApplicationController`) defines a method called `redirect_to`, which performs an HTTP redirect. To redirect to another site, you can pass it a URL as a string. To redirect to a different action in your application, pass it a hash that specifies the controller, action, and ID.

Here's a BureaucracyController that shuffles incoming requests to and fro between various actions, finally sending the client to an external site:

```
class BureaucracyController < ApplicationController
  def index
    redirect_to :controller => 'bureaucracy', :action => 'reservation_window'
  end

  def reservation_window
    redirect_to :action => 'claim_your_form', :id => 123
  end

  def claim_your_form
    redirect_to :action => 'fill_out_your_form', :id => params[:id]
  end

  def fill_out_your_form
    redirect_to :action => 'form_processing'
  end

  def form_processing
    redirect_to "http://www.dmv.org/"
  end
end
```

If you run the Rails server and hit *http://localhost:3000/bureaucracy/* in your browser, you'll end up at *http://www.dmv.org/*. The Rails server log will show the chain of HTTP requests you made to get there:

```
"GET /bureaucracy HTTP/1.1" 302
"GET /bureaucracy/reservation_window HTTP/1.1" 302
"GET /bureaucracy/claim_your_form/123 HTTP/1.1" 302
"GET /bureaucracy/fill_out_your_form/123 HTTP/1.1" 302
"GET /bureaucracy/form_processing HTTP/1.1" 302
```

You don't need to create view templates for all of these actions, because the body of an HTTP redirect isn't displayed by the web browser.

Discussion

The redirect_to method uses smart defaults. If you give it a hash that doesn't specify a controller, it assumes you want to move to another action in the same controller. If you leave out the action, it assumes you are talking about the index action.

From the simple redirects given in the Solution, you might think that calling redirect_to actually stops the action method in place and does an immediate HTTP redirect. This is not true. The action method continues to run until it ends or you call return. The redirect_to method doesn't do a redirect: it tells Rails to do a redirect once the action method has finished running.

Here's an illustration of the problem. You might think that the call to `redirect_to` below prevents the method do_something_dangerous from being called.

```
class DangerController < ApplicationController
  def index
    redirect_to (:action => 'safety') unless params[:i_like_danger]
    do_something_dangerous
  end

  # ...
end
```

But it doesn't. The only way to stop an action method from running all the way to the end is to call return.* What you really want to do is this:

```
class DangerController < ApplicationController
  def index
    redirect_to (:action => 'safety') and return unless params[:i_like_danger]
    do_something_dangerous
  end
end
```

Notice the and return at the end of `redirect_to`. It's very rare that you'll want to execute code after telling Rails to redirect the user to another page. To avoid problems, make a habit of adding and return at the end of calls to `redirect_to` or `render`.

See Also

- The generated RDoc for the methods `ApplicationController::Base#redirect_to` and `ApplicationController::Base#url_for`

15.5 Displaying Templates with Render

Problem

Rails's default mapping of one action method to one view template is not flexible enough for you. You want to customize the template that gets rendered for a particular action by calling Rails's rendering code directly.

Solution

Rendering happens in the `ActionController::Base#render` method. Rails's default behavior is to call `render` after the action method runs, mapping the action to a corresponding view template. The foo action gets mapped to the `foo.rhtml` template.

---

* You could throw an exception, but then your redirect wouldn't happen: the user would see an exception screen instead.

You can call render from within an action method to make Rails render a different template. This controller defines two actions, both of which are rendered using the shopping_list.rhtml template:

```
class ListController < ApplicationController
  def index
    @list = ['papaya', 'polio vaccine']
    render :action => 'shopping_list'
  end

  def shopping_list
    @list = ['cotton balls', 'amino acids', 'pie']
  end
end
```

By default, render assumes that you are talking about the controller and action that are running when render is called. If you call render with no arguments, Rails will work the same way it usually does. But specifying 'shopping_list' as the view overrides this default, and makes the index action use the shopping_list.rhtml template, just like the shopping_list action does.

Discussion

Although they use the same template, visiting the index action is not the same as visiting the shopping_list action. They display different lists, because index defines a different list from shopping_list.

Recall from Recipe 15.4 that the redirect method doesn't perform an immediate HTTP redirect. It tells Rails to do a redirect once the current action method finishes running. Similarly, the render method doesn't do the rendering immediately. It only tells Rails which template to render when the action is complete.

Consider this example:

```
class ListController < ApplicationController
  def index
    render :action => 'shopping_list'
    @budget = 87.50
  end

  def shopping_list
    @list = ['lizard food', 'baking soda']
  end
end
```

You might think that calling index sets @list but not @budget. Actually, the reverse is true. Calling index sets @budget but not @list.

The @budget variable gets set because render does not stop the execution of the current action. Calling render is like sealing a message in an envelope that gets opened by Rails at some point in the future. You're still free to set instance variables and make other method calls. Once your action method returns, Rails will open the envelope and use the rendering strategy contained within.

The @list variable does *not* get set because the render call does not call the shopping_list action. It just makes the existing action, index, use the shopping_list.rhtml template instead of the index.rhtml template. There doesn't even need to *be* a shopping_list action: there just has to be a template named shopping_list.rhtml.

If you do want to invoke one action from another, you can invoke the action method explicitly. This code will make index set both @budget and @list:

```
class ListController < ApplicationController
  def index
    shopping_list and render :action => 'shopping_list'
    @budget = 87.50
  end
end
```

Another consequence of this "envelope" behavior is that you must never call render twice within a single client request (the same goes for render's cousin redirect_to, which also seals a message in an envelope).

If you write code like the following, Rails will complain. You're giving it two sealed envelopes, and it doesn't know which to open:

```
class ListController < ApplicationController
  def plain_and_fancy
    render :action => 'plain_list'
    render :action => 'fancy_list'
  end
end
```

But the following code is fine, because any given request will only trigger one branch of the if/else clause. Whatever happens, render will only be called once per request.

```
class ListController < ApplicationController
  def plain_or_fancy
    if params[:fancy]
      render :action => 'fancy_list'
    else
      render :action => 'plain_list'
    end
  end
end
```

With redirect_to, if you want to force your action method to stop running, you can put a return statement immediately after your call to render. This code does not set the @budget variable, because execution never gets past the return statement:

```
class ListController < ApplicationController
  def index
    render :action => 'shopping_list' and return
    @budget = 87.50           # This line won't be run.
  end
end
```

See Also

- Recipe 15.4, "Redirecting to a Different Location"
- Recipe 15.14, "Refactoring the View into Partial Snippets of Views," shows examples of calling render within a view template

15.6   Integrating a Database with Your Rails Application

Problem

You want your web application to store persistent data in a relational database.

Solution

The hardest part is setting things up: creating your database and hooking Rails up to it. Once that's done, database access is as simple as writing Ruby code.

To tell Rails how to access your database, open your application's config/database.yml file. Assuming your Rails application is called mywebapp, it should look something like this:

```
development:
adapter: mysql
database: mywebapp_development
host: localhost
username: root
password:

test:
adapter: mysql
database: mywebapp_test
host: localhost
username: root
password:

production:
adapter: mysql
database: mywebapp
host: localhost
username: root
password:
```

For now, just make sure the development section contains a valid username and password, and that it mentions the correct adapter name for your type of database (see Chapter 13 for the list).

Now create a database table. As with so much else, Rails does a lot of the database work automatically if you follow its conventions. You can override the conventions if necessary, but for now it's easiest to go along with them.

The name of the table must be a pluralized noun: for instance, "people", "tasks", "items".

The table must contain an auto-incrementing primary key field called id.

For this example, use a database tool or a CREATE DATABASE SQL command to create a mywebapp_development database (see the chapter introduction for Chapter 13 if you need help doing this). Then create a table in that database called people. Here's the SQL to create a people table in MySQL; you can adapt it for your database.

```
use mywebapp_development;

DROP TABLE IF EXISTS 'people';
CREATE TABLE 'people' (
'id' INT(11) NOT NULL AUTO_INCREMENT,
'name' VARCHAR(255),
'email' VARCHAR(255),
PRIMARY KEY (id)
) ENGINE=InnoDB;
```

Now go to the command line, change into the web application's root directory, and type ./script/generate model Person. This generates a Ruby class that knows how to manipulate the people table.

```
$ ./script/generate model Person
exists app/models/
exists test/unit/
exists test/fixtures/
create app/models/person.rb
create test/unit/person_test.rb
create test/fixtures/people.yml
```

Notice that your model is named Person, even though the table was named people. If you abide by its conventions, Rails automatically handles these pluralizations for you (see Recipe 15.7 for details).

Your web application now has access to the people table, via the Person class. Again from the command line, run this command:

```
$ ./script/runner 'Person.create(:name => "John Doe", \
:email => "john@doe.com")'
```

That code creates a new entry in the people table. (If you've read Recipe 13.11, you'll recognize this as ActiveRecord code.)

To access this person from your application, create a new controller and a view to go along with it:

```
$ ./script/generate controller people list
exists app/controllers/
```

```
exists app/helpers/
create app/views/people
exists test/functional/
create app/controllers/people_controller.rb
create test/functional/people_controller_test.rb
create app/helpers/people_helper.rb
create app/views/people/list.rhtml
```

Edit *app/view/people/list.rhtml* so it looks like this:

```
<!-- list.rhtml -->
<ul>
<% Person.find(:all).each do |person| %>
<li>Name: <%= person.name %>, Email: <%= person.email %
></li>
<% end %>
</ul>
```

Start the Rails server, visit *http://localhost:3000/people/list/*, and you'll see John Doe listed.

The Person model class is accessible from all parts of your Rails application: your controllers, views, helpers, and mailers.

Discussion

Up until now, the applications created in these recipes have been using only controllers and views.* The Person class, and its underlying database table, give us for the first time the Model portion of the Model-View-Controller triangle.

A relational database is usually the best place to store real-world models, but it's difficult to program a relational database directly. Rails uses the ActiveRecord library to hide the people table behind a Person class. Methods like Person.find let you search the person database table without writing SQL; the results are automatically converted into Person objects. The basics of ActiveRecord are covered in Recipe 13.11.

The Person.find method takes a lot of optional arguments. If you pass it an integer, it will look for the person entry whose unique ID is that integer, and return an appropriate Person object. The :all and :first symbols grab all entries from the table (an array of Person objects), or only the first person that matches. You can limit or order your dataset by specifying :limit or :order; you can even set raw SQL conditions via :conditions.

Here's how to find the first five entries in the people table that have email addresses. The result will be a list containing five Person objects, ordered by their name fields.

```
Person.find(:all,
    :limit => 5,
```

---

* More precisely, our models have been embedded in our controllers, as ad hoc data structures like hardcoded shopping lists.

```
          :order => 'name',
          :conditions => 'email IS NOT NULL')
```

The three different sections of config/database.yml specify the three different databases used at different times by your Rails application:

Development database
> The database you use when working on the application. Generally filled with test data.

Test database
> A scratch database used by the unit testing framework when running tests for your application. Its data is populated automatically by the unit testing framework.

Production database
> The database mode to use when your web site is running with live data.

Unless you explicitly setup Rails to run in production or test mode, it defaults to development mode. So to get started, you only need to make sure the development portion of database.yml is set up correctly.

See Also

- Chapter 13
- Recipe 13.11, "Using Object Relational Mapping with ActiveRecord"
- Recipe 13.13, "Building Queries Programmatically"
- Recipe 13.14, "Validating Data with ActiveRecord"
- ActiveRecord can't do everything that SQL can. For complex database operations, you'll need to use DBI or one of the Ruby bindings to specific kinds of database; these topics too are covered in Recipe 13.15, "Preventing SQL Injection Attacks," which gives more on the format of the database.yml file

15.7 Understanding Pluralization Rules

Problem

You want to understand and customize Rails's rules for automatically pluralizing nouns.

Solution

You can use Rails' pluralization functionality in any part of your application, but ActiveRecord is the only major part of Rails that does pluralization automatically. ActiveRecord generally expects table names to be pluralized noun phrases and the corresponding model classes to be singular versions of the same noun phrases.

So when you create a model class, you should always use a singular name. Rails automatically pluralizes:

- The corresponding table name for the model
- has_many relations
- has_and_belongs_to_many relations

For example, if you create a LineItem model, the table name automatically becomes line_items. Note also that the table name has been lowercased, and the word break indicated by the original camelcase is now conveyed with an underscore.

If you then create an Order model, the corresponding table needs to be called orders. If you want to describe an order that has many line items, the code would look like this:

```
class Order < ActiveRecord::Base
  has_many :line_items
end
```

Like the name of the table it references, the symbol used in the has_many relation is pluralized and underscored. The same goes for the other relationships between tables, like has_and_belongs_to_many.

Discussion

ActiveRecord pluralizes these names to make your code read more like an English sentence: has_many :line_items can be read "has many line items". If pluralization confuses you, you can disable it by setting ActiveRecord::Base.pluralize_table_names to false. In Rails, the simplest way to do this is to put the following code in config/environment.rb:

```
Rails::Initializer.run do |config|
  config.active_record.pluralize_table_names = false
end
```

If your application knows specific words that ActiveRecord does not know how to pluralize, you can define your own pluralization rules by manipulating the Inflector class. Let's say that the plural of "foo" is "fooze", and you've build an application to manage fooze. In Rails, you can specify this transformation by putting the following code in config/environment.rb:

```
Inflector.inflections do |inflect|
  inflect.plural /^(foo)$/i, '\1ze'
  inflect.singular /^(foo)ze/i, '\1'
end
```

In this case, it's simpler to use the irregular method:

```
Inflector.inflections do |inflect|
  inflect.irregular 'foo', 'fooze'
end
```

If you have nouns that should never be inflected (usually because they are mass nouns, or because their plural form is the same as their singular form), you can pass them into the uncountable method:

```
Inflector.inflections do |inflect|
  inflect.uncountable ['status', 'furniture', 'fish', 'sheep']
end
```

The Inflector class is part of the activesupport gem, and you can use it outside of ActiveRecord or Rails as a general way of pluralizing English words. Here's a stand-alone Ruby program:

```
require 'rubygems'
require 'active_support/core_ext'

'blob'.pluralize                             # => "blobs"
'child'.pluralize                            # => "children"
'octopus'.pluralize                          # => "octopi"
'octopi'.singularize                         # => "octopus"
'people'.singularize                         # => "person"

'goose'.pluralize                            # => "gooses"
Inflector.inflections { |i| i.irregular 'goose', 'geese' }
'goose'.pluralize                            # => "geese"

'moose'.pluralize                            # => "mooses"
Inflector.inflections { |i| i.uncountable 'moose' }
'moose'.pluralize                            # => "moose"
```

See Also

- Recipe 13.11, "Using Object Relational Mapping with ActiveRecord"

15.8 Creating a Login System

Problem

You want your application to support a login system based on user accounts. Users will log in with a unique username and password, as in most commercial and community web sites.

Solution

Create a users table that contains nonnull username and password fields. The SQL to create this table should look something like this MySQL example:

```
use mywebapp_development;
DROP TABLE IF EXISTS `users`;
CREATE TABLE `users` (
  `id` INT(11) NOT NULL AUTO_INCREMENT,
  `username` VARCHAR(255) NOT NULL,
```

```
    `password` VARCHAR(40) NOT NULL,
    PRIMARY KEY (`id`)
);
```

Enter the main directory of the application and generate a User model corresponding to this table:

```
$ ./script/generate model User
      exists  app/models/
      exists  test/unit/
      exists  test/fixtures/
      create  app/models/user.rb
      create  test/unit/user_test.rb
      create  test/fixtures/users.yml
```

Open the generated file *app/models/user.rb* and edit it to look like this:

```
class User < ActiveRecord::Base
  validates_uniqueness_of :username
  validates_confirmation_of :password, :on => :create
  validates_length_of :password, :within => 5..40

  # If a user matching the credentials is found, returns the User object.
  # If no matching user is found, returns nil.
  def self.authenticate(user_info)
    find_by_username_and_password(user_info[:username],
                                  user_info[:password])
  end
end
```

Now you've got a User class that represents a user account, and a way of validating a username and password against the one stored in the database.

Discussion

The simple User model given in the Solution defines a method for doing username/password validation, and some validation rules that impose limitations on the data to be stored in the users table. These validation rules tell User to:

- Ensure that each username is unique. No two users can have the same username.
- Ensure that, whenever the password attribute is being set, the password_confirmation attribute has the same value.
- Ensure that the value of the password attribute is between 5 and 40 characters long.

Now let's create a controller for this model. It'll have a login action to display the login page, a process_login action to check the username and password, and a logout action to deauthenticate a logged-in session. So that the user accounts will actually do something, we'll also add a my_account action:

```
$ ./script/generate controller user login process_login logout my_account
      exists  app/controllers/
      exists  app/helpers/
```

```
        create  app/views/user
        exists  test/functional/
        create  app/controllers/user_controller.rb
        create  test/functional/user_controller_test.rb
        create  app/helpers/user_helper.rb
        create  app/views/user/login.rhtml
        create  app/views/user/process_login.rhtml
        create  app/views/user/logout.rhtml
```

Edit *app/controllers/user_controller.rb* to define the three actions:

```
class UserController < ApplicationController
  def login
    @user = User.new
    @user.username = params[:username]
  end

  def process_login
    if user = User.authenticate(params[:user])
      session[:id] = user.id # Remember the user's id during this session
      redirect_to session[:return_to] || '/'
    else
      flash[:error] = 'Invalid login.'
      redirect_to :action => 'login', :username => params[:user][:username]
    end
  end

  def logout
    reset_session
    flash[:message] = 'Logged out.'
    redirect_to :action => 'login'
  end

  def my_account
  end
end
```

Now for the views. The process_login and logout actions just redirect to other actions, so we only need views for login and my_account. Here's a view for login:

```
<!-- app/views/user/login.rhtml -->
<% if @flash[:message] %><div><%= @flash[:message] %></div><% end %>
<% if @flash[:error] %><div><%= @flash[:error] %></div><% end %>

<%= form_tag :action => 'process_login' %>
 Username: <%= text_field "user", "username" %>&#x00A;
  Password: <%= password_field "user", "password" %>&#x00A;
   <%= submit_tag %>
<%= end_form_tag %>
```

The @flash instance variable is a hashlike object used to store temporary messages for the user between actions. When the logout action sets flash[:message] and redirects to login, or process_login sets flash[:error] and redirects to login, the results are available to the view of the login action. Then they get cleared out.

Here's a very simple view for my_account:

```
<!-- app/views/user/my_account.rhtml -->
<h1>Account Info</h1>

<p>Your username is <%= User.find(session[:id]).username %>
```

Create an entry in the users table, start the server, and you'll find that you can log in from *http://localhost:3000/user/login*, and view your account information from *http://localhost:3000/user/my_account*.

```
$ ./script/runner 'User.create(:username => "johndoe", \
                               :password => "changeme")'
```

There's just one missing piece: you can visit the my_account action even if you're not logged in. We don't have a way to close off an action to unauthenticated users. Add the following code to your *app/controllers/application.rb* file:

```
class ApplicationController < ActionController::Base
  before_filter :set_user

protected
  def set_user
    @user = User.find(session[:id]) if @user.nil? && session[:id]
  end

  def login_required
    return true if @user
    access_denied
    return false
  end

  def access_denied
    session[:return_to] = request.request_uri
    flash[:error] = 'Oops. You need to login before you can view that page.'
    redirect_to :controller => 'user', :action => 'login'
  end
end
```

This code defines two filters, set_user and login_required, which you can apply to actions or controllers. The set_user filter is run on every action (because we pass it into before_filter in ApplicationController, the superclass of all our controllers). The set_user method sets the instance variable @user if the user is logged in. Now information about the logged-in user (if any) is available throughout your application. Action methods and views can use this instance variable like any other. This is useful even for actions that don't require login: for instance, your main layout view might display the name of the logged-in user (if any) on every page.

You can prohibit unauthenticated users from using a specific action or controller by passing the symbol for the login_required method into before_filter. Here's how to protect the my_account action defined in *app/controllers/user_controller.rb*:

```
class UserController < ApplicationController
  before_filter :login_required, :only => :my_account
end
```

Now if you try to use the my_account action without being logged in, you'll be redirected to the login page.

See Also

- Recipe 13.14, "Validating Data with ActiveRecord"
- Recipe 15.6, "Integrating a Database with Your Rails Application"
- Recipe 15.9, "Storing Hashed User Passwords in the Database"
- Recipe 15.11, "Setting and Retrieving Session Information"
- Rather than doing this work yourself, you can install the login_generator gem and use its login generator: it will give your application a User model and a controller that implements a password-based authentication system; see *http://wiki. rubyonrails.com/rails/pages/LoginGenerator*; also see *http://wiki.rubyonrails.com/ rails/pages/AvailableGenerators* for other generators (including the more sophisticated model_security_generator)

15.9   Storing Hashed User Passwords in the Database

Problem

The database table defined in Recipe 15.8 stores users' passwords as plain text. This is a bad idea: if someone compromises the database, she will have all of your users' passwords. It's best to store a secure hash of the password instead. That way, you don't have the password (so no one can steal it), but you can verify that a user knows his password.

Solution

Recreate the users table from Recipe 15.8 so that instead of a password field, it has a hashed_password field. Here's some MySQL code to do that:

```
use mywebapp_development;
DROP TABLE IF EXISTS `users`;
CREATE TABLE `users` (
  `id` INT(11) NOT NULL AUTO_INCREMENT,
  `username` VARCHAR(255) NOT NULL,
  `hashed_password` VARCHAR(40) NOT NULL,
  PRIMARY KEY (id)
);
```

Open the file *app/models/user.rb* created in Recipe 15.8, and edit it to look like this:

```
require 'sha1'

class User < ActiveRecord::Base
  attr_accessor :password
  attr_protected :hashed_password
  validates_uniqueness_of :username
```

```
    validates_confirmation_of :password,
      :if => lambda { |user| user.new_record? or not user.password.blank? }
    validates_length_of :password, :within => 5..40,
      :if => lambda { |user| user.new_record? or not user.password.blank? }

    def self.hashed(str)
      SHA1.new(str).to_s
    end

    # If a user matching the credentials is found, returns the User object.
    # If no matching user is found, returns nil.
    def self.authenticate(user_info)
      user = find_by_username(user_info[:username])
      if user && user.hashed_password == hashed(user_info[:password])
        return user
      end
    end

    private
    before_save :update_password

    # Updates the hashed_password if a plain password was provided.
    def update_password
      if not password.blank?
        self.hashed_password = self.class.hashed(password)
      end
    end
  end
```

Once you do this, your application will work as before (though you'll have to convert any preexisting user accounts to the new password format). You don't need to modify any of the controller or view code, because the User.authenticate method works the same way it did before. This is one of the benefits of separating business logic from presentation logic.

Discussion

There are now three pieces to our user model. The first is the enhanced validation code. The user model now:

- Provides getters and setters for the password attribute.
- Makes sure that the hashed_password field in the database can't be accessed from the outside.
- Ensures that each user has a unique username.

When a new user is created, or when the password is changed, User ensures:

- That the value of the password_confirmation attribute is equal to the value of the password attribute.
- That the password is between 5 and 40 characters long.

The second section of code defines User class methods as before. We add one new class-level method, hashed, which performs the hashing function on a plaintext password. If we want to change hashing mechanisms in the future, we only have to change this method (and migrate any existing passwords).

The third piece of code in the model is a private instance method, update_password, which synchronizes the plaintext password attribute with the hashed version in the database. The call to before_save sets up this method to be called before a User object is saved to the database. This way you can change a user's password by setting password to its plaintext value, instead of doing the hash yourself.

See Also

- Recipe 13.14, "Validating Data with ActiveRecord"
- Recipe 15.8, "Creating a Login System"

15.10 Escaping HTML and JavaScript for Display

Problem

You want to display data that might contain HTML or JavaScript without making browsers render it as HTML or interpret the JavaScript. This is especially important when displaying data entered by users.

Solution

Pass a string of data into the h( ) helper function to escape its HTML entities. That is, instead of this:

```
<%= @data %>
```

Write this:

```
<%=h @data %>
```

The h( ) helper function converts the following characters into their HTML entity equivalents: ampersand (&), double quote ("), left angle bracket (<), and right angle bracket (>).

Discussion

You won't find the definition for the h( ) helper function anywhere in the Rails source code, because it's a shortcut for ERb's built-in helper function html_escape( ).

JavaScript is deployed within HTML tags like <SCRIPT>, so escaping an HTML string will neutralize any JavaScript in the HTML. However, sometimes you need to escape just the JavaScript in a string. Rails adds a helper function called escape_javascript( ) that you can use. This function doesn't do much: it just turns line breaks into the string "\n", and adds backslashes before single and double quotes. This is handy when you want to use arbitrary data in your own JavaScript code:

```
<!-- index.rhtml -->
<script lang="javascript">
var text = "<%= escape_javascript @javascript_alert_text %>";
alert(text);
</script>
```

See Also

- Chapter 11

15.11 Setting and Retrieving Session Information

Problem

You want to associate some data with each distinct web client that's using your application. The data needs to persist across HTTP requests.

Solution

You can use cookies (see Recipe 15.12) but it's usually simpler to put the data in a user's session. Every visitor to your Rails site is automatically given a session cookie. Rails keys the value of the cookie to a hash of arbitrary data on the server.

Throughout your entire Rails application, in controllers, views, helpers, and mailers, you can access this hash by calling a method called session. The objects stored in this hash are persisted across requests by the same web browser.

This code in a controller tracks the time of a client's first visit to your web site:

```
class IndexController < ApplicationController
  def index
    session[:first_time] ||= Time.now
  end
end
```

Within your view, you can write the following code to display the time:*

```
<!-- index.rhtml -->
You first visited this site on <%= session[:first_time] %>.

That was <%= time_ago_in_words session[:first_time] %> ago.
```

---

* The helper function time_ago_in_words( ) calculates how long it's been since a certain time and returns English text such as "about a minute" or "5 hours" or "2 days". This is a nice, easy way to give the user a perspective on what a date means.

Discussion

Cookies and sessions are very similar. They both store persistent data about a visitor to your site. They both let you implement stateful operations on top of HTTP, which has no state of its own. The main difference between cookies and sessions is that with cookies, all the data is stored on your visitors' computers in little cookie files. With sessions, all the data is stored on the web server. The client only keeps a small session cookie, which contains a unique ID that's tied to the data on the server. No personal data is ever stored on the visitor's computer.

There are a number of reasons why you might want to use sessions instead of cookies:

- A cookie can only store four kilobytes of data.
- A cookie can only store a string value.
- If you store personal information in a cookie, it can be intercepted unless all of a client's requests are encrypted with SSL. Even then, cross-site scripting attacks may be able to read the client cookie and retrieve the sensitive information.

On the other hand, cookies are useful when:

- The information is not sensitive and not very large.
- You don't want to store session information about each visitor on your server.
- You need speed from your application, and not every page needs to access the session data.

Generally, it's a better idea to use sessions than to store data in cookies.

You can include model objects in your session: this can save a lot of trouble over retrieving the same objects from the database on every request. However, if you are going to do this, it's a good idea to list in your application controller all the models you'll be putting into the session. This reduces the risk that Rails won't be able to deserialize the objects when retrieving them from the session store.

```
class ApplicationController < ActionController::Base
  model :user, :ticket, :item, :history
end
```

Then you can put ActiveRecord objects into a session:

```
class IndexController < ApplicationController
  def index
    session[:user] ||= User.find(params[:id])
  end
end
```

If your site doesn't need to store any information in sessions, you can disable the feature by adding the following code to your app/controllers/application.rb file:

```
class ApplicationController < ActionController::Base
  session :off
end
```

As you may have guessed, you can also use the `session` method to turn sessions off for a single controller:

```
class MyController < ApplicationController
  session :off
end
```

You can even bring it down to an action level:

```
class MyController < ApplicationController
  session :off, :only => ['index']

  def index
    #This action will not have any sessions available to it
  end
end
```

The session interface is intended for data that persists over many actions, possibly over the user's entire visit to the site. If you just need to pass an object (like a status message) to the next action, it's simpler to use the `flash` construct described in Recipe 15.8:

```
flash[:error] = 'Invalid login.'
```

By default, Rails sessions are stored on the server via the `PStore` mechanism. This mechanism uses `Marshal` to serialize session data to temporary files. This approach works well for small sites, but if your site will be getting a lot of visitors or you need to run your Rails application concurrently on multiple servers, you should explore some of the alternatives.

The three main alternatives are `ActiveRecordStore`, `DRbStore`, and `MemCacheStore`. `ActiveRecordStore` keeps session information in a database table: you can set up the table by running `rake create_sessions_table` on the command line. Both `DRbStore` and `MemCacheStore` create an in-memory hash that's accessible over the network, but they use different libraries.

Ruby comes with a standard library called `DRb` that allows you to share objects (including hashes) over the network. Ruby also has a binding to the Memcached daemon, which has been used to help scale web sites like Slashdot and LiveJournal. Memcached works like a direct store into RAM, and can be distributed automatically over various computers without any special configuration.

To change the session storing mechanism, edit your *config/environment.rb* file like this:

```
Rails::Initializer.run do |config|
  config.action_controller.session_store = :active_record_store
end
```

See Also

- Recipe 15.8, "Creating a Login System," has an example using `flash`
- Recipe 15.12, "Setting and Retrieving Cookies"
- Recipe 16.10, "Sharing a Hash Between Any Number of Computers"

- Recipe 16.16, "Storing Data on Distributed RAM with MemCached"
- *http://wiki.rubyonrails.com/rails/pages/HowtoChangeSessionOptions*

15.12 Setting and Retrieving Cookies

Problem

You want to set a cookie from within Rails.

Solution

Recall from Recipe 15.11 that all Rails controllers, views, helpers, and mailers have access to a method called sessions that returns a hash of the current client's session information. Your controllers, helpers, and mailers (but not your views) also have access to a method called cookies, which returns a hash of the current client's HTTP cookies.

To set a cookie for a user, simply set a key/value pair in that hash. For example, to keep track of how many pages a visitor has looked at, you might set a "visits" cookie:

```
class ApplicationController < ActionController::Base
  before_filter :count_visits

  private

  def count_visits
    value = (cookies[:visits] || '0').to_i
    cookies[:visits] = (value + 1).to_s
    @visits = cookies[:visits]
  end
end
```

The call to before_filter tells Rails to run this method before calling any action method. The private declaration makes sure that Rails doesn't think the count_ visits method is itself an action method that the public can view.

Since cookies are not directly available to views, count_visits makes the value of the :visits cookie available as the instance variable @visits. This variable can be accessed from a view:

```
<!-- index.rhtml -->
You've visited this website's pages <%= @visits %> time(s).
```

HTTP cookie values can only be strings. Rails can automatically convert some values to strings, but it's safest to store only string values in cookies. If you need to store objects that can't easily be converted to and from strings, you should probably store them in the session hash instead.

Discussion

There may be times when you want more control over your cookies. For instance, Rails cookies expire by default when the user closes their browser session. If you want to change the browser expiration time, you can give cookies a hash that contains an :expires key and a time to expire the cookie. The following cookie will expire after one hour:*

```
cookies[:user_id] = { :value => '123', :expires => Time.now + 1.hour}
```

Here are some other options for a cookie hash passed into cookies.

The domain to which this cookie applies:

```
:domain
```

The URL path to which this cookie applies (by default, the cookie applies to the entire domain: this means that if you host multiple applications on the same domain, their cookies may conflict):

```
:path
```

Whether this cookie is secure (secure cookies are only transmitted over HTTPS connections; the default is false):

```
:secure
```

Finally, Rails provides a quick and easy way to delete cookies:

```
cookies.delete :user_id
```

Of course, every Ruby hash implements a delete method, but the cookies hash is a little different. It includes special code so that not only does calling delete remove a key-value pair from the cookies hash, it removes the corresponding cookie from the user's browser.

See Also

- Recipe 3.5, "Doing Date Arithmetic"
- Recipe 15.11, "Setting and Retrieving Session Information," has a discussion of when to use cookies and when to use session

---

* Rails extends Ruby's numeric classes to include some very helpful methods (like the hour method shown here). These methods convert the given unit to seconds. For example, Time.now + 1.hour is the same as Time. now + 3600, since 1.hour returns the number of seconds in an hour. Other helpful methods include minutes, hours, days, months, weeks, and years. Since they all convert to numbers of seconds, you can even add them together like 1.week + 3.days.

15.13 Extracting Code into Helper Functions

Problem

Your views are getting cluttered with Ruby code.

Solution

Let's create a controller with a fairly complex view to see how this can happen:

```
$ ./scripts/generate controller list index
      exists  app/controllers/
      exists  app/helpers/
      create  app/views/list
      exists  test/functional/
      create  app/controllers/list_controller.rb
      create  test/functional/list_controller_test.rb
      create  app/helpers/list_helper.rb
      create  app/views/list/index.rhtml
```

Edit app/controllers/list_controller.rb to look like this:

```
class ListController < ApplicationController
  def index
    @list = [1, "string", :symbol, ['list']]
  end
end
```

Edit app/views/list/index.rhtml to contain the following code. It iterates over each element in @list, and prints out its index and the SHA1 hash of its object ID:

```
<!-- app/views/list/index.rhtml -->
<ul>
<% @list.each_with_index do |item, i| %>
  <li class="<%= i%2==0 ? 'even' : 'odd' %>"><%= i %>:
    <%= SHA1.new(item.id.to_s) %></li>
<% end %>
</ul>
```

This is pretty messy, but if you've done much web programming it should also look sadly familiar.

To clean up this code, we're going to move some of it into the *helper* for the controller. In this case, the controller is called list, so its helper lives in app/helpers/list_helper.rb.

Let's create a helper function called create_li. Given an object and its position in the list, this function creates an <LI> tag suitable for use in the index view:

```
module ListHelper
  def create_li(item, i)
    %{<li class="#{ i%2==0 ? 'even' : 'odd' }">#{i}:
      #{SHA1.new(item.id.to_s)}</li>}
  end
end
```

The list controller's views have access to all the functions defined in ListHelper. We can clean up the index view like so:

```
<!-- app/views/list/index.rhtml -->
<ul>
<% @list.each_with_index do |item, i| %>
  <%= create_li(item, i) %>
<% end %>
</ul>
```

Your helper functions can do anything you can normally do from within a view, so they are a great way to abstract out the heavy lifting.

Discussion

The purpose of helper functions is to create more maintainable code, and to enforce a good division of labor between the programmers and the UI designers. Maintainable code is easier for the programmers to work on, and when it's in helper functions it's out of the way of the designers, who can tweak the HTML here and there without having to sifting through code.

A good rule of thumb for when to use helpers is to read the code aloud. If it sounds like nonsense to someone familiar with HTML, or it makes up more than a short English sentence, hide it in a helper.

The flip side of this is that you should minimize the amount of HTML generated from within the helpers. That way the UI designers, or other people familiar with HTML, won't wander your code, wondering where to find the bit of HTML that needs tweaking.

Although helper functions are useful and used very often, Rails also provides *partials*, another way of extracting code into smaller chunks.

See Also

• Recipe 15.14, "Refactoring the View into Partial Snippets of Views," has more on partials

15.14 Refactoring the View into Partial Snippets of Views

Problem

Your view doesn't contain a lot of Ruby code, but it's still becoming more complicated than you'd like. You'd like to refactor the view logic into separate, reusable templates.

Solution

You can refactor a view template into multiple templates called partials. One template can include another by calling the render method, first seen in Recipe 15.5.

Let's start with a more complex version of the view shown in Recipe 15.5:

```
<!-- app/views/list/shopping_list.rhtml -->
<h2>My shopping list</h2>

<ul>
<% @list.each do |item| %>
 <li><%= item.name %> -
   <%= link_to 'Delete', {:action => 'delete', :id => item.id},
              :post => true %>
 </li>
<% end %>
</ul>

<h2>Add a new item</h2>

<%= form_tag :action => 'new' %>
 Item: <%= text_field "product", "name" %>&#x00A;
 <%= submit_tag "Add new item" %>
<%= end_form_tag %>
```

Here's the corresponding controller class, and a dummy `ListItem` class to serve as the model:

```
# app/controllers/list_controller.rb
class ListController < ActionController::Base
  def shopping_list
    @list = [ListItem.new(4, 'aspirin'), ListItem.new(199, 'succotash')]
  end

  # Other actions go here: add, delete, etc.
  # ...
end

class ListItem
  def initialize(id, name)
    @id, @name = id, name
  end
end
```

The view has two parts: the first part lists all the items, and the second part prints a form to add a new item. An obvious first step is to split out the new item form.

We can do this by creating a partial view to print the new item form. To do this, create a new file within *app/views/list/* called *_new_item_form.rhtml*. The underscore in front of the filename indicates that it is a partial view, not a full-fledged view for an action called new_item_form. Here's the partial file.

```
<!-- app/views/list/_new_item_form.rhtml -->

<%= form_tag :action => 'new' %>
Item: <%= text_field "item", "value" %>&#x00A;
<%= submit_tag "Add new item" %>
<%= end_form_tag %>
```

To include a partial, call the render method from within a template. Here is the _new_
item_form partial integrated into the main view. The view looks exactly the same, but
the code is better organized.

```
<!-- app/views/list/shopping_list.rhtml -->
<h2>My shopping list</h2>

<ul>
<% @list.each do |item| %>
 <li><%= item.name %> -
  <%= link_to 'Delete', {:action => 'delete', :id => item.id},
            :post => true %>
 </li>
<% end %>
</ul>
<%= render :partial => 'new_item_form' %>
```

Even though the filename starts with an underscore, when you call the partial, you
omit the underscore.

Discussion

Partial views inherit all the instance variables provided by the controller, so they have
access to the same instance variables as the parent view. That's why we didn't have
to change any of the form code for the _new_item_form partial.

We can create a second partial to factor out the code that prints the <LI> tag for
each list item. Here's *list_item.rhtml*:

```
<!-- app/views/list/_list_item.rhtml -->
<li><%= list_item.name %> -
<%= link_to 'Delete', {:action => 'delete', :id => list_item.id},
          :post => true %>
</li>
```

And here's the revised main view:

```
<!-- app/views/list/shopping_list.rhtml -->
<h2>My shopping list</h2>

<ul>
<% @list.each do |item| %>
  <%= render :partial => 'list_item', :locals => {:list_item => item} %>
<% end %>
</ul>

<%= render :partial => 'new_item_form' %>
```

Partial views do *not* inherit local variables from their parent view, so the `item` variable needs to be passed in to the partial, in a special hash called `:locals`. It's accessible in the partial as `list_item`, because that's the name it was given in the hash.

This scenario, iterating over an `Enumerable` and rendering a partial for each element, is very common in web applications, so Rails provides a shortcut. We can simplify our main view even more by passing our array into `render` (as the `:collection` parameter) and having it do the iteration for us:

```
<!-- app/views/list/shopping_list.rhtml -->
<h2>My shopping list</h2>

<ul>
 <%= render :collection => @list, :partial => 'list_item' %>
</ul>

<%= render :partial => 'new_item_form' %>
```

The partial is rendered once for every element in `@list`. Each list element is made available as the local variable `list_item`. In case you haven't guessed, this name comes from the name of the partial itself: `render` automatically gives `_foo.rhtml` a local variable called `foo`.

`list_item_counter` is another variable that is set automatically (again, the name mirrors the name of the template). `list_item_counter` is the current item's index in the collection undergoing iteration. This variable can be handy if you want alternating list items to show up in different styles:

```
<!-- app/views/list/_list_item.rhtml -->
<li><%= list_item.name %> -
<% css_class = list_item_counter % 2 == 0 ? 'a' : 'b' %>
<%= link_to 'Delete', {:action => 'delete', :id => list_item.id},
            {'class' => css_class}, :post => true %>
</li>
```

When there's no collection present, you can pass a single object into a partial by specifying an `:object` argument to `render`. This is simpler than creating a whole hash of `:locals` just to pass one object. As with `:collection`, the object will be made available as a local variable whose name is based on the name of the partial.

Here's an example: we'll send the shopping list into the `new_item_form.rhtml` partial, so that the new item form can print a more verbose message. Here's the change to `shopping_list.rhtml`:

```
<%= render :partial => 'new_item_form', :object => @list %>
```

Here's the new version of `_new_item_form.rhtml`:

```
<!-- app/views/list/_new_item_form.rhtml -->
<h2>Add a new item to the <%= new_item_form.size %> already in this
list</h2>
```

```
<%= form_tag :action => 'new' %>
 Item: <%= text_field "product", "name" %>
 <%= submit_tag "Add new item" %>
<%= end_form_tag %>
```

See Also

- Recipe 15.5, "Displaying Templates with Render"

15.15 Adding DHTML Effects with script.aculo.us

Problem

You want to add fancy effects such as fades to your application, without writing any JavaScript.

Solution

Every Rails application comes bundled with some JavaScript libraries that allow you to create Ajax and DHTML effects. You don't even have to write JavaScript to enable DHTML in your Rails web site.

First edit your main layout template (see Recipe 15.3) to call javascript_include_tag within your <HEAD> tag:

```
<!-- app/views/layouts/application.rhtml -->

<html>
  <head>
    <title>My Web App</title>
    <%= javascript_include_tag "prototype", "effects" %>
  </head>
  <body>
    <%= @content_for_layout %>
  </body>
</html>
```

Now within your views you can call the visual_effect method to accomplish the DHTML tricks found in the script.aculo.us library.

Here's an example of the "highlight" effect:

```
<p id="important">Here is some important text, it will be highlighted
when the page loads.</p>

<script type="text/javascript">
<%= visual_effect(:highlight, "important", :duration => 1.5) %>
</script>
```

Here's an example of the "fade" effect:

```
<p id="deleted">Here is some old text, it will fade away when the page
loads.</p>
```

```
<script type="text/javascript">
<%= visual_effect(:fade, "deleted", :duration => 1.0) %>
</script>
```

Discussion

The sample code snippets above are triggered when the page loads, because they're enclosed in <SCRIPT> tags. In a real application, you'll probably display text effects in response to user actions: deleted items might fade away, or the selection of one item might highlight related items. Here's an image that gets squished when you click the link below it:

```
<img id="to-squish" src="bug.jpg">
<%=link_to_function("Squish the bug!", visual_effect(:squish, "to-squish"))%>
```

The JavaScript code generated by the visual_effect method looks a lot like the arguments you passed into the method. For instance, this piece of a Rails view:

```
<script type="text/javascript">
<%= visual_effect(:fade, 'deleted-text', :duration => 1.0) %>
</script>
```

Generates this JavaScript:

```
<script type="text/javascript">
new Effect.Fade("deleted-text", {duration:1.0});
</script>
```

This similarity means that documentation for the script.aculo.us library is almost directly applicable to visual_effect. It also means that if you feel more comfortable writing straight JavaScript, your code will still be fairly understandable to someone who knows visual_effect.

The following table lists many of the effects available in Rails 1.0.

JavaScript initialization	Rails initialization
new Effect.Highlight	visual_effect(:highlight)
new Effect.Appear	visual_effect(:appear)
new Effect.Fade	visual_effect(:fade)
new Effect.Puff	visual_effect(:puff)
new Effect.BlindDown	visual_effect(:blind_down)
new Effect.BlindUp	visual_effect(:blind_up)
new Effect.SwitchOff	visual_effect(:switch_off)
new Effect.SlideDown	visual_effect(:slide_down)
new Effect.SlideUp	visual_effect(:slide_up)
new Effect.DropOut	visual_effect(:drop_out)
new Effect.Shake	visual_effect(:shake)
new Effect.Pulsate	visual_effect(:pulsate)

JavaScript initialization	Rails initialization
new Effect.Squish	visual_effect(:squish)
new Effect.Fold	visual_effect(:fold)
new Effect.Grow	visual_effect(:grow)
new Effect.Shrink	visual_effect(:shrink)
new Effect.ScrollTo	visual_effect(:scroll_to)

See Also

- The script.aculo.us demo (*http://wiki.script.aculo.us/scriptaculous/show/CombinationEffectsDemo*)
- Recipe 15.3, "Creating a Layout for Your Header and Footer," has more on layout templates
- Recipe 15.17, "Creating an Ajax Form"

15.16 Generating Forms for Manipulating Model Objects

Problem

You want to define actions that let a user create or edit objects stored in the database.

Solution

Let's create a simple model, and then build forms for it. Here's some MySQL code to create a table of key-value pairs:

```
use mywebapp_development;
DROP TABLE IF EXISTS items;
CREATE TABLE `items` (
  `id` int(11) NOT NULL auto_increment,
  `name` varchar(255) NOT NULL default '',
  `value` varchar(40) NOT NULL default '[empty]',
  PRIMARY KEY (`id`)
);
```

Now, from the command line, create the model class, along with a controller and views:

```
$ ./script/generate model Item
      exists  app/models/
      exists  test/unit/
      exists  test/fixtures/
      create  app/models/item.rb
      create  test/unit/item_test.rb
      create  test/fixtures/items.yml
      create  db/migrate
      create  db/migrate/001_create_items.rb
```

```
$ ./script/generate controller items new create edit
      exists  app/controllers/
      exists  app/helpers/
      create  app/views/items
      exists  test/functional/
      create  app/controllers/items_controller.rb
      create  test/functional/items_controller_test.rb
      create  app/helpers/items_helper.rb
      create  app/views/items/new.rhtml
      create  app/views/items/edit.rhtml
```

The first step is to customize a view. Let's start with *app/views/items/new.rhtml*. Edit it to look like this:

```
<!-- app/views/items/new.rhtml -->

<%= form_tag :action => "create" %>
 Name: <%= text_field "item", "name" %><br />
 Value: <%= text_field "item", "value" %><br />
 <%= submit_tag %>
<%= end_form_tag %>
```

All these method calls generate HTML: form_tag opens a <FORM> tag, submit_tag generates a submit button, and so on. You can type out the same HTML by hand and Rails won't care, but it's easier to make method calls, and it makes your templates neater.

The text_field call is a little more involved. It creates an <INPUT> tag that shows up in the HTML form as a text entry field. But it also binds the value of that field to one of the members of the @item instance variable. This code creates a text entry field that's bound to the name member of @item:

```
<%= text_field "item", "name" %>
```

But what's the @item instance variable? Well, it's not defined yet, because we're still using the generated controller. If you try to access the page /items/new page right now, you may get an error complaining about an unexpected nil value. The nil value is the @item variable, which gets used (in text_field calls) without ever being defined.

Let's customize the ItemsController class so that the new action sets the @item instance variable properly. We'll also implement the create action so that something actually happens when the user hits the submit button on our generated form.

```
class ItemsController < ApplicationController
  def new
    @item = Item.new
  end

  def create
    @item = Item.create(params[:item])
    redirect_to :action => 'edit', :id => @item.id
  end
end
```

Now if you access the /items/new page, you'll see what you'd expect: a form with two text entry fields. The "Name" field will be blank, and the "Value" field will contain the default database value of "[empty]".

Fill out the form and submit, and a new row will be created in the items table. You'll be redirected to the edit action, which doesn't exist yet. Let's create it now. Here's the controller part (note the similarity between ItemsController#edit and ItemsController#create above):

```
class ItemsController < ApplicationController
  def edit
    @item = Item.find(params[:id])

    if request.post?
      @item.update_attributes(params[:item])
      redirect_to :action => 'edit', :id => @item.id
    end
  end
end
```

In fact, the edit action is so similar to the create action that its form can be almost identical. The only differences are in the arguments to form_tag:

```
<!-- app/views/items/edit.rhtml -->

<%= form_tag :action => "edit", :id => @item.id %>
 Name: <%= text_field "item", "name" %><br />
 Value: <%= text_field "item", "value" %><br />
 <%= submit_tag %>
<%= end_form_tag %>
```

Discussion

This is probably the most common day-to-day task faced by web developers. It's so common that Rails comes with a tool called scaffold that generates this kind of code for you. If you'd invoked generate this way instead of with the arguments given above, Rails would have generate code for the actions given in the Solution, plus a few more:

```
$ ./script/generate scaffold Items
```

Starting off with scaffolding doesn't mean you can get away with not knowing how Rails form generation works, because you'll definitely want to customize the scaffolding code.

There are two places in our code where magic happens. The first is the text_field call in the view, which is explained in the Solution. It binds a member of an object (@item.name, for instance) to an HTML form control. If you view the source of the /items/new page, you will see that the form fields look something like this:

```
Name: <input type="text" name="item[name]" value="" /><br />
Value <input type="text" name="item[value]" value="[empty]" /><br />
```

These special field names are used by the second piece of magic, located in the calls to Item.create (in new) and Item#update_attributes. In both cases, an Item object is fed a hash of new values for its members. This hash is embedded into the params hash, which contains CGI form values.

The names of the HTML form fields (item[name] and item[value]) translate into a params hash that looks like this:

```
{
  :item => {
    :name => "Name of the item",
    :value => "Value of the item"
  },
  :controller => "items",
  :action => "create"
}
```

So this line of code:

```
Item.create(params[:item])
```

is effectively the same as this line:

```
Item.create(:name => "Name of the item", :value => "Value of the item")
```

The call to Item#update_attributes in the edit action works exactly the same way.

As mentioned above, the views for edit and new are very similar, differing only in the destination of the form. With some minor refactoring, we can remove one of the view files completely.

A call to <%= form_tag %> without any parameters at all sets the form destination to the current URL. Let's change the *new.rhtml* file appropriately:

```
<!-- app/views/items/new.rhtml -->
<%= form_tag %>

Name: <%= text_field "item", "name" %>&#x00A;
Value: <%= text_field "item", "value" %>&#x00A;

<%= submit_tag %>
<%= end_form_tag %>
```

Now the new.rhtml view is suitable for use by both new and edit. We just need to change the new action to call the create method (since the form doesn't go there anymore), and change the edit action to render new.rhtml instead of edit.rhtml (which can be removed):

```
class ItemsController < ApplicationController
  def new
    @item = Item.new
    create if request.post?
  end
```

```
    def edit
      @item = Item.find(params[:id])

      if request.post?
        @item.update_attributes(params[:item])
        redirect_to :action => 'edit', :id => @item.id and return
      end
      render :action => 'new'
    end
  end
```

Remember from Recipe 15.5 that a render call only specifies the template file to be used. The render call in edit won't actually call the new method, so we don't need to worry about the new method overwriting our value of @item.

In real life, there would be enough differences in the content surrounding the add and edit forms to a separate view for each action. However, there's usually enough similarity between the forms themselves that they can be refactored into a single partial view (see Recipe 15.14) which both views share. This is a great example of the DRY (Don't Repeat Yourself) principle. If there is a single form for both the add and edit views, it's easier and less error-prone to maintain that form as the database schema changes.

See Also

- Recipe 15.5, "Displaying Templates with Render"
- Recipe 15.14, "Refactoring the View into Partial Snippets of Views"

15.17 Creating an Ajax Form

Problem

You want to build a web application that's responsive and easy to use. You don't want your users to spend lots of time waiting around for the browser to redraw the screen.

Solution

You can use JavaScript to make the browser's XMLHTTPRequest object send data to the server, without dragging the user through the familiar (but slow) page refresh. This technique is called Ajax,* and Rails makes it easy to use Ajax without writing or knowing any JavaScript.

---

* This doesn't quite stand for Asynchronous JavaScript and XML. The origins of the term Ajax are now a part of computing mythology, but it is not an acronym.

Before you can do Ajax in your web application, you must edit your application's main layout template so that it calls the javascript_include_tag method within its <HEAD> tag. This is the same change made in Recipe 15.15:

```
<!-- app/views/layouts/application.rhtml -->

<html>
  <head>
    <title>My Web App</title>
    <%= javascript_include_tag "prototype", "effects" %>
  </head>
  <body>
    <%= @content_for_layout %>
  </body>
</html>
```

Let's change the application from Recipe 15.16 so that the new action is AJAX-enabled (if you followed that recipe all the way through, and made the edit action use new.rhtml instead of edit.rhtml, you'll need to undo that change and make edit use its own view template).

We'll start with the view template. Edit *app/views/items/new.rhtml* to look like this:

```
<!-- app/views/items/new.rhtml -->
<div id="show_item"></div>

      <%= form_remote_tag :url => { :action => :create },
      :update => "show_item",
      :complete => visual_effect(:highlight, "show_item") %>

  Name: <%= text_field "item", "name" %><br />
  Value: <%= text_field "item", "value" %><br />
  <%= submit_tag %>
  <%= end_form_tag %>
```

Those small changes make a standard HTML form into an Ajax form. The main difference is that we call form_remote_tag instead of form_tag. The other differences are the arguments we pass into that method.

The first change is that we put the :action parameter inside a hash passed into the :url option. Ajax forms have more options associated with them than a normal form, so you can't describe its form action as simply as you can with form_tag.

When the user clicks the submit button, the form values are serialized and sent to the destination action (in this case, create) in the background. The create action processes the form submission as before, and returns a snippet of HTML.

What happens to this HTML? That's what the :update option is for. It tells Rails to take the result of the form submission, and stick it into the element with the HTML ID of "show_item". This is why we added that <div id="show_item"> tag to the top of the template: that's where the response from the server goes.

The last change to the new.rhtml view is the :complete option. This is a callback argument: it lets you specify a string of JavaScript code that will be run once an Ajax request is complete. We use it to highlight the response from the server once it shows up.

That's the view. We also need to modify the create action in the controller so that when you make an Ajax form submission, the server returns a snippet of HTML. This is the snippet that's inserted into the "show_item" element on the browser side. If you make a regular (nonAjax) form submission, the server can behave as it does in Recipe 15.16, and send an HTTP redirect.* Here's what the controller class needs to look like:

```
class ItemsController < ApplicationController
  def new
    @item = Item.new
  end

  def create
    @item = Item.create(params[:item])
    if request.xml_http_request?
    render :action => 'show', :layout => false
    else
    redirect_to :action => 'edit', :id => @item.id
    end
  end

  def edit
    @item = Item.find(params[:id])

    if request.post?
      @item.update_attributes(params[:item])
      redirect_to :action => 'edit', :id => @item.id
    end
  end
end
```

This code references a new view, show. It's the tiny HTML snippet that's returned by the server, and stuck into the "show_element" tag by the web browser. We need to define it:

```
<!-- app/views/items/show.rhtml -->

Your most recently created item:<br />
Name: <%= @item.name %><br />
Value: <%= @item.value %><br />
<hr>
```

Now when you use *http://localhost:3000/items/new* to add new items to the database, you won't be redirected to the edit action. You'll stay on the new page, and the

---

* This will happen if someone's using your application with JavaScript turned off.

results of your form submission will be displayed above the form. This makes it easy to create many new items at once.

Discussion

Recipe 15.16 shows how to submit data to a form in the traditional way: the user clicks a "submit" button, the browser sends a request to the server, the server returns a response page, and the browser renders the response page.

Recently, sites like Gmail and Google Maps have popularized techniques for sending and receiving data without a page refresh. Collectively, these techniques are called Ajax. Ajax is a very useful tool for improving your application's response time and usability.

An Ajax request is a real HTTP request to one of your application's actions, and you can deal with it as you would any other request. Most of the time, though, you won't be returning a full HTML page. You'll just be returning a snippet of data. The web browser will be sending the Ajax request in the context of a full web page (which you served up earlier) that knows how to handle the response snippet.

You can define JavaScript callbacks at several points throughout the lifecycle of an Ajax request. One callback, :complete, was used above to highlight the snippet after inserting it into the page. This table lists the other callbacks.

Callback name	Callback description
:loading	Called when the web browser begins to load the remote document.
:loaded	Called when the browser has finished loading the remote document.
:interactive	Called when the user can interact with the remote document, even if it has not finished loading.
:success	Called when the XMLHttpRequest is completed, and the HTTP status code is in the 2XX range.
:failure	Called when the XMLHttpRequest is completed, and the HTTP status code is not in the 2XX range.
:complete	Called when the XMLHttpRequest is complete. If :success and/or :failure are also present, runs after they do.

15.18 Exposing Web Services on Your Web Site

Problem

You want to offer SOAP and XML-RPC web services from your web application.

Solution

Rails comes with a built-in web service generator that makes it easy to expose a controller's actions as web services. You don't have to spend time writing WSDL files or even really know how SOAP and XML-RPC work.

Here's a simple example. First, follow the directions in Recipe 15.16 to create a database table named items, and to generate a model for that table. Don't generate a controller.

Now, run this from the command line:

```
./script/generate web_service Item add edit fetch
      create  app/apis/
      exists  app/controllers/
      exists  test/functional/
      create  app/apis/item_api.rb
      create  app/controllers/item_controller.rb
      create  test/functional/item_api_test.rb
```

This creates an item controller that supports three actions: add, edit, and fetch. But instead of web application actions with .rhtml views, these are web service actions that you access with SOAP or XML-RPC.

A Ruby method doesn't care about the data types of the objects it accepts as arguments, or the data type of its return value. But a SOAP or XML-RPC web service method does care. To expose a Ruby method through a SOAP or XML-RPC interface, we need to define type information for its signature. Open up the file *app/apis/item_api.rb* and edit it to look like this:

```
class ItemApi < ActionWebService::API::Base
  api_method :add, :expects => [:string, :string], :returns => [:int]
  api_method :edit, :expects => [:int, :string, :string], :returns => [:bool]
  api_method :fetch, :expects => [:int], :returns => [Item]
end
```

Now we need to implement the actual web service interface. Open *app/controllers/item_controller.rb* and edit it to look like this:

```
class ItemController < ApplicationController
  wsdl_service_name 'Item'

  def add(name, value)
    Item.create(:name => name, :value => value).id
  end

  def edit(id, name, value)
    Item.find(id).update_attributes(:name => name, :value => value)
  end

  def fetch(id)
    Item.find(id)
  end
end
```

Discussion

The `item` controller now implements SOAP and XML-RPC web services for the `items` table. This controller can live alongside an `items` controller that implements a traditional web interface.[*]

The URL to the XML-RPC API is *http://www.yourserver.com/item/api*, and the URL to the SOAP API is *http://www.yourserver.com/item/service.wsdl*. To test these services, here's a short Ruby script that calls the web service methods through a SOAP client:

```
require 'soap/wsdlDriver'

wsdl = "http://localhost:3000/item/service.wsdl"
item_server = SOAP::WSDLDriverFactory.new(wsdl).create_rpc_driver

item_id = item_server.add('foo', 'bar')

if item_server.edit(item_id, 'John', 'Doe')
  puts 'Hey, it worked!'
else
  puts 'Back to the drawing board...'
end
# Hey, it worked!

item = item_server.fetch(item_id)
item.class                                  # => SOAP::Mapping::Object
item.name                                   # => "John"
item.value                                  # => "Doe"
```

Here's the XML-RPC equivalent:

```
require 'xmlrpc/client'
item_server = XMLRPC::Client.new2('http://localhost:3000/item/api')

item_id = item_server.call('Add', 'foo', "bar")
if item_server.call('Edit', item_id, 'John', 'Doe')
  puts 'Hey, it worked!'
else
  puts 'Back to the drawing board...'
end
# Hey, it worked!

item = item_server.call('Fetch', item_id)
# => {"name"=>"John", "id"=>2, "value"=>"Doe"}
item.class                                  # => Hash
```

[*] You can even add your web interface actions to the `ItemController` class. Then a single controller will implement both the traditional web interface and the web service interface. But you can't define a web application action with the same name as a web service action, because a controller class can contain only one method with a given name.

See Also

- Matt Biddulph's article "REST on Rails" describes how to create REST-style web services on top of Rails (*http://www.xml.com/pub/a/2005/11/02/rest-on-rails.html*)
- Recipe 16.3, "Writing an XML-RPC Client," and Recipe 16.4, "Writing a SOAP Client"
- Recipe 16.5, "Writing a SOAP Server," shows a nonRails implementation of SOAP web services

15.19 Sending Mail with Rails

Problem

You want to send an email from within your Rails application: perhaps a confirmation of an order, or notification that some action has been taken on a user's behalf.

Solution

The first is to generate some mailer infrastructure. Go to the application's base directory and type this command:

```
./script/generate mailer Notification welcome
      exists  app/models/
      create  app/views/notification
      exists  test/unit/
      create  test/fixtures/notification
      create  app/models/notification.rb
      create  test/unit/notification_test.rb
      create  app/views/notification/welcome.rhtml
      create  test/fixtures/notification/welcome
```

We're giving the name "Notification" to the mailing center of the application; it's somewhat analogous to a controller in the web interface. The mailer is set up to generate a single email, called "welcome": this is analagous to an action with a view template.

Now open app/models/notification.rb and edit it to look like this:

```
class Notification < ActionMailer::Base
  def welcome(user, sent_at=Time.now)
    @subject =  'A Friendly Welcome'
    @recipients = user.email
    @from =  'admin@mysite.com'
    @sent_on =    sent_at
    @body = {
      :user => user,
      :sent_on => sent_at
    }
```

```
        attachment 'text/plain' do |a|
          a.body = File.read('rules.txt')
        end
      end
    end
```

The subject of the email is "A Friendly Welcome", and it's sent to the user's email address from the address "*admin@mysite.com*". It's got an attachment taken from the disk file `rules.txt` (relative to the root directory of your Rails application).

Although the file `notification.rb` is within the `models/` directory, it acts like a controller in that each of its email messages has an associated view template. The view for the welcome email is in `app/views/notification/welcome.rhtml`, and it acts almost the same as the view of a normal controller.

The most important difference is that mailer views do not have access to the instance variables of the mailer. To set instance variables for mailers, you pass a hash of those variables to the body method. The keys become instance variable names and the values become their values. In `notification.rb`, we make two instance variables available to the welcome view, `@user` and `@sent_on`. Here's the view itself:

```
<!-- app/views/notification/welcome.rhtml -->

Hello, <%= @user.name %>, and thanks for signing up at <%= @sent_on
%>. Please print out the attached set of rules and keep them in a
prominent place; they help keep our community running smoothly. Be
sure to pay special attention to sections II.4 ("Assignment of
Intellectual Property Rights") and XIV.21.a ("Dispute Resolution
Through Ritual Combat").
```

To send the welcome email from your Rails application, add the following code to either a controller, a model, or an observer:

```
Notification.deliver_welcome(user)
```

Here, the user variable can be any object that implements `#name` and `#email`, the two methods called in the `welcome` method and in the template.

Discussion

You never call the `Notification#welcome` method directly. In fact, `Notification#welcome` is not even available, since it's an instance method, and you never instantiate a `Notification` object directly. The `ActionMailer::Base` class defines a `method_missing` implementation that looks at all calls to undefined class methods. This is why you call `deliver_welcome` even though you never defined it.

The `welcome.rhtml` template given above generates plaintext email. To send HTML emails, simply add the following code to `Notification#welcome`:

```
content_type 'text/html'
```

Now your templates can generate HTML; email clients will recognize the format of the email and render it appropriately.

Sometimes you'll want more control over the delivery process—for example, when you're unit-testing your ActionMailer classes. Instead of calling deliver_welcome to send out an email, you can call create_welcome to get the email as a Ruby object. These "create" methods return TMail objects, which you can examine or manipulate as necessary.

If your local web server is incapable of sending email, you can modify environment.rb to contact a remote SMTP server:

```
Rails::Initializer.run do |config|
  config.action_mailer.server_settings = {
    :address => 'someserver.com',
    :user_name => 'uname',
    :password => 'passwd',
    :authentication => 'cram_md5'
  }
end
```

See Also

- Recipe 10.8, "Responding to Calls to Undefined Methods"
- Recipe 14.5, "Sending Mail," has more on ActionMailer and SMTP settings

15.20 Automatically Sending Error Messages to Your Email

Problem

You want to receive a descriptive email message every time one of your users encounters an application error.

Solution

Any errors that occur while running your application are sent to the ActionController::Base#log_error method. If you've set up a mailer (as shown in Recipe 15.19) you can override this method and have it send mail to you. Your code should look something like this:

```
class ApplicationController < ActionController::Base

private
  def log_error(exception)
    super
    Notification.deliver_error_message(exception,
      clean_backtrace(exception),
      session.instance_variable_get("@data"),
```

```
            params,
            request.env
        )
    end
end
```

That code rounds up a wide variety of information about the state of the Rails request at the time of the failure. It captures the exception object, the corresponding backtrace, the session data, the CGI request parameters, and the values of all environment variables.

The overridden log_error calls Notification.deliver_error_messsage, which assumes you've created a mailer called "Notification", and defined the method Notification.error_message. Here's the implementation:

```
class Notification < ActionMailer::Base
  def error_message(exception, trace, session, params, env, sent_on = Time.now)
    @recipients       = 'me@mydomain.com'
    @from             = 'error@mydomain.com'
    @subject          = "Error message: #{env['REQUEST_URI']}"
    @sent_on          = sent_on
    @body = {
      :exception => exception,
      :trace => trace,
      :session => session,
      :params => params,
      :env => env
    }
  end
end
```

The template for this email looks like this:

```
<!-- app/views/notification/error_message.rhtml -->

Time: <%= Time.now %>
Message: <%= @exception.message %>
Location: <%= @env['REQUEST_URI'] %>
Action: <%= @params.delete('action') %></td></tr>
Controller: <%= @params.delete('controller') %></td></tr>
Query: <%= @env['QUERY_STRING'] %></td></tr>
Method: <%= @env['REQUEST_METHOD'] %></td></tr>
SSL: <%= @env['SERVER_PORT'].to_i == 443 ? "true" : "false" %>
Agent: <%= @env['HTTP_USER_AGENT'] %>

Backtrace
<%= @trace.to_a.join("</p>\n<p>") %>

Params
<% @params.each do |key, val| -%>
* <%= key %>: <%= val.to_yaml %>
<% end -%>
```

```
Session
<% @session.each do |key, val| -%>
* <%= key %>: <%= val.to_yaml %>
<% end -%>

Environment
<% @env.each do |key, val| -%>
* <%= key %>: <%= val %>
<% end -%>
```

Discussion

ActionController::Base#log_error gives you the flexibility to handle errors however you like. This is especially useful if your Rails application is hosted on a machine to which you have limited access: you can have errors sent to you, instead of written to a file you might not be able to see. Or you might prefer to record the errors in a database, so that you can look for patterns.

The method ApplicationController#log_error is declared private to avoid confusion. If it weren't private, all of the controllers would think they had a log_error action defined. Users would be able to visit /<controller>/log_error and get Rails to act strangely.

See Also

• Recipe 15.19, "Sending Mail with Rails"

15.21 Documenting Your Web Site

Problem

You want to document the controllers, models, and helpers of your web application so that the developers responsible for maintaining the application can understand how it works.

Solution

As with any other Ruby program, you document a Rails application by adding specially-formatted commands to your code. Here's how to add documentation to the FooController class and one of its methods:

```
# The FooController controller contains miscellaneous functionality
# rejected from other controllers.
class FooController < ApplicationController
  # The set_random action sets the @random_number instance variable
  # to a random number.
  def set_random
    @random_number = rand*rand
  end
end
```

The documentation for classes and methods goes before their declaration, not after.

When you've finished adding documentation comments to your application, go to your Rails application's root directory and issue the `rake appdoc` command:

```
$ rake appdoc
```

This Rake task runs RDoc for your Rails application and generates a directory called `doc/app`. This directory contains a web site with the aggregate of all your documentation comments, cross-referenced against the source code. Open the `doc/app/index.rhtml` file in any web browser, and you can browse the generated documentation.

Discussion

Your RDoc comments can contain markup and special directives: you can describe your arguments in definition lists, and hide a class or method from documentation with the `:nodoc:` directive. This is covered in Recipe 17.11.

The only difference between Rails applications and other Ruby programs is that Rails comes with a Rakefile that defines an `appdoc` task. You don't have to find or write one yourself.

You probably already put inline comments *inside* your methods, describing the action as it happens. Since the RDoc documentation contains a formatted version of the original source code, these comments will be visible to people going through the RDoc. These comments are formatted as Ruby source code, though, not as RDoc markup.

See Also

- Recipe 17.11, "Documenting Your Application"
- Chapter 19, especially Recipe 19.2, "Automatically Generating Documentation"
- The RDoc for RDoc (*http://rdoc.sourceforge.net/doc/index.html*)

15.22 Unit Testing Your Web Site

Problem

You want to create a suite of automated tests that test the functionality of your Rails application.

Solution

Rails can't write your test code any more than it can write your views and controllers for you, but it does make it easy to organize and run your automated tests.

When you use the ./script/generate command to create controllers and models, not only do you save time, but you also get a generated framework for unit and functional tests. You can get pretty good test coverage by filling in the framework with tests for the functionality you write.

So far, all the examples in this chapter have run against a Rails application's development database, so you only needed to make sure that the development section of your *config/database.yml* file was set up correctly. Unit test code runs on your application's test database, so now you need to set up your test section as well. Your mywebapp_test database doesn't have to have any tables in it, but it must exist and be accessible to Rails.

When you generate a model with the generate script, Rails also generates a unit test script for the model in the *test* directory. It also creates a *fixture*, a YAML file containing test data to be loaded into the mywebapp_test database. This is the data against which your unit tests will run:

```
./script/generate model User
      exists  app/models/
      exists  test/unit/
      exists  test/fixtures/
      create  app/models/user.rb
      create  test/unit/user_test.rb
      create  test/fixtures/users.yml
      create  db/migrate
      create  db/migrate/001_create_users.rb
```

When you generate a controller with generate, Rails creates a functional test script for the controller:

```
./script/generate users list
      exists  app/controllers/
      exists  app/helpers/
      create  app/views/users
      exists  test/functional/
      create  app/controllers/users_controller.rb
      create  test/functional/users_controller_test.rb
      create  app/helpers/users_helper.rb
      create  app/views/users/list.rhtml
```

As you write code in the model and controller classes, you'll write corresponding tests in these files.

To run the unit and functional tests, invoke the rake command in your home directory. The default Rake task runs all of your tests. If you run it immediately after generating your test files, it'll look something like this:

```
$ rake
(in /home/lucas/mywebapp)
/usr/bin/ruby1.8 "test/unit/user_test.rb"
Started
.
Finished in 0.048702 seconds.
```

```
1 tests, 1 assertions, 0 failures, 0 errors
/usr/bin/ruby1.8 "test/functional/users_controller_test.rb"
Started
.
Finished in 0.024615 seconds.

1 tests, 1 assertions, 0 failures, 0 errors
```

Discussion

All the lessons for writing unit tests in other languages and in other Ruby programs (see Recipe 17.7) apply to Rails. Rails does some accounting for you, and it defines some useful new assertions (see below), but you still have to do the work. The rewards are the same, too: you can modify and refactor your code with confidence, knowing that if something breaks, your tests will break. You'll hear about the problem immediately and you'll be able to fix it more quickly.

Let's see what Rails has generated for us. Here's a generated *test/unit/user_test.rb*:

```
require File.dirname(__FILE__) + '/../test_helper'

class UserTest < Test::Unit::TestCase
  fixtures :users

  # Replace this with your real tests.
  def test_truth
    assert true
  end
end
```

A good start, but `test_truth` is kind of tautological. Here's a slightly more realistic test:

```
class UserTest
  def test_first
    assert_kind_of User, users(:first)
  end
end
```

This code fetches the first element from the users table, and asserts that ActiveRecord turns it into a `User` object. This isn't testing our `User` code (we haven't written any) so much as it's testing Rails and ActiveRecord, but it shows you the kind of assertion that makes for good unit tests.

But how does `users(:first)` return anything? The test suite runs against the mywebapp_test database, and we didn't even put any tables in it, much less sample data.

We didn't, but Rails did. When you run the test suite, Rails copies the schema of the development database to the test database. Instead of running every test against whatever data happens to exist in the development database, Rails loads special test data from YAML files called fixtures. The fixture files contain whatever database data you need to test: objects that only exist to be deleted by a test, strange relationships between rows in different tables, or anything else you need.

In the example above, the fixture for the users table was loaded by the line `fixtures`
`:users`. Here's the generated fixture for the User model, in *test/fixtures/users.yml*:

```
first:
  id: 1
another:
  id: 2
```

Before running the unit tests, Rails reads this file, creates two rows in the users table,
and defines aliases for them (`:first` and `:another`) so you can refer to them in your
unit tests. It then defines the users method (like so much else, this method name is
based on the name of the model). In `test_first`, the call to `users(:first)` retrieves
the User object corresponding to `:first` in the fixture: the object with ID 1.

Here's another unit test:

```
class UserTest
  def test_another
    assert_kind_of User, users(:another)
    assert_equal 2, users(:another).id
    assert_not_equal users(:first), users(:another)
  end
end
```

Rails adds the following Rails-specific assertions to Ruby's `Test::Unit`:

- `assert_dom_equal`
- `assert_dom_not_equal`
- `assert_generates`
- `assert_no_tag`
- `assert_recognizes`
- `assert_redirected_to`
- `assert_response`
- `assert_routing`
- `assert_tag`
- `assert_template`
- `assert_valid`

See Also

- "Testing the Rails" is a guide to unit and functional testing in Rails (*http://manuals.rubyonrails.com/read/book/5*)
- Rails 1.1 supports integration testing as well, for testing the interactions between controllers and actions; see *http://rubyonrails.com/rails/classes/ActionController/IntegrationTest.html* and *http://jamis.jamisbuck.org/articles/2006/03/09/integration-testing-in-rails-1-1*

- The ZenTest library inclues Test::Rails, which lets you write separate tests for your views and controllers (*http://rubyforge.org/projects/zentest/*)
- Read about fixtures at *http://ar.rubyonrails.org/classes/Fixtures.html*
- Read about the assertions that Rails adds to Test::Unit at *http://rails.rubyonrails. com/classes/Test/Unit/Assertions.html*
- Recipe 15.6, "Integrating a Database with Your Rails Application"
- Recipe 17.7, "Writing Unit Tests"
- Chapter 19

15.23 Using breakpoint in Your Web Application

Problem

Your Rails application has a bug that you can't find using log messages. You need a heavy-duty debugging tool that lets you inspect the full state of your application at any given point.

Solution

The breakpoint library lets you stop the flow of code and drop into irb, an interactive Ruby session. Within irb you can inspect the variables local to the current scope, modify those variables, and resume execution of the normal flow of code. If you have ever spent hours trying to track down a bug by placing logging messages everywhere, you'll find that breakpoint gives you a much easier and more straightforward way to debug.

But how can you run an interactive console program from a web application? The answer is to have a console program running beforehand, listening for calls from the Rails server.

The first step is to run ./script/breakpointer on the command line. This command starts a server that listens over the network for breakpoint calls from the Rails server. Keep this program running in a terminal window: this is where the irb session will start up:

```
$ ./script/breakpointer
No connection to breakpoint service at druby://localhost:42531
Tries to connect will be made every 2 seconds...
```

To trigger an irb session, you can call the breakpoint method anywhere you like from your Rails application—within a model, controller, or helper method. When execution reaches that point, processing of the incoming client request will stop, and an irb session will start in your terminal. When you quit the session, processing of the request will resume.

Discussion

Here's an example. Let's say you've written the following controller, and you're having trouble modifying the name attribute of an `Item` object.

```
class ItemsController < ApplicationController
  def update
    @item = Item.find(params[:id])
    @item.value = '[default]'
    @item.name = params[:name]
    @item.save
    render :text => 'Saved'
  end
end
```

You can put a breakpoint call in the `Item` class, like this:

```
class Item < ActiveRecord::Base
  attr_accessor :name, :value

  def name=(name)
    super
    breakpoint
  end
end
```

Accessing the URL *http://localhost:3000/items/update/123?name=Foo* calls `Item-Controller#update`, which finds `Item` number 123 and then calls its `name=` method. The call to `name=` triggers the breakpoint. Instead of rendering the text "Saved", the site seems to hang and become unresponsive to requests.

But if you return to the terminal running the breakpointer server, you'll see that an interactive Ruby session has started. This session allows you to play with all the local variables and methods at the point where the breakpoint was called:

```
Executing break point "Item#name=" at item.rb:4 in `name='
  irb:001:0> local_variables
  => ["name", "value", "_", "__"]
  irb:002:0> [name, value]
  => ["Foo", "[default]"]
 irb:003:0> [@name, @value]
  => ["Foo", "[default]"]
  irb:004:0> self
  => #<Item:0x292fbe8 @name="Foo", @value="[default]">
  irb:005:0> self.value = "Bar"
  => "Bar"
  irb:006:0> save
 => true
  irb:006:0> exit

 Server exited. Closing connection...
```

Once you finish, type `exit` to terminate the interactive Ruby session. The Rails application continues running at the place it left off, rendering "Saved" as expected.

By default, breakpoints are named for the method in which they appear. You can pass a string into breakpoint to get a more descriptive name. This is especially helpful if one method contains several breakpoints:

```
breakpoint "Trying to set Item#name, just called super"
```

Instead of calling breakpoint directly, you can also call assert, a method which takes a code block. If the block evaluates to false, Ruby calls breakpoint; otherwise, things continue as normal. Using assert lets you set breakpoints that are only called when something goes wrong (called "conditional breakpoints" in traditional debuggers):

```
1.upto 10 do |i|
  assert { Person.find(i) }
  p = Person.find(i)
  p.update_attribute(:name, 'Lucas')
end
```

If all of the required Person objects are found, the breakpoint is never called, because Person.find always returns true. If one of the Person objects is missing, Ruby calls the breakpoint method and you get an irb session to investigate.

Breakpoint is a powerful tool that can vastly simplify your debugging process. It can be hard to understand the true power of it until you try it yourself, so go through the solution with your own code to toy around with it.

See Also

- Recipe 17.10, "Using breakpoint to Inspect and Change the State of Your Application," covers breakpoint in more detail.
- *http://wiki.rubyonrails.com/rails/show/HowtoDebugWithBreakpoint*

CHAPTER 16

Web Services and Distributed Programming

Distributed programming is like network programming—only the audience is different. The point of network programming is to let a human control a computer across the network. The point of distributed programming is to let computers communicate between themselves.

Humans use networking software to get data and use algorithms they don't have on their own computers. With distributed programming, automated programs can get in on this action. The programs are (one hopes) designed for the ultimate benefit of humans, but an end user doesn't see the network usage or even neccessarily know that it's happening.

The simplest and most common form of distributed programming is the web service. Web services work on top of HTTP: they generally involve sending an HTTP request to a certain URL (possibly including an XML document), and getting a response in the form of another XML document. Rather than showing this document to an end user the way a web browser would, the web service client parses the XML response document and does something with it.

We start the chapter with a number of recipes that show how to provide and use web services. We include generic recipes like Recipe 16.3, and recipes for using specific, existing web services like Recipes 16.1, 16.6, and 16.9. The specific examples are useful in their own right, but they should also help you see what kind of features you should expose in your own web services.

There are three main approaches to web services: REST-style services,* XML-RPC, and SOAP. You don't need any special tools to offer or use REST-style services. On the client end, you just need a scriptable web client (Recipe 14.1) and an XML parser

---

* Why am I saying "REST-style" instead of REST? Because REST is a design philosophy, not a technology standard. REST basically says: use the technologies of the web the way they were designed to work. A lot of so-called "REST Web Services" fall short of the REST philosophy in some respect (the Amazon web service, covered in Recipe 16.1, is the most famous example). These might more accurately be called "HTTP+XML" services, or "HTTP+POX" (Plain Old XML) services. Don't get too hung up on the exact terminology.

(Recipes11.2 and 11.3). On the server side, you just write a web application that knows how to generate XML (Recipe 11.9). We cover some REST philosophy while exploring useful services in Recipe 16.1 and Recipe 16.2.

REST *is* HTTP; XML-RPC and SOAP are protocols that run on top of HTTP. We've devoted several recipes to Ruby's SOAP client: Recipes 16.4 and 16.7 are the main ones. Ruby's standalone SOAP server is briefly covered in Recipe 16.5. Rails provides its own SOAP server (Recipe 15.18), which incidentally also acts as an XML-RPC server.

XML-RPC isn't used much nowadays, so we've just provided a client recipe (Recipe 16.3). If you want to write a standalone XML-RPC server, check out the documentation at *http://www.ntecs.de/projects/xmlrpc4r/server.html*.

You can use a web service to store data on a server or change its state, but web service clients don't usually use the server to communicate with *each other*. Web services work well when there's a server with some interesting data and many clients who want it. It works less well when you want to get multiple computers to cooperate, or distribute a computation across multiple CPUs.

This is where DRb (Distributed Ruby) comes in. It's a network protocol that lets Ruby programs share objects, even when they're running on totally different computers. We cover a number of the possibilities, from simple data structure sharing (Recipe 16.10) to a networked application (Recipe 16.18) that, after the initial connection, has no visible networking code at all.

Distributed programming with DRb is a lot like multithreaded programming, except the "threads" are actually running on multiple computers. This can be great for performance. On a single CPU, multithreading makes it look like two things are happening at once, but it's just an illusion. Run two "threads" on different computers, and you can actually do twice as much work in the same time. You just need to figure out a way to split up the work and combine the results.

That's the tricky part. When you start coordinating computers through DRb, you'll run into concurrency problems and deadlock: the same problems you encounter when you share data structures between threads. You can address these problems using the same techniques that worked in Recipes 20.4 and 20.11. You'll also encounter brand new problems, like the tendency of machines to drop off the network at unfortunate times. These are more troublesome, and the solutions usually depend on the specific tasks you've assigned the machines. Recipe 16.10, the first DRb recipe, provides a brief introduction to these problems.

16.1 Searching for Books on Amazon

Problem

You want to incorporate information about books or other cultural artifacts into your application.

Solution

Amazon.com exposes a web service that gives you access to all kinds of information on books, music, and other media. The third-party Ruby/Amazon library provides a simple Ruby interface to the Amazon web service.

Here's a simple bit of code that searches for books with Ruby/Amazon, printing their new and used prices.

```
require 'amazon/search'

$AWS_KEY = 'Your AWS key goes here' # See below.

def price_books(keyword)
  req = Amazon::Search::Request.new($AWS_KEY)
  req.keyword_search(keyword, 'books', Amazon::Search::LIGHT) do |product|
    newp = product.our_price || 'Not available'
    usedp = product.used_price || 'not available'
    puts "#{product.product_name}: #{newp} new, #{usedp} used."
  end
end

price_books('ruby cookbook')
# Ruby Cookbook (Cookbooks (O'Reilly)): $31.49 new, not available used.
# Rails Cookbook (Cookbooks (O'Reilly)): $25.19 new, not available used.
# Ruby Ann's Down Home Trailer Park Cookbook: $10.85 new, $3.54 used.
# Ruby's Low-Fat Soul-Food Cookbook: Not available new, $12.43 used.
# ...
```

To save bandwidth, this code asks Amazon for a "light" set of search results. The results won't include things like customer reviews.

Discussion

What's going on here? In one sense, it doesn't matter. Ruby/Amazon gives us a Ruby method that somehow knows about books and their Amazon prices. It's getting its information from a database somewhere, and all we need to know is how to query that database.

In another sense, it matters a lot, because this is just one example of a REST-style web service. By looking under the cover of the Amazon web services, you can see how to use other REST-style services like the ones provided by Yahoo! and Flickr.

REST-style web services operate directly on top of HTTP. Each URL in a REST system designates a resource or a set of them. When you call keyword_search, Ruby/Amazon retrieves a URL that looks something like this:

```
http://xml.amazon.com/onca/xml3?KeywordSearch=ruby+cookbook&mode=books...
```

This URL designates a set of Amazon book records that match the keywords "ruby cookbook". Ruby/Amazon uses the Net::HTTP library to send a GET request to this

URL. Amazon returns a representation of the resource, an XML document that looks something like this:

```
<?xml version="1.0" encoding="UTF-8"?>
<ProductInfo xmlns:xsi="http://www.w3.org/2001/XMLSchema-instance"
 xsi:noNamespaceSchemaLocation="http://xml.amazon.com/schemas3/dev-lite.xsd">
...
 <TotalResults>11</TotalResults>
  <TotalPages>2</TotalPages>

    <Details url="http://www.amazon.com/exec/obidos/ASIN/0596523696/">
       <ProductName>Ruby Cookbook</ProductName>
       <Catalog>Book</Catalog>
       <Authors>
         <Author>Lucas Carlson</Author>
         <Author>Leonard Richardson</Author>
       </Authors>
       <ReleaseDate>September, 2006</ReleaseDate>
       <Manufacturer>O'Reilly Media</Manufacturer>
...
    </Details>
...
</ProductInfo>
```

Ruby/Amazon uses REXML to parse this XML data and turn it into `Amazon::Product` objects. An `Amazon::Product` is a lot like a Ruby `Struct`: it's got a bunch of member methods for getting information about the object (you can list these methods by calling `Product#properties`). All that information is derived from the original XML.

A REST web service works like a web site designed for a software program instead of a human. The web is good for publishing and modifying documents, so REST clients make HTTP GET requests to retrieve data, and POST requests to modify server state, just like you'd do from a web browser with an HTML form. XML is good for describing documents, so REST servers usually give out XML documents that are easy to read and parse.

How does REST relate to other kinds of web services? REST is a distinct design philosophy, but not all "REST-style" web services take it as gospel.* There's a sense in which "REST" is a drive for simpler web services, a reaction to the complexity of SOAP and the WS-* standards. There's no reason why you can't use SOAP in accordance with the REST philosophy, but in practice that never seems to happen.

---

* Amazon's web services are a case in point. They use GET requests exclusively, even when they're modifying data like the items in a shopping cart. This is very unRESTful because "put the Ruby Cookbook in my shopping cart" is a command, not an object the way a set of books is an object. To avoid the wrath of the pedant I refer to Amazon Web Services as a "REST-style" service. It would be more RESTful to define a separate resource (URL) for the shopping cart, and allow the client to POST a message to that resource saying "Hey, shopping cart, add the Ruby Cookbook to yourself."

Like REST, XML-RPC and SOAP web services run atop HTTP.[*] But while REST services expect clients to operate on a large URL space, XML-RPC and SOAP services are generally bound to a single "server" URL. If you have a "resource" to specify, you include it in the document you send to the server. REST, XML-RPC, and SOAP all serve XML documents, but XML-RPC and SOAP serve serialized versions of data structures, and REST usually serves RDF, Atom, or Plain Old XML.

If there were no Ruby/Amazon library, it wouldn't be hard to do the work yourself with Net::HTTP and REXML. It'd be more difficult to write a Ruby XML-RPC client without xmlrpc4r, and *much* more difficult to write a SOAP client without SOAP::RPC::Driver.

The downside of this flexibility is that, at least for now, every REST service is different. Everyone arranges their resources differently, and everyone's response documents need to be parsed with different code. Ruby/Amazon won't help you at all if you want to use some other REST service: you'll need to find a separate library for that service, or write your own using Net::HTTP and REXML.

See Also

- Like Google's web services and others, Amazon's can only be used if you sign up for an identifying key. You can sign up for an AWS key at the Amazon Web Services site (*http://www.amazon.com/gp/browse.html?node=3435361*)
- Get Ruby/Amazon at *http://www.caliban.org/ruby/ruby-amazon.shtml*: you can download it as a tarball and run setup.rb to install it; the same site hosts generated RDoc for the library; see especially *http://www.caliban.org/ruby/ruby-amazon/classes/Amazon.html*
- The Amazon Web Services documentation (*http://www.amazon.com/gp/browse.html/103-8028883-0351026?node=3435361*)
- Recipe 11.2, "Extracting Data from a Document's Tree Structure"
- Recipe 14.1, "Grabbing the Contents of a Web Page"
- Recipe 16.2, "Finding Photos on Flickr"
- Recipe 16.4, "Writing a SOAP Client"

16.2   Finding Photos on Flickr

Problem

You want to use Ruby code to find freely reusable photos: perhaps to automatically illustrate a piece of text.

---

[*] SOAP services can run over other protocols, like email. But almost everyone uses HTTP. After all, they're "web services," not "Internet services."

Solution

The Flickr photo-sharing web site has a huge number of photos and provides web services for searching them. Many of the photos are licensed under Creative Commons licenses, which give you permission to reuse the photos under various restrictions.

There are several Ruby bindings to Flickr's various web service APIs, but its REST API is so simple that I'm just going to use it directly. Given a tag name (like "elephants"), this code will find an appropriate picture, and return the URL to a thumbnail version of the picture.

First, a bit of setup. As with Amazon and Google, to use the Flickr API at all you'll need to sign up for an API key (see below for details).

```
require 'open-uri'
require 'rexml/document'
require 'cgi'

FLICKR_API_KEY = 'Your API key here'
```

The first method, flickr_call, sends a generic query to Flickr's REST web service. It doesn't do anything special: it just makes an HTTP GET request and parses the XML response.*

```
def flickr_call(method_name, arg_map={}.freeze)
  args = arg_map.collect {|k,v| CGI.escape(k) + '=' + CGI.escape(v)}.join('&')
  url = "http://www.flickr.com/services/rest/?api_key=%s&method=%s&%s" %
    [FLICKR_API_KEY, method_name, args]
  doc = REXML::Document.new(open(url).read)
end
```

Now comes pick_a_photo, a method that uses flickr_call to invoke the flickr.photos.search web service method. That method returns a REXML Document object containing a <photo> element for each photo that matched the search criteria. I use XPath to grab the first <photo> element, and pass it into small_photo_url (defined below) to turn it into an image URL.

```
def pick_a_photo(tag)
  doc = flickr_call('flickr.photos.search', 'tags' => tag, 'license' => '4',
                    'per_page' => '1')
  photo = REXML::XPath.first(doc, '//photo')
  small_photo_url(photo) if photo
end
```

Finally, I'll define the method, small_photo_url. Given a <photo> element, it returns the URL to a smallish version of the appropriate Flickr photo.

```
def small_photo_url(photo)
  server, id, secret = ['server', 'id', 'secret'].collect do |field|
```

---

* Some of Flickr's APIs let you do things like upload photos and add comments. You'll need to use POST requests to make these calls, since they modify the state of the site. More importantly, you'll also need to authenticate against your Flickr account.

```
    photo.attribute(field)
  end
 "http://static.flickr.com/#{server}/#{id}_#{secret}_m.jpg"
  end
```

Now I can find an appropriate photo for any common word (Figure 16-1):

```
pick_a_photo('elephants')
# => http://static.flickr.com/32/102580480_506d5865d0_m.jpg

pick_a_photo('what-will-happen-tomorrow')
# => nil
```

Figure 16-1. A photo of elephants by Nick Scott-Smith

Discussion

It's nice if there's a predefined Ruby binding available for a particular REST-style web service, but it's usually pretty easy to roll your own. All you need to do is to craft an HTTP request and figure out how to process the response document. It's usually an XML document, and a well-crafted XPath statement should be enough to grab the data you want.

Note the clause license=4 in pick_a_photo's arguments to flickr_call. I wanted to find a picture that I could publish in this book, so I limited my search to pictures made available under a Creative Commons "Attribution" license. I can reproduce that picture of the elephants so long as I credit the person who took the photo. (Nick Scott-Smith of London. Hi, Nick!)

Flickr has a separate API call that lists the available licenses (flickr.licenses.getInfo), but once I looked them up and found that "Creative Commons Attribution" was number four, it was easier to hardcode the number than to look it up every time.

See Also

- The first few recipes in Chapter 11 demonstrate different ways of extracting data from XML documents; XPath (Recipe 11.4) and Rubyful Soup (Recipe 11.5) let you extract data without writing much code
- Recipe 14.1, "Grabbing the Contents of a Web Page"
- Sign up for a Flickr API key at *http://www.flickr.com/services/api/key.gne*

- Flickr provides REST, XML-RPC, and SOAP interfaces, and comprehensive documentation of its API (*http://www.flickr.com/services/api/*)
- The Flickr URL documentation shows how to turn a <photo> element into a URL (*http://www.flickr.com/services/api/misc.urls.html*)
- Flickr.rb (*http://redgreenblu.com/flickr/*; available as the flickr gem), the libyws project (*http://rubyforge.org/projects/libyws*; check out from CVS repository), and rflickr (*http://rubyforge.org/projects/rflickr/*; available as the rflickr gem)
- A brief explanation of the Creative Commons licences (*http://creativecommons. org/about/licenses/meet-the-licenses*)

16.3   Writing an XML-RPC Client

Credit: John-Mason Shackelford

Problem

You want to call a remote method through the XML-RPC web service protocol.

Solution

Use Michael Neumann's xmlrpc4r library, found in Ruby's standard library.

Here's the canonical simple XML-RPC example. Given a number, it looks up the name of a U.S. state in an alphabetic list:

```
require 'xmlrpc/client'
server = XMLRPC::Client.new2('http://betty.userland.com/RPC2')
server.call('examples.getStateName', 5)                        # => "California"
```

Discussion

XML-RPC is a language-independent solution for distributed systems that makes a simple alternative to SOAP (in fact, XML-RPC is an ancestor of SOAP). Although it's losing ground to SOAP and REST-style web services, XML-RPC is still used by many blogging engines and popular web services, due to its simplicity and relatively long history.

A XML-RPC request is sent to the server as a specially-formatted HTTP POST request, and the XML-RPC response is encoded in the HTTP response to that request. Since most firewalls allow HTTP traffic, this has the advantage (and disadvantage) that XML-RPC requests work through most firewalls. Since XML-RPC requests are POST requests, typical HTTP caching solutions (which only cache GETs) can't be used to speed up XML-RPC requests or save bandwidth.

An XML-RPC request consists of a standard set of HTTP headers, a simple XML document that encodes the name of a remote method to call, and the parameters to pass to that method. The xmlrpc4r library automatically converts between most

XML-RPC data types and the corresponding Ruby data types, so you can treat XML-RPC calls almost like local method calls. The main exceptions are date and time objects. You can pass a Ruby Date or Time object into an XML-RPC method that expects a dateTime.iso8601 parameter, but a method that returns a date will always be represented as an instance of XMLRPC::DateTime.

Table 16-1 lists the supported data types of the request parameters and the response.

Table 16-1. Supported data types

XML-RPC data type	Description	Ruby equivalent
int	Four-byte signed integer	Fixnum or Bignum
boolean	0 (false) or 1 (true)	TrueClass or FalseClass
string	Text or encoded binary data; only the characters < and & are disallowed and rendered as HTML entities	String
double	Double-precision signed floating point number	Float
dateTime.iso8601	Date/time in the format YYYYMMDDTHH:MM:SS (where T is a literal)	XMLRPC::DateTime
base64	base64-encoded binary data	String
struct	An unordered set of key value pairs where the name is always a String and the value can be any XML-RPC data type, including netsted a nested struct or array	Hash
array	A series of values that may be of any of XML-RPC data type, including a netsted struct or array; multiple data types can be used in the context of a single array	Array

Note that nil is not a supported XML-RPC value, although some XML-RPC implementations (including xmlrpc4r) follow an extension that allows it.

An XML-RPC response is another XML document, which encodes the return value of the remote method (if you're lucky) or a "fault" (if you're not). xmlrpc4r parses this document and transforms it into the corresponding Ruby objects.

If the remote method returned a fault, xmlrpc4r raises an XMLRPC::FaultException. A fault contains an integer value (the fault code) and a string containing an error message. Here's an example:

```
begin
  server.call('noSuchMethod')
rescue XMLRPC::FaultException => e
  puts "Error: fault code #{e.faultCode}"
  puts e.faultString
end
# Error: fault code 7
# Can't evaluate the expression because the name "noSuchMethod" hasn't been defined.
```

Here's a more interesting XML-RPC example that searches an online UPC database:

```
def lookup_upc(upc)
  server = XMLRPC::Client.new2('http://www.upcdatabase.com/rpc')
```

```
  begin
    response = server.call('lookupUPC', upc)
    return response['found'] ? response : nil
  rescue XMLRPC::FaultException => e
    puts "Error: "
    puts e.faultCode
    puts e.faultString
  end
end

product = lookup_upc('018787765654')
product['description']                 # => "Dr Bronner's Peppermint Oil Soap"
product['size']                        # => "128 fl oz"

lookup_upc('no such UPC')              # => nil
```

See Also

- Michael Neumann's xmlrpc4r—HOWTO (*http://www.ntecs.de/projects/xmlrpc4r/howto.html*)
- The XML-RPC Specification (*http://www.xmlrpc.com/spec*)
- The extension to XML-RPC that lets it represent nil values (*http://ontosys.com/xml-rpc/extensions.php*)
- The *Ruby Developer's Guide*, published by Syngress and edited by Michael Neumann, contains over 20 pages devoted to implementing XML-RPC clients and servers with xmlrpc4r.
- Recipe 15.8, "Creating a Login System," shows how to serve XML-RPC requests from within a Rails application

16.4   Writing a SOAP Client

Credit: Kevin Marshall

Problem

You need to call a remote method through a SOAP-based web service.

Solution

Use the SOAP RPC Driver in the Ruby standard library.

This simple program prints a quote of the day. It uses the SOAP RPC Driver to connect to the SOAP web service at codingtheweb.com.

```
require 'soap/rpc/driver'
driver = SOAP::RPC::Driver.new(
            'http://webservices.codingtheweb.com/bin/qotd',
            'urn:xmethods-qotd')
```

Once the driver is set up, we define the web service method we want to call (getQuote). We can then call it like a normal Ruby method and display the result:

```
driver.add_method('getQuote')

puts driver.getQuote
# The holy passion of Friendship is of so sweet and steady and
# loyal and enduring a nature that it will last through a whole
# lifetime, if not asked to lend money.
# Mark Twain (1835 - 1910)
```

Discussion

SOAP is a heavyweight protocol for web services, a distant descendant of XML-RPC. As with XML-RPC, a SOAP client sends an XML representation of a method call to a server, and gets back an XML representation of a return value. The whole process is more complex than XML-RPC, but Ruby's built-in SOAP library handles the low-level details for you, leaving you free to focus on using the results in your program.

There are only a few things you need to know to build useful SOAP clients (as I run through them, I'll build another SOAP client; this one is to get stock quotes):

1. The location of the web service (known as the endpoint URL) and the namespace used by the service's documents.

   ```
   require 'soap/rpc/driver'
   driver = SOAP::RPC::Driver.new(
       'http://services.xmethods.net/soap/',      # The endpoint url
       'urn:xmethods-delayed-quotes')             # The namespace
   ```

2. The name of the SOAP method you want to call, and the names of its parameters.

   ```
   driver.add_method('getQuote', 'symbol')
   ```

   Behind the scenes, that call to add_method actually defines a new method on the SOAP::RPC::Driver object. The SOAP library uses metaprogramming to create custom Ruby methods that act like SOAP methods.

3. The details about the results you expect back.

   ```
   puts 'Stock price: %.2f' % driver.getQuote('TR')
   # Stock price: 28.78
   ```

   We expect the stock quote service in the example to return a floating-point value, which we simply display. With more complex result sets, you'll probably assign the results to a variable, which you'll treat as an array or class instance.

See Also

- Recipe 16.6, "Searching the Web with Google's SOAP Service," provides a more complex example
- Recipe 16.7, "Using a WSDL File to Make SOAP Calls Easier"

16.5   Writing a SOAP Server

Credit: Kevin Marshall

Problem

You want to host a SOAP-based web service using a standalone server (that is, not as part of a Rails application).

Solution

Building your own SOAP server really only requires three simple steps:

1. Subclass the SOAP::StandaloneServer class. In the constructor, register the methods you want to expose and the arguments they should take. Here we expose a method sayhelloto method that expects one parameter, username:

```
require 'soap/rpc/standaloneServer'

class MyServer < SOAP::RPC::StandaloneServer
  def initialize(*args)
    super
    add_method(self, 'sayhelloto', 'username')
  end
end
```

2. Define the methods you exposed in step 1:

```
class MyServer
  def sayhelloto(username)
    "Hello, #{username}."
  end
end
```

3. Finally, set up and start your server. Our example server runs on port 8888 on localhost. Its name is "CoolServer" and its namespace is "urn:mySoapServer":

```
server = MyServer.new('CoolServer','urn:mySoapServer','localhost',8888)
trap('INT') { server.shutdown }
server.start
```

   We trap interrupt signals so that we can stop our server from the command line.

Discussion

We've now built a complete SOAP server. It uses the SOAP StandaloneServer and hosts one simple sayhelloto method that can be accessed at "*http://localhost:8888/sayhelloto*" with a namespace of "urn:mySoapServer".

To test your service, start your server in one Ruby session and then use the simple script below in another Ruby session to call the method it exposes:

```
require 'soap/rpc/driver'
driver = SOAP::RPC::Driver.new('http://localhost:8888/', 'urn:mySoapServer')
driver.add_method('sayhelloto', 'username')
driver.sayhelloto('Kevin')                          # => "Hello, Kevin."
```

See Also

- Recipe 15.18, "Exposing Web Services on Your Web Site," shows how to use the XML-RPC/SOAP server that comes with Rails
- For information on building web service *clients*, see Recipes 16.2 through 16.4 and 16.7.
- *Ruby on Rails* by Bruce A. Tate and Curt Hibbs (O'Reilly)

16.6 Searching the Web with Google's SOAP Service

Problem

You want to use Google's web services to perform searches and grab their results within your Ruby application.

Solution

Google exposes a SOAP API to its search functionality, and some other miscellaneous methods like spellcheck. Call these methods with the SOAP client that comes with Ruby's standard library:

```
$KCODE = 'u' # This lets us parse UTF characters
require 'soap/wsdlDriver'

class Google
  @@key = 'JW/JqyXMzCsv7k/dxqR9E9HF+jiSgbDL'
# Get a key at http://www.google.com/apis/
  @@driver = SOAP::WSDLDriverFactory.
    new('http://api.google.com/GoogleSearch.wsdl').create_rpc_driver

 def self.search(query, options={})
    @@driver.doGoogleSearch(
      @@key,
      query,
      options[:offset] || 0,
      options[:limit] || 10,        # Note that this value cannot exceed 10
      options[:filter] || true,
      options[:restricts] || ' ',
      options[:safe_search] || false,
      options[:lr] || ' ',
      options[:ie] || ' ',
      options[:oe] || ' '
    )
  end

  def self.count(query, options={})
    search(query, options).estimatedTotalResultsCount
  end
```

```
      def self.spell(phrase)
        @@driver.doSpellingSuggestion(@@key, phrase)
      end
    end
```

Here it is in action:

```
Google.count "Ruby Cookbook site:oreilly.com"
# => 368

results = Google.search "Ruby Cookbook site:oreilly.com", :limit => 7
results.resultElements.size
# => 7

results.resultElements.first["title"]
# => "oreilly.com -- Online Catalog: <b>Ruby Cookbook</b>..."

results.resultElements.first["URL"]
# => "http://www.oreilly.com/catalog/rubyckbk/"

results.resultElements.first["snippet"]
# => "The <b>Ruby Cookbook</b> is a new addition to ..."

Google.spell "tis is te centence"
# => "this is the sentence"
```

Discussion

Each of the options defined in Google.search corresponds to an option in the Google search API.

Name	Description
key	Unique key provided when you sign up with Google's web services.
query	The search query.
limit	How many results to grab; the maximum is 10.
offset	Which result in the list to start from.
filter	Whether or not to let Google group together similar results.
restricts	Further restrict search results to those containing this string.
safe_search	Whether or not to enable the SafeSearch filtering feature.
lr	Language restriction: lets you search for pages in specific languages.
ie	Input encoding: lets you choose the character encoding for the query.
oe	Output encoding: lets you choose the character encoding for the returned results.

See Also

- For a simpler API, see Recipe 16.7, "Using a WSDL File to Make SOAP Calls Easier"
- *http://www.google.com/apis/reference.html*
- *http://www.google.com/help/refinesearch.html*

16.7 Using a WSDL File to Make SOAP Calls Easier

Credit: Kevin Marshall

Problem

You need to create a client for a SOAP-based web service, but you don't want to type out the definitions for all the SOAP methods you'll be calling.

Solution

Most web services provide a WSDL file: a machine-readable description of the methods they offer. Ruby's SOAP WSDL Driver can parse a WSDL file and make the appropriate methods available automatically.

This code uses the *xmethods.com* SOAP web service to get a stock price. In Recipe 16.7, we defined the getQuote method manually. Here, its name and signature are loaded from a hosted WSDL file. You still have to know that the method is called getQuote and that it takes one string, but you don't have to write any code telling Ruby this.

```
require 'soap/wsdlDriver'
wsdl = 'http://services.xmethods.net/soap/urn:xmethods-delayed-quotes.wsdl'
driver = SOAP::WSDLDriverFactory.new(wsdl).create_rpc_driver

puts "Stock price: %.2f" % driver.getQuote('TR')
# Stock price: 28.78
```

Discussion

According to the World Wide Web Consortium (W3), "WSDL service definitions provide documentation for distributed systems and serve as a recipe for automating the details involved in applications communication."

What this means to you is that you don't have to tell Ruby which methods a web service provides, and what arguments it expects. If you feed a WSDL file in to the Driver Factory, Ruby will give you a Driver object with all the methods already defined.

There are only a few things you need to know to build useful SOAP clients with a WSDL file. I'll illustrate with some code that performs a Google search and prints out the results.

1. Start with the URL to the WSDL file:

   ```
   require 'soap/wsdlDriver'
   wsdl = 'http://api.google.com/GoogleSearch.wsdl'
   driver = SOAP::WSDLDriverFactory.new(wsdl).create_rpc_driver
   ```

2. Next you need the name of the SOAP method you want to call, and the expected types of its parameters:

   ```
   my_google_key = 'get yours from https://www.google.com/accounts'
   my_query = 'WSDL Ruby'
   ```

```
XSD::Charset.encoding = 'UTF8'
result = driver.doGoogleSearch(my_google_key, my_query, 0, 10, false,
                          '', false, '', '', '')
```

Without WSDL, you need to tell Ruby that methods a web service exposes, and what parameters it takes. With WSDL, Ruby loads this information from the WSDL file. Of course, *you* still need to know this information so you can write the method call. In this case, you'll also need to sign up for an API key that lets you use the web service.

The Google search service returns data encoded as UTF-8, which may contain special characters that cause mapping problems to Ruby strings. That's what the call to `XSD::Charset.encoding = 'UTF8'` is for. The Soap4r and WSDL Factory libraries rely on the XSD library to handle the data type conversions from web services to native Ruby types. By explicitly telling Ruby to use UTF-8 encoding, you'll ensure that any special characters are properly escaped within your results so you can treat them as proper Ruby Strings.

```
result.class
# => SOAP::Mapping::Object

(result.methods - SOAP::Mapping::Object.instance_methods).sort
# => ["directoryCategories", "directoryCategories=", "documentFiltering",
#     ...
#     "searchTips", "searchTips=", "startIndex", "startIndex="]
```

3. Here's how to treat the result object you get back:

```
"Query for: #{my_query}"
# => "Query for: WSDL Ruby"
"Found: #{result['estimatedTotalResultsCount']}"
# => "Found: 159000"
"Query took about %.2f seconds" % result['searchTime']
# => "Query took about 0.05 seconds"

result["resultElements"].each do |rec|
  puts "Title: #{rec["title"]}"
  puts "URL: #{rec["URL"]}"
  puts "Snippet: #{rec["snippet"]}"
  puts
end
# Title: <b>wsdl</b>: <b>Ruby</b> Standard Library Documentation
# URL: http://www.ruby-doc.org/stdlib/libdoc/wsdl/rdoc/index.html
# Snippet: #<SOAP::Mapping::Object:0xb705f560>
#
# Title: how to make SOAP4R read <b>WSDL</b> files?
# URL: http://www.ruby-talk.org/cgi-bin/scat.rb/ruby/ruby-talk/37623
# Snippet: Subject: how to make SOAP4R read <b>WSDL</b> files? <b>...</b>
# ...
```

We expect the Google search service to return a complex SOAP type. The XSD library will convert it into a Ruby hash, containing some keys like `EstimatedTotalResultsCount` and `resultElements`—the latter points to an array of search results. Every search result is itself a complex type, and XSD maps it to a hash as well: a hash with keys like snippet and URL.

See Also

- Recipe 16.4, "Writing a SOAP Client," provides a more generic example of a SOAP client
- Recipe 16.6, "Searching the Web with Google's SOAP Service," shows what searching Google would be like without WSDL
- *https://www.google.com/accounts* to get an access key to Google Web APIs

16.8 Charging a Credit Card

Problem

You want to charge a credit card from within your Ruby application.

Solution

To charge credit cards online, you need an account with a credit card merchant. Although there are many to choose from, Authorize.Net is one of the best and most widely used. The payment library encapsulates the logic of making a credit card payments with Authorize.Net, and soon it will support other gateways as well. It's available as the payment gem.

```
require 'rubygems'
require 'payment/authorize_net'

transaction = Payment::AuthorizeNet.new(
  :login           => 'username',
  :transaction_key => 'my_key',
  :amount          => '49.95',
  :card_number     => '4012888818888',
  :expiration      => '0310',
  :first_name      => 'John',
  :last_name       => 'Doe'
)
```

The submit method sends a payment request. If there's a problem with your payment (probably due to an invalid credit card), the submit method will raise a Payment::PaymentError:

```
begin
  transaction.submit
  puts "Card processed successfully: #{transaction.authorization}"
rescue Payment::PaymentError
  puts "Card was rejected: #{transaction.error_message}"
end
# Card was rejected: The merchant login ID or password is invalid
# or the account is inactive.
```

Discussion

Some of the information sent during initialization of the `Payment::AuthorizeNet` class represent your account with Authorize.Net, and will never change (at least, not for the lifetime of the account). You can store this information in a YAML file called *.payment.yml* in your home directory, and have the payment library load it automatically. A *.payment.yml* file might look like this:

```
login: username
transaction_key: my_key
```

That way you don't have to hardcode `login` and `transaction_key` within your Ruby code.

If you're using the payment library from within a Rails application, you might want to put your YAML hash in the *config* directory with other configuration files, instead of in your home directory. You can override the location for the defaults file by specifying the `:prefs` key while initializing the object:

```
payment = Payment::AuthorizeNet
    .new(:prefs => "#{RAILS_ROOT}/config/payment.yml")
payment.amount = 20
payment.card_number = 'bogus'
payment.submit rescue "That didn't work"
```

Notice that after the `Payment::AuthorizeNet` object has been initialized, you can change its configuration with accessor methods.

Like most online merchants, Authorize.Net uses its own XML-formatted responses to do transactions over HTTPS. Some merchants, such as Payflow Pro, use proprietary interfaces to their backend that require a bridge with their Java or C libraries. If you're using Ruby, this approach can be cumbersome and difficult. It's worth investing some time into researching how flexible the backend is before you decide on a merchant platform for your Ruby application.

See Also

* Recipe 2.17, "Checking a Credit Card Checksum"
* The online RDoc for the payment library (*http://payment.rubyforge.org/*)
* *http://authorize.net/*

16.9 Finding the Cost to Ship Packages via UPS or FedEx

Problem

You want to calculate the cost to ship any item with FedEx or UPS. This is useful if you're running an online store.

Solution

FedEx and UPS provide web services that can query information on pricing as well as retrieve shipping labels. The logic for using these services has been encapsulated within the shipping gem:

```
require 'rubygems'
require 'shipping'

ship = Shipping::Base.new(
  :fedex_url => 'https://gatewaybeta.fedex.com/GatewayDC',
  :fedex_account => '123456789',
  :fedex_meter => '387878',

  :ups_account => '7B4F74E3075AEEFF',
  :ups_user => 'username',
  :ups_password => 'password',

  :sender_zip => 10001               # It's shipped from Manhattan.
)

ship.weight = 2                      # It weighs two pounds.
ship.city = 'Portland'
ship.state = 'OR'
ship.zip = 97202

ship.ups.price                       # => 8.77
ship.fedex.price                     # => 5.49
ship.ups.valid_address?              # => true
```

If you have a UPS account or a FedEx account, but not both, you can omit the account information you don't have, and instantiate a Shipping::UPS or a Shipping:: FedEx object.

Discussion

You can either specify your account information during the initialization of the object (as above) or in a YAML hash. It's similar to the payment library described in Recipe 16.8. If you choose to use the YAML hash, you can specify the account information in a file called *.shipping.yml* within the home directory of the user running the Ruby program:

```
fedex_url: https://gatewaybeta.fedex.com/GatewayDC
fedex_account: 1234556
fedex_meter: 387878

ups_account: 7B4F74E3075AEEFF
ups_user: username
ups_password: password
```

But your directory is not a good place to keep a file being used by a Rails application. Here's how to move the *.shipping* file into a Rails application:

```
ship = Shipping::FedEx.new(:prefs => "#{RAILS_ROOT}/config/shipping.yml")

ship.sender_zip = 10001
ship.zip = 97202
ship.state = 'OR'
ship.weight = 2

ship.price > ship.discount_price                       # => true
```

Notice the use of ship.discount_price to find the discounted price; if you have an account with FedEx or UPS, you might be eligible for discounts.

See Also

- *http://shipping.rubyforge.org/*
- Recipe 16.8, "Charging a Credit Card"

16.10 Sharing a Hash Between Any Number of Computers

Credit: James Edward Gray II

Problem

You want to easily share some application data with remote programs. Your needs are as trivial as, "What if all the computers could share this hash?"

Solution

Ruby's built-in DRb library can share Ruby objects across a network. Here's a simple hash server:

```
#!/usr/local/ruby -w
# drb_hash_server.rb
require 'drb'

# Start up DRb with a URI and a hash to share
shared_hash = {:server => 'Some data set by the server' }
DRb.start_service('druby://127.0.0.1:61676', shared_hash)
puts 'Listening for connection...'
DRb.thread.join  # Wait on DRb thread to exit...
```

Run this server in one Ruby session, and then you can run a client in another:

```
require 'drb'

# Prep DRb
DRb.start_service
# Fetch the shared object
shared_data = DRbObject.new_with_uri('druby://127.0.0.1:61676')
```

```
# Add to the Hash
shared_data[:client] = 'Some data set by the client'
shared_data.each do |key, value|
  puts "#{key} => #{value}"
end
# client => Some data set by the client
# server => Some data set by the server
```

Discussion

If this looks like magic, that's the point. DRb hides the complexity of distributed programming. There are some complications (covered in later recipes), but for the most part DRb simply makes remote objects look like local objects.

The solution given above may meet your needs if you're working with a single server and client on a trusted network, but applications aren't always that simple. Issues like thread-safety and security may force you to find a more robust solution. Luckily, that doesn't require too much more work.

Let's take thread-safety first. Behind the scenes, a DRb server handles each client connection in a separate Ruby thread. Ruby's Hash class is not automatically thread-safe, so we need to do a little extra work before we can reliably share a hash between multiple concurrent users.

Here's a library that uses delegation to implement a thread-safe hash. A ThreadsafeHash object delegates all its method calls to an underlying Hash object, but it uses a Mutex to ensure that only one thread (or DRb client) can have access to the hash at a time.

```
# threadsafe_hash.rb
require 'rubygems'
require 'facet/basicobject'          # For the BasicObject class
require 'thread'                     # For the Mutex class
```

We base our thread-safe hash on the BasicObject class in the Facets More library (available as the facets_more gem). A BasicObject is an ordinary Ruby object, except it defines no methods at all—not even the methods of Object. This gives us a blank slate to work from. We can make sure that every single method of ThreadsafeHash gets forwarded to the underlying hash, even methods like inspect, which are defined by Object and which wouldn't normally trigger method_missing.

```
# A thread-safe Hash that delegates all its methods to a real hash.
class ThreadsafeHash < BasicObject
  def initialize(*args, &block)
    @hash = Hash.new(*args, &block)  # The shared hash
    @lock = Mutex.new                # For thread safety
  end

  def method_missing(method, *args, &block)
    if @hash.respond_to? method      # Forward Hash method calls...
      @lock.synchronize do           # but wrap them in a thread safe lock.
        @hash.send(method, *args, &block)
```

```
          end
       else
          super
       end
     end
   end
```

The next step is to build a RemoteHash using BlankSlate. The implementation is trivial. Just forward method calls onto the Hash, but wrap each of them in a synchronization block in order to ensure only one thread can affect the object at a time.

Now that we have a thread-safe RemoteHash, we can build a better server:

```
#!/usr/bin/ruby -w
# threadsafe_hash_server.rb

require 'threadsafe_hash'  # both sides of DRb connection need all classes
require 'drb'
```

We begin by pulling in our RemoteHash library and DRb:

```
$SAFE = 1  # Minimum acceptable paranoia level when sharing code!
```

The $SAFE = 1 line is *critical*! Don't put any code on a network without a minimum of $SAFE = 1. It's just too dangerous. Malicious code, like obj.instance_eval("`rm -rf / *`"), must be controlled. Feel free to raise $SAFE even higher, in fact.

```
# Start up DRb with a URI and an object to share.
DRb.start_service('druby://127.0.0.1:61676', Threadsafe.new)
puts 'Listening for connection...'
DRb.thread.join  # wait on DRb thread to exit...
```

We're now ready to start the DRb service, which we do with a URI and an object to share. If you don't want to allow external connections, you may want to replace "127.0.0.1" with "localhost" in the URI.

Since DRb runs in its own threads, the final line of the server is needed to ensure that we don't exit before those threads have done their job.

Run that code, and then you can run this client code to share a hash:

```
#!/usr/bin/ruby
# threadsafe_hash_client.rb

require 'remote_hash'  # Both sides of DRb connection need all classes
require 'drb'

# Prep DRb
DRb.start_service

# Fetch the shared hash
$shared_data = DRbObject.new_with_uri('druby://127.0.0.1:61676')

puts 'Enter Ruby commands using the shared hash $shared_data...'
require 'irb'
IRB.start
```

Here again we pull in the needed libraries and point DRb at the served object. We store that object in a variable so that we can continue to access it as needed.

Then, just as an example of what can be done, we enter an IRb session, allowing you to manipulate the variable any way you like. Remember, any number of clients can connect and share this hash.

Let's illustrate some sample sessions. In the first one, we add some data to the hash:

```
$ ruby threadsafe_hash_client.rb
Enter Ruby commands using the shared hash $shared_data...
irb(main):001:0> $shared_data.keys
=> []
irb(main):002:0> $shared_data[:terminal_one] = 'Hello other terminals!'
=> "Hello other terminals!"
```

Let's attach a second client and see what the two of them find:

```
$ ruby threadsafe_hash_client.rb
Enter Ruby commands using the shared hash $shared_data...
irb(main):001:0> $shared_data.keys
=> [:terminal_one]
irb(main):002:0> $shared_data[:terminal_one]
=> "Hello other terminals!"
irb(main):003:0> $shared_data[:terminal_two] = 'Is this thing on?'
=> "Is this thing on?"
```

Going back to the first session, we can see the new data:

```
irb(main):003:0> $shared_data.each_pair do |key, value|
irb(main):004:1*   puts "#{key} => #{value}"
irb(main):005:1> end
terminal_one => Hello other terminals!
terminal_two => Is this thing on?
```

Notice that, as you'd hope, the DRb magic can even cope with a method that takes a code block.

See Also

- There is a good beginning tutorial for DRb at *http://www.rubygarden.org/ ruby?DrbTutorial*
- There is a helpful DRb presentation by Mark Volkmann in the "Why Ruby?" repository at *http://rubyforge.org/docman/view.php/251/216/DistributedRuby.pdf*
- The standard library documentation for DRb can be found at *http://www.ruby- doc.org/stdlib/libdoc/drb/rdoc/index.html*
- For more on the internal workings of the thread-safe hash, see Recipe 8.8, "Delegating Method Calls to Another Object," and Recipe 20.4, "Synchronizing Access to an Object"
- Recipe 20.11, "Avoiding Deadlock," for another common problem with multi-threaded programming

16.11 Implementing a Distributed Queue

Credit: James Edward Gray II

Problem

You want to use a central server as a workhorse, queueing up requests from remote clients and handling them one at a time.

Solution

Here's a method that shares a Queue object with clients. Clients put job objects into the queue, and the server handles them by yielding them to a code block.

```
#!/usr/bin/ruby
# queue_server.rb

require 'thread'      # For Ruby's thread-safe Queue
require 'drb'

$SAFE = 1             # Minimum acceptable paranoia level when sharing code!

def run_queue(url='druby://127.0.0.1:61676')
  queue = Queue.new  # Containing the jobs to be processed

  # Start up DRb with URI and object to share
  DRb.start_service(url, queue)
  puts 'Listening for connection...'
  while job = queue.deq
    yield job
  end
end
```

Have your server call run_queue, passing in a code block that handles a single job. Every time one of your clients puts a job into the server queue, the server passes the job into the code block. Here's a sample code block that can handle a fast-running job ("Report") or a slow-running job ("Process"):

```
run_queue do |job|
  case job['request']
  when 'Report'
    puts "Reporting for #{job['from']}...  Done."
  when 'Process'
    puts "Processing for #{job['from']}..."
    sleep 3           # Simulate real work
    puts 'Processing complete.'
  end
end
```

If we get a couple of clients sending in requests, output might look like this:

```
$ ruby queue_server.rb
Listening for connection...
```

```
Processing for Client 1...
Processing complete.
Processing for Client 2...
Processing complete.
Reporting for Client 1...  Done.
Reporting for Client 2...  Done.
Processing for Client 1...
Processing complete.
Reporting for Client 2...  Done.
...
```

Discussion

A client for the queue server defined in the Solution simply needs to connect to the DRB server and add a mix of "Report" and "Process" jobs to the queue. Here's a client that connects to the DRb server and adds 20 jobs to the queue at random:

```
#!/usr/bin/ruby
# queue_client.rb

require 'thread'
require 'drb'

# Get a unique name for this client
NAME = ARGV.shift or raise "Usage:  #{File.basename($0)} CLIENT_NAME"

DRb.start_service
queue = DRbObject.new_with_uri("druby://127.0.0.1:61676")

20.times do
  queue.enq('request' => ['Report', 'Process'][rand(2)], 'from' => NAME)
  sleep 1 # simulating network delays
end
```

Everything from Recipe 16.10 applies here. The major difference is that Ruby ships with a thread-safe Queue. That saves us the trouble of building our own.

See Also

- Recipe 16.10

16.12 Creating a Shared "Whiteboard"

Credit: James Edward Gray II

Problem

You want to create the network equivalent of a whiteboard. Remote programs can place Ruby objects up on the board, examine objects on the board, or remove objects from the board.

Solution

You could just use a synchronized hash (as in Recipe 16.10), but Rinda[*] provides a data structure called a TupleSpace that is optimized for distributed programming. It works well when you have some clients putting data on the whiteboard, and other clients processing the data and taking it down.

Let's create an application that lets clients on different parts of the network translate each others' sentences, and builds a translation dictionary as they work.

It's easier to see the architecture of the server if you see the clients first, so here's a client that adds some English sentences to a shared TupleSpace:

```ruby
#!/usr/bin/ruby -w
# english_client.rb
require 'drb'
require 'rinda/tuplespace'

# Connect to the TupleSpace...
DRb.start_service
tuplespace = Rinda::TupleSpaceProxy.new(
  DRbObject.new_with_uri('druby://127.0.0.1:61676')
)
```

The English client's job is to split English sentences into words and to add each sentence to the whiteboard as a tuple: [unique id, language, words].

```ruby
counter = 0
DATA.each_line do |line|
  tuplespace.write([(counter += 1), 'English', line.strip.split])
end

__END__
Ruby programmers have more fun
Ruby gurus are obsessed with ducks
Ruby programmers are happy programmers
```

Here's a second client. It creates a loop that continually reads all the English sentences from the TupleSpace and puts up word-for-word translations into Pig Latin. It uses Tuplespace#read to read English-language tuples off the whiteboard without removing them.

```ruby
require 'drb'
require 'rinda/tuplespace'
require 'set'

DRb.start_service
tuplespace = Rinda::TupleSpaceProxy.new(
  DRbObject.new_with_uri('druby://127.0.0.1:61676')
)
```

---

[*] Rinda is a companion library to DRb. It's a Ruby port of the Linda distributed computing environment, which is based on the idea of the tuplespace. It's similar to JavaSpaces.

```
# Track of the IDs of the sentences we've translated
translated = Set.new

# Continually read English sentences off of the board.
while english = tuplespace.read([Numeric, 'English', Array])
  # Skip anything we've already translated.
  next if translated.member? english.first
  translated << english.first

  # Translate English to Pig Latin.
  pig_latin = english.last.map do |word|
    if word =~ /^[aeiou]/i
      "#{word}way"
    elsif word =~ /^([^aeiouy]+)(.+)$/i
      "#{$2}#{$1.downcase}ay"
    end
  end

  # Write the Pig Latin translation back onto the board
  tuplespace.write([english.first, 'Pig Latin', pig_latin])
end
```

Finally, here's the language server: the code that exposes a TupleSpace for the two clients to use. It also acts as a third client of the TupleSpace: it continually takes non-English sentences down off of the whiteboard (using the destructive TupleSpace#take method) and matches them word-for-word with the corresponding English sentences (which it also removes from the whiteboard). In this way it gradually builds an English-to-Pig Latin dictionary, which it serializes to disk with YAML:

```
#!/usr/bin/ruby -w
# dictionary_building_server.rb
require 'drb'
require 'yaml'
require 'rinda/tuplespace'

# Create a TupleSpace and serve it to the world.
tuplespace = Rinda::TupleSpace.new
DRb.start_service('druby://127.0.0.1:61676', tuplespace)

# Create a dictionary to hold the terms we have seen.
dictionary = Hash.new
# Remove non-English sentences from the board.
while translation = tuplespace.take([Numeric, /^(?!English)/, Array])
  # Match each with its English equivalent.
  english = tuplespace.take([translation.first, 'English', Array])
  # Match up the words, and save the dictionary.
  english.last.zip(translation.last) { |en, tr| dictionary[en] = tr }
  File.open('dictionary.yaml', 'w') { |file| YAML.dump(dictionary, file) }
end
```

If you run the server and then the two clients, the server will spit out a dictionary.yaml file that shows how much it has already learned:

```
$ ruby dictionary_building_server.rb &
$ ruby english_client.rb
$ ruby pig_latin_client.rb &

$ cat dictionary.yaml
---
happy: appyhay
programmers: ogrammerspray
Ruby: ubyray
gurus: urusgay
ducks: ucksday
obsessed: obsessedway
have: avehay
are: areway
fun: unfay
with: ithway
more: oremay
```

Discussion

Rinda's TupleSpace class is pretty close to the network equivalent of a whiteboard. A "tuple" is just an ordered sequence—in this case, an array of Ruby objects. A TupleSpace holds these sequences and provides an interface to them.

You can add sequences of objects to the TupleSpace using TupleSpace#write. Later, the same or different code can query the object using TupleSpace#read or TupleSpace#take. The only difference is that TupleSpace#take is destructive; it removes the object from the TupleSpace as it's read.

You can select certain tuples by passing TupleSpace#read or TupleSpace#take a *template* that matches the tuples you seek. A template is just another tuple. In the example code, we used templates like [Numeric, 'English', Array]. Each element of a tuple is matched against the corresponding element of a template with the === operator, the same operator used in Ruby case statements.

That particular template will match any three-element tuple whose first element is a Numeric object, whose second element is the literal string 'English', and whose third element is an Array object: that is, all the English sentences currently on the whiteboard.

You can create templates containing any kind of object that will work with the === operator: for instance, a Regexp object in a template can match against strings in a tuple. Any nil slot in a template is a wildcard slot that will match anything.

See Also

- The DRb presentation by Mark Volkmann in the "Why Ruby?" repository at *http://rubyforge.org/docman/view.php/251/216/DistributedRuby.pdf* has some material on TupleSpaces
- Clients can also choose to be notified of TupleSpace events; you can see an example at *http://ruby-talk.org/cgi-bin/scat.rb/ruby/ruby-talk/159065*

16.13 Securing DRb Services with Access Control Lists

Credit: James Edward Gray II

Problem

You want to keep everybody in the world (literally!) from having access to your DRb service. Instead you want to control which hosts can, and cannot, connect.

Solution

Here's the simple shared hash from Recipe 16.10, only this time it's locked down with DRb's ACL (access control list) class:

```ruby
#!/usr/bin/ruby
# acl_hash_server.rb

require 'drb'
require 'drb/acl'

# Setup the security--remember to call before DRb.start_service()
DRb.install_acl(ACL.new(%w{ deny all
                            allow 192.168.1.*
                            allow 127.0.0.1 } ) )

# Start up DRb with a URI and a hash to share
shared_hash = {:server => 'Some data set by the server' }
DRb.start_service("druby://127.0.0.1:61676", shared_hash)
puts 'Listening for connection...'
DRb.thread.join  # Wait on DRb thread to exit...
```

Discussion

If you bind your DRb server to localhost, it'll only be accessible to other Ruby processes on your computer. That's not very distributed. But if you bind your DRb server to some other hostname, anyone on your local network (if you've got a local network) or anyone on the Internet at large will be able to share your Ruby objects. You're probably not feeling that generous.

DRb's ACL class provides simple white/blacklist security similar to that used by the Unix /etc/hosts.allow and /etc/hosts.deny files. The ACL constructor takes an array of strings. The first string of a pair is always "allow" or "deny", and it's followed by the address or addresses to allow or deny access.

String addresses can include wildcards ("*"), as shown in the solution, to allow or deny an entire range of addresses. The ACL class also understands the term "all," and your first address should be either "deny all" or (less likely) "allow all". Subsequent entries can relax or restrict access, as needed.

In the Solution above, the default is to deny access. Exceptions are carved out afterwards for anyone on the local IP network (192.168.1.**) and anyone on the same host as the server itself (127.0.0.1). A public DRb server might allow access by default, and deny access only to troublesome client IPs.

See Also

- Recipe 16.10, "Sharing a Hash Between Any Number of Computers"

16.14 Automatically Discovering DRb Services with Rinda

Credit: James Edward Gray II

Problem

You want to distribute Ruby code across your local network without hardcoding the clients with the addresses of the servers.

Solution

Using Ruby's standard Rinda library, it's easy to provide zero-configuration networking for clients and services. With Rinda, machines can discover DRb services without providing any addresses. All you need is a running RingServer on the local network:

```
#!/usr/bin/ruby
# rinda_server.rb

require 'rinda/ring'        # for RingServer
require 'rinda/tuplespace'  # for TupleSpace

DRb.start_service

# Create a TupleSpace to hold named services, and start running.
Rinda::RingServer.new(Rinda::TupleSpace.new)

DRb.thread.join
```

Discussion

The RingServer provides automatic service detection for DRb servers. Any machine on your local network can find the local RingServer without knowing its address. Once it's found the server, a client can look up services and use them, not having to know the addresses of the DRb servers that host them.

To find the Rinda server, a client broadcasts a UDP packet asking for the location of a RingServer. All computers on the local network will get this packet, and if a computer is running a RingServer, it will respond with its address. A server can use the RingServer to register services; a client can use the RingServer to look up services.

A RingServer object keeps a service listing in a shared TupleSpace (see Recipe 16.12). Each service has a corresponding tuple with four members:

- The literal symbol :name, which indicates that the tuple is an entry in the RingServer namespace.
- The symbol of a Ruby class, indicating the type of the service.
- The DRbObject shared by the service.
- A string description of the service.

By retrieving this TupleSpace remotely, you can look up services as tuples and advertise your own services. Let's advertise an object (a simple TupleSpace) through the RingServer under the name :TupleSpace:

```
#!/usr/bin/ruby
# share_a_tuplespace.rb

require 'rinda/ring'       # for RingFinger and SimpleRenewer
require 'rinda/tuplespace' # for TupleSpace

DRb.start_service
ring_server = Rinda::RingFinger.primary

# Register our TupleSpace service with the RingServer
ring_server.write( [:name, :TupleSpace, Rinda::TupleSpace.new, 'Tuple Space'],
                   Rinda::SimpleRenewer.new )

DRb.thread.join
```

The SimpleRenewer sent in with the namespace listing lets the RingServer periodically check whether the service has expired.

Now we can write clients that find this service by querying the RingServer, without having to know which machine it lives on. All we need to know is the name of the service:

```
#!/usr/bin/ruby
# use_a_tuplespace.rb

require 'rinda/ring'       # for RingFinger
require 'rinda/tuplespace' # for TupleSpaceProxy

DRb.start_service
ring_server = Rinda::RingFinger.primary

# Ask the RingServer for the advertised TupleSpace.
ts_service = ring_server.read([:name, :TupleSpace, nil, nil])[2]
tuplespace = Rinda::TupleSpaceProxy.new(ts_service)

# Now we can use the object normally:
tuplespace.write([:data, rand(100)])
puts "Data is #{tuplespace.read([:data, nil]).last}."
# Data is 91.
```

These two programs locate each other without needing hardcoded IP addresses. Addresses are still being used under the covers, but the address to the Rinda server is discovered automatically through UDP, and all the other addresses are kept in the Rinda server.

`Rinda::RingFinger.primary` stores the first `RingServer` to respond to your Ruby process's UDP packet. If your local network is running more than one `RingServer`, the first one to respond might not be the one with the service you want, so you should probably only run one `RingServer` on your network. If you do have more than one `RingServer`, you can iterate over them with `Rinda::RingFinger#each`.

See Also

- Recipe 16.12, "Creating a Shared "Whiteboard""
- Recipe 16.18, "A Remote-Controlled Jukebox"
- Eric Hodel has a Rinda::RingServer tutorial at *http://segment7.net/projects/ruby/ drb/rinda/ringserver.html*

16.15 Proxying Objects That Can't Be Distributed

Credit: James Edward Gray II

Problem

You want to allow classes to connect to your DRb server, without giving the server access to the class definition. Perhaps you've given clients an API to implement, and you don't want to make everyone send you the source to their implementations just so they can connect to the server.

...OR...

You have some code that is tied to local resources: database connections, log files, or even just the closure aspect of Ruby's blocks. You want this code to interact with a DRb server, but it must be run locally.

...OR...

You want to send an object to a DRb server, perhaps as a parameter to a method; but you want the server to notice changes to that object as your local code modifies it.

Solution

Rather than sending an object to the server, you can ask DRb to send a proxy instead. When the server acts on the proxy, a description of the act will be sent across the network. The client end will actually perform the action. In effect, you've partially switched the roles of the client and the server.

You can set up a proxy in two simple steps. First, make sure your client code includes the following line before it interacts with any server objects:

```
DRb.start_service  # The client needs to be a DRb service too.
```

That's generally just a good habit to get into with DRb client code, because it allows DRb to magically support some constructs (like Ruby's blocks) by sending a proxy object when necessary. If you're intentionally trying to send a proxy, it becomes essential.

As long as your client is a DRb service of its own, you can proxy all objects made from a specific class or individual objects by including the DRbUndumped module:

```
class MyLocalClass
  include DRbUndumped  # The magic line.  All objects of this type are proxied.
  # ...
end

# ... OR ...

my_local_object.extend DRbUndumped  # Proxy just this object.
```

Discussion

Under normal circumstances, DRb is very simple. A method call is packaged up (using Marshal) as a target object, method name, and some arguments. The resulting object is sent over the wire to the server, where it's executed. The important thing to notice is that the server receives copies of the original arguments.

The server unmarshals the data, invokes the method, packages the result, and sends it back. Again, the result objects are copied to the client.

But that process doesn't always work. Perhaps the server needs to pass a code block into a method call. Ruby's blocks cannot be serialized. DRb notices this special case and sends a proxy object instead. As the server interacts with the proxy, the calls are bundled up and sent back to you, just as described above, so everything just works.

But DRb can't magically notice all cases where copying is harmful. That's why you need DRbUndumped. By extending an object with DRbUndumped, you can force DRb to send a proxy object instead of the real object, and ensure that your code stays local.

If all this sounds confusing, a simple example will probably clear it right up. Let's code up a trivial hello server:

```
#!/usr/bin/ruby
# hello_server.rb
require 'drb'

# a simple greeter class
class HelloService
  def hello(in_stream, out_stream)
    out_stream.puts 'What is your name?'
    name = in_stream.gets.strip
```

```
      out_stream.puts "Hello #{name}."
   end
end

# start up DRb with URI and object to share
DRb.start_service('druby://localhost:61676', HelloService.new)
DRb.thread.join  # wait on DRb thread to exit...
```

Now we try connecting with a simple client:

```
#!/usr/bin/ruby
# hello_client.rb
require 'drb'

# fetch service object and ask it to greet us...
hello_service = DRbObject.new_with_uri('druby://localhost:61676')
hello_service.hello($stdin, $stdout)
```

Unfortunately, that yields an error message. Obviously, `$stdin` and `$stdout` are local resources that won't be available from the remote service. We need to pass them by proxy to get this working:

```
#!/usr/bin/ruby
# hello_client2.rb
require 'drb'

DRb.start_service  # make sure client can serve proxy objects...
# and request that the streams be proxied
$stdin.extend   DRbUndumped
$stdout.extend DRbUndumped

# fetch service object and ask it to greet us...
hello_service = DRbObject.new_with_uri('druby://localhost:61676')
hello_service.hello($stdin, $stdout)
```

With that client, DRb has remote access to the streams (through the proxy objects) and can read and write them as needed.

See Also

- Recipe 16.10, "Sharing a Hash Between Any Number of Computers"
- Eric Hodel's "Introduction to DRb" covers DRbUndumped (*http://segment7.net/projects/ruby/drb/introduction.html*)
- The DRb presentation by Mark Volkmann in the "Why Ruby?" repository at *http://rubyforge.org/docman/view.php/251/216/DistributedRuby.pdf* has some material on DRbUndumped

16.16 Storing Data on Distributed RAM with MemCached

Credit: Ben Bleything with Michael Granger

Problem

You need a lightweight, persistent storage space, and you have systems on your network that have unused RAM.

Solution

memcached provides a distributed in-memory cache. When used with a Ruby client library, it can be used to store almost any Ruby object. See the Discussion section below for more information, and details of where to get memcached.

In this example, we'll use Michael Granger's Ruby-MemCache library, available as the Ruby-MemCache gem.

Assume you have a memcached server running on the machine at IP address 10.0.1.201. You can use the memcache gem to access the cache as though it were a local hash. This Ruby code will store a string in the remote cache:

```
require 'rubygems'
require 'memcache'

MC = MemCache.new '10.0.1.201'

MC[:test] = 'This string lives in memcached!'
```

The string has been placed in your memcached with the key :test. You can fetch it from a different Ruby session:

```
require 'rubygems'
require 'memcache'

MC = MemCache.new '10.0.1.201'

MC[:test]                           # => "This string lives in memcached!"
```

You can also place more complex objects in memcached. In fact, any object that can be serialized with Marshal.dump can be placed in memcached. Here we store and retrieve a hash:

```
hash = {
  :roses   => 'are red',
  :violets => 'are blue'
}

MC[:my_hash] = hash
MC[:my_hash][:roses]                # => "are red"
```

Discussion

memcached was originally designed to alleviate pressure on the database servers for LiveJournal.com. For more information about how memcached can be used for this kind of purpose, see Recipe 16.17.

memcached provides a lightweight, distributed cache space where the cache is held in RAM. This makes the cache extremely fast, and it never blocks on disk I/O. When effectively deployed, memcached can significantly reduce the load on your database servers by farming out storage to unused RAM on other machines.

To start using memcached, you'll need to download the server (see below). You can install it from source, or get it via most *nix packaging systems.

Next, find some machines on your network that have extra RAM. Install memcached on them, then start the daemon with this command:

```
$ memcached -d -m 1024
```

This starts up a memcached instance with a 1024-megabyte memory cache (you can, of course, vary the cache size as appropriate for your hardware). If you run this command on the machine with IP address 10.0.1.201, you can then access it from other machines on your local network, as in the examples above.

memcached also supports more advanced functions, such as conditional sets and expiration times. You can also combine multiple machines into a single virtual cache. For more information about these possibilities, refer to the memcached documentation and to the documentation for the Ruby library that you're using.

See Also

- Recipe 13.2, "Serializing Data with Marshal"
- Recipe 16.7, "Using a WSDL File to Make SOAP Calls Easier"
- The memcached homepage, located at *http://danga.com/memcached/*, contains further information about memcached, documentation, and links to client libraries for other languages; there is also a mailing list at *http://lists.danga.com/mailman/listinfo/memcached*
- The Ruby-MemCache homepage is at *http://deveiate.org/projects/RMemCache*; if you install Ruby-MemCache from source, you'll also need to install IO::Reactor (*http://deveiate.org/projects/IO-Reactor*)
- The Robot Co-op has released their own memcached library, memcache-client, available at *http://dev.robotcoop.com/Libraries/* or via the memcache-client gem; it is reported to be API-compatible with Ruby-MemCache

16.17 Caching Expensive Results with MemCached

Credit: Michael Granger with Ben Bleything

Problem

You want to transparently cache the results of expensive operations, so that code that triggers the operations doesn't need to know how to use the cache. The memcached program, described in Recipe 16.16, lets you use other machines' RAM to store key-value pairs. The question is how to hide the use of this cache from the rest of your code.

Solution

If you have the luxury of designing your own implementation of the expensive operation, you can design in transparent caching from the beginning. The following code defines a get method that delegates to expensive_get if it can't find an appropriate value in the cache. In this case, the expensive operation that gets cached is the (relatively inexpensive, actually) string reversal operation:

```ruby
require 'rubygems'
require 'memcache'

class DataLayer

  def initialize(*cache_servers)
    @cache = MemCache.new(*cache_servers)
  end

  def get(key)
    @cache[key] ||= expensive_get(key)
  end
  alias_method :[], :get

  protected
  def expensive_get(key)
    # ...do expensive fetch of data for 'key'
    puts "Fetching expensive value for #{key}"
    key.to_s.reverse
  end
end
```

Assuming you've got a memcached server running on your local machine, you can use this DataLayer as a way to cache the reversed versions of strings:

```ruby
layer = DataLayer.new( 'localhost:11211' )

3.times do
  puts "Data for 'foo': #{layer['foo']}"
end
```

```
# Fetching expensive value for foo
# Data for 'foo': oof
# Data for 'foo': oof
```

Discussion

That's the easy case. But you don't always get the opportunity to define a data layer from scratch. If you want to add memcaching to an existing data layer, you can create a caching strategy and add it to your existing classes as a mixin.

Here's a data layer, already written, that has no caching:

```
class MyDataLayer
  def get(key)
    puts "Getting value for #{key} from data layer"
    return key.to_s.reverse
  end
end
```

The data layer doesn't know about the cache, so all of its operations are expensive. In this instance, it's reversing a string every time you ask for it:

```
layer = MyDataLayer.new

"Value for 'foo': #{layer.get('foo')}"
# Getting value for foo from data layer
# => "Value for 'foo': oof"

"Value for 'foo': #{layer.get('foo')}"
# Getting value for foo from data layer
# => "Value for 'foo': oof"

"Value for 'foo': #{layer.get('foo')}"
# Getting value for foo from data layer
# => "Value for 'foo': oof"
```

Let's improve performance a little by defining a caching mixin. It'll wrap the get method so that it only runs the expensive code (the string reversal) if the answer isn't already in the cache:

```
require 'memcache'

module GetSetMemcaching
  SERVER = 'localhost:11211'

  def self::extended(mod)
    mod.module_eval do
      alias_method :__uncached_get, :get
      remove_method :get

      def get(key)
        puts "Cached get of #{key.inspect}"
        get_cache()[key] ||= __uncached_get(key)
      end
```

```
    def get_cache
      puts "Fetching cache object for #{SERVER}"
      @cache ||= MemCache.new(SERVER)
    end
  end
  super
end

def self::included(mod)
  mod.extend(self)
  super
end
end
```

Once we mix GetSetMemcaching into our data layer, the same code we ran before will magically start to use use the cache:

```
# Mix in caching to the pre-existing class
MyDataLayer.extend(GetSetMemcaching)

"Value for 'foo': #{layer.get('foo')}"
# Cached get of "foo"
# Fetching cache object for localhost:11211
# Getting value for foo from data layer
# => "Value for 'foo': oof"

"Value for 'foo': #{layer.get('foo')}"
# Cached get of "foo"
# Fetching cache object for localhost:11211
# => "Value for 'foo': oof"

"Value for 'foo': #{layer.get('foo')}"
# Cached get of "foo"
# Fetching cache object for localhost:11211
# => "Value for 'foo': oof"
```

The examples above are missing a couple features you'd see in real life. Their API is very simple (just get methods), and they have no cache invalidation—items will stay in the cache forever, even if the underlying data changes.

The same basic principles apply to more complex caches, though. When you need a value that's expensive to find or calculate, you first ask the cache for the value, keyed by its identifying feature. The cache might map a SQL query to its result set, a primary key to the corresponding database object, an array of compound keys to the corresponding database object, and so on. If the object is missing from the cache, you fetch it the expensive way, and put it in the cache.

See Also

- The Ruby on Rails wiki has a page full of memcached examples at *http://wiki.rubyonrails.com/rails/pages/MemCached*; this should give you more ideas on how to use memcached to speed up your application

---

16.18 A Remote-Controlled Jukebox

What if you had a jukebox on your main computer that played random or selected items from your music collection? What if you could search your music collection and add items to the jukebox queue from a laptop in another room of the house?

Ruby can help you realize this super-geek dream—the software part, anyway. In this recipe, I'll show you how to write a jukebox server that can be programmed from any computer on the local network.

The jukebox will consist of a client and a server. The server broadcasts its location to a nearby Rinda server so clients on the local network can find it without knowing the address. The client will look up the server with Rinda and then communicate with it via DRb.

What features should the jukebox have? When there are no clients interfering with its business, the server will pick random songs from a predefined playlist and play them. It will call out to external Unix programs to play songs on the local computer's audio system (if you have a way of broadcasting songs through streaming audio, say, an IceCast server, it could use that instead).

A client can query the jukebox, stop or restart it, or request that a particular song be played. The jukebox will keep requests in a queue. Once it plays all the requests, it will resume playing songs at random.

Since we'll be running subprocesses to access the sound card on the computer that runs the jukebox, the Jukebox object can't be distributed to another machine. Instead, we need to proxy it with DRbUndumped.

The first thing we need to do is start a RingServer somewhere on our local network. Here's a reprint of the RingServer program from Recipe 16.14:

```ruby
#!/usr/bin/ruby
# rinda_server.rb

require 'rinda/ring'        # for RingServer
require 'rinda/tuplespace'  # for TupleSpace

DRb.start_service

# Create a TupleSpace to hold named services, and start running.
Rinda::RingServer.new(Rinda::TupleSpace.new)

DRb.thread.join
```

Here's the jukebox server file. First, we'll define the Jukebox server class, and set up its basic behavior: to play its queue and pick randomly when the queue is empty.

```ruby
#!/usr/bin/ruby -w
# jukebox_server.rb
require 'drb'
```

```
require 'rinda/ring'
require 'rinda/tuplespace'
require 'thread'
require 'find'

DRb.start_service

class Jukebox
  include DRbUndumped
  attr_reader :now_playing, :running

  def initialize(files)
    @files = files
    @songs = @files.keys
    @now_playing = nil
    @queue = []
  end

  def play_queue
    Thread.new(self) do
      @running = true
      while @running
        if @queue.empty?
          play songs[rand(songs.size)]
        else
          play @queue.shift
        end
      end
    end
  end
end
```

Next, we'll write the methods that a client can use:

```
# Adds a song to the queue. Returns the new size of the queue.
def <<(song)
  raise ArgumentError, 'No such song' unless @files[song]
  @queue.push song
  return @queue.size
end

# Returns the current queue of songs.
def queue
  return @queue.clone.freeze
end

# Returns the titles of songs that match the given regexp.
def songs(regexp=/.*/)
  return @songs.grep(regexp).sort
end

# Turns the jukebox on or off.
def running=(value)
  @running = value
  play_queue if @running
end
```

Finally, here's the code that actually plays a song, by calling out to a preinstalled program—either mpg123 or ogg123, depending on the extension of the song file:

```
private

# Play the given through this computer's sound system, using a
# previously installed music player.
def play(song)
  @now_playing = song

  path = @files[song]
  player = path[-4..path.size] == '.mp3' ? 'mpg123' : 'ogg123'
  command = %{#{player} "#{path}"}
  # The player and path both come from local data, so it's safe to
  # untaint them.
  command.untaint
  system(command)
end
end
```

Now we can use the Jukebox class in a script. This one treats ARGV as a list of directories. We descend each one looking for music files, and feed the results into a Jukebox:

```
if ARGV.empty?
  puts "Usage: #{__FILE__} [directory full of MP3s and/or OGGs] ..."
  exit
else
  songs = {}
  Find.find(*ARGV) do |path|
    if path =~ /\.(mp3|ogg)$/
      name = File.split(path)[1][0..-5]
      songs[name] = path
    end
  end
end
```

```
jukebox = Jukebox.new(songs)
```

So far there hasn't been much distributed code, and there won't be much total. But we do need to register the Jukebox object with Rinda so that clients can find it:

```
# Set safe before we start accepting connections from outside.
$SAFE = 1
puts "Registering..."
# Register the Jukebox with the local RingServer, under its class name.
ring_server = Rinda::RingFinger.primary
ring_server.write([:name, :Jukebox, jukebox, "Remote-controlled jukebox"],
                  Rinda::SimpleRenewer.new)
```

Start the jukebox running, and we're in business:

```
jukebox.play_queue
DRb.thread.join
```

Now we can query and manipulate the jukebox from an irb session on another computer:

```
require 'rinda/ring'
require 'rinda/tuplespace'

DRb.start_service
ring_server = Rinda::RingFinger.primary
jukebox = ring_server.read([:name, :Jukebox, nil, nil])[2]

jukebox.now_playing                          # => "Chickadee"
jukebox.songs(/D/)
# => ["ID 3", "Don't Leave Me Here (Over There Would Be Fine)"]

jukebox << 'ID 3'                            # => 1
jukebox << "Attack of the Good Ol' Boys from Planet Honky-Tonk"
# ArgumentError: No such song
jukebox.queue                                # => ["ID 3"]
```

But it'll be easier to use if we write a real client program. Again, there's almost no DRb programming in the client, which is as it should be. Once we have the remote Jukebox object, we can use it just like we would a local object.

First, we have some preliminary argument checking:

```
#!/usr/bin/ruby -w
# jukebox_client.rb

require 'rinda/ring'

NO_ARG_COMMANDS = %w{start stop now-playing queue}
ARG_COMMANDS = %w{grep append grep-and-append}
COMMANDS = NO_ARG_COMMANDS + ARG_COMMANDS

def usage
  puts "Usage: #{__FILE__} [#{COMMANDS.join('|')}] [ARG]"
  exit
end

usage if ARGV.size < 1 or ARGV.size > 2

command = ARGV[0]
argument = nil
usage unless COMMANDS.index(command)

if ARG_COMMANDS.index(command)
  if ARGV.size == 1
    puts "Command #{command} takes an argument."
    exit
  else
    argument = ARGV[1]
  end
```

```
  elsif ARGV.size == 2
    puts "Command #{command} takes no argument."
    exit
  end
```

Next, the only distributed code in the client: the fetch of the Jukebox object from the Rinda server.

```
DRb.start_service
ring_server = Rinda::RingFinger.primary

jukebox = ring_server.read([:name, :Jukebox, nil, nil])[2]
```

Now that we have the Jukebox object (rather, a proxy to the real Jukebox object on the other computer), we can apply the user's desired command to it:

```
case command
when 'start' then
  if jukebox.running
    puts 'Already running.'
  else
    jukebox.running = true
    puts 'Started.'
  end
when 'stop' then
  if jukebox.running
    jukebox.running = false
    puts 'Jukebox will stop after current song.'
  else
    puts 'Already stopped.'
  end
when 'now-playing' then
  puts "Currently playing: #{jukebox.now_playing}"
when 'queue' then
  jukebox.queue.each { |song| puts song }
when 'grep'
  jukebox.songs(Regexp.compile(argument)).each { |song| puts song }
when 'append' then
  jukebox << argument
  jukebox.queue.each { |song| puts song }
when 'grep-and-append' then
  jukebox.songs(Regexp.compile(argument)).each { |song| jukebox << song }
  jukebox.queue.each { |song| puts song }
end
```

Some obvious enhancements to this program:

- Combine the server with the ID3 parser from Recipe 6.17 to provide more reliable title information, as well as artist and other metadata.

- Make the ID3 metadata searchable, so that you can search for songs by a particular band.

- Make the @songs data structure capable of handling multiple distinct songs with the same name.

- Make the selection keep track of song history, so that it doesn't choose to play the same song twice in the row.

- Have the jukebox send its selections to a program that streams audio over the network, rather than to programs that play the music locally. This way you can listen to the jukebox from any computer in your house. Without this step, you need to wire your whole house for sound, or have really loud speakers, or a really small house (like mine).

See Also

- Recipe 6.17, "Processing a Binary File"
- Recipe 16.14, "Automatically Discovering DRb Services with Rinda"
- Recipe 16.15, "Proxying Objects That Can't Be Distributed"

Testing, Debugging, Optimizing, and Documenting

The recipes in previous chapters focus on writing code to do what you want. This chapter focuses on verifying that your code really works, and on fixing it when it breaks. We start off simple and move to more advanced debugging techniques.

What happens when your program has a bug? The best-case scenario is that you discover the bug before it affects anyone, including other developers. That's the goal of unit tests (Recipe 17.7). Ruby and the Ruby community promote a philosophy of writing automated tests as (or even before) you write the corresponding functionality. At every stage of development, you know that your program works, and if you make a change that breaks something, you know about it immediately. These tests can replace much boring manual testing and bug hunting.

Suppose a bug slips past your tests, and you only discover it in production. How's it going to manifest itself? If you're lucky, you'll see an exception: a notification from some piece of Ruby code that something is wrong.

Exceptions interrupt the normal flow of execution, and, if not handled, will crash the program. The good news is that they give you a place in the code to start debugging. It's worse if a bug *doesn't* cause an exception, because you'll only notice its byproducts: corrupt data or even security violations. We show code for handling exceptions (Recipes 17.3 and 17.4) and for creating your own (Recipe 17.2).

Successful debugging means reproducing the bug in an environment where you can poke at it. This may mean dropping from a running program into an `irb` session (Recipe 17.10), or it may be as simple as adding diagnostic messages that make the program show its work (Recipe 17.1).

Even a program that has no noticeable bugs may run too slowly or use too many resources. Ruby provides two tools for doing performance optimization: a profiler (Recipe 17.12) and a benchmarking suite (Recipe 17.13). It's easy to create your own analysis tools by writing a trace function that hooks into the Ruby interpreter as it runs. The call graph tracker presented at chapter's end (Recipe 17.15) exploits this feature.

17.1 Running Code Only in Debug Mode

Problem

You want to print out debugging messages or run some sanity-checking code, but only while you're developing your application;, not when you're running it in production.

Solution

Run the code only if the global variable $DEBUG is true. You can trigger debug mode by passing in the --debug switch to the Ruby interpreter, or you can set the variable $DEBUG to true within your code.

Here's a Ruby program to divide two random numbers. It contains a trivial bug. It usually runs to completion, but sometimes it crashes. A line of debug code has been added to give some more visibility into the internal workings of the program:

```
#!/usr/bin/env ruby
# divide.rb
numerator = rand(100)
denominator = rand(10)
$stderr.puts "Dividing #{numerator} by #{denominator}" if $DEBUG
puts numerator / denominator
```

When run with the --debug flag, the debug message is printed to standard error:

```
$ ./divide.rb --debug
Dividing 64 by 9
7

$ ./divide.rb --debug
Dividing 93 by 2
46

$ ./divide.rb --debug
Dividing 54 by 0
Exception `ZeroDivisionError' at divide_buggy.rb:6 - divided by 0
divide_buggy.rb:6:in `/': divided by 0 (ZeroDivisionError)
        from divide_buggy.rb:6
```

Once the bug is fixed, you can go back to running the script normally, and the debug message won't show up:

```
$ ./divide.rb
24
```

Discussion

This is a common technique when a "real" debugger is too much trouble. It's usually used to send debug messages to standard error, but you can put any code at all within a $DEBUG conditional. For instance, many Ruby libraries have their own "verbose", "debug level", or "debug mode" settings: you can choose to set these other variables appropriately only when $DEBUG is true.

```
require 'fileutils'
FileUtils.cp('source', 'destination', $DEBUG)
```

If your code is running deep within a framework, you may not have immediate access to the standard error stream of the process. You can always have your debug code write to a temporary logfile, and monitor the file.

Use of $DEBUG costs a little speed, but except in tight loops it's not noticeable. At the cost of a little more speed, you can save yourself some typing by defining convenience methods like this one:

```
def pdebug(str)
  $stderr.puts('DEBUG: ' + str) if $DEBUG
end

pdebug "Dividing #{numerator} by #{denominator}"
```

Once you've fixed the bug and you no longer need the debugging code, it's better to put it into a conditional than to simply remove it. If the problem recurs later, you'll find yourself adding the debugging code right back in.

Sometimes commenting out the debugging code is better than putting it into a conditional. It's more difficult to hunt down all the commented-out code, but you can pick and choose which pieces of code to uncomment. With the $DEBUG technique, it's all or nothing.

It doesn't *have* to be all or nothing, though. $DEBUG starts out a boolean but it doesn't have to stay that way: you can make it a numeric "debug level". Instead of doing something if $DEBUG, you can check whether $DEBUG is greater than a certain number. A very important piece of debug code might be associated with a debug level of 1; a relatively unused piece might have a debug level of 5. Setting $DEBUG to zero would turn off debugging altogether.

Here are some convenience methods that make it easy to use $DEBUG as either a boolean or a numeric value:

```
def debug(if_level)
  yield if ($DEBUG == true) || ($DEBUG && $DEBUG >= if_level)
end

def pdebug(str, if_level=1)
  debug(if_level) { $stderr.puts "DEBUG: " + str }
end
```

One final note: make sure that you put the --debug switch on the command line *before* the name of your Ruby script. It's an argument to the Ruby interpreter, not to your script.

See Also

- Recipe 17.5, "Adding Logging to Your Application," demonstrates a named system of debug levels; in fact, if your debug messages are mainly diagnostic, you might want to implement them as log messages

17.2 Raising an Exception

Credit: Steve Arneil

Problem

An error has occurred and your code can't keep running. You want to indicate the error and let some other piece of code handle it.

Solution

Raise an *exception* by calling the Kernel#raise method with a description of the error. Calling the raise method interrupts the flow of execution.

The following method raises an exception whenever it's called. Its second message will never be printed:

```
def raise_exception
  puts 'I am before the raise.'
  raise 'An error has occurred.'
  puts 'I am after the raise.'
end

raise_exception
# I am before the raise.
# RuntimeError: An error has occurred
```

Discussion

Here's a method, inverse, that returns the inverse of a number x. It does some basic error checking by raising an exception unless x is a number:

```
def inverse(x)
  raise "Argument is not numeric" unless x.is_a? Numeric
  1.0 / x
end
```

When you pass in a reasonable value of x, all is well:

```
inverse(2)                          # => 0.5
```

When x is not a number, the method raises an exception:

```
inverse('not a number')
# RuntimeError: Argument is not numeric
```

An exception is an object, and the Kernel#raise method creates an instance of an exception class. By default, Kernel#raise creates an exception of RuntimeError class, which is a subclass of StandardError. This in turn is a subclass of Exception, the superclass of all exception classes. You can list all the standard exception classes by starting a Ruby session and executing code like this:

```
ObjectSpace.each_object(Class) do |x|
  puts x if x.ancestors.member? Exception
end
```

This variant lists only the better-known exception classes:

```
ObjectSpace.each_object(Class) { |x| puts x if x.name =~ /Error$/ }
# SystemStackError
# LocalJumpError
# EOFError
# IOError
# RegexpError
# ...
```

To raise an exception of a specific class, you can pass in the class name as an argument to raise. RuntimeError is kind of generic for the inverse method's check against x. The problem is there is actually a problem with one of the arguments passed into the method. A more aptly named exception class for that check would be ArgumentError:

```
def inverse(x)
  raise ArgumentError, 'Argument is not numeric' unless x.is_a? Numeric
  1.0 / x
end
```

To be even more specific about an error, you can define your own Exception subclass:

```
class NotInvertibleError < StandardError
end
```

The implementation of inverse method would then become:

```
def inverse(x)
  raise NotInvertibleError, 'Argument is not numeric' unless x.is_a? Numeric
  1.0 / x
end

inverse('not a number')
# NotInvertibleError: Argument is not numeric
```

In some other programming languages, exceptions are "thrown." In Ruby, they are not thrown but "raised." Ruby does have a Kernel#throw method, but it has nothing to do with exceptions. See Recipe 7.8 for an example of throw, as opposed to raise.

See Also

- Recipe 7.8, "Stopping an Iteration"
- Recipe 17.2, "Raising an Exception"
- Recipe 17.3, "Handling an Exception"

17.3 Handling an Exception

Credit: Steve Arneil

Problem

You want to handle or recover from a raised exception.

Solution

Rescue the exception with a begin/rescue block. The code you put into the rescue clause should handle the exception and allow the program to continue executing.

This code demonstrates the rescue clause:

```
def raise_and_rescue
  begin
    puts 'I am before the raise.'
    raise 'An error has occurred.'
    puts 'I am after the raise.'
  rescue
    puts 'I am rescued!'
  end
  puts 'I am after the begin block.'
end

raise_and_rescue
# I am before the raise.
# I am rescued!
# I am after the begin block.
```

The exception doesn't stop the program from running to completion, but the code that was interrupted by the exception never gets run. Once the exception is handled, execution continues immediately after the begin block that spawned it.

Discussion

You can handle an exception with a rescue block if you know how to recover from the exception, if you want to display it in a nonstandard way, or if you know that the exception is not really a problem. You can solve the problem, present it to the end user, or just ignore it and forge ahead.

By default, a rescue clause rescues exceptions of class StandardError or its subclasses. Mentioning a specific class in a rescue statement will make it rescue exceptions of that class and its subclasses.

Here's a method, do_it, that calls the Kernel#eval method to run some Ruby code passed to it. If the code cannot be run (because it's not valid Ruby), eval raises an exception—a SyntaxError. This exception is not a subclass of StandardError; it's a subclass of ScriptError, which is a subclass of Exception.

```
def do_it(code)
  eval(code)
rescue
  puts "Cannot do it!"
end

do_it('puts 1 + 1')
# 2

do_it('puts 1 +')
# SyntaxError: (eval):1:in `do_it': compile error
```

That rescue block never gets called because SyntaxError is not a subclass of StandardError. We need to tell our rescue block to rescue us from SyntaxError, or else from one of its superclasses, ScriptError and Exception:

```
def do_it(code)
  eval(code)
rescue SyntaxError
  puts "Cannot do it!"
end

do_it('puts 1 +')
# Cannot do it!
```

You can stack rescue clauses in a begin/rescue block. Exceptions not handled by one rescue clause will trickle down to the next:

```
begin
 # ...
rescue OneTypeOfException
 # ...
rescue AnotherTypeOfException
 # ...
end
```

If you want to interrogate a rescued exception, you can map the Exception object to a variable within the rescue clause. Exception objects have useful methods like message and backtrace:

```
begin
  raise 'A test exception.'
rescue Exception => e
  puts e.message
  puts e.backtrace.inspect
end
# ["(irb):33:in `irb_binding'",
#  "/usr/lib/ruby/1.8/irb/workspace.rb:52:in `irb_binding'",
#  ":0"]
```

You can also use the special variable $! within a rescue block to refer to the most recently raised Exception. If you do a require 'English', you can use the $ERROR_INFO variable, which is easier to remember.

```
require 'English'
begin
  raise 'Another test exception.'
rescue Exception
  puts $!.message
  puts $ERROR_INFO.message
end
# Another test exception.
# Another test exception.
```

Since $! is a global variable, and might be changed at any time by another thread, it's safer to map each Exception object you rescue to an object.

See Also

- Recipe 17.2, "Raising an Exception"
- Recipe 17.4, "Rerunning After an Exception"

17.4 Rerunning After an Exception

Credit: Steve Arneil

Problem

You want to rerun some code that raised an exception, having (hopefully) fixed the problem that caused it in the first place.

Solution

Retry the code that failed by executing a retry statement within a rescue clause of a code block. retry reruns the block from the beginning.

Here's a demonstration of the retry statement. The first time the code block runs, it raises an exception. The exception is rescued, the problem is "fixed," and the code runs to completion the second time:

```
def rescue_and_retry
  error_fixed = false
  begin
    puts 'I am before the raise in the begin block.'
    raise 'An error has occurred!' unless error_fixed
    puts 'I am after the raise in the begin block.'
  rescue
    puts 'An exception was thrown! Retrying...'
    error_fixed = true
    retry
  end
  puts 'I am after the begin block.'
end
```

```
rescue_and_retry
# I am before the raise in the begin block.
# An exception was thrown! Retrying...
# I am before the raise in the begin block.
# I am after the raise in the begin block.
# I am after the begin block.
```

Discussion

Here's a method, check_connection, that checks if you are connected to the Internet. It will try to connect to a url up to max_tries times. This method uses a retry clause to retry connecting until it successfully completes a connection, or until it runs out of tries:

```
require 'open-uri'

def check_connection(max_tries=2, url='http://www.ruby-lang.org/')
  tries = 0
  begin
    tries += 1
    puts 'Checking connection...'
    open(url) { puts 'Connection OK.' }
  rescue Exception
    puts 'Connection not OK!'
    retry unless tries >= max_tries
  end
end

check_connection
# Checking connection...
# Connection OK.

check_connection(2, 'http://this.is.a.fake.url/')
# Checking connection...
# Connection not OK!
# Checking connection...
# Connection not OK!
```

See Also

- Recipe 17.2, "Raising an Exception"
- Recipe 17.3, "Handling an Exception"

17.5   Adding Logging to Your Application

Problem

You want to make your application log events or diagnostic data to a file or stream. You want verbose logging when your application is in development, and more taciturn logging when in production.

Solution

Use the `logger` library in the Ruby standard library. Use its `Logger` class to send logging data to a file or other output stream.

In most cases, you'll share a single `Logger` object throughout your application, as a global variable or module constant:

```
require 'logger'
$LOG = Logger.new($stderr)
```

You can then call the instance methods of `Logger` to send messages to the log at various levels of severity. From least to most severe, the instance methods are `Logger#debug`, `Logger#info`, `Logger#warn`, `Logger#error`, and `Logger#fatal`.

This code uses the application's logger to print a debugging message, and (at a higher severity) as part of error-handling code.

```
def divide(numerator, denominator)
  $LOG.debug("Numerator: #{numerator}, denominator #{denominator}")
  begin
    result = numerator / denominator
  rescue Exception => e
    $LOG.error "Error in division!: #{e}"
    result = nil
  end
  return result
end

divide(10, 2)
# D, [2006-03-31T19:35:01.043938 #18088] DEBUG -- : Numerator: 10, denominator 2
# => 5

divide(10, 0)
# D, [2006-03-31T19:35:01.045230 #18088] DEBUG -- : Numerator: 10, denominator 0
# E, [2006-03-31T19:35:01.045495 #18088] ERROR -- : Error in division!: divided by 0
# => nil
```

To change the log level, simply assign the appropriate constant to `level`:

```
$LOG.level = Logger::ERROR
```

Now our logger will ignore all log messages except those with severity `ERROR` or `FATAL`:

```
divide(10, 2)
# => 5

divide(10, 0)
# E, [2006-03-31T19:35:01.047861 #18088] ERROR -- : Error in division!: divided by 0
# => nil
```

Discussion

Ruby's standard logging system works like Java's oft-imitated Log4J. The `Logger` object centralizes all the decisions about whether a particular message is important

---

enough to be written to the log. When you write code, you simply assume that all the messages will be logged. At runtime, you can get a more or a less verbose log by changing the log level. A production application usually has a log level of Logger::INFO or Logger::WARN.

The DEBUG log level is useful for step-by-step diagnostics of a complex task. The ERROR level is often used when handling exceptions: if the program can't solve a problem, it logs the exception rather than crash and expects a human administrator to deal with it. The FATAL level should only be used when the program cannot recover from a problem, and is about to crash or exit.

If your log is being stored in a file, you can have Logger rotate or replace the log file when it get too big, or once a certain amount of time has elapsed:

```
# Keep data for the current month only
Logger.new('this_month.log', 'monthly')

# Keep data for today and the past 20 days.
Logger.new('application.log', 20, 'daily')

# Start the log over whenever the log exceeds 100 megabytes in size.
Logger.new('application.log', 0, 100 * 1024 * 1024)
```

If the default log entries are too verbose for you, you have a couple of options. The simplest is to set datetime_format to a more concise date format. This code gets rid of the milliseconds:

```
$LOG.datetime_format = '%Y-%m-%d %H:%M:%S'
$LOG.error('This is a little shorter.')
# E, [2006-03-31T19:35:01#17339] ERROR -- : This is a little shorter.
```

If that's not enough for you, you can replace the call method that formats a message for the log:

```
class Logger
  class Formatter
    Format = "%s [%s] %s %s\n"
    def call(severity, time, progname, msg)
      Format % [severity, format_datetime(time), progname, msg]
    end
  end
end

$LOG.error('This is much shorter.')
# ERROR [2006-03-31T19:35:01.058646 ]  This is much shorter.
```

See Also

- The standard library documentation for the logger library

17.6 Creating and Understanding Tracebacks

Problem

You are debugging a program, and need to understand the stack traces that come with Ruby exceptions. Or you need to see which path the Ruby interpreter took to get to a certain line of code.

Solution

You can call the Kernel#caller method at any time to look at the Ruby interpreter's current call stack. The call stack is represented as a list of strings.

This Ruby program simulates a company with a top-down management style: one method delegates to another, which calls yet another. The method at the bottom can use caller to look upwards and see the methods that called it:

```
1   #!/usr/bin/ruby -w
2   # delegation.rb
3   class CEO
4     def CEO.new_vision
5       Manager.implement_vision
6     end
7   end
8
9   class Manager
10    def Manager.implement_vision
11      Engineer.do_work
12    end
13  end
14
15  class Engineer
16    def Engineer.do_work
17      puts 'How did I get here?'
18      first = true
19      caller.each do |c|
20        puts %{#{(first ? 'I' : ' which')} was called by "#{c}"}
21        first = false
22      end
23    end
24  end
25
26  CEO.new_vision
```

Running this program illustrates the path the interpreter takes to Engineer.do_work:

```
$ ./delegation.rb
How did I get here?
I was called by "delegation.rb:11:in `implement_vision'"
 which was called by "delegation.rb:5:in `new_vision'"
 which was called by "delegation.rb:26"
```

Discussion

Each string in a traceback shows which line of Ruby code made some method call. The first bit of the traceback given above shows that `Engineer.do_work` was called by `Manager.implement_vision` on line 11 of the program. The second line shows how `Manager.implement_vision` was called, and so on.

Remember the stack trace displayed when a Ruby script raises an exception? It's the same one you can get any time by calling `Kernel#caller`. In fact, if you rescue an exception and assign it to a variable, you can get its traceback as an array of strings—the equivalent of calling `caller` on the line that triggered the exception:

```
def raise_exception
  raise Exception, 'You wanted me to raise an exception, so...'
end

begin
  raise_exception
rescue Exception => e
  puts "Backtrace of the exception:\n #{e.backtrace.join("\n ")}"
end
# Backtrace of the exception:
# (irb):2:in `raise_exception'
# (irb):5:in `irb_binding'
# /usr/lib/ruby/1.8/irb/workspace.rb:52:in `irb_binding'
# :0
```

Note the slight differences between a backtrace generated from a Ruby script and one generated during an `irb` session.

If you've used languages like Python, you might long for "real" backtrace objects. About the best you can do is to parse the strings of a Ruby backtrace with a regular expression. The `parse_caller` method below extracts the files, lines, and method names from a Ruby backtrace. It works in both Ruby programs and `irb` sessions.

```
CALLER_RE = /(.*):([0-9]+)(:in \`(.*)')?/
def parse_caller(l)
  l.collect do |c|
    captures = CALLER_RE.match(c)
    [captures[1], captures[2], captures[4]]
  end
end

begin
  raise_exception
rescue Exception => e
  puts "Exception history:"
  first = true
  parse_caller(e.backtrace).each do |file, line, method|
    puts %{ #{first ? "L" : "because l"}ine #{line} in "#{file}"} +
         %{ called "#{method}" }
    first = false
```

```
      end
    end
# Exception history:
#  Line 2 in "(irb)" called "raise_exception"
#  because line 24 in "(irb)" called "irb_binding"
#  because line 52 in "/usr/lib/ruby/1.8/irb/workspace.rb" called "irb_binding"
#  because line 0 in "" called ""
```

See Also

• Recipe 17.3, "Handling an Exception"

17.7 Writing Unit Tests

Credit: Steve Arneil

Problem

You want to write some unit tests for your software, to guarantee its correctness now and in the future.

Solution

Use Test::Unit, the Ruby unit testing framework, from the Ruby standard library.

Consider a simple class for storing the name of a person. The Person class shown below stores a first name, a last name, and an age: a person's full name is available as a computed value. This code might go into a Ruby script called app/person.rb:

```
# app/person.rb
class Person
  attr_accessor :first_name, :last_name, :age

  def initialize(first_name, last_name, age)
    raise ArgumentError, "Invalid age: #{age}" unless age > 0
    @first_name, @last_name, @age = first_name, last_name, age
  end

  def full_name
    first_name + ' ' + last_name
  end
end
```

Now, let's write some unit tests for this class. By convention, these would go into the file test/person_test.rb.

First, require the Person class itself and the Test::Unit framework:

```
# test/person_test.rb
require File.join(File.dirname(__FILE__), '..', 'app', 'person')
require 'test/unit'
```

Next, extend the framework class `Test::Unit::TestCase` with a class to contain the actual tests. Each test should be written as a method of the test class, and each test method should begin with the prefix test. Each test should make one or more *assertions*: statements about the code which must be true for the code to be correct. Below are three test methods, each making one assertion:

```ruby
class PersonTest < Test::Unit::TestCase
  def test_first_name
    person = Person.new('Nathaniel', 'Talbott', 25)
    assert_equal 'Nathaniel', person.first_name
  end

  def test_last_name
    person = Person.new('Nathaniel', 'Talbott', 25)
    assert_equal 'Talbott', person.last_name
  end

  def test_full_name
    person = Person.new('Nathaniel', 'Talbott', 25)
    assert_equal 'Nathaniel Talbott', person.full_name
  end

  def test_age
    person = Person.new('Nathaniel', 'Talbott', 25)
    assert_equal 25, person.age
    assert_raise(ArgumentError) { Person.new('Nathaniel', 'Talbott', -4) }
    assert_raise(ArgumentError) { Person.new('Nathaniel', 'Talbott', 'four') }
  end
end
```

This code is somewhat redundant; see below for a way to fix that issue. For now, let's run our four tests, by running `person_test.rb` as a script:

```
$ ruby test/person_test.rb
Loaded suite test/person_test
Started
....
Finished in 0.008837 seconds.

4 tests, 6 assertions, 0 failures, 0 errors
```

Great! All the tests passed.

Discussion

The `PersonTest` class defined above works, but it's got some redundant and inefficient code. Each of the four tests starts by creating a `Person` object, but they could all share the same `Person` object. The `test_age` method needs to create some additional, invalid `Person` objects to verify the error checking, but there's no reason why it can't share the same "normal" `Person` object as the other three test methods.

`Test::Unit` makes it possible to refactor shareable code into a method named setup. If a test class has a `setup` method, it will be called before any of the assertion methods. Conversely, any clean-up code that is required *after* each test method runs can be placed in a method named teardown.

Here's a new implementation of PersonTest that uses setup and class constants to remove the duplicate code:

```ruby
# person2.rb
require File.join(File.dirname(__FILE__), '..', 'app', 'person')
require 'test/unit'

class PersonTest < Test::Unit::TestCase
  FIRST_NAME, LAST_NAME, AGE = 'Nathaniel', 'Talbott', 25

  def setup
    @person = Person.new(FIRST_NAME, LAST_NAME, AGE)
  end

  def test_first_name
    assert_equal FIRST_NAME, @person.first_name
  end

  def test_last_name
    assert_equal LAST_NAME,  @person.last_name
  end

  def test_full_name
    assert_equal FIRST_NAME + ' ' + LAST_NAME, @person.full_name
  end

  def test_age
    assert_equal 25, @person.age
    assert_raise(ArgumentError) { Person.new(FIRST_NAME, LAST_NAME, -4) }
    assert_raise(ArgumentError) { Person.new(FIRST_NAME, LAST_NAME, 'four') }
  end
end
```

There are lots of assertion methods besides the assert_equal and assert_raise method used in the test classes above: assert_not_equal, assert_nil, and more exotic methods like assert_respond_to. All the assertion methods are defined in the Test::Unit::Assertions module, which is mixed into the Test::Unit::TestCase class.

The simplest assertion method is just plain assert. It causes the test method to fail unless it's passed a value other than false or nil:

```ruby
def test_first_name
  assert(FIRST_NAME == @person.first_name)
end
```

assert is the most basic assertion method. All the other assertion methods can be defined in terms of it:

```ruby
def assert_equal(expected, actual)
  assert(expected == actual)
end
```

So, if you can't decide (or remember) which particular assertion method to use, you can always use assert.

See Also

- `ri Test::Unit`
- The documentation for the Test::Unit library is also online at *http://www.ruby-doc.org/stdlib/libdoc/test/unit/rdoc/index.html*
- Recipe 15.22, "Unit Testing Your Web Site"
- Recipe 17.8, "Running Unit Tests"
- Recipe 19.1, "Automatically Running Unit Tests"

17.8 Running Unit Tests

Credit: Steve Arneil

Problem

You want to run some or all of the unit tests you've written.

Solution

This solution uses the example test class `PersonTest` from the previous recipe, Recipe 17.7. In that scenario, this code lives in a file test/person_test.rb, and the code to be tested lives in app/person.rb. Here's test/person_test.rb again:

```
# person_test.rb
require File.join(File.dirname(__FILE__), '..', 'app', 'person')
require 'test/unit'

class PersonTest < Test::Unit::TestCase
  FIRST_NAME, LAST_NAME, AGE = 'Nathaniel', 'Talbott', 25

  def setup
    @person = Person.new(FIRST_NAME, LAST_NAME, AGE)
  end

  def test_first_name
    assert_equal FIRST_NAME, @person.first_name
  end

  def test_last_name
    assert_equal LAST_NAME,  @person.last_name
  end

  def test_full_name
    assert_equal FIRST_NAME + ' ' + LAST_NAME, @person.full_name
  end
```

```
  def test_age
    assert_equal 25, @person.age
    assert_raise(ArgumentError) { Person.new(FIRST_NAME, LAST_NAME, -4) }
    assert_raise(ArgumentError) { Person.new(FIRST_NAME, LAST_NAME, 'four') }
  end
end
```

As seen in the previous recipe, the simplest solution is to run the script that contains the tests as a Ruby script:

```
$ ruby test/person_test.rb
Loaded suite test/person_test
Started
....
Finished in 0.008955 seconds.

4 tests, 6 assertions, 0 failures, 0 errors
```

But the person_test.rb script also accepts command-line arguments. You can use the --name option to choose which test methods to run, and the --verbose option to print each test method as it's run:

```
$ ruby test/person_test.rb --verbose --name test_first_name \
  --name test_last_name
Loaded suite test/person_test
Started
test_first_name(PersonTest): .
test_last_name(PersonTest): .

Finished in 0.012567 seconds.

2 tests, 2 assertions, 0 failures, 0 errors
```

Discussion

How do the tests run when person_test.rb doesn't appear to do anything but define a class? How can person_test.rb accept command-line arguments? We wrote that file, and we didn't put in any command-line parsing code.

It all happens behind the scenes. When we required the Test::Unit framework, it passed a block into the method method Kernel#at_exit. This block is guaranteed to be called before the Ruby interpreter exits. It looks like this:

```
$ tail -5 /usr/local/lib/ruby/1.8/test/unit.rb
at_exit do
  unless $! || Test::Unit.run?
    exit Test::Unit::AutoRunner.run
  end
end
```

Once the code in person_test.rb defines its test class, the Ruby interpreter exits: but first, it runs that block, which triggers the AutoRunner test runner. This does the command-line parsing, the execution of the tests in PersonTest, and all the rest of it.

Here are a few more helpful options to a unit test script.

The `--name` option can be used with a regular expression to choose the test methods to run.

```
$ ruby test/person_test.rb --verbose --name '/test_f/'
Loaded suite test/person_test
Started
test_first_name(PersonTest): .
test_full_name(PersonTest): .

Finished in 0.014891 seconds.

2 tests, 2 assertions, 0 failures, 0 errors
```

The `Test::Unit` framework can be also be loaded alone to run tests in the current directory and its subdirectories. Use the `--pattern` option with a regular expression to select the test files to run:

```
$ ruby -rtest/unit -e0 -- --pattern '/_test/'
Loaded suite .
Started
...
Finished in 0.009329 seconds.

4 tests, 6 assertions, 0 failures, 0 errors
```

To list all the available `Test::Unit` options, use the `--help` option:

```
$ ruby test/person_test.rb --help
```

Additional options are available when the `Test::Unit` framework is run standalone. Again, use the `--help` option:

```
$ ruby -rtest/unit -e0 -- --help
```

See Also

- `ri Test::Unit`
- Recipe 15.22, "Unit Testing Your Web Site"
- Recipe 17.7, "Writing Unit Tests"
- Recipe 19.1, "Automatically Running Unit Tests"

17.9 Testing Code That Uses External Resources

Credit: John-Mason Shackelford

Problem

You want to test code without triggering its real-world side effects. For instance, you want to test a piece of code that makes an expensive network connection, or irreversibly modifies a file.

Solution

Sometimes you can set up an alternate data source to use for testing (Rails does this for the application database), but doing that makes your tests slower and imposes a setup burden on other developers. Instead, you can use Jim Weirich's FlexMock library, available as the `flexmock` gem.

Here's some code that performs a destructive operation on a live data source:

```
class VersionControlMaintenance

  DAY_SECONDS = 60 * 60 * 24

  def initialize(vcs)
    @vcs = vcs
  end

  def purge_old_labels(age_in_days)
    @vcs.connect
    old_labels = @vcs.label_list.select do |label|
      label['date'] <= Time.now - age_in_days * DAY_SECONDS
    end
    @vcs.label_delete(*old_labels.collect{|label| label['name']})
    @vcs.disconnect
  end
end
```

This code would be difficult to test by conventional means, with the vcs variable pointing to a live version control repository. But with FlexMock, it's simple to define a mock vcs object that can impersonate a real one.

Here's a unit test for VersionControlMaintenance#purge_old_labels that uses Flex-Mock, instead of modifying a real version control repository. First, we set up some dummy labels:

```
require 'rubygems'
require 'flexmock'
require 'test/unit'

class VersionControlMaintenanceTest < Test::Unit::TestCase

  DAY_SECONDS = 60 * 60 * 24
  LONG_AGO = Time.now - DAY_SECONDS * 3
  RECENT   = Time.now - DAY_SECONDS * 1
  LABEL_LIST = [
                 { 'name' => 'L1', 'date' => LONG_AGO },
                 { 'name' => 'L2', 'date' => RECENT   }
               ]
```

We use FlexMock to define an object that expects a certain series of method calls:

```
def test_purge
  FlexMock.use("vcs") do |vcs|
    vcs.should_receive(:connect).with_no_args.once.ordered
```

```
vcs.should_receive(:label_list).with_no_args.
    and_return(LABEL_LIST).once.ordered

vcs.should_receive(:label_delete).
    with('L1').once.ordered

vcs.should_receive(:disconnect).with_no_args.once.ordered
```

Then we pass our mock object into the class we want to test, and call purge_old_labels normally:

```
v = VersionControlMaintenance.new(vcs)
v.purge_old_labels(2)

# The mock calls will be automatically varified as we exit the
# @FlexMock.use@ block.
    end
  end
end
```

Discussion

FlexMock lets you script the behavior of an object so that it acts like the object you don't want to actually call. To set up a mock object, call FlexMock.use, passing in a textual label for the mock object, and a code block. Within the code block, call should_receive to tell the mock object to expect a call to a certain method.

You can then call with to specify the arguments the mock object should expect on that method call, and call and_returns to specify the return value. A call to #once indicates that the tested code should call the method only one time, and #ordered indicates that the tested code must call these mock methods in the order in which they are defined.

After the code block is executed, FlexMock verifies that the mock object's expectations were met. If they weren't (the methods weren't called in the right order, or they were called with the wrong arguments), it raises a TestFailedError as any Test::Unit assertion would.

The example above tells Ruby how we expect purge_old_labels to work. It should call the version control system's connect method, and then label_list. When this happens, the mock object returns some dummy labels. The code being tested is then expected to call label_delete with "L1" as the sole parameter.

This is the crucial point of this test. If purge_old_labels is broken, it might decide to pass both "L1" and "L2" into label_delete (even though "L2" is too recent a label to be deleted). Or it might decide not to call label_delete at all (even though "L1" is an old label that ought to be deleted). Either way, FlexMock will notice that purge_old_labels did not behave as expected, and the test will fail. This works without you having to write any explicit Test::Unit assertions.

FlexMock lives up to its name. Not only can you tell a mock object to expect a given method call is expected once and only once, you have a number of other options, summarized in Tables 17-1 and 17-2.

Table 17-1. From the RDoc

Specifier	Meaning	Modifiers allowed?
`zero_or_more_times`	Declares that the message may be sent zero or more times (default, equivalent to `at_least.never`)	No
`once`	Declares that the message is only sent once	Yes
`twice`	Declares that the message is only sent twice	Yes
`never`	Declares that the message is never sent	Yes
`times(n)`	Declares that the message is sent n times	Yes

Table 17-2. From the RDoc

Modifier	Meaning
`at_least`	Modifies the immediately following message count declarator to mean that the message must be sent at least that number of times; for instance, `at_least.once` means that the message is expected at least once but may be sent more than once
`at_most`	Similar to `at_least`, but puts an upper limit on the number of messages

Both the `at_least` and `at_most` modifiers may be specified on the same expectation.

Besides listing a mock method's expected parameters using `with(arglist)`, you can also use `with_any_args` (the default) and `with_no_args`. With `should_ignore_missing`, you can indicate that it's okay for the tested code to call methods that you didn't explicitly define on the mock object. The mock object will respond to the undefnied method, and return `nil`.

Especially handy is `FlexMock`'s support for specifying return values as a block. This allows us to simulate an exception, or complex behavior on repeated invocations.

```
# Simulate an exception in the mocked object.
mock.should_receive(:connect).and_return{ raise ConnectionFailed.new }

# Simulate a spotty connection: the first attempt fails
# but when the exception handler retries, we connect.
i = 0
mock.should_receive(:connect).twice.
  and_return{ i += 1; raise ConnectionFailed.new unless i > 1 }
end
```

Test-driven development usually produces a design that makes it easy to substitute mock objects for external dependencies. But occasionally, circumstances call for special magic. In such cases Jim Weirich's `class_intercepter.rb` is a welcome ally.

The class below instantiates an object which connects to an external data source. We can't touch this data source when we're testing the code.

```
class ChangeHistoryReport
  def date_range(label1, label2)
    vc = VersionControl.new
    vc.connect
    dates = [label1, label2].collect do |label|
      vc.fetch_label(label).files.sort_by{|f|f['date']}.last['date']
    end
    vc.disconnect
    return dates
  end
end
```

How can we test this code? We could refactor it—introduce a factory or a dependency injection scheme. Then we could substitute in a mock object (although in this case, we'd simply move the complex operations to another method). But if we are sure we "aren't going to need it" (as the saying goes) and since we are programming in Ruby and not a less flexible language, we can test the code as is.

As before, we call `FlexMock.use` to define a mock object:

```
require 'class_intercepter'
require 'test/unit'
class ChangeHistoryReportTest < Test::Unit::TestCase
  def test_date_range
    FlexMock.use('vc') do |vc|
    # initialize the mock
    vc.should_receive(:connect).once.ordered
    vc.should_receive(:fetch_label).with(LABEL1).once.ordered
    vc.should_receive(:fetch_label).with(LABEL2).once.ordered
    vc.should_receive(:disconnect).once.ordered
    vc.should_receive(:new).and_return(vc)
```

Here's the twist: we reach into the `ChangeHistoryReport` class and tell it to use our mock class whenever it wants to use the `VersionControl` class:

```
ChangeHistoryReport.use_class(:VersionControl, vc) do
```

Now we can use a `ChangeHistoryReport` object without worrying that it will operate against any real version control repository. As before, the FlexMock framework takes care of making the actual assertions.

```
        c = ChangeHistoryReport.new
        c.date_range(LABEL1, LABEL2)
      end
    end
  end
end
```

See Also

- The `FlexMock` generated RDoc (*http://onestepback.org/software/flexmock/*)
- `class_intercepter.rb` (*http://onestepback.org/articles/depinj/ci/class_intercepter_rb.html*)

- Alternatives to FlexMock include RSpec (*http://rspec.rubyforge.org/*) and Test:: Unit::Mock (*http://www.deveiate.org/projects/Test-Unit-Mock/*)
- Jim Weirich's presentation on Dependency Injection is closely related to testing with mock objects (*http://onestepback.org/articles/depinj/*)
- Kent Beck's classic *Test Driven Development: By Example* (Addison-Wesley) is a must read; even the seasoned TD developer will benefit from Kent's helpful patterns section at the back of the book

17.10 Using breakpoint to Inspect and Change the State of Your Application

Problem

You're debugging an application, and would like to be able to stop the program at any point and inspect the application's state (variables, data structures, etc.). You'd also like to be able to modify the application's state before restarting it.

Solution

Use the breakpoint library, available as the ruby-breakpoint gem.

Once you require 'breakpoint', you can call the breakpoint method from anywhere in your application. When the execution hits the breakpoint call, the application turns into an interactive Ruby session.

Here's a short Ruby program:

```ruby
#!/usr/bin/ruby -w
# breakpoint_test.rb
require 'rubygems'
require 'breakpoint'

class Foo
  def initialize(init_value)
    @instance_var = init_value
  end

  def bar
    test_var = @instance_var
    puts 'About to hit the breakpoint!'
    breakpoint
    puts 'HERE ARE SOME VARIABLES:'
    puts "test_var: #{test_var}, @instance_var: #{@instance_var}"
  end
end

f = Foo.new('When in the course')
f.bar
```

When you run the application, you quickly hit the call to breakpoint in Foo#bar. This drops you into an irb session:

```
$ ruby breakpoint_test.rb
About to hit the breakpoint!
Executing break point at breakpoint_test.rb:14 in `bar'
irb(#<Foo:0xb7452464>):001:0>
```

Once you quit the irb session, the program continues on its way:

```
irb(#<Foo:0xb7452a18>):001:0> quit
HERE ARE SOME VARIABLES:
test_var: When in the course, @instance_var: When in the course
```

But there's a lot you can do within that irb session before you quit. You can look at the array local_variables, which enumerates all variables local to the current method. You can also look at and modify any of the variables that are currently in scope, including instance variables, class variables, and globals:

```
$ ruby breakpoint_test.rb
About to hit the breakpoint!
Executing break point at breakpoint_test.rb:14 in `bar'
irb(#<Foo:0xb7452464>):001:0> local_variables
=> ["test_var", "_"]
irb(#<Foo:0xb7452428>):002:0> test_var
=> "When in the course"
irb(#<Foo:0xb7452428>):003:0> @instance_var
=> "When in the course"
irb(#<Foo:0xb7452428>):004:0> @instance_var = 'of human events'
=> "of human events"
```

As before, once you quit the irb session, the program continues running:

```
irb(#<Foo:0xb7452428>):005:0> quit
HERE ARE SOME VARIABLES:
test_var: When in the course, @instance_var: of human events
```

Because we changed the variable @instance_variable within our breakpoint, the puts in the program reports the new value after we leave the breakpoint session.

Discussion

There is another way to access a breakpoint. Instead of calling breakpoint directly, you can pass a code block into assert. If the block evaluates to false, assert executes a breakpoint. Let's say you want to execute a breakpoint only if the instance variable @instance_variable has a certain value. Here's how:

```
#!/usr/bin/ruby -w
# breakpoint_test_2.rb
require 'rubygems'
require 'breakpoint'

class Foo
  def initialize(init_value)
```

```
    @instance_var = init_value
  end

  def bar
    test_var = @instance_var
    puts 'About to hit the breakpoint! (maybe)'
    assert { @instance_var == 'This is another fine mess' }
    puts 'HERE ARE SOME VARIABLES:'
    puts "test_var: #{test_var}, @instance_var: #{@instance_var}"
  end
end

Foo.new('When in the course').bar        # This will NOT cause a breakpoint
Foo.new('This is another fine mess').bar # This will NOT cause a breakpoint

$ ruby breakpoint_test_2.rb
About to hit the breakpoint! (maybe)
HERE ARE SOME VARIABLES:
test_var: When in the course, @instance_var: When in the course
About to hit the breakpoint! (maybe)
Assert failed at breakpoint_test_2.rb:14 in `bar'. Executing implicit breakpoint.
irb(#<Foo:0xb7452450>):001:0> @instance_var
=> "This is another fine mess"
irb(#<Foo:0xb7452450>):002:0> quit
HERE ARE SOME VARIABLES:
test_var: This is another fine mess, @instance_var: This is another fine mess
```

By using assert, you can enter an interactive irb session only when the state of your application is worth inspecting.

17.11 Documenting Your Application

Problem

You want to create a set of API documentation for your application. You might want to go so far as to keep all your documentation in the same files as your source code.

Solution

It's good programming practice to preface each of your methods, classes, and modules with a comment that lets the reader know what's going on. Ruby rewards this behavior by making it easy to transform those comments into a set of HTML pages that document your code. This is similar to Java's JavaDoc, Python's PyDoc, and Perl's Pod.

Here's a simple example. Suppose your application contains only one file, sum.rb, which defines only one method:

```
def sum(*terms)
  terms.inject(0) { |sum, term| sum + term}
end
```

To document this application, use Ruby comments to document the method, and also to document the file as a whole:

```
# Just a simple file that defines a sum method.

# Takes any number of numeric terms and returns the sum.
#    sum(1, 2, 3)                           # => 6
#    sum(1, -1, 10)                         # => 10
#    sum(1.5, 0.2, 0.3, 1)                  # => 3.0
def sum(*terms)
  terms.inject(0) { |sum, term| sum + term}
end
```

Change into the directory containing the sum.rb file, and run the rdoc command.

```
$ rdoc
sum.rb: .
Generating HTML...

Files:    1
Classes:  0
Modules:  0
Methods:  1
Elapsed:  0.101s
```

The rdoc command creates a doc/ subdirectory beneath the current directory. It parses every Ruby file it can find in or below the current directory, and generates HTML files from the Ruby code and the comments that document it.

The index.html file in the doc/ subdirectory is a frameset that lets users navigate the files of your application. Since the example only uses one file (sum.rb), the most interesting thing about its generated documentation is what RDoc has done with the comments (Figure 17-1).

Discussion

RDoc parses a set of Ruby files, cross-references them, and generates a web site that captures the class and module structure, and the comments you wrote while you were coding.

Generated RDoc makes for a useful reference to your classes and methods, but it's not a substitute for handwritten examples or tutorials. Of course, RDoc comments can *contain* handwritten examples or tutorials. This will help your users and also help you keep your documentation together with your code.

Notice that when I wrote examples for the sum method, I indented them a little from the text above them:

```
# Takes any number of numeric terms and returns the sum.
#    sum(1, 2, 3)                           # => 6
```

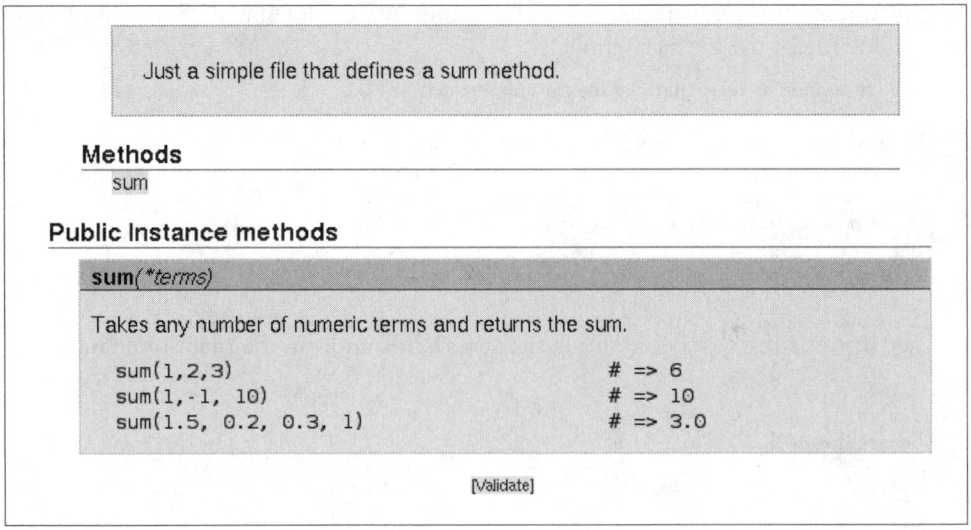

```
        Just a simple file that defines a sum method.
```

Methods
    sum

Public Instance methods

sum(*terms*)

Takes any number of numeric terms and returns the sum.

```
    sum(1,2,3)                              # => 6
    sum(1,-1, 10)                           # => 10
    sum(1.5, 0.2, 0.3, 1)                   # => 3.0
```

[Validate]

Figure 17-1. RDoc comments

RDoc picked up on this extra indentation and displayed my examples as Ruby code, in a fixed-width font. This is one of many RDoc conventions for improving the looks of the rendered HTML. As with wiki markup, the goal of the RDoc conventions is to allow text to render nicely as HTML while being easy to read and edit as plain text (Figure 17-2).

```
# =A whirlwind tour of SimpleMarkup
#
# ==You can mark up text
#
# * *Bold* a single word <b>or a section</b>
# * _Emphasize_ a single word <i>or a section</i>
# * Use a <tt>fixed-width font</tt> for a section or a +word+
# * URLs are automatically linked: https://www.example.com/foo.html
#
# ==Or create lists
#
# Types of lists:
# * Unordered lists (like this one, and the one above)
# * Ordered lists
#    1. Line
#    2. Square
#    3. Cube
```

```
# * Definition-style labelled lists (useful for argument lists)
#   [pos] Coordinates of the center of the circle ([x, y])
#   [radius] Radius of the circle, in pixels
# * Table-style labelled lists
#   Author:: Sophie Aurus
#   Homepage:: http://www.example.com
```

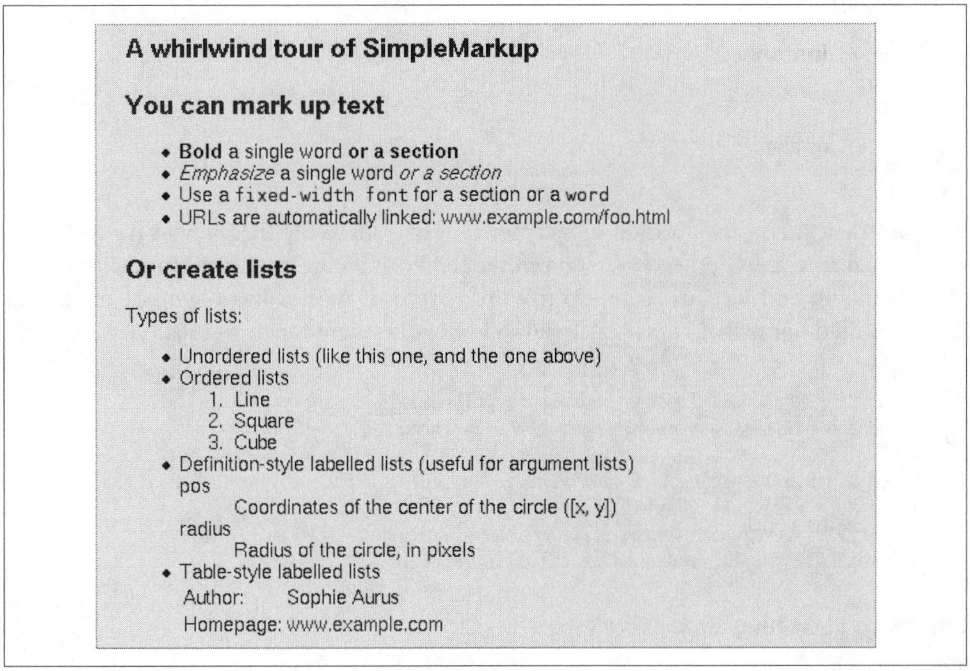

A whirlwind tour of SimpleMarkup

You can mark up text

- **Bold** a single word **or a section**
- *Emphasize* a single word *or a section*
- Use a `fixed-width` font for a section or a word
- URLs are automatically linked: www.example.com/foo.html

Or create lists

Types of lists:

- Unordered lists (like this one, and the one above)
- Ordered lists
    1. Line
    2. Square
    3. Cube
- Definition-style labelled lists (useful for argument lists)
  pos
        Coordinates of the center of the circle ([x, y])
  radius
        Radius of the circle, in pixels
- Table-style labelled lists
  Author: Sophie Aurus
  Homepage: www.example.com

Figure 17-2. Plain text

There are also several special RDoc directives that go into comments on the same line as a method, class, or module definition. The most common is :nodoc:, which is used if you want to hide something from RDoc. You can and should put an RDoc-style comment even on a :nodoc: method or class, so that people reading your Ruby code will know what it does.

```
# This class and its contents are hidden from RDoc; here's what it does:
# ...
#
class HiddenClass # :nodoc:
  # ...
end
```

Private methods don't show up in RDoc generated documentation—that would usually just mean clutter. If you want one particular private method to show up in the documentation (probably for the benefit of people subclassing your class), use the :doc: directive; it's the opposite of the :nodoc: directive:*

```
class MyClass
  private

  def hidden_method
  end

  def visible_method # :doc:
  end
end
```

If a comment mentions another class, method, or source file, RDoc will try to locate and turn it into a hyperlinked cross-reference. To indicate that a method name is a method name and not just a random word, prefix it with a hash symbol or use its fully qualified name (MyClass.class_method or MyClass#instance_method:

```
# The SimplePolynomial class represents polynomials in one variable
# and can perform most common operations on them.
#
# See especially #solve and #derivative. For multivariate polynomials,
# see MultivariatePolynomial (especially
# MultivariatePolynomial#simplify, which may return a
# SimplePolynomial), and much of calculus.rb.
```

Other ways of creating RDoc

The Ruby gem installation process generates a set of RDoc files for every gem it installs. If you package your software as a gem, anyone who installs it will automatically get the RDoc files as well.

You can also create RDoc files programatically from a Ruby program, by creating and scripting RDoc objects. The rdoc command itself is nothing more than Ruby code such as the following, along with some error handling:

```
#!/usr/bin/ruby
# rdoc.rb
require 'rdoc/rdoc'
RDoc::RDoc.new.document(ARGV)
```

---

* If you want all private methods to show up in the documentation, pass the --all argument to the rdoc command. The rdoc command supports many command-line arguments, giving you control over the rules for generating the documentation and the layout of the results.

See Also

- Recipe 18.5, "Reading Documentation for Installed Gems"
- The RDoc documentation covers all the markup conventions and directives in detail (*http://rdoc.sourceforge.net/doc/*)
- *http://rdoc.sourceforge.net/doc/files/markup/simple_markup_rb.html*

17.12 Profiling Your Application

Problem

You want to find the slowest parts of your application, and speed them up.

Solution

Include the Ruby profiler in your application with include 'profile' and the profiler will start tracking and timing every subsequent method call. When the application exits, the profiler will print a report to your program's standard error stream.

Here's a program that contains a performance flaw:

```
#!/usr/bin/env ruby
# sequence_counter.rb
require 'profile'

total = 0
# Count the letter sequences containing an a, b, or c.
('a'..'zz').each do |seq|
  ['a', 'b', 'c'].each do |i|
    if seq.index(i)
      total += 1
      break
    end
  end
end
puts "Total: #{total}"
```

When the program is run, the profiler shows the parts of the program that are most important to optimize:

```
$ ruby sequence_counter.rb
Total: 150
  %   cumulative   self              self     total
 time   seconds   seconds    calls  ms/call  ms/call  name
54.55     0.30      0.30      702     0.43     0.50   Array#each
32.73     0.48      0.18        1   180.00   550.00   Range#each
 7.27     0.52      0.04     1952     0.02     0.02   String#index
 3.64     0.54      0.02      702     0.03     0.03   String#succ
 1.82     0.55      0.01      150     0.07     0.07   Fixnum#+
...
```

The program takes about 0.3 seconds to run, and most of that is spent in Array#each. What if we replaced that code with an equivalent regular expression?

```
#!/usr/bin/env ruby
# sequence_counter2.rb
require 'profile'

total = 0
# Count the letter sequences containing an a, b, or c.
('a'..'zz').each {|seq| total +=1 if seq =~ /[abc]/ }
puts "Total: #{total}"
```

Running this program yields a much better result:

```
$ ruby sequence_counter2.rb
Total: 150
  %   cumulative   self              self     total
 time   seconds   seconds    calls  ms/call  ms/call  name
 83.33    0.05      0.05         1    50.00    60.00   Range#each
 16.67    0.06      0.01       150     0.07     0.07   Fixnum#+
  0.00    0.06      0.00         1     0.00     0.00   Fixnum#to_s
 ...
```

The new version takes only 0.05 seconds to run, and as near as the profiler can measure, it's running nearly as fast as an empty iterator over the range 'a'..'zz'.

Discussion

You might think that regex_counter2.rb has a performance problem of its own. After all, it initializes the regular expression /[abc]/ within a loop, which seems to indicate that it's being initialized multiple times. The natural instinct of the optimizing programmer is to move that definition outside the loop; surely that would be more efficient.

```
re = /[abc]/
('a'..'zz').each {|seq| total +=1 if seq =~ re }
```

But it's not (try it!). The profiler actually shows a *decrease* in performance when the regular expression is assigned to a variable outside the loop. The Ruby interpreter is doing some optimization behind the scenes, and the code with an "obvious" performance problem beats the more complex "optimized" version.* There is a general lesson here: the problem is often not where you think it is, and empirical data always beats guesswork.

Ruby's profiler is a fairly blunt tool (it's written in only about 60 lines of Ruby), and to instrument it for anything but a simple command-line application, you'll need to do some work. It helps if your code has unit tests, because profiler tests require a lot

---

* Of course, a regular expression is a pretty simple object. If you've got a loop that builds a million-element data structure, or reads the same file over and over, the Ruby interpreter can't help you. Move that sucker out of the loop. If you make this kind of mistake, it'll show up in the profiler.

of the same scaffolding as unit tests. You can even build up a library of profiler test scripts to go with your unit tests, although the profiler output is difficult to analyze automatically.

If you know that some particular operation is slow, you can write code that stress-tests that operation (the way you might write a unit test), and run only that code with the profiler. To stress-test sequence_counter2.rb, you might change it to operate on a larger range like ('a'..'zzzz'). Big datasets make performance problems more visible.

If you don't know which operations are slow, pick the most common operations and instrument them on large datasets. If you're writing an XML library, write a profiler script that loads and parses an enormous file, and one that turns an enormous data structure into XML. If you've got no ideas at all, run the profiler on your unit test suite and look for problems. The tests that run slowly may be exercising problematic parts of your program.

The profiler results are ordered with the most time-consuming method calls first. To optimize your code, go from the top of the profiler results and address each call in turn. See why your script led to so many calls of that method, and what you can do about it. Either change the underlying code path so it doesn't call that method so many times, or optimize the method itself. If the method is one you wrote, you can optimize it by profiling it in isolation.

The timing data given by the profiler isn't terribly accurate,* but it should be good enough to find problem areas. If you want a more reliable estimate of how long some code takes to run, try the benchmark library, or run your script using the Unix time command.

The Ruby profiler sets the interpreter's trace function (by passing a code block into Kernel#set_trace_func), so if your program uses a trace function of its own, using the profiler will overwrite the old function. This probably won't affect you, because the trace function is mainly used by profilers and other analysis tools.

See Also

- If the profiler says your problem is in a commonly-called method like Array#each, you need to somehow figure out which calls to the method are the problematic ones; see Recipe 17.15, "Who's Calling That Method? A Call Graph Analyzer"

---

* Note the timing inconsistencies in the examples above. Somehow the entire original sequence_counter.rb runs in 0.30 seconds, but when you ignore all the Array#each calls, the cumulative time jumps up to 0.48 seconds.

17.13 Benchmarking Competing Solutions

Problem

You want to see which of two solutions to a problem is faster. You might want to compare two different algorithms, or two libraries that do the same thing.

Solution

Use the benchmark library to time the tasks you want to run. The `Benchmark.bm` method gives you an object that can report on how long it takes for code blocks to run.

Let's explore whether the `member?` method is faster on arrays or hashes. First, we create a large array and a large hash with the same data, and define a method that exercises the `member?` method:

```
RANGE = (0..1000)
array = RANGE.to_a
hash = RANGE.inject({}) { |h,i| h[i] = true; h }

def test_member?(data)
  RANGE.each { |i| data.member? i }
end
```

Next, we call `Benchmark.bm` to set up a series of timing tests. The first test calls `test_member?` on the array; the second one calls it on the hash. The results are printed in a tabular form to standard error:

```
require 'benchmark'

Benchmark.bm(5) do |timer|
  timer.report('Array') { test_member?(array) }
  timer.report('Hash') { test_member?(hash) }
end
#        user      system     total        real
# Array  0.260000  0.060000   0.320000 (  0.332583)
# Hash   0.010000  0.000000   0.010000 (  0.001242)
```

As you'd expect, `member?` is much faster on a hash.

Discussion

What do the different times mean? The real time is "wall clock" time: the number of seconds that passed in the real world between the start of the test and its completion. This time is actually not very useful, because it includes time during which the CPU was running some other process. If your system is operating under a heavy load, the Ruby interpreter will get less of the CPU's attention and the real times won't reflect the actual performance of your benchmarks. You only need real times when you're measuring user-visible performance on a running system.

The user time is time actually spent running the Ruby interpreter, and the system time is time spent in system calls spawned by the interpreter. If your test does a lot of I/O, its system time will tend to be large; if it does a lot of processing, its user time will tend to be large. The most useful time is probably total, the sum of the user and system times.

When two operations take almost exactly the same time, you can make the difference more visible by putting a times loop within the code block passed to report. For instance, array lookup and hash lookup are both very fast operations that take too little time to measure. But by timing thousands of lookup operations instead of just one, we can see that hash lookups are a tiny bit slower than array lookups:

```
Benchmark.bm(5) do |timer|
  timer.report('Array') { 1000.times { RANGE.each { |i| array[i] } } }
  timer.report('Hash') { 1000.times { RANGE.each { |i| hash[i] } } }
end
#           user      system      total            real
# Array   0.950000    0.210000    1.160000  (   1.175042)
# Hash    1.010000    0.210000    1.220000  (   1.221090)
```

If you want to measure one operation instead of comparing several operations to each other, use Benchmark#measure. It returns an object that you can interrogate to get the times, or print out to get a listing in the same format as Benchmark.bm. This code demonstrates that I/O-bound code has a larger system time:

```
def write_to_file
  File.open('out', 'w') { |f| f.write('a') }
end

puts Benchmark.measure { 10000.times { write_to_file } }
# 0.120000   0.360000   0.480000 (   0.500653)
```

Recall that the real time can be distorted by the CPU doing things other than running your Ruby process. The user and system times can also be distorted by the Ruby interpreter doing things besides running your program. For instance, time spent doing garbage collection is counted by benchmark as time spent running Ruby code.

To get around these problems, use the Benchmark.bmbm method. It runs each of your timing tests twice. The first time is just a rehearsal to get the interpreter into a stable state. Nothing can completely isolate the time spent running benchmarks from other tasks of the Ruby interpreter, but bmbm should be good enough for most purposes.

See Also

- The standard library documentation for the benchmark library has lots of information about varying the format of benchmark reports

17.14 Running Multiple Analysis Tools at Once

Problem

You want to combine two analysis tools, like the Ruby profiler and the Ruby tracer. But when one tool calls set_trace_func, it overwrites the trace function left by the other.

Solution

Change set_trace_func so that it keeps an array of trace functions instead of just one. Here's a library called multitrace.rb that makes it possible:

```
# multitrace.rb
$TRACE_FUNCS = []

alias :set_single_trace_func :set_trace_func
def set_trace_func(proc)
  if (proc == nil)
    $TRACE_FUNCS.clear
  else
    $TRACE_FUNCS << proc
  end
end

trace_all = Proc.new do |event, file, line, symbol, binding, klass|
  $TRACE_FUNCS.each { |p| p.call(event, file, line, symbol, binding, klass)}
end
set_single_trace_func trace_all

def unset_trace_func(proc)
  $TRACE_FUNCS.delete(proc)
end
```

Now you can run any number of analysis tools simultaneously. However, when one of the tools stops, they will all stop:

```
#!/usr/bin/ruby -w
# paranoia.rb
require 'multitrace'
require 'profile'
require 'tracer'

Tracer.on
puts "I feel like I'm being watched."
```

This program's nervousness is well-justified, since its every move is being tracked by the Ruby tracer *and* timed by the Ruby profiler:

```
$ ruby paranoia.rb
#0:./multitrace.rb:9:Array:<:     $TRACE_FUNCS << proc
#0:./multitrace.rb:11:Object:<: end
#0:paranoia.rb:9::-: puts "I feel like I'm being watched."
#0:paranoia.rb:9:Kernel:>: puts "I feel like I'm being watched."
```

```
...
   %   cumulative   self               self    total
  time    seconds   seconds    calls  ms/call  ms/call  name
  0.00      0.00      0.00         1    0.00     0.00  Kernel.require
  0.00      0.00      0.00         1    0.00     0.00  Fixnum#==
  0.00      0.00      0.00         1    0.00     0.00  String#scan
...
```

Without the `include 'multitrace'` at the beginning, only the profiler will run: its trace function will override the tracer's.

Discussion

This example illustrates yet again how you can benefit by replacing some built-in part of Ruby. The `multitrace` library creates a drop-in replacement for `set_trace_func` that lets you run multiple analyzers at once. You probably don't really want to run the tracer and the analyzer simultaneously, since they're both monolithic tools. But if you've written some smaller, more modular analysis tools, you're more likely to want to run more than one during a single run of a program.

The standard way of stopping a tracer is to pass `nil` into `set_trace_func`. Our new `set_trace_func` will accept `nil`, but it has no way of knowing which trace function you want to stop.* It has no choice but to remove all of them. Of course, if you're writing your own trace functions, and you know `multitrace` will be in place, you don't need to pass `nil` into `set_trace_func`. You can call `unset_trace_func` to remove one particular trace function, without stopping the rest.

See Also

* The tracer function created in Recipe 17.15, "Who's Calling That Method? A Call Graph Analyzer," is the kind of lightweight analysis tool I'd like to see more of: one that it makes sense to run in conjunction with others

17.15 Who's Calling That Method? A Call Graph Analyzer

Suppose you're profiling a program such as the one in Recipe 17.12, and the profiler says that the top culprit is Array#each. That is, your program spends more time iterating over arrays than doing any one other thing:

```
   %   cumulative   self               self    total
  time    seconds   seconds    calls  ms/call  ms/call  name
 12.19     2.74      2.74      4930    0.56     0.77  Array#each
```

---

* Well, you could do this by taking a snapshot of the call stack every time `set_trace_func` was called with a `Proc` object. When `set_trace_func` was called with `nil`, you could look at the call stack at that point (see Recipe 17.6), and only remove the `Proc` object(s) inserted by the same file. For instance, if a `nil` call comes in from `profiler.rb`, you could remove only the `Proc` object(s) inserted by calls coming from `profiler.rb`. This is probably not worth the trouble.

This points you in the right direction, but where do you go from here? Most programs are full of calls to Array#each. To optimize your program, you need to know which lines of code are responsible for most of the Array#each calls. Ruby's profiler can't give tell you which line of code called a problem method, but it's easy to write a different profiler that can.

The heart of any Ruby profiler is a Proc object passed into the Kernel#set_trace_func method. This is a hook into the Ruby interpreter itself: if you set a trace function, it's called every time the Ruby interpreter does something interesting like call a method.

Here's the start of a CallTracker class. It initializes a hash-based data structure that tracks "interesting" classes and methods. It assumes that we pass a method tally_calls into set_trace_func; we'll define tally_calls a little later.

```ruby
class CallTracker

  # Initialize and start the trace.
  def initialize(show_stack_depth=1)
    @show_stack_depth = show_stack_depth
    @to_trace = Hash.new { |h,k| h[k] = {} }
    start
    at_exit { stop }
  end

  # Register a class/method combination as being interesting. Subsequent calls
  # to the method will be tallied by tally_calls.
  def register(klass, method_symbol)
    @to_trace[klass][method_symbol] = {}
  end

  # Tells the Ruby interpreter to call tally_calls whenever it's about to
  # do anything interesting.
  def start
    set_trace_func method(:tally_calls).to_proc
  end

  # Stops the profiler, and prints a report of the interesting calls made
  # while it was running.
  def stop(out=$stderr)
    set_trace_func nil
    report(out)
  end
end
```

Now let's define the missing methods tally_calls and report. The Proc object passed into set_trace_func needs to take six arguments, but this analyzer only cares about three of them:

event
  Lets us know what the interpreter is doing. We only care about "call" and "c-call" events, which let us know that the interpreter is calling a Ruby method or a C method.

klass

> The Class object that defines the method being called.

symbol

> The name of the method as a Symbol.

The `tally_calls` method looks up the class and name of the method being called to see if it's one of the methods being tracked. If so, it grabs the current call stack with `Kernel#caller`, and notes where in the execution path the method was called:

```
# If the interpreter is about to call a method we find interesting,
# increment the count for that method.
def tally_calls(event, file, line, symbol, binding, klass)
  if @to_trace[klass] and @to_trace[klass][symbol] and
  (event == 'call' or event =='c-call')
    stack = caller
    stack = stack[1..(@show_stack_depth ? @show_stack_depth : stack.size)]
    @to_trace[klass][symbol][stack] ||= 0
    @to_trace[klass][symbol][stack] += 1
  end
end
```

All that's left is the method that prints the report. It sorts the results by execution path (as indicated by the stack traces), so the more often a method is called from a certain line of code, the higher in the report that line of code will show up:

```
# Prints a report of the lines of code that called interesting
# methods, sorted so that the the most active lines of code show up
# first.
def report(out=$stderr)
  first = true
  @to_trace.each do |klass, symbols|
    symbols.each do |symbol, calls|
      total = calls.inject(0) { |sum, ct| sum + ct[1] }
      padding = total.to_s.size
      separator = (klass.is_a? Class) ? '#' : '.'
      plural = (total == 1) ? '' : 's'
      stack_join = "\n" + (' ' * (padding+2))
      first ? first = false : out.puts
      out.puts "#{total} call#{plural} to #{klass}#{separator}#{symbol}"
      (calls.sort_by { |caller, times| -times }).each do |caller, times|
        out.puts " %#{padding}.d #{caller.join(stack_join)}" % times
      end
    end
  end
end
```

Here's the analyzer in action. It analyses my use of the Rubyful Soup HTML parser (which I was working on optimizing) to see which lines of code are responsible for calling `Array#each`. It shows three main places to look for optimizations:

```
require 'rubygems'
require 'rubyful_soup'
```

```
tracker = CallTracker.new
tracker.register(Array, :each)

BeautifulSoup.new(open('test.html') { |f| f.read })
tracker.stop($stdout)
# 4930 calls to Array#each
# 1671 ./rubyful_soup.rb:715:in `pop_to_tag'
# 1631 ./rubyful_soup.rb:567:in `unknown_starttag'
# 1627 ./rubyful_soup.rb:751:in `smart_pop'
#    1 ./rubyful_soup.rb:510:in `feed'
```

By default, the CallTracker shows only the single line of code that called the "interesting" method. You can get more of the call stack by passing a larger show_stack_depth into the CallTracker initializer.

See Also

- Recipe 17.6, "Creating and Understanding Tracebacks"
- Recipe 17.12, "Profiling Your Application"

Packaging and Distributing Software

No matter how productive it makes you, a programming language won't save you any time if you can't take advantage of a body of code written by other people. A community works faster than any one person, and it's usually easier to install and learn a library than to write and debug the same code yourself.

That is, if you can find the library in the first place. And if you're not sucked into an mess of dependencies that grow and grow, making you want to write the code yourself just so you can be doing some real programming.

The success of Perl's CPAN archive has made the Ruby community work on our own centralized code repository and packaging system. Whatever you think of Perl, you must admit that a Perl programmer can find just about any library they need in CPAN. If you write your own Perl library, you know where to send it: CPAN. This is not really a technical aspect of Perl, but it's a powerful component of that language's popularity.

The problem of packaging is more a logistical problem than a technical one. It's a matter of coordination: getting everyone to agree on a single mechanism for installing packages, and a single place to go to find those packages. For Ruby, the installation mechanism is Ruby gems (or rubygems or just "gems"), and rubyforge.org is the place to go to find gems (packaged libraries and programs).

In many recipes in this book, we tell you to use a gem for some task: the alternative is often to show you pages and pages of code. This chapter covers how to find the gems you need, install them, and package your own software as gems so that others can benefit from your work.

You may need to find and install the Ruby gems system itself. It comes installed by default on Windows, but not on Unix. You can download it from this URL:

```
http://rubyforge.org/frs/?group_id=126
```

To install the Ruby gems package, unzip the tarball or ZIP file, and run the setup.rb script within. You can then use the gem command to search for and install gems, as described in Recipes 18.1 and 18.2. You can also build your own gems from "gem-spec" files, as described in Recipe 18.6, and upload it to RubyForge or some other site (Recipe 18.7).

An older installation system called setup.rb is still in use (for instance, to install the Ruby gems package itself). We cover this mechanism briefly in Recipe 18.8.

Neither Ruby gems nor setup.rb play well with a Unix distribution's native package installers. If you use a system like Debian or Red Hat, you may find that some packages (like Rails) are available both as gems and in your native package format. These issues are still being resolved; in the meantime, you should use your native package format whenever possible.

18.1 Finding Libraries by Querying Gem Respositories

Problem

You want to find new gems to install on your system, or see which gems you already have installed.

Solution

From the command line, use gem's query command:

```
$ gem query
*** LOCAL GEMS ***

sources (0.0.1)
    This package provides download sources for remote gem installation

$ gem query --remote
*** REMOTE GEMS ***
actionmailer (1.1.1, 1.0.1, 1.0.0, 0.9.1, 0.9.0, 0.8.1, ...)
    Service layer for easy email delivery and testing.

actionpack (1.10.1, 1.9.1, 1.9.0, 1.8.1, 1.8.0, 1.7.0, ...)
    Web-flow and rendering framework putting the VC in MVC.

[... Much more output omitted ....]
```

From Ruby code, use Gem::cache to query your locally installed gems, and Gem::RemoteInstaller#search to query the gems on some other site. Gem::cache can be treated as an Enumerable full of tasty Gem::Specification objects. Gem::RemoteInstaller#search returns an Array containing an Array of Gem::Specification objects for every remote source it searched. Usually there will only be one remote source—the main gem repository on rubyforge.org.

This Ruby code iterates over the locally installed gems:

```
require 'rubygems'

Gem::cache.each do |name, gem|
  puts %{"#{gem.name}" gem version #{gem.version} is installed.}
end
# "sources" gem version 0.0.1 is installed.
```

The `format_gems` method defined below gives a convenient way of looking at a large set of `Gem::Specification` objects. It groups the gems by name and version, then prints a formatted list:

```
require 'rubygems/remote_installer'
require 'yaml'

def format_gems(gems)
  gem_versions = gems.inject({}) { |h, gem| (h[gem.name] ||= []) << gem; h}
  gem_versions.keys.sort.each do |name|
   versions = gem_versions[name].collect { |gem| gem.version.to_s }
    puts "#{name} is available in these versions: #{versions.join(', ')}"
  end
end
```

Here it is being run on the gems available from RubyForge:

```
format_gems(Gem::RemoteInstaller.new.search(/.*/).flatten)
# Asami is available in these versions: 0.04
# Bangkok is available in these versions: 0.1.0
# Bloglines4R is available in these versions: 0.1.0
# BlueCloth is available in these versions: 0.0.2, 0.0.3, 0.0.4, 1.0.0
# ...
```

Discussion

Not only are Ruby gems a convenient packaging mechanism, they're an excellent way to find out about new pieces of Ruby code. The gem repository at rubyforge.org is the canonical location for Ruby libraries, so you've got one place to find new code.

You can query the gems library for gems whose names match a certain regular expression:

```
$ gem query --remote --name-matches "test"
** REMOTE GEMS ***

lazytest (0.1.0)
    Testing and benchmarking for lazy people

test-unit-mock (0.30)
    Test::Unit::Mock is a class for conveniently building mock objects
    in Test::Unit test cases.

testunitxml (0.1.4, 0.1.3)
    Unit test suite for XML documents
```

```
ZenTest (3.1.0, 3.0.0)
   == FEATURES/PROBLEMS
```

Or, from Ruby code:

```
format_gems(Gem::RemoteInstaller.new.search(/test/i).flatten)
# ZenTest is available in these versions: 3.0.0, 3.1.0
# lazytest is available in these versions: 0.1.0
# test-unit-mock is available in these versions: 0.30
# testunitxml is available in these versions: 0.1.3, 0.1.4
```

This method finds gems that are newer than a certain date. It has to keep around both a Date and a Time object for comparisons, because RubyForge stores some gems' dates as Date objects, some as Time objects, and some as string representations of dates.[*]

```
require 'date'

def gems_newer_than(date, query=/.*/)
  time = Time.local(date.year, date.month, date.day, 0, 0, 0)
  gems = Gem::RemoteInstaller.new.search(query).flatten
  gems.reject do |gem|
    gem_date = gem.date
    gem_date = DateTime.parse(gem_date) if gem_date.respond_to? :to_str
    gem_date < (gem_date.is_a?(Date) ? date : time)
  end
end

todays_gems = gems_newer_than(Date.today-1)
todays_gems.size                                      # => 7
format_gems(todays_gems)
# filament is available in these versions: 0.3.0
# mechanize is available in these versions: 0.4.1
# mongrel is available in these versions: 0.3.12.1, 0.3.12.1
# rake is available in these versions: 0.7.1
# rspec is available in these versions: 0.5.0
# tzinfo is available in these versions: 0.2.0
```

By default, remote queries look only at the main gem repository on rubyforge.org:

```
Gem::RemoteInstaller.new.sources          # => ["http://gems.rubyforge.org"]
```

To query a gem repository other than rubyforge.org, pass in the URL to the repository as the `--source` argument from the command line. This code starts a gem server on the local machine (it can serve all of your installed gems to other machines), and queries it:

```
$ gem_server &

$ gem query --remote --source http://localhost:8808
# *** REMOTE GEMS ***
```

---

[*] This is because of differences in the underlying gem specification files. Different people build their gemspecs in different ways.

```
# Updating Gem source index for: http://localhost:8808
# sources (0.0.1)
#    This package provides download sources for remote gem installation
```

From Ruby code, modify the Gem.sources variable to retrieve gems from another source:

```
Gem.sources.replace(['http://localhost:8808'])
format_gems(Gem::RemoteInstaller.new.search(/.*/).flatten)
# sources is available in these versions: 0.0.1
```

See Also

- Recipe 18.7, "Distributing Your Gems," for more on hosting your own gem repository
- The Ruby Application Archive is a companion to rubyforge.org: rather than hosting Ruby projects, it links to Ruby packages hosted all around the Web; you're more likely to see projects on the RAA that aren't packaged as gems (see Recipe 18.8 for tips on installing them)

18.2 Installing and Using a Gem

Problem

You want to install a gem, then use the code it provides in your programs.

Solution

You can install the latest version of a gem with the gem install command. This command looks for an uninstalled gem file on your local system; if it can't find one, it calls out to an external source (gems.rubyforge.org, unless you specify otherwise) asking for a gem file. Since gem install changes the system-wide Ruby installation, you'll need to have superuser access to run it.

```
$ gem install RedCloth
Attempting local installation of 'RedCloth'
Local gem file not found: RedCloth*.gem
Attempting remote installation of 'RedCloth'
Successfully installed RedCloth-3.0.4
```

A gem contains standard Ruby code files, and once you install the gem, you can require those files normally and use the classes and modules they define. However, gems are not installed in the same path as the standard Ruby libraries, so you'll need to tell Ruby to supplement its normal library path with the path to the gems. The simplest way is to require 'rubygems' in any program that uses a gem, before you write any require statements for libraries installed via gems. This is the solution we use throughout this book.

```
# This code assumes the "redcloth" gem has been installed, as in the
# code above.
require 'redcloth'
# LoadError: no such file to load -- redcloth

require 'rubygems'
require 'redcloth'
parser = RedCloth::CommandParser.new
# ...
```

For a solution that works across Ruby scripts, you'll need to change your Ruby run-time environment, either by setting the RUBYOPT environment variable to rubygems, or by aliasing your ruby command so that it always passes in a -rubygems option to the interpreter.

```
$ ruby -e "require 'redcloth'; puts 'Success'"
-e:1:in `require': no such file to load -- redcloth (LoadError)
        from -e:1

$ ruby -rubygems -e "require 'redcloth'; puts 'Success'"
Success

# On Unix:
$ export RUBYOPT=rubygems
$ ruby -e "require 'redcloth'; puts 'Success'"
Success

# On Windows:
$ set RUBYOPT=rubygems
$ ruby -e "require 'redcloth'; puts 'Success'"
Success
```

Discussion

Once you've installed a gem, you can upgrade it to the latest version with the gem update command. Even if you've already got the latest version, you'll see output like this:

```
$ gem update RedCloth
# Upgrading installed gems...
# Attempting remote upgrade of RedCloth
# Attempting remote installation of 'RedCloth'
# Successfully installed RedCloth-3.0.4
# Gems: [redcloth] updated
```

You might install a gem for your own use, or because it's required by a program you want to run. If you want to use a gem in your own programs, there's no reason not to always use the latest version. Some programs, though, impose version constraints that force you to install a particular version of a gem.

Ruby's gem system can keep multiple versions of the same gem installed at once. You can satisfy one program's archaic dependencies while still being able to use the latest version of a gem in your own programs. To install a specific version of a gem, append the version number to the name, or specify a --version argument to gem install.

```
$ gem install RedCloth-3.0.4
$ gem install RedCloth --version "3.0.4"
```

Use the technique described in Recipe 18.3 to require the one that's right for your program.

A program that imposes a version constraint doesn't usually tell you which specific version of a gem you need to install. Instead, it crashes with an error that tells you which contraint string you need to meet. Again, you can see Recipe 18.3 for more on constraint strings, but they look like > 2.0 or <= 1.6. You can install a version of a gem that satisfies a constraint string by passing the contraint as a --version argument to gem install. The gem command will find and install the latest version that meets that constraint.

```
$ ruby -e "require 'rubygems'; require_gem 'units', '~>1.0' puts 'Units'"
/usr/local/lib/site_ruby/1.8/rubygems.rb:204:in `report_activate_error':
Could not find RubyGem units (~> 1.0) (Gem::LoadError)

$ gem install units --version "~> 1.0"
Attempting remote installation of 'units'
Successfully installed units-1.0.1
Installing RDoc documentation for units-1.0.1...

$ ruby -e "require 'rubygems'; require_gem 'units', '~>1.0'; puts 'Units'"
Units!
```

Whether you run the gem install command, or install a gem from Ruby code that you write, you'll need to have the proper permissions to write to your gem directory.

When you install a gem from the command line, the gem command will offer you a chance to install all other gems on which it depends. You can have gem install the dependencies without prompting by passing in the --include-dependencies flag. This invocation installs the rubyful_soup gem and the htmltools gem on which it depends:

```
$ gem install rubyful_soup --include-dependencies
Attempting local installation of 'rubyful_soup'
Local gem file not found: rubyful_soup*.gem
Attempting remote installation of 'rubyful_soup'
Successfully installed rubyful_soup-1.0.4
Successfully installed htmltools-1.09
Installing RDoc documentation for rubyful_soup-1.0.4...
Installing RDoc documentation for htmltools-1.09...
```

You can install a gem from Ruby code by creating a Gem::Installer or Gem::RemoteInstaller object, and calling its install method. The install method will return an array containing a Gem::Specification object for the gem that was installed.

Here's a simple method that mimics the behavior of the gem install command, looking for a local copy of a gem before going out to the network:

```
require 'rubygems/installer'
require 'rubygems/remote_installer'

def install_gem(gem_name)
  if File.file? gem_name:
    Gem::Installer.new(gem_name).install
  else
    Gem::RemoteInstaller.new.install(gem_name)
  end
end

install_gem('redcloth')
# Updating Gem source index for: http://gems.rubyforge.org
# => [#<Gem::Specification:0xb5fc7dbc
#     @loaded_from="/usr/lib/ruby/gems/1.8/specifications/redcloth-2.0.0.gemspec"]
# ...
```

To install a gem from Ruby code, you must first go through all of its dependencies and install them, too.

See Also

- Recipe 18.3, "Requiring a Specific Version of a Gem"

18.3 Requiring a Specific Version of a Gem

Problem

Your program depends on an interface or feature of a gem found only in particular versions of the library. If a user tries to run your program with the wrong version installed, you want to tell them which version you require, so they can upgrade.

Solution

The rubygems library defines a method, Kernel#require_gem, which is a kind of assertion method for gems. It will raise a Gem::LoadError if the given gem is not installed, or if no installed version of a gem meets your requirements.

The easiest solution is to allow any version of a gem; you don't need to use require_gem at all:

```
require 'rubygems'
require 'cmdparse'                                   # => true
```

This is equivalent to requiring a minimum version of 0.0.0:

```
require_gem 'nosuchgem'
# Gem::LoadError: Could not find RubyGem nosuchgem (> 0.0.0)
```

If you can't use just any version of a gem, it's usually safe to require a minimum version, relying on future versions to be backwards-compatible:[*]

```
require_gem 'cmdparse', '>= 1.0'                            # => false
require_gem 'cmdparse', '>= 2.0.3'
# Gem::LoadError: RubyGem version error: cmdparse(2.0.0 not >= 2.0.3)
```

Discussion

Although you may already be familiar with it, a brief review of the structure of version numbers is useful here. A version number for a Ruby gem (and most other pieces of open source software) has three parts: a major version number, a minor version number, and a revision number or build number (Figure 18-1).

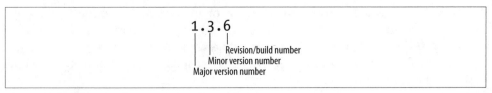

Figure 18-1. Anatomy of a version number

Some packages have only a major and minor version number (such as 2.0 or 1.6), and some have additional numbers after the revision number, but the three-number convention is the accepted standard for numbering Ruby gems.

The revision number is incremented at every new public release of the software. If the revision contains more than minor changes, or changes the public API in a backwards-compatible way, the author increments the minor version and resets the revision number to zero. When a release contains large changes, especially ones that change the public API in backwards-incompatible ways, the author usually increments the major version number, and resets the minor version and revision number to zero.

Version numbers are not decimal numbers: version 1.10 is more recent than version 1.1, not the same. Version numbers should be represented as a string or an array of integers, not as a floating-point number or `BigDecimal`.

The `require_gem` method takes the name of a gem and an optional version requirement. A version requirement is a string containing a comparison operator and a version number: for instance, `"< 2.4"`. A version requirement can use any of the comparison operators usable in Ruby code, including =, !=, <, >, <=, and =>.

RubyGems uses the comparison operator to compare the installed version of a gem to the required version. The assertion is met if the installed version has the given

---

[*] The first `require_gem` command in this code snippet returns false not because the `cmdparse` gem isn't there, but because we've already loaded the `cmdparse` library (in the very first code snippet of this recipe). The require method only returns true the first time it loads a library.

relationship with the required version. For instance, if version 1.1.4 is installed, and the version requirement is "> 0.9", the two version numbers are compared with an expression similar to "1.1.4 > 0.9", which evaluates to true (the installed major version, 1, is greater than the required major version, 0).

A version requirement can also use the special ~> comparison operator, which restricts certain parts of the version number while leaving the others alone. You'll usually use it to restrict the installed version of a gem to a particular minor version, but allowing any revision number. For instance, the version requirement ~> 2.0 will match any version with a major number of 2 and a minor number of 0: 2.0, 2.0.1, 2.0.2, and 2.0.20 will all be accepted. ~> 2 will match any version whose major number is 2; 2.0, 2.1, and 2.10 will all be accepted.

A library is supposed to increment its major or minor version whenever the published API changes, so ~> is designed to let you require a particular version of a library's API. This is slightly more restrictive than requiring a minimum version, and is useful if the API changes drastically between versions, or if you anticipate incompatible changes in the future.

Since a single Ruby installation can have multiple versions of a single gem installed at once, there's no technical reason (other than disk space) why you can't make your users install the exact same versions of the gems you used to develop your program:

```
require_gem 'gem_1' '= 1.0.1'
require_gem 'gem_2' '= 2.6'
require_gem 'gem_3' '= 1.3.2'
```

However, it's usually not necessary, and such draconian specificity imposes burdens on the programmers as well as the users. It's usually better to use >= or ~>.

If a particular version of a library has an awful bug in it, you can refuse to use it with code like this:

```
require_gem 'buggy' '!=1.0.3'
```

You can combine comparison operators by making multiple calls to require_gem. For instance, you can simulate ~> with two calls:

```
require_gem 'my_gem' '>= 2.0'
require_gem 'my_gem' '< 3'
```

See Also

- Recipe 18.2, "Installing and Using a Gem," for information on using the version requirement strings to install the appropriate version of a gem
- The Facets Core library defines a String#natcmp that can compare version numbers: that is, "1.10.0" will show up as being less than "1.2.0"

18.4   Uninstalling a Gem

Problem

You want to remove an installed gem from your Ruby installation.

Solution

From the command line, use the gem uninstall command:

```
$ gem uninstall blinkenlights
Attempting to uninstall gem 'blinkenlights'
Successfully uninstalled blinkenlights version 0.0.2
```

From Ruby code, the most reliable way to uninstall a gem is to simulate a command-line invocation with the Gem::GemRunner class. This code installs a gem, then immediately removes it:

```
require 'rubygems'
require 'rubygems/installer'
require 'rubygems/remote_installer'
Gem::RemoteInstaller.new.install('blinkenlights')

require 'rubygems/gem_runner'
require 'rubygems/doc_manager'
Gem.manage_gems
Gem::GemRunner.new.run(['uninstall', 'blinkenlights'])
# Successfully uninstalled blinkenlights version 0.0.4
```

Uninstalling a gem can disrupt the normal workings of your Ruby programs, so I recommend you only uninstall gems from the command line. That way, there's less chance of a bug wiping out all your gems.

Discussion

Since rubygems can manage multiple installed versions of the same gem, you won't usually have to remove old copies of gems. There are three main reasons to remove gems:

1. You find out that a particular version of a gem is buggy, and you want to make sure it never gets used.
2. You want to save disk space.
3. You want to clean up the list of installed gems so that it's more obvious which gems you actually use.

If uninstalling a gem would leave another installed gem with an unmet dependency, you'll be told about the dependency and asked whether you want to go through with the uninstall anyway. You'll get this interactive prompt whether you run the gem uninstall command or whether you use the Gem::Uninstaller class from Ruby code.

```
Gem::Uninstaller.new('actionpack', {}).uninstall
# You have requested to uninstall the gem:
```

```
#        actionpack-1.8.1
# actionmailer-0.9.1 depends on [actionpack (= 1.8.1)]
# If you remove this gem, the dependency will not be met.
# Uninstall anyway? [yN]
```

The sources gem is a special gem that tells rubygems to look for remotely installable gems at *http://gems.rubyforge.org/* by default. If you uninstall this gem, you won't be able to install any more gems, except through complicated hacks of the classes in the Gem module. Just don't do it. Not even if you never plan to install any gems from rubyforge.org. Not even if you'd never thought of doing it until I brought it up in this recipe, and now you're curious.

You did it, didn't you? Now you'll have to reinstall rubygems by rerunning its `setup.rb` script.

18.5 Reading Documentation for Installed Gems

Problem

You want to read the RDoc documentation for the gems you have installed. Although some gem projects provide human-written documentation like tutorials, the generated RDoc documentation isn't usually available online.

Solution

RDoc documentation isn't usually available online because when you install a gem, Ruby generates your very own HTML copy of the RDoc documentation and installs it along with the software. The documentation you need is probably already on your computer.

The simplest way to browse the documentation for your installed gems is to run the `gem_server` command, then visit *http://localhost:8808/*. You'll see all your installed gems in a table form, and be able to browse the generated documentation of each gem that provides any.

Otherwise, you can find your Rubygems documentation directory, and browse the installed documentation with local filesystem tools.

Discussion

The generated rdoc for a gem is kept in the doc/ subdirectory of the base directory in which the gem was installed. For instance, on my computer, gems are installed in /usr/lib/ruby/gems/1.8/. For every gem that has RDoc, the generated HTML documentation will be kept in the directory /usr/lib/ruby/gems/1.8/doc/[gem name]/rdoc/. If I were to install one particular gem to another directory, the documentation for the gem would be in a doc/ subdirectory of that directory.

Here's some code that prints out the location of the RDoc files for every installed gem. Unless you've installed specific gems in nonstandard locations, they'll all be in the doc/ subdirectory of Gem.dir. This code snippet also shows off some of the capabilities of Gem::DocManager, the Ruby class you can use to manipulate a gem's RDoc.

```ruby
require 'rubygems'
Gem.manage_gems

def show_gem_rdoc
  puts "Your generated docs are all probably in #{File.join(Gem.dir, "doc")}"

  puts "Just to be safe, I'll print out every gem's RDoc location:"
  specifications_dir = File.join(Gem.dir, 'specifications')
  lacking_rdoc = []
  Gem::SourceIndex.from_installed_gems(specifications_dir).each do |path, spec|
    manager = Gem::DocManager.new(spec)
    if manager.rdoc_installed?
      doc_path = File.join(spec.installation_path, 'doc', spec.full_name)
      puts " #{spec.full_name} => #{doc_path}"
    else
      lacking_rdoc << spec.full_name
    end
  end

  unless lacking_rdoc.empty?
    puts "\nThese installed gems have no RDoc installed:"
    puts " #{lacking_rdoc.join("\n ")}"
  end
end

show_gem_rdoc
# Your generated RDoc is probably all in /usr/lib/ruby/gems/1.8/doc
# Just to be safe, I'll print out every gem's RDoc location:
#  flexmock-0.1.7 => /usr/lib/ruby/gems/1.8/doc/flexmock-0.1.7
#  simple-rss-1.1 => /usr/lib/ruby/gems/1.8/doc/simple-rss-1.1
#  classifier-1.3.0 => /usr/lib/ruby/gems/1.8/doc/classifier-1.3.0
#  actionmailer-1.1.5 => /usr/lib/ruby/gems/1.8/doc/actionmailer-1.1.5
# ...
#
# These installed gems have no RDoc installed:
#  Ruby-MemCache-0.0.1
#  RedCloth-3.0.4
#  sources-0.0.1
# ...
```

RDoc is generated for most gems whether or not the author was careful to add RDoc descriptions to all their Ruby code. At minimum, a gem's RDoc will list the classes and methods present in the gem, which is useful in a bare-bones way.

If you don't want to generate RDoc when you install a gem, pass in the --no-rdoc argument to the gem install command. The only real reason to do this is a concern for disk space.

The flip side of reading a gem's documentation is writing it. When you're writing your gemspec (see Recipe 18.6), you should set spec.has_rdoc = true. This will let the end user's gem installer know that your gem was written with RDoc in mind. It doesn't do much except suppress a warning during the installation of your gem.

See Also

- The Ruby Standard Library Documentation collection (*http://www.ruby-doc.org/ stdlib/*) contains generated HTML for the RDoc of all the packages in the Ruby standard library: it includes everything in lib/ruby/, but it doesn't include the core application
- Recipe 17.11, "Documenting Your Application"
- Recipe 18.6, "Packaging Your Code as a Gem"
- Recipe 19.2, "Automatically Generating Documentation"

18.6 Packaging Your Code as a Gem

Problem

You want to package a program you wrote as a Ruby gem, possibly to distribute it on the main gem server at rubyforge.org.

Solution

First, you must write a specification file. This file consists of a few lines of Ruby code that instantiate a Gem::Specification object and populate it with information about your program. Assuming that all of your program's files are in a subdirectory called lib/, the following might make a good specification file:

```
# shielding.gemspec
require 'rubygems'
spec = Gem::Specification.new do |spec|
  spec.name = 'shielding'
  spec.summary = 'A library for calculating the strength of duophasic shielding'
  spec.description = %{This library calculates to high precision the
  physical and electrostatic strength of a duophasic shield. It knows
  about most real-world shield configurations, as well as many
  theoretical arrangements not yet built.}
  spec.author = 'Bob Zaff'
  spec.email = 'zaff@example.com'
  spec.homepage = 'http://www.example.com/software/shielding/'
  spec.files = Dir['lib/*.rb']
  spec.version = '1.0.0'
end
```

You can then use the gem build command to create the actual gem from its specification file:

```
$ gem build shielding.gemspec
Attempting to build gem spec 'shielding.gemspec'
  Successfully built RubyGem
  Name: shielding
  Version: 1.0.0
  File: shielding-1.0.0.gem

$ ls
shield.gemspec  shielding-1.0.0.gem
```

Then install the gem normally:

```
$ gem install ./shielding-1.0.0.gem
Attempting local installation of './shielding-1.0.0.gem'
Successfully installed shielding, version 1.0.0
Installing RDoc documentation for shielding-1.0.0...
WARNING: Generating RDoc on .gem that may not have RDoc.
```

You can also build a gem from within Ruby code by passing the completed Gem::Specification into a Gem::Builder object.

```
require 'rubygems/builder'
builder = Gem::Builder.new(spec).build
# Successfully built RubyGem
# Name: shielding
# Version: 1.0.0
# File: shielding-1.0.0.gem
# => "shielding-1.0.0.gem"
```

Gem::Builder is useful as a starting point for automating your releases, but if you're interested in doing that, you should use Rake (see Chapter 19, especially Recipe 19.4).

Discussion

Other recipes in this chapter query gem repositories for information and get it back in the form of Gem::Specification objects. To create your own Ruby gem, you need to create a Gem::Specification object from scratch. A file that defines a Gem::Specification object is called a "gemspec" and it usually has a .gemspec extension.

To make a Gem::Specification object that can be turned into a gem, you must define the four attributes name, summary, version, and files. The version attribute should be a string of the form "[major version].[minor version].[revision]"; this is the recommended form for version numbers of software products packaged as gems (see Recipe 18.3).

I recommend you also define author, email, description, and possibly homepage. The description attribute advertises your gem, and the other three attributes give a way for your users to get in touch with you.

Some other tips on creating your gemspec:

- If you want a user to be able to require a file from their own Ruby code, put it into the lib/ subdirectory of your project. If you put it into some other directory, you'll need to add the name of that directory to the require_paths attribute.

- If you want a user to be able to run a file as a Ruby script, put it into the bin/ subdirectory of your project. If you put it into some other directory, you'll need to change the bindir attribute.

- If the code in your gem has associated unit tests, put the names of the test files into an array as the test_files attribute. It's also a good idea to keep those files together in a test/ subdirectory. Once the gem is installed, you can run its tests by issuing the command gem check -t [gem name].

- Ruby automatically generates a set of RDoc HTML pages for all the Ruby classes and files in your gem. Unless you set the has_rdoc attribute, when you install the gem you'll get a "WARNING: Generating RDoc on .gem that may not have RDoc."

  You can take advantage of the RDoc generation by linking nonRDoc files from the RDoc site: just name those files in the array extra_rdoc_files. If your gem comes with a README file or other nonRDoc documentation, it's a good idea to include that with the RDoc, since that's where most people will look first for documentation.

- The files attribute should be an array that includes every file you want to be packaged in the gem. If you included any files in test_files or extra_rdoc_files, you must include them again here or they won't actually be installed. The simplest way to do this is to define files last of all, and stick test_files and extra_rdoc_files inside:

  ```
  spec.test_files = Dir['test/*.rb']
  spec.extra_rdoc_files = ['README']
  spec.files = Dir['lib/*.rb'] + spec.test_files + spec.extra_rdoc_files
  ```

- If your gem requires another gem to work, the spec file is where you define the dependency. Use the Gem::Specification#add_dependency method rather than modifying the dependencies attribute directly. The add_dependency method accepts an optional version restriction, in a format that should be familiar to you if you've read other recipes in this chapter. You can use a version restriction to make sure your gem is only used with certain versions of another gem.

  ```
  spec.add_dependency('another_gem')
  spec.add_dependency('yet_another_gem', '~> 3.0')
  # Any version will do.
  # Must be 3.0.x series.
  ```

See Also

- The Gemspec reference (*http://docs.rubygems.org/read/chapter/20*)
- Recipe 18.3, "Requiring a Specific Version of a Gem"
- Recipe 18.7, "Distributing Your Gems"
- Recipe 19.4, "Automatically Building a Gem"

18.7 Distributing Your Gems

Problem

You've packaged your software as a Ruby gem, but nobody knows about it. You want to make your gem easy to find and install, so that your genius does not go unrecognized.

Solution

The simplest solution (for you, at least) is to upload your .gem file to a web site or FTP site. Your users can download the .gem file, then install it by passing the filename into the gem install command:

```
$ wget http://www.example.com/gems/my_gem-1.0.4.gem
--10:40:10--  http://www.example.com/gems/my_gem-1.0.4.gem
           => `my_gem-1.0.4.gem'
Resolving gems.example.com... 204.127.202.4
Connecting to gems.example.com|204.127.202.4|:80... connected.
HTTP request sent, awaiting response... 200 OK
Length: 40,823 (40K) [text/plain]

100%[====================================>] 40,823        46.96K/s

10:40:11 (46.85 KB/s) - `my_gem-1.0.4.gem' saved [40823/40823]

$ gem install ./my_gem-1.0.4.gem
Attempting local installation of './my_gem-1.0.4.gem'
Successfully installed my_gem, version 1.0.4
Installing RDoc documentation for my_gem-1.0.4...
```

If your gem has dependencies, the end user must separately install the dependencies before installing a downloaded gem, or the gem command will become confused and die. This will happen even if the user specifies the --include-dependencies flag:

```
$ gem install --include-dependencies ./my_gem_with_dependency-1.0.0.gem
Attempting local installation of './my_gem_with_dependency.1.0.0.gem'
ERROR: Error installing gem ./my_gem_with_dependency-1.0.0.gem[.gem]:
  my_gem_with_dependency requires my_dependency > 0.0.0
```

If you distribute your gem from a web site, be sure to set the homepage attribute in your gemspec file.

Discussion

Gems are usually distributed through HTTP. A web server might serve standalone .gem files intended for download by the end user, or it might also serve some metadata that allows the gem command to download and install gems on its own.

There are several ways of setting up gems for distribution. In general you must negotiate a tradeoff between the developer's (your) convenience and the end user's ease of installation. The Rubygems package makes it easy to install and manage third-party Ruby packages, but the developers of those packages have to jump through some hoops if they want to make the installation process as transparent as possible.

Simply uploading the raw gem files to your web site is the simplest solution from your point of view (assuming you already have a web site), but it's less convenient for your users. This is especially true if your gem has dependencies. The most convenient solution for the end user is for you to upload your gem to the rubyforge.org site. Whenever you upload a .gem file to a project on this site, it is automatically mirrored to the canonical rubygems repository at *http://gems.rubyforge.org/gems/*. This is where the rubygems package looks for gems by default.

However, getting your gem onto rubyforge.org is more complicated than uploading a gem to your own web site. You must first sign up for a RubyForge account, giving the administrators your personal information. You must then submit a project (the name of the project should go into the rubyforge_project attribute in your gemspec) and have it approved by the site administrators.

Once your RubyForge project is set up, you can use the web interface to "create a new release" for your project, then upload your prebuilt gem to your project's file repository. Within a few minutes to a few hours, your gem will be mirrored to the main gem repository. From that point on, anybody with the rubygems package and Internet access can install your gem, along with any dependencies, simply by running gem install your_gem --include-dependencies. But for your smaller projects, the work you have to do to get to this point may seem like overkill.

A compromise is to host the gem yourself on an existing web server, and also host the YAML metadata that lets the gem command locate, download, and install gems on its own. You can generate the YAML metadata with the generate_yaml_index.rb script that comes with the rubygems package. Put all your gems into a *gems/* directory somewhere in your webspace, and pass in the parent of the *gems/* directory as the --dir argument to generate_yaml_index.rb.

```
$ cd ~/public_html/
$ mkdir gems
$ cp ~/mygem-1.0.0.gem gems/
$ generate_yaml_index.rb --dir=~/public_html/ --verbose
Building yaml file
   ... adding mygem-1.0.0
```

```
Building yaml.Z file
$ ls yaml*
yaml  yaml.Z
```

The yaml and yaml.Z files are intended for download by the various gem commands. Simply tell your users to pass in an appropriate `--source` argument to gem, and they'll be able to install gems from your web space just as they can from the canonical repository at RubyForge

The `--source` argument should correspond to the directory in your webspace that contains the yaml and yaml.Z files. For instance, if your *~/public_html/* directory in the example above corresponds to the URL *http://www.example.com/~leonardr/*, you should ask your users to install your gems with `gem install --source=http://www.example.com/~leonardr/`. Passing in a `--source` is more work than just getting everything from RubyForge, but once the user knows the URL, it's not *much* more.

Note, however, that one invocation of the gem `install` command can only load gems from a single source. If you're hosting a gem that depends on other gems, you must assume the user has already installed the dependencies, or else provide copies of the dependency gems in the same *gems/* directory as your own gems. If gem `install` is given a `--source` argument, it won't know to look at gems.rubyforge.org as a backup.

If you don't already have a web site, you can run a special web server that only serves gems. The rubygems package comes with an application called gem_server that acts as a web server providing copies of all the gems installed on your system. The best way to use this is as a private gem repository that distributes in-house Ruby gems throughout your team or organization.

See Also

- Recipe 18.2, "Installing and Using a Gem"
- Recipe 18.6, "Packaging Your Code as a Gem"
- A tutorial for running a gem server as a Windows service (*http://rubyforge.org/docman/view.php/85/126/gemserver_tutorial.txt*)

18.8 Installing and Creating Standalone Packages with setup.rb

Problem

You want to install a Ruby package that includes a setup.rb script instead of being packaged as a Ruby gem. Or, you want to make it possible for people to install your software package without having to install Ruby gems.

Solution

To install a `setup-rb`–based Ruby package as root or the administrative user, simply run the `setup.rb` script:

```
$ ruby setup.rb
```

By default, `setup.rb` installs a package into your *site_ruby* directory. If you don't have root access or only want to install the package for your own use, you can install the package into your home directory, like this:

```
$ ruby setup.rb all --installdirs=home
```

That command installs the package into the *lib/ruby/* subdirectory of your home directory. Make sure you have that directory included in your `RUBYLIB` environment variable, or Ruby won't know to look there when you `require` a library. You can check your library path with the special `$:` global variable:

```
$:
# => ["/home/leonardr/lib/ruby", "/usr/local/lib/site_ruby/1.8", ... ]
require 'installed_via_setup'
# => true
```

Discussion

Because Ruby gems are not yet part of the standard Ruby library, some people prefer to package their software releases as self-contained archives. A package that includes a `setup.rb` installation script contains all the code and data necessary for installation; it might have dependencies, but it doesn't rely on another component just to get itself installed. The `rubygems` package itself is installed via `setup.rb`, since it can't assume that the system already supports gem-based installations.

You might also use a `setup.rb` script instead of a Ruby gem if you want to add Ruby hook scripts to the installation procedure. For instance, you might want to create a new database when your package is installed. Once the Rubygems package is included in the Ruby standard library, this will be just about the only reason left not to package all your software as Ruby gems. Even native C extensions can be included in a Ruby gem and built as part of the gem installation.

Ruby gems and `setup.rb` impose similar file structures on your package: your Ruby libraries go into a `lib/` subdirectory, command-line applications go into a `bin/` subdirectory, and unit tests go into a *tests/* subdirectory.

To use `setup.rb`, simply arrange your package to conform with its file stucture, and copy the `setup.rb` file itself into the top-level directory of your package.

`setup.rb` works kind of like a Unix Makefile: it has various tasks like `test`, `clean`, `install`, and `all` that are triggered when the user runs `setup.rb` with certain options. You can put a pre- or post-hook into any task by creating a Ruby script called "pre-[task].rb" or "post-[task].rb". All such files will be run before or after the appropriate task.

Here's a simple example. I've created a small package with the following layout:

```
setup.rb
post-clean.rb
lib/
lib/installed_via_setup.rb
lib/pre-config.rb
bin/
bin/command.rb
```

I've got a library, a command-line script, a hook script `pre-config.rb` that needs to run before the `config` task, and a second hook script `post-clean.rb` that needs to run after the `clean` task. The hook scripts simply print out the messages "Pre-config hook called" and "Post-clean hook called".

When I run the clean task, with the command `ruby setup.rb clean`, I see the following output:

```
$ ruby setup.rb clean
---> bin
<--- bin
---> lib
<--- lib
Post-clean hook called.
rm -f .config
rm -f InstalledFiles
```

When I run `setup.rb` without specifying a task, I see the following output:

```
$ ruby setup.rb
...
Pre-configuration hook called.
...
rm -f InstalledFiles
---> bin
mkdir -p /usr/bin/
install command.rb /usr/bin/
<--- bin
---> lib
mkdir -p /usr/local/lib/site_ruby/1.8/
install installed_via_setup.rb /usr/local/lib/site_ruby/1.8/
```

My command-line program gets installed into /usr/bin/, and my library file into site_ruby. The preconfiguration hook script gets called because the default task, `all`, simply runs three other tasks: `config` (triggering the hook script), `setup`, and `install`.

Once I've run `ruby setup.rb`, I am free to `require 'installed_via_setup'` from within any Ruby program, and to invoke `command.rb` from the command line.

There's no easy way to uninstall a package installed with `setup.rb`; you need to delete the files manually.

One final thing to watch out for: standalone Ruby packages created before about 2004 may be installed via a script called install.rb. This script works much the same way as setup.rb. The two scripts were both written by Minero Aoki and are both part of the setup.rb package, but install.rb was intended for smaller-scale installations. As of late 2003, the two scripts were merged, so now you only have to worry about setup.rb.

See Also

- Many of the packages on the Ruby Application Archive use setup.rb, while most of the packages on rubyforge.org are packaged as gems (*http://raa.ruby-lang.org/*)

- The "setup.rb User Manual" describes how to run and create setup.rb scripts (*http://i.loveruby.net/en/projects/setup/doc/*)

- If you want to write setup.rb hook scripts, see the hook script API at *http://i.loveruby.net/en/projects/setup/doc/hookapi.html*

Automating Tasks with Rake

Even when your software is written, tested, and packaged, you're still not done. You've got to start working on the next version, and the next... Every release you do, in some cases every change you make to your code, will send you running through a maze of repetitive tasks that have nothing to do with programming.

Fortunately, there's a way to automate these tasks, and the best part is that you can do it by writing more Ruby code. The answer is Rake.

Rake is a build language, Ruby's answer to Unix make and Java's Ant. It lets you define *tasks*: named code bocks that carry out specific actions, like building a gem or running a set of unit tests. Invoke Rake, and your predefined tasks will happily do the work you once did: compiling C extensions, splicing files together, running unit tests, or packaging a new release of your software. If you can define it, Rake can run it.

Rake is available as the rake gem; if you've installed Rails, you already have it. Unlike most gems, it doesn't just install libraries: it installs a command-line program called rake, which contains the logic for actually performing Rake tasks. For ease of use, you may need to add to your PATH environment variable the directory containing the rake script: something like /usr/lib/ruby/gems/1.8/gems/rake-0.6.2/bin/. That way you can just run rake from the command line.

A Rakefile is just a Ruby source file that has access to some special methods: task, file, directory, and a few others. Calling one of these methods defines a task, which can be run by the command-line rake program, or called as a dependency by other tasks.

The most commonly used method is the generic one: task. This method takes the name of the task to define, and a code block that implements the task. Here's a simple Rakefile that defines two tasks, cross_bridge and build_bridge, one of which depends on the other. It designates cross_bridge as the default task by defining a third task called default which does nothing except depend on cross_bridge.

```
# Rakefile
desc "Cross the bridge."
task :cross_bridge => [:build_bridge] do
```

```
    puts "I'm crossing the bridge."
  end

  desc "Build the bridge"
  task :build_bridge do
    puts 'Bridge construction is complete.'
  end

  task :default => [:cross_bridge]
```

Call this file Rakefile, and it'll be automatically picked up by the rake command
when you run the command in its directory. Here are some sample runs:

```
$ rake
Bridge construction is complete.
I'm crossing the bridge.

$ rake build_bridge
Bridge construction is complete.
```

Note all the stuff I didn't have to do. I didn't have to write code to process command-
line options and run the appropriate tasks: the rake command does that. The rake
command also takes care of loading the Rake libraries, so I didn't have to recite
require statements at the beginning of my Rakefile. I certainly didn't have to learn a
whole new programming language or a new file format: just one new Ruby method
and its arguments.

Adapt the recipes in this chapter to your project's Rakefile, and a lot of the auxilliary
work that surrounds a software project will simply disappear. You won't have to
remember to run unit tests or generate documentation after every change, because it
will happen as a side effect of things you do anyway. If your unit tests fail, so will
your attempt to release your project, and you won't be embarrassed by bugs.

Whenever you ask yourself: "What was the command to ...?", just invoke rake with
the -T option. It will print a list of available tasks and a description of each:

```
$ rake -T
(in /home/leonardr/my_project/)
rake build_bridge  # Build the bridge.
rake cross_bridge  # Cross the bridge.
```

Nothing says you can only use Rake in Ruby projects. Most Rake tasks simply run
external programs and move disk files around: the same things tasks do in other build
languages. You can use Rake as a replacement for make, build static web sites with it, or
automate any other repetitive action made up of smaller, interlocking actions.

Here are some more resources for automating tasks with Ruby:

- The site *http://docs.rubyrake.org/* provides a tutorial, a user guide, and examples
  for Rake.
- The generated RDoc for Rake has a good overview of the special methods available to Rakefiles (*http://rake.rubyforge.org/files/doc/rakefile_rdoc.html*)

19.1 Automatically Running Unit Tests

Credit: Pat Eyler

Problem

You want to make it easy to run your project's unit test suite. You also want the tests to run automatically before you do a new release of your project.

Solution

Require the `rake/testtask` library and create a new `Rake::TestTask`. Save the following code in a file called `Rakefile` in the project's top-level directory (or add it to your existing Rakefile).

```
require 'rake/testtask'

Rake::TestTask.new('test') do |t|
  t.pattern = 'test/**/tc_*.rb'
  t.warning = true
end
```

This Rakefile makes two assumptions:

1. The `Test::Unit` test cases live in files under the `test` directory (and its subdirectories). The names of these files start with `tc_` and end in `.rb`.

2. The Ruby libraries to be tested live under the `lib` directory. Rake automatically appends this directoy to Ruby's load path, the list of directories that Ruby searches when you try to require a library.

To execute your test cases, run the command `rake test` in the project's top-level directory. The tests are loaded by a new Ruby interpreter with warnings enabled. The output is the same as you'd see from `Test::Unit`'s console runner.

Discussion

If it's easy to trigger the test process, you'll run your tests more often, and you'll detect problems sooner. Rake makes it really convenient to run your tests.

We can make the test command even shorter by defining a *default* task. Just add the following line to the Rakefile. The position within the file doesn't matter, but to keep things clear, you should put it before other task definitions:

```
task "default" => ["test"]
```

Now, whenever we run rake without an argument, it will invoke the test task. If your Rakefile already has a default task, you should be able to just add the test task to its list of prerequisites. Similarly, if you have a task that packages a new release of your software (like the one defined in Recipe 19.4), you can make the test task a prerequisite. If your tests fail, your package won't be built and you won't release a buggy piece of software.

The `Rake::TestTask` has a special attribute, `libs`; the entries in this array are added to Ruby's load path. As mentioned above, the default value is `["lib"]`, making it possible for your tests to require files in your project's `lib/` subdirectory. Sometimes this default is not enough. Your Ruby code might not be in the `lib/` subdirectory. Or worse, your test code might change the current working directory. Since `lib/` is a relative path, the default value of `libs` would start out as a valid source for library files, and then stop being valid when the test code changed the working directory.

We can solve this problem by specifying the absolute path to the project's lib directory in the `Rakefile`. Using an absolute path is generally more stable. In this sample `Rakefile`, we give the load path the absolute path to the `lib` and `test` subdirectories. Adding the test directory to the load path is useful if you need to require a library full of test utility methods:

```
require 'rake/testtask'

lib_dir = File.expand_path('lib')
test_dir = File.expand_path('test')

Rake::TestTask.new("test") do |t|
    t.libs = [lib_dir, test_dir]
    t.pattern = "test/**/tc_*.rb"
    t.warning = true
end
```

Test suites

As a project grows, it takes longer and longer to run all the test cases. This is bad for the habit we're trying to inculcate, where you run the tests whenever you make a change. To solve this problem, group the test cases into *test suites*. Depending on the project, you might have a test suite of all test cases concerning file I/O, another suite for the console interface, and so on.

Let's say that when you're working on the `DataFile` class, you can get away with only running the file I/O test suite. But before releasing a new version of the software, you need to run all the test cases.

To create a Rake test suite, instantiate a `Rake::TestTask` instance, and set the `test_files` attribute to something other than the complete list of test files. This sample `Rakefile` splits up the test files into two suites.

```
require 'rake/testtask'

Rake::TestTask.new('test-file') do |t|
    t.test_files = ['test/tc_datafile.rb',
                    'test/tc_datafilewriter.rb',
                    'test/tc_datafilereader.rb']
```

```
        t.warning = true
    end

    Rake::TestTask.new('test-console') do |t|
        t.test_files = ['test/tc_console.rb',
                        'test/tc_prettyprinter.rb']
        t.warning = true
    end
```

Invoking rake test-file runs the tests related to file I/O, and invoking rake test-console tests the console interface. The only thing missing is a task that runs all tests. You can either use the all-inclusive task from the Rakefile given in the Solution, or you can create a task that has all the test suites as prerequisites:

```
    task 'test' => ['test-file', 'test-console']
```

When this test task is invoked, Rake runs the test-file suite and then the test-console suite. Each suite is run in its own Ruby interpreter.

See Also

- Recipe 17.8, "Running Unit Tests"
- For a guide to the options available to the TestTask class, consult its RDoc; it's available at, for instance, *http://rake.rubyforge.org/classes/Rake/TestTask.html*

19.2   Automatically Generating Documentation

Credit: Stefan Lang

Problem

You want to automatically create HTML pages from the RDoc formatted comments in your code, and from other RDoc formatted files.

Solution

Within your Rakefile, require the rake/rdoctask library and create a new Rake:: RDocTask. Here's a typical example:

```
    require 'rake/rdoctask'

    Rake::RDocTask.new('rdoc') do |t|
      t.rdoc_files.include('README', 'lib/**/*.rb')
      t.main = 'README'
      t.title = "MyLib API documentation"
    end
```

Now you can run the command rake rdoc from a shell in your project's top-level directory. This particular Rake task creates API documentation for all files under the *lib* directory (and its subdirectories) whose names end in .rb. Additionally, the

RDoc-formatted contents of the top-level README file will appear on the front page of the documentation.

The HTML output files are written under your project's *%(filename)html%* directory. To read the documentation, point your browser to *%(filename)html/index.html%*. The browser will show "MyLib API documentation" (that is, the value of the task's `title`) as the page title.

Discussion

It is common practice among authors of Ruby libraries to document a library's API with RDoc-formatted text. Since Ruby 1.8.1, a standard Ruby installation contains the rdoc tool, which extracts the RDoc comments from source code and creates nicely formatted HTML pages.

Unlike the tasks you define from scratch with the `task` method, but like the `TestTask` covered in Recipe 19.1, `Rake::RDocTask.new` takes a code block, which is executed immediately at task definition time. The code block lets you customize how your RDoc documentation should look. After running your code block, the `Rake::RDocTask` object defines *three* new Rake tasks:

rdoc
    Updates the HTML documentation by running RDoc.

clobber_rdoc
    Removes the directory and its contents created by the rdoc task.

rerdoc
    Force a rebuild of the HTML-documentation. Has the same effect as running clobber_rdoc followed by rdoc.

Now we know enough to integrate the `Rake::RDocTask` into a more useful Rakefile. Suppose we want a task that uploads the documentation to RubyForge (or another site), and a general cleanup task that removes the generated HTML-documentation as well as all backup files in the project directory. To keep the example simple, I've inserted comments instead of the actual commands for uploading and removing the files; see Recipes 19.3 and 19.8 for more realistic examples.

```
require 'rake/rdoctask'

Rake::RDocTask.new('rdoc') do |t|
  t.rdoc_files.include('README', 'lib/**/*.rb')
  t.main = 'README'
  t.title = "MyLib API documentation"
end

desc 'Upload documentation to RubyForge.'
task 'upload' => 'rdoc' do
    # command(s) to upload html/ and contents to RubyForge
end
```

```
desc 'Remove generated and backup files.'
task 'clobber' => 'clobber_rdoc' do
    # command(s) to remove all files ending in ~ or .bak
end
```

Finally, we make the default task dependent on the rdoc task, so that RDoc gets built automatically when you invoke rake with no task. If there already is a default task, this code will simply add another dependency to the existing task:

```
task :default => ['rdoc']
```

Available attributes

Here's a list of attributes that can be set in the block given to Rake::RDocTask.new.

rdoc_dir
> Name of the directory where the produced HTML files go. Defaults to *html*.

title
> A title for the produced HTML pages.

main
> Name of the input file whose contents should appear at the initial page of the HTML output.

template
> Name of the template to be used by RDoc.

rdoc_files
> Initialized to an empty filelist. Just call the include method with the names of files to be documented, or glob patterns matching multiple files.

options
> An array of arguments to be passed directly to rdoc. Use this if none of the other attributes fits your needs. Run rdoc --help for a list of available options.

See Also

- Recipe 19.3, "Cleaning Up Generated Files"
- Recipe 19.8, "A Generic Project Rakefile"
- The RDoc documentation for the Rake::RDocTask class (*http://rake.rubyforge.org/classes/Rake/RDocTask.html*)

19.3 Cleaning Up Generated Files

Credit: Stefan Lang

Problem

You want to clean up files that aren't actually part of your project: generated files, backup files, and so on.

Solution

Within your Rakefile, require the rake/clean library to get access to the clean and clobber tasks. Put glob patterns for all your generated files in the CLOBBER FileList. Put glob patterns for all other scratch files in the CLEAN FileList.

By default, CLEAN also includes the patterns **/*~, **/*.bak, and **/core. Here's a typical set of CLOBBER and CLEAN files:

```
require 'rake/clean'

# Include the "pkg" and "doc" directories and their contents.
# Include all files ending in ".o" in the current directory
#  and its subdirectories (recursively).
CLOBBER.include('pkg', 'doc', '**/*.o')

# Include InstalledFiles and .config: files created by setup.rb.
# Include temporary files created during test run.
CLEAN.include('InstalledFiles', '.config', 'test/**/*.tmp')
```

Run rake clean to remove all files specified by the CLEAN filelist, and rake clobber to remove the files specified by *both* file lists.

Discussion

The rake/clean library initializes the constants CLEAN and CLOBBER to new Rake:: FileList instances. It also defines the tasks clean and clobber, making clean a prerequisite of clobber. The idea is that rake clean removes any files that might need to be recreated once your program changes, while rake clobber returns your source tree to a completely pristine state.

Other Rake libraries define cleanup tasks that remove certain products of their main tasks. An example: the packaging libraries create a task called clobber_package, and make it a prerequisite of clobber. Running rake clobber on such a project removes the package files: you don't have to explicitly include them in your CLOBBER list.

You can do the same thing for your own tasks: rather than manipulate CLEAN and CLOBBER, you can create a custom cleanup task and make it a prerequisite of clean or clobber. The following code is a different way of making sure that rake clobber removes any precompiled object files:

```
desc 'Remove all object files.'
task 'clobber_objects' do
  rm_f FileList['**/*.o']
end

# Make clobber_objects a prerequisite of the preexisting clobber task
task 'clobber' => 'clobber_objects'
```

Now you can run rake clobber_objects to remove all object files, and rake clobber to remove all other unwanted files as well.

See Also

- The documentation for the `Dir.glob` method describes the format for the patterns accepted by `FileList#include`; it's accessible via `ri Dir.glob`
- Online documentation for the `rake/clean` library (*http://rake.rubyforge.org/files/lib/rake/clean_rb.html*)

19.4   Automatically Building a Gem

Credit: Stefan Lang

Problem

You want to automatically build a gem package for your application or library whenever you do a release.

Solution

Require the rake/gempackagetask library within your Rakefile, and create a Gem::Specification instance that describes your project. Feed it to the Rake::GemPackageTask constructor, which automatically defines a number of gem-related tasks:

```
require 'rake/gempackagetask'

# Create a gem specification
gem_spec = Gem::Specification.new do |s|
  s.name = 'docbook'
  s.version = '1.0.0'
  s.summary = 'DocBook formatting program and library.'

  # Files containing Test::Unit test cases.
  s.test_files = FileList['tests/**/*']

  # Executable scripts under the "bin" directory.
  s.executables = ['voc']

  # List of other files to be included.
  s.files = FileList['README', 'ChangeLog', 'lib/**/*.rb']
end

Rake::GemPackageTask.new(gem_spec) do |pkg|
  pkg.need_zip = false
  pkg.need_tar = false
end
```

Run the command rake package, and (assuming those files actually exist), Rake will build a gem file docbook-1.0.0.gem under the pkg/ directory.

Discussion

The RubyGems library provides the `Gem::Specification` class, and Rake provides the `Rake::GemPackageTask` class that uses it. Creating a new `Rake::GemPackageTask` object automatically defines the three tasks: package, `clobber_package`, and repackage.

The package task builds a gem inside the project's *pkg/* directory. The `clobber_package` task removes the *pkg/* directory and its contents. The repackage task just invokes `clobber_package` to remove any old package file, and then invokes package to rebuild them from scratch.

The example above sets to false the attributes `need_zip` and `need_tar` of the `Rake::GemPackageTask`. If you set them to true, then in addition to a gem you'll get a ZIP file and a gzipped tar archive containing the same files as the gem. Note that Rake uses the zip and tar command-line tools, so if your system doesn't provide them (the way a standard Windows installation doesn't), the package task won't be able to create these ZIP or tar archives.

The package task recreates a package file only if it doesn't already exist, or if you've updated one of your input files since you last built the package. The most common problem you'll run into here is that you'll decide to stop packaging a certain file. Rake won't recognize the change (since the file is gone), and running rake package won't do anything. To force a rebuild of your package file(s), run rake repackage.

See Also

- Recipe 18.6, "Packaging Your Code as a Gem"
- The `Gem::Specification` reference describes everything you can do when creating a gem (*http://docs.rubygems.org/read/chapter/20*)
- The Rake alternative Rant can build gems, ZIP files, and tarballs without calling out to external tools; point your browser to *http://make.ruby-co.de*

19.5 Gathering Statistics About Your Code

Credit: Stefan Lang

Problem

You want to gather statistics about your Ruby project, like the total number of lines of code.

Solution

Here's a class that parses Ruby source files and gathers statistics. Put this in `scriptlines.rb` in your project's top-level directory.

```ruby
# scriptlines.rb
# A ScriptLines instance analyses a Ruby script and maintains
# counters for the total number of lines, lines of code, etc.
class ScriptLines

  attr_reader :name
  attr_accessor :bytes, :lines, :lines_of_code, :comment_lines

  LINE_FORMAT = '%8s %8s %8s %8s   %s'

  def self.headline
    sprintf LINE_FORMAT, "BYTES", "LINES", "LOC", "COMMENT", "FILE"
  end

  # The 'name' argument is usually a filename
  def initialize(name)
    @name = name
    @bytes = 0
    @lines = 0      # total number of lines
    @lines_of_code = 0
    @comment_lines = 0
  end

  # Iterates over all the lines in io (io might be a file or a
  # string), analyses them and appropriately increases the counter
  # attributes.
  def read(io)
    in_multiline_comment = false
    io.each { |line|
      @lines += 1
      @bytes += line.size
      case line
      when /^=begin(\s|$)/
        in_multiline_comment = true
        @comment_lines += 1
      when /^=end(\s|$)/:
        @comment_lines += 1
        in_multiline_comment = false
      when /^\s*#/
        @comment_lines += 1
      when /^\s*$/
        # empty/whitespace only line
      else
        if in_multiline_comment
          @comment_lines += 1
        else
          @lines_of_code += 1
        end
      end
    }
  end

  # Get a new ScriptLines instance whose counters hold the
  # sum of self and other.
```

```
      def +(other)
        sum = self.dup
        sum.bytes += other.bytes
        sum.lines += other.lines
        sum.lines_of_code += other.lines_of_code
        sum.comment_lines += other.comment_lines
        sum
      end

      # Get a formatted string containing all counter numbers and the
      # name of this instance.
      def to_s
        sprintf LINE_FORMAT,
          @bytes, @lines, @lines_of_code, @comment_lines, @name
      end
    end
```

To tie the class into your build system, give your Rakefile a stats task like the following. This task assumes that the Rakefile and scriptlines.rb are in the same directory:

```
task 'stats' do
  require 'scriptlines'

  files = FileList['lib/**/*.rb']

  puts ScriptLines.headline
  sum = ScriptLines.new("TOTAL (#{files.size} file(s))")

  # Print stats for each file.
  files.each do |fn|
    File.open(fn) do |file|
      script_lines = ScriptLines.new(fn)
      script_lines.read(file)
      sum += script_lines
      puts script_lines
    end
  end

  # Print total stats.
  puts sum
end
```

Discussion

ScriptLines performs a very basic parsing of Ruby code: it divides a source file into blank lines, comment lines, and lines containing Ruby code. If you want more detailed information, you can include each file and get more information about the defined classes and methods with reflection or an extension like ParseTree.

Invoke the stats task to run all the Ruby scripts beneath your lib/ directory through ScriptLines. The following example output is for the highline library:

```
$ rake stats
(in /usr/local/lib/ruby/gems/1.8/gems/highline-1.0.1)
```

```
BYTES  LINES   LOC  COMMENT  FILE
18626    617   360      196  lib/highline.rb
12745    375   168      181  lib/highline/menu.rb
15760    430   181      227  lib/highline/question.rb
  801     25     7       14  lib/highline/import.rb
47932   1447   716      618  TOTAL (4 scripts)
```

BYTES is the file size in bytes, LINES the number of total lines in each file, LOC stands for "Lines Of Code," and COMMENT is the number of comment-only lines.

These simple metrics are good for gauging the complexity of a project, but don't use them as a measure of day-to-day progress. Complexity is not the same as progress, and a good day's work might consist of replacing a hundred lines of code with ten.

See Also

- `ri Kernel#sprintf`
- The RDoc documentation for Rake's `FileList` class (*http://rake.rubyforge.org/ classes/Rake/FileList.html*)
- The `ParseTree` extension (*http://rubyforge.org/projects/parsetree/*)

19.6 Publishing Your Documentation

Credit: Stefan Lang

Problem

You want to automatically update your project's web site on RubyForge (or some other site) with generated documentation or custom pages.

Solution

As seen in Recipe 19.2, Rake provides a `RDocTask` for generating RDoc documentation:

```
require 'rake/rdoctask'

html_dir = 'doc/html'
library = 'MyLib'
Rake::RDocTask.new('rdoc') do |t|
  t.rdoc_files.include('README', 'lib/**/*.rb')
  t.main = 'README'
  t.title = "#{library} API documentation"
  t.rdoc_dir = html_dir
end
```

To upload your generated documentation to RubyForge, use this task along with the upload-docs task defined below. The Unix scp command-line tool does the actual work of uploading:

```
# Define your RubyForge username and your project's Unix name here:
rubyforge_user = 'user'
rubyforge_project = 'project'
```

```
rubyforge_path = "/var/www/gforge-projects/#{rubyforge_project}/"
desc 'Upload documentation to RubyForge.'
task 'upload-docs' => ['rdoc'] do
    sh "scp -r #{html_dir}/* " +
        "#{rubyforge_user}@rubyforge.org:#{rubyforge_path}"
end
```

Discussion

Set off the publishing process by invoking rake upload-docs. The upload-docs task has the rdoc task as a prerequisite, so the HTML pages under doc/html/ will be created if necessary.

Then scp prompts for your RubyForge account password. Enter it, and all files under doc/html/ and its subdirectories will be uploaded to RubyForge. The docs will become available under *http://project.rubyforge.org/*, where "project" is the Unix name of your project. Now your users can read your RDoc online without having to generate it themselves. Your documentation will also show up in web search results.

Rake's sh method starts an instance of the OS's standard shell. This feature is used to run the scp command-line tool. This means that this recipe will only work if scp is installed on your system.

The scp command copies all the files that the RDoc placed under doc/html/, to the root of your project's web site on the RubyForge server. In effect, the main page of the API documentation will appear as your project's homepage. Some RubyForge projects don't have a custom homepage, so this is a good place to put the RDoc. If you want a custom homepage, just copy the RDoc into a different directory by changing rubyforge_path:

```
rubyforge_path = "/var/www/gforge-projects/#{rubyforge_project}/rdoc/"
```

You'll have to manually create the rdoc directory before you can use the scp shortcut. After that, the generated RDoc will show up at *http://project.rubyforge.org/rdoc/*, and you can link to it from your custom homepage with a relative link to rdoc/.

You can make Rake upload your custom homepage as well, of course. Just add an upload-site task that uploads your custom homepage and other web content. Make upload-site and upload-docs prerequisites of an overarching publish task:

```
website_dir = 'site'
desc 'Update project website to RubyForge.'
task 'upload-site' do
  sh "scp -r #{website_dir}/* " +
    "#{rubyforge_user}@rubyforge.org:/var/www/gforge-projects/project/"
end

desc 'Update API docs and project website to RubyForge.'
task 'publish' => ['upload-docs', 'upload-site']
```

Now you can run rake publish to update the generated API documentation, and upload it together with the rest of the web site to RubyForge. The publish task can be just one more prerequisite for an overarching release task.

Of course, you can use this same technique if you're using a web host other than RubyForge: just change the destination host of the scp command.

See Also

- Recipe 17.11, "Documenting Your Application," covers writing RDoc documentation
- Recipe 19.2, "Automatically Generating Documentation"

19.7 Running Multiple Tasks in Parallel

Problem

Your build process takes too long to run. Rake finishes copying one set of files only to start copying another set. You could save time by running these tasks in parallel, instead of stringing them one after another.

Solution

Define a task using the multitask function instead of task. Each of that task's prerequisites will be run in a separate thread.

In this code, I'll define two long-running tasks:

```
task 'copy_docs' do
  # Simulate a large disk copy.
  sleep 5
end

task 'compile_extensions' do
  # Simulate a C compiler compiling a bunch of files.
  sleep 10
end

task 'build_serial' => ['copy_docs', 'compile_extensions']
multitask 'build_parallel' => ['copy_docs', 'compile_extensions']
```

The build_serial task runs in about 15 seconds, but the build_parallel task does the same thing in about 10 seconds.

Discussion

A multitask runs just like a normal task, except that each of its dependencies runs in a separate thread. When running the dependencies of a multitask, Rake first finds any common secondary dependencies of these dependencies, and runs them first. It then spawns a separate thread for each dependency, so that they can run simultaneously.

Consider three tasks, ice_cream, cheese, and yogurt, all of which have a dependency on buy_milk. You can run the first three tasks in separate threads with a multitask, but Rake will run buy_milk before creating the threads. Otherwise, ice_cream, cheese, and yogurt would *all* trigger buy_milk, wasting time.

When your tasks spend a lot of time blocking on I/O operations (as many Rake tasks do), using a multitask can speed up your builds. Unfortunately, it can also cause the same problems you'll see with any multithreaded code. If you've got a fancy Rakefile, in which the tasks keep state inside Ruby data structures, you'll need to synchronize access to those data structures to prevent multithreading problems.

You may also have problems converting a task to a multitask if your dependencies are set up incorrectly. Take the following example:

```
task 'build' => ['compile_extensions', 'run_tests', 'generate_rdoc']
```

The unit tests can't run if the compiled extensions aren't available, so :compile_extensions shouldn't be in this list at all: it should be a dependency of :run_tests. You might not notice this problem as long as you're using task (because :compile_extensions runs before :run_tests anyway), but if you switch to a multitask your tests will start failing. Fixing your dependencies will solve the problem.

The multitask method is available only in Rake 0.7.0 and higher.

See Also

- Chapter 20

19.8 A Generic Project Rakefile

Credit: Stefan Lang

Every project's Rakefile is different, but most Ruby projects can be handled by very similar Rakefiles. To close out the chapter, we present a generic Rakefile that includes most of the tasks covered in this chapter, and a few (such as compilation of C extensions) that we only hinted at.

This Rakefile will work for pure Ruby projects, Ruby projects with C extensions, and projects that are *only* C extensions. It defines an overarching task called publish that builds the project, runs tests, generates RDoc, and releases the whole thing on Ruby-Forge. It's a big file, but you don't have to use all of it. The publish task is made entirely of smaller tasks, and you can pick and choose from those smaller tasks to build your own Rakefile. For a simple project, you can just customize the settings at the beginning of the file, and ignore the rest. Of course, you can also extend this Rakefile with other tasks, like the stats task presented in Recipe 19.5.

This Rakefile assumes that you follow the directory layout conventions laid down by the setup.rb script, even if you don't actually use setup.rb to install your project. For instance, it assumes you put your Ruby files in lib/ and your unit tests in test/.

First, we include Rake libraries that make it easy to define certain kinds of tasks:

```
# Rakefile
require "rake/testtask"
require "rake/clean"
require "rake/rdoctask"
require "rake/gempackagetask"
```

You'll need to configure these variables:

```
# The name of your project
PROJECT = "MyProject"

# Your name, used in packaging.
MY_NAME = "Frodo Beutlin"

# Your email address, used in packaging.
MY_EMAIL = "frodo.beutlin@my.al"

# Short summary of your project, used in packaging.
PROJECT_SUMMARY = "Commandline program and library for ..."

# The project's package name (as opposed to its display name). Used for
# RubyForge connectivity and packaging.
UNIX_NAME = "my_project"

# Your RubyForge user name.
RUBYFORGE_USER = ENV["RUBYFORGE_USER"] || "frodo"

# Directory on RubyForge where your website's files should be uploaded.
WEBSITE_DIR = "website"

# Output directory for the rdoc html files.
# If you don't have a custom homepage, and want to use the RDoc
# index.html as homepage, just set it to WEBSITE_DIR.
RDOC_HTML_DIR = "#{WEBSITE_DIR}/rdoc"
```

Now we start defining the variables you probably won't have to configure. The first set is for your project includes C extensions, to be compiled with extconf.rb, these variables let Rake know where to find the source and header files, as well as extconf.rb itself:

```
# Variable settings for extension support.
EXT_DIR = "ext"
HAVE_EXT = File.directory?(EXT_DIR)
EXTCONF_FILES = FileList["#{EXT_DIR}/**/extconf.rb"]
EXT_SOURCES = FileList["#{EXT_DIR}/**/*.{c,h}"]
# Eventually add other files from EXT_DIR, like "MANIFEST"
EXT_DIST_FILES = EXT_SOURCES + EXTCONF_FILES
```

This next piece of code automatically finds the current version of your project, so long as you define a file my_project.rb, which defines a module MyProject containing a constant VERSION. This is convenient because you don't have to change the version number in your gemspec whenever you change it in the main program.

```
REQUIRE_PATHS = ["lib"]
REQUIRE_PATHS << EXT_DIR if HAVE_EXT
$LOAD_PATH.concat(REQUIRE_PATHS)
# This library file defines the MyProject::VERSION constant.
require "#{UNIX_NAME}"
PROJECT_VERSION = eval("#{PROJECT}::VERSION") # e.g., "1.0.2"
```

If you don't want to set it up this way, you can:

- Have the Rakefile scan a source file for the current version.
- Use an environment variable.

Hardcode PROJECT_VERSION here, and change it whenever you do a new version.

These variables here are for the rake clobber tasks: they tell Rake to clobber files generated when you run setup.rb or build your C extensions.

```
# Clobber object files and Makefiles generated by extconf.rb.
CLOBBER.include("#{EXT_DIR}/**/*.{so,dll,o}", "#{EXT_DIR}/**/Makefile")
# Clobber .config generated by setup.rb.
CLOBBER.include(".config")
```

Now we start defining file lists and options for the various tasks. If you have a non-standard file layout, you can change these variables to reflect it.

```
# Options common to RDocTask AND Gem::Specification.
#   The --main argument specifies which file appears on the index.html page
GENERAL_RDOC_OPTS = {
  "--title" => "#{PROJECT} API documentation",
  "--main" => "README.rdoc"
}

# Additional RDoc formatted files, besides the Ruby source files.
RDOC_FILES = FileList["README.rdoc", "Changes.rdoc"]
# Remove the following line if you don't want to extract RDoc from
# the extension C sources.
RDOC_FILES.include(EXT_SOURCES)

# Ruby library code.
LIB_FILES = FileList["lib/**/*.rb"]

# Filelist with Test::Unit test cases.
TEST_FILES = FileList["test/**/tc_*.rb"]

# Executable scripts, all non-garbage files under bin/.
BIN_FILES = FileList["bin/*"]

# This filelist is used to create source packages.
# Include all Ruby and RDoc files.
```

```
DIST_FILES = FileList["**/*.rb", "**/*.rdoc"]
DIST_FILES.include("Rakefile", "COPYING")
DIST_FILES.include(BIN_FILES)
DIST_FILES.include("data/**/*", "test/data/**/*")
DIST_FILES.include("#{WEBSITE_DIR}/**/*.{html,css}", "man/*.[0-9]")
# Don't package files which are autogenerated by RDocTask
DIST_FILES.exclude(/^(\.\/)?#{RDOC_HTML_DIR}(\/|$)/)
# Include extension source files.
DIST_FILES.include(EXT_DIST_FILES)
# Don't package temporary files, perhaps created by tests.
DIST_FILES.exclude("**/temp_*", "**/*.tmp")
# Don't get into recursion...
DIST_FILES.exclude(/^(\.\/)?pkg(\/|$)/)
```

Now we can start defining the actual tasks. First, a task for running unit tests:

```
# Run the tests if rake is invoked without arguments.
task "default" => ["test"]

test_task_name = HAVE_EXT ? "run-tests" : "test"
Rake::TestTask.new(test_task_name) do |t|
  t.test_files = TEST_FILES
  t.libs = REQUIRE_PATHS
end
```

Next a task for building C extensions:

```
# Set an environment variable with any configuration options you want to
# be passed through to "setup.rb config".
CONFIG_OPTS = ENV["CONFIG"]
if HAVE_EXT
  file_create ".config" do
    ruby "setup.rb config #{CONFIG_OPTS}"
  end

  desc "Configure and make extension. " +
    "The CONFIG variable is passed to `setup.rb config'"
  task "make-ext" => ".config" do
    # The -q option suppresses messages from setup.rb.
    ruby "setup.rb -q setup"
  end

  desc "Run tests after making the extension."
  task "test" do
    Rake::Task["make-ext"].invoke
    Rake::Task["run-tests"].invoke
  end
end
```

A task for generating RDoc:

```
# The "rdoc" task generates API documentation.
Rake::RDocTask.new("rdoc") do |t|
  t.rdoc_files = RDOC_FILES + LIB_FILES
  t.title = GENERAL_RDOC_OPTS["--title"]
```

```
    t.main = GENERAL_RDOC_OPTS["--main"]
    t.rdoc_dir = RDOC_HTML_DIR
  end
```

Now we define a gemspec for the project, using the customized variables from the beginning of the file. We use this to define a task that builds a gem.

```
GEM_SPEC = Gem::Specification.new do |s|
  s.name = UNIX_NAME
  s.version = PROJECT_VERSION
  s.summary = PROJECT_SUMMARY
  s.rubyforge_project = UNIX_NAME
  s.homepage = "http://#{UNIX_NAME}.rubyforge.org/"
  s.author = MY_NAME
  s.email = MY_EMAIL
  s.files = DIST_FILES
  s.test_files = TEST_FILES
  s.executables = BIN_FILES.map { |fn| File.basename(fn) }
  s.has_rdoc = true
  s.extra_rdoc_files = RDOC_FILES
  s.rdoc_options = GENERAL_RDOC_OPTS.to_a.flatten
  if HAVE_EXT
    s.extensions = EXTCONF_FILES
    s.require_paths << EXT_DIR
  end
end

# Now we can generate the package-related tasks.
Rake::GemPackageTask.new(GEM_SPEC) do |pkg|
  pkg.need_zip = true
  pkg.need_tar = true
end
```

Here's a task to publish RDoc and static HTML content to RubyForge:

```
desc "Upload website to RubyForge. " +
  "scp will prompt for your RubyForge password."
task "publish-website" => ["rdoc"] do
  rubyforge_path = "/var/www/gforge-projects/#{UNIX_NAME}/"
  sh "scp -r #{WEBSITE_DIR}/* " +
    "#{RUBYFORGE_USER}@rubyforge.org:#{rubyforge_path}",
    :verbose => true
end
```

Here's a task that uses the `rubyforge` command to log in to RubyForge and publish the packaged software as a release of the project:

```
task "rubyforge-setup" do
  unless File.exist?(File.join(ENV["HOME"], ".rubyforge"))
    puts "rubyforge will ask you to edit its config.yml now."
    puts "Please set the `username' and `password' entries"
    puts "to your RubyForge username and RubyForge password!"
    puts "Press ENTER to continue."
    $stdin.gets
    sh "rubyforge setup", :verbose => true
```

```
      end
  end

  task "rubyforge-login" => ["rubyforge-setup"] do
    # Note: We assume that username and password were set in
    # rubyforge's config.yml.
    sh "rubyforge login", :verbose => true
  end

  task "publish-packages" => ["package", "rubyforge-login"] do
    # Upload packages under pkg/ to RubyForge
    # This task makes some assumptions:
    # * You have already created a package on the "Files" tab on the
    #   RubyForge project page. See pkg_name variable below.
    # * You made entries under package_ids and group_ids for this
    #   project in rubyforge's config.yml.  If not, eventually read
    #   "rubyforge --help" and then run "rubyforge setup".
    pkg_name = ENV["PKG_NAME"] || UNIX_NAME
    cmd = "rubyforge add_release #{UNIX_NAME} #{pkg_name} " +
          "#{PROJECT_VERSION} #{UNIX_NAME}-#{PROJECT_VERSION}"
    cd "pkg" do
    sh(cmd + ".gem", :verbose => true)
      sh(cmd + ".tgz", :verbose => true)
      sh(cmd + ".zip", :verbose => true)
    end
  end
```

Now we're in good shape to define some overarching tasks. The prepare-release task makes sure the code works, and creates a package. The top-level publish task does all that and also performs the actual release to RubyForge:

```
# The "prepare-release" task makes sure your tests run, and then generates
# files for a new release.
desc "Run tests, generate RDoc and create packages."
task "prepare-release" => ["clobber"] do
  puts "Preparing release of #{PROJECT} version #{VERSION}"
  Rake::Task["test"].invoke
  Rake::Task["rdoc"].invoke
  Rake::Task["package"].invoke
end

# The "publish" task is the overarching task for the whole project. It
# builds a release and then publishes it to RubyForge.
desc "Publish new release of #{PROJECT}"
task "publish" => ["prepare-release"] do
  puts "Uploading documentation..."
  Rake::Task["publish-website"].invoke
  puts "Checking for rubyforge command..."
  `rubyforge --help`
  if $? == 0
    puts "Uploading packages..."
    Rake::Task["publish-packages"].invoke
    puts "Release done!"
```

```
    else
      puts "Can't invoke rubyforge command."
      puts "Either install rubyforge with 'gem install rubyforge'"
      puts "and retry or upload the package files manually!"
    end
  end
```

To get an overview of this extensive Rakefile, run rake -T:

```
$ rake -T
rake clean            # Remove any temporary products.
rake clobber          # Remove any generated file.
rake clobber_package  # Remove package products
rake clobber_rdoc     # Remove rdoc products
rake package          # Build all the packages
rake prepare-release  # Run tests, generate RDoc and create packages.
rake publish          # Publish new release of MyProject
rake publish-website  # Upload website to RubyForge. scp will prompt for your
                      # RubyForge password.
rake rdoc             # Build the rdoc HTML Files
rake repackage        # Force a rebuild of the package files
rake rerdoc           # Force a rebuild of the RDOC files
rake test             # Run tests for test
```

Here's the idea behind prepare-release and publish: suppose you get a bug report and you need to do a new release. You fix the bug and add a test case to make sure it stays fixed. You check your fix by running the tests with rake (or rake test). Then you edit a library file and bump up the project's version number.

Now that you're confident the bug is fixed, you can run rake publish. This task builds your package, tests it, packages it, and uploads it to RubyForge. You didn't have to do any work besides fix the bug and increment the version number.

The rubyforge script is a command-line tool that performs common interactions with RubyForge, like the creation of new releases. To use the publish task, you need to install the rubyforge script and do some basic setup for it. The alternative is to use the prepare-release task instead of publish, and upload all your new packages manually.

Note that Rake uses the zip and tar command-line tools to create the ZIP file and tarball packages. These tools are not available on most Windows installations. If you're on windows, set the attributes need_tar and need_zip of the Rake::GemPackageTask to false. With these attributes, the package task only creates a gem package.

See Also

- Recipe 19.4, "Automatically Building a Gem"
- You can download the rubyforge script from *http://rubyforge.org/projects/codeforpeople/*

Multitasking and Multithreading

You can't concentrate on more than What's six times nine? one thing at once. You won't get very far reading this book if someone is interrupting you every five seconds asking you to do arithmetic problems. But any computer with a modern operating system can do many things at once. More precisely, it can simulate that ability by switching very quickly back and forth between tasks.

In a multitasking operating system, each program, or process, gets its own space in memory and a share of the CPU's time. Every time you start the Ruby interpreter, it runs in a new process. On Unix-based systems, your script can spawn subprocesses: this feature is very useful for running external command-line programs and using the results in your own scripts (see Recipes 20.8 and 20.9, for instance).

The main problem with processes is that they're expensive. It's hard to read while people are asking you to do arithmetic, not because either activity is particularly difficult, but because it takes time to switch from one to the other. An operating system spends a lot of its time as overhead, switching between processes, trying to make sure each one gets a fair share of the CPU's time.

The other problem with processes is that it's difficult to get them to communicate with each other. For simple cases, you can use techniques like those described in Recipe 20.8. You can implement more complex cases with Inter-Process Communication and named pipes, but we say, don't bother. If you want your Ruby program to do two things at once, you're better off writing your code with threads.

A thread is a sort of lightweight process that runs inside a real process. One Ruby process can host any number of threads, all running more or less simultaneously. It's faster to switch between threads than to switch between processes, and since all of a process's threads run in the same memory space, they can communicate simply by sharing variables.

Recipe 20.3 covers the basics of multithreaded programming. We use threads throughout this book, except when only a subprocess will work (see, for instance,

Recipe 20.1). Some recipes in other chapters, like Recipes 3.12 and 14.4, show threads used in context.

Ruby implements its own threads, rather than using the operating system's implementation. This means that multithreaded code will work exactly the same way across platforms. Code that spawns subprocesses generally work only on Unix.

If threads are faster and more portable, why would anyone write code that uses subprocesses? The main reason is that it's easy for one thread to stall all the others by tying up an entire process with an uninterruptible action. One such action is a system call. If you want to run a system call or an external program in the background, you should probably fork off a subprocess to do it. See Recipe 16.18 for a vivid example of this—a program that we need to spawn a subprocess instead of a subthread, because the subprocess is going to play a music file.

20.1 Running a Daemon Process on Unix

Problem

You want to run a process in the background with minimal interference from users and the operating system.

Solution

In Ruby 1.9, you can simply call `Process.daemon` to turn the current process into a daemon. Otherwise, the most reliable way is to use the `Daemonize` module. It's not available as a gem, but it's worth downloading and installing, because it makes it easy and reliable to write a daemon:

```ruby
#!/usr/bin/ruby -w
# daemonize_daemon.rb
require 'tempfile'
require 'daemonize'
include Daemonize          # Import Daemonize::daemonize into this namespace

puts 'About to daemonize.'
daemonize                  # Now you're a daemon process!
log = Tempfile.new('daemon.log')
loop do
  log.puts "I'm a daemon, doin' daemon things."
  log.flush
  sleep 5
end
```

If you run this code at the command line, you'll get back a new prompt almost immediately. But there will still be a Ruby process running in the background, writing to a temporary file every five seconds:

```
$ ./daemonize_daemon.rb
About to daemonize.
```

```
$ ps x | grep daemon
 4472 ?        S      0:00 ruby daemonize_daemon.rb
 4474 pts/2    S+     0:00 grep daemon

$ cat /tmp/daemon.log4472.0
I'm a daemon, doin' daemon things.
I'm a daemon, doin' daemon things.
I'm a daemon, doin' daemon things.
```

Since it runs an infinite loop, this daemon process will run until you kill it:

```
$ kill 4472

$ ps x | grep daemon
 4569 pts/2    S+     0:00 grep daemon
```

A different daemon might run until some condition is met, or until it receives a Unix signal, or a "stop" message through some interface.

Discussion

A daemon process is one that runs in the background, without any direct user interface at all. Servers are usually daemon processes, but you might also write a daemon to do monitoring or task scheduling.

Rather than replacing your process with a daemon process, you may want to spawn a daemon while continuing with your original work. The best strategy for this is to spawn a subprocess with Kernel#fork.

Ruby's fork implementation takes a code block to be run by the subprocess. The code defined after the block is run in the original process. So pass your daemonizing code into fork, and continue with your work in the main body of the code:

```
#!/usr/bin/ruby -w
# daemon_spawn.rb
require 'tempfile'
require 'daemonize'
include Daemonize

puts "About to daemonize."
fork do
  daemonize
  log = Tempfile.new('daemon.log')
  loop do
    log.puts "I'm a daemon, doin' daemon things."
    log.flush
    sleep 5
  end
end

puts 'The subprocess has become a daemon.'
puts "But I'm going to stick around for a while."
sleep 10
puts "Okay, now I'm done."
```

The Daemonize code fits in a single file, and it's licensed under the same terms as Ruby. If you don't want to require your users to download and install it, you can just include it with your program. Because the code is short, you can even copy-and-paste the code into a file in your own program.

However, there's also some (less fancy) daemonizing code in the Ruby 1.8 standard library. It's the WEBrick::Daemon class.

```
#!/usr/bin/ruby
# webrick_daemon.rb
require 'tempfile'
require 'webrick'

puts 'About to daemonize.'
WEBrick::Daemon.start do
  log = Tempfile.new('daemon.log')
  loop do
    log.puts "I'm a daemon, doin' daemon things."
    log.flush
    sleep 5
  end
end
```

It's worth examining the simpler daemonizing code in WEBrick::Daemon so that you can see what's going on. Here's the method in question:

```
def Daemon.start
  exit!(0) if fork
  Process::setsid
  exit!(0) if fork
  Dir::chdir("/")
  File::umask(0)
  STDIN.reopen("/dev/null")
  STDOUT.reopen("/dev/null", "w")
  STDERR.reopen("/dev/null", "w")
  yield if block_given?
end
```

A daemonizer works by forking a new process, letting the original one die, and closing off some of the resources that were available to the original.

Process::setsid disconnects the daemon from the terminal that spawned it. This is why, when your process becomes a daemon process, you get your command line back immediately. We close the original standard input, output, and error and replace them with null streams. We set the working directory and file umask to sensible defaults, regardless of what the daemon inherited from the parent. Then we run the daemon code.

Daemonize::daemonize also sets up signal handlers, calls srand so that the daemon process has a new random number seed, and (optionally) closes any open filehandles left around by the original process. It can also retry the fork if it fails because the operating system is running too many processes to create another one.

The fork method, and methods like `daemonize` that depend on it, are only available on Unix-like systems. On Windows, the `win32-process` extension provides Windows implementations of methods like `fork`. The `win32-process` implementation of `fork` isn't perfect, but it's there if you need it. For cross-platform code, we recommend you spawn a thread and run your daemon code in the thread.

See Also

- The `Daemonize` package (*http://grub.ath.cx/daemonize/*)
- If you want to run an Internet server, you might want to use `gserver` from Ruby's standard library; see Recipe 14.14, "Writing an Internet Server"
- A service is the Windows equivalent of a daemon process; see Recipe 20.2, "Creating a Windows Service"
- Recipe 20.3, "Doing Two Things at Once with Threads"
- Both `win32-process` and `win32-service` were written by Daniel J. Berger; you can download them from his win32utils project at *http://rubyforge.org/projects/win32utils/*
- Get `win32-process` from *http://rubyforge.org/projects/win32utils/*

20.2 Creating a Windows Service

Credit: Bill Froelich

Problem

You want to write a self-contained Ruby program for Windows that performs a task in the background.

Solution

Create a Windows service using the `win32-service` library, available as the `win32-service` gem.

Put all the service code below into a Ruby file called *rubysvc.rb*. It defines a service that watches for the creation of a file `c:\findme.txt`; if it ever finds that file, it immediately renames it.

The first step is to register the service with Windows. Running `ruby rubysrvc.rb register` will create the service.

```
# rubysrvc.rb
require 'rubygems'
require 'win32/service'
include Win32

SERVICE_NAME = "RubySvc"
SERVICE_DISPLAYNAME = "A Ruby Service"
```

```
if ARGV[0] == "register"
  # Start the service.
  svc = Service.new
  svc.create_service do |s|
    s.service_name = SERVICE_NAME
    s.display_name = SERVICE_DISPLAYNAME
    s.binary_path_name = 'C:\InstantRails-1.3\ruby\bin\ruby ' +
      File.expand_path($0)
    s.dependencies = []
  end
  svc.close
  puts "Registered Service - " + SERVICE_DISPLAYNAME
```

When you're all done, you can run `rubysrvc.rb stop` to stop the service and remove it from Windows:

```
elsif ARGV[0] == "delete"
  # Stop the service.
  if Service.status(SERVICE_NAME).current_state == "running"
    Service.stop(SERVICE_NAME)
  end
  Service.delete(SERVICE_NAME)
  puts "Removed Service - " + SERVICE_DISPLAYNAME
else
```

If you run `rubysrvc.rb` with no arguments, nothing will happen, but it will remind you what parameters you can use:

```
if ENV["HOMEDRIVE"]!=nil
  # We are not running as a service, but the user didn't provide any
  # command line arguments. We've got nothing to do.
  puts "Usage: ruby rubysvc.rb [option]"
  puts "   Where option is one of the following:"
  puts "       register - To register the Service so it " +
      "appears in the control panel"
  puts "       delete   - To delete the Service from the control panel"
  exit
end
```

But when Windows runs `rubysrvc.rb` as a service, the real action starts:

```
# If we got this far, we are running as a service.
class Daemon
  def service_init
    # Give the service time to get everything initialized and running,
    # before we enter the service_main function.
    sleep 10
  end

  def service_main
    fileCount = 0   # Initialize the file counter for the rename
    watchForFile = "c:\\findme.txt"
    while state == RUNNING
      sleep 5
      if File.exists? watchForFile
```

```
            fileCount += 1
            File.rename watchForFile, watchForFile + "." + fileCount.to_s
        end
      end
    end
  end
  d = Daemon.new
  d.mainloop
end
```

Once you run `ruby rubysrvc.rb register`, the service will show up in the Services Control Panel as "A Ruby Service". To see it, go to Start → Control Panel → Administrative Tools → Services (Figure 20-1). Start the service by clicking the service name in the list and clicking the start button.

Figure 20-1. The Services Control Panel

To test the service, create a file in `c:\` called *findme.txt*.

```
$ echo "test" > findme.txt
```

Within seconds, the file you just created will be renamed to *findme.txt*:

```
$ dir findme*
# Volume in drive C has no label.
# Volume Serial Number is 7C61-E72E
# Directory of c:\
# 04/14/2006  02:29 PM                    9 findme.txt.1
```

To remove the service, run `ruby rubysrvc.rb delete`.

Discussion

There's no reason why the code that registers `rubysrvc.rb` as a Windows service has to be in `rubysrvc.rb` itself, but it makes things much simpler. When you run `ruby rubysrvc.rb register`, the script tells Windows to run `rubysrvc.rb` again, only as a service. The key is the `binary_path_name` defined on the `Service` object: this is the command for Windows to run as a service. In this case, it's an invocation of the ruby interpreter with the service script passed as an input. But you could have run the same code from an `irb` session: then, `rubysrvc.rb` would only have been invoked once, by Windows, when running it as a service.

The code above assumes that your Ruby interpreter is located in `c:InstantRails-1.3\ruby\bin\ruby`. Of course, you can change this to point to your Ruby interpreter if it's somewhere else: perhaps `c:\ruby\bin\ruby`. If you've got the Ruby interpreter in your path, you just do this:

```
s.binary_path_name = 'ruby ' + File.expand_path($0)
```

When you create a service, you specify both a service name and a display name. The service name is shorter, and is used when referring to the service from within Ruby code. The display name is the one shown in the Services Control Panel.

Our example service checks every five seconds for a file with a certain name. Whenever it finds that file, it renames it by appending a number to the filename. To keep things simple, it does no error checking to see if the new filename already exists; nor does it do any file locking to ensure that the file is completely written before renaming it. Real services should include at least some basic high-level error handling:

```
def service_main
  begin
    while state == RUNNING
      # Do my work
    end
    # Finish my work
  rescue StandardError, Interrupt => e
    # Handle the error
  end
end
```

In addition to the `service_main` method, your service can define additional methods to handle the other service events (`stop`, `pause`, and `restart`). The `win32-service` gem comes with a useful example script, `daemon_test.rb`, which provides sample implementations of these methods.

See Also

- The win32-service library was written by Daniel J. Berger, and is part of the win32utils project (*http://rubyforge.org/projects/win32utils/*)
- Recipe 6.13, "Locking a File," and Recipe 6.14, "Backing Up to Versioned Filenames," demonstrate more robust renaming and filelocking strategies
- Recipe 20.1, "Running a Daemon Process on Unix," for similar functionality on Unix
- Recipe 23.2, "Managing Windows Services"

20.3 Doing Two Things at Once with Threads

Problem

You want your program to run two or more pieces of code in parallel.

Solution

Create a new thread by passing a code block into `Thread.new`. That block will run simultaneously with any code you write after the call to `Thread.new`.

The following code features two competing threads. One continually decrements a variable by one, while the main program's thread busily incrementing the same variable by three. The decrementing thread starts its work earlier, but the incrementing thread always wins in the end, because it increments the counter by a larger number:

```
x = 0
Thread.new do
  while x < 5
    x -= 1
    puts "DEC: I decremented x to #{x}\n"
  end
  puts "DEC: x is too high; I give up!\n"
end

while x < 5
  x += 3
  puts "INC: I incremented x to #{x}\n"
end
# DEC: I decremented x to -1
# DEC: I decremented x to -2
# DEC: I decremented x to -3
# DEC: I decremented x to -4
# INC: I incremented x to -1
# DEC: I decremented x to -2
# INC: I incremented x to 1
# DEC: I decremented x to 0
# INC: I incremented x to 3
# DEC: I decremented x to 2
# INC: I incremented x to 5
# DEC: x is too high; I give up!

x                              # => 5
```

Discussion

A Ruby process starts out running only one thread: the main thread. When you call `Thread#new`, Ruby spawns another thread and starts running it alongside the main thread. The operating system divides CPU time among all the running processes, and the Ruby interpreter further divides its alotted CPU time among all of its threads.

The block you pass into `Thread.new` is a closure (see Recipe 7.4), so it has access to all the variables that were in scope at the time you instantiated the thread. This means that threads can share variables; as a result, you don't need complex communication schemes the way you do to communicate between processes. However, it also means that your threads can step on each other's toes unless you're careful to synchronize any shared objects. In the example above, the threads were *designed* to step on each other's toes, providing head-to-head competition, but usually you don't want that.

Once a thread's execution reaches the end of its code block, the thread dies. If your main thread reaches the end of *its* code block, the process will exit and all your other threads will die prematurely. If you want your main thread to stall and wait for some other thread to finish, you can call Thread#join on the thread in question.

This code spawns a subthread to count to one million. Without the call to Thread#join, the counter only gets up to a couple hundred thousand before the process exits:

```
#!/usr/bin/ruby -w
# counter_thread.rb
counter = 0
counter_thread = Thread.new do
  1.upto(1000000) { counter += 1; }
end

counter_thread.join unless ARGV[0]
puts "The counter was able to count up to #{counter}."
$ ./counter_thread.rb
The counter was able to count up to 1000000.

$ ./counter_thread.rb dont_call_join
The counter was able to count up to 172315.
```

You can get a list of the currently active thread objects with Thread.list:

```
Thread.new { sleep 10 }
Thread.new { x = 0; 10000000.times { x += 1 } }
Thread.new { sleep 100 }
Thread.list
# => [#<Thread:0xb7d19ae0 sleep>, #<Thread:0xb7d24cec run>,
#      #<Thread:0xb7d31cf8 sleep>, #<Thread:0xb7d68748 run>]
```

Here, the two running threads are the main irb thread and the thread running the counter loop. The two sleeping threads are the ones currently running sleep calls.

20.4   Synchronizing Access to an Object

Problem

You want to make an object accessible from only one thread at a time.

Solution

Give the object a Mutex member (a semaphore that controls whose turn it is to use the object). You can then use this to synchronize activity on the object.

This code gives every object a synchronize method. This simulates the behavior of Java, in which synchronize is a keyword that can be applied to any object:

```
require 'thread'
class Object
  def synchronize
    mutex.synchronize { yield self }
  end

  def mutex
    @mutex ||= Mutex.new
  end
end
```

Here's an example. The first thread gets a lock on the list and then dawdles for a while. The second thread is ready from the start to add to the list, but it doesn't get a chance until the first thread releases the lock.

```
list = []
Thread.new { list.synchronize { |l| sleep(5); 3.times { l.push "Thread 1" } } }
Thread.new { list.synchronize { |l| 3.times { l.push "Thread 2" } } }
sleep(6)
list
# => ["Thread 1", "Thread 1", "Thread 1", "Thread 2", "Thread 2", "Thread 2"]
```

Object#synchronize only prevents two synchronized code blocks from running at the same time. Nothing prevents a wayward thread from modifying the object without calling synchronize first:

```
list = []
Thread.new { list.synchronize { |l| sleep(5); 3.times { l.push "Thread 1" } } }
Thread.new { 3.times { list.push "Thread 2" } }
sleep(6)
list
# => ["Thread 2", "Thread 2", "Thread 2", "Thread 1", "Thread 1", "Thread 1"]
```

Discussion

One of the big advantages of multithreaded programs is that different threads can share data. But where there is data sharing, there is the possibility for corruption. When two threads operate on the same object at the same time, the results can vary wildly depending on when the Ruby interpreter decides to switch between threads. To get predictable behavior, you need to have one thread lock the object, so other threads can't use it.

When every object has a synchronize method, it's easier to share an object between threads: if you want to work alone with the object, you put that code within a synchronize block. Of course, you may find yourself constantly writing synchronization code whenever you call certain methods of an object.

It would be nice if you could to do this synchronization implicitly, the way you can in Java: you just designate certain methods as "synchronized," and the interpreter won't start running those methods until it can obtain an exclusive lock on the corresponding object. The simplest way to do this is to use aspect-oriented programming. The RAspect library described in Recipe 10.15 can be used for this.

The following code defines an Aspect that can wrap methods in synchronization code. It uses the Object#mutex method defined above, but it could easily be changed to define its own Mutex objects:

```
require 'aspectr'
require 'thread'

class Synchronized < AspectR::Aspect
  def lock(method_sym, object, return_value, *args)
    object.mutex.lock
  end

  def unlock(method_sym, object, return_value, *args)
    object.mutex.unlock
  end
end
```

Any AspectR aspect method needs to take three arguments: the symbol of the method being called, the object it's being called on, and (if the aspect method is being called after the original method) the return value of the method.

The rest of the arguments are the arguments to the original method. Since this aspect is very simple, the only argument we need is object, the object we're going to lock and unlock.

Let's use the Synchronized aspect to create an array where you can only call push, pop, or each once you get an exclusive lock.

```
array = %w{do re mi fa so la ti}
Synchronized.new.wrap(array, :lock, :unlock, :push, :pop, :each)
```

The call to wrap tells AspectR to modify our array's implementation of push, pop, and each with generated singleton methods. Synchronized#lock is called before the old implementation of those methods is run, and Synchronized#unlock is called afterward.

The following example creates two threads to work on our synchronized array. The first thread iterates over the array, and the second thread destroys its contents with repeated calls to pop. When the first thread calls each, the AspectR-generated code calls lock, and the first thread gets a lock on the array. The second thread starts and it wants to call pop, but pop has been modified to require an exclusive lock on the array. The second thread can't run until the first thread finishes its call to each, and the AspectR-generated code calls unlock.

```
Thread.new { array.each { |x| puts x } }
Thread.new do
  puts 'Destroying the array.'
  array.pop until array.empty?
  puts 'Destroyed!'
end
# do
# re
# mi
```

```
# fa
# so
# la
# ti
# Destroying the array.
# Destroyed!
```

See Also

- See Recipe 10.15, "Doing Aspect-Oriented Programming," especially for information on problems with AspectR when wrapping operator methods in aspects
- Recipe 13.17, "Adding Hooks to Table Events," demonstrates the aspect-oriented programming features of the Glue library, which are simpler than AspectR (but actually, in my experience, more difficult to use)
- Recipe 16.10, "Sharing a Hash Between Any Number of Computers," has an alternate solution: it defines a delegate class (ThreadsafeHash) whose method_ missing implementation synchronizes on a mutex and then delegates the method call; this is an easy way to synchronize *all* of an object's methods
- Recipe 20.11, "Avoiding Deadlock"

20.5 Terminating a Thread

Problem

You want to kill a thread before the end of the program.

Solution

A thread terminates if it reaches the end of its code block. The best way to terminate a thread early is to convince it to reach the end of its code block. This way, the thread can run cleanup code before dying.

This thread runs a loop while the instance variable continue is true. Set this variable to false, and the thread will die a natural death:

```
require 'thread'

class CounterThread < Thread
  def initialize
    @count = 0
    @continue = true

    super do
      @count += 1 while @continue
      puts "I counted up to #{@count} before I was cruelly stopped."
    end
  end

  def stop
    @continue = false
```

```
    end
  end

counter = CounterThread.new
sleep 2
counter.stop
# I counted up to 3413544 before I was cruelly stopped.
```

If you need to stop a thread that doesn't offer a stop-like function, or you need to stop an out-of-control thread *immediately*, you can always call Thread#terminate. This method stops a thread in its tracks:

```
t = Thread.new { loop { puts 'I am the unstoppable thread!' } }
# I am the unstoppable thread!
# I am the unstoppable thread!
# I am the unstoppable thread!
# I am the unstoppable thread!
t.terminate
```

Discussion

It's better to convince someone they should do something than to force them to do it. The same is true of threads. Calling Thread.terminate is a bit like throwing an exception: it interrupts the normal flow of execution in an unpredictable place. Worse, there's no equivalent of a begin/ensure construct for thread termination, so calling Thread.terminate may corrupt your data or leave your program in an inconsistent state. If you plan to stop a thread before the program is over, you should build that capability into the thread object itself.

A common type of thread implements a loop: threads that process requests from a queue, or that periodically poll for new data. In these, the end of an iteration forms a natural stopping point. These threads can benefit from some simple VCR-style controls: pause, unpause, and stop.

Here's a Thread subclass which implements a loop that can be paused or stopped in a predictable way. A code block passed into the Thread constructor would implement the entire loop, but the code block passed into the LoopingThread constructor should implement only one iteration of the loop. Setup and cleanup code should be handled in the methods before_loop and after_loop.

```
class LoopingThread < Thread
  def initialize
    @stopped = false
    @paused = false
    super do
      before_loop
      until @stopped
        yield
        Thread.stop if @paused
      end
```

```
        after_loop
      end
    end

    def before_loop; end
    def after_loop; end

    def stop
      @stopped = true
    end

    def paused=(paused)
      @paused = paused
      run if !paused
    end
  end
end
```

Here's the CounterThread class from the Solution, implemented as a LoopingThread. I've added a reader method for count so we can peek at its value when the thread is paused:

```
class PausableCounter < LoopingThread
  attr_reader :count

  def before_loop
    @count = 0
  end

  def initialize
    super { @count += 1 }
  end

  def after_loop
    puts "I counted up to #{@count} before I was cruelly stopped."
  end
end

counter = PausableCounter.new
sleep 2
counter.paused = true
counter.count                                    # => 819438
sleep 2
counter.count                                    # => 819438
counter.paused = false
sleep 2
counter.stop
# I counted up to 1644324 before I was cruelly stopped.
counter.count                                    # => 1644324
```

20.6 Running a Code Block on Many Objects Simultaneously

Problem

Rather than iterating over the elements of a data structure one at a time, you want to run some function on all of them simultaneously.

Solution

Spawn a thread to handle each element of the data structure.

Here's a simple equivalent of Enumerable#each that runs a code block against every element of a data structure simultaneously.[*] It returns the Thread objects it spawned so that you can pause them, kill them, or join them and wait for them to finish:

```
module Enumerable
  def each_simultaneously
    threads = []
    each { |e| threads << Thread.new { yield e } }
    return threads
  end
end
```

Running the following high-latency code with Enumerable#each would take 15 seconds. With our new Enumerable#each_simultaneously, it takes only five seconds:

```
start_time = Time.now
[7,8,9].each_simultaneously do |e|
  sleep(5) # Simulate a long, high-latency operation
  print "Completed operation for #{e}!\n"
end
# Completed operation for 8!
# Completed operation for 7!
# Completed operation for 9!
Time.now - start_time                    # => 5.009334
```

Discussion

You can save time by doing high-latency operations in parallel, since it often means you pay the latency price only once. If you're doing nameserver lookups, and the nameserver takes five seconds to respond to a request, you're going to be waiting at least five seconds. If you need to do 10 nameserver lookups, doing them in series will take 50 seconds, but doing them all at once might only take 5.

This technique can also be applied to the other methods of Enumerable. You could write a collect_simultaneously, a find_all_simultaneously, and so on. But that's a

---

[*] Well, more or less. The thread for the first element will start running before the thread for the last element does.

lot of methods to write. All the methods of Enumerable are based on each. What if we could just convince those methods to use each_simultaneously instead of each?

It would be too much work to replace all the existing methods of Enumerable, but we can swap out an individual Enumerable object's each implementation for another, by wrapping it in an Enumerable::Enumerator. Here's how it would work:

```ruby
require 'enumerator'

array = [7, 8, 9]
simultaneous_array = array.enum_for(:each_simultaneously)
simultaneous_array.each do |e|
  sleep(5) # Simulate a long, high-latency operation
  print "Completed operation for #{e}!\n"
end
# Completed operation for 7!
# Completed operation for 9!
# Completed operation for 8!
```

That call to enum_for returns an Enumerable::Enumerator object. The Enumerator implements all of the methods of Enumerable as the original array would, but its each method uses each_simultaneously under the covers.

Do we now have simultaneous versions of all the Enumerable methods? Not quite. Look at this code:

```ruby
simultaneous_array.collect { |x| sleep 5; x * -1 }          # => []
```

What happened? The collect method returns before the threads have a chance to complete their tasks. When we were using each_simultaneously on its own, this was a nice feature. Consider the following idealized code, which starts three infinite loops in separate threads and then goes on to other things:

```ruby
[SSHServer, HTTPServer, IRCServer].each_simultaneously do |server|
  server.serve_forever
end

# More code goes here...
```

This is not such a good feature when we're calling an Enumerable method with a return value. We need an equivalent of each_simultaneously that doesn't return until all of the threads have run:

```ruby
require 'enumerator'
module Enumerable
  def all_simultaneously
    if block_given?
      collect { |e| Thread.new { yield(e) } }.each { |t| t.join }
      self
    else
      enum_for :all_simultaneously
    end
  end
end
```

You wouldn't use this method to spawn infinite loops (they'd all spawn, but you'd never regain control of your code). But you can use it to create multithreaded versions of collect and other Enumerable methods:

```
array.all_simultaneously.collect { |x| sleep 5; x * -1 }
# => [-7, -9, -8]
```

That's better, but the elements are in the wrong order: after all, there's no guarantee which thread will complete first. This doesn't usually matter for Enumerable methods like find_all, grep, or reject, but it matters a lot for collect. And each_with_index is simply broken:

```
array.all_simultaneously.each_with_index { |x, i| sleep 5; puts "#{i}=>#{x}" }
# 0=>8
# 0=>7
# 0=>9
```

Here are thread-agnostic implementations of Enumerable#collect and Enumerable#each_with_index, which will work on normal Enumerable objects, but will also work in conjunction with all_simultaneously:

```
module Enumerable
  def collect
    results = []
    each_with_index { |e, i| results[i] = yield(e) }
    results
  end

  def each_with_index
    i = -1
    each { |e| yield e, i += 1 }
  end
end
```

Now it all works:

```
array.all_simultaneously.collect { |x| sleep 5; x * -1 }
# => [-7, -8, -9]

array.all_simultaneously.each_with_index { |x, i| sleep 5; puts "#{i}=>#{x}" }
# 1=>8
# 0=>7
# 2=>9
```

See Also

• Recipe 7.9, "Looping Through Multiple Iterables in Parallel"

20.7 Limiting Multithreading with a Thread Pool

Problem

You want to process multiple requests in parallel, but you don't necessarily want to run all the requests simultaneously. Using a technique like that in Recipe 20.6 can create a huge number of threads running at once, slowing down the average response time. You want to set a limit on the number of simultaneously running threads.

Solution

You want a thread pool. If you're writing an Internet server and you want to service requests in parallel, you should build your code on top of the gserver module, as seen in Recipe 14.14: it has a thread pool and many TCP/IP-specific features. Otherwise, here's a generic ThreadPool class, based on code from gserver.

The instance variable @pool contains the active threads. The Mutex and the ConditionVariable are used to control the addition of threads to the pool, so that the pool never contains more than @max_size threads:

```
require 'thread'

class ThreadPool
  def initialize(max_size)
    @pool = []
    @max_size = max_size
    @pool_mutex = Mutex.new
    @pool_cv = ConditionVariable.new
  end
```

When a thread wants to enter the pool, but the pool is full, the thread puts itself to sleep by calling ConditionVariable#wait. When a thread in the pool finishes executing, it removes itself from the pool and calls ConditionVariable#signal to wake up the first sleeping thread:

```
  def dispatch(*args)
    Thread.new do
      # Wait for space in the pool.
      @pool_mutex.synchronize do
        while @pool.size >= @max_size
          print "Pool is full; waiting to run #{args.join(',')}...\n" if $DEBUG
          # Sleep until some other thread calls @pool_cv.signal.
          @pool_cv.wait(@pool_mutex)
        end
      end
```

The newly-awakened thread adds itself to the pool, runs its code, and then calls ConditionVariable#signal to wake up the *next* sleeping thread:

```
      @pool << Thread.current
      begin
        yield(*args)
```

```
        rescue => e
          exception(self, e, *args)
        ensure
          @pool_mutex.synchronize do
            # Remove the thread from the pool.
            @pool.delete(Thread.current)
            # Signal the next waiting thread that there's a space in the pool.
            @pool_cv.signal
          end
        end
      end
    end
  end

  def shutdown
    @pool_mutex.synchronize { @pool_cv.wait(@pool_mutex) until @pool.empty? }
  end

  def exception(thread, exception, *original_args)
    # Subclass this method to handle an exception within a thread.
    puts "Exception in thread #{thread}: #{exception}"
  end
end
```

Here's a simulation of five incoming jobs that take different times to run. The pool ensures no more than three jobs run at a time. The job code doesn't need to know anything about threads or thread pools; that's all handled by ThreadPool#dispatch.

```
$DEBUG = true
pool = ThreadPool.new(3)

1.upto(5) do |i|
  pool.dispatch(i) do |i|
    print "Job #{i} started.\n"
    sleep(5-i)
    print "Job #{i} complete.\n"
  end
end
# Job 1 started.
# Job 3 started.
# Job 2 started.
# Pool is full; waiting to run 4...
# Pool is full; waiting to run 5...
# Job 3 complete.
# Job 4 started.
# Job 2 complete.
# Job 5 started.
# Job 5 complete.
# Job 4 complete.
# Job 1 complete.

pool.shutdown
```

Discussion

When should you use a thread pool, and when should you just send a swarm of threads after the problem? Consider why this pattern is so common in Internet servers that it's built into Ruby's gserver library. Internet server requests are usually I/O bound, because most servers operate on the filesystem or a database. If you run high-latency requests in parallel (like requests for filesystem files), you can complete multiple requests in about the same time it would take to complete a single request.

But Internet server requests can use a lot of memory, and any random user on the Internet can trigger a job on your server. If you create and start a thread for every incoming request, it's easy to run out of resources. You need to find a tradeoff between the performance benefit of multithreading and the performance hazard of thrashing due to insufficient resources. The simplest way to do this is to limit the number of requests that can be processed at a given time.

A thread pool isn't a connection pool, like you might see with a database. Database connections are often pooled because they're expensive to create. Threads are pretty cheap; we just don't want a lot of them actively running at once. The example in the Solution creates five threads at once, but only three of them can be active at any one time. The rest are asleep, waiting for a notification from the condition variable pool_cv.

Calling ThreadPool#dispatch with a code block creates a new thread that runs the code block, but not until it finds a free slot in the thread pool. Until then, it's waiting on the condition variable @pool_cv. When one of the threads in the pool completes its code block, it calls signal on the condition variable, waking up the first thread currently waiting on it.

The shutdown method makes sure all the jobs complete by repeatedly waiting on the condition variable until no other threads want access to the pool.

See Also

- Recipe 14.14, "Writing an Internet Server"

20.8 Driving an External Process with popen

Problem

You want to execute an external command in a subprocess. You want to pass some data into its standard input stream, and read its standard output.

Solution

If you don't care about the standard input side of things, you can just use the %x{} construction. This runs a string as a command in an operating system subshell, and returns the standard output of the command as a string.

```
%x{whoami}                                        # => "leonardr\n"
puts %x{ls -a empty_dir}
# .
# ..
```

If you want to pass data into the standard input of the subprocess, do it in a code
block that you pass into the IO.popen method. Here's IO.popen used on a Unix system to invoke tail, a command that prints to standard output the last few lines of its
standard input:

```
IO.popen('tail -3', 'r+') do |pipe|
  1.upto(100) { |i| pipe << "This is line #{i}.\n" }
  pipe.close_write
  puts pipe.read
end
# This is line 98.
# This is line 99.
# This is line 100.
```

Discussion

IO.popens pawns a subprocess and creates a pipe: an IO stream connecting the Ruby
interpreter to the subprocess. IO.popen makes the pipe available to a code block, just
as File.open makes an open file available to a code block. Writing to the IO object
sends data to the standard input of the subprocess; reading from it reads data from
its standard output.

IO.popen takes a file mode, just like File.open. To use both the standard input and
output of a subprocess, you need to open it in read-write mode ("r+").

A command that accepts standard input won't really start running until its input
stream is closed. If you use popen to run a command like tail, you must call pipe.
close_write before you read from the pipe. If you try to read the subprocess' standard output while the subprocess is waiting for you to send it data on standard
input, both processes will hang forever.

The %{} construct and the popen technique work on both Windows and Unix, but
scripts that use them won't usually be portable, because it's very unlikely that the
command you're running exists on all platforms.

On Unix systems, you can also use popen to spawn a Ruby subprocess. This is like
calling fork, except that the parent gets a read-write filehandle that's hooked up to
the standard input and output of the child. Unlike with Kernel#fork (but like C's
implementation of fork), the same code block is called for the parent and the child.
The presence or absence of the filehandle is the only way to know whether you're the
parent or the child:

```
IO.popen('-', 'r+') do |child_filehandle|
  if child_filehandle
    $stderr.puts "I am the parent: #{child_filehandle.inspect}"
    child_filehandle.puts '404'
```

```
    child_filehandle.close_write
    puts "My child says the square root of 404 is #{child_filehandle.read}"
  else
    $stderr.puts "I am the child: #{child_filehandle.inspect}"
    number = $stdin.readline.strip.to_i
    $stdout.puts Math.sqrt(number)
  end
end
# I am the child: nil
# I am the parent: #<IO:0xb7d25b9c>
# My child says the square root of 404 is 20.0997512422418
```

See Also

- Recipe 20.1, "Running a Daemon Process on Unix"
- Recipe 20.9, "Capturing the Output and Error Streams from a Unix Shell Command"
- Recipe 20.10, "Controlling a Process on Another Machine"

20.9 Capturing the Output and Error Streams from a Unix Shell Command

Problem

You want to run an external program as in Recipe 20.8, but you also want to capture the standard error stream. Using popen only gives you access to the standard output.

Solution

Use the open3 library in the Ruby standard library. Its popen3 method takes a code block, to which it passes three IO streams: one each for standard input, output, and error.

Suppose you perform the Unix ls command to list a nonexistent directory. ls will rightly object to this and write an error message to its standard error stream. If you invoked ls with IO.popen or the %x{} construction, that error message is passed right along to the standard error stream of your Ruby process. You can't capture it or suppress it:

```
%x{ls no_such_directory}
# ls: no_such_directory: No such file or directory
```

But if you use popen3, you can grab that error message and do whatever you want with it:

```
require 'open3'

Open3.popen3('ls -l no_such_directory') { |stdin, stdout, stderr| stderr.read }
# => "ls: no_such_directory: No such file or directory\n"
```

Discussion

The same caveats in the previous recipe apply to the IO streams returned by popen3. If you're running a command that accepts data on standard input, and you read from stdout before closing stdin, your process will hang.

Unlike IO.popen, the popen3 method is only implemented on Unix systems. However, the win32-open3 package (part of the Win32Utils project) provides a popen3 implementation.

See Also

- Recipe 20.8, "Driving an External Process with popen"
- Like many other Windows libraries for Ruby, win32-open3 is available from *http://rubyforge.org/projects/win32utils*

20.10 Controlling a Process on Another Machine

Problem

You want to run a process on another machine, controlling its input stream remotely, and reading its output and error streams.

Solution

The ruby-ssh gem, first described in Recipe 14.10, provides a popen3 method that works a lot like Ruby's built-in popen3, except that the process you spawn runs on another computer.

Here's a method that runs a Unix command on another computer and yields its standard I/O streams to a code block on your computer. All traffic going between the computers is encrypted with SSL. To authenticate yourself against the foreign host, you'll either need to provide a username and password, or set up an SSL key pair ahead of time.

```
require 'rubygems'
require 'net/ssh'

def run_remotely(command, host, args)
  Net::SSH.start(host, args) do |session|
    session.process.popen3(command) do |stdin, stdout, stderr|
      yield stdin, stdout, stderr
    end
  end
end
```

Here it is in action:

```
run_remotely('ls -l /home/leonardr/dir', 'example.com', :username=>'leonardr',
             :password => 'mypass') { |i, o, e| puts o.read }
```

```
# -rw-rw-r--    1 leonardr leonardr       33 Dec 29 20:40 file1
# -rw-rw-r--    1 leonardr leonardr      102 Dec 29 20:40 file2
```

Discussion

The Net::SSH library implements a low-level interface to the SSH protocol, but most of the time you don't need all that power. You just want to use SSH as a way to spawn and control processes on a remote computer. That's why Net:SSH also provides a popen3 interface that looks a lot like the popen3 you use to manipulate processes on your own computer.

Apart from the issue of authentication, there are a couple of differences between Net::SSH.popen3 and Open3.popen3. With Open3.popen3, you must be careful to close the standard input stream before reading from the output or error streams. With the Net::SSH version of popen3, you can read from the output or error streams as soon as the process writes any data to it. This lets you interleave stdin writes and stdout reads:

```
run_remotely('cat', 'example.com', :username=>'leonardr',
              :password => 'mypass') do |stdin, stdout, stderr|
  stdin.puts 'Line one.'
  puts stdout.read
  stdin.puts 'Line two.'
  puts stdout.read
end
# "Line one."
# "Line two."
```

Another potential pitfall is that the initial working directory for an SSH session is the filesystem root (/). If you've used the ssh or scp commands, you may be accustomed to starting out in your home directory. To compensate for this, you can change to your home directory within your command: issue a command like cd; ls or cd /home/[user name]/; ls instead of just plain ls.

See Also

- The Net::SSH manual at: *http://net-ssh.rubyforge.org/*
- Recipe 14.2, "Making an HTTPS Web Request," has information on installing the OpenSSL extension that is a prerequisite of ruby-ssh
- Recipe 14.10, "Being an SSH Client covers the basic rules of SSH"
- Recipe 20.8, "Driving an External Process with popen," and Recipe 20.9, "Capturing the Output and Error Streams from a Unix Shell Command," cover the basic features of the popen family of methods

20.11 Avoiding Deadlock

Problem

Your threads are competing for exclusive access to the same resources. With no coordination between threads, you'll end up with deadlock. Thread A will be blocking, waiting for a resource held by thread B, and thread B will be blocking, waiting for a resource held by thread A. Neither thread will ever be seen again.

Solution

There's no simple mix-in solution to this problem. You need to come up with some rules for how your threads acquire locks, and make sure your code always abides by them.

Basically, you need to guarantee that all your threads acquire locks in the same order. Impose an ordering (formally or informally) on all the locks in your program and make sure that your threads always acquire locks in ascending numerical order.

Here's how it would work. The standard illustration of deadlock is the Dining Philosophers problem. A table of philosophers are sharing a plate of rice and some chopsticks, but there aren't enough utensils to go around. When there are only two chopsticks, it's easy to see the problem. If philosopher A is holding one chopstick (that is, has a lock on it), and philosopher B is holding the other, then nobody can eat.

In this scenario, you'd designate the the lock on one chopstick as lock #1, and the lock on the other chopstick as lock #2. If you guarantee that no philosopher will pick up chopstick #2 unless they're already picked up the chopstick #1, deadlock is impossible. You can guarantee this by simply making all the philosophers implement the same behavior:

```
require 'thread'
$chopstick1 = Mutex.new
$chopstick2 = Mutex.new

class Philosopher < Thread
  def initialize(name)
    super do
      loop do
        $chopstick1.synchronize do
          puts "#{name} has picked up one chopstick."
          $chopstick2.synchronize do
            puts "#{name} has picked up two chopsticks and eaten a " +
                 "bite of tasty rice."
          end
        end
      end
    end
  end
end
```

```
Philosopher.new('Moore')
Philosopher.new('Anscombe')
# Moore has picked up one chopstick.
# Moore has picked up two chopsticks and eaten a bite of tasty rice.
# Anscombe has picked up one chopstick.
# Anscombe has picked up two chopsticks and eaten a bite of tasty rice.
# Moore has picked up one chopstick.
# Moore has picked up two chopsticks and eaten a bite of tasty rice.
# ...
```

Discussion

It's hard to come up with an ordering of resources that isn't totally arbitrary. Why is chopstick #1 designated #1 and not #2? It just is. When you've got more than a few locks, it's hard to remember the order.

But if you keep a list of the locks in the proper order, you can have Ruby handle the locking order for you. The lock_all method defined below takes an unordered list of locks, and makes sure they get locked in the "right" order, as defined in the global hash $lock_order:

```ruby
require 'thread'
pool_lock, lion_lock, penguin_lock, cabbage_lock = (1..4).collect { Mutex.new }
locks = [pool_lock, lion_lock, penguin_lock, cabbage_lock]
$lock_order = {}
locks.each_with_index { |lock, i| $lock_order[lock] = i }

def lock_all(*locks)
  ordered_locks = locks.sort_by { |x| $lock_order[x] }
  ordered_locks.each do |lock|
    puts "Locking #{$lock_order[lock]}." if $DEBUG
    lock.lock
  end
  begin
    yield
  ensure
    ordered_locks.reverse_each do |lock|
      puts "Unlocking #{$lock_order[lock]}." if $DEBUG
      lock.unlock
    end
  end
end
```

Now you can simply pass the locks you want to get into lock_all, without having to keep track of an arbitrary order:

```ruby
$DEBUG = true
lock_all(penguin_lock, pool_lock) do
  puts "I'm putting the penguin in the pool."
end
# Locking 0.
# Locking 2.
# I'm putting the penguin in the pool.
# Unlocking 2.
# Unlocking 0.
```

When lock_all encounters a mutex that's already locked, the thread blocks until the mutex becomes available. A less greedy alternative is to drop all of the mutexes already obtained and try again from the start. This makes deadlock less likely even when not all of the code respects the order of the locks.

There are two locking-related problems that you can't solve by imposing a lock ordering. The first is resource starvation. In the context of the dining philosophers, this would mean that one philosopher continually puts down chopstick #1 and immediately takes it up again, preventing anyone else from eating.

The thread library prevents this problem by keeping a list of the threads that are waiting for a lock to be released. Once it's released, Ruby wakes up the first thread in line. So threads get the lock in the order they asked for it, rather than it being a free-for-all. You can see this if you create a bunch of Philosopher objects using the example from the Solution. Even if there are 20 philosophers and only one pair of chopsticks, the philosophers will take turns using the chopsticks in the order they were created, not randomly depending on the whims of the Ruby interpreter.

The second problem is harder to solve: a thread can "deadlock" with itself. The following code looks unobjectionable (why shouldn't you be able to lock what you already have?), but it creates a thread that sleeps forever:

```
require 'thread'
$lock = Mutex.new
Thread.new do
  $lock.synchronize { $lock.synchronize { puts 'I synchronized twice!' } }
end
```

The first time you call lock.synchronize, everything works fine: the Mutex isn't locked, and the thread gets a lock on it. The second time, the Mutex *is* locked, so the thread stops to wait until it gets unlocked.

The problem is, the thread B that's stopping to wait is the same thread as thread A, which has the lock. Thread A is supposed to wake up thread B once it's done, but it never does, because it *is* thread B, and it's asleep. A thread can't wake itself up.

That looks like a contrived example, but it's pretty easy to get there by accident. If you're synchronizing an object, as described in Recipe 20.4, there's a chance you'll go too far and synchronize two methods that call each other. Calling one method will synchronize and call the other, which will synchronize and put the thread to sleep forever. Short of hacking Mutex to keep track of which thread has the lock, the only way to avoid this problem is to be careful.

See Also

- Recipe 6.13, "Locking a File," shows an alternate way of avoiding deadlock when the resource under contention is a file

User Interface

Ruby has libraries for attaching programs to the three main types of user interface. The web interface, Ruby's most popular, is covered in depth in Chapters 15, 16, and (to a lesser extent) 14. This chapter covers the other two interfaces: the terminal or console interface, and the graphical (GUI) interface. We also cover some unorthodox interfaces (Recipe 21.11).

The terminal interface is is a text-based interface usually invoked from a command line. It's used by programs like irb and the Ruby interpreter itself. The terminal interface is usually seen on Unix systems, but all modern operating systems support it.

In the classic Unix-style "command-line program," the user interface consists of the options used to invoke the program (Recipe 21.3); and the program's standard input, output, and error streams (Recipe 21.1; also see Recipe 6.16). The Ruby interpreter is a good example of this kind of program. You can invoke the ruby program with arguments like -d and --version, but once the interpreter starts, your options are limited to typing in a Ruby program and executing it.

The advantage of this simple interface is that you can use Unix shell tools like redirection and pipes to connect these programs to each other. Instead of manually typing a Ruby program into the interpreter's standard input, you can send it a file with the Unix command ruby < file.rb. If you've got another program that generates Ruby code and prints it to standard output, you can pipe the generated code into the interpreter with generator | ruby.

The disadvantage is that these programs are not very user-friendly. Libraries like Curses (Recipe 21.5), Readline, and HighLine can add color and sophistication to your terminal programs. The irb interactive interpreter uses Readline to offer interactive line editing instead of the simpler interface offered by the Unix shell (Recipe 21.10).

The graphical user interface is the most common interface in the world. Even a web interface is usually interpreted within a GUI on the client end. However, there's not much that's Ruby-specific about GUI programming. All the common GUI libraries (like Tk, GTK, and QT) are written in C, and Ruby's bindings to them look a lot like the bindings for other dynamic languages such as Perl and Python.

All the GUI libraries work pretty much the same way. You create objects corresponding to GUI elements, or "widgets," attach chunks of code to them as callbacks (so that something will happen when, for instance, the user clicks a button), and then "pack" them into a frame for display. Because it's easiest to do the GUI layout work in a tool like Glade, and write only the callbacks in regular Ruby, this chapter contains only a few sample recipes on GUI programming.

Resources

HighLine, written by James Edward Gray II and Gregory Brown, is available as the highline gem. The Curses and Readline libraries come preinstalled with Ruby (even on Windows, if you use the one-click installer). If you're using Windows and don't have Curses, you can get the library and the Ruby bindings from *http://www.dave. burt.id.au/ruby/curses.zip*.

Ncurses is an improved version of Curses (allowing things like colored text), and most modern Unix systems have it installed. You can get Ncurses bindings for Ruby from *http://ncurses-ruby.berlios.de/*. It's also available as the Debian package libncurses-ruby.

The Tk binding for Ruby comes preinstalled with Ruby, assuming you've installed Tk itself. Ruby bindings for the most common GUI toolkits have been written:

- GTK (*http://ruby-gnome2.sourceforge.jp/*)
- QT (*http://sfns.u-shizuoka-ken.ac.jp/geneng/horie_hp/ruby/index.html*)
- wxRuby (*http://wxruby.rubyforge.org/*)

wxRuby is interesting because it's cross-platform and uses native widgets on each platform. You can write a Ruby program with wxRuby that runs on Unix, Windows, and Mac OS X, and looks like a native application on all three platforms.

On Mac OS X, all the tools you need to build a Ruby GUI application come with the operating system, including a GUI builder. If you're using GTK, your life will be easier if you download the Glade GUI builder (*http://glade.gnome.org/*).

21.1 Getting Input One Line at a Time

Problem

You're writing an interactive console program, and you want to get line-based input from the user. You present the user with a prompt, and he types some data before hitting enter.

Solution

Instead of reading standard input all at once, read it a line at a time with gets or readline.

This method populates a data structure with values obtained from user input:

```
def confirmation_hearings
  questions = [['What is your name?', :name],
               ['How old are you?', :age],
               ['Why would you like to be Secretary of the Treasury?', :why]]
  answers = questions.inject({}) do |answers, qv|
    question, value = qv
    print question + ' '
    answers[value] = gets.chomp
    answers
  end
  puts "Okay, you're confirmed!"
  return answers
end

confirmation_hearings
# What is your name?                                    # <= Leonard Richardson
# How old are you?                                      # <= 27
# Why would you like to be Secretary of the Treasury? # <= Mainly for the money
# Okay, you're confirmed!
# => {:age=>"26", :why=>"Mainly for the money", :name=>"Leonard Richardson"}
```

Discussion

Most console programs take their input from command-line switches or from a file passed in on standard input. This makes it easy to programatically combine console programs: you can pipe cat into grep into last without any of the programs having to know that they're connected to each other. But sometimes it's more user-friendly to ask for input interactively: in text-based games, or data entry programs with workflow.

The only difference between this technique and traditional console applications is that you're writing to standard output before you're completely done reading from standard input. You can pass an input file into a program like this, and it'll still work. In this example, a Ruby program containing the questionnaire code seen in the Solution is fed by an input file:

```
$ ./confirmation_hearings.rb < answers
# => What is your name? How old are you? Why would you like to be
#    Secretary of the Treasury? Okay, you're confirmed!
```

The program works, but the result looks different—even though the standard output is actually the same. When a human is running the program, the newline created when they hit enter is echoed to the screen, making the second question appear on a separate line from the first. Those newlines don't get echoed when they're read from a file.

The HighLine library requires that you install a gem (highline), but it makes sophisticated line-oriented input much easier. You can make a single method call to print a prompt, retrieve the input, and validate it. This code works the same way as the code above, but it's shorter, and it makes sure you enter a reasonable age for the question "How old are you?"

```ruby
require 'rubygems'
require 'highline/import'

def confirmation_hearings
  answers = {}
  answers[:name] = ask('What is your name? ')
  answers[:age] = ask('How old are you? ', Integer) { |q| q.in = 0..120 }
  answers[:why] = ask('Why would you like to be Secretary of the Treasury? ')
  puts "Okay, you're confirmed!"
  return answers
end

confirmation_hearings
# What is your name?                                   # <= Leonard Richardson
# How old are you?                                     # <= twenty-seven
# You must enter a valid Integer.
# ?                                                    # <= 200
# Your answer isn't within the expected range (included in 0..120)
# ?                                                    # <= 27
# ...
```

See Also

- Recipe 21.2, "Getting Input One Character at a Time"
- Recipe 21.9, "Reading a Password"
- The examples/basic_usage.rb script in the HighLine library has many more examples of data validation with HighLine
- If you want your program to treat its command-line arguments as filenames and read from the files one line at a time, see Recipe 21.3, "Parsing Command-Line Arguments," for a shortcut

21.2   Getting Input One Character at a Time

Problem

You're writing an interactive application or a terminal-based game. You want to read a user's input from standard input a single character at a time.

Solution

Most Ruby installations on Unix come with the the Curses extension installed. If Curses has the features you want to write the rest of your program, the simplest solution is to use it.

This simple Curses program echoes every key you type to the top-left corner of the screen. It stops when you hit the escape key (\e).[*]

```
#!/usr/bin/ruby -w
# curses_single_char_input.rb
require 'curses'
include Curses

# Setup: create a curses screen that doesn't echo its input.
init_screen
noecho

# Cleanup: restore the terminal settings when the program is exited or
# killed.
trap(0) { echo }

while (c = getch) != ?\e do
  setpos(0,0)
  addstr("You typed #{c.chr.inspect}")
end
```

If you don't want Curses to take over your program, you can use the HighLine library instead (available as the highline gem). It does its best to define a get_character method that will work on your system. The get_character method itself is private, but you can access it from within a call to ask:

```
require 'rubygems'
require 'highline/import'

while (c = ask('') { |q| q.character = true; q.echo = false }) != "\e" do
  print "You typed #{c.inspect}"
end
```

Be careful; ask echoes a newline after every character it receives.[†] That's why I use a print statement in that example instead of puts.

Of course, you can avoid this annoyance by hacking the HighLine class to make get_character public:

```
class HighLine
  public :get_character
end
```

---

[*] This code will also work in irb, but it'll look strange because Curses will be fighting with irb for control of the screen.

[†] This actually happens at the end of HighLine.get_response, which is called by ask.

```
input = HighLine.new
while (c = input.get_character) != ?\e do
  puts "You typed #{c.chr.inspect}"
end
```

Discussion

This is a huge and complicated problem that (fortunately) is completely hidden by
Curses and HighLine. Here's the problem: Unix systems know how to talk to a lot of
historic and modern terminals. Each one has a different feature set and a different
command language. HighLine (through the Termios library it uses on Unix) and
Curses hide this complexity.

Windows doesn't have to deal with a lot of terminal types, but Windows programs
don't usually read from standard input either (much less one character at a time). To
do single-character input on Windows, HighLine makes raw Windows API calls.
Here's some code based on HighLine's, which you can use on Windows if you don't
want to require HighLine:

```
require 'Win32API'

def getch
  @getch ||= Win32API.new('crtdll', '_getch', [], 'L')
  @getch.call
end

while (c = getch) != ?\e
  puts "You typed #{c.chr.inspect}"
end
```

HighLine also has two definitions f get_character for Unix; you can copy one of
these if you don't want to require HighLine. The most reliable implementation is
fairly complicated, and requires the termios gem. But if you need to require the
termios gem, you might as well require the highline gem as well, and use HighLine's
implementation as is. So if you want to do single-character input on Unix without
requiring any gems, you'll need to rely on the Unix command stty:

```
def getch
  state = `stty -g`
  begin
    `stty raw -echo cbreak`
    $stdin.getc
  ensure
    `stty #{state}`
  end
end

while (c = getch) != ?\e
  puts "You typed #{c.chr.inspect}"
end
```

All of the HighLine code is in the main *highline.rb* file; search for "get_character".

See Also

- Recipe 21.5, "Setting Up and Tearing Down a Curses Program"
- Recipe 21.8, "Changing Text Color"

21.3 Parsing Command-Line Arguments

Problem

You want to make your Ruby script take command-line arguments, the way most Unix utilities and scripts do.

Solution

If you want to treat your command-line arguments as a simple list of strings, you can just iterate over the ARGV array.

Here's a Ruby version of the Unix command cat; it takes a list of files on the command line, opens each one, and prints its contents to standard output:

```
#!/usr/bin/ruby -w
# cat.rb

ARGV.each { |filename| IO.readlines(filename).each { |line| puts line } }
```

If you want to treat your command-line arguments as a list of files, *and* you plan to open each of those files and iterate over them line by line, you can use ARGF instead of ARGV. The following cat implementation is equivalent to the first one.*

```
#!/usr/bin/ruby -w
# cat_argf.rb

ARGF.each { |line| puts line }
```

If you want to treat certain command-line arguments as switches, or as anything other than a homogenous list of strings, use the OptionParser class in the optparse library. Don't write the argument parsing code yourself; there are too many edge cases to think about.

Discussion

The OptionParser class can parse any command-line arguments you're likely to need, and it includes a lot of Unix know-how that would take a long time to write yourself. All you have to do is define the set of arguments your script accepts, and write code that reacts to the presence of each argument on the command line. Here, I'll

---

* It's actually a little better, because ARGF will iterate over standard input if there are no files given in ARGV.

use OptionParser to write cat2.rb, a second Ruby version of cat that supports a few of the real cat's command-line arguments.

The first phase is turning any command-line arguments into a data structure that I can easily consult during the actual program. The CatArguments class defined below is a hash that uses OptionParser to populate itself from a list of command-line arguments.

For each argument accepted by cat2.rb, I've added a code block to be run as a callback. When OptionParser sees a particular argument in ARGV, it runs the corresponding code block, which sets an appropriate value in the hash:

```ruby
#!/usr/bin/ruby
# cat2.rb
require 'optparse'

class CatArguments < Hash
  def initialize(args)
    super()
    self[:show_ends] = ''

    opts = OptionParser.new do |opts|
      opts.banner = "Usage: #$0 [options]"
      opts.on('-E', '--show-ends [STRING]',
              'display [STRING] at end of each line') do |string|
        self[:show_ends] = string || '$'
      end

      opts.on('-n', '--number', 'number all output lines') do
        self[:number_lines] = true
      end

      opts.on_tail('-h', '--help', 'display this help and exit') do
        puts opts
        exit
      end
    end

    opts.parse!(args)
  end
end

arguments = CatArguments.new(ARGV)
```

At this point in the code, our CatArguments object contains information about which command-line arguments were passed in. If the user passed in a command-line switch -E or --show-ends, then arguments[:show_ends] contains a string to be shown at the end of each line.

What's more, the command-line arguments handled by OptionParser have been stripped from ARGV. The only things left in ARGV can be assumed to be the names of files the user wants to concatenate. This means we can now use the ARGF shortcut to iterate over those files line by line. All we need is a little extra code to actually implement the command-line arguments:

```
counter = 0
eol =
ARGF.each do |line|
  line.sub!(/$/, arguments[:show_ends])
  print '%6.d ' % (counter += 1) if arguments[:number_lines]
  print line
end
```

Here's a shell session showing off the robustness that optparse brings to even a simple script. The help message is automatically generated, multiple combined flags are handled correctly, nonexistent flags are rejected, and you can disable flag processing altogether with the -- argument. In general, it works like you expect a Unix command-line tool to work.

```
$ ./cat2.rb --help
Usage: ./cat2.rb [options]
    -E, --show-ends [STRING]        display STRING at end of each line
    -n, --number                    number all output lines
    -h, --help                      display this help and exit

$ ./cat2.rb file1 file2
This is file one.
Another line in file one.
This is file two.
I'm a lot more interesting than file one, I'll tell you that!

$ ./cat2.rb file1 -E$ -n file2
     1  This is file one.$
     2  Another line in file one.$
     3  This is file two.$
     4  I'm a lot more interesting than file one, I'll tell you that!$

$ ./cat2.rb --nosuchargument
/usr/lib/ruby/1.8/optparse.rb:1445:in `complete': invalid option: --nosuchargument
(OptionParser::InvalidOption)

$ ./cat2.rb --show-ends=" STOP" -- --argument-looking-file
The name of this file STOP
looks just like an argument STOP
for some odd reason. STOP
```

With a little more work, you can make OptionParser validate argument data for you—parse strings as numbers, restrict option values to values from a list. The documentation for the OptionParser class has a much more complex example that shows off these advanced features.

See Also

- ri OptionParser

21.4 Testing Whether a Program Is Running Interactively

Problem

You want to see whether there's another person on the other end of your program, or whether the program has been hooked up to a file or the output of another program.

Solution

STDIN.tty? returns true if there's a terminal hooked up to your program's original standard input. Since only humans use terminals, this will suffice. This code works on Unix and Windows:

```
#!/usr/bin/ruby -w
# interactive_or_not.rb
if STDIN.tty?
  puts "Let me be the first to welcome my human overlords."
else
  puts "How goes the revolution, brother software?"
end
```

Running this program in different ways gives different results:

```
$ ./interactive_or_not.rb
Let me be the first to welcome my human overlords.

$ echo "Some data" | interactive_or_not.rb
How goes the revolution, brother software?

$ ./interactive_or_not.rb < input_file
How goes the revolution, brother software?
```

Discussion

An interactive application can be more user friendly than one that runs solely off its command-line arguments and input streams. By checking STDIN.tty? you can make your program have an interactive and a noninteractive mode. The noninteractive mode can be chained together with other programs or used in shell scripts.

21.5 Setting Up and Tearing Down a Curses Program

Problem

To write a program that uses Curses or Ncurses, you have to write a lot of setup and cleanup code. You'd like to factor that out.

Solution

Here's a wrapper method that sets up the Curses library and passes the main screen object into a code block:

```
require 'curses'

module Curses
  def self.program
    main_screen = init_screen
    noecho
    cbreak
    curs_set(0)
    main_screen.keypad = true
    yield main_screen
  end
end
```

Here's a simple Ruby program that uses the wrapper method to fill up the screen with random placements of a given string:

```
Curses.program do |scr|
  str = ARGV[0] || 'Test'
  max_x = scr.maxx-str.size+1
  max_y = scr.maxy
  100.times do
    scr.setpos(rand(max_y), rand(max_x))
    scr.addstr(str)
  end
  scr.getch
end
```

Discussion

The initialization, which is hidden in Curses.program, does the following things:

- Stops keystrokes from being echoed to the screen (noecho)
- Hides the cursor (curs_set(0))
- Turns off buffered input so keys can be processed as they're typed (cbreak)
- Makes the keyboard's arrow keys generate recognizable key events (keypad = true)

The code is a little different if you're using the third-party ncurses binding instead of the curses library that comes with Ruby. The main difference is that with ncurses, you must write some of the cleanup code that the curses library handles automatically. A wrapper method is also a good place to set up the ncurses color code if you plan to use colored text (see Recipe 21.8 for more on this).

Here's an Ncurses.program method that's equivalent to Curses.program, except that it performs its cleanup manually by registering an at_exit block to run just before the interpreter exits. This wrapper also turns on color and initializes a few default color pairs. If your terminal has no color support, the color code will run but it won't do anything.

```ruby
require 'ncurses'

module Ncurses
  COLORS = [COLOR_BLACK, COLOR_RED, COLOR_GREEN, COLOR_YELLOW, COLOR_BLUE,
            COLOR_MAGENTA, COLOR_CYAN, COLOR_WHITE]

  def self.program
    stdscr = Ncurses.initscr

    # Run ncurses cleanup code when the program exits.
    at_exit do
      echo
      nocbreak
      curs_set(1)
      stdscr.keypad(0)
      endwin
    end

    noecho
    cbreak
    curs_set(0)
    stdscr.keypad(1)
    start_color

    COLORS[1...COLORS.size].each_with_index do |color, i|
      init_pair(i+1, color, COLOR_BLACK)
    end

    yield stdscr
  end
end
```

Here's the ncurses equivalent of the curses program given earlier:

```ruby
Ncurses.program do |scr|
  str = ARGV[0] || 'Test'
  max_y, max_x = [], []
  scr.getmaxyx(max_y, max_x)
  max_y = max_y[0]
  max_x = max_x[0] - str.size + 1
  100.times do
    scr.mvaddstr(rand(max_y), rand(max_x), str)
  end
  scr.getch
end
```

See Also

- See this chapter's introduction for information on installing Ncurses
- "Writing Programs with NCURSES" is a good general overview of the Ncurses library; it's written for C programmers, but it's useful for Rubyists because Ruby's interfaces to Curses and Ncurses are little more than wrappers (*http://dickey.his.com/ncurses/ncurses-intro.html*)

21.6 Clearing the Screen

Problem

You're writing a console application, and you want it to clear the screen.

Solution

Capture the output of the Unix clear command as a string and print it whenever you want to clear the screen:

```
#!/usr/bin/ruby -w
# clear_console.rb
clear_code = %x{clear}

puts 'Press enter to clear the screen.'
$stdin.gets
print clear_code
puts "It's cleared!"
```

Discussion

The clear command prints an escape code sequence to standard output, which the Unix terminal interprets as a clear-screen command. The exact string depends on your terminal, but it's probably an ANSI escape sequence, like this:

```
%x{clear}                    # => "\e[H\e[2J"
```

Your Ruby script can print this escape code sequence to standard output, just as the clear command can, and clear the screen.

On Windows, the command is cls, and you can't just print its standard output to clear the screen. Every time you want to clear the screen, you need to call out to cls with Kernel#system:

```
# clear_console_windows.rb

puts 'Press enter to clear the screen.'
$stdin.gets
system('cls')
puts "It's cleared!"
```

If you've made your Windows terminal support ANSI (see Recipe 21.8), then you can print the same ANSI escape sequence used on Unix.

The Curses library makes this a lot more straightforward. A Curses application can clear any of its windows with `Curses::Window#clear`. `Curses::clear` will clear the main window:

```
#!/usr/bin/ruby -w
# curses_clear.rb
require 'curses'

Curses.init_screen
Curses.setpos(0,0)
Curses::addstr("Type all you want. 'C' clears the screen, Escape quits.\n")

begin
  c = nil
  begin
    c = Curses.getch
  end until c == ?C or c == ?\e
  Curses.clear
end until c == ?\e
```

But, as always, Curses takes over your whole application, so you might want to just use the escape sequence trick.

21.7 Determining Terminal Size

Problem

Within a terminal-based application, you want to find the size of the terminal: how many rows and columns are available for you to draw on.

Solution

This is easy if you're using the Curses library. This example uses the `Curses.program` wrapper described in Recipe 21.5:

```
Curses.program do |scr|
  max_y, max_x = scr.maxy, scr.maxx

  scr.setpos(0, 0)
  scr.addstr("Your terminal size is #{max_x}x#{max_y}. Press any key to exit.")
  scr.getch
end
```

It's a little less easy with Ncurses: you have to pass in two arrays to the underlying C libraries, and extract the numbers from the arrays. Again, this example uses the Ncurses wrapper from Recipe 21.5:

```
Ncurses.program do |scr|
  max_y, max_x = [], []
```

```
    scr.getmaxyx(max_y, max_x)
    max_y, max_x = max_y[0], max_x[0]

    str = "Your terminal size is #{max_x}x#{max_y}. Press any key to exit."
    scr.mvaddstr(0, 0, str)
    scr.getch
  end
```

If you're not using a Curses-style library, it's not easy at all.

Discussion

If you plan to simulate graphical elements on a textual terminal, subdivide it into virtual windows, or print justified output, you'll need to know the terminal's dimensions. For decades, the standard terminal size has been 25 rows by 80 columns, but modern GUIs and high screen resolutions let users create text terminals of almost any size. It's okay to enforce a minimum terminal size, but it's a bad idea to assume that the terminal is any specific size.

The terminal size is a very useful piece of information to have, but it's not an easy one to get. The Curses library was written to solve this kind of problem, but if you're willing to go into the operating system API, or if you're on Windows where Curses is not a standard feature, you can find the terminal size without letting a Curses-style library take over your whole application.

On Unix systems (including Mac OS X), you can make an ioctl system call to get the terminal size. Since you're calling out to the underlying operating system, you'll need to use strange constants and C-like structures to carry the response:

```
TIOCGWINSZ = 0x5413               # For an Intel processor
# TIOCGWINSZ = 0x40087468         # For a PowerPC processor

def terminal_size
 rows, cols = 25, 80
  buf = [ 0, 0, 0, 0 ].pack("SSSS")
  if STDOUT.ioctl(TIOCGWINSZ, buf) >= 0 then
    rows, cols, row_pixels, col_pixels = buf.unpack("SSSS")[0..1]
  end
  return rows, cols
end

terminal_size                            # => [21, 80]
```

Here, the methods pack and unpack convert between a four-element array and a string that is modified in-place by the ioctl call. After the call, the first two elements of the array contain the number of rows and columns for the terminal. Note that the first argument to ioctl is architecture-dependent.

The Windows version works the same way, although you must jump through more hoops and the system call returns a much bigger data structure:

```
STDOUT_HANDLE = 0xFFFFFFF5
def terminal_size
```

```
    m_GetStdHandle = Win32API.new('kernel32', 'GetStdHandle', ['L'], 'L')
    m_GetConsoleScreenBufferInfo = Win32API.new ('kernel32',
                                            'GetConsoleScreenBufferInfo',
                                            ['L', 'P'], 'L' )
    format = 'SSSSSsssssSS'
    buf = ([0] * format.size).pack(format)
    stdout_handle = m_GetStdHandle.call(STDOUT_HANDLE)

    m_GetConsoleScreenBufferInfo.call(stdout_handle, buf)
    (bufx, bufy, curx, cury, wattr,
     left, top, right, bottom, maxx, maxy) = buf.unpack(format)
    return bottom - top + 1, right - left + 1
end

terminal_size                          # => [25, 80]
```

If all else fails, on Unix systems you can call out to the stty command:

```
def terminal_size
  %x{stty size}.split.collect { |x| x.to_i }
end

terminal_size                          # => [21, 80]
```

See Also

- The ioctl code is based on code posted to ruby-talk by Paul Brannan (*http:// blade.nagaokaut.ac.jp/cgi-bin/rcat.rb/ruby/ruby-talk/40350*)
- The Windows code is based on code in the Win32API_Console library, a simple Ruby wrapper around Windows' console-related API calls (*http://rb-w32mod. sourceforge.net/*)
- Recipe 21.5, "Setting Up and Tearing Down a Curses Program"

21.8 Changing Text Color

Problem

You want to display multicolored text on the console.

Solution

The simplest solution is to use HighLine. It lets you enclose color commands in an ERb template that gets interpreted within HighLine and printed to standard output. Try this colorful bit of code to test the capabilities of your terminal:

```
require 'rubygems'
require 'highline/import'

say(%{Here's some <%= color('dark red text', RED) %>.})
say(%{Here's some <%= color('bright red text on a blue background',
                     RED+BOLD+ON_BLUE) %>.})
```

```
say(%{Here's some <%= color('blinking bright cyan text', CYAN+BOLD+BLINK) %>.})
say(%{Here's some <%= GREEN+UNDERLINE %>underlined dark green text<%=CLEAR%>.})
```

Some of these features (particularly the blinking and underlining) aren't supported on all terminals.

Discussion

The HighLine#color method encloses a display string in special command strings, which start with an escape character and a left square bracket:

```
HighLine.new.color('Hello', HighLine::GREEN)
# => "\e[32mHello\e[0m"
```

These are ANSI escape sequences. Instead of displaying the string "\e[32m", an ANSI-compatible terminal treats it as a command: in this case, a command to start printing characters in green-on-black. The string "\e[0m" tells the terminal to go back to white-on-black.

Most modern Unix terminals support ANSI escape sequences, including the Mac OS X terminal. You should be able to get green text in your irb session just by calling puts "\e[32mHello\e[0m" (try it!), but HighLine makes it easy to get color without having to remember the ANSI sequences.

Windows terminals don't support ANSI by default, but you can get it to work by loading ANSI.SYS (see below for a relevant Microsoft support article).

An alternative to HighLine is the Ncurses library.* It supports color terminals that use a means other than ANSI, but these days, most color terminals get their color support through ANSI. Since Ncurses is much more complex than HighLine, and not available as a gem, you should only use Ncurses for color if you're already using it for its other features.

Here's a rough equivalent of the HighLine program given above. This program uses the Ncurses::program wrapper described in Recipe 21.5. The wrapper sets up Ncurses and initializes some default color pairs:

```
Ncurses.program do |s|
  # Define the red-on-blue color pair used in the second string.
  # All the default color pairs use a black background.
  Ncurses.init_pair(8, Ncurses::COLOR_RED, Ncurses::COLOR_BLUE)

  Ncurses::attrset(Ncurses::COLOR_PAIR(1))
  s.mvaddstr(0,0, "Here's some dark red text.")

  Ncurses::attrset(Ncurses::COLOR_PAIR(8) | Ncurses::A_BOLD)
  s.mvaddstr(1,0, "Here's some bright red text on a blue background.")
```

---

* Standard Curses doesn't support color because it was written in the 1980s, when monochrome ruled the world.

```
      Ncurses::attrset(Ncurses::COLOR_PAIR(6) | Ncurses::A_BOLD |
                       Ncurses::A_BLINK)
      s.mvaddstr(2,0, "Here's some blinking bright cyan text.")

      Ncurses::attrset(Ncurses::COLOR_PAIR(2) | Ncurses::A_UNDERLINE)
      s.mvaddstr(3,0, "Here's some underlined dark green text.")

      s.getch
    end
```

An Ncurses program can draw from a palette of color pairs—combinations of foreground and background colors. `Ncurses::program` sets up a default palette of the seven basic ncurses colors (red, green, yellow, blue, magenta, cyan, and white), each on a black background. You can change this around if you like, or define additional color pairs (like the red-on-blue defined in the example). The following Ncurses program prints out a color chart of all foreground-background pairs. It makes the text of the chart bold, so that the text doesn't become invisible when the background is the same color.

```
    Ncurses.program do |s|
      pair = 0
      Ncurses::COLORS.each_with_index do |background, i|
        Ncurses::COLORS.each_with_index do |foreground, j|
          Ncurses::init_pair(pair, foreground, background) unless pair == 0
          Ncurses::attrset(Ncurses::COLOR_PAIR(pair) | Ncurses::A_BOLD)
          s.mvaddstr(i, j*4, "#{foreground},#{background}")
          pair += 1
        end
      end
      s.getch
    end
```

You can modify a color pair by combining it with an Ncurses constant. The most useful constants are `Ncurses::A_BOLD`, `Ncurses::A_BLINK`, and `Ncurses::A_UNDERLINE`. This works the same way (and, on an ANSI system, uses the same ANSI codes) as HighLine's `BOLD`, `BLINK`, and `UNDERLINE` constants. The only difference is that you modify an Ncurses color with the OR operator (|), and you modify a HighLine color with the addition operator.

See Also

- Recipe 1.3, "Substituting Variables into an Existing String," has more on ERb
- *http://en.wikipedia.org/wiki/ANSI_escape_code* has technical details on ANSI color codes
- The `examples/ansi_colors.rb` file in the HighLine gem
- You can get a set of Ncurses bindings for Ruby at *http://ncurses-ruby.berlios.de/*; it's also available as the Debian package `libncurses-ruby`

- If you want something more lightweight than the highline gem, try the term-ansicolor gem instead: it defines methods for generating the escape sequences for ANSI colors, and nothing else
- "How to Enable ANSI.SYS in a Command Window" (*http://support.microsoft.com/?id=101875*)

21.9 Reading a Password

Problem

You want to prompt the user for a password, or otherwise capture input without echoing it to the screen for all to see.

Solution

The ruby-password library makes this easy, but it's not available as a Ruby gem. The HighLine library is available as a gem, and it can do this almost as well. You just have to turn off the terminal echo feature:

```
require 'rubygems'
require 'highline/import'

def get_password(prompt='Password: ')
  ask(prompt) { |q| q.echo = false}
end

get_password("What's your password? ")
# What's your password?
# => "buddy"
```

Discussion

In 2000, President Bill Clinton signed into law the Electronic Signatures Bill, which makes electronic signatures as binding as handwritten signatures. He signed the law by hand and then signed it electronically. As he typed the password to his electronic signature, it was was echoed to the screen. Everyone in the world saw that his password was the name of his pet dog, Buddy. Don't let this happen to you: turn off echoing when gathering passwords.

Turning off echoing altogether is the safest way to gather a password, but it might make your users think your program has stopped responding to input. It's more user-friendly to echo a mask character, like an asterisk, for every character the user types. You can do this in HighLine by setting echo to the mask character instead of false:

```
def get_password(prompt='Password: ', mask='*')
  ask(prompt) { |q| q.echo = mask }
end
```

```
get_password
# Password: *****
# => "buddy"

get_password('Password: ', false)
# Password:
# => "buddy"
```

See Also

- The ruby-password third-party library also provides ways of generating, encrypting, and test-cracking passwords (*http://www.caliban.org/ruby/ruby-password.shtml*)

21.10 Allowing Input Editing with Readline

Problem

You want to let your users edit their lines of input as they write them, the way irb does.

Solution

Use the readline library. Instead of reading directly from standard input, pass a prompt string into Readline.readline. The user will be able to edit their input using the same shortcut keys you can use in the irb Ruby interpreter (assuming their terminal supports those keys).

```
#!/usr/bin/ruby -w
# readline.rb
require 'readline'
vegetable = Readline.readline("What's your favorite vegetable?> ")
puts "#{vegetable.capitalize}? Are you crazy?"
```

Note that you don't have to chomp the result of Readline.readline:

```
$ ruby readline.rb
What's your favorite vegetable?> okra
Okra? Are you crazy?
```

On Windows, this isn't necessary because the cmd shell provides any console program with many of readline's features. The example given above will work on both Windows and Unix, but if you're writing a Windows-specific program, you don't need readline:

```
# readline_windows.rb
print "What's your favorite vegetable?> "
puts gets.chomp.capitalize + "? Are you crazy?"
```

Discussion

In a Unix program that accepts data from standard input, the user can use their backspace key to correct typing mistakes, one character at a time. Backspace is a *control character*: it's a real character, just like "1" and "m" (its Ruby string representation is `"\010"`), but it's not usually interpreted as data. Instead, it's treated as a command: it erases one character from the input buffer.

With the backspace key, you can correct errors one character at a time. But what if you want to insert text into the middle of a line, or delete the whole thing and start over? That's where `readline` comes in. It's a Ruby interface to the Readline library used by many Unix programs, and it recognizes many control characters besides the backspace.

In a `readline` program, you can use the left and right arrow keys to move back and forth in the input string before submitting it. If you're familiar with the Readline shortcut keys from Emacs or other Unix programs, you can perform more sophisticated text editing operations, including cut and paste.

The `readline` library also supports command history: that's the feature of `irb` that lets you revisit commands you've already typed. To add this feature to your program, pass `true` as the second argument to `Readline.readline`. When the user enters a line, her input will be added to the command history. The next time your code calls `Readline.readline`, the user can hit the up arrow key to recall previous lines of input.

Here's a simple Ruby interpreter that has all the line-editing capabilities of `irb`, including command history:

```
#!/usr/bin/ruby -w
# mini_irb.rb
require 'readline'
line = 0
loop do
  eval Readline.readline('%.3d> ' % line, true)
  line += 1
end
```

See Also

- Recipe 1.5, "Representing Unprintable Characters"
- If your `irb` session *doesn't* support `readline` commands, make sure you have the latest version of Ruby installed, and try invoking it as `irb --readline`; this is an especially common problem on Mac OS X

21.11 Making Your Keyboard Lights Blink

Problem

You want to control the three standard keyboard LEDs (num lock, caps lock, and scroll lock) from a Ruby script.

Solution

Use the Blinkenlights library, available as the `blinkenlights` gem. It works on Windows or Linux (but not on Mac OS X), and it lets you toggle the lights individually or in patterns:

```
require 'rubygems'
require 'blinkenlights'

# Turn individual lights on or off.
BlinkenLights.open do |lights|
  lights.left = true
  lights.middle = true
  lights.right = true

  lights.scr = false
  lights.cap = false
  lights.num = false
end

# Display a light show.
BlinkenLights.open do |lights|
  lights.left_to_right
  10.times { lights.random }
  lights.right_to_left
end
```

Discussion

The keyboard lights are an often-overlooked user interface. They were originally designed to reflect information about the state of the keyboard itself, but they can be manipulated from the computer to display more interesting things. Each light can continually display one bit of information (such as whether you have new email), or can flash over time to indicate a rate (such as your computer's use of incoming or outgoing bandwidth).

BlinkenLights works by writing special command codes to the Unix keyboard device (/dev/tty8 is the default, but /dev/console should also work). Usually, you can only write to these devices when running as root.

On Windows, BlinkenLights works by sending key events that make Windows think you actually hit the corresponding key. This means that if you tell BlinkenLights on

Windows to turn on your caps lock light, caps lock itself is also enabled. The state of the light can't be disconnected from the state of the keyboard.

When you pass a code block into `Blinkenlights.open`, BlinkenLights runs the block and then restores the original state of the lights. This avoids confusing those users who use their lights to keep track of the state of their keyboards. If you want your setting of the lights to persist until they're changed again, then use the return value of `Blinkenlights.open` instead of passing in a code block.

This code will turn on the first two lights to represent the number six in binary. Until they're changed again, whether through the keyboard or through code, they'll stay on. Even the end of your program won't restore the original state of the lights.

```ruby
# Display the binary number 6 (that is, 110):
BlinkenLights.new.set(6)
```

Here's a program that converts an alphanumeric message to Morse code and displays it on the keyboard lights:

```ruby
#!/usr/bin/ruby -w
# blink_morse.rb
require 'rubygems'
require 'blinkenlights'

class String

  # Morse code representations for 0-9 and A-Z.
  MORSE_TABLE = %w{01111 00111 00011 00001 00000 10000 11000 11100 11110 11111
                   01 1000 1010 100 0 0010 110 0000 00 0111 101 0100 11
                   10 111 0110 1101 010 000 1 001 0001 011 1001 1011 1100}

  def to_morse(dit_time = 0.3)
    a = "A"[0]
    zero = "0"[0]
    words = upcase.gsub(/[^A-Z0-9\s]/, "").split
    BlinkenLights.open do |lights|
      words.each do |word|
        word.each_byte do |letter|
          code = MORSE_TABLE[letter - (letter < a ? zero : a-10)]
          code.each_byte do |signal|
            lights.flash(dit_time * (signal == zero ? 1 : 3))
            sleep(dit_time)          # Space between parts of a letter.
          end
          sleep(dit_time * 3)        # Space between letters.
        end
        sleep(dit_time * 5)          # Space between words.
      end
    end
  end
end

ARGV.shift.to_s.to_morse if $0 == __FILE__
```

See Also

- The BlinkenLights homepage at *http://blinkenlights.rubyforge.org/*; see especially the generated RDoc at *http://blinkenlights.rubyforge.org/doc/index.html*, which lists the many light patterns defined by the library
- The examples subdirectory of the installed gem contains sample programs that control the keyboard lights based on your system load or network activity
- The name "Blinkenlights" is explained at *http://www.catb.org/jargon/html/B/blinkenlights.html*
- An explanation of Morse code (*http://en.wikipedia.org/wiki/Morse_code*)
- The idea for the blink_morse.rb program comes from Neal Stephenson's novel *Cryptonomicon*

21.12 Creating a GUI Application with Tk

Credit: Kevin Marshall

Problem

You need to create a program that has a graphical user interface (GUI).

Solution

Use the Tk library. It's language-independent, cross-platform, and best of all, it comes standard with most Ruby distributions.

With Tk you create GUI elements, or "widgets", and then bind code blocks to them. When something happens (like the user clicking a widget), Tk runs the appropriate code block.

Ruby provides a class for each type of Tk widget. This simple Tk program creates a "root" widget (the application window), and a "label" widget within the window. The program then waits for events (although it can't respond to any).

```
require 'tk'
root = TkRoot.new { title "Tiny Tk Application" }
label = TkLabel.new(root) { text "You are a trout!" }
label.pack
Tk.mainloop
```

When run, it looks like Figure 21-1.

Figure 21-1. You are a trout

Discussion

The simple application above shows most of the basic features of GUI programming in Tk and other modern GUI toolkits. We'll use the techniques to build a more complex application.

Tk GUI development and layout take a parent/child approach. Most widgets are children of other widgets: depending on the widget, this nesting can go arbitrarily deep. The exception to this rule is the TkRoot widget: it's always the top-level widget, and it's represented as the application window.

Child widgets are "packed" inside their parents so they can be displayed. A system called the geometry manager controls where on the screen the widgets actually show up. The default geometry manager is the "placer" manager, which lets you place widgets in relation to each other.

Tk applications are event-driven, so the final step is to start a main event loop which tells our program to listen for events to be fired on our widgets.

To further illustrate, let's make a simple stopwatch program to demostrate a real-world use of Tk.

To start, we'll create four simple methods that will be bound to our widgets. These are the nonGUI core of the program:

```ruby
#!/usr/bin/ruby
# stopwatch.rb
require 'tk'

class Stopwatch

  def start
    @accumulated = 0 unless @accumulated
    @elapsed = 0
    @start = Time.now

    @mybutton.configure('text' => 'Stop')
    @mybutton.command { stop }
    @timer.start
  end

  def stop
    @mybutton.configure('text' => 'Start')
    @mybutton.command { start }
    @timer.stop
    @accumulated += @elapsed
  end

  def reset
    stop
    @accumulated, @elapsed = 0, 0
    @mylabel.configure('text' => '00:00:00.0')
  end
```

```
def tick
  @elapsed = Time.now - @start
  time = @accumulated + @elapsed
  h = sprintf('%02i', (time.to_i / 3600))
  m = sprintf('%02i', ((time.to_i % 3600) / 60))
  s = sprintf('%02i', (time.to_i % 60))
  mt = sprintf('%1i', ((time - time.to_i)*10).to_i)
  newtime = "#{h}:#{m}:#{s}:#{mt}"
  @mylabel.configure('text' => newtime)
end
```

Next, we set up our GUI. This consists of six simple widgets. As before, the TkRoot is our application window, and contains all our other widgets:

```
def initialize
  root = TkRoot.new { title 'Tk Stopwatch' }
```

The TkMenuBar corresponds to the menu bar at the top of the screen in most modern GUI programs. It's an easy way to group a set of program features and make them available across our application. The menu layout of a TkMenuBar is defined by a nested array containing the menu items, and the code blocks to run when a menu item is selected:

```
menu_spec = [
              [
                ['Program'],
                ['Start', lambda { start } ],
                ['Stop', lambda { stop } ],
                ['Exit', lambda { exit } ]
              ],
              [
                ['Reset'], ['Reset Stopwatch', lambda { reset } ]
              ]
            ]

@menubar = TkMenubar.new(root, menu_spec, 'tearoff' => false)
@menubar.pack('fill'=>'x', 'side'=>'top')
```

The TkFont is used only as a configuration option for our TkLabel, which in turn is only used to display the value of our stopwatch:

```
@myfont = TkFont.new('size' => 16, 'weight' => 'bold')

@mylabel = TkLabel.new(root)
@mylabel.configure('text' => '00:00:00.0', 'font' => @myfont)
@mylabel.pack('padx' => 10, 'pady' => 10)
```

Apart from the menu bar, the TKButton is the only part of the GUI that the user can directly manipulate. The code block passed into its command method is run when the user clicks the button. Recall how the start and stop methods call this method to modify the behavior of the button. This makes the button act like the toggle on a physical stopwatch:

```
@mybutton = TkButton.new(root)
@mybutton.configure('text' => 'Start')
@mybutton.command { start }
@mybutton.pack('side'=>'left', 'fill' => 'both')
```

The TkAfter event is an especially interesting widget because it has no direct visual representation in our program. Instead, it runs in the background firing our tick method every millisecond:

```
@timer = TkAfter.new(1, -1, proc { tick })
```

Finally, we'll start up the main Tk event loop. This call loads the GUI and starts listening for events:

```
    Tk.mainloop
  end
end

Stopwatch.new
```

Figure 21-2 shows the final product.

Figure 21-2. The stopwatch in action

This recipe only scratches the surface of the Tk library, not to mention GUI design in general. The Tk library includes dozens of widgets with lots of options and features. Entire books have been written about how to use the library. You should refer to the Ruby Tk documentation or other Tk references for complete details.

See Also

- If your Ruby distribution doesn't include Tk, you can obtain the binary or source from *http://www.tcl.tk*; you may then need to rebuild Ruby from the source distribution once you have the Tk extension; on Debian GNU/Linux, you can just install the libtk-ruby package
- Ruby's Tk documentation is not very complete; fortunately, its Tk binding is similar to Perl's, so you can get a lot of information from the Perl/Tk documentation; one location for this is *http://perlhelp.web.cern.ch/PerlHelp/*
- *Tcl and Tk* by Brent B. Welch and Ken Jones with Jeffrey Hobbs (Prentice Hall)
- *Perl/Tk Pocket Reference* by Stephen Lidie (O'Reilly)
- The next few recipes (21.13 and 21.15) reproduce the simple GUI application and the stopwatch with the Ruby bindings to various other GUI libraries

21.13 Creating a GUI Application with wxRuby

Problem

You want to write a portable GUI application that looks better than a Tk application.

Solution

Use the wxRuby library, available as a third-party download. It uses native GUI widgets on Windows, Unix, and Mac OS X. It's got many more features than the Tk library, and even greater complexity.

Here's a very simple wxRuby application (Figure 21-3):

```ruby
#!/usr/bin/ruby -w
# wxtrout.rb

require 'wxruby'
class TroutApp < Wx::App
  def on_init
    frame = Wx::Frame.new(nil, -1, 'Tiny wxRuby Application')
    panel = Wx::StaticText.new(frame, -1, 'You are a trout!',
                               Wx::Point.new(-1,1), Wx::DEFAULT_SIZE,
                               Wx::ALIGN_CENTER)

    frame.show
  end
end

TroutApp.new.main_loop
```

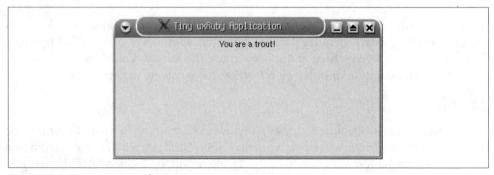

Figure 21-3. You are a wxRuby trout

Discussion

The simple wxRuby application has the same basic structure as its Tk cousin (see Recipe 21.12). A top-level widget is created (here called a Frame) and a label (StaticText) widget is added to it. The application then goes into an event loop, listening for and retrieving events like mouse clicks.

A wxRuby version of the Tk stopwatch program is also similar, although much longer. wxRuby code tends to be more verbose and less idiomatic than Ruby Tk code.

The core methods are nearly unchanged, because they have little to do with the GUI:

```ruby
#!/usr/bin/ruby -w
# wx_stopwatch.rb
require 'wxruby'

class StopwatchApp < Wx::App

  def start
    @start = Time.now
    @button.set_label('Stop')
    @button.refresh
    @frame.evt_button(@button.get_id) { stop }
    @timer.start(100) # The timer should tick every 100 milliseconds.
  end

  def stop
    @button.set_label('Start')
    @button.refresh
    @frame.evt_button(@button.get_id) { start }
    @timer.stop
    @accumulated += @elapsed
  end

  def reset
    stop
    @accumulated, @elapsed = 0, 0
    @label.set_label('00:00:00.0')
    @frame.layout
  end

  def tick
    @elapsed = Time.now - @start
    time = @accumulated + @elapsed
    h = sprintf('%02i', (time.to_i / 3600))
    m = sprintf('%02i', ((time.to_i % 3600) / 60))
    s = sprintf('%02i', (time.to_i % 60))
    mt = sprintf('%1i', ((time - time.to_i)*10).to_i)
    newtime = "#{h}:#{m}:#{s}:#{mt}"
    @label.set_label(newtime)
    @frame.layout
  end
```

The menu bar takes a lot more code in wxRuby than in Tk. Every widget in a wxRuby program has a unique ID, which must be passed in when you register an event handler. I've defined a hardcoded ID for each menu item, so that after I create the "menu item" widget, I can pass its unique ID into the event-handler registration method, evt_menu. You can really sense the underlying C code here:

```ruby
# Constants for the IDs of the menu items.
START_MENU = 10
```

```
STOP_MENU = 11
EXIT_MENU = 12
RESET_MENU = 13

# Constant for the ID of the timer widget, used below.
TIMER_ID = 14

def on_init
  @accumulated, @elapsed = 0, 0
  @frame = Wx::Frame.new(nil, -1, 'wxRuby Stopwatch')

  menu_bar = Wx::MenuBar.new

  program_menu = Wx::Menu.new
  menu_bar.append(program_menu, '&Program')
  program_menu.append(START_MENU, '&Start', 'Start the stopwatch')
  @frame.evt_menu(START_MENU) { start }
  program_menu.append(STOP_MENU, 'S&top', 'Stop the stopwatch')
  @frame.evt_menu(STOP_MENU) { stop }
  menu_exit = program_menu.append(EXIT_MENU, "E&xit\tAlt-X",
                                  'Exit the program')
  @frame.evt_menu(EXIT_MENU) { exit }

  reset_menu = Wx::Menu.new
  menu_bar.append(reset_menu, '&Reset')
  reset_menu.append(RESET_MENU, '&Reset', 'Reset the stopwatch')
  @frame.evt_menu(RESET_MENU) { reset }
  @frame.set_menu_bar(menu_bar)
```

wxRuby uses Sizer objects to pack widgets into their display areas. The BoxSizer
object used below arranges widgets within the frame vertically, so that the label will
be above the stopwatch button.

```
sizer = Wx::BoxSizer.new(Wx::VERTICAL)

@label = Wx::StaticText.new(@frame, -1, '00:00:00.0')
font = Wx::FontData.new.get_chosen_font
font.set_point_size(16)
font.set_weight(Wx::FONTWEIGHT_BOLD)
@label.set_font(font)
sizer.add(@label, 1, Wx::ALIGN_CENTER)
```

The button and the timer work more or less like their Tk equivalents. The call to
@frame.set_sizer tells the root widget to use our vertical BoxSizer when deciding
how to arrange widgets on the screen (Figure 21-4).

```
@button = Wx::Button.new(@frame, -1, 'Start')
@frame.evt_button(@button.get_id) { start }
sizer.add(@button, 0, Wx::ALIGN_CENTER, 2)

@frame.set_sizer(sizer)
@frame.show
```

```
    @timer = Wx::Timer.new(@frame, TIMER_ID)
    @frame.evt_timer(TIMER_ID) { tick }
  end
end

StopwatchApp.new.main_loop
```

Figure 21-4. The wxRuby stopwatch looks more like a native application than the Tk one

See Also

- You need to download (and, on Unix systems, compile) wxRuby as a Ruby extension; you can get it from *http://wxruby.rubyforge.org/*; the wxRuby developers provide a good installation guide at *http://wxruby.rubyforge.org/wiki/wiki. pl?Installation*

- The wxRuby wiki has a lot of useful information, including a simple tutorial at *http://wxruby.rubyforge.org/wiki/wiki.pl?Getting_Started*; the wxRuby distribution also comes with many good sample applications in its samples/ directory

- The web site for wxWidgets (the underlying library to which wxRuby is a binding) also has lots of good reference material: *http://www.wxwidgets.org/*; you just have to be able to translate the C++-style class and method names into Ruby style (for instance, WxLabel::SetLabel becomes Wx::Label#set_label)

21.14 Creating a GUI Application with Ruby/GTK

Problem

You want to write a GUI application that uses the GTK widget library, perhaps so you can integrate it with the Gnome desktop environment.

Solution

Use the Ruby bindings to Gnome's GTK widget library, available as a third-party download. Here's a simple Ruby/GTK application (Figure 21-5).

```
#!/usr/bin/ruby -w
# gtktrout.rb
require 'gtk2'

Gtk.init
window = Gtk::Window.new 'Tiny Ruby/GTK Application'
label = Gtk::Label.new 'You are a trout!'
window.add label
window.signal_connect('destroy') { Gtk.main_quit }
window.show_all
Gtk.main
```

Figure 21-5. You are a GTK trout

Discussion

Gnome is one of the two most popular Unix desktop suites. The Ruby-Gnome2 project provides and documents Ruby bindings to Gnome's vast array of C libraries. You can write Ruby applications that fully integrate with the Gnome desktop, but in this recipe I'm going to focus on the basics of the Gnome GUI library GTK.

Although the details are different, the sample program above is basically the same as it would be with Tk (Recipe 21.12) or the wxRuby library (Recipe 21.13). You create two widgets (a window and a label), attach the label to the window, and tell the GUI library to display the window. As with Tk and wxRuby, the application goes into a display loop, capturing user events like mouse clicks.

The sample program won't actually respond to any user events, though, so let's create a Ruby/GTK version of the stopwatch program seen in previous GUI recipes.

The core methods, the ones that actually implement the stopwatch, are basically the same as the corresponding methods in the Tk and wxRuby recipes. Since GTK doesn't have a timer widget, I've implemented a simple timer as a separate thread. The other point of interest is the HTML-like markup that GTK uses to customize the font size and weight of the stopwatch text.

```
#!/usr/bin/ruby -w
# gtk_stopwatch.rb
require 'gtk2'

class Stopwatch

  LABEL_MARKUP = '<span font_desc="16" weight="bold">%s</span>'

  def start
    @accumulated ||= 0
```

```
    @elapsed = 0
    @start = Time.now

    @mybutton.label = 'Stop'
    set_button_handler('clicked') { stop }
    @timer_stopped = false
    @timer = Thread.new do
      until @timer_stopped do
        sleep(0.1)
        tick unless @timer_stopped
      end
    end
  end

  def stop
    @mybutton.label = 'Start'
    set_button_handler('clicked') { start }
    @timer_stopped = true
    @accumulated += @elapsed
  end

  def reset
    stop
    @accumulated, @elapsed = 0, 0
    @mylabel.set_markup(LABEL_MARKUP % '00:00:00.0')
  end

  def tick
    @elapsed = Time.now - @start
    time = @accumulated + @elapsed
    h = sprintf('%02i', (time.to_i / 3600))
    m = sprintf('%02i', ((time.to_i % 3600) / 60))
    s = sprintf('%02i', (time.to_i % 60))
    mt = sprintf('%1i', ((time - time.to_i)*10).to_i)
    @mylabel.set_markup(LABEL_MARKUP % "#{h}:#{m}:#{s}:#{mt}")
  end
```

Now begins the GUI setup. Ruby uses VBox and HBox objects to pack widgets into the display area. The stopwatch application will give its main window a single VBox containing three widgets arranged from top to bottom: a menu bar, a label (displaying the stopwatch time), and a button (to start and stop the stopwatch):

```
  def initialize
    Gtk.init
    root = Gtk::Window.new('GTK Stopwatch')

    accel_group = Gtk::AccelGroup.new
    root.add_accel_group(accel_group)
    root.set_border_width 0

    box = Gtk::VBox.new(false, 0)
    root.add(box)
```

The program's menu bar consists of many nested MenuBar, Menu, and MenuItem objects. Rather than create these objects ourselves, we define the parameters of our menu bar in a nested array, and pass it into an ItemFactory object:

```
menu_factory = Gtk::ItemFactory.new(Gtk::ItemFactory::TYPE_MENU_BAR,
                                    '<main>', nil)
menu_spec = [
              ['/_Program'],
              ['/Program/_Start', '<Item>', nil, nil, lambda { start } ],
              ['/Program/S_top', '<Item>', nil, nil, lambda { stop } ],
              ['/Program/_Exit', '<Item>', nil, nil,
               lambda { Gtk.main_quit } ],
              ['/_Reset'],
              ['/Reset/_Reset Stopwatch', '<Item>', nil, nil,
               lambda { reset } ]
            ]
menu_factory.create_items(menu_spec)
menu_root = menu_factory.get_widget('<main>')
box.pack_start(menu_root)
```

The label and the button are pretty simple: just define them and pack them into the VBox:

```
@mylabel = Gtk::Label.new
@mylabel.set_markup(LABEL_MARKUP % '00:00:00.0')
box.pack_start(@mylabel)

@mybutton = Gtk::Button.new('Start')
set_button_handler('clicked') { start }
box.pack_start(@mybutton)

root.signal_connect('destroy') { Gtk.main_quit }
root.show_all

Gtk.main
end
```

I've been calling a nonexistent method Stopwatch#set_button_handler whenever I want to modify the code that runs when the user clicks the button. I close out the Stopwatch class by defining that method (Figure 21-6):

```
  def set_button_handler(event, &block)
    @mybutton.signal_handler_disconnect(@mybutton_handler) if @mybutton_handler
    @mybutton_handler = @mybutton.signal_connect(event, &block)
  end
end

Stopwatch.new
```

In the Tk recipe, I simply called a button's command method whenever I needed to change the code block that runs when the user clicks the button. So why this set_button_handler code? Why not just call signal_connect whenever I need to change what the button does here? I can't do that because GTK lets you associate multiple

Figure 21-6. The GTK stopwatch

code blocks with a single event. This doesn't usually come up, but it's a problem here because I'm changing the function of a button.

If the button is set up to call start when you click it, and you call signal_connect('clicked', proc { stop }), then clicking on the button will call start and *then* call stop. You've added a second code block to the "clicked" event, when what you want is to replace the old "clicked" code with the new code. To avoid this problem, set_button_handler removes any old handler from the button before installing the new handler. The set_button_handler method tracks the internal ID of the newly installed handler, so that *it* can be removed if the user clicks the button yet again.

See Also

- You can download the Ruby bindings to GTK from the project homepage (*http://ruby-gnome2.sourceforge.jp/*); the GTK homepage itself is at *http://www.gtk.org*; Debian GNU/Linux users can install the libgtk2-ruby package

- The Ruby GTK bindings are documented on the Ruby-GNOME2 Wiki at *http://ruby-gnome2.sourceforge.jp/hiki.cgi?Ruby%2FGTK*; there's also a tutorial at *http://ruby-gnome2.sourceforge.jp/hiki.cgi?tut-gtk*

- Don't confuse the Ruby-GNOME2 project with its predecessor, Ruby-GNOME; the documentation for the older project is still online and will mislead you if you go to the wrong web site

21.15 Creating a Mac OS X Application with RubyCocoa

Credit: Alun ap Rhisiart

Problem

You want to create a native Mac OS X program with a graphical user interface.

Solution

Use the Mac OS X Cocoa library along with RubyCocoa and the Interface Builder application. RubyCocoa creates real OS X applications and provides a GUI interface for building GUIs, as opposed to other libraries, which make you define the GUI with Ruby code. RubyCocoa is a free download, and the Cocoa development tools are on the Mac OS X installation DVD.

Interface Builder is very powerful: you can create simple applications without writing any code. In fact, it takes longer to explain what to do than to do it. Here's how to create a simple application with Interface Builder:

1. Start the Xcode application and create a new project from the File menu. Choose "Cocoa-Ruby Application" from the "New Project" list, hit the Next button, give your project a name and location on disk, and click Finish.

   XCode will create a project that looks like Figure 21-7.

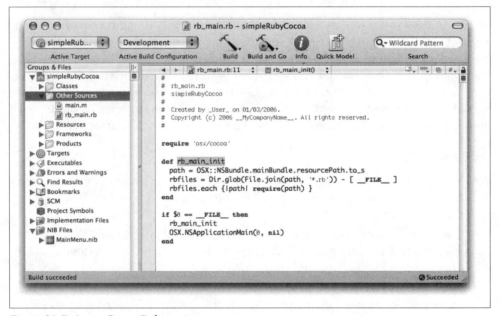

Figure 21-7. A new Cocoa-Ruby project

The Cocoa-Ruby project template comes with two files: main.m (an Objective-C file) and rb_main.rb (a RubyCocoa file). For a simple application, this is all the code you need.

2. Open the NIB Files group and doubleclick MainMenu.nib to open Interface Builder. You get a new application window, into which you can drag and drop GUI widgets, and a menubar labeled MainMenu.nib (English) – MainMenu.

   You'll also see a palette window with a selection of GUI objects; a nib document window named MainMenu.nib (English), containing classes, instances, images and sounds; and an inspector. If the inspector is not open, select Show Inspector from the Tools menu.

The screenshot in Figure 21-8 shows what we're going to do to our new application window (seen in the upper left).

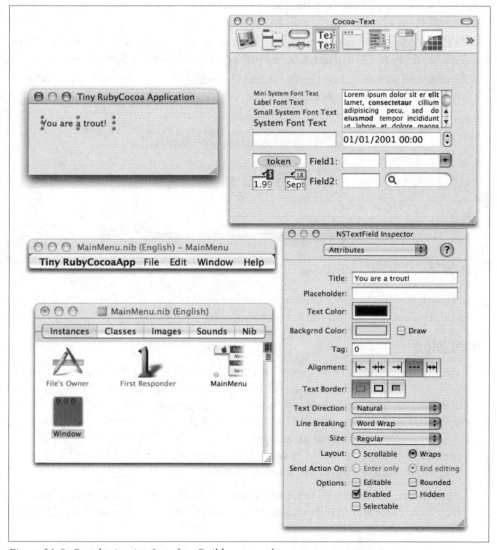

Figure 21-8. Our destination Interface Builder screenshot

1. Select the new application window and set the application's title. Type "Tiny RubyCocoa Application" in the inspector's Window Title field (you need to select the "Attributes" tab to see this field).

2. Add a text label to the application window. Select the Text palette in the palette window. The visible controls are all text fields, with only slight differences

between them. We'll use the control called System Font Text: drag this control into your application window.

3. Double-click the new text field in the application window and type "You are a trout!"

4. For completeness, go through the menus in the menubar and change "New Application" to "Tiny RubyCocoaApp" wherever it occurs. Save your nib.

5. Go back to Xcode. Click the Build and Go button. Your application should now run; it will look like Figure 21-9.

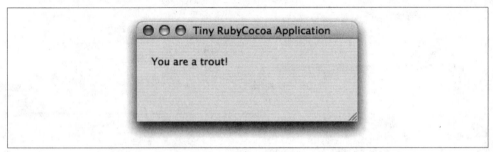

Figure 21-9. You are a Mac OS X trout

A compiled, doubleclickable version of the application will be found in your project build folder—usually within the project subfolder.

Discussion

This simple application doesn't show much about RubyCocoa, but it gives a glimpse of the power of the Cocoa framework. The NSApplication class gives you a lot of functionality for free: spellchecking, printing, application hiding, and so on. Ruby-Cocoa creates an instance of NSApplication, which deals with the run loop, handling events from the operating system, and more. You could have created this GUI application entirely in code (it would have looked something like the Tk example), but in practice, programmers always use Interface Builder.

For a more realistic example, we'll need to write some code that interacts with the interface. Like Rails and many other modern frameworks, Cocoa uses a Model-View-Controller pattern.

- The view layer consists of the windows and widgets: NSView and its subclasses, such as NSTextField. These are built using Interface Builder.

- The model layer is coded by the programmer, based on NSObject or a more specialised subclass.

- The Controller layer can be dealt with in Interface Builder using subclasses of NSController (these are in the Controllers palette), or in code.

Let's create a RubyCocoa version of the Stopwatch program seen in previous GUI recipes like Recipe 21.12. First, we need to create a new Cocoa-Ruby Application project in Xcode, and once more open the MainMenu.nib file in Interface Builder. Because RubyCocoa makes it easy, we'll display the time on the stopwatch two ways: as a digital readout *and* as an analog clock face (Figure 21-10).

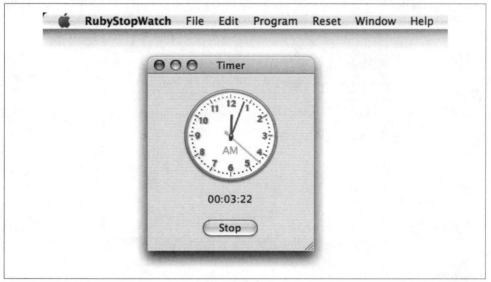

Figure 21-10. The RubyCocoa stopwatch in analog mode

1. Create a new Cocoa-Ruby application. Select the new application window and change its title in the inspector to Timer.

2. Create the clock. From the Text palette we used before, drag a NSDatePicker (a label that displays a date and time) into the application window. In the inspector, change the style to "Graphical", date selection to "None", and time selection to "Hour, Minute, and Second". The NSDatePicker now shows up as a clock.

3. Create the digital readout. Drag an NSTextField ("System Font Text", as in the previous example) onto the window below the clock. Now drag a date formatter (marked with a small calendar in the palette) onto the NSTextField. The Inspector changes to show a list of possible formats; select %H:%M:%S.

4. Create the stopwatch button. Switch to the button palette and drag a normal, rounded, NSButton to the application window. In the Inspector, change the title to "Start" and make sure its type is "Push Button".

5. Build the menu bar. Change to the menus palette and drag Submenu objects onto the "MainMenu" menubar. Double-click them to change their titles (to "Program" and "Reset"), and drag Item objects onto the menu objects to add items to the menu. As in the stopwatch examples for other GUI libraries, our "Program"

menu will contain menu items for "Start" and "Stop". The "Reset" menu will have a single menu item: "Reset Stopwatch". Unlike in the other examples, the application menus will contain no menu item for "Exit". This is because Mac OS X already provides a way to exit any program from the apple menu.

6. Now we have all our interface elements in place. We need a model object to actually do the work. Click on Classes in the MainMenu.nib window, to bring up the class browser (Figure 21-11).

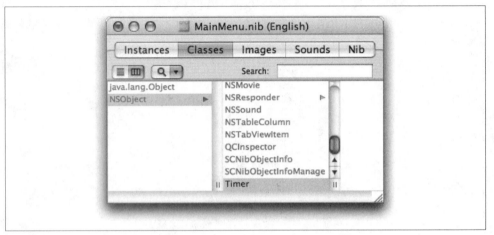

Figure 21-11. The class browser

Select NSObject and then "Subclass NSObject" from the Classes menu. Change the name of the new class to Timer. This class will implement the stopwatch code.

We need to tell Interface Builder about the interface to this class. Start by specifying three methods. In the inspector, with the new class still selected in the class browser, make sure that the Attributes-Actions tab is selected and hit the Add button three times. Name the methods reset:, start:, and stop:. These are the methods that will be called from the button and menus.

The model class we are creating also needs to know about some interface elements; for instance, it needs to know about the time controls so it can change the displayed time. The model class accesses Interface Builder widgets through instance variables called *outlets*. Switch to the "Attributes-Outlets" tab and click Add three times. Name the outlets clock, timeField, and button.

1. With the model object declared and all the interface elements in place, we can connect everything together. Recall that Interface Builder deals with instances of objects; we have a Timer class that implements the stopwatch functionality, but as of yet we have no instance of the class. Keeping the Timer class selected in the class browser, choose "Instantiate Timer" from the Classes menu. The window switches to the Instances tab, with a new icon representing the Timer instance.

To make a connection between two objects, we drag *from* the object that needs to know, *to* the object it needs to know about. First, let's deal with the actions.

When we click the Start button, we want the start method on our Timer class to be called. The button needs to know about the start: method. Control drag from the Start button to the Timer instance icon. The Inspector changes to show the methods of Timer, and automatically selects the start: method for you (it matches the button label). Click the Connect button to make the connection.

Make the same connection *from* the menu item "Program/Start" *to* the Timer, and then from "Program/Stop" to the stop: method. Connect "Reset/Reset Stopwatch" to the reset: method.

2. The controls now know which Ruby methods they trigger. We need to tell our Timer class which interface elements are accessible from its outlets (instance variables). Now the connections are made *from* the Timer class *to* the interface controls it needs to know about. Control-drag the Timer instance to the clock control: the inspector changes to show the outlets tab for Timer. Select clock and click the Connect button.

Connect the textField and button outlets to the digital time control and the start button. Save the nib file as Timer.rb.

Back in Xcode, we are finally ready to write the Ruby code that actually implements the stopwatch. Choose "New File..." from the File menu, and then select "Ruby-Cocoa NSObject subclass" from the list. The core model object code is very similar to the Tk recipe, with some small differences:

```
require 'osx/cocoa'
include OSX

ZeroDate = NSDate.dateWithString('2000-01-01 00:00:00 +0000')

class Timer < NSObject
    ib_outlets :clock, :timeField, :button

    def initialize
        @timer = NSTimer.
        scheduledTimerWithTimeInterval_target_selector_userInfo_repeats(
        1.0, self, :tick, nil, true)
    end
```

First, we call the ib_outlets decorator to specify instance variables that are matched up with the objects specified in Interface Builder.

In the other GUI examples, we displayed a plaintext label and formatted the time as a string for display. Here, the label has its own date formatter, so we can tell it to display an NSDate object and have it figure out the formatting on its own.

NSTimer is a Cocoa class we can use to tap into the Mac OS X user-event loop and call a method at a certain interval. We can get submillisecond time intervals from

NSTimer, but there's not much point because NSDate won't display fractions of a second. So we set it up to call the tick method once a second.[*]

Now we define the start method, triggered when the end user pushes the "Start" button:

```
def start(sender)
    @running = true
    @start = NSDate.date
    @accumulated = 0 unless @accumulated
    @elapsed = 0.0
    @button.setTitle('Stop')
    @button.setAction(:stop)
end
```

One thing to note here: NSTimer hooks into the operating system's event loop, which means it can't be switched off. We define a @running variable so we know to ignore the timer when we are not running the stopwatch.

The rest of the code is similar to the other GUI examples:

```
def stop(sender)
    @running = false
    @accumulated += @elapsed
    @button.setTitle('Start')
    @button.setAction(:start)
end

def reset(sender)
    stop(nil)
    @accumulated, @elapsed = 0.0, 0.0
    @clock.setDateValue(ZeroDate)
    @timeField.setObjectValue(ZeroDate)
end

def tick( )
  if @running
        @elapsed = NSDate.date.timeIntervalSinceDate(@start)
        d = ZeroDate.addTimeInterval(@elapsed + @accumulated)
        @clock.setDateValue(d)
        @timeField.setObjectValue(d)
    end
  end
end
```

This recipe is pretty long-winded compared to the other GUI recipes, but that's because it takes more words to explain how to use a GUI application than to explain how a block of Ruby code works. Once you're familiar with Interface Builder, you can create complex Cocoa applications very quickly.

---

[*] If, as in the other GUI recipes, we'd decided to format the time ourselves and display it as a string, we could set a shorter interval and make the fractions of a second whiz by.

The combination of Ruby and Cocoa can make you very productive. Cocoa is a very big class library, and the GUI part, called AppKit, is only a part of it. There are classes for speech recognition, Bluetooth, disc recording, HTML rendering (Web-Kit), database (Core Data), graphics, audio, and much more. The disadvantage is that a RubyCocoa program is tied to Mac OS X, unlike Tk or wxRuby, which will work on Windows and Linux as well.

With Apple's recent change to Intel processors, you'll want to create "universal binaries" for your application, so that your users can run it natively whether they have a PowerPC or an Intel Mac. The Ruby code doesn't need to change, because Ruby is an interpreted language; but a RubyCocoa application also contains Objective-C code, which must be compiled separately for each architecture.

To make a universal binary, select the top-most group in the "Groups & Files" list in Xcode (the one with the name of your project). Get Info on this (Command-I), go to the "Build" tab, select "Architectures", and click the Edit button. Select both the PowerPC and Intel checkboxes, and your packaged application will include compiled code for both architectures.

See Also

- While Ruby, Xcode, and Interface Builder come as standard with all Macintoshes, RubyCocoa does not (yet!); there is a standard installer, available from *http://rubycocoa.sourceforge.net*, which includes both the framework classes and the Xcode project templates
- RubyCocoa comes with some documentation and a number of examples; however, once you know how to translate Objective-C messages to RubyCocoa messages, you can reference the huge amount of Cocoa documentation available via Xcode's Help menu, and a large number of examples: there are also many useful and free add-on libraries and Interface Builder palettes, for instance from The Omni Group
- *Cocoa Programming for Mac OS X* by Aaron Hillegass (Addison-Wesley)
- *Cocoa Programming* by Scott Anguish, Erik M. Buck, and Donald A. Yacktman (Sams)

21.16 Using AppleScript to Get User Input

Problem

On Mac OS X, AppleScript makes it easy to add simple graphical interface elements to programs. You want to use AppleScript from a Ruby program.

Solution

Use the AppleScript library, written by John Butler and available as the `applescript` gem. It lets you talk to AppleScript from Ruby.

Here's a script that uses the `AppleScript` class to get input through AppleScript. It also shows off the `AppleScript.say` method, which uses Mac OS X's text-to-speech capabilities:

```
require 'rubygems'
require 'applescript'

name = AppleScript.gets("What's your name?")

AppleScript.puts("Thank you!")

choice = AppleScript.choose("So which of these is your name?",
                            ["Leonard", "Mike", "Lucas", name])

if name == choice
  AppleScript.say "You are right!"
  picture = AppleScript.choose_file("Find a picture of yourself")

  if File.exists?(picture)
    AppleScript.say "Thanks, I will now post it on Flickr for you."
    # Exercise for the reader: upload the file to Flickr
  end
else
  AppleScript.say "But you just said your name was #{name}!"
end
```

Discussion

The AppleScript library is just a simple wrapper around the `osascript` command-line interface to AppleScript. If you already know AppleScript, you can execute raw AppleScript code with `AppleScript.execute`:

```
script = 'tell application "Finder" to display dialog "Hello World!" ' +
         'buttons {"OK"}'
AppleScript.execute(script)
```

See Also

- The manpage for `osascript`, available online at *http://developer.apple.com/documentation/Darwin/Reference/ManPages/man1/osascript.1.html*

Extending Ruby with Other Languages

When you decide to use an interpreted language such as Ruby, you're trading raw speed for ease of use. It's far easier to develop a program in a higher-level language, and you get a working program faster, but you sacrifice some of the speed you might get by writing the program in a lower-level language like C and C++.

That's the simplified view. Anyone who's spent any serious amount of time working with higher-level languages knows that the truth is usually more complex. In many situations, the tradeoff doesn't really matter: if the program is only going to be run once, who cares if it takes twice as long to do its job? If a program is complex enough, it might be prohibitively hard to implement in a low-level language: you might never actually get it working right without using a language like Ruby.

But even Ruby zealots must admit that there are still situations where it's useful to be able to call code written in another language. Maybe you need a particular part of your program to run blazingly fast, or maybe you want to use a particular library that's implemented in C or Java. When that happens you'll be grateful for Ruby's extension mechanism, which lets you call C code from a regular Ruby program; and the JRuby interpreter, which runs atop the Java Virtual Machine and uses Java classes as though they were Ruby classes.

Compared to other dynamic languages, it's pretty easy to write C extensions in Ruby. The interfaces you need to understand are easy to use and clearly defined in just a few header files, there are numerous examples available in the Ruby standard library itself, and there are even tools that can help you access C libraries without writing any C code at all.

So let's break out that trusty C compiler and learn how to drop down under the hood of the Ruby interpreter, because you just never know when your next program will to turn into one of those situations where a little bit of C code is the only solution to the problem.

—Garrett Rooney

22.1 Writing a C Extension for Ruby

Credit: Garrett Rooney

Problem

You want to implement part of your Ruby program in C. This might be the part of your program that needs to run really fast, it might contain some very platform-specific code, or you might just have a C implementation already, and you don't want to also write one in Ruby.

Solution

Write a C extension that implements that portion of your program. Compile it with extconf.rb and require it in your Ruby program as though it were a Ruby library. You'll need to have the Ruby header files installed on your system.

Here's a simple Ruby program that requires a library called example. It instantiates an instance of Example::Class from that library, and calls a method on that library:

```
require 'example'
e = Example::Class.new
e.print_string("Hello World\n")
# Hello World
```

What would the example library look like if it were written in Ruby? Something like this:

```
# example.rb
module Example
  class Class
    def print_string(s)
      print s
    end
  end
end
```

Let's implement that same functionality in C code. This small C library, example.c, defines a Ruby module, class, and method using the functions made available by ruby.h:

```
#include <ruby.h>
#include <stdio.h>

static VALUE rb_mExample;
static VALUE rb_cClass;

static VALUE
print_string(VALUE class, VALUE arg)
{
  printf("%s", RSTRING(arg)->ptr);
  return Qnil;
}
```

```
void
Init_example()
{
  rb_mExample = rb_define_module("Example");

  rb_cClass = rb_define_class_under(rb_mExample, "Class", rb_cObject);

  rb_define_method(rb_cClass, "print_string", print_string, 1);
}
```

To build the extension, you also need to create an extconf.rb file:

```
# extconf.rb
require 'mkmf'

dir_config('example')
create_makefile('example')
```

Then you can build your library by running extconf.rb, then make:

```
$ ls
example.c  extconf.rb

$ ruby extconf.rb
creating Makefile

$ make
gcc -fPIC -Wall -g -O2 -fPIC -I. -I/usr/lib/ruby/1.8/i486-linux
  -I/usr/lib/ruby/1.8/i486-linux -I.   -c example

gcc -shared  -L"/usr/lib" -o example.so example.o  -lruby1.8
  -lpthread -ldl -lcrypt -lm   -lc

$ ls
Makefile  example.c  example.o  example.so  extconf.rb
```

The example.so file contains your extension. As long as it's in your Ruby include path (and there's no example.rb that might mask it), you can use it like any other Ruby library:

```
require 'example'
e = Example::Class.new
e.print_string("Hello World\n")
# Hello World
```

Discussion

Most programs can be implemented using plain old Ruby code, but occasionally it turns out that it's better to implement part of the program in C. The example library above simply provides an interface to C's printf function, and Ruby already has a perfectly good IO#printf method.

Perhaps you need to perform a calculation hundreds of thousands of times, and implementing it in Ruby would be too slow (the Example::Class#print_string method is faster than IO#printf). Or maybe you need to interact with some platform-specific API that's not exposed by the Ruby standard library. There are a number of reasons you might want to fall back to C code, so Ruby provides you with a reasonably simple way of doing it.

Unfortunately, the fact that it's easy doesn't always mean it's a good idea. You must remember that when writing C-level code, you're playing with fire. The Ruby interpreter does its best to limit the damage you can do if you write bad Ruby code. About the worst you can do is cause an exception: another part of your program can catch the exception, handle it, and carry on. But C code runs outside the Ruby interpreter, and an error in C code can crash the Ruby interpreter.

With that in mind, let's go over some of the details you need to know to write a C extension.

A Ruby extension is just a small, dynamically loadable library, which the Ruby interpreter loads via dlopen or something similar. The entry point to your extension is via its Init function. For our example module, we defined an Init_example function to set everything up. Init_example is the first function to be called by the Ruby interpreter when it loads our extension.

The Init_example function uses a number of functions provided by the Ruby interpreter to declare modules, classes, and methods, just as you might in Ruby code. The difference, of course, is that here the methods are implemented in C. In this example, we used rb_define_module to create the Example module, then rb_define_class_under to define the Example::Class class (which inherits from Object), and finally rb_define_method to give Example::Class a print_string method.

The first thing to notice in the C code is all the VALUE variables lying around. A VALUE is the C equivalent of a Ruby reference, and it can point to any Ruby object. Ruby provides you with a number of functions and macros for manipulating VALUEs.

The rb_cObject variable is a VALUE, a reference to Ruby's Object class. When we pass it into rb_define_class_under, we're telling the Ruby interpreter to define a new subclass of Object. The ruby.h header file defines similar variables for many other Ruby-level modules (named using the rb_mFoo convention) and classes (the convention is rb_cFoo).

To manipulate a VALUE, you need to know something about it. It makes no more sense in C code than in Ruby code to call a method of File on a value that refers to a string. The simplest way to check a Ruby object's type is to use the Check_Type macro, which lets you see whether or not a VALUE points to an instance of a particular Ruby class. For convenience, the ruby.h file defines constants T_STRING, T_ARRAY, and so on, to denote built-in Ruby classes.

But that's not what we'd do in Ruby code. Ruby enforces duck typing, in which objects are judged on the methods they respond to, rather than the class they instantiate. C code can operate on Ruby objects the same way. To check whether an object responds to a particular message, use the function rb_respond_to. To send the message, use rb_funcall. It looks like this:

```
static VALUE
write_string(VALUE object, VALUE str)
{
  if (rb_respond_to(object, rb_intern("<<")))
  {
    rb_funcall(object, rb_intern("<<"), 1, str);
  }
  return Qnil;
}
```

That's the C-level equivalent of the following Ruby code:

```
def write_string(object, str)
  object << str if object.respond_to?('<<')
  return nil
end
```

A few more miscellaneous tips: the rb_intern function takes a symbol name as a C string and returns the corresponding Ruby symbol ID. You use this with functions like rb_respond_to and rb_funcall to refer to a Ruby method. Qnil is just the C-level name for Ruby's special nil object. There are a few similar constants, like Qfalse and Qtrue, which do just about what you'd think they'd do.

There are a number of other C level functions that let you create and manipulate strings (look in for functions that start with rb_str), arrays (rb_ary), and hashes (rb_hash). These APIs are pretty self-explanatory, so we won't go into them in depth here, but you can find them in the Ruby header files, specifically ruby.h and intern.h.

Ruby also defines some macros to do convenient things with common data types. For example, the StringValuePtr macro takes a VALUE that refers to a ruby String and returns a C-style char pointer. This can be useful for interacting with C-level APIs. You can find this and other similar helpers in the ruby.h header.

See Also

- The file README.EXT file in the Ruby source tree
- Recipe 22.2, "Using a C Library from Ruby"

22.2   Using a C Library from Ruby

Credit: Garrett Rooney

Problem

You'd like to use a library in your Ruby program, but the library's implemented in C and there are no bindings.

Solution

Write a Ruby extension that wraps the C library with Ruby classes and methods.

Let's say we want to give a Ruby interface to C's file methods (yes, the File class already does this, but this makes a good example). We want to make it possible to open a disk file and read from it a byte at a time.

Just as in Recipe 22.1, you'll need a C file that implements the actual extension. This one is called stdio.c. It's got an Init_stdio function that defines a Ruby module (Stdio), a Ruby class (Stdio::File), and some methods for that class.

The file_allocate function corresponds to the Stdio::File constructor. Because it's a constructor, we must also define some hook functions to create and destroy the underlying resources (in this case, a filehandle and the memory it uses):

```c
#include "stdio.h"
#include "ruby.h"

static VALUE rb_mStdio;
static VALUE rb_cStdioFile;

struct file
{
  FILE *fhandle;
};

static VALUE
file_allocate(VALUE klass)
{
  struct file *f = malloc(sizeof(*f));
  f->fhandle = NULL;
  return Data_Wrap_Struct(klass, file_mark, file_free, f);
}

static void
file_mark(struct file *f)
{
}

static void
file_free(struct file *f)
{
  fclose(f->fhandle);
  free(f);
}
```

The file_open function implements the Stdio::File#open method:

```c
static VALUE
file_open(VALUE object, VALUE fname)
{
  struct file *f;
  Data_Get_Struct(object, struct file, f);
```

```
    f->fhandle = fopen(RSTRING(fname)->ptr, "r");
    return Qnil;
  }
```

file_readbyte implements the Stdio::File#readbyte method:

```
static VALUE
file_readbyte(VALUE object)
{
  char buffer[2] = { 0, 0 };
  struct file *f;

  Data_Get_Struct(object, struct file, f);

  if (! f->fhandle)
    rb_raise(rb_eRuntimeError, "Attempt to read from closed file");

  fread(buffer, 1, 1, f->fhandle);

  return rb_str_new2(buffer);
}
```

Finally, our Init_ method defines the Stdio module, the File class, and the three methods defined for the File class:

```
void
Init_stdio()
{
  rb_mStdio = rb_define_module("Stdio");
  rb_cStdioFile = rb_define_class_under(rb_mStdio, "File", rb_cObject);

  rb_define_alloc_func(rb_cStdioFile, file_allocate);
  rb_define_method(rb_cStdioFile, "open", file_open, 1);
  rb_define_method(rb_cStdioFile, "readbyte", file_readbyte, 0);
}
```

As before, you'll need an extconf.rb file that knows how to compile your C library:

```
# extconf.rb
require 'mkmf'
dir_config("stdio")
create_makefile("stdio")
```

Once the C library is compiled, you can use it from Ruby as though it were a Ruby library:

```
open('foo.txt', 'w') { |f| f << 'foo' }

require 'stdio'
f = Stdio::File.new
f.open('foo.txt')
f.readbyte                              # => "f"
f.readbyte                              # => "o"
f.readbyte                              # => "o"
```

Discussion

The basic idea when writing a Ruby extension is to create a C data structure and wrap it in a Ruby object. The C data structure gives you someplace to store whatever data you need, so you can access it in your C methods. You're creating a primitive form of object-oriented programming in C.

Ruby provides some macros to help with this. `Data_Wrap_Struct` wraps a C data structure in a Ruby object. It takes a pointer to your data structure, along with a few pointers to callback functions, and returns a VALUE. The `Data_Get_Struct` macro takes that VALUE and gives you back a pointer to your C data structure.

You usually use `Data_Wrap_Struct` inside your class's `allocate` function (called by the constructor), and `Data_Get_Struct` inside its instance methods. In the example above, the `file_allocate` function creates a C struct (containing a variable of type `FILE`) and passes it into `Data_Wrap_Struct` to get a VALUE. The functions for the instance methods, `file_open` and `file_readbyte`, both take a VALUE as an argument, and pass it into `Data_Get_Struct` to get a C struct.

So what about those callback functions? There are three of them: an "allocate" function, a "mark" function, and a "free" function. The "allocate" function is called whenever an object is created. The other two have to do with garbage collection.

Ruby's garbage collector uses a mark-and-sweep algorithm: it runs through all the "live" objects in the system, marking them to note that it was able to reach them. Then it destroys every object that it couldn't reach: by definition, those objects are no longer in use, and don't need to be kept around in memory. To make this work, you need to provide two callbacks: one that marks an object as reachable, and one that frees the underlying resources for all unreachable objects.

In this case, both functions are simple. The "free" callback simply closes the filehandle and calls the C `free` function. The "mark" callback doesn't need to do anything, since this object doesn't refer to any other Ruby objects.

If your object does contain references to other Ruby objects, all you need to do is explicitly mark them (by calling the `rb_gc_mark` function) in your "mark" callback. This example goes a bit further than it needs to by defining an empty mark callback; it could accomplish the same thing by passing in a NULL function pointer.

To summarize: if your library doesn't define its own data structures, define your own C struct. Implement methods that translate Ruby arguments into their C equivalents, call the library functions you're interested in, then translate the return values back into Ruby data structures, so that the rest of the Ruby program can use it.

See Also

- The README.EXT file in the Ruby source tree
- Recipe 22.1, "Writing a C Extension for Ruby"
- Recipe 22.3, "Calling a C Library Through SWIG," might do what you want with less complication

22.3   Calling a C Library Through SWIG

Credit: Garrett Rooney

Problem

You want to use a C library in your Ruby code, but you don't want to have to write any C code to do it.

Solution

Use SWIG to generate the C extension for you. SWIG is a programming tool that takes as its input a file containing the information about C functions. It produces source code that lets you access those C functions from a variety of programming languages, including Ruby.

All you you need to write is an interface file, containing the prototypes for the C functions you want to call. The interface file also contains a few directives to control things like the name of the resulting module. Process that file with the `swig` command-line tool, build your extension, and you're up and running.

Let's build a SWIG extension that lets Ruby access functions from the standard C library. It'll provide access to enough functionality that you can read data from one file and write it to another. In Recipe 22.1, we wrote the C code for a similar extension ourselves, but here we'll let SWIG do it.

First we'll need a SWIG interface file, `libc.i`:

```
%module libc

FILE *fopen(const char *, const char *);

int fread(void *, size_t, size_t, FILE *);
int fwrite(void *, size_t, size_t, FILE *);
int fclose(FILE *);

void *malloc(size_t);
```

This file specifies the name of our extension as "libc". For SWIG Ruby extensions, this means the extension will be named "libc", and the code will be contained in a Ruby module claled `Libc`. This file also provides the prototypes for the functions we're going to want to call.

You'll also need an extconf.rb program, similar to the one we used in the previous two recipes:

```
# extconf.rb
require 'mkmf'
dir_config('tcl')
dir_config('libc')
create_makefile('libc')
```

To generate the C extension, we process the header file with the swig command-line tool. We then run Ruby's extconf.rb program to generate a makefile, and run make to compile the extension:

```
$ swig -ruby libc.i
$ ls
extconf.rb  libc.i  libc_wrap.c

$ ruby extconf.rb --with-tcl-include=/usr/include/tcl8.4
creating Makefile

$ make
...


$ ls
Makefile extconf.rb  libc.i  libc.so  libc_wrap.c  libc_wrap.o
```

Once the module is compiled, we can use it just like any other Ruby extension. This code uses a Ruby interface to prepopulate a file with random data, then uses the C interface to copy the contents of that file to another file:

```
random_data = ""
10000.times { random_data << rand(255) }
open('source.txt', 'w') { |f| f << random_data }

require 'libc'
f1 = Libc.fopen('source.txt', 'r')
f2 = Libc.fopen('dest.txt', 'w+')

buffer = Libc.malloc(1024)

nread = Libc.fread(buffer, 1, 1024, f1)

while nread > 0
  Libc.fwrite(buffer, 1, nread, f2)
  nread = Libc.fread(buffer, 1, 1024, f1)
end
Libc.fclose(f1)
Libc.fclose(f2)

# dest.txt now contains the same random data as source.txt.
random_data == open('dest.txt') { |f| f.read }
# => true
```

There you have it: without writing a line of C code, we've been able to call into a C library from Ruby.

Discussion

The great advantage of SWIG over writing your own interface to a C library is that you don't have to write your own interface to a C library. The disadvantage is that you get the exact same interface (or a subset) as the C library. The Libc module exposes a Ruby module that's nothing more than a collection of C functions. If you want a friendlier interface, you need to write it yourself on top of the SWIG-generated module.

In addition to the actual function prototypes, the interface file needs to have a little metadata about your extension. At the minimum, you'll need a %module line that tells SWIG what to call the extension it generates. Depending on your C code, you might also need to tell SWIG how to handle C constructs that don't map directly to Ruby; see the SWIG documentation on %typemap for details.

There are two main ways to create an interface file. The simplest way is simply to copy the prototypes for your C functions right from your header file into your SWIG interface file. Alternatively, you can use the %import filename directive to include a C header file in a SWIG interface file.

One more thing: note the references to tcl in the extconf.rb file and in the command-line invocation of extconf.rb. Our Libc module has nothing to do with Tcl, but SWIG's Ruby bindings always generate code that relies on the Tcl libraries. Unless your Tcl header files live in one of your system's standard include directory, you need to tell extconf.rb where to find them.

See Also

- *http://www.swig.org/*
- On Debian GNU/Linux systems, you can install SWIG as the swig package

22.4 Writing Inline C in Your Ruby Code

Credit: Garrett Rooney

Problem

You want to implement small portions of your program in C without going to the trouble of creating a C extension to Ruby.

Solution

Embed C code right in your Ruby program, and let RubyInline (available as the rubyinline gem) create an extension automatically.

For example, if you want to use C's stdio functions to copy a file, you can write RubyInline code like this:*

```
#!/usr/bin/ruby -w
# copy.rb
require 'rubygems'
require 'inline'

class Copier
  inline do |builder|
    builder.c <<END
  void copy_file(const char *source, const char *dest)
  {
    FILE *source_f = fopen(source, "r");
    if (!source_f)
    {
      rb_raise(rb_eIOError, "Could not open source : '%s'", source);
    }

    FILE *dest_f = fopen(dest, "w+");
    if (!dest_f)
    {
      rb_raise(rb_eIOError, "Could not open destination : '%s'", dest);
    }

    char buffer[1024];

    int nread = fread(buffer, 1, 1024, source_f);
    while (nread > 0)
    {
      fwrite(buffer, 1, nread, dest_f);
      nread = fread(buffer, 1, 1024, source_f);
    }
  }
END
  end
end
```

The C function copy_file now exists as an instance method of Copier:

```
open('source.txt', 'w') { |f| f << 'Some text.' }
Copier.new.copy_file('source.txt', 'dest.txt')
puts open('dest.txt') { |f| f.read }
```

Run this Ruby script, and you'll see it copy the string "Some text." from source.txt to dest.txt.

---

* RubyInline won't work from within irb, so this is a standalone program.

Discussion

RubyInline is a framework that lets you embed other languages inside your Ruby code. It defines the `Module#inline` method, which returns a builder object. You pass the builder a string containing code written in a language other than Ruby, and the builder transforms it into something that you can call from Ruby.

When given C or C++ code (the two languages supported in the default RubyInline install), the builder objects writes a small extension to disk, compiles it, and loads it. You don't have to deal with the compilation yourself, but you can see the generated code and compiled extensions in the `.ruby_inline` subdirectory of your home directory.

There are some limitations you should be aware of, though.

First, RubyInline only understands a limited subset of C and C++. The functions you embed can only accept and return arguments of the types `char`, `unsigned`, `unsigned int`, `char *`, `int`, `long`, and `unsigned long`.

If you need to use other types, RubyInline won't be able to automatically generate the wrapper functions. You'll have to work around the problem using the `inline.c_raw` function to embed code that conforms to the Ruby C API, just like any other extension.

Second, if you're going to just run a script that uses RubyInline, you'll need to have the Ruby development libraries and headers installed, along with a C/C++ compiler to actually build the extension.

There's a way around this, though: RubyInline lets you generate a RubyGem package with a precompiled extension. See the RubyInline docs on the `inline_package` script for details.

As always, be careful to make sure that it's actually worth the trouble to write C code. You should only rewrite part of a Ruby program in C if you've actually determined that Ruby spends a lot of time there. You should benchmark before and after your change, to make sure that you're making things better rather than worse. Writing C code within your Ruby code is much easier than writing a separate extension, but writing Ruby code is easier still.

See Also

- *http://www.zenspider.com/ZSS/Products/RubyInline/*
- *http://rubyforge.org/projects/rubyinline/*
- Recipe 17.12, "Profiling Your Application"
- Recipe 17.13, "Benchmarking Competing Solutions"

22.5   Using Java Libraries with JRuby

Credit: Thomas Enebo

Problem

Java offers many class libraries that would be useful to a Ruby programmer; you'd like to use one of those libraries from within Ruby. A Java JDBC database may allow you to connect to a database for which Ruby has no connector. Or perhaps you need to use an obscure Java library that has no Ruby counterpart.

Solution

JRuby provides an alternate implementation of the Ruby programming language that runs atop the Java Virtual Machine. When you interpret a Ruby program with JRuby instead of using the default Ruby interpreter, you can load and use Java classes from within the Ruby code.

The first step to using JRuby is to install it:

1. Download the latest copy of JRuby (see below for the address).
2. Unzip the JRuby package into the directory where you'd like to install it.
3. Add to your PATH environment variable the `bin/` subdirectory of your JRuby installation.
4. Unless you've already installed it, download the Java Runtime Environment from Sun's Java web site and install it. You'll need the JRE version 1.4.x or higher.

Now you can invoke the JRuby interpreter with the `jruby` command and use it to run Ruby code. Here's a simple example that imports and uses Java's built-in `Random` class:

```
#!/usr/bin/env jruby
# random.jrb
require 'java'
include_class 'java.util.Random'

r = Random.new(123)
puts "Some random number #{r.nextInt % 10}"
r.seed = 456
puts "Another random number #{r.nextInt % 10}"
```

Heres a run of this program:

```
$ jruby random.jrb
Some random number 9
Another random number 0
```

Discussion

JRuby generally behaves like Ruby. The jruby interpreter supports a common subset of Ruby's command-line options, and includes a subset of common core libraries. As JRuby is developed, it will eventually end up with all of Ruby's options and libraries.

The first step in a JRuby program is to load the Java support classes. If you don't do this, you can still use the JRuby interpreter, but you'll be limited to a subset of the Ruby core libraries: you might as well just use the C implementation.

The statement require 'java' updates Ruby's Object class with an include_class method, which you can use to import Java classes. When we call include_class to include a class like java.util.Random, Ruby inserts a class called Random into the current namespace. This class is really a Ruby class that proxies method calls to the underlying Java class.

The Random class proxies a constructor call to the java.util.Random constructor. Random#nextInt becomes a call to java.util.Random#nextInt. Random#seed= becomes a call to java.util.Random#setSeed; JRuby creates seed= as a Ruby convenience method, to make the Java classes feel more like Ruby.

If you're including a Java class whose name conflicts with an existing constant in your namespace, then include_class will throw a ConstantAlreadyExistsError. This is problematic if you want to use Java classes like java.lang.String, whose names conflict with the names of built-in Ruby classes. Fortunately, you can customize the name of the proxy class created by include_class. This piece of code loads 'java.lang.String' as the class JString instead of String:

```
include_class('java.lang.String') { |package,name| "J" + name }
```

It's worth noting that JRuby implicitly translates primitive types between Ruby and Java. In the Random constructor, the Fixnum argument 123 gets implicitly converted to a Java primitive long, since that's what the java.util.Random constructor takes.

Ruby type	Java type
String	char, String
Fixnum	long, int, java.lang.Long, java.lang.Integer
Float	float, double, Java.lang.Float, java.lang.Double
Boolean	java.lang.Boolean, boolean

This automatic conversion creates some amount of ambiguity, because Java supports method overloading and Ruby doesn't. Suppose you have a Java class which defines two methods with the same name:

```
class Foo
{
  public void bar(int arg) {...}
  public void bar(long arg) {...}
}
```

If you import that class into JRuby and call Foo#bar, to which method should the proxy class dispatch your call?

```
Foo.new.bar(5)
```

In JRuby, the exact heuristic is undefined. In practice, this is not a huge problem, since methods that define same-named methods are semantically equivalent. If you do encounter an ambiguous case, you can work around ambiguity using Java's reflection APIs.

Convenience methods

JRuby tries to make Java classes and objects seem as unobtrusive to Ruby as it can. In our earlier example, we saw how a setter:

```
setSeed(value);
```

Can be called from Ruby as:

```
seed = value
```

JRuby supports the following additional Ruby method name shortcuts:

Java	Ruby
obj.getFoo( )	obj.foo
obj.setFoo(value)	obj.foo = value
obj.isFoo(value)	obj.foo? value

The original name still exists, so if you like you can use getFoo and setFoo from Ruby. Of course, if Java already has a method by the same shorthand name (e.g., obj.foo), Ruby won't create the shorthand name.

JRuby also provides some Ruby methods that make Java classes seem more like Ruby classes. Here is a list as of Ruby 0.8.3:

- All of Java's Map, Set, and List types define each
- java.lang.Comparable defines <=>
- List defines <<, sort, and sort!

JRuby is still a project under development, so expect to see more added as developers discover more candidates.

See Also

- JRuby is available from *http://jruby.sourceforge.net/*
- You can download the JRE from Sun's Java site at *http://java.sun.com/*

System Administration

Once you start using Ruby, you'll want to use it everywhere. Well, nothing's stopping you. This chapter shows you how to use Ruby in command-line programs that solve general everyday problems. It also demonstrates patterns that you can use to solve your own, more specific everyday problems.

System administration scripts are usually private scripts, disposable or lightly reusable. Ruby scripts are easy to write, so you can get the job done quickly and move on. You won't feel bad if your script is less rigorous than your usual work, and you won't feel invested in a huge program that you only needed once.

Ruby's syntax makes it easy to write, but for system administration, it's the libraries that make Ruby powerful. Most of the recipes in this chapter combine ideas from recipes elsewhere in the book to solve a real-world problem. The most commonly used idea is the Find.find technique first covered in Recipe 6.12. Recipes 23.5, 23.6, 23.7, 23.8, and 23.9 all give different twists on this technique.

The major new feature introduced in this chapter is Ruby's standard etc library. It lets you query a Unix system's users and groups. It's used in Recipe 23.10 to look up a user's ID given their username. Recipe 23.9 uses it to find a user's home directory and to get the members of Unix groups.

Although these recipes focus mainly on Unix system administration, Ruby is perhaps even more useful for Windows administration. Unix has a wide variety of standard shell tools and an environment that makes it easy to combine them. If Ruby and other high-level languages didn't exist, Unix administrators would still have tools like find and cut, and they'd use those tools like they did throughout the 1980s. On Windows, though, languages like Ruby are useful even for simple administration tasks: Ruby is easier to use than VBScript or batch files.

If you're trying to administer a Windows machine with Ruby, there are many third-party libraries that provide Ruby hooks into Windows internals: see especially the "win32utils" project at *http://rubyforge.org/projects/win32utils/*. Another useful library is Ruby's standard Win32OLE library, which lets you do things like query Active Directory.

Libraries are also available for the more esoteric parts of Unix systems. See, for instance, Recipe 23.10, which uses the third-party library sys-proctable to gain access to the kernel's process table.

23.1 Scripting an External Program

Problem

You want to automatically control an external program that expects to get terminal input from a human user.

Solution

When you're running a program that only needs a single string of input, you can use IO.popen, as described in Recipe 20.8. This method runs a command, sends it a string as standard input, and returns the contents of its standard output:

```
def run(command, input='')
  IO.popen(command, 'r+') do |io|
    io.puts input
    io.close_write
    return io.read
  end
end

run 'wc -w', 'How many words are in this string?'        # => "7\n"
```

This technique is commonly used to invoke a command with sudo, which expects the user's password on standard input. This code obtains a user's password and runs a command on his behalf using sudo:

```
print 'Enter your password for sudo: '
sudo_password = gets.chomp
run('sudo apachectl graceful', user_password)
```

Discussion

IO.popen is a good way to run noninteractive commands—commands that read all their standard input at once and produce some output. But some programs are interactive; they send prompts to standard output, and expect a human on the other end to respond with more input.

On Unix, you can use Ruby's standard PTY and expect libraries to spawn a command and impersonate a human on the other end. This code scripts the Unix passwd command:

```
require 'expect'
require 'pty'

print 'Old password:'
old_pwd = gets.chomp
```

```
print "\nNew password:"
new_pwd = gets.chomp

PTY.spawn('passwd') do |read,write,pid|
  write.sync = true
  $expect_verbose = false

  # If 30 seconds pass and the expected text is not found, the
  # response object will be nil.
  read.expect("(current) UNIX password:", 30) do |response|
    write.print old_pwd + "\n" if response
  end

  # You can use regular expressions instead of strings. The code block
  # will give you the regex matches.
  read.expect(/UNIX password: /, 2) do |response, *matches|
    write.print new_pwd + "\n" if response
  end

  # The default value for the timeout is 9999999 seconds
  read.expect("Retype new UNIX password:") do |response|
    write.puts new_pwd + "\n" if response
  end
end
```

The read and write objects in the PTY#spawn block are IO objects. The expect library defines the IO#expect method found throughout this example.

See Also

- Recipe 20.8, "Driving an External Process with popen"
- Recipe 21.9, "Reading a Password," shows how to obtain a password without echoing it to the screen

23.2 Managing Windows Services

Credit: Bill Froelich

Problem

You want to interact with existing system services on the Windows platform.

Solution

User the win32-service library, available as the gem of the same name. Its Service module gives you an interface to work with services in Windows 2000 or XP Pro.

You can use this to print a list of the currently running services on your machine:

```
require 'rubygems'
require 'win32/service'
include Win32
```

```
puts 'Currently Running Services:'
Service.services do |svc|
  if svc.current_state == 'running'
    puts "#{svc.service_name}\t-\t#{svc.display_name}"
  end
end
# Currently Running Services:
# ACPI      -         Microsoft ACPI Driver
# AcrSch2Svc    -         Acronis Scheduler2 Service
# AFD       -     AFD Networking Support Environment
# agp440   -       Intel AGP Bus Filter
# ...
```

This command checks whether the DNS client service exists on your machine:

```
Service.exists?('dnscache')                          # => true
```

Service.status returns a Win32ServiceStatus struct describing the current state of a service:

```
Service.status('dnscache')
# => #<struct Struct::Win32ServiceStatus
#       service_type="share process", current_state="running",
#       controls_accepted=["netbind change", "param change", "stop"],
#       win32_exit_code=0, service_specific_exit_code=0, check_point=0,
#       wait_hint=0, :interactive?=false, pid=1144, service_flags=0>
```

If a service is not currently running, you can start it with Service.start:

```
Service.stop('dnscache')
Service.status('dnscache').current_state            # => "stopped"
Service.start('dnscache')
Service.status('dnscache').current_state            # => "running"
```

Discussion

Services are typically accessed using their service_name attribute, not by their display name as shown in the Services Control Panel. Fortunately, Service provides helpful methods to convert between the two:

```
Service.getdisplayname('dnscache')                  # => "DNS Client"
Service.getservicename('DNS Client')                # => "dnscache"
```

In addition to getting information about the status and list of services available, the win32-service gem lets you start, pause, and stop services. In the example below, replace the "foo" service with a valid service_name that responds to each of the commands.

```
Service.start('foo')
Service.pause('foo')
Service.resume('foo')
Service.stop('foo')
```

You can check whether a service supports pause or resume by checking the controls_ accepted member of its Win32ServiceStatus struct. As seen below, the dnscache command can't be paused or resumed:

```
Service.status('dnscache').controls_accepted
# => ["netbind change", "param change", "stop"]
```

Stopping system services may cause Windows to behave strangely, so be careful.

See Also

- The win32-service library was written by Daniel J. Berger; it's part of his win32utils project (*http://rubyforge.org/projects/win32utils/*)
- The win32-service API reference at *http://rubyforge.org/docman/view.php/85/29/ service.txt*; see especially the member list for the Win32Service struct yielded by Service.services
- You can also use win32-service to make your own services; see Recipe 20.2, "Creating a Windows Service"

23.3 Running Code as Another User

Problem

While writing a Ruby script that runs as root, you need to take some action on behalf of another user: say, run an external program or create a file.

Solution

Simply set Process.euid to the UID of the user. When you're done, set it back to its previous value (that is, root's UID). Here's a method Process.as_uid that runs a code block under a different user ID and resets it at the end:

```
module Process
  def as_uid(uid)
    old_euid, old_uid = Process.euid, Process.uid
    Process.euid, Process.uid = uid, uid
    begin
      yield
    ensure
      Process.euid, Process.uid = old_euid, old_uid
    end
  end
  module_function(:as_uid)
end
```

Discussion

When a Unix process tries to do something that requires special permissions (like access a file), the permissions are checked according to the "effective user ID" of the process. The effective user ID starts out as the user ID you used when you started the process, but if you're root you can change the effective user ID with `Process.euid=`. The operating system will treat you as though you were really that user.

This comes in handy when you're administering a system used by others. When someone asks you for help, you can write a script that impersonates them and runs the commands they don't know how to run. Rather than creating files as root and using chown to give them to another user, you can create the files as the other user in the first place.

Here's an example. On my system the account *leonardr* has UID 1000. When run as root, this code will create one directory owned by root and one owned by *leonardr*:

```
Dir.mkdir("as_root")
Process.as_uid(1000) do
  Dir.mkdir("as_leonardr")
  %x{whoami}
end
# => "leonardr\n"
```

Here are the directories:

```
$ ls -ld as_*
drwxr-xr-x  2 leonardr root 4096 Feb  2 13:06 as_leonardr/
drwxr-xr-x  2 root     root 4096 Feb  2 13:06 as_root/
```

When you're impersonating another user, your permissions are restricted to what that user can do. I can't remove the as_root directory as a nonroot user, because I created it as root:

```
Process.as_uid(1000) do
  Dir.rmdir("as_root")
end
# Errno::EPERM: Operation not permitted - as_root

Dir.rmdir("as_root")                              # => 0
```

On Windows, you can do something like this by splitting your Ruby script into two, and running the second one through `runas.exe`:

```
# script_one.rb
system 'runas /user:frednerk ruby script_two.rb'
```

See Also

- Recipe 6.2, "Checking Your Access to a File"
- If you want to pass in the name of the user to impersonate, instead of their UID, you can adapt the technique shown in Recipe 23.10, "Killing All Processes for a Given User"

23.4 Running Periodic Tasks Without cron or at

Problem

You want to write a self-contained Ruby program that performs a task in the background at a certain time, or runs repeatedly at a certain interval.

Solution

Fork off a new process that sleeps until it's time to run the Ruby code.

Here's a program that waits in the background until a certain time, then prints a message:

```ruby
#!/usr/bin/ruby
# lunchtime.rb

def background_run_at(time)
  fork do
    sleep(1) until Time.now >= time
    yield
  end
end

today = Time.now
noon = Time.local(today.year, today.month, today.day, 12, 0, 0)
raise Exception, "It's already past lunchtime!" if noon < Time.now

background_run_at(noon) { puts "Lunchtime!" }
```

The fork command only works on Unix systems. The win32-process third-party add-on gives Windows a fork implementation, but it's more idiomatic to run this code as a Windows service with win32-service.

Discussion

With this technique, you can write self-contained Ruby programs that act as though they were spawned by the at command. If you want to run a backgrounded code block at a certain interval, the way a cronjob would, then combine fork with the technique described in Recipe 3.12.

```ruby
#!/usr/bin/ruby
# reminder.rb
def background_every_n_seconds(n)
  fork do
    loop do
      before = Time.now
      yield
      interval = n-(Time.now-before)
      sleep(interval) if interval > 0
    end
```

```
      end
   end

   background_every_n_seconds(15*60) { puts 'Get back to work!' }
```

Forking is the best technique if you want to run a background process *and* a foreground process. If you want a script that immediately returns you to the command prompt when it runs, you might want to use the `Daemonize` module instead; see Recipe 20.1.

See Also

- Both the `win32-process` and the `win32-service` libraries are available at *http://rubyforge.org/projects/win32utils/*
- Recipe 3.12, "Running a Code Block Periodically"
- Recipe 20.1, "Running a Daemon Process on Unix"

23.5   Deleting Files That Match a Regular Expression

Credit: Matthew Palmer

Problem

You have a directory full of files and you need to remove some of them. The patterns you want to match are too complex to represent as file globs, but you can represent them as a regular expression.

Solution

The `Dir.entries` method gives you an array of all files in a directory, and you can iterate over this array with #each. A method to delete the files matching a regular expression might look like this:

```
def delete_matching_regexp(dir, regex)
  Dir.entries(dir).each do |name|
    path = File.join(dir, name)
    if name =~ regex
      ftype = File.directory?(path) ? Dir : File
      begin
        ftype.delete(path)
      rescue SystemCallError => e
        $stderr.puts e.message
      end
    end
  end
end
```

Here's an example. Let's create a bunch of files and directories beneath a temporary directory:

```
require 'fileutils'
tmp_dir = 'tmp_buncha_files'
files = ['A', 'A.txt', 'A.html', 'p.html', 'A.html.bak']
directories = ['text.dir', 'Directory.for.html']

Dir.mkdir(tmp_dir) unless File.directory? tmp_dir
files.each { |f| FileUtils.touch(File.join(tmp_dir,f)) }
directories.each { |d| Dir.mkdir(File.join(tmp_dir, d)) }
```

Now let's delete some of those files and directories. We'll delete a file or directory if its name starts with a capital letter, and if its extension (the string after its last period) is at least four characters long. This corresponds to the regular expression /^[A-Z].*\.[^.]{4,}$/:

```
Dir.entries(tmp_dir)
# => [".", "..", "A", "A.txt", "A.html", "p.html", "A.html.bak",
#     "text.dir", "Directory.for.html"]

delete_matching_regexp(tmp_dir, /^[A-Z].*\.[^.]{4,}$/)

Dir.entries(tmp_dir)
# => [".", "..", "A", "A.txt", "p.html", "A.html.bak", "text.dir"]
```

Discussion

Like most good things in Ruby, Dir.entries takes a code block. It yields every file and subdirectory it finds to that code block. Our particular code block uses the regular expression match operator =~ to match every real file (no subdirectories) against the regular expression, and File.delete to remove offending files.

File.delete won't delete directories; for that, you need Directory.delete. So delete_matching_regexp uses the File predicates to check whether a file is a directory. We also have error reporting, to report cases when we don't have permission to delete a file, or a directory isn't empty.

Of course, once we've got this basic "find matching files" thing going, there's no reason why we have to limit ourselves to deleting the matched files. We can move them to somewhere new:

```
def move_matching_regexp(src, dest, regex)
  Dir.entries(dir).each do |name|
    File.rename(File.join(src, name), File.join(dest, name)) if name =~ regex
  end
end
```

Or we can append a suffix to them:

```
def append_matching_regexp(dir, suffix, regex)
  Dir.entries(dir).each do |name|
    if name =~ regex
      File.rename(File.join(dir, name), File.join(dir, name+suffix))
    end
  end
end
```

Note the common code in both of those implementations. We can factor it out into yet another method that takes a block:

```
def each_matching_regexp(dir, regex)
  Dir.entries(dir).each { |name| yield name if name =~ regex }
end
```

We no longer have to tell `Dir.each` how to match the files we want; we just need to tell each_matching_regexp what to do with them:

```
def append_matching_regexp(dir, suffix, regex)
  each_matching_regexp(dir, regex) do |name|
    File.rename(File.join(dir, name), File.join(dir, name+suffix))
  end
end
```

This is all well and good, but these methods only manipulate files directly beneath the directory you specify. "I've got a whole *tree* full of files I want to get rid of!" I hear you cry. For that, you should use `Find.find` instead of `Dir.each`. Apart from that change, the implementation is nearly identical to delete_matching_regexp:

```
def delete_matching_regexp_recursively(dir, regex)
  Find.find(dir) do |path|
    dir, name = File.split(path)
    if name =~ regex
      ftype = File.directory?(path) ? Dir : File
      begin
        ftype.delete(path)
      rescue SystemCallError => e
        $stderr.puts e.message
      end
    end
  end
end
```

If you want to recursively delete the contents of directories that match the regular expression (even if the contents themselves don't match), use `FileUtils.rm_rf` instead of `Dir.delete`.

See Also

- `Dir.delete` will only remove an empty directory; see Recipe 6.18 for information on how to remove one that's not empty
- Recipe 6.20, "Finding the Files You Want"

23.6 Renaming Files in Bulk

Problem

You want to rename a bunch of files programmatically: for instance, to normalize the filename case or to change the extensions.

Solution

Use the `Find` module in the Ruby standard library. Here's a method that renames files according to the results of a code block. It returns a list of files it couldn't rename, because their proposed new name already existed:

```
require 'find'

module Find
  def rename(*paths)
    unrenamable = []
    find(*paths) do |file|
      next unless File.file? file # Skip directories, etc.
      path, name = File.split(file)
      new_name = yield name

      if new_name and new_name != name
        new_path = File.join(path, new_name)
        if File.exists? new_path
          unrenamable << file
        else
          puts "Renaming #{file} to #{new_path}" if $DEBUG
          File.rename(file, new_path)
        end
      end
    end
    return unrenamable
  end
  module_function(:rename)
end
```

This addition to the `Find` module makes it easy to do things like convert all filenames to lowercase. I'll create some dummy files to demonstrate:

```
require 'fileutils'
tmp_dir = 'tmp_files'
Dir.mkdir(tmp_dir)
['CamelCase.rb', 'OLDFILE.TXT', 'OldFile.txt'].each do |f|
  FileUtils.touch(File.join(tmp_dir, f))
end

tmp_dir = File.join(tmp_dir, 'subdir')
Dir.mkdir(tmp_dir)
['i_am_SHOUTING', 'I_AM_SHOUTING'].each do |f|
  FileUtils.touch(File.join(tmp_dir, f))
end
```

Now let's convert these filenames to lowercase:

```
$DEBUG = true
Find.rename('./') { |file| file.downcase }
# Renaming ./tmp_files/subdir/I_AM_SHOUTING to ./tmp_files/subdir/i_am_shouting
# Renaming ./tmp_files/OldFile.txt to ./tmp_files/oldfile.txt
# Renaming ./tmp_files/CamelCase.rb to ./tmp_files/camelcase.rb
# => ["./OldFile.txt", "./dir/i_am_SHOUTING"]
```

Two of the files couldn't be renamed, because `oldfile.txt` and `subdir/i_am_shouting` were already taken.

Let's add a ".txt" extension to all files that have no extension:

```
Find.rename('./') { |file| file + '.txt' unless file.index('.') }
# Renaming ./tmp_files/subdir/i_am_shouting to ./tmp_files/subdir/i_am_shouting.txt
# Renaming ./tmp_files/subdir/i_am_SHOUTING to ./tmp_files/subdir/i_am_SHOUTING.txt
# => []
```

Discussion

Renaming files in bulk is a very common operation, but there's no standard command-line application to do it because renaming operations are best described algorithmically.

The `Find.rename` method makes several simplifying assumptions. It assumes that you want to rename regular files and not directories. It assumes that you can decide on a new name for a file based solely on its filename, not on its full path. It assumes that you'll handle in some other way the files it couldn't rename.

Another implementation might make different assumptions: it might yield both `path` and `name`, and use autoversioning to guarantee that it can rename every file, although not necessary to the exact filename returned by the code block. It all depends on your needs.

Perhaps the most common renaming operation is modifying the extensions of files. Here's a method that uses `Find.rename` to make this kind of operation easier:

```
module Find
  def change_extensions(extension_mappings, *paths)
    rename(*paths) do |file|
      base, extension = file.split(/(.*)\./)[1..2]
      new_extension = extension
      extension_mappings.each do |re, ext|
        if re.match(extension)
          new_extension = ext
          break
        end
      end
      "#{base}.#{new_extension}"
    end
  end
  module_function(:change_extensions)
end
```

This code uses `Find.change_extensions` to normalize a collection of images. All JPEG files will be given the extension ".jpg", all PNG files the extension ".png", and all GIF files the extension ".gif".

Again, we'll create some dummy image files to test:

```
tmp_dir = 'tmp_graphics'
Dir.mkdir(tmp_dir)
```

```
['my.house.jpeg', 'Construction.Gif', 'DSC1001.JPG', '52.PNG'].each do |f|
  FileUtils.touch(File.join(tmp_dir, f))
end
```

Now, let's rename:

```
Find.change_extensions({/jpe?g/i => 'jpg',
                        /png/i => 'png',
                        /gif/i => 'gif'}, tmp_dir)
# Renaming tmp_graphics/52.PNG to tmp_graphics/52.png
# Renaming tmp_graphics/DSC1001.JPG to tmp_graphics/DSC1001.jpg
# Renaming tmp_graphics/Construction.Gif to tmp_graphics/Construction.gif
# Renaming tmp_graphics/my.house.jpeg to tmp_graphics/my.house.jpg
```

See Also

- Some Unix installations come with a program or Perl script called rename, which can do your renaming if you can represent it as a string substitution or a regular expression; you may not need anything else
- Recipe 6.14, "Backing Up to Versioned Filenames"
- Recipe 6.20, "Finding the Files You Want"

23.7 Finding Duplicate Files

Problem

You want to find the duplicate files that are taking up all the space on your hard drive.

Solution

The simple solution is to group the files by size and then by their MD5 checksum. Two files are presumed identical if they have the same size and MD5 sum.

The following program takes a list of directories on the command line, and prints out all sets of duplicate files. You can pass a different code block into each_set_of_duplicates for different behavior: for instance, to prompt the user about which of the duplicates to keep and which to delete.

```
#!/usr/bin/ruby
# find_duplicates.rb

require 'find'
require 'digest/md5'

def each_set_of_duplicates(*paths)
  sizes = {}
  Find.find(*paths) do |f|
    (sizes[File.size(f)] ||= []) << f if File.file? f
  end
```

```
   sizes.each do |size, files|
     next unless files.size > 1
     md5s = {}
     files.each do |f|
       digest = Digest::MD5.hexdigest(File.read(f))
       (md5s[digest] ||= []) << f
     end
     md5s.each { |sum, files| yield files if files.size > 1 }
   end
 end

 each_set_of_duplicates(*ARGV) do |f|
   puts "Duplicates: #{f.join(", ")}"
 end
```

Discussion

This is one task that can't be handled with a simple Find.find code block, because it's trying to figure out which files have certain relationships *to each other*. Find.find takes care of walking the file tree, but it would be very inefficient to try to make a single trip through the tree and immediately spit out a set of duplicates. Instead, we group the files by size and then by their MD5 checksum.

The MD5 checksum is a short binary string used as a stand-in for the contents of a file. It's commonly used to verify that a huge file was downloaded without errors. It's not impossible for two different files to have an MD5 sum, but unless someone is deliberately trying to trick you, it's almost impossible to have two files with the same size *and* the same MD5 sum.

Calculating a MD5 sum is very expensive: it means performing a mathematical calculation on the entire contents of the file. Grouping the files by size beforehand greatly reduces the number of sums that must be calculated, but that's still a lot of I/O. Even if two similarly sized files differ in the first byte, the code above will read the entire files.

Here's a different version of the same program that takes an incremental approach like that seen in Recipe 6.10. When it thinks a set of files might contain duplicates, it makes repeated calls to a method called eliminate_non_duplicates. The duplicates are yielded and the nonduplicates discarded over the course of these calls.

```
#!/usr/bin/ruby
# find_duplicates2.rb

require 'find'
BLOCK_SIZE = 1024*8

def each_set_of_duplicates(*paths, &block)
  sizes = Hash.new {|h, k| h[k] = [] }
  Find.find(*paths) { |f| sizes[File.size(f)] << f if File.file? f }

  sizes.each_pair do |size, files|
    next unless files.size > 1
```

```
      offset = 0
      files = [files]
      while !files.empty? && offset <= size
        files = eliminate_non_duplicates(files, size, offset, &block)
        offset += BLOCK_SIZE
      end
    end
  end
end
```

The method `eliminate_non_duplicates` takes lists of files that might contain duplicates. It reads each file an eight-kilobyte block at a time, and compares just one block of each file. Files whose blocks don't match the corresponding blocks of any other file are discarded; they're not duplicates. All files with the same block are put into a new list of *possible* duplicates, and sent back to each_set_of_duplicates.

If two files are not duplicates, `eliminate_non_duplicates` will eventually find a block where they differ. Otherwise, it will eventually read the last block of each file and confirm them as duplicates.

```
def eliminate_non_duplicates(partition, size, offset)
  possible_duplicates = []
  partition.each do |possible_duplicate_set|
    blocks = Hash.new {|h, k| h[k] = [] }
    possible_duplicate_set.each do |f|
      block = open(f, 'rb') do |file|
        file.seek(offset)
        file.read(BLOCK_SIZE)
      end
      blocks[block || ''] << f
    end
    blocks.each_value do |files|
      if files.size > 1
        if offset+BLOCK_SIZE >= size
          # We know these are duplicates.
          yield files
        else
          # We suspect these are duplicates, but we need to compare
          # more blocks of data.
          possible_duplicates << files
        end
      end
    end
  end
  return possible_duplicates
end

each_set_of_duplicates(*ARGV) do |f|
  puts "Duplicates: #{f.join(", ")}"
end
```

This code is more complicated, but in real-world situations, it's considerably faster. Most files of the same size are not duplicates, and it's cheaper to find this out by reading eight kilobytes than by reading many megabytes and then performing two

MD5 sums. This solution also eliminates any last possibility that each_set_of_
duplicates will claim two files are duplicates when they're not.

See Also

- Recipe 6.10, "Comparing Two Files"
- Recipe 6.12, "Walking a Directory Tree"

23.8 Automating Backups

Problem

You want to make a dated archive of a directory to burn to CD or otherwise store on
backup media.

Solution

This script copies a directory to a timestamped backup. It reuses the File.versioned_
filename method defined in Recipe 6.14, so you can create multiple backups in the
same time period:

```
require 'fileutils'

def backup(from_dir, to_dir, time_format="-%Y%m%d")
  from_path, from_name = File.split(from_dir)
  now = Time.now.strftime(time_format)
  Dir.mkdir(to_dir) unless File.exists? to_dir
  unless File.directory? to_dir
    raise ArgumentError, "Not a directory: #{to_dir}"
  end
  to = File.versioned_filename(File.join(to_dir, from_name + now))
  FileUtils.cp_r(from_dir, to, :preserve=>true)
  return to
end

# This method copied from "Backing Up to Versioned Filenames"
class File
  def File.versioned_filename(base, first_suffix=".0")
    suffix = nil
    filename = base
    while File.exists?(filename)
      suffix = (suffix ? suffix.succ : first_suffix)
      filename = base + suffix
    end
    return filename
  end
end

# Create a dummy directory
Dir.mkdir('recipes')
```

```
# And back it up.
backup('recipes', '/tmp/backup')           # => "/tmp/backup/recipes-20061031"
backup('recipes', '/tmp/backup')           # => "/tmp/backup/recipes-20061031.0"
backup('recipes', '/tmp/backup', '-%Y%m%d-%H.%M.%S')
# => "/tmp/backup/recipes-20061031-20.48.56"
```

Discussion

The backup method recursively copies the contents of a directory into another directory, possibly on another filesystem. It uses the time-based scheme you specify along with versioned_filename to uniquely name the destination directory.

As written, the backup method uses a lot of space: every time you call it, it creates an entirely new copy of every file in the source directory. Fortunately, the technique has many variations. Instead of copying the files, you can make a timestamped tarball with the techniques from Recipe 12.10. You can archive the files to another computer with the techniques from Recipe 14.11 (although to save space, you should use the rsync program instead). You could even automatically check your work into a version control system every so often; this works better with text than with binary files.

See Also

- Recipe 6.14, "Backing Up to Versioned Filenames"
- Recipe 12.10, "Compressing and Archiving Files with Gzip and Tar"
- Recipe 14.11, "Copying a File to Another Machine"

23.9 Normalizing Ownership and Permissions in User Directories

Problem

You want to make make sure your users' home directories don't contain world-writable directories, directories owned by other users, or other potential security problems.

Solution

Use the etc library to look up a user's home directory and UID from the username. Then use Find.find to walk the directory trees, and File methods to check and modify access to each file.

We are looking out for any case where one user's home directory can be modified by some other user. Whenever we find such a case, we fix it with a File.chmod or File.chown call. In this program, the actual calls are commented out, so that you don't accidentally change your permissions when you just want to test out the program.

```
#!/usr/bin/ruby -w
# normalize_homes.rb

require 'etc'
require 'find'
require 'optparse'

def normalize_home(pwd_entry, maximum_perms=0775, dry_run=true)
  uid, home = pwd_entry.uid, pwd_entry.dir
  username = pwd_entry.name

  puts "Scanning #{username}'s home of #{home}."

  Find.find(home) do |f|
  next unless File.exists? f
    stat = File.stat(f)
    file_uid, file_gid, mode = stat.uid, stat.gid, stat.mode
```

The most obvious thing we want to check is whether the user owns every file in their home directory. With occasional exceptions (such as files owned by the web server), a user should own the files in his or her home directory:

```
    # Does the user own the file?
    if file_uid != uid
      begin
        current_owner = Etc.getpwuid(file_uid).name
      rescue ArgumentError # No such user; just use UID
        current_owner = "uid #{file_uid}"
      end
      puts " CHOWN #{f}"
      puts "   Current owner is #{current_owner}, should be #{username}"
      # File.chown(uid, nil, f) unless dry_run
    end
```

A less obvious check involves the Unix group that owns the file. A user can let other people work on a file in their home directory by giving ownership to a user group. But you can only give ownership to a group if you're a member of that group. If a user's home directory contains a file owned by a group the user doesn't belong to, something fishy is probably going on.

```
    # Does the user belong to the group that owns the file?
    begin
      group = Etc.getgrgid(file_gid)
      group_name = group.name
    rescue ArgumentError # No such group
      group_name = "gid #{file_gid}"
    end
    unless group && (group.mem.member?(username) || group.name == username)
      puts " CHGRP #{f}"
      puts "   Current group is #{group_name}, and #{username} doesn't belong."
      # File.chown(nil, uid, f) unless dry_run
    end
```

Finally, we'll check each file's permissions and make sure they are no more permissive than the value passed in as maximum_perms. The default value of 0775 allows any kind of file except a world-writable file. If normalize_home finds a world-writable file, it will flip the world-writable bit and leave the rest of the permissions alone:

```
      # Does the file have more than the maximum allowed permissions?
      perms = mode & 0777              # Drop non-permission bits
      should_be = perms & maximum_perms
      if perms != should_be
        puts " CHMOD #{f}"
        puts "  Current perms are #{perms.to_s(8)}, " +
             "should be #{should_be.to_s(8)}"
        # File.chmod(perms & maximum_perms, f) unless dry_run
      end
    end
  end
end
```

All that's left to do is a simple command-line interface to the normalize_home method:

```
dry_run = false
opts = OptionParser.new do |opts|
  opts.on("-D", "--dry-run",
          "Display changes to be made, don't make them.") do
    dry_run = true
  end

  opts.on_tail("-h", "--help", "display this help and exit") do
    puts opts
    exit
  end
end
opts.banner = "Usage: #{__FILE__} [--dry-run] username [username2, ...]"
opts.parse!(ARGV)

# Make sure all the users exist.
pwd_entries = ARGV.collect { |username| Etc.getpwnam(username) }

# Normalize all given home directories.
pwd_entries.each { |p| normalize_home(p, 0775, dry_run ) }
```

Discussion

Running this script on my home directory shows over 2,500 problems. These are mostly files owned by root, files owned by UIDs that don't exist on my system (these come from tarballs), and world-writable files. Below I give a sample of the embarrassment:

```
$ ruby -D normalize_homes.rb leonardr

Scanning leonardr's home of /home/leonardr.
 CHOWN /home/leonardr/writing/Ruby Cookbook/sys-proctable-0.7.3/proctable.so
  Current owner is root, should be leonardr
 CHGRP /home/leonardr/writing/Ruby Cookbook/sys-proctable-0.7.3/proctable.so
```

```
      Current group is root, and leonardr doesn't belong.
  ...
  CHOWN /home/leonardr/writing/Ruby Cookbook/rubygems-0.8.4/lib/rubygems.rb
    Current owner is uid 501, should be leonardr
  CHGRP /home/leonardr/writing/Ruby Cookbook/rubygems-0.8.4/lib/rubygems.rb
    Current group is gid 501, and leonardr doesn't belong.
  ...
  CHMOD /home/leonardr/SORT/gogol-home-2002/mail
    Current perms are 722, should be 720
  ...
```

Running the script as root (and with the `File.chmod` and `File.chown` calls uncommented) fixes all the problems.

You can run the script as yourself to check your own home directory, and it'll fix permission problems on files you own. But if a file is owned by someone else, you can't take it back just because it's in your home directory—that's part of the problem with having a file owned by someone else in your home directory.

As usual with system administration scripts, `normalize.homes.rb` is only a starting point. You'll probably need to adapt this program to your specific purposes. For instance, you may want to leave certain files alone, especially files owned by root (who can modify anyone's home directory anyway) or by system processes such as the web server (usually user apache, `httpd`, or nobody).

See Also

- Recipe 2.6, "Converting Between Numeric Bases"
- Recipe 6.2, "Checking Your Access to a File"
- Recipe 6.3, "Changing the Permissions on a File"
- Recipe 6.12, "Walking a Directory Tree"

23.10 Killing All Processes for a Given User

Problem

You want an easy way to kill all the running processes of a user whose processes get out of control.

Solution

You can send a Unix signal (including the deadly SIGTERM or the even deadlier SIGKILL) from Ruby with the `Process.kill` method. But how to get the list of processes for a given user? The simplest way is to call out to the unix `ps` command and parse the output. Running `ps -u#{username}` gives us the processes for a particular user.

```
#!/usr/bin/ruby -w
# banish.rb
```

```
def signal_all(username, signal)
  lookup_uid(username)
  killed = 0
  %x{ps -u#{username}}.each_with_index do |proc, i|
    next if i == 0                    # Skip the header provided by ps
    pid = proc.split[0].to_i
    begin
      Process.kill(signal, pid)
    rescue SystemCallError => e
      raise e unless e.errno == Errno::ESRCH
    end
    killed += 1
  end
  return killed
end
```

There are a couple things to look out for here.

- ps dumps a big error message if we pass in the name of a nonexistent user. It would look better if we could handle that error ourselves. That's what the call to lookup_uid will do.

- ps prints out a header as its first line. We want to skip that line because it doesn't represent a process.

- Killing a process also kills all of its children. This can be a problem if the child process shows up later in the ps list: killing it again will raise a SystemCallError. We deal with that possibility by catching and ignoring that particular SystemCallError. We still count the process as "killed," though.

Here's the implementation of lookup_id:

```
def lookup_uid(username)
  require 'etc'
  begin
    user = Etc.getpwnam(username)
  rescue ArgumentError
    raise ArgumentError, "No such user: #{username}"
  end
  return user.uid
end
```

Now all that remains is the command-line interface:

```
require 'optparse'
signal = "SIGHUP"
opts = OptionParser.new do |opts|
  opts.banner = "Usage: #{__FILE__} [-9] [USERNAME]"
  opts.on("-9", "--with-extreme-prejudice",
          "Send an uncatchable kill signal.") { signal = "SIGKILL" }
end
opts.parse!(ARGV)

if ARGV.size != 1
  $stderr.puts opts.banner
```

```
    exit
  end

username = ARGV[0]
if username == "root"
  $stderr.puts "Sorry, killing all of root's processes would bring down the system."
  exit
end
puts "Killed #{signal_all(username, signal)} process(es)."
```

As root, you can do some serious damage with this tool:

```
$ ./banish.rb peon
5 process(es) killed
```

Discussion

The main problem with banish.rb as written is that it depends on an external program. What's worse, it depends on parsing the human-readable output of an external program. For a quick script this is fine, but this would be more reliable as a self-contained program.

You can get a Ruby interface to the Unix process table by installing the sys-proctable library. This makes it easy to treat the list of currently running processes as a Ruby data structure. Here's an alternate implementation of signal_all that uses sys-proctable instead of invoking a separate program. Note that, unlike the other implementation, this one actually uses the return value of lookup_uid:

```
def signal_all(username, signal)
  uid = lookup_uid(username)
  require 'sys/proctable'
  killed = 0
  Sys::ProcTable.ps.each do |proc|
    if proc.uid == uid
      begin
        Process.kill(signal, proc.pid)
      rescue SystemCallError => e
        raise e unless e.errno == Errno::ESRCH
      end
      killed += 1
    end
  end
  return killed
end
```

See Also

- sys-proctable is in the RAA at *http://raa.ruby-lang.org/project/sys-proctable/*; it's one of the sysutils packages: see *http://rubyforge.org/projects/sysutils* for the others
- To write an equivalent program for Windows, you'd either use WMI through Ruby's win32ole standard library, or install a native binary of GNU's ps and use win32-process

Index

Symbols

:: (double-colon) operator, 308
<< operator, arrays, 124
@ prefix, variables, 270

A

abstract methods, creating, 299–302
Accept-Language HTTP header, 504–506
Access Control lists, 644–645
accessor methods, attributes, 283–284
ActionMailer library, 508–512
ActiveRecord
    object relational mapping in
        databases, 473–477
    transactions and, 490–492
    validation and, 485–487
ActiveRecord::Validations module, 485
add_text method, 391
Ajax, Rails and, 592–594
    forms creation, 598–601
algorithm-diff gem, 212
alias command, 362
aliases, methods, 361–364
Amazon books, searching for, 617–619
analysis tools, multiple, 696–697
annotate method, 413
appending to files, overwriting and, 205
applications
    documentation, 686–691
    Mac OS X, RubyCocoa and, 807–815
    profiler, 691–693

Rails
    code files, 559
    database integration, 570–573
    system status, 557–560
archiving files, 433–436
arguments
    code blocks, 238
        binding to variables, 244–246
        default values, 239
    command-line, parsing, 779–781
    keyword, simulating, 295–297
    methods, 2
    passing, variable number, 293–295
    validation, 367–370
arithmetic, date and time and, 102–104
array, 124
Array#collect! method, 126
Array#each method, 16
Array#grep method, 467
Array#join method, 5
Array#map! method, 126
Array#shuffle method, 144
Array#size method, 124
Array#slice method, 149
Array#sort method, 133
Array#sort_by method, 135
Array#to_midi method, 444
Array#unique method, 131
arrays, 123
    << operator, 124
    brackets, 123
    elements
        duplicate, stripping, 130
        largest, 145–147

We'd like to hear your suggestions for improving our indexes. Send email to *index@oreilly.com*.

declarations, constants, 307–309
decorator methods, 271
defining methods, undefining, 358–361
degrees, converting to radians, 58
delegate library, 285
deleting files, 231–232
delimiters, stripping, 203
deliver_simple_message method, 509
DHTML, 592–594
    Rails and, 592–594
diff.rb package, 212
Diff::LCS library, 210
diff-lcs gem, 210
Dir.chdir method, 235
Dir.entries method, 198–201
Dir.foreach method, 198–201
Dir.getwd method, 235
directories
    common operations, 187
    current, finding and changing, 235
    listing contents, 198–201
    ownership, 849–852
    permissions, 849–852
    recursively processing, 214–216
distributed programming
    introduction, 616
    objects, proxying, 647–649
    RAM, data storage, 650–651
    web services and, 616
distributed queues,
        implementation, 639–640
distribution, 701
    gems, 717–719
DNS#each_address method, 507
DNS, queries, 506–508
do keyword, 237
do...end syntax, 238
documentation, 686–691
    gems, 712–714
    Rake
        generating automatically, 727–729
        publishing, 735–737
    web sites, Rails, 608–609
documents
    HTML
        extracting URLs, 398–401
        web site text summary, 402–405
        navigating, XPath and, 377–380
    XML
        converting to hashes, 382–385
        creating, 390–393
        encoding, converting, 396–397

encoding, guessing, 395–396
    modifying, 390–393
    validation, 385–387
    whitespace, 394–395
double quotes, 6
double-colon operator (::), 308
downcase method, 20
Draw#annotate method, 414
DRb (Distributed Ruby), 617
DRb library, 635
DRb services
    Access Control lists, 644–645
    Rinda and, 645–647
DTDs, validation and, 385
duck typing, 267
    class typing and, 275
duplicate files, 845–848
duplicate values, hash keys, 170
dynamic typing, 267

E

each method, 248, 323
echoing characters, 777
editing input, readline and, 792–793
Element#delete_attribute method, 392
Element#text= method, 391
elements
    arrays, 123
        duplicate, stripping, 130
        largest, 145–147
        random order, 143–145
        smallest, 145–147
        sorting by, 141–143
        summing, 140–141
    hashes
        adding to, 164–166
        removing, 166–168
email
    addresses, validation, 33–36
    checking for messages, 514
    forwarding messages to cell phone, 515,
        518
    headers, 514
    Rails, 604–606
        user error and, 606–608
    reading messages
        IMAP server and, 512–516
        POP3 and, 516–520
    sending messages, RubyMail
        library, 508–512
    UIDs for messages, 514

hashes (*continued*)
    weighted lists, 179–181
    XML documents, converting, 382–385
headers
    email messages, 514
    HTTP requests, 504–506
    layout, Rails, 563–565
helper functions, extracting code
        to, 587–588
here documents style, strings, 3
Highline library, 776
    text color, 788
HighLine#color method, 789
histograms
    building, 181–183
    hashes and, 181–183
HTML
    converting plain text to, 401–402
    documents
        extracting URLs, 398–401
        web site text summary, 402–405
    Rails, escaping, 581–582
htmltools gem, 381
HTTP
    clients, 551–554
    response headers, 540, 542
    REST-style web services, 618
HTTP request, headers, 504–506
HTTP#get_response_method, 501
HTTPResponse#code method, 501
HTTPS web requests, 502–504

I

I/O, buffered, 205
iconv library, 397
Image#columns method, 410
Image#rows method, 410
ImageMagick, 409
    image files, formats, 416
images
    captions, 412–415
    copyright statements, 412–415
    formats, converting among, 415–417
    text, 412–415
    thumbnails, 409–412
IMAP, reading email messages, 512–516
implementation
    class methods, 309–311
    Enumerable module, 322–324
    single methods, 309–311

indexes, arrays, 124
indexing
    Ferret, 459–463
    SimpleSearch and, 458–459
inheritance, multiple, simulating, 315–319
inherited classes, writing, 277–279
initialization
    instance variables, automatic, 351–352
    mixins, automatic, 330–332
initialize method, 279
initializes, 698
inject method, 141
inline C, writing, 827–829
input
    AppleScript and (Mac), 815–816
    editing, readline and, 792–793
    redirecting, 225–226
installation
    gems, 705–708
    packages, setup.rb and, 719–722
    rails gem, 558
    Ruby, xxv
instance variables
    access simulation, 282
    defining, 271
    initialization, automatic, 351–352
    modules and, 329–330
    Object#instance_variable_get method
        and, 271
    prefixes, 272
    setter methods and, 281
instances, managing data, 269–272
instantiation
    class variables and, 273
    code blocks, 238
Integer#upto method, 126
international encodings, 24
Internet server, writing, 532–534
interosculate method, 259
interpolation, triggering, 7
interrupting code, 121–122
invalid markup, extracting, 380–382
inverting hashes, 177–178
invoking code blocks, 240–241
IO#read method, 201–204
IO#readlines method, 202
IO#write method, 204
IO.popen method, 834
isdst method, 109
iteration
    arrays, 125–128
    building strings and, 4–6

prime, generating, 81–85
rational, 48
Roman, math with, 73–78
standard deviation, 57

O

object relational mapping, databases
    ActiveRecord and, 473–477
    Og and, 477–481
Object#class method, 334
Object#clone method, 305
Object#dup method, 305
Object#extend method, 319–321
Object#inspect method, 291
Object#instance_methods method, 335
Object#instance_variable_get method, 271
Object#instance_variable_set, 271
Object#instance_variables method, 345
Object#method method, 335, 339–341
Object#must_have_instance_variables
        method, 346
Object#singleton_methods method, 335
objects
    access, synchronizing, 754–757
    attributes, checking for, 345–347
    classes, finding, 334–335
    converting to different types, 287–291
    copying, 304–307
    DateTime, 89
    extending, modules and, 319–321
    freezing, 302–304
    impersonating another, 284
    Matrix, 60
    methods
        listing, 335–337
        listing unique, 337–339
    print outs, 291–293
    proxying, 647–649
    Queue, 639–640
    Rails, editing, 594–598
    Rational, 48
    string like, 22
    superclasses, finding, 334–335
    Symbol, 15
    to_str method, 22
    variables, associating, 269–272
    whiteboard, 640–643
objectsThreadsafeHash, 636
Og library
    object relational mapping in
        databases, 477–481
    taggable tables, 495–498

open-uri library, 500–502
OrderedHash class, 174
orderedhash library, 174
output
    capturing from Unix shell
        command, 767–768
    redirecting, 225–226
outside variables, code blocks, 246
overloading methods, 279–281
ownership, directories, 849–852

P

packages
    code as gems, 714–717
    diff.rb, 212
    standalone, setup.rb and, 719–722
packaging, 701
parentheses, 2
parse methods, 94
parseexcel library, 431
parsing
    arguments, command-line, 779–781
    comma-separated data, 426–429
    csv library and, 426
    dates, 93–96
    Excel spreadsheets, 431–433
    extracting data during, 376–377
    numbers from strings, 40–43
    text strings, 429–431
    URLs, 534–537
    XML files to data structure, 374–376
partial views, 589
passing arguments, variable
        number, 293–295
passwords
    Rails, hashed, storing in
        database, 579–581
    reading, 791–792
pattern matching, strings, 30
pausing program, 118–120
payment gem, 632
Payment::AuthorizeNet class, 633
Payment::PaymentError, 632
PDF files, generating, 439–443
PDF::Writer library, 439
periodic tasks, 839–840
permissions
    directories, 849–852
    files, changing, 193–196
persistence, Madeleine and, 455–457
ping library, 531–532
Ping.pingecho method, 531–532

About the Authors

Lucas Carlson is a professional Ruby programmer who specializes in Rails web development. He has authored a half-dozen libraries and contributed to many others, including Rails and RedCloth. He lives in Portland, Oregon and maintains a web site at *http://rufy.com/*.

Leonard Richardson has been programming since he was eight years old. Recently, the quality of his code has improved somewhat. He is responsible for libraries in many languages, including Rubyful Soup. A California native, he now works in New York and maintains a web site at *http://www.crummy.com/*.

Colophon

The animal on the cover of *Ruby Cookbook* is a side-striped jackal (*Canis adustus*), found mostly in central and southern Africa. These jackals avoid the open, preferring thickly wooded areas on the edge of savannas and forests. They occasionally make their way into cities. Side-striped jackals are rare but not considered endangered. There are reserves for these jackals at the Serengeti National Park in Tanzania and at the Akagera National Park in Rwanda.

Side-striped jackals are about 15 inches tall and weigh between 16 and 26 pounds. This jackal has a light grey coat with a white stripe from shoulder to hip, and a white-tipped tail. The diet of side-striped jackals consists largely of wild fruits, small mammals, and insects. They also eat carrion and are adept scavengers; they will follow a lion or other big cat to a kill. The jackals usually live singly or in pairs, but they sometimes gather in family units of up to six members. Their lifespan is about 10 to 12 years.

Jackals have been an object of superstition because of their association with carrion and death, and because of their eerie nocturnal noises: they hoot, yap, and make a kind of screaming yell. Perhaps because jackals were often found prowling and hunting the edges of the desert near cemeteries, the ancient Egyptian god of embalming and gatekeeper of the path of the dead, Anubis, was depicted as a jackal-headed man. Anubis served as a *psychopomp*, conducting souls to the underworld, where he weighed their hearts on a scale to determine whether they would be admitted to the underworld or cast to the crocodile-headed demon, Ammit.

The cover image is from *Lydekker's Royal History*. The cover font is Adobe ITC Garamond. The text font is Linotype Birka; the heading font is Adobe Myriad Condensed; and the code font is LucasFont's TheSans Mono Condensed.

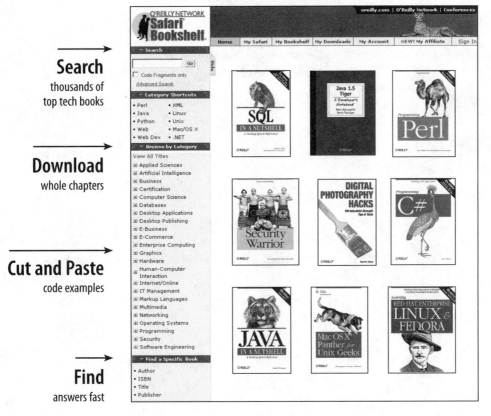

Related Titles from O'Reilly

O'REILLY®

Our books are available at most retail and online bookstores.

To order direct: 1-800-998-9938 • *order@oreilly.com* • *www.oreilly.com*

Online editions of most O'Reilly titles are available by subscription at *safari.oreilly.com*